Fodor's 2009

NEW ZEALAND

Where to Stay and Eat
for All Budgets

Must-See Sights
and Local Secrets

Ratings You Can Trust

Fodor's Travel Publications   New York, Toronto, London, Sydney, Auckland
www.fodors.com

FODOR'S NEW ZEALAND 2009

Editor: Stephanie E. Butler, Josh McIlvain

Contributors: Sue Farley, Jessica Kany, Alia Levine, Bob Marriott, Kathy Ombler, Richard Pamatatau

Editorial Production: Tom Holton
Maps & Illustrations: David Lindroth, Mark Stroud, *cartographers*; Bob Blake, Rebecca Baer, and William Wu *map editors*
Design: Fabrizio LaRocca, *creative director*; Guido Caroti, Siobhan O'Hare, *art directors*; Tina Malaney, Chie Ushio, Ann McBride, *designers*; Melanie Marin, *senior picture editor*; Moon Sun Kim, *cover designer*
Cover Photo: (Mount Cook National Park, Canterbury): Jeremy Bright/Robert Harding
Production/Manufacturing: Angela L. McLean

ISBN 978–1–4000–1952–6

ISSN 1531–0450

SPECIAL SALES
This book is available at special discounts for bulk purchases for sales promotions or premiums. Special editions, including personalized covers, excerpts of existing books, and corporate imprints, can be created in large quantities for special needs. For more information, write to Special Markets/Premium Sales, 1745 Broadway, MD 6-2, New York, New York 10019, or e-mail specialmarkets@randomhouse.com.

AN IMPORTANT TIP & AN INVITATION
Although all prices, opening times, and other details in this book are based on information supplied to us at press time, changes occur all the time in the travel world, and Fodor's cannot accept responsibility for facts that become outdated or for inadvertent errors or omissions. So **always confirm information when it matters,** especially if you're making a detour to visit a specific place. Your experiences—positive and negative—matter to us. If we have missed or misstated something, **please write to us.** We follow up on all suggestions. Contact the New Zealand editor at editors@fodors.com or c/o Fodor's at 1745 Broadway, New York, NY 10019.

PRINTED IN THE UNITED STATES OF AMERICA

10 9 8 7 6 5 4 3 2 1

Be a Fodor's Correspondent

Your opinion matters. It matters to us. It matters to your fellow Fodor's travelers, too. And we'd like to hear it. In fact, we need to hear it.

When you share your experiences and opinions, you become an active member of the Fodor's community. That means we'll not only use your feedback to make our books better, but we'll publish your names and comments whenever possible. Throughout our guides, look for "Word of Mouth," excerpts of your unvarnished feedback.

Here's how you can help improve Fodor's for all of us.

Tell us when we're right. We rely on local writers to give you an insider's perspective. But our writers and staff editors—who are the best in the business—depend on you. Your positive feedback is a vote to renew our recommendations for the next edition.

Tell us when we're wrong. We're proud that we update most of our guides every year. But we're not perfect. Things change. Hotels cut services. Museums change hours. Charming cafés lose charm. If our writer didn't quite capture the essence of a place, tell us how you'd do it differently. If any of our descriptions are inaccurate or inadequate, we'll incorporate your changes in the next edition and will correct factual errors at fodors.com immediately.

Tell us what to include. You probably have had fantastic travel experiences that aren't yet in Fodor's. Why not share them with a community of like-minded travelers? Maybe you chanced upon a beach or bistro or B&B that you don't want to keep to yourself. Tell us why we should include it. And share your discoveries and experiences with everyone directly at fodors.com. Your input may lead us to add a new listing or highlight a place we cover with a "Highly Recommended" star or with our highest rating, "Fodor's Choice."

Give us your opinion instantly at our feedback center at www.fodors.com/feedback. You may also e-mail editors@fodors.com with the subject line "New Zealand Editor." Or send your nominations, comments, and complaints by mail to New Zealand Editor, Fodor's, 1745 Broadway, New York, NY 10019.

You and travelers like you are the heart of the Fodor's community. Make our community richer by sharing your experiences. Be a Fodor's correspondent.

Happy traveling!

Tim Jarrell, Publisher

CONTENTS

ABOUT THIS BOOK

Our Ratings

Sometimes you find terrific travel experiences and sometimes they just find you. But usually the burden is on you to select the right combination of experiences. That's where our ratings come in.

As travelers we've all discovered a place so wonderful that its worthiness is obvious. And sometimes that place is so experiential that superlatives don't do it justice: you just have to be there to know. These sights, properties, and experiences get our highest rating, **Fodor's Choice**, indicated by orange stars throughout this book.

Black stars highlight sights and properties we deem **Highly Recommended**, places that our writers, editors, and readers praise again and again for consistency and excellence.

By default, there's another category: any place we include in this book is by definition worth your time, unless we say otherwise. And we will.

Disagree with any of our choices? Care to nominate a place or suggest that we rate one more highly? Visit our feedback center at www.fodors.com/feedback.

Budget Well

Hotel and restaurant price categories from ¢ to $$$$ are defined in the opening pages of each chapter. For attractions, we always give standard adult admission fees; reductions are usually available for children, students, and senior citizens. Want to pay with plastic? **AE, D, DC, MC, V** following restaurant and hotel listings indicate if American Express, Discover, Diners Club, MasterCard, and Visa are accepted.

Restaurants

Unless we state otherwise, restaurants are open for lunch and dinner daily. We mention dress only when there's a specific requirement and reservations only when they're essential or not accepted—it's always best to book ahead.

Hotels

Hotels have private bath, phone, TV, and air-conditioning and operate on the European Plan (aka EP, meaning without meals), unless we specify that they use the Continental Plan (CP, with a Continental breakfast), Breakfast Plan (BP, with a full breakfast), or Modified American Plan (MAP, with breakfast and dinner) or are all-inclusive (including all meals and most activi-

ties). We always list facilities but not whether you'll be charged an extra fee to use them, so when pricing accommodations, find out what's included.

Many Listings
- ★ Fodor's Choice
- ★ Highly recommended
- ⊠ Physical address
- ✛ Directions
- ⌂ Mailing address
- ☎ Telephone
- 🖷 Fax
- ⊕ On the Web
- ✆ E-mail
- ☑ Admission fee
- ☉ Open/closed times
- Ⓜ Metro stations
- ▭ Credit cards

Hotels & Restaurants
- 🏨 Hotel
- ➦ Number of rooms
- ⌂ Facilities
- ¶◎¶ Meal plans
- ✕ Restaurant
- ⌕ Reservations
- ↘ Smoking
- ₷₽ BYOB
- ✕🖾 Hotel with restaurant that warrants a visit

Outdoors
- 🏌 Golf
- ⛺ Camping

Other
- ☾ Family-friendly
- ⇨ See also
- ⊠ Branch address
- ☞ Take note

WHAT'S WHERE

New Zealand consists of three main islands: the North Island (44,197 square mi), the South Island (58,170 square mi), and Stewart Island (676 square mi). The country also includes the Subantarctic Islands, composed of five island groups, and the 10 Chatham Islands—the first inhabited land in the world to greet the sun. New Zealand is relatively small—if the country were stretched out along the west coast of the United States, it would extend from Los Angeles to Seattle. No point is more than 112 km (70 mi) from the sea, and rivers tend to be short, swift, and broad. Much of the country is made up of hilly, expansive, green fields occupied by some 40 million sheep and 5 million cattle.

More than 70% of the total population lives on the North Island, where industry and government are concentrated. The South Island is dominated by the Southern Alps, a spine of mountains running almost two-thirds the length of the island close to the West Coast.

NORTH ISLAND

Cataclysmic geological events and earth-spewing uproars have shaped this country. Volcanic activity created features you will see all around the North Island—the Māori pā, black-sand beaches, and Lake Taupo (catch trout from a caldera!). Even Napier's art deco can be attributed to "terra-ble" times: in 1931 an earthquake triggered a fire that decimated the city, and the city was rebuilt with the architecture in vogue. You roll your eyes: yes, 1931 was like a million years ago (don't tell grandma that), but volcanic shenanigans are occurring in New Zealand even as you read this sentence. The North Island is a land of active volcanoes. Don't show up with a mixing bowl over your head, they are *active* not *erupting*. (But if you're skiing on the slopes of Mt. Ruapehu and you hear an alarm, you had best take heed.)

Let's start at the top: From the lighthouse at Cape Reinga you can see where the Tasman Sea and Pacific Ocean have an ongoing meeting (they don't say much, just keep waving at each other). Cape Reinga is the beginning of State Highway One. Ninety Mile Beach gives way to the revered and mighty 1,200-year-old kauri (*cow*-ree) trees of Northland. The miles of island-strewn coastline of the Coromandel Peninsula are a perfect foil for the bustle of Auckland, New Zealand's largest city. One Tree Hill (nicknamed None Tree Hill) was a pā built upon a volcanic cinder cone (it's the world's largest

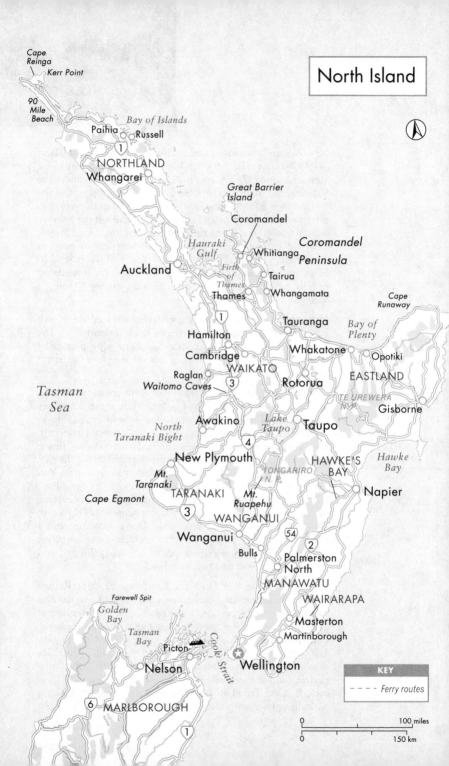

earth fort). You'll need to fortify yourself when you boat over to Whakaari Island, home to the country's only live marine volcano. Mid-island, Rotorua oozes with surreal and smelly geothermal activity. Parklands at Tongariro and Mt. Taranaki offer outstanding hiking, while world-renowned trout-fishing is at Lake Taupo (Australasia's largest). In the agriculturally bountiful Waikato region, caves are home to entrancing glowworms. Townies revel in the famous wine-producing Hawke's Bay region, while the nation's capital city, Wellington, remains an arts and culinary haven.

SOUTH ISLAND

Along a stretch of road at the base of the Lindis Pass, you will encounter a strange phenomenon. Hundreds of cairns have been built there, seemingly haphazardly. Some are carefully constructed towers, and some a mere squat pyramid of four or five stones, dwarfed by pink lupines. There's something about this vista that stirs drivers to get out and build. A little *I was here* in this great big scheme of things. And the South Island *is* the Great Big Scheme: Milford Sound will have your jaw dropping; Queenstown will have your stomach dropping; on Rakiura you'll step in penguin droppings.

Let's start at the top: Kayaking the emerald waters of Abel Tasman could be a highlight of your trip. Marlborough offers the Treat Triumvirate: vino, sun, and vittles. On the wild West Coast, Hokitika gives new meaning to "may contain nuts" at the annual Wildfoods Festival. Across the Canterbury Plain is the gracious city of Christchurch. Back inland you will find Alpha Centauri and other galactic jewels, visible from the observatory in Lake Tekapo. Fly to one of the West Coast glaciers, and walk on the ancient ice mass. There are no words for the sounds of Fiordland: Milford and Doubtful sounds are a must (you will find words for the sandflies there, unprintable, filthy words). Continue south: pert roadside signs advertising fresh cherries and apricots give way to hand-painted boards announcing the on-site sale of manure, dags, and swedes (a local turnip). By now you have presumably worn a body harness and jumped from great heights in Queenstown. Head out on the Otago Peninsula to see the Royal Albatross. Swing south and west along the Catlins toward Invercargill, stopping at Curio Bay to ponder the fossilized Jurassic forest. From Invercargill, head farther south to the end of the road. Jump on the ferry here, and brave Foveaux Strait to reach extraordinary Stewart Island.

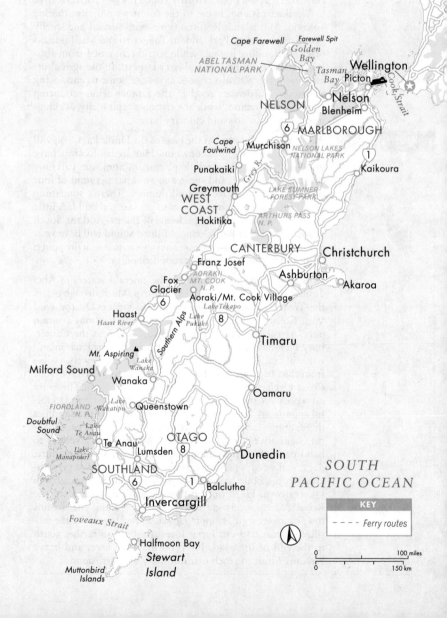

South Island

NORTH ISLAND

Cape Farewell
Farewell Spit
Golden Bay
ABEL TASMAN NATIONAL PARK
Tasman Bay
Wellington
Picton
Cook Strait
NELSON
Nelson
Blenheim
MARLBOROUGH
Cape Foulwind
Murchison
NELSON LAKES NATIONAL PARK
Punakaiki
Grey R.
Kaikoura
Greymouth
LAKE SUMNER FOREST PARK
WEST COAST
ARTHURS PASS N. P.
Hokitika
CANTERBURY
Christchurch
Franz Josef
AORAKI MT. COOK N. P.
Ashburton
Akaroa
Fox Glacier
Aoraki/Mt. Cook Village
Lake Tekapo
Haast
Haast River
Lake Pukaki
Southern Alps
Timaru
Mt. Aspiring
Lake Wanaka
Milford Sound
Wanaka
FIORDLAND N. P.
Lake Wakatipu
Queenstown
Oamaru
Doubtful Sound
Lake Te Anau
Te Anau
OTAGO
Lake Manapouri
Lumsden
Dunedin
SOUTHLAND
SOUTH PACIFIC OCEAN
Balclutha
Invercargill
Foveaux Strait
KEY
- - - Ferry routes
Halfmoon Bay
Stewart Island
Muttonbird Islands
0   100 miles
0   150 km

QUINTESSENTIAL NEW ZEALAND

Matariki

Meet the whānau (extended family). There is more to Māori culture than the fierce haka performed by the All Blacks prior to rugby games. Places like Rotorua and Waitangi have huge significance for Māori history and culture, and the collection of taonga (treasures) at Te Papa museum in Wellington is well worth a visit. The story of the Māori is fascinating and still unfolding; this indigenous culture has not been relegated to the pages of history. Travel anywhere in New Zealand and see evidence that Māori culture is a vital part of this country. The architectural centerpiece of many communities is the beautiful marae—the Māori meeting place. Look up as you enter, the pare (door lintel) is an example of intricate Māori carving. The Māori have their own political party, and there is a Māori-language TV station. Restaurants around New Zealand offer traditional Māori dishes such as lamb and kūmara pie, roast muttonbird, or rewena (potato bread). Many of the meals are baked in a *hāngi,* a traditional Māori earth oven, in which food is cooked underground with hot stones. If you visit New Zealand in June you can celebrate Matariki, the Māori New Year, which is marked by the rising of the Pleiades.

Wine Country

When you land and reset your watch, there's an hour that might not be on your dial yet. Many Kiwis observe wine o'clock, which occurs any time from around 4 PM onwards, depending on the day and the drinker. Older generations recall sipping sherry in their uni dorms, but the past decades have seen a surge in wine production, pride, and appreciation. Even some of the saltiest sea dogs in the deepest southern pubs might be found quaffing a glass of pinot noir. New

Zealand wines are reasonably priced and very, very good. Sauvignon blanc has been internationally prized, and pinot noir is a favorite red. Riesling, chardonnay, pinot gris, malbec, sparkling wines, and many other types are produced here, too. If you want to see where it comes from and do the wine tour thing, visit Marlborough, Hawke's Bay, Gisborne, East Cape, Wairarapa, and Central Otago. Wine has always been paired with crayfish, venison, lamb, and other cuisine, and wineries increasingly have been pairing their product with music: vineyards host musicians or all-day concerts featuring the likes of Hayley Westerna, Brooke Fraser, and Bic Runga. Surrounded by grapes, gorgeous scenery, gourmet food, mellow music, and sunshine, you'll soon discover why the typical response to an offered drop is wine-not.

Close Encounters with Sealife

There's a reason why dolphin-, whale-, and seal-lovers treasure the coastal and island regions of New Zealand. Every time you're on a boat, you're likely to spot these beautiful animals frolicking in the waves, sometimes right alongside your ferry. Bottlenose dolphins are the most commonly sighted, but during certain seasons you might be lucky enough to spy an orca, or a rare Hector's dolphin, the world's smallest, near Kaikoura or off the Banks Peninsula.

If it's an up-close-and-personal encounter you're after, you'll find that many east-coast towns in the North and South islands offer day tours, where you're invited to jump in the water and swim among seals and dolphins. Paihia (in Northland), Tauranga and Whakatane (in the Bay of Plenty), Kaikoura (in Marlborough Sounds), and Abel Tasman

National Park have such tours. Many of them guarantee a sighting of marine mammals, and offer a free trip the next day if the animals are not spotted.

The seas off the South Island are known stomping grounds for giant squid, but they are rarely captured on film. Keen marine scientists throw squid gonads overboard to lure these elusive sea critters to their cameras. Chances are you won't have the same resources.

Kiwi-Spotting
There are some simple ways to "meet the locals." Do a farmstay, or lodge at a B&B. Check local notice boards for sausage sizzles or garden shows. Local A & P shows are wonderful social events when hard-working country Kiwis come out of the woodwork. As they say down here, "Get amongst it," and join in the fun. If you think you can pitchfork a water-soaked hay bale over the high wire, go for it.

Don't be put off by a grumpy exterior if you see a grizzled old fisherman fiddling with pots on a wharf; ask him questions. The worst that can happen is he's a true grumpus who barks, "Piss off!" You'll laugh about it later. (Don't apply this approach to members of the Mongrel Mob; you *won't* laugh about it later.) Lots of country pubs hold quiz nights, which are always a hoot.

Finally, when you're booking activities, ask around among the locals who the best guide might be, or tell the i-Site agent that you'd prefer a private, truly local guiding company. Your tour will be a more interesting and intimate experience, and you'll have a chance to see the country through native eyes. (Your fishing guide might turn out to be the grumpus, now he *has* to talk to you!)

IF YOU LIKE

Beaches

New Zealand has more than 15,000 km (9,300 mi) in coastline, which ripples and zigzags to create bays, coves, fjords, and countless beaches. These run the gamut from surfing hot spots to quiet, sheltered lagoons to rugged, boulder-studded strands. All are open to the public, and few are crowded. The greatest hazards are sunburn—the lack of smog and a subequatorial location mean the sun is **strong**—and strong currents.

On the North Island, Coromandel's eastern shore and the Bay of Plenty—especially busy **Mount Maunganui**—are favorites during summer "time off." The black "iron sand" on the West Coast of the North Island is a result of volcanic activity. **Karekare Beach,** west of Auckland, is the striking, cliff-backed beach that was made famous in Jane Campion's film *The Piano.* The dunes at **90 Mile Beach,** in Northland are spectacular, and nearby **Doubtless Bay** has some of the country's loveliest caramel-colored beaches. New Zealand's most famous surf breaks are located west of Hamilton in the laid-back town of **Raglan;** you can "hang-ten" here or at **Piha** near Auckland.

South Island beaches are captivating, particularly in **Abel Tasman National Park** and neighboring **Golden Bay.** The sands are golden, and the water is jade green. Westerly winds carry driftwood, buoys, entire trees, and a fascinating variety of flotsam from as far away as South America to Stewart Island's **Mason Bay,** making this dramatic sweep of sand a beachcomber's paradise. The sand is crisscrossed with the tracks of kiwis (the birds) that reside in the area by the thousands.

Bushwalking

The traditional way to hike in New Zealand is freedom walking. Freedom walkers carry their own provisions, sleeping bags, food, and cooking gear and sleep in basic huts. A more refined alternative—usually on more popular trails—is the guided walk, on which you trek with just a light day pack, guides do the cooking, and you sleep in heated lodges.

The most popular walks are in the Southern Alps. The **Milford Track** is a four-day walk through breathtaking scenery to the edge of Milford Sound. The **Queen Charlotte Track** (68 km [42 mi]) winds along the jagged coast of the Marlborough Sounds region; you can see seals and sometimes orcas from the waterside cliffs.

The hard-core hiker will be challenged on remote Rakiura National Park's **North West Circuit.** The 10- to 12-day trek will sometimes feel more like mud wrestling than walking, but the scenic rewards are immeasurable, as is the pint of beer waiting at the South Sea Pub when it's over. If you would like to experience Rakiura, do the three-day **Rakiura Track,** or have a water taxi drop you along one of the many coastal trails and walk back.

The North Island has plenty of wonders of its own. The Coromandel Peninsula has forests of gigantic 1,200-year-old kauri trees, 80-foot-tall tree ferns, a gorgeous coastline, and well-marked trails. You can hike among active volcanic peaks in **Tongariro National Park.** And on a nub of the West Coast formed by volcanic activity hundreds of years ago, sits the majestic, Fuji-like **Mt. Taranaki.** If time is short, at least put aside a few hours for trekking in the **Waitakerei Ranges,** just a short drive from Auckland city.

Boating

There are boating and fishing options to match any mood.

If you're feeling cruisy, rent a kayak and paddle around the crystal green pools of the Abel Tasman, or the penguin-filled waters of Paterson Inlet. Take a canoe on the Whanganui River, or sail the Bay of Islands. Feeling really lazy? Just charter a boat and captain and take in the scenery of the Marlborough Sounds or busy Auckland Harbour. Fly fish a trout from a caldera in Lake Taupo, or one of the many pristine rivers and lakes throughout the country.

If you want some fun and a bit of a rush, much of the fishing in the South is simple rod or hand-lining for groper (grouper), trumpeter, and greenbone. Northerners argue their snapper is superior to the succulent Stewart Island blue cod; sample both to weigh in on this tasty debate. Go on a creaky wooden boat for the local old-school experience (some skippers will fry your catch), or opt for a sleeker vessel and a bird tour and let your heart soar with the mollymawks.

Up North ups the excitement, with big game fishing out of Russell and Paihia for big fish such as striped marlin. Tuna is always a challenging catch, and the **Hokitika Trench** off Greymouth is one of the few places in the world where the three species of bluefin tuna gather.

If you want a major adrenaline buzz, go jet-boating on the **Shotover River** near Queenstown, or raft the North Island's **Kaituna River**, near Rotorua, which has the highest commercially rafted waterfall (22 feet) in the southern hemisphere. Or get off the boat and go spearfishing for moki in the kelp forests beneath the waves.

Birds

It is one thing to read "9.6 feet" here in ink, but it is quite another sensation to watch the magnificent royal albatross spread its wings and soar through your field of vision. You don't have to be a twitcher (bird-watching nut) to appreciate New Zealand's feathered population—this country will turn you into a bird nerd. The birds of New Zealand are extraordinary to behold: a raft of thousands of sooty shearwaters (aka muttonbirds or titi) move like smoke over the water; a yellow-eyed penguin pops like a cork from the bright green surf and waddles up the beach; fantails squeak and follow you through the forest; the soft cry of the morepork (owl) is interrupted by the otherworldly call of the kiwi. Pelagic birds such as the royal albatross will take your breath away; the Otago Peninsula colony (off Dunedin) is the only mainland breeding colony for these perfect flying machines. It may be ornithologically incorrect to say so, but many of the native birds are simply hilarious. Penguins always make people smile, and New Zealand is home to the little blue (or fairy), the extremely rare hoiho (or yellow-eyed), and the yellow-tweedled Fiordland-crested penguin. The kea and its cousin the kaka are wild parrots whose antics crack people up—these birds like to hang upside down from gutters and regard you with bright beady eyes. And, of course, there is the star of the bird show: the kiwi. You won't ever see another bird like this funny flightless brown bird, and to glimpse a kiwi is an unforgettable and joyful experience. Hot bird spots include Kapiti Island off the North Island and Stewart Island way down south.

GREAT ITINERARIES

INTRODUCTION TO NORTH ISLAND

8 to 10 days

Auckland

2 days. After a long international flight, stretch your legs and invigorate your circulation with a walk around the city center, with perhaps stops at Auckland Museum and Auckland Domain Park or Albert Park. Head to the harbor (or "harbour") and take a ferry ride round-trip between Auckland and Devonport for a great view of the city from the water. Have an early dinner and turn in to get over the worst of the jet lag.

On your second day, you'll have more wind in your sails to explore the City of Sails. Depending on your interests, head to Kelly Tarlton's Underwater World and Antarctic Encounter, the New Zealand National Maritime Museum, the Auckland Art Gallery, or the Parnell neighborhood for window-shopping. If you're feeling energetic, you can even do a bit of kayaking (or just sunbathing) at Mission Bay or Karekare Beach.

Waitomo & Rotorua

1 or 2 days. Waitomo is known for what's beneath the surface—intricate limestone caves filled with stalactites, stalagmites, and galaxies of glowworms. If this is up your alley, get an early start from Auckland to arrive here before 11 AM and sign up for a cave tour. Afterward, continue on to Rotorua, which seethes with geothermal activity. In the late afternoon you should have time for a walk around the town center, strolling through the Government Gardens and perhaps also Kuirau Park. If you decide to skip the Waitomo worms, you can zip straight down from

Auckland to Rotorua. In addition to the town proper, visit some of the eye-popping thermal areas nearby, such as Waiotapu. At night, be a guest at a *hāngi*, a Māori feast accompanied by a cultural performance. On the next day, you can either see some of the outlying thermal areas or continue south to Taupo.

Taupo

1 day. Midway between Auckland and Wellington, the resort town of Taupo, on its giant namesake lake, is the perfect base for a day full of aquatic activities. If you're at all interested in trout fishing, this is the place to do it.

Napier

1 day. This small town is an art deco period piece; after a devastating Richter 7.9 earthquake in 1931, the center of town was rebuilt in the distinctive style, and it's been carefully preserved ever since. Take a guided or self-guided walk around the Heritage (historically significant) neighborhood. If you have a car, drive out of town and visit one of the 30-odd wineries around Hawke's Bay. In the afternoon, take a drive to the top of Te Mata Peak, or visit nearby towns Hastings or Havelock North. Otherwise, hang out at the waterfront or visit the aquarium.

Wellington

2 days. New Zealand's capital, Wellington, is a terrific walking city, and there's even a cable car to help you with the hills. The big cultural draw is Te Papa Tongarewa—the Museum of New Zealand, which, with five floors and great interactive activities for kids, can take several hours to explore. You may wish to spend the rest of your first day here along the waterfront, winding up with dinner in the area. Be sure to check out the entertainment listings, too; you could be in town during one of the many festivals or catch a cool local band. On your second day, explore more of the urban highlights, like the City Gallery and the Museum of Wellington, City & Sea, followed by a bit of browsing on the main shopping drags or a trip up into the hills to the Botanic Garden. If you'd prefer more time out in the country and have a car, drive up the Kapiti Coast and book to visit Kapiti Island Nature Reserve, or sip acclaimed pinot noir in the wine center of Martinborough.

Other Top Options

1 or 2 days. With at least one more day at your disposal, you could squeeze in one of the following destinations. The Tongariro Crossing, a challenging but spectacular daylong hike, could be added to your Taupo stay. You'll "tramp" up-close to three volcanoes: Tongariro, Ngauruhoe, and Ruapehu. If you have two days and are keen on swimming with dolphins or doing some diving, loop up to Paihia, a small seaside town and gateway to the Bay of Islands, after your initial two days in Auckland. You can dip into the mellow, rural Coromandel Peninsula, perhaps the gateway town of Thames, before going south to Rotorua. Most places on the Coromandel are within 1 to 1½ hours' drive from the Thames township.

By Public Transportation

Bus service links all major North Island destinations. You'll ride InterCity Coachlines or Newmans Coach Lines. Contact Tranz Scenic for rail tickets on the Overlander, between Auckland and Wellington or the Capital Connection, between Wellington and Palmerston North.

Tips & Logistics

Summer in New Zealand—winter in North America—is the best time to visit the North Island. From Christmas through January's end, schools are out—it's the "Silly Season"—and you'll be competing for reservations at hotels, so book ahead. During the cold-weather months, rates are cheaper, crowds thin out, and the weather is actually quite mild; there's the frequent rain, but that just means the countryside looks even greener.

INTRODUCTION TO SOUTH ISLAND

10 to 13 days
Picton & Blenheim

2 days. Hop or drive onto the ferry from Wellington to Picton. This small seaside township is the Marlborough region's main commercial port, and the gateway to the gorgeously jagged coastline of Marlborough Sounds. Hop on a mail boat, which makes stops at coves and islands along the Sounds; take a day-walk along the famous Queen Charlotte Track for spectacular water views; or join a kayak tour (you might just see some seals and dolphins as you paddle around). Have dinner along the foreshore and turn in early.

The next morning, head out of town to the Blenheim region, where the rolling hills are covered with grapevines and dotted with scores of wineries. Stop in for tastings at esteemed spots like the Seresin Estate, Cloudy Bay, and Allan Scott Wines; if you've prebooked, you might also be able to dine at Herzog or Hunter's Vineyard Restaurant. Be sure to pick up a few bottles of wine and olive oil to take with you.

Kaikoura

1 day. Get an early start and continue down the South Island's eastern coast to the seaside settlement of Kaikoura, where you can go whale-watching, reef diving, swimming with dolphins or seals, or stay on land and indulge in a big crayfish lunch ("Kaikoura" actually means "meal of crayfish" in the Māori language).

Christchurch

1 or 2 days. Although Christchurch, "The Garden City," is the South Island's largest city, it's still a relaxing place to be. Depending on when you get here from Kaikoura, you can stroll through the city center, visit the Arts Centre (especially fun during the weekend market), the Botanic Gardens, or one of the city's museums or galleries. For a two-day stay, fit in a couple of hours at the International Antarctic Centre after a ride on the Christchurch Gondola. You might enjoy a cruise to see the endangered Hector's dolphins. The next morning, get an early start to make the push to Queenstown.

Queenstown

2 or 3 days. Depending on your appetite for adventure, Queenstown may be the locus of your South Island trip. Take the plunge with AJ Hackett Bungy, free-fall on the Shotover Canyon Swing, try a jet-boat ride, or go rafting. As the town is set on Lake Wakatipu with the jagged peaks of the Remarkables mountains around it, you won't lack for scenic distractions. If you're interested in the area's gold-mining history, detour to nearby Arrowtown and see the Lakes District Museum. If the area looks familiar, you're not dreaming: many scenes from the *Lord of the Rings* film trilogy were shot here.

Fiordland National Park

2 days. Follow your extreme sports adventure with some extremely beautiful landscapes. At Milford and Doubtful sounds in Fiordland National Park, deep green slopes fall steeply down to crystalline waters. Rare species live in the unique underwater environment here, so try to visit the Milford Deep Underwater Observatory. Drink in the views by catamaran, by kayak, or by flightseeing. Whatever

you do, don't forget your rain gear and bug repellent! If pressed, you could make a trip to Milford Sound a long day's trip from Queenstown.

Other Top Options

2 or 3 days. With more time in your schedule, build in a couple of low-key days to offset the thrills-and-chills outdoor activities. After you arrive at Picton, you can drive or take a bus to Nelson, a relaxed waterfront town that's a good base for arts and crafts shopping and wine tasting. One fun stop is the World of Wearable Art & Collectable Cars Museum. If ice is on your mind and you're willing to brave rainy conditions, push on down the rugged West Coast, stopping at the Pancake Rocks—columns of limestone resembling stacks of pancakes—on your way to the Fox or Franz Josef glaciers in Westland National Park. Their flow rates are up to 10 times the speed of most valley glaciers. (To do this, plan on three days, as it's a long drive and you'll want at least one full day at the glaciers.)

By Public Transportation

Buses run between all major South Island destinations, but in the Southern Alps trips can take several hours. You may want to consider a short-hop flight between Christchurch and Queenstown. Consider a couple of train options, too, with the TranzAlpine train linking Christchurch and Greymouth on the West Coast and the TransCoastal train connecting Christchurch with Kaikoura and Picton.

Tips & Logistics

If you're planning to do some bushwalking on this island—and some of New Zealand's greatest "Great Walks" are here, including the Milford Track and Queen Charlotte Track—it's best to visit in the New Zealand spring, summer, or fall. Most tracks at the northern tip are open all year, while those positioned at higher altitudes—such as Milford, Kepler, and Routeburn—remain open when weather and track conditions permit.

When driving South Island roads, which really are "those less traveled," use caution. Some roads don't have center divider lines, which can make it easy to get disoriented—especially when you're not used to driving on the left-hand side of the road.

WHEN TO GO

New Zealand is in the southern hemisphere, which means that the seasons are reversed—it's winter Down Under during the American and European summer. The ideal months for comfortable all-round travel are October through April, especially if you want to participate in adventure activities. Avoid school holidays, when highways may be congested and accommodations are likely to be scarce and more expensive. Summer school holidays (the busiest) fall between mid-December and the end of January; other holiday periods are mid-May to the end of May, early July to mid-July, and late August to mid-September.

Climate

Climate in New Zealand varies from subtropical in the north to temperate in the south. Summer (December–March) is generally warm, with an average of seven to eight hours of sunshine per day throughout the country. Winter (June–September) is mild at lower altitudes in South Island, but heavy snowfalls are common, particularly on the peaks of the Southern Alps. Strong southerly winds bring a blast of Antarctica. Rain can pour at any time of the year. (Some areas on the West Coast of South Island receive an annual rainfall of more than 100 inches.)

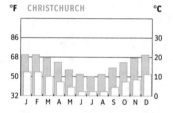

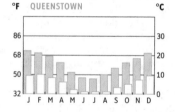

ON THE CALENDAR

Sports feature heavily in New Zealand's festival calendar. Horse and boat races, triathlons, and fishing competitions are prominent; although there are also arts festivals, and those celebrating the country's food and wine. Just about every town holds a yearly agricultural and pastoral (A&P) show, and these proud displays of local crafts, produce, livestock, and wood-chopping and sheep-shearing prowess provide a memorable look at rural New Zealand. An annual calendar of New Zealand special events can be found on the Web at ⊕ *www.newzealand.com.*

SUMMER Last Mon. in Jan.	For the **Auckland Anniversary Day Regatta** (☎ *0800/734–2882* ⊕ *www.regatta.org.nz*), Auckland's birthday party, the City of Sails takes to the water.
Feb. 6	**Waitangi Day,** New Zealand's national day, commemorates the signing of the Treaty of Waitangi between Europeans and Māori in 1840. The focus of the celebration is, naturally enough, the town of Waitangi in the Bay of Islands.
Feb. 9–10	**Speights Coast to Coast** (☎ *03/326–5493* ⊕ *www.coasttocoast.co.nz*) is the ultimate Ironman challenge—a two-day, 238-km (148-mi) marathon, "World Multisport Championship," of cycling, running, and kayaking that crosses South Island from west to east.
Feb. 17–18	**The Devonport Food & Wine Festival** (☎ *09/353–4026* ⊕ *www.devonportwinefestival.co.nz*), the first of its kind in New Zealand, showcases some of the country's best restaurants. It's reached by a ferry trip from Auckland.
Mid-Feb.	The **Festival of Flowers & Romance** (☎ *03/365–5403* ⊕ *www.festivalofflowers.co.nz*) is held in Christchurch—the city where lovers can stroll through an old English garden and enjoy a punt ride on the Avon River. Admission is free and you'll see the Christchurch Cathedral Floral Carpet and Wearable Flowers Parade. **HERO Festival** (⊕ *www.hero.org.nz*) is Auckland's annual GayPride event with big-scale festivities such as the HERO Party.
Feb. 15–19	Napier's **Art Deco Weekend** (☎ *06/835–1191* ⊕ *www.artdeconapier.com*) celebrates the city's style with wining, dining, house tours, vintage car displays, and more.

AUTUMN	
1st Thurs.–Sat. of Mar.	**Golden Shears International Sheep Shearing and Wool Handling Championships** (☎*06/378–8008* ⊕*www.goldenshears.co.nz*) is a three-day event, the world's premier competition, that pits men armed with shears against the fleecy sheep in Masterton, north of Wellington.
2nd Sat. in Mar.	Screw up your courage to try some unusual bush tucker like grubs and "Westcargots" (local snails), possum pies, and gorse-flower wine at Hokitika's **Wildfoods Festival** (☎*03/755–8321* ⊕*www.wildfoods.co.nz*).
MidMar.	Some people take the wine tasting along the route of the **Martinborough Round the Vines Fun Walk/Run** (☎*06/306–9330* ⊕*www.roundthevines.org.nz*) much more seriously than the running. Fancy dress isn't compulsory, but you'll feel far more a part of the proceedings if you at least wear a funny hat. The **Pasifika Festival** (☎*09/379–2020* ⊕*www.aucklandcity.govt.nz/whatson/events/pasifika/default.asp*) highlights the many Pacific Island cultures found in Auckland with plenty of color, music, and dance. It's the South Pacific's largest Pacific Islands community event, and it's free. The main activity is at Western Springs Lakeside and Stadium near the Auckland Zoo. The festival is extremely popular and crowded, so don't try to find parking. Check local newspapers for special bus services on the day.
Late Mar.	Easter weekend brings **Warbirds Over Wanaka 2008,** the southern hemisphere's most spectacular warbird air show. (⊕*www.warbirdsoverwanaka.co.nz*). Up, up and away! About 30 hot-air balloons from around the world take part in the **Genesis Wairarapa International Balloon Festival** (☎*04/473–8039* ⊕*www.nzballoons.co.nz*). The event finishes with a night glow, where balloons are lighted to show off their colors, and fireworks in Masterton's Solway Showgrounds. Auckland's **Round the Bays Run** (☎*09/360–3190* ⊕*www.roundthebays.co.nz*) is one of the world's largest 8.4-km (5.2-mi) fun runs. A few people are hard core but 70,000 participants run or walk the course in their own time. The event starts in the city, follows Tamaki Drive around the waterfront, and finishes in the plush suburb of St. Heliers.

Mar. or Apr.	The **Easter** holiday weekend lasts from Good Friday through Easter Monday. The **Royal Easter Show** (☎09/623–7724 ⊕*www.royaleastershow.co.nz*) is held at Auckland's Showgrounds over the holiday. It's the country's largest and most varied family festival.
Apr. 25	**Anzac Day** honors the soldiers, sailors, and airmen and women who fought and died for the country. This public holiday is marked by dawn parades around the country.
Late Apr.	The **Bluff Oyster and Southland Seafood Festival** (☎0800/272–687 ⊕*www.bluffoysterfest.co.nz*) stars the local specialty, the Bluff oyster.
Early May	The **Lion Foundation Rotorua Marathon** (☎09/570–2222 ⊕*www.rotoruamarathon.co.nz*) around Lake Rotorua is New Zealand's premier long-distance event at 42.2 km (26.2 mi). There's a fun run, too, or you can walk the course.
WINTER Late May–early June	The **Out Takes Gay & Lesbian Film Festival** (☎04/972–6775 ⊕*www.outtakes.org.nz*) is held in theaters in Auckland, Wellington, Dunedin, and Christchurch. The **Queen's Birthday** is celebrated nationwide on the first Monday in June.
Late July	At the **Queenstown Winter Festival** (☎03/441–2453 ⊕*www.winterfestival.co.nz*) the winter-sports capital hits the slopes for a week of competition by day and entertainment by night. The southern hemisphere's ultimate winter party takes place at Coronet Peak, Earnslaw Park, and Queenstown Bay; there are free and ticketed events.
Late Aug.	At the **Stewart Island Singles' Ball** (☎03/219–1400 ⊕*www.singlesball.co.nz*) Cinderella might find her handsome prince and her missing glass…gumboot? Rakiura residents throw a party at the community hall each August, replete with live music, a seafood smorgasbord, and a chance to meet your soul mate. So far no lasting relationships have resulted.
SPRING Mid-Sept.	The **42 Below Cocktail World Cup** (⊕*www.42below.com*) in Queenstown brings cocktail bar staff from top bars worldwide to mix it up in "extreme" cocktail making. Cocktails are stirred and shaken while the mixologists bungy (New Zealand spelling for bungee) jump, jet boat, and more. Tickets to Wellington's free-spirited **Montana World of WearableArt Awards** (⊕*www.worldofwearableart.com*) sell like hotcakes.

Last weekend in Oct.	**Dunedin Rhododendron Festival** (☎ *03/474–5162* ⊕ *www.rhododunedin.co.nz*) opens the city's gardens for tours and offers lectures and plant sales.
Oct. 23	**Labour Day** is observed throughout the country.
Late Oct.–early Nov.	**Taranaki Rhododendron & Garden Festival** (☎ *0800/746–363* ⊕ *www.rhodo.co.nz*) showcases gardens approved by the New Zealand Gardens Trust. As many as 45 private gardens are open to the public in cities including New Plymouth and Stratford, plus plant-o-philes can partake of guided walks, seminars, and other related events.
2nd week in Nov.	The **Canterbury Agricultural and Pastoral Show** (☎ *03/343–3033* ⊕ *www.theshow.co.nz*) spotlights the farmers and graziers of the rich countryside surrounding Christchurch.
Nov.	**Ellerslie Flower Show** (☎ *09/309–5000 tickets, 09/579–6260 info* ⊕ *www.ellerslieflowershow.co.nz*) in Auckland is one of the headline events on New Zealand's gardening calendar. It is modeled on London's Chelsea Flower Show. In a confusing twist, the show moved in 1998 from the suburb of Ellerslie to the Botanic Gardens at Manurewa, farther south, while retaining its old name. The city of Blenheim's six-day-long **Hunter's Garden Marlborough** (☎ *0800/627–527* ⊕ *www.garden-marlborough.co.nz*) has local garden tours and a Garden Fête with products for sale. Meet gardening luminaries and celebrity chefs, too. **Toast Martinborough Wine, Food & Music Festival** (☎ *04/473–4838* ⊕ *www.toastmartinborough.co.nz*) pours new releases and previously sold-out vintages that you pair with gourmet cuisine from the region's finest restaurants. Groove to top-flight music, too. Tickets are held for foreign guests.

Auckland

WORD OF MOUTH

"Our first activity was a visit to the Sky Tower. Since we are avid photographers it was fun to take photos all around the observation deck. We marveled at the courage of those who did the Sky Jump and the Sky Screamer that was next to the hotel."

—jeep61

"Drove over to the gannet colony and to Bethell's Beach, where apparently Xena was filmed. The black iron sands retain heat and also sparkle with bits of gold (pyrite I assume). Very beautiful and worth the drive."

—mlgb

Updated
by Richard
Pamatatau

AUCKLAND IS CALLED THE CITY OF SAILS, and visitors flying in will see why. On the East Coast is the Waitemata Harbour—a Māori word meaning sparkling waters—which is bordered by the Hauraki Gulf, an aquatic playground dotted with small islands where many Aucklanders can be found "mucking around in boats." Not surprising, Auckland City has some 70,000 boats. About one in four households in Auckland city has a seacraft of some kind and there are 102 beaches within an hour's drive; during the week many are quite empty. Even the airport is by the water; it borders the Manukau Harbour, which takes its name as well from the Māori language and means solitary bird.

According to Māori tradition, the Auckland isthmus was originally peopled by a race of giants and fairy folk. When Europeans arrived in the early 19th century, however, the Ngāti-Whatua tribe was firmly in control of the region. The British began negotiations with the Ngāti-Whatua in 1840 to purchase the isthmus and establish the colony's first capital. In September of that year the British flag was hoisted to mark the township's foundation, and Auckland remained the capital until 1865, when the seat of government was moved to Wellington. Aucklanders expected to suffer from the shift; it hurt their pride, but not their pockets. As the terminal for the South Sea shipping routes, Auckland was already an established commercial center. Since then the urban sprawl has made this city of approximately 1.3 million people one of the world's largest geographically.

A couple of days in the city will reveal just how developed and sophisticated Auckland is, though those seeking a New York in the South Pacific will be disappointed. Auckland is more get up and go outside rather than get dressed up and go out. That said, most shops are open daily, central bars and a few nightclubs buzz well into the wee hours especially Thursday through Saturday, and a mix of Māori, Pacific people, Asians, and Europeans contributes to the cultural milieu. Auckland has the world's largest single population of Pacific Islanders living outside their home countries, though many of them live outside the mainstream parts of the city and in Manukau to the south. Most Pacific people came to New Zealand seeking a better life, but when the plentiful, low-skilled work that attracted them here dried up, the dream soured and its population has suffered with poor health and poor education. Fortunately, policies are now addressing that and change is slowly being made. The Pacifica Festival in March though remains the region's biggest cultural event, attracting thousands to Western Springs.

At the geographical center of Auckland city is the 1,082-foot Sky Tower, a convenient landmark for those exploring on foot and some say a visible sign of the city's naked aspiration. It has earned nicknames like the needle and of course the Big Penis—a counterpoint perhaps to a verse in a poem by acclaimed New Zealand poet James K. Baxter who refers to Rangitoto, an island in the gulf, as a clitoris in the harbor.

The Waitemata Harbour has become better known since New Zealand staged its first defense of the America's Cup in 2000. The regatta was a catalyst for major redevelopment of the waterfront. The area, where

TOP REASONS TO GO

Boating & Sailing: Auckland is dubbed "City of Sails," and the population is crazy about boating and any other sea-related recreation. A variety of ferries and high-speed catamarans operate on Waitemata Harbour. Even better, go for a leisurely sail on the *Pride of Auckland,* or experience a genuine match race on America's Cup yachts with Sail NZ.

Cuisine & Café Culture: Some of the finest restaurants in the country reside in Auckland—and not just fine dining. The restaurant scene thrives from top-end down to bistro-cum-bars. Neighborhoods such as Ponsonby are crammed with vibrant eateries and cafés, their tables spilling onto the pavement, turning out fine fare for the discerning locals.

Year-Round Golf: Frank Nobilo's hometown, Auckland, has more than 20 golf courses, from informal and easygoing to challenging championship level designed by the likes of Sir Bob Charles and Alister MacKenzie. Most have beautiful scenery, some with views of the Hauraki Gulf. Golf is played year-round here, and the green fees are among the cheapest anywhere.

Gorgeous Beaches: The West Coast's black-sand beaches are best for surfing, whereas the safest swimming is on the East Coast. Beaches that have a reputation for large waves and rips are patrolled in the summer, so swim between the flags. The ozone layer is weak above New Zealand, so slap on the sunscreen.

many of the city's most popular bars, cafés, and restaurants are found, is now known as Viaduct Basin or, more commonly, the Viaduct. On New Year's Eve it becomes a sea of people getting very kissy.

These days, Auckland is considered too bold and brash for its own good by many Kiwis who live "south of the Bombay Hills," the geographical divide between Auckland and the rest of New Zealand (barring Northland). "Jafa," an acronym for "just another f—ing Aucklander," has entered the local lexicon; there's even a book out called *Way of the Jafa: A Guide to Surviving Auckland and Aucklanders.* A common complaint is that Auckland absorbs the wealth from the hard work of the rest of the country. Most Aucklanders, on the other hand, shrug and see it as the parochial envy of those who live in small towns. But these internal identity squabbles aren't your problem. You can enjoy a well-made coffee in almost any café, or take a walk on a beach—knowing that within 30 minutes' driving time you could be cruising the spectacular harbor, playing a round at a public golf course, or even walking in subtropical forest while listening to the song of a native *tūī bird.*

ORIENTATION & PLANNING

GETTING ORIENTED

The Auckland region is geographically diverse, and Auckland City sits on an isthmus between the Waitemata and Manukau harbors. At its narrowest point the isthmus is only 1 km (½ mi) wide. The Orakei and Panmure basins are actually large explosion craters that have been invaded by the sea. Like many parts of the country, there's plenty of rural activity on the easy rolling terrain outside the central suburban areas. The many islands of the Hauraki Gulf offer the chance to explore by sea.

The drive from the airport, once you pass some industrial parks, presents the other image of New Zealand—clean and green with the landscape dominated by the city's 50 or so volcanic hills, many set aside as parks with their grassy flanks shorn by sheep. And reading the highway signs will begin to give you a taste of the unusual and sometimes hard-to-say Māori place-names.

Central Business District. Aucklanders see the central business district as beginning at the waterfront and around Queen Street.

Parnell. To the east of the city center and bounded by Newmarket and Hobson Bay, this district has a wealth of historic buildings, chic restaurants, and urban and water views. Along with Ponsonby, this is the neighborhood where you'll most likely spot someone famous—one of the many film actors who slip into Auckland or a local celebrity.

Ponsonby. Narrow streets are lined with wooden Victorian villas that were once home to the working classes and now owned by many with big mortgages and nostalgia for old buildings. Its main strip is lined with cafés, bars, and restaurants.

Karangahape Road. To the west of the center and merging with the expensive gentrified suburbs of St. Mary's Bay and Herne Bay, is Karangahape Road, or K Road, which has a colorful mix of shops and cheap eateries. What once was seedy is now quite trendy with a host of clubs for those seeking evening activity from trance and hip-hop to lip-synching gender-surfing transvestites. Auckland's gay nightclubs are around here, too.

Newmarket. This is one of the better areas for buying local and overseas designers. Nearby is the Domain—a significant city park with good walking and a range of sculpture.

Remuera. Close to the Domain is the tony suburb of Remuera where people who style themselves as "old money" like to live.

North Shore. The Auckland Harbour Bridge spans the Waitemata Harbour, connecting the city with the highway and the North Shore, where more suburbs sprawl along a coast of safe swimming beaches. Those who live "on the shore" see themselves as more relaxed than their city counterparts, and with more industry on this side of the Harbour Bridge they can work closer to home.

AUCKLAND PLANNER

WHEN TO GO

Auckland's weather can be unpredictable and there's a song by New Zealand band Crowded House that sums it up—*Four Seasons in One Day*. But don't let that put you off; there is always something to do whatever the weather. As a rule of thumb, the warmest months are December through April and a sun hat is a good idea. Winter kicks in about July running through October. It can be humid in summer and quite chilly in winter. It often rains, so be prepared.

GETTING HERE & AROUND

BY AIR

Auckland International Airport (AKL) lies 21 km (13 mi) southwest of the city center, about a 30-minute drive away. It has adopted a "quiet airport" policy, so it doesn't use loudspeakers to announce boarding times. Look for flight info.

A free inter-terminal bus links the international and domestic terminals, with frequent departures in each direction, 6 AM–10 PM. Otherwise, the walk between the two terminals takes about 10 minutes. Luggage for flights aboard the two major domestic airlines, Air New Zealand and Qantas Airways, can be checked at the international terminal.

Air New Zealand and Qantas are the main domestic carriers serving Auckland. Air New Zealand connects with about 25 domestic cities a day, and makes about 10 flights a day to Australia. Qantas connects with five domestic cities daily and crosses the Tasman 20 times a day. Air Tahiti Nui stops off in Auckland on its L.A. and New York runs.

Airport **Auckland International Airport** (✉ *Fred Thomas Dr., Manukau* ☎ *09/275-0789* ⊕ *www.auckland-airport.co.nz*).

AIRPORT TRANSFERS The Airbus costs $15 one-way and $22 round-trip and leaves the international terminal every 20 minutes between 6 AM and 6 PM, then every 30 minutes until 10 PM. The route between the airport and the Ferry Building at 180 Quay Street includes, on request, a stop at any bus stop, hotel, or motel along the way. The trip takes 60 minutes. Returning from the city, the bus leaves the Ferry Building at 20-minute intervals between 5 AM and 6 PM, and then every 30 minutes until 8:50 PM.

Hallmark Limousines and Tours operates Ford LTD limousines between the airport and the city for approximately $110, and Lincoln limousines for around $280.

Super Shuttle has service between the airport and any address in the city center. The cost is $22 for a single traveler and $5 extra for each additional person. The Shuttle picks up several parties on the way to the airport, so allow an hour's traveling time.

Taxi fare to the city is around $45 to $50. There are always plenty of taxis waiting at the ranks directly outside the terminal.

Contacts **Airbus** (☎ *0508/247–287* ⊕ *www.airbus.co.nz*). **Hallmark Limousines and Tours** (☎ *09/629–0940*). **Super Shuttle** (☎ *09/522–5100*).

BY BOAT & FERRY

Various companies serve Waitemata Harbour; one of the best and least expensive is Fullers. The ferry terminal is on the harbor side of the Ferry Building on Quay Street, near the corner of Albert Street. Boats leave here for Devonport Monday–Thursday 6:15 AM–11 PM, Friday and Saturday 6:15 AM–1 AM, and Sunday 7:15 AM–10 PM at half-hour intervals, except for one 45-minute interval between the 9:15 AM and 10 AM sailings. From 8 PM Monday through Thursday and from 7 PM on Sunday they sail on the hour. The cost is $9 round-trip. However, a better deal is to buy the Auckland Day Pass for $10, which gets you a return sailing and unlimited travel on Link buses to boot. Ferries also make the 35-minute run to Waiheke Island from 5:30 AM to 11:45 PM at a cost of $26 round-trip. Return ferries leave every hour on the hour, and every half hour at peak commuter times. SeaLink runs car and passenger ferries to Waiheke, leaving from Half Moon Bay to the east of the city. The round-trip fare is $113 per car, plus $28.50 for each adult.

Contacts **Fullers Booking Office** (✉ *Ferry Bldg., Quay St.* ☎ *09/367-9111* ⊕ *www.fullers.co.nz*). **SeaLink** (✉ *Ara-Tai Dr., Half Moon Bay* ☎ *09/300-5900* ⊕ *www.sealink.co.nz*).

BY BUS

AROUND AUCKLAND
The Sky City Coach Terminal is Auckland's hub for the two main bus lines, InterCity Coaches and Newmans Coaches. The terminal has secure storage lockers and a café next door. InterCity links Auckland to most other major cities at least once a day. Newmans goes to Wellington daily via Hamilton and Taupo, and to Rotorua and Napier daily. Auckland is also a jumping-off point for several of InterCity's special travel pass routes, with daily departures for trips such as "Forests, Islands, and Geysers" and "New Zealand Pathfinder."

Kiwi Experience goes to many more out-of-the-way destinations such as the East Cape. You can get a "Funky Chicken" round-trip pass that allows you to hop on and off where you please along the route. The buses depart Auckland from the Parnell office.

The Northliner Express goes to both Kaitaia and Kaikohe twice daily. It departs from 172 Quay Street, opposite the Ferry Building.

Bus Depot **Sky City Coach Terminal** (✉ *102 Hobson St., City Center* ☎ *09/300-6130*).

Bus Lines **InterCity Coaches** (☎ *09/623-1503* ⊕ *www.intercitycoach.co.nz*). **Kiwi Experience** (✉ *195-197 Parnell Rd., Parnell* ☎ *09/366-9830* ⊕ *www.kiwi experience.co.nz*). **Newmans Coaches** (☎ *09/623-1504* ⊕ *www.newmanscoach. co.nz*). **Northliner Express** (☎ *09/307-5873* ⊕ *www.northliner.co.nz*).

WITHIN AUCKLAND
The easily recognizable white Link Buses circle the inner city, including many of the most popular stops for visitors, every 10 minutes between 6 AM and 7 PM weekdays, and then every 15 minutes until about 11:30 PM. The same service applies on weekends but starts at 7 AM and runs to 6 PM. The route includes the Britomart Centre between Customs Street and Quay Street, and buses stop at Queen Street, Parnell, Newmar-

ket (near the Auckland Museum), Ponsonby, and Karangahape Road, among other places. The fare anywhere on the route is $1.50, payable as you get onto the bus; you should have change or small notes. A free red-color bus circuits the inner city between Britomart, the university, and the Sky Tower every 10 minutes between 8 AM and 6 PM daily.

To travel farther afield, take a Stagecoach Bus, which is run by the same company as the Link Buses and has services as far north as Orewa on the Hibiscus Coast and south to Pukekohe. An Auckland Day Pass at $11 for unlimited travel is easily the best value for anyone planning extensive use of the buses (both Link and Stagecoach), particularly because it is also valid for travel on Link ferries between the city and the North Shore. The Discovery Pass ($14) also includes the local trains. You can buy the passes from the ferry office or the bus drivers. The information office at Britomart provides information, maps, and timetables, or you can call Maxx for transit details.

Contacts **Information Office** (⊠ *Britomart Transport Centre, Queen Elizabeth Sq., Queen and Quay Sts., City Center*). **Maxx** (☎ *09/366–6400* ⊕ *www.maxx.co.nz*).

BY CAR

Local rush hours last from 7 to 9 AM and 4:30 to 6:30 PM. The main motorways all have convenient city turnoffs, but watch the signs to make sure you are in the correct lane. When changing lanes, flick on your indicator promptly, as New Zealanders are not always the most obliging when it comes to merging.

City-center parking meters are cheaper than the covered lots, but make sure you have a wide selection of coins and be aware that the meters are well policed. Meter time is generally limited to an hour in the city center, two hours in outer areas. For parking lots, a good one to try is the underground Civic lot by the Aotea Centre, Town Hall, Sky City Metro Centre, and the Civic Theatre. Drive in from Greys Avenue or Albert Street, right behind the Aotea Centre. After 5 PM you pay a flat rate of $8; before 5, the rate is approximately $4.50 per hour. The Downtown lot, opposite the Viaduct and Princes Wharf, has the same rates as the Civic. The entrance is at Customs Street West.

Avis, Budget, and Hertz have offices inside the Auckland International Airport. They stay open for all incoming flights.

Parking Lots **Civic Car Park** (⊠ *Greys Ave. and Mayoral Dr.* ☎ *09/379–6035*). **Downtown Car Park** (⊠ *31 Customs St. W* ☎ *09/309–6007*).

Rental Agencies **Avis** (☎ *09/275–7239*). **Budget** (☎ *09/256–8451*). **Hertz** (☎ *09/256–8695*).

BY TAXI

Auckland taxi rates vary with the company. Most are around $2 per kilometer (½ mi), but some charge as much as $4. Flag-fall, when the meters start, is usually $2. The rates are listed on the driver's door. Most taxis accept major credit cards.

Taxi Companies **Alert Taxis** (☎09/309–2000). **Auckland Cooperative Taxi Service** (☎09/300–3000). **Corporate Cabs** (☎09/377–0773). **Eastern Taxis** (☎09/527–7077).

BY TRAIN

The terminal for all InterCity train services is the Britomart Transport Centre at Queen Elizabeth Square, on the harbor end of Queen Street. There's a booking office at Britomart.

Contact **Britomart Transport Centre** (✉Queen Elizabeth Sq., Queen and Quay Sts. ☎09/374–3873).

EMERGENCIES

For off-hours over-the-counter needs, hit the After-Hours Pharmacy, which stays open weekdays from 6 PM to 1 AM and weekends 9 AM to 1 AM.

Emergency Services **Fire, police, and ambulance** (☎111).

Hospitals **Auckland Hospital** (✉Park Rd., Grafton ☎09/367–0000). **MercyAscot Hospital** (✉90 Greenland Rd. E, Remuera ☎09/520–9555 or 09/520–9500).

Late-Night Pharmacy **After-Hours Pharmacy** (✉60 Broadway, Newmarket ☎09/520–6634).

VISITOR INFORMATION

The main bureau of Auckland's visitor center is open 8 to 8 daily. The branch in the airport opens daily at 5 AM and stays open until the last flight arrives. The branch at the Viaduct Harbour is open 9 to 5 daily. The Devonport visitor center is open weekdays 8 to 5, and 8:30 to 5 on weekends.

The Thursday *Auckland Tourist Times* is a free newspaper with the latest information on tours, exhibitions, and shopping. The paper is available from hotels and from visitor centers.

For information on the Hauraki Gulf islands, marine reserves, and other conservation areas, check in with the Department of Conservation Visitor Centre, open on weekdays from 9:30 to 5.

Contacts **Auckland International Airport Visitor Centre** (✉Ground fl., International Airport Terminal ☎09/275–6467 🖷09/256–8942). **Auckland i-Site Visitor Centre** (✉Atrium, Sky City, Victoria and Federal Sts. ☎09/363–7182 🖷09/363–7181 ⊕www.aucklandnz.com). **Department of Conservation Visitor Centre** (✉Ferry Bldg., Quay St. ☎09/379–6476 ⊕www.doc.govt.nz). **Devonport i-Site Visitor Centre** (✉3 Victoria Rd., Devonport ☎09/446–0677 ⊕www. tourismnorthshore.org.nz). **Takapuna i-Site Visitor Centre** (✉49 Hurstmere Rd., Takapuna ☎09/486–8670 ⊕www.tourismnorthshore.org.nz). **New Zealand Visitor Centre** (✉Princes Wharf ☎09/367–6009 ⊕www.aucklandnz.com). **Arataki Visitor Centre** (✉5 km [3 mi] past Titirangi town center ☎09/817–0077 ⊕www.arc. govt.nz). **Kumeu and District Visitor Centre** (✉Main Rd., Kumeu ☎09/412–9886 ⊕www.kumeuinfo.co.nz).

EXPLORING AUCKLAND

You can get around city center——close to the harbor, Ponsonby, Devonport, and Parnell——on foot, by bus, and by ferry. Elsewhere, Auckland is not as easy to explore. The neighborhoods and suburbs sprawl from the Waitemata and Manukau harbors to rural areas, and you can get confused by complicated roads and heavy traffic. It's best to have a car for getting around between neighborhoods, and even between some city-center sights. What might look like easy walking distances on maps can turn out to be 20- to 30-minute treks, and stringing a few of those together can get frustrating.

If you're nervous about driving on the left, especially when you first arrive, purchase a one-day Link Bus Pass that covers the inner-city neighborhoods or, for a circuit of the main sights, an Explorer Bus Pass, and take a bus to get acquainted with the city layout. Getting around Auckland by bus is easy and inexpensive. The region's bus services are coordinated through the Maxx Service, which also coordinates trains and ferries; its Web site can provide you with door-to-door information, including bus route numbers. For trips around the central business district (CBD) and close suburbs there is the Link bus service. For journeys farther afield buses can be boarded in all the main suburban centers and at bus stops along the way.

CITY CENTER & PARNELL

Auckland's city center includes the port area, much of it reclaimed from the sea in the latter half of the 19th century. You'll find a market close to the foot of town on weekends. Successive city administrators neglected Auckland's older buildings, so Queen Street and its surrounds are a mix of glass tower office buildings and a dwindling number of older, some say more gracious, buildings. Tucked away in Lorne and High streets, running parallel with Queen Street, are good examples of the city's early architecture, now home to the shops of some of New Zealand's leading fashion designers. The central business district (CBD) has been energized by a residential surge since the late 1990s, boosted by apartment development and an influx of Asian students. The Auckland Domain and Parnell areas are where you'll find the city's preeminent museums as well as historic homes and shops. Parnell was Auckland's first suburb, established in 1841, and is a good place to look for arts and crafts or sample some of Auckland's most popular cafés, bars, and restaurants.

A dozen "city ambassadors" patrol the city center on weekdays between 8:30 and 5; they can give you directions and field questions you might have. They're identified by their yellow and gray uniforms with "ambassador" written on their tops in red.

WHAT TO SEE

❹ Albert Park. These 15 acres of formal gardens, fountains, and statue-studded lawns are a favorite for Aucklanders who pour out of nearby office buildings and the university and polytechnic to eat lunch and

TOURING THE TOWN

Several companies offer city orientation tours or special-interest excursions outside town.

BOAT TOURS

Fullers (☎09/367–9111 ⊕www.fullers.co.nz) cruises around the harbor and to the islands of Hauraki Gulf. The 1½-hour Auckland Harbor cruise ($31), with commentary and bar, departs daily at 10:30 and 1:30. There's also a Waiheke Island Explorer tour, for $42, which stops at Onetangi Beach, and a Waiheke Vineyard Explorer trip for $85. Some trips are seasonal; reservations are essential in summer. Boats leave from the Ferry Building.

The **Pride of Auckland Company** (☎09/373–4557 ⊕www.pride ofauckland.com) sails the inner harbor. The 1½-hour lunch cruise ($73) departs at 1, and the 2½-hour dinner cruise ($95) departs at 7 from the Maritime Museum, near Princes Wharf.

BUS TOURS

The white double-decker **Explorer Bus** (☎0800/439–756 ⊕www.explorerbus.co.nz) travels in a circuit, stopping at nine city attractions; you can hop on and off anywhere along the way. Buses begin at the Ferry Building between 9 and 4 daily. Buy tickets from the driver or at the Fullers office in the Ferry Building. A day pass is $30.

Scenic Tours (☎09/307–7880 ⊕www.scenictours.co.nz) operates a three-hour Auckland Highlights guided bus tour that leaves from Quay Street, just across from the Ferry Building, at 9:15, and tickets are $55.

WILDERNESS TOURS

Auckland Adventures (☎09/379–4545 or 0274/855–856 ⊕www.aucklandadventures.co.nz) has one half-day ($85) and two daylong tours ($120) that go to the summit of Mt. Eden, head out west to visit at least one winery and then on to Muriwai beach to see a gannet colony.

Bush and Beach Ltd. (☎09/575–1458 ⊕www.bushandbeach.co.nz) runs daily afternoon tours ($110) through the Waitakere Ranges and out to a west-coast beach, such as Karekare Beach. A daylong tour ($155) spends the morning visiting Auckland highlights before heading out to the Waitakere Ranges.

Harvey's Safaris (⌖ Auckland ☎0800/VEG–OIL toll-free in New Zealand, 0064-27/383–7603 ⊕www.harveysafaris.com) offer tours of Auckland and its West Coast beaches in a luxury, seven-seater, biofuel-powered coach.

WINE TOURS

Auckland Wine Tours (☎09/575–1958 ⊕www.aucklandwinetours.co.nz) run about four hours and are based around wine-growing areas to Auckland's north and west plus Waiheke Island.

Fine Wine Tours (☎09/849–4519 or 021/626–529 ⊕www.insidertouring.co.nz), offers a four-hour West Auckland tour ($139) that takes in three wineries and includes a picnic lunch, and a full-day Matakana tour ($239) with four wineries and lunch at the Ascension winery café.

lounge under trees on sunny days. Good cafés in the university make a range of take-away food and coffee. The park is built on the site of a garrison from the 1840s and '50s that protected settlers from neighboring Māori tribes. There are remnants of its stone walls (with rifle slits) behind university buildings on the park's east side. ⊠ *Bounded by Wellesley St. W, Kitchener St., Waterloo Quad, City Center.*

❸ ★ Auckland Art Gallery Toi o Tāmaki. The Auckland Art Gallery has some 14,000 items in it dating from the 12th century. The châteaulike main gallery, built in the 1880s and now being renovated, holds many of the historic paintings, whereas the **New Gallery** across the street shows temporary exhibitions. With the renovations underway this will be home to much of the collection and exhibitions. Portraits of Māori chiefs by C.F. Goldie and Gottfried Lindauer offer an ethnocentric view of people who some say were seen too one-sidedly as a fiercely martial people. Goldie used sitters introduced to him by friends, often using the same sitters repeatedly—odd, considering he aimed to document what he considered a dying race. Keep an eye out for *The Arrival of the Māoris in New Zealand,* which Goldie painted with his teacher, Louis John Steele, basing the work on Theodore Géricault's *Raft of the Medusa.* The big painting is full of inaccuracies—the figures are not like Māori and they're in a type of *waka* (war canoe) not built until they settled in New Zealand—but it was a hit at the time and launched Goldie's career. New Zealand artists to keep an eye out for are Frances Hodgkins, Doris Lusk, and Colin McCahon. There are free collection tours daily at 2 pm. ⊠ *5 Kitchener St., at Wellesley St. E, City Center* ☎ *09/307-7700* ⊕ *www.aucklandartgallery.govt.nz* ⊠ *Heritage Gallery free, except for special exhibits; New Gallery $7. Both galleries free Mon.* ⊙ *Daily 10–5.*

NEED A BREAK?
Reflect on your gallery visit from one of the balconies virtually suspended in the treetops at **Reuben** (⊠ *New Gallery, Kitchener and Wellesley Sts.* ☎ *09/302-0226* ⊙ *Closed Sun.*). Bite into a fried-egg sandwich with *harissa* (Tunisian hot-chili paste) and crispy pancetta, or the classic Reuben. Glasses of wine are reasonably priced.

⓫ Auckland Domain. Saturday cricketers, Sunday picnickers, and morning runners are three types of Aucklanders you'll see enjoying the rolling, 340-acre park—not to mention loads of walkers, particularly the "Remuera Bobs," women with husbands earning fat salaries who like their wives trim and young looking. Watch the local paper for free summer weekend-evening concerts, which usually include opera and fireworks displays. Take a bottle of wine and a basket of something tasty and join in with the locals—up to 300,000 of them per show. Within the Domain, the domed **Wintergardens** (open daily 10–4) house a collection of tropical plants and palms and seasonally displayed hothouse plants—a good stop for the horticulturally inclined. There is some magnificent sculpture in the Domain. ⊠ *Entrances at Stanley St., Park Rd., Carlton Gore Rd., and Maunsell Rd.* ⊠ *Free* ⊙ *24 hrs.*

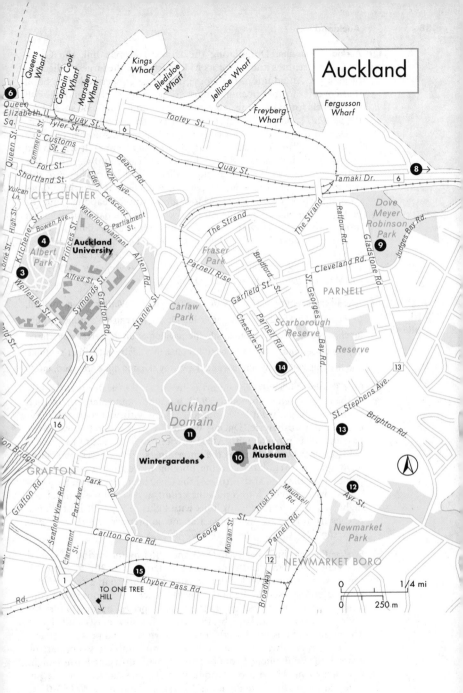

⑩ Auckland Museum. Dominating the Domain atop a hill, the Greek
★ Revival museum is known for its Māori artifacts, the largest collection
☺ of its kind. An addition, the Dome, is a large copper-and-glass hood
that covers a former open-air court in the center of the building with
three levels for exhibitions, entertainment, and lectures. Be sure to see
the *pātaka,* or storehouse; these structures were a fixture in Māori villages, and this pātaka is one of the finest examples. Another must-see
is "Te Toki a Tapiri," the last great Māori *waka* (canoe). It was carved
from a single log, and, at 85 feet long, could carry 100 warriors. The
figurehead shows off their carving abilities. To delve further into this
culture, attend one of the Māori performances held at least three times
daily; the show demonstrates Māori song, dance, weaponry, and the
haka (a ceremonial dance the All Blacks rugby team has adopted as an
intimidating pregame warm-up). The museum offers a changing menu
of world-class exhibitions and is strong on Pacific material. There's also
an extensive collection of musical instruments. ✉*Auckland Domain,
Park Rd.* ☎*09/309–0443* ⊕*www.aucklandmuseum.com* ✐*$5; $15
for Māori cultural performance* ⊙*Daily 10–5.*

**NEED A
BREAK?**
Take in the scenery at **The Pavilion on Domain** (✉*Wintergarden Pavilion,
Domain Dr., Auckland Domain* ☎*09/303–0627*). You can have brunch, a light
lunch, or coffee from a table inside the pavilion or on the terrace overlooking the duck ponds. Try the smoked fish dish in a pastry with other seafood,
and the chips with mayonnaise and the crispy skinned duck are good, too.

❶ Civic Theatre. This extravagant art nouveau movie theater was the talk
★ of the town when it opened in 1929, but nine months later the owner,
Thomas O'Brien, went bust and fled, taking with him the week's rev-
enues and an usherette. During World War II a cabaret show in the
basement was popular with Allied servicemen in transit to the battlefields of the Pacific. One of the entertainers, Freda Stark, is said to
have appeared regularly wearing nothing more than a coat of gold
paint—now the café at the front of the Civic bears her name. Sit down
to a show or movie, look up to the ceiling and you'll see a simulated
night sky, and on stage giant lions with lights for eyes. It hosts dance
parties from time to time as well as movie premieres. ✉*Queen and
Wellesley Sts., City Center* ☎*09/307–5075.*

⑫ Ewelme Cottage. Built between 1863 and 1864 by the curiously named
Reverend Vicesimus Lush (*vicesimus* is Latin for "20th," his birth
order) and inhabited by his descendants for more than a century, this
historic cottage stands behind a picket fence. The house was constructed of kauri, a resilient timber highly prized by the Māori for
their war canoes and later by Europeans for ship masts and floors.
The home contains much of the original furniture and personal effects
of the Lush family. You have to duck as you climb the steep, narrow
stairs to the small pitched-roof bedrooms, made up as the Lushes might
have left them. The drawing room, veranda, and garden appeared in
Jane Campion's film *The Piano.* ✉*14 Ayr St., Parnell* ☎*09/379–0202*
✐*$7.50* ⊙*Fri.–Sun. 10:30–noon and 1–4:30.*

6 **Ferry Building.** This magnificent Edwardian building continues to stand out on Auckland's waterfront. The 1912 building is still used for its original purpose, and it's here that you can catch the ferry to Devonport as well as to Waiheke and other Hauraki Gulf islands. The building also houses bars and restaurants—more recent additions. Nearby, and easily seen from the Ferry Building, is Marsden Wharf, where French frogmen bombed and sank the Greenpeace vessel *Rainbow Warrior* in 1985. ⊠ *Quay St., City Center.*

8 **Kelly Tarlton's Underwater World and Antarctic Encounter.** The creation of New Zealand's most celebrated undersea explorer and treasure hunter *(see the Kelly Tarlton CloseUp box)*, this harborside marine park offers a fish's-eye view of the sea. A transparent tunnel, 120 yards long, makes a circuit past moray eels, lobsters, sharks, and stingrays. In Antarctic Encounter, you enter a reproduction of explorer Robert Falcon Scott's 1911 Antarctic hut at McMurdo Sound, then circle around a deep-freeze environment aboard a heated Sno-Cat (snowmobile) that winds through a penguin colony and an aquarium exhibiting marine life of the polar sea. You emerge at Scott Base 2000, where you can see a copy of the Antarctic Treaty and flags of all the countries involved, as well as some scientific research equipment currently used in Antarctica. You can also dive with the sharks after taking a course and also feed various fish. ⊠ *Orakei Wharf, 23 Tamaki Dr., 5 km (3 mi) east of downtown Auckland* ☎ *09/528–0603* ⊕ *www.kellytarltons.co.nz* ☞ *$29.50* ☺ *Daily 9–6, last admission at 5.*

Fodor's Choice
★

15 **Lionzone.** Lion Beer doesn't have the international recognition of Guinness or Budweiser, but it's a Kiwi icon all the same. A tour takes you through the brewing process and the bottling and packaging hall. There's a chance to taste the company's Lion Red or Steinlager at the end of the tour. ⊠ *380 Khyber Pass Rd., Newmarket* ☎ *09/358–8366* ⊕ *www. lionzone.co.nz* ☞ *$15* ☺ *Tours Mon.–Sat. at 9:30, 12:15, and 3.*

7 **National Maritime Museum.** Plunge into New Zealand's rich seafaring history in this marina complex on Auckland Harbour. Experience what it was like to travel steerage class in the 1800s in a simulated rocking cabin, or check out a reproduction of a shipping office from the turn of the last century. There are detailed exhibits on early whaling and a superb collection of yachts, ship models, and Polynesian outriggers—not to mention *KZ1*, the 133-foot racing sloop built for the America's Cup challenge in 1988. A scow conducts short harbor trips twice a day on Tuesday, Thursday, and weekends and there's a wharf-side eatery. You can also wander to the adjacent Viaduct Basin and look at the yachts of the seriously rich people moored there. This is where the software magnate Larry Ellison kept his boat during the America's Cup race series. ⊠ *Eastern Viaduct, Quay St., City Center* ☎ *09/373–0800* ⊕ *www.nzmaritime.org* ☞ *$12, harbor trip $15 extra* ☺ *Oct.–Easter, daily 9–6; Easter–Sept., daily 9–5.*

One Tree Hill. The largest of Auckland's extinct volcanoes and one of the best lookout points, One Tree Hill, or Maungakiekie, was the site of three Māori *pā* (fortifications). The hill is not as distinctive as it once

Kelly Tarlton

"Diver, dreamer, explorer, inventor, instigator, worker, storyteller, father, a man who linked us all with his love of the sea." This inscription on the bust of the celebrated figure that stands in the eponymous Kelly Tarlton's Underwater World reveals something of the man whose charisma and vision knit together a team of fellow adventurers.

In 1956 Kelly Tarlton was set to join a climbing expedition to the Andes. When political unrest in Peru canceled the trip, he was left at loose ends. Bored, he went to see the Jacques Cousteau film *Silent World* and thought diving looked like more fun than climbing, with no politics to worry about. With typical Kiwi No. 8 fencing wire ingenuity (aka a do-it-yourself mentality), he built much of his own diving gear, got an underwater camera, and devised housings for the camera and flash.

In the 1960s, Tarlton focused on photographing marine life. In 1967 a trip to the Three Kings Islands to photograph and collect marine specimens whetted his appetite for treasure hunting. He and companion Wade Doak found the wreck of the *Elingamite*, which had foundered on the islands in 1902 with thousands of pounds in gold bullion on board, much of which they recovered.

One of Tarlton's most celebrated finds was the jewels of Isodore Rothschild on the *Tasmania*, which had sunk in 1897. Through his characteristic detailed research, Tarlton pinpointed the whereabouts of the wreck and succeeded in salvaging most of the jewelry in the late 1970s. The treasure was put on display in his now defunct Museum of Shipwrecks in Paihia but was then stolen by a staff member.

Though the thief was imprisoned, he has never revealed the jewelry's fate.

Tarlton's interest broadened to marine archaeology. His first major success was finding the first de Surville anchor. Jean François Marie de Surville sailed the *St. Jean Baptiste* into Doubtless Bay in the Far North in 1769, where three of his anchors were lost in a storm. Tarlton plotted their whereabouts from crew accounts of the ship's dangerous proximity to a "big rock" and its position "a pistol shot" from shore, and by calculating the magnetic variations and wind directions from the original maps. The anchor is now in Wellington's Te Papa Museum.

But Tarlton is perhaps best known for the aquarium he built on Auckland's waterfront. Not having the funds to buy ready-molded acrylic to build his planned transparent viewing tunnels, Tarlton said that if he could mold his own camera housings, he could create his own tunnels, too. And do it he did, with a team of skilled and loyal friends, building an "oven" for the molding and inventing a new gluing technique to form the curving tunnels.

Opened in January 1985, the aquarium was a huge success. After only seven weeks Tarlton shook the hand of the 100,000th visitor, an image captured in the last photo of him. Tragically, he died that very night, at the age of 47, of a heart complication.

–Toni Mason

was, though; its signature lone pine was attacked several times by activists who saw it as a symbol of colonialism, and in 2000 it was taken down. Sir John Logan Campbell, founding father of the city, is buried on the summit. There is fantastic walking and running in the parklands with avenues of oaks, a kauri plantation, and an old olive grove. Free electronic barbecue sites are also on offer. Because the park is a working farm of sheep and cattle, paths take you through the fields and at times you'll need to be wary of the cows with their calves. There's also a cricket club with old-style seating if you want to sit and watch a game in summer and a pavilion where you can buy refreshments. ⊠ *Greenlane Rd. W.*

⑨ **Parnell Rose Gardens.** When you tire of boutiques and cafés, take a 10-minute stroll to gaze upon and sniff this collection of some 5,000 rosebushes. The main beds contain mostly modern hybrids, with new introductions being planted regularly. The adjacent **Nancy Steen Garden** is the place to admire the antique varieties. And don't miss the garden's incredible trees. There is a 200-year-old *pohutukawa* (puh-hoo-too-*ka*-wa) whose weighty branches touch the ground and rise up again, and a *kanuka* that is one of Auckland's oldest trees. In summer it's a popular site for wedding photographs. ⊠ *Parnell* 🖾 *Free* ☉ *Daily dawn–dusk.*

⑭ **Parnell Village.** The pretty Victorian timber villas along the slope of
★ Parnell Road have been transformed into antiques shops, designer boutiques, cafés, and restaurants. Parnell Village is the creation of Les Harvey, who saw the potential of the old, run-down shops and houses and almost single-handedly snatched them from the jaws of the developers' bulldozers in the early 1960s by buying them, renovating them, and leasing them out. Harvey's vision has paid handsome dividends, and today this village of trim pink-and-white timber facades is one of the most delightful parts of the city. At night, the area's restaurants and bars attract Auckland's upmarket set. There are some very good jewelry stores in Parnell including Hartfields in the center of the main strip. ⊠ *Parnell Rd. between St. Stephen's Ave. and Augustus Rd., Parnell.*

⑬ **St. Mary's Church in Holy Trinity.** Gothic Revival wooden churches don't get much finer than this one. Built in 1886, it was commissioned by the early Anglican missionary Bishop Selwyn. The craftsmanship inside the kauri church is remarkable, down to the hand-finished columns. One of the carpenters left his trademark, an owl, sitting in the beams to the right of the pulpit. If you stand in the pulpit and clasp the lectern, you'll feel something lumpy under your left hand—a mouse, the trademark of another of the craftsmen who made the lectern, the so-called Mouse Man of Kilburn. The story of the church's relocation is also remarkable. St. Mary's originally stood on the other side of Parnell Road, and in 1982 the entire structure was moved across the street to be next to the new church, the Cathedral of the Holy Trinity. ⊠ *Parnell Rd. and St. Stephen's Ave., Parnell* ☉ *Daily 8–6.*

❷ **Sky City Metro Centre.** With design concepts that could be from a science-fiction movie (actually, some are), the Metro Centre is worth a

Volcano Views

Auckland is built on and around 48 volcanoes, and the tops provide sweeping views of the city. **One Tree Hill,** the largest of Auckland's extinct volcanoes, was the site of an early Māori settlement. **Mt. Eden,** the highest volcano on the Auckland isthmus, is probably the most popular, and several bus tours include this central site. **Rangitoto Island** has an even better vista. This volcano emerged from the sea 600 years ago, no doubt much to the wonder of the Māori people living next door on Motutapu Island. Take a ferry to the island; then either a short ride or an hour's walk to the top will give you a 360-degree view of the city and the Hauraki Gulf islands. It's thought that Māori settled on the volcanoes beginning in the 14th century, taking advantage of the fertile soils. There's evidence that in the 16th century, the Māori used the cones as defensive *pā* (fortified villages). Evidence of complex earthworks can be seen on Mt. Eden and One Tree Hill where Māori cleared volcanic stone to develop garden plots and formed the terraces that are features of *pā*.

look even if you don't intend to partake in its entertainment. Spiral staircases, bridges designed to look like film, and elevators in the shape of rockets regularly attract design and architecture students—as well as hordes of teenagers. The Metro Centre incorporates a 13-screen cineplex, an international food court with good food, especially Asian, and several bars, including the **Playhouse Pub,** an English-style tavern with a Shakespearean theme. A video arcade, bookstore, and photo developer add to the mix. ✉ *291–297 Queen St., City Center* ☉ *Daily 9 AM–midnight.*

⑤ Sky Tower. This 1,082-foot beacon is the first place many Aucklanders take visiting friends to give them a view of the city. Up at the main observation level, the most outrageous thing is the glass floor panels—looking down at your feet, you see the street hundreds of yards below. Adults step gingerly onto the glass, and kids delight in jumping up and down on it. There's also an outdoor observation level. Through glass panels in the floor of the elevator you can see the counterweight fly up to pass you. For an adrenaline rush you can even take a controlled leap off **Sky Jump,** a 630-foot observation deck, for a steep $195. ✉ *Victoria and Federal Sts., City Center* ☎ *09/912–6000* 🎫 *$18* ☉ *Sun.–Thurs. 8:30 AM–11 PM, last elevator 10:30 PM; Fri. and Sat. 8:30 AM–midnight, last elevator 11:30 PM.*

WESTERN SPRINGS

Auckland Zoo. Since the 1990s, this zoo has focused on providing its animals with the most natural habitats possible, as well as on breeding and conservation. The primates area, sea lion and penguin shores, and the Pridelands section, where lions, giraffes, zebra, springbok, rhino, and ostriches range in savannalike grasslands, best exemplify this approach. To catch a glimpse of New Zealand flora and fauna, spend time in the New Zealand Native Aviary, where you walk among the birds, and the

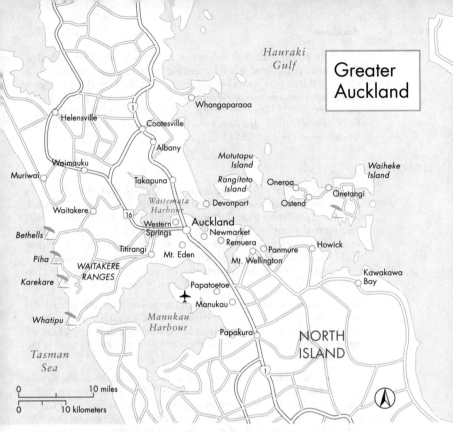

Kiwi and Tuatara Nocturnal House, which are at opposite ends of the zoo. In 2004, an enterprising Asian elephant escaped by dropping a tree on an electric fence and took herself for a walk in the neighboring park. She was coaxed home after 45 minutes, and the zoo's fences are now elephant-proof. In 2007 an otter escaped and its sightings dominated local media for weeks until it was captured. The Cheetah Experience lets visitors enter the enclosure of the big cats with a handler to eventually touch them. By car, take Karangahape Road (which turns into Great North Road) west out of the city, past Western Springs. Take a right onto Motions Road. Buses from the city stop opposite Motions Road. ⊠ *Motions Rd., Western Springs* ✛ *6 km (4 mi) west of Auckland* ☎ *09/360–3819* ⊕ *www.aucklandzoo.co.nz* ✉ *$16* ⊗ *Sept.–May, daily 9:30–5:30; June–Aug., daily 9:30–5.*

⌕ **Museum of Transport & Technology.** This is a fantastic place for anyone with a technical bent of any kind. There's a fascinating collection of vehicles, telephones, cameras, locomotives, steam engines, and farm equipment that's a tribute to Kiwi ingenuity. The aviation collection includes the only surviving Solent flying boat. One of the most intriguing exhibits is the remains of an aircraft built by Robert Pearse. There is a reproduction of another he built in which he made a successful powered flight around the time the Wright brothers first took to the skies.

The flight ended inauspiciously when his plane crashed into a hedge. But Pearse, considered a wild eccentric by his farming neighbors, is recognized today as a mechanical genius. MOTAT, as the museum is called, also has the scooter Prime Minister Helen Clark rode to her university. ✉825 Great North Rd., off Northwestern Motorway, Rte. 16, Western Springs ✛6 km (4 mi) west of Auckland ☎09/846–0199 ⊕www.motat.org.nz ⊠$14 ⊙Daily 10–5.

DEVONPORT

The 20-minute ferry to Devonport across Waitemata Harbour provides a fine view of Auckland's busy harbor. Originally known as Flagstaff, after the signal station on the summit of Mt. Victoria, Devonport was the first settlement on the north side of the harbor. Later the area drew some of the city's wealthiest traders, who built their homes where they could watch their sailing ships arriving with cargo from Europe. Aucklanders have fixed up and repopulated its great old houses, laying claim to the suburb's relaxed and moneyed seaside atmosphere.

The Esplanade Hotel is one of the first things you'll see as you leave the ferry terminal. It stands at the harbor end of Victoria Road, a pleasant street for stopping at a shop, a bookstore, or a café; or picking up some fish-and-chips to eat under the giant Moreton Bay fig tree on the green across the street.

Long before European settlement, the ancient volcano of **Mt. Victoria** was the site of a Māori *pā* (fortified village) of the local Kawerau tribe. On the northern and eastern flanks of the hill you can still see traces of the terraces once protected by palisades of sharpened stakes. Don't be put off by its name—this is more molehill than mountain. The climb is easy, but the views are outstanding. Mt. Victoria is signposted on Victoria Road, a few minutes' walk from the Esplanade Hotel. ✉Kerr St. off Victoria Rd.

New Zealand's navy is hardly a menacing global force, but the small **Navy Museum** has interesting exhibits on the early exploration of the country. Displays of firearms, swords, and memorabilia will likely grab former navy men far more than the uninitiated. The museum is five blocks west of Victoria Wharf and next to the naval base. ✉Queens Parade ☎09/445–5186 ⊕www.navymuseum.mil.nz ⊠Small donation ⊙Daily 10–4:30.

The position of **North Head**, an ancient Māori defense site, jutting out from Devonport into Auckland's harbor, was enough to convince the European settlers that they, too, should use the head for strategic purposes. Rumor has it that veteran aircraft are still stored in the dark, twisting tunnels under North Head, but plenty of curious explorers have not found any. You can still get into most tunnels (they're safe), climb all over the abandoned antiaircraft guns, and get great views of Auckland and the islands to the east. North Head is a 20-minute walk east of the ferry terminal on King Edward Parade, left onto Cheltenham Street, and then out Takarunga Road. The visitor information center will tell you what night the local folk-music club has events in one of the old bunkers, and it's one of the best places to watch yacht racing on the harbor. A few quiet beaches are off the coastal walk. ✉ *Takarunga Rd.*

HAURAKI GULF ISLANDS

More than 50 islands lie in the Hauraki Gulf, forming the Hauraki Gulf Marine Park, managed by the Department of Conservation (DOC). Many of the islands are nature reserves, home to endangered plants and birds, and public access to these is restricted. Others are public reserves that can be reached by ferry, and a few are privately owned. Great Barrier Island, the largest in the gulf, has a population of around 1,100, and is mostly agricultural. It's popular with surfers—particularly Awana Beach. Motuihe, a popular swimming spot, was a prisoner-of-war camp during World War I and the scene of a daring escape: Count Felix Von Luckner, known as the "Sea Devil," commandeered the camp commander's boat and got as far as the Kermadec Islands before being recaptured.

You can see rare native birds up close at **Tiritiri Matangi,** a bird sanctuary open to the public. A gentle walk on well-maintained and signposted tracks takes you to the top of the island and the oldest lighthouse in the gulf, still in operation. The island is free from predators, and the birds are unafraid. Tiritiri is home to at least 18 *takahe,* large blue and green flightless birds with red beaks. You can usually spot them eating grass near the lighthouse. The grave of Mr. Blue, the hand-reared male of the first pair on the island, is marked by a plaque at his favorite spot near the lighthouse.

To get the full scoop on the various islands, or the country's entire National Conservation Park network, stop by Auckland's **Department of Conservation Visitor Centre** (✉ *Ferry Bldg., Quay St.* ☎ *09/379–6476* ⊕ *www.doc.govt.nz*).

RANGITOTO ISLAND

When Rangitoto Island emerged from the sea in a series of fiery eruptions 600 years ago, it had an audience. Footprints in the ash on its close neighbor Motutapu Island prove that Māori people watched Rangitoto's birth. It is now the largest and youngest of about 50 volcanic cones and craters in the Auckland volcanic field, though scientists are confident that it will not blow again. During the 1920s and 1930s hundreds of prisoners built roads and trails on the island, some of which are still used as walkways. Small beach houses were also erected by families on the island in the early 20th century. Many were pulled down in the 1970s until their historical significance was recognized. Thirty-two remain, and a few are still used by lease-holders who are allowed to use them during their lifetimes. (Afterward, they'll be relinquished to the DOC.)

Rangitoto is covered with a hardy *pohutukawa* forest. When the flowers bloom around Christmastime, the slopes are a sea of red (hence the tree's popular name, the New Zealand Christmas tree). The most popular activity on the island is the one-hour summit walk, beginning at Rangitoto Wharf and climbing through lava fields and forest to the peak. At the top, walkers are rewarded with panoramic views of Auckland and the Hauraki Gulf. Short detours will lead to lava caves and even to the remnants of a botanical park planned in 1915, and you can walk around the rim of the crater. Carry water with you because parts of the walk are on exposed lava flows, which are hot in the sun. You can also swim at Islington Bay and at the Rangitoto wharf in a specially made pool.

GETTING HERE   **Fullers Booking Office** (☎09/367–9111 ⊕www.fullers.co.nz) operates ferries year-round to Rangitoto daily at 9:15 and 12:15, departing the island at 12:45 and 3:30. The fare is $20 round-trip; boats leave from the Ferry Building. Fullers also arrange Volcanic Explorer tours, which include a guided ride to the summit in a covered carriage. It's $30, or $50 for the tour and ferry ride, and you must book in advance.

WAIHEKE ISLAND

Waiheke was once a sleepy spot, summer vacation retreat and hippie haven, with beach houses dotting its edges. Waiheke now sports the holiday homes of affluent city dwellers and many wealthy foreigners, raising housing costs in their wake. The island is earning a reputation for its vineyards, and local cafés sometimes stock wines unavailable elsewhere. The annual Waiheke Jazz Festival at Easter attracts renowned overseas performers.

From the ferry landing at Matiatia Wharf you can walk five minutes to the small town of **Oneroa,** the island's hub, with its shops, cafés, bars, and real estate agents. Another minute's walk gets you to **Oneroa Beach,** one of the most accessible beaches. The north-facing beaches—sheltered bays with little surf—are the best for swimming. The most popular is **Palm Beach,** 10 minutes by bus from Oneroa. Around the rocks to the left is **Little Palm Beach,** one of Auckland's three nudist beaches. Another great beach on Waiheke is **Onetangi,** on the north side of the island, 20 minutes from Matiatia by bus. **Whakanewha Regional Park,** on the south side of the island, is a lovely bush reserve leading down to a half-moon bay. You can go hiking and picnic here, and the wetlands is home to rare birds such as the New Zealand dotterel. You can get to the park from Oneroa by shuttle bus.

GETTING HERE & AROUND

Fullers ferries (☎09/367–9111) go between the Ferry Building and Waiheke at least a dozen times a day, even on Sunday. However, crossings can be canceled if the seas are rough. The return fare is $28.50. Buses meet ferries at the Waiheke terminal and loop the island.

You can also take a shuttle to beaches or vineyards; **Waiheke Shuttles** (☎09/372–7262) has reliable service. The best way to get to Whakanewha Regional Park is by shuttle.

If you're planning on going farther afield on the island, you can purchase an all-day bus pass from **Fullers Booking Office** (☎09/367–9111)

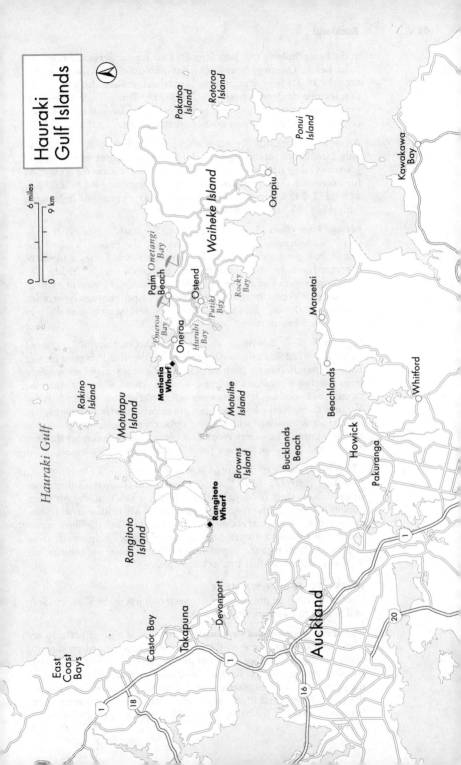

at the Ferry Building on Quay Street ($8 for regular service: to Oneroa, Palm Beach, Onetangi, and Rocky Bay). To use the pass, you need to take the 10 AM ferry. Return time is optional. Fullers also offers tours that include the ferry fee *(see the Touring the Town box)*. After either tour, on the same day, passengers may use their ticket to travel free on regular island buses to visit additional attractions.

VINEYARDS   Around 35 vineyards are on Waiheke Island, but some are new, so only 20-odd are producing wine. First to plant grapes were Kim and Jeanette Goldwater, whose eponymous wines have earned a reputation for excellence. The **Goldwater Estate** (⊠ *18 Causeway Rd., Putiki Bay* ☎ *09/372–7493* ⊕ *www.goldwaterwine.com*) is open only in January, daily 11–4. It's best to call ahead.

Passage Rock Wines (⊠ *438 Orapiu Rd., Te Matuku Bay* ☎ *09/372–7257* ⊕ *www.passagerockwines.co.nz*), on the eastern end of the island, has good-value wines. The Passage Rock Forté, a blend of cabernet franc, merlot, and cabernet sauvignon, is rated highly. The café is open every day and makes delicious thin-crust pizzas in a wood-fired oven. It's open for tastings on weekends April through November, Wednesday through Sunday in December and March, and daily in January and February.

Stephen White's **Stonyridge Vineyard** (⊠ *80 Onetangi Rd., Ostend* ☎ *09/372–8822* ⊕ *www.stonyridge.com*) has the island's highest profile. Its wines have followers from all over, and the Stonyridge Larose, made from the classic bordeaux varieties, is world class. Call before you visit, he may have nothing left to taste or sell. Reservations for lunch at the Veranda Café, overlooking the vines, are essential; but if it's booked, you may be accommodated with antipasto platters and wine on a blanket in the olive grove. The winery is open for tastings daily December through March, and Thursday through Tuesday April through November.

The friendly Dunleavy family of **Te Motu Vineyard** (⊠ *76 Onetangi Rd., Onetangi* ☎ *09/372–6884* ⊕ *www.temotu.co.nz*) started planting vines in 1989. Now their Te Motu bordeaux blend, which is made only when conditions are right, is on the wine list at many Michelin-starred restaurants in France—a great endorsement. The restaurant, the Shed, serves wonderful food in a Tuscan setting. Everything is made on-site from scratch and bookings are essential. The winery is open for tastings, but its best to call ahead first to check for times.

WHERE TO EAT IN WAIHEKE
For information on price categories, see the charts in the Where to Stay and Where to Eat sections, below.

$$$$ ✕**Mudbrick Vineyard and Restaurant.** Mudbrick is a good place to try wines that never make it to the mainland. The vineyard produces a small portfolio of whites and reds and serves them along with those of other tiny producers. Because bordeaux varieties predominate on the island, the food emphasis is on red meat; particular favorites are the rack of lamb and Black Angus eye fillet. The front terrace is the best spot to take in the harbor views. Mudbrick is open for lunch and

dinner daily, year-round, and many people like to arrive by helicopter. ⊠*Church Bay Rd., Oneroa* ☎*09/372–9050* ⊕*www.mudbrick.co.nz* ⊟*AE, DC, MC, V.*

$$$–$$$$ ✕**Te Whau Vineyard and Café.** With a wine list of more than 600 of the
Fodor's Choice best New Zealand and international wines, this restaurant has been
★ described as one of the best in the world for wine lovers. Owners Tony and Moira Forsyth have many vintages that are no longer available anywhere else. Spectacularly perched atop a finger of land, the restaurant commands a nearly 360-degree view. Te Whau's own bordeaux blend is much praised; you'll be able to try their chardonnay only here. You'll always get fresh seafood like the salmon house-smoked over oak and *manuka* (a native tea tree) wood. They also cook duck, beef, and venison to rave reviews. ⊠*218 Te Whau Dr., Te Whau Point* ☎*09/372–7191* ⊕*www.tewhau.com* ⊟*AE, MC, V* ⊗*Closed Tues. Nov.–Easter, and weekdays Easter–late Oct. No dinner.*

$$–$$$ ✕**Vino Vino.** Waiheke's longest-running restaurant perches on Oneroa's main street, with a large all-weather deck overlooking the bay. The platters—Mediterranean, grilled (with Italian sausages and calamari), or seafood—are perennial favorites. Or try something with a North African spin, such as the dry-marinated chicken over a red-pepper-and-tomato salad. ⊠*3/153 Ocean View Rd., Oneroa* ☎*09/372–9888* ⊕*www.vinovino.co.nz* ⌑*Reservations essential* ⊟*AE, MC, V.*

WHERE TO STAY IN WAIHEKE

$$$$ ▦**Boatshed.** An internal spiral staircase leads to the Lighthouse, a two-
★ story suite on the top floor of a turret. The glass doors of the dayroom fold open onto a wraparound deck overlooking the golden sands of Oneroa Bay, where boats moor and the swimming is great. From the bedroom on the first floor the view is equally spectacular. A long central room, with doors onto the sail-covered deck, divides this boutique hotel and gives onto a cozy sunken lounge. In the Bridge Room, up a flight of stairs, bifold windows off the sun porch frame a view of the bay. If you go for one of the three Boatshed Rooms, leave the louvered doors to your private deck open, for fresh sea air as you sleep. Owner Jonathan Scott, a former chef, prepares dinners by arrangement. **Pros:** Beautiful location, lovely rooms. **Con:** Some say the cooking is not always up to scratch. ⊠*Tawa and Huia Sts., Little Oneroa* ☎*09/372–3242* ⊟*09/372–3262* ⊕*www.boatshed.co.nz* ▱*4 rooms, 1 suite* ⌂*In-room: DVD, Wi-Fi. In-hotel: spa, no elevator* ⊟*AE, DC, MC, V* ⦿*BP.*

$$$ ▦**The Moorings.** From the bright guest rooms of this L-shaped Mediterranean farmhouse-style home, you can look outward or inward: out onto the bay or into a sheltered courtyard with lavender hedges and lemon trees. Each room has a king-size bed, a spacious seating area, and a small deck. Below the decks a terraced path leads to the bay. **Pros:** Clean, informal, lovely location. **Con:** The furniture appears cheap. ⊠*9 Oceanview Rd., Oneroa* ☎⊟*09/372–8283* ⊕*www. themoorings.gen.nz* ▱*2 rooms* ⌂*In-room: kitchen, dial-up. In-hotel: no elevator* ⊟*MC, V* ⦿*CP.*

$$$ ▦**Winemaker's Loft.** From the dining area of this apartment-style loft, you can look onto the vines of Cable Bay vineyard and beyond to

Church Bay. Standing a short distance from the owners' home, this is a private retreat, yet it's only five minutes from the relative bustle of Oneroa. In keeping with the wine theme, all the right wineglasses are provided, and you can start with the complimentary bottle. One-night stays incur a $50 surcharge. **Pros:** Friendly hosts, clean, lovely views. **Con:** You'll need to take a cab to town. ⊠*20 Nick Johnston Dr., Oneroa* ☎*09/372–9384* 🖷*09/372–5869* ⊕*www.winemakersloft. co.nz* ↩*1 suite* ⅁*In-room: kitchen, DVD, dial-up. In-hotel: no elevator* ▤*MC, V* ⅃◯⅃*CP.*

WHERE TO EAT

Princes Wharf and adjoining Viaduct Quay, an easy stroll from the city's major thoroughfare, Queen Street, offer dozens of eateries in every style from cheap-and-cheerful to superposh. High Street, running parallel to Queen Street on the Albert Park side of town, has developed into a busy café and restaurant strip over the last few years. You can get between Queen and High streets via Vulcan Lane, which has some attractive bars itself. Asian immigrants have created a market for a slew of cheap noodle and sushi bars throughout the inner city and the rule of thumb is the more crowded, the better.

Away from the city center, the top restaurant areas are on Ponsonby and Parnell roads, a 10-minute bus or cab ride from the city center. Dominion and Mt. Eden roads in the city, as well as Hurstmere Road in the seaside suburb of Takapuna, just over the Harbour Bridge, are also worth exploring. The mix is eclectic—Indian, Chinese, Japanese, Italian, and Thai eateries sit alongside casual taverns, pizzerias, and high-end restaurants. At hole-in-the-wall spots in and around the city center a few dollars will buy you anything from fish-and-chips to nachos, noodles, or naan bread.

To the west, out toward the Waitakere Ranges, the suburb of Titirangi has earned a reputation as a dining village, with everything from low-key pizza, Middle Eastern, and Southeast Asian places to wine bars and upscale restaurants with harbor views.

Traveling east there are many ethnic restaurants that are inexpensive—in particular the Panmure shopping center, about 20 minutes from central Auckland, has outstanding Malaysian and Indian restaurants. What look like very down-at-heel premises often have kitchens staffed by cooks who turn out super food for mostly ethnic and very knowing customers. Driving a little farther east will bring you into the Botany Downs area, which also, despite the bleak look of the new houses, has some good restaurants that escape the mainstream food critics.

WHAT TO EXPECT

New Zealand chefs are cultivating an innovative style that has often been tagged "Pacific Rim" or "fusion," but they are most concerned about the best combinations of the freshest ingredients and people coming back for more. Auckland has a wide mix of cafés, restaurants, brasseries, and bars, but proximity to the city center is not the only marker for quality. Many good eateries are in the suburbs.

Predominant local styles at smart restaurants segue between Mediterranean and Asian flavors but with very firm European roots. Seafood is a strong suit. Don't miss delicacies like Bluff oysters (in season March–August; farmed Pacific oysters are available year-round); salmon from Akaroa, Marlborough, or the McKenzie Country; Greenshell mussels (also known as green-lipped or New Zealand green mussels); scallops; crayfish; and two clamlike shellfish, *pipi* and *tuatua*.

In spring, many restaurants feature whitebait, known to Māori as *inanga,* which are the juvenile of several fish species. They are eaten whole, usually in an omeletlike fritter—the less egg and flour with a pinch of salt and pepper, the better the fritter. You'll also encounter *kumara,* a local sweet potato that has several varieties and is a staple in the traditional Māori diet.

Peak dinnertime in Auckland is between 8 and 9, but most kitchens stay open until at least 10 PM. Many restaurants, particularly in Ponsonby and Parnell, serve food all day, some with a limited menu between 3 and 6 PM; some still close between their lunch and dinner services. On Sunday and Monday, check whether a place is open. Only in the most formal restaurants do men need to wear a jacket. BYOB policies have become limited mainly to ethnic restaurants such as Thai and Indian. There's usually a few dollars per-person corkage fee. Some restaurants have started charging a 15% surcharge on public holidays, reflecting their need to pay their staff higher holiday wages.

WHAT IT COSTS IN NEW ZEALAND DOLLARS					
	¢	$	$$	$$$	$$$$
Restaurants	under $10	$10–$15	$15–$20	$20–$30	over $30

Prices are per person for a main course at dinner, or the equivalent.

CITY CENTER

$$$$　✕**The French Café.** It's not really a café, and it's not strictly French, but
Fodor'sChoice　don't let that put you off—this is one of Auckland's very best restau-
★　rants. Simon Wright's light touch translates into focused flavors, harmonizing in such dishes as pot-au-feu of organic chicken and crayfish with spring vegetables, lemon aioli, and basil bouillon. The menu changes frequently, but you will always find the best ingredients in perfectly executed dishes. The wine list includes a few finds, and the excellent staff makes well-informed recommendations. ✉*210B Symonds St., near Kyber Pass Rd., Eden Terrace* ☎*09/377–1911* ⊕*www.thefrench cafe.co.nz* ▤*AE, DC, MC, V* ⊘*Closed Sun. and Mon.*

$$$$　✕**Harbourside Seafood Bar and Grill.** Overlooking the water from the upper level of the restored Ferry Building, this sprawling seafood restaurant is an Auckland institution. Some of the finest New Zealand fish and shellfish, including tuna, salmon, snapper, pipi, and tuatua, appear on a menu with a fashionably Mediterranean approach. You can also select crayfish direct from the tank. Nonfish-eaters have their choice of lamb, eye fillet (beef tenderloin), and perhaps *cervena* (farmed venison). On warm nights, reserve a table outside on the balcony where you can watch the ferries come and go. ⊠ *Ferry Bldg., Quay St., City Center* ☎ *09/307–0486* ⊕ *www.harboursiderestaurant.co.nz* ⊟ *AE, DC, MC, V.*

$$$$
Fodor's Choice
★

✕ **White.** This restaurant looks like it stepped out of the pages of a 1990s design magazine. Vast windows mark the boundary between the harbor and the alabaster decor. Fittingly, New Zealand seafood dominates, with dishes such as scampi and salmon tortellini served with arugula and caper-butter sauce or *hapuka* (grouper) in a crust of hazelnut and *horopito* (an indigenous pepper) served with baby turnips and pearl onions. If you come for lunch, bring your sunglasses because the light that bounces off the walls from the water can shock the eyes. ⊠ *Hilton Auckland, Princes Wharf, 147 Quay St.* ☎ *09/978–2000* ⊟ *AE, DC, MC, V.*

$$$–$$$$

✕ **Cin Cin on Quay.** Auckland's original seaside brasserie is popular with the after-work crowd on Thursday and Friday and has just been renovated. The menu makes good use of local produce, such as creamy Clevedon coast oysters and fried shallots in a champagne vinaigrette, and Waimarino free-range pork served with kūmara (New Zealand sweet potato), apple syrup, and toasted-fennel jus. The extensive wine list has several vintages of local icons such as Kumeu River. If you're in town on the weekend, reserve an outside table overlooking the harbor for brunch. The service can get patchy when things get busy, especially when the after-work crowd is in for drinks. ⊠ *Ferry Bldg., Quay St., City Center* ☎ *09/307–6966* ⊟ *AE, DC, MC, V.*

$$$–$$$$
Fodor's Choice
★

✕ **Dine by Peter Gordon.** New Zealand's most celebrated chef and fusion cuisine pioneer, Peter Gordon, opened this signature restaurant—his first in the country since the 1980s—in 2005, in the city's newest major hotel. He oversees the restaurant from London, where he runs the Providores, and visits regularly. As you would expect from a chef of his standing, the refined food delights with surprises such as the wasabi-*tobiko* (flying-fish roe) spiked avocado cream served with the truffled yellowfin tuna, or the roast five-spice pork belly and rum-roast pineapple that accompanies sautéed scallops. ⊠ *Sky City Grand Hotel, 90 Federal St., City Center* ☎ *09/363–7030* ⊟ *AE, DC, MC, V.*

$$$–$$$$

✕ **Kermadec.** This complex's two restaurants are owned by a major fishing company, so naturally, the chefs lean on seafood. Both places have harborside views and dramatic Pacific-theme decor. In the more casual brasserie, which can get very noisy, seek the kitchen's advice on the catch of the day. The adjacent restaurant prepares great sashimi, or you could try orange roughy steamed and served with sesame-ginger Chinese greens. Can't decide? Share a platter—it will probably include smoked salmon, scallops, prawns, mussels, smoked eel, scampi, John Dory, and snapper. ⊠ *1st fl., Viaduct Quay Bldg., Quay and Lower Hobson Sts., City Center* ☎ *09/309–0413 brasserie, 09/309–0412 restaurant* ⊕ *www.kermadec.co.nz* ⊟ *AE, DC, MC, V.*

$$$–$$$$ ✕**Number 5 Restaurant.** The sign outside declares, "Life is too short to drink bad wine." Accordingly, the wine list here is designed to prevent such a mishap, with a vast selection by the glass and the bottle. Unlike most high-end restaurants, Number 5 is happy to serve just a small dish with a glass of wine. But you shouldn't pass up the main courses, such as individual beef Wellingtons, or venison steak with mashed kūmara and truffled mushrooms and syrah reduction. ⊠ *5 City Rd., City Center* ☎ *09/309–9273* ▤ *AE, DC, MC, V* ☻ *Closed Sun. No lunch.*

$$$–$$$$ ✕**O'Connell Street Bistro.** The former bank vault, on one of the city's
★ fashionable backstreets, is chic yet serene, and has a cozy bar from which you can watch passersby through thin venetian blinds. Loyal diners keep coming back for the roasted pork piccata on butter-bean cassoulet, or duck two ways—roast duck breast, and confit duck leg on a pepper-and-red-onion stew with fried *haloumi* (a salty, Middle Eastern–style sheep's milk cheese)—served on tables covered in crisp white linen. On the wine list you will find varieties rarely seen elsewhere, such as Waiheke's sought-after Stonyridge Larose cabernets. ⊠ *3 O'Connell St., City Center* ☎ *09/377–1884* ▤ *AE, DC, MC, V* ☻ *Closed Sun. No lunch Mon. and Sat.*

$$$–$$$$ ✕**Soul Bar and Bistro.** On the terrace at Soul, center stage in the Viaduct, you're close enough to the moorings to study the paintwork on the yachts and when it gets crowded to see which of the patrons (both men and women) have been to see Dr. Botox. When you do decide to study the menu, be prepared to muse on which type of fish you'd like—perhaps John Dory, snapper, yellowfin tuna, or Chatham Island blue cod—then how to have it prepared. You might go for grilled, with a side of sage-fried potatoes and a coriander-walnut vinaigrette, or blackened served on a parsnip *skordalia* (pureed with garlic, lemon, vinegar, and olive oil) with a broccolini and parsley salad. At night, the bar and outside tables are packed with a polished and often noisy crowd and the wine list is sensational. ⊠ *Viaduct Harbour, City Center* ☎ *09/356–7249* ▤ *AE, DC, MC, V.*

$$$ ✕**La Zeppa.** *Zeppa* is Italian for "wedge," but you won't get the thin end here. Tapas-style dishes are served in this cavernous warehouselike space that, despite its size, is always lively. It's very popular with the after-work set and on a Friday and Saturday can be packed with people either on the way home from work, or on the way out to something. Mediterranean flavors come in dishes such as porcini-and-Parmesan risotto balls, and espresso-cured lamb loin with *machiatto* dressing— served on sweet-potato salad in a New Zealand twist—but Asian influences abound. Freshly smoked salmon with a lemon glaze and added zing of wasabi caviar is delivered to your table on its individual slab of cedar fresh from the hot plate. And the miso-cured pork on a salad of glass onion and sugar snap peas is inclined to be fought over. ⊠ *33 Drake St., Victoria Park Market, City Center* ☎ *09/379–8167* ▤ *AE, DC, MC, V* ☻ *Closed Sun. and Mon. No lunch Sat.*

$$$ ✕**Mecca on the Viaduct.** This restaurant in the center of the Viaduct is
Fodor's Choice the flagship for the Mecca Group of seven restaurants. It offers a New
★ Zealand cuisine with a Middle Eastern twist. It's open all day and is designed to cope with anything from tables for two to larger groups in a relaxed environment. The food is always fresh and the two signature

dishes are lamb shanks slow cooked in a fragrant tomato gravy and fish baked with fresh vegetables, garlic, and chilies. People have been trying to get the shank recipe out of the owner for years. Like many of the Viaduct places it can get busy—they do take bookings but a limited number and the menu changes at least four times a year. The restaurant is also a popular place for first Internet dates. The wine list while not adventurous offers a good overview of the bigger New Zealand producers. ⊠ *Viaduct Harbour, City Center* ☎ *09/358–1093* ▤ *AE, DC, MC, V.*

$$$ ╳ **Prime.** Diners can gaze out at the harbor over lunch in this slick, sparely designed restaurant opposite Princes Wharf. Most dishes are offered at appetizer or main course sizes, and you're welcome to simply linger over some tapas—as in small dishes, though not particularly Spanish—with a glass of wine. For something more substantial, try the perennial favorite, braised rabbit pappardelle with *rimu* wood–smoked bacon and walnut-watercress pesto. The menu suggests pairing it with the Rabbit Ranch pinot noir from central Otago. Tapas only are served from 3 to 6:30. ⊠ *188 Quay St.* ☎ *09/357–0188* ▤ *AE, DC, MC, V* ⊘ *Closed weekends. No dinner.*

$$–$$$ ╳ **Mexican Café.** The worn red paint on the steps leading to this lively favorite says it all. Get to this restaurant at least a half hour ahead of time and join the crowds at the bar. People go as much for the noisy, friendly atmosphere as they do for the food and it can be outrageously noisy. The menu is packed with traditional choices such as nachos, tacos, and enchiladas. Don't get tucked away in a corner table. ⊠ *67 Victoria St. W, City Center* ☎ *09/373–2311* ▤ *AE, DC, MC, V.*

$$ ╳ **Galbraith's Ale House.** Brew lovers and Brits craving a taste of home head straight for Keith Galbraith's alehouse, as do many Kiwis before a rugby match a nearby Eden Park. The English-style ales are made on the premises and served at proper cellar temperature. Keith learned the art of brewing in the United Kingdom and sticks religiously to the style. Order a pint and dig into bangers and mash (seriously good sausages made by a local butcher with meat marinated in the Grafton Porter ale atop creamy mashed potatoes). People also come for the smoked fish platter—a selection of fish and seafood smoked at the Coromandel smokehouse. There's also a reasonable selection of whiskey. ⊠ *2 Mt. Eden Rd., Eden Terrace* ☎ *09/379–3557* ⊕ *www.alehouse.co.nz* ▤ *AE, DC, MC, V.*

$–$$ ╳ **C.A.C. Bar and Eaterie.** C.A.C. is housed in a historic 1920s blue-
★ stone building that once housed the Colonial Ammunition Company and has become a firm fixture in Auckland's dining scene in an understated way. There is an extensive wine and beer list and they now carry the acclaimed Greystone wines from Waipara in the South Island. But people go for the food, which is based around sharing lots of small plates. It's popular with people who are after flavorsome food but don't want to be restricted to a main-size meal. Try the pork and veal meatballs, the duck sausage, or the chicken salad with currants, parsley, and orange. There is also live music on Tuesday and Thursday, and if the crowd is right there can be quite a fun vibe—without visitors feeling like they need to be hyper-trendy to fit in. ⊠ *2r Normandy Rd., Mt. Eden* ☎ *09/630–5790* ⊕ *www.cacbar.co.nz* ▤ *AE, DC, MC, V.*

DEVONPORT

$$$-$$$$ ✕**Esplanade Hotel.** The cooking in this landmark hotel overlooking the pier is enough to lure citysiders, who are notoriously reluctant to visit the shore. But they can see the city from the conservatory-like dining room before enjoying contemporary dishes with a Mediterranean spin, such as baked chicken stuffed with chervil and ricotta. The Esplanade also houses a branch of Mecca—a chain of restaurants known for its lamb shanks and baked fish dishes. There are elegant rooms upstairs, befitting its Edwardian heritage. ⊠*1 Victoria Rd., Devonport* ☎*09/445–1291* ⊕*www.esplanadehotel.co.nz* ▤*AE, DC, MC, V.*

$$-$$$ ✕**Manuka.** Sitting on a corner on Devonport's main street makes for perfect people-watching. Manuka is a relaxed spot with bare wooden tables and stacks of newspapers and magazines. Weekend brunch is its busiest time when the locals turn out but tables turn over quickly. Wood-fired pizzas are available all day, with toppings ranging from classic pepperoni to smoked chicken, Brie, and roasted cashews. You could also nibble on a delicious salad or slice into a meaty offering such as venison with blueberry-and-onion marmalade. ⊠*49 Victoria Rd., Devonport* ☎*09/445–7732* ▤*AE, DC, MC, V.*

PARNELL

$$$$ ✕**Antoine's.** Owners Tony and Beth Astle have run this stately institu-
Fodor'sChoice tion for more than a quarter century, and it still enjoys a reputation as
★ one of *the* special-occasion spots in town though it also has its regulars. The decor is considered, the service immaculate, and the food delicious—and expensive. Tony is still at the stove, and his "table menu" reads as if it were designed by a chef half his age. On his "nostalgic menu" classics such as braised duckling with orange and Grand Marnier sauce remain, along with inventive dishes such as the appetizer of Bloody Mary jelly (just as it sounds: a jelly made from Bloody Mary ingredients) with prosciutto, artichokes, asparagus, and citrus-infused olive oil; or sautéed spiced watermelon, grilled scallops, and wasabi flying-fish roe topped with a lime-and-pink-peppercorn vinaigrette. The wine list is extensive. ⊠*333 Parnell Rd., Parnell* ☎*09/379–8756* ⊕*www.antoinesrestaurant.co.nz* ▤*AE, DC, MC, V* ☾*Closed Sun. No lunch Sat.*

$$$-$$$$ ✕**Cibo.** Italian for "good food," *cibo* is an apt name for this restaurant with Mediterranean- and Asian-influenced dishes. The smart crowd has made this a second home, coming for the adventurous and sound cuisine of chef Kate Fay served by slick but relaxed staff led by co-owner Jeremy Turner who is possibly Auckland's best maître d' and an avid triathlete. In an old chocolate factory, the restaurant opens onto a quiet courtyard where you can dine by a fishpond lined with rushes. Or take a table in the interior where palms grow toward the high skylights. They cook a steak with aplomb or try the spiced duck leg confit with rocket and mascarpone risotto, or duck parfait with grilled plum. In season, you can't pass up the whitebait fritter, served with lemon beurre blanc. The staff is excellent. ⊠*91 St. Georges Bay Rd., Parnell* ☎*09/303–9660* ▤*AE, DC, MC, V* ☾*Closed Sun. No lunch Sat.*

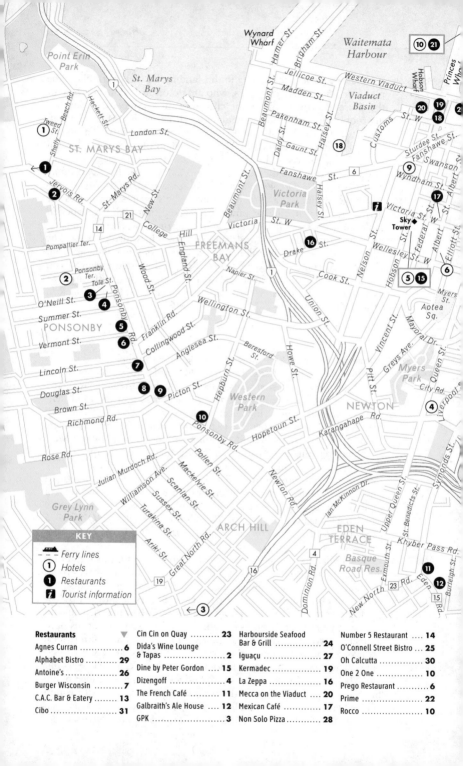

KEY

- Ferry lines
- ① Hotels
- ❶ Restaurants
- ℹ Tourist information

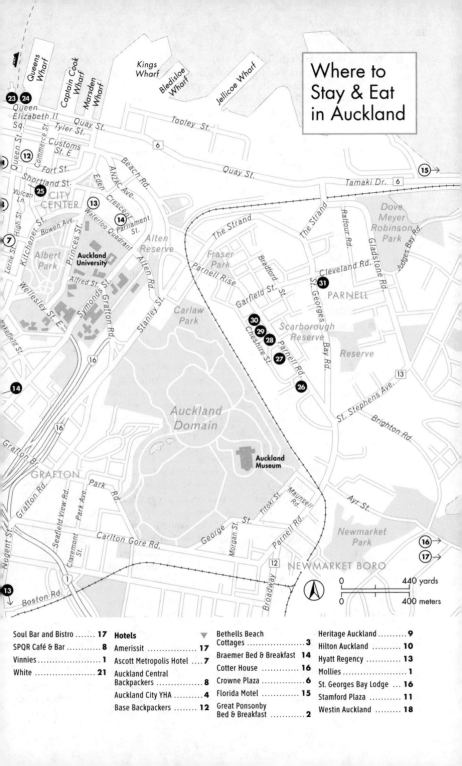

Where to Stay & Eat in Auckland

$$$–$$$$ ✕ **Non Solo Pizza.** This uncompromisingly Italian eatery offers pasta as
★   a single serving or in table-sharing bowls that feed four or more and
is very consistent. It's popular with the lunch crowd who head for a
table in the lush Italianate courtyard or ladies starting a night on the
town. The spaghetti with fresh shellfish in chili and white wine, and
osso buco *di cervo* (venison braised in white wine served with creamy
truffled polenta) are good. There's always pizza with traditional top-
pings followed by a masterfully prepared green salad. The same team
runs the popular Toto, on the other side of town, so if you can't get
a seat here, ask if the sister restaurant has room. ⊠ *259 Parnell Rd.,
Parnell* ☎ *09/379–5358* ▭ *AE, DC, MC, V.*

$$$ ✕ **Iguaçú.** With flares blazing near the entrance, a terra-cotta-tile floor,
enormous mirrors in Mexican metalwork frames, and a pair of chan-
deliers made from copper tubing, the decor is eclectic and the menu
follows suit. The kitchen goes nationalistic with battered fish-and-chips
with tartar sauce which is very popular, plus there are staples like venison rubbed with *Dukkah* (an Egyptian nut-and-spice blend), topped
with a lemongrass-and-tamarind sauce. ⊠ *269 Parnell Rd., Parnell*
☎ *09/309–4124* ▭ *AE, DC, MC, V.*

$$ ✕ **Oh Calcutta.** When executive chef Meena Anand moved to New Zea-
★   land, she applied her traditional cooking skills to new produce, focus-
ing on fresh seafood and vegetables. The results are fantastic and you'll
find plenty of traditional dishes—it would be hard to beat her butter
chicken—but her interpretations, such as prawn *malabari* (fat shelled
prawns sautéed with onions, peppers, coriander, and fresh coconut
cream), are light and brimming with flavor. Her fish tikka, made with
deep-sea kingfish and served with a sharp mint chutney, is another
standout. This is widely considered among the best Indian restaurants
in town, and on Friday and Saturday nights you need to reserve ahead.
The wine list is average, but they do have a bring-your-own license,
though they charge each person a corkage fee. ⊠ *149–155 Parnell Rd.,
Parnell* ☎ *09/377–9090* ⊕ *www.ohcalcutta.co.nz* ▭ *AE, DC, MC, V.*

¢–$$ ✕ **Alphabet Bistro.** Take a table on the sidewalk for the best breakfast
and brunch on the strip. Classics such as eggs Benedict and boiled eggs
with "toast soldiers" (strips of toasted bread for dipping) are done just
right, and the coffee is great. Bigger appetites might go for the red-flan-
nel hash, with two types of sausage (pork-and-fennel, and garlic) or
panfried lamb's kidneys. Lunch is good, too, with a small but perfectly
formed blackboard menu offering salads, pasta, and steak sandwiches.
⊠ *193 Parnell Rd., Parnell* ☎ *09/307–2223* ▭ *AE, MC, V.*

PONSONBY

$$$–$$$$ ✕ **Vinnies.** This shop-front restaurant has a warm, intimate feel, with
★   long filmy curtains and velvet-covered chairs. Specialty local produce
prepared with elegant flair is Chef Geoff Scott's trademark. Start with
savory cones filled with smoked eel pâté, beef *bresaola* (Italian-cured
and air-dried beef) and cantaloupe, and ostrich carpaccio. Or perhaps
with Clevedon coast oysters chased with a lemon-and-vodka-sour
shooter. If fish is your thing, try the main course of seared hapuka

served with spinach, ruby grapefruit, Sicilian pasta, crab, and coconut cream. It's right on the border of Ponsonby. ⊠*166 Jervois Rd., Herne Bay* ☎*09/376–5597* ⊕*www.vinnies.co.nz* ⊟*AE, DC, MC, V* ☉*Closed Sun. and Mon. No lunch.*

$$$ ✕**GPK.** The initials stand for Gourmet Pizza Kitchen or Gourmet Pizza Konnection—take your pick. This corner eatery was the city's pioneer posh-pizza place and soon afterward spawned a sister establishment at 234 Dominion Road, Mt. Eden, and another in Takapuna at 162 Hurstmere Road. Some of the toppings would make a traditionalist squirm (tandoori chicken with banana and yogurt), but there are plenty of more traditional toppings, and they cook a great steak. The wine and beer list is impressive. ⊠*262 Ponsonby Rd., Ponsonby* ☎*09/360–1113* ♟*Reservations not accepted* ⊟*AE, DC, MC, V.*

$$$ ✕**Rocco.** That it's slightly away from the heaviest foot traffic on Pon-
★ sonby Road doesn't deter the crowds that come for the glorious Mediterranean food in this old house. Spanish flavors pepper a menu that lets favorites survive changes, so you'll always find the squid-ink noodles with seafood and the roast pork chop filled with chorizo, pancetta, and apple, with garlic-and-honey aioli—a fiendish dish that tempts you to eat beyond capacity. The wine list has a good sampling of New Zealand's best at reasonable prices, and the restaurant's only fault is the staff can be quite aloof. This is not a place for intimate dining; the buoyant crowd sees to that, and the toilets are up quite a steep set of stairs. ⊠*23 Ponsonby Rd., Ponsonby* ☎*09/360–6262* ⊕*www. rocco.co.nz* ♟*Reservations essential* ⊟*AE, DC, MC, V* ☉*Closed Sun. No lunch Sat.*

$$$ ✕**SPQR Cafe & Bar.** There's no better vantage point for people-watching
★ on Ponsonby Road than the tables outside this longtime local favorite; if you want to fit in, wear black and big sunglasses. Should outdoors not be an option, you can sit in the minimalist concrete interior of what was once a motorcycle shop. You can keep your shades on there, too; with the eclectic clientele, the people-watching is just as good inside. The excellent food is largely Italian, and the place is known for its thin-crust pizzas and for the attitude of the staff who sometimes forget that the customers are more important. The food mostly makes up for service. The bar cranks up as the sun goes down, and on weekend mornings aspiring celebrities and the "love your work set" can be seen having a late breakfast in public. A lot of air-kissing goes on at SPQR. ⊠*150 Ponsonby Rd., Ponsonby* ☎*09/360–1710* ♟*Reservations not accepted* ⊟*AE, MC, V.*

$$–$$$ ✕**Prego Restaurant.** It's no mean feat being the longest-running restau-
FodorsChoice rant in Ponsonby, a trendy area whose inhabitants count eating out
★ among the necessities of life. The comprehensive Italian menu includes wood-fired pizzas and pasta prepared just as it should be, but many can't go past the fish of the day, usually panfried and served over a risotto with a delicate sauce or zesty salsa. You may strain to hear your companions over the din, unless you sit in the courtyard shaded by the robinia tree. Prego is always full and lively, but the expert staff will usher you to the bar and secure a table within about 20 minutes. The wine list is comprehensive. ⊠*226 Ponsonby Rd., Ponsonby* ☎*09/376–3095* ♟*Reservations not accepted* ⊟*AE, DC, MC, V.*

$$ ✕**Dida's Wine Lounge & Tapas.** In 1941 a grocer's shop stood on this site, run by a Croatian, Joseph Jakicevich, who also made his own wine. Today, three generations on, his descendants run this lively wine and tapas bar in the same building, alongside one of the wineshops in their Glengarry chain. A photo of *Dida,* Croatian for "Grandfather," hangs on the wall in the company of many family photos, and it is likely you'll be served by one of his great-grandchildren. Befitting such wine specialists, more than 100 wines are offered by the glass to accompany a menu of around 18 tapas, such as chorizo sausage cooked in merlot and bay leaf, meatballs in sherry tomato sauce, and salt-cod croquets. Locals love it, so you may need to arrive early to get a table inside or outside. ⊠ *54 Jervois Rd., Ponsonby* ☎ *09/376–2813* ⌂ *Reservations not accepted* ☰ *AE, DC, MC, V.*

¢–$ ✕**Agnes Curran.** Named after the grandmother of the founder Cameron
★ Woodcock, this small café just off Ponsonby Road tries to recall a time when home baking was served for afternoon tea on plates lined with doilies. You can choose from a counter selection of classic antipodean homemade cakes and cookies, which are duly served with lashings of thick cream and style. Breakfast is a choice between croissants and brioches, and for lunch, filled rolls and chicken mustard pie. As well as tea they do serve a mean coffee. A bank of shelves holds quirky finds for sale: cookware, glassware, and assorted treasures. You can spot a local Oscar-winning designer here from time to time. ⊠ *181 Franklin Rd., Ponsonby* ☎ *09/360–1551* ☰ *MC, V* ⊙ *No dinner.*

¢–$ ✕**Dizengoff.** The food is Jewish, though hardly kosher. The most popular breakfast dish is scrambled eggs and veal sausages with homemade pesto and French bread followed by toast and an unbelievably creamy lemon curd spread. At lunch try the beet salad—baby beets with fava beans in a balsamic dressing, topped with pesto and shaved Parmesan—or the salad made with shredded poached chicken, parsley, and lemon. The coffee is among the best around and there is an ever-changing selection of New Zealand art. ⊠ *256 Ponsonby Rd., Ponsonby* ☎ *09/360–0108* ☰ *AE, DC, MC, V* ⊙ *No dinner.*

¢–$ ✕**One 2 One.** Chris Priestley was a Ponsonby pioneer, and he still runs one of the best coffee bars on the strip. There's food for vegetarians, vegans, macrobiotics, and meat eaters. A couple of cats like to mosey about the place. Children are catered to in the outside courtyard, where scattered toys and other distractions like the sandpit keep them amused while you nibble on rice or salads, followed by coffee made from beans roasted on the premises. The decor is bohemian, and the service is supercasual. Ordering at the counter can be a lengthy affair while the diet-conscious make their choices. There is occasional live music including ukulele enthusiasts. ⊠ *121 Ponsonby Rd., Ponsonby* ☎ *09/376–4954* ☰ *No credit cards* ⛄*BYOB* ⊙ *No dinner.*

¢ ✕**Burger Wisconsin.** This is one of the best places to get a burger and often where people who are working late will grab a bite before heading back to meet a deadline. The bunned delights include chicken breast with cream cheese and apricot sauce, Malaysian satay, bacon and beef with coconut mayonnaise, and a vegetarian soy-and-sesame-seed burger plus one with blue cheese. There is also a traditional Kiwi-style burger with beetroot, and their chunky french fries—Kiwis call them chips—are delicious. At this branch you can order your burger to go, then wander over to nearby **Western Park** or drive to nearby **Westhaven Marina** and watch the boats. You will find other Burger Wisconsin outlets in a few other suburbs. ⊠*168 Ponsonby Rd., Ponsonby* ☎*09/360–1894* ▤*AE, DC, MC, V.*

OTHER SUBURBS

$–$$$$ ✕**Scalinis Italian Restaurant and Pizzeria.** This restaurant in the corner of the St. Heliers Bay carpark is one of Auckland's best hidden gems. The chef and owner Joe Lam is Samoan Chinese, but if you didn't know that you'd think he was born and bred in Italy based on the food. The well-heeled residents of St. Heliers and the surrounding suburbs are good customers, so it pays to book ahead although they do make outstanding pizza to go. The tasting platter with its mix of Pacific-style raw fish, Italian salami, and preserves always delights and the slow-roasted pork belly will leave you with a smile. The wine list is good and the vibe charming. Mr. Lam often brings the dishes out to the table to assist the waiting staff. ⊠ *429 Tamaki Dr., St. Heliers* ☎*575–9810* ▤*AE, MC, V.*

$$–$$$ ✕**Akdeniz.** "Mediterranean" stretches to its widest sense at this North Shore restaurant. Greek salad and Turkish dishes join the pizzas and pasta. Best of all is the seafood *guvech* (fish, mussels, calamari, and prawns cooked in a clay dish in the wood-fired oven, topped with tomato sauce and grilled mozzarella). If it's a cold night, reserve a table near the open fire; Akdeniz is popular before and after the movies. ⊠*34 Anzac St., Takapuna* ☎*09/486–4900* ▤*AE, DC, MC, V.*

$$–$$$ ✕**The Hardware Cafe.** Don't let the name fool you—this joint does everything from coffee and a range of superb breakfast things to excellent evening meals. The Thai-style chicken curry is excellent as is the bread and dips selection. It was set up in an old hardware shop and over the years has become a firm favorite not only with the Titirangi locals, but also the many surfers who pass through on their way out to the West Coast beaches. The Hardware is where you are likely to be seated next to a famous artist, a politician, or mountain bikers and cyclists getting a caffeine injection after riding the hard Waitakere Hills, or hard-out surfer types boasting about the waves they caught having "an early" or morning surf before heading to work in the city. ⊠*404 Titirangi Rd., Titirangi* ☎*09/817–5059* ▤*AE, MC, V.*

$$–$$$ ✕**Takahe Restaurant.** Perched on a steep hillside overlooking native bush, this restaurant stands out with its corrugated iron and polished timber exterior. The menu undergoes radical changes from time to time, according to the season and it is popular with people after a more formal meal. In summer you find the likes of seafood pasta, tuna niçoise, and classic Caesar salad, whereas winter brings more rib-sticking fare such as lamb shanks. You don't have far to go if you want to walk it off in the Waitakere Ranges. On Sunday afternoons you can forgo the walk and listen to live jazz. ⊠*421 Titirangi Rd., Titirangi* ☎*09/817–5057* ▤*AE, MC, V* ☉*Closed Mon.*

¢–$ ✕ **Sri Puteri.** Panmure is one of Auckland's down-at-heel suburbs that is starting to come into its own as petrol prices rise and people realize it's on the train line. And the Malaysian restaurant run by recent migrants from that country is a surprising hit in a suburb where many people are unemployed or living on low wages. You will eat the best selection of curries within 15 km (9 mi) with the friendliest service. It gets really busy and you might be forced to share a table with other customers who might not speak English. The Sirop Limau, a rose-and-lime-syrup drink, is a refreshing starter before ordering Malaysian style noodles or more traditional curries. The fish head curry is unbelievable and the prices very cheap for the quality of the food. ⊠ *59 Queen's Rd., Panmure* ☎*574–6775* ♺*Reservations* ⊟*No credit cards*

WHERE TO STAY

As New Zealand's gateway city, Auckland has all the large international chain hotels you'd expect, but it also has plenty of comfortable bed-and-breakfasts, mom-and-pop motels, and other individually owned places. Many of the large flashy hotels cluster around the central business district (CBD), whereas B&Bs tend to congregate in the nearby or trendier neighborhoods. Many of the best are found in suburbs close to the city center like Devonport and Ponsonby. You'll find your hosts quite chatty and keen to recommend local sights but equally happy to offer you privacy if you want it.

November to March are the busiest months for Auckland hotels, so it pays to book by August to ensure you get your first choice. Hotel rooms are usually equipped with TVs, hair dryers, ironing boards, and basic toiletries. All the major hotels have parking at a price. A number of the B&Bs offer parking, an especially useful perk since they're usually in narrow city-center streets. Better yet, B&Bs generally don't charge for parking. High-speed Internet access is becoming standard in hotels and B&Bs, and a computer is almost always available if you didn't bring a laptop. B&B owners can generally be relied on for insider knowledge on what's best close by, and many will make reservations or other arrangements for you. Only the hotels tend to have air-conditioning, but this isn't a problem when you can fling open the windows and let in the fresh air in.

WHAT IT COSTS IN NEW ZEALAND DOLLARS				
	¢	$	$$	$$$	$$$$
Hotels	under $75	$75–$125	$125–$200	$200–$300	over $300

Prices are for a standard double room in high season, including 12.5% tax.

CITY CENTER, PARNELL & REMUERA

$$$$ ▥ **Ascott Metropolis Hotel.** Auckland's old Magistrate's Courthouse was
★   transformed into an elegant lobby with a stunning onyx ceiling, restaurant, and bar for this all-suites hotel. The guest rooms are in a

Manhattan-inspired tower built just behind the court. Though most rooms have decent views, the best sea views are higher up on the east side of the hotel, at a slightly higher price. On a clear day you can see across the harbor to the Coromandel Peninsula. The stylish apartments are either one- or two-bedroom with sliding doors separating the living area; most have balconies, and all come with a kitchenette, including dishwasher, and washing machine and dryer. **Pros:** Grand building, nice facilities. **Con:** Service sometimes slack. ⊠*1 Courthouse La., City Center* ☎*09/300–8800* 📠*09/300–8899* ⊕*www.the-ascott.com* 🛏*145 suites* ♿*In-room: safe, kitchen, Ethernet. In-hotel: restaurant, bar, pool, gym, public Internet, parking (fee)* 🖮*AE, DC, MC, V.*

$$$$
Fodor'sChoice
★

Cotter House. This 1847 Regency mansion, the fifth-oldest house in Auckland, is the kind of place rock stars have been known to retreat to after mishaps on tropical islands. The home has been refurbished in original style, with classic features such as egg-and-dart molding, recessed arches, and narrow shutters on the high windows and is very private with security gates. Colombian-French owner Gloria Poupard-Walbridge loves to spoil people, which she is able to do because Cotter House cannot take large numbers of guests. Predinner drinks are served in the two refined lounges, and she bakes brioches and croissants herself as part of the four-course breakfast. Cotter House is elegant and a showcase for art collected over the two decades when Gloria was a diplomat's wife. The art shares the rooms with a significant collection of antiques, from antique writing desks, vanities, and armoires to the French scallop-shaped bath in the suite. Table d'hôte dinners are available by arrangement. **Pro:** Like staying in a charming, private country house. **Con:** Grounds are a little small. ⊠*4 St. Vincent Ave., Remuera* ☎*09/529–5156* 📠*09/529–5186* ⊕*www.cotterhouse.com* 🛏*2 rooms, 1 suite* ♿*In-room: no a/c, safe, DVD, Wi-Fi. In-hotel: spa, public Internet* 🖮*AE, DC, MC, V* ⦿*BP.*

$$$$

Heritage Auckland. Transforming one of Auckland's landmark buildings, the Farmers Department Store, this hotel added a tower wing, making it New Zealand's largest hotel. The size hasn't detracted from its character—the main building has retained its original 1920s art deco design, including high ceilings, large jarrah-wood columns, and native timber floors. The tower wing includes New Zealand art especially commissioned for the rooms and public areas. Ask for a harbor-view room. **Pros:** Close to city center, clean, good views from some rooms. **Con:** Decor is a little tired. ⊠*35 Hobson St., City Center* ☎*09/379–8553* 📠*09/379–8554* ⊕*www.heritagehotels.co.nz* 🛏*224 rooms, 243 suites* ♿*In-room: safe, Ethernet. In-hotel: 3 restaurants, bar, tennis court, pools, gym, spa, public Wi-Fi* 🖮*AE, DC, MC, V.*

$$$$
Fodor'sChoice
★

Hilton Auckland. Perched on the end of Princes Wharf, the Hilton resembles the cruise ships that dock alongside it. White walls and neutral furnishings in the chic, clean-lined rooms let your eyes drift to the view, best in the bow and starboard. Each room has a piece of original art—and a teddy bear. The hallways are painted chocolate on one side and white on the other, presumably to aid navigation. The hotel's restaurant, White, is one of the best in town, and the Viaduct Basin is within a five-minute walk. **Pros:** Lovely views, good rooms.

Con: Ships mooring nearby can be noisy. ⊠*Princes Wharf, 147 Quay St., City Center* ☎*09/978–2000* 🖷*09/978–2001* ⊕*www.hilton.com* ↘*160 room, 6 suites, 35 apartments* ⚸*In-room: safe, Ethernet. In-hotel: restaurant, bar, pool, gym, public Wi-Fi* ⊟*AE, DC, MC, V.*

$$$$ 🏨 **Hyatt Regency.** This branch of the international chain has been keeping up with the Joneses. The Residence tower has brighter and larger rooms, and all rooms have balconies and at least partial harbor views. Corner suites have large wraparound balconies. There is also a hushed, luxurious spa; among its treatments is a detoxifying wrap in Rotorua mud. For a more energetic pursuit, splash along the 25-meter indoor lap pool, which has a retractable roof. **Pros:** Close to city center, reliable service, some rooms have views. **Cons:** Dated foyer, average café. ⊠*Princes St. and Waterloo Quadrant, City Center* ☎*09/355–1234* 🖷*09/303–2932* ⊕*www.auckland.regency.hyatt.com* ↘*254 rooms, 140 suites* ⚸*In-room: dial-up, Ethernet, Wi-Fi. In-hotel: pool, gym, spa, public Wi-Fi* ⊟*AE, DC, MC, V.*

$$$$ 🏨 **Sky City Grand Hotel.** The specially commissioned works of top
★ New Zealand artists hanging in the soaring lobby of Auckland's latest major hotel are testimony to the attention to design throughout—even the staff uniforms were designed by local fashion leaders. Rooms are decked in light, contemporary hues, with red bed throws and iconic New Zealand prints by late photographer Robin Morrison. Rooms on the west side have views of the neighboring Sky Tower and beyond to the harbor. On the top floor, the Grand Suite is the size of four standard rooms and even has a butler's pantry. The excellent main restaurant, Dine, is run by acclaimed Kiwi chef Peter Gordon. **Pros:** Close to the city center and casino, good restaurant. **Cons:** No views, looks ugly from the outside. ⊠*90 Federal St., City Center* ☎*09/363–7000* 🖷*09/363–7010* ⊕*www.skycitygrand.co.nz* ↘*296 rooms, 20 suites* ⚸*In-room: Ethernet, Wi-Fi (some). In-hotel: 2 restaurants, bar, pool, gym, spa, laundry service, public Internet, public Wi-Fi* ⊟*AE, DC, MC, V.*

$$$$ 🏨 **Stamford Plaza.** Constant upgrades, noteworthy service, and attention to detail keep this mid-city hotel at the top of its game. Standard rooms are large and furnished extensively with natural fabrics and native woods in an updated art deco style. The best rooms are on the harbor side—the higher the better. If you've got something to celebrate, head to the Yanrepé champagne bar. **Pros:** Close to town, good service. **Con:** Work needed on refreshing the foyer and entry court. ⊠*Albert St. and Swanson St., City Center* ☎*09/309–8888* 🖷*09/379–6445* ⊕*www.stamford.com.au* ↘*329 rooms* ⚸*In-room: safe, Ethernet. In-hotel: 2 restaurants, bar, pool* ⊟*AE, DC, MC, V.*

$$$$ 🏨 **Westin Auckland Hotel.** This waterfront hotel is Auckland's latest and it presents the customer with both luxury plus a friendly environment with many rooms offering views of the ever-changing Vviaduct Basin. It was opened in 2007 and word-of-mouth has already put it on the map. The rooms are beautifully appointed with very pleasant views of either the basin. Each room has Wi-Fi Internet access and the entire hotel is non-smoking. The Harbour View corner rooms with their floor-to-ceiling windows are particularly in demand. At this writing the

restaurant was still getting through a few teething problems and service was bumpy, but that is being worked on. Travelers used to the Westin style of hospitality will not be disappointed. **Pros:** New, close to the Viaduct, excellent rooms. **Con:** Viaduct area can be noisy. ⊠*21 Viaduct Harbour Av., City Center* ☎*09/909–9000* ⊕ *www.westin.com* ⬑*172 suites* ⬙*In-room: safe, Wi-Fi. In-hotel: restaurant, bar, pool, gym, public Internet, parking (fee)* ▤*AE, DC, MC, V.*

$$$–$$$$ **Crowne Plaza.** An escalator connects the atrium of this hotel to the "Atrium on Elliot" shopping complex, a short walk from Queen Street. However, with 10 conference and banquet rooms, the hotel plays host to many large functions. Guest rooms begin on the 16th floor; all have city views, and there is even a menu for pillow choice. The suites on the 28th floor have great views and bigger bathrooms for just a slightly higher price. **Pros:** Close to town, well priced, good café. **Cons:** Often frequented by conference goers, shopping center is drab. ⊠*128 Albert St., City Center* ☎*09/302–1111* 🖷*09/302–3111* ⊕*www.crowne plaza.co.nz* ⬑*352 rooms* ⬙*In-room: Ethernet. In-hotel: restaurant, bar, gym, public Internet, public Wi-Fi* ▤*AE, DC, MC, V.*

$$–$$$ **Amerissit.** At the end of a quiet cul-de-sac overlooking rooftops and Mt. Hobson, this architecturally modern, cedar B&B is a quiet home away from home yet close to the restaurants of Parnell and shops in Newmarket. White walls and bed linen and soft charcoal carpet throughout add to the peacefulness. The two upstairs rooms have private decks, and one has a whirlpool bath. Owner Barbara McKain serves breakfast in the semicircular conservatory-style dining room, and will give you a tour of the city to help you get your bearings. **Pros:** Quiet environment, well tended. **Con:** Coin-operated washing machine and dryer is ridiculous. ⊠*20 Buttle St., Remuera* ☎*09/522–9297* ⊕*www.amerissit.co.nz* ⬑*3 rooms* ⬙*In-room: no a/c, DVD, Ethernet. In-hotel: parking (no fee), no elevator* ▤*AE, DC, MC, V* ⦿*BP.*

$$–$$$ **Braemar Bed & Breakfast.** This beautiful bed-and-breakfast is in an
★   Edwardian town house in the heart of the city opposite the High Court. It's close to parks, art galleries, and the museum. The house was bought by its owners to save it from demolition, and they've made it a very elegant and comfortable place to stay. It has lovely furniture and the menu is mostly organic. The owners know about restaurants close by and are happy to make reservations and point you in the direction of good tours and places to visit. Braemar is quite busy so contact them well in advance. **Pros:** Beautiful historic building, charming hosts. **Cons:** None really. ⊠*7 Parliament St., Central City* ☎*09/377–5463* 🖷*09/377–3056* ⊕*www.parliamentstreet.co.nz* ⬑*3 rooms* ⬙*In-room: no a/c, DVD. In-hotel: public Internet* ▤*AE, MC, V* ⦿*BP.*

¢–$ **Auckland Central Backpackers.** The best-equipped budget place in
★   town, this hostel manages to keep the lid on its rates despite a Queen Street locale. It has air-conditioning and a security system that you would normally expect to pay a lot more for. Accommodation varies from a six-bed bunk room to family rooms with bath. The lounge and Internet café area act as the hostel's social hub, where you'll also find a travel center and even a New Zealand job-search service, should you be compelled to cancel your return flight. **Pros:** Inexpensive, secure,

range of rooms. **Cons:** Noisy and not private. ✉ *229 Queen St., City Center* ☎*09/358–4877* 🖷*09/358–4872* ⊕*www.stayatbase.com* 📞*71 rooms, 35 with bath* ♿*In-room: kitchen. In-hotel: 2 restaurants, bar, laundry facilities* ▭*MC, V.*

¢–$ 🏨**Base Backpackers.** Just off the harbor end of Queen Street you'll find
★ this popular new arrival on the backpacker circuit. Double rooms come with small bathrooms, security lockers, and an extra single bed. A floral scent signals you've arrived at the women-only Sanctuary floor; this has a few extra frills, including hair dryers in the bathrooms. The rooftop deck looks over office buildings out to the harbor. The café is open in the morning and evening, serving meals such as fish-and-chips, lasagna, and spaghetti Bolognese. A lively bar has happy hour from 5 to 8 every evening. **Pros:** Women-only floor, inexpensive, close to town, in-house bar. **Con:** Fort Street is seedy. ✉ *16–20 Fort St., City Center* ☎*09/300–9999* 🖷*09/302–0065* ⊕*www.basebackpackers.com* 📞*37 rooms, 39 dorm rooms with shared bath* ♿*In-room: kitchen. In-hotel: restaurant, bar, laundry facilities, public Internet* ▭*MC, V.*

¢   🏨**Auckland City YHA.** Hotels with much higher room rates must envy this hostel's location just behind upper Queen Street. It's a few minutes' walk from the lively area of Karangahape Road and close to the bus circuit. Most rooms have a view over Auckland toward the harbor, but the best outlook is from the sundeck and common room. All share bathrooms. Bunk rooms take three to six people, and there are single, twin-bed, and double-bed rooms, too. Luggage storage and tour booking are available. **Pros:** Close to K Road, well priced, harbor views. **Con:** Lack of privacy. ✉ *City Rd. at Liverpool St., City Center* ☎*09/309–2802* 🖷*09/373–5083* ⊕*www.yha.co.nz* 📞*162 beds* ♿*In-room: no a/c, no TV. In-hotel: restaurant, public Internet* ▭*AE, MC, V.*

PONSONBY

$$$$ 🏨**Mollies.** Music lovers will have extra reason to admire this boutique
FodorśChoice hotel. It's run by Frances Wilson, a voice coach who taught at New
★ York's Metropolitan Opera. Her husband, Stephen Fitzgerald, was a theater set designer and also renovated New York City apartments before transforming this two-story 1870 villa. Each individually decorated suite has a mix of antiques and stylish modern furnishings and there are nice gardens. After dinner, by request, Frances goes to the Steinway grand piano in the drawing room and a butler reveals himself to be one of her pupils by joining her for a recital. Actress Tilda Swinton has stayed here and it is popular with the fashion set. **Pros:** Private and sedate. **Con:** Some might find it a bit pretentious and frou frou. ✉ *6 Tweed St., St. Mary's Bay* ☎*09/376–3489* 🖷*09/378–6592* ⊕*www.mollies.co.nz* 📞*12 suites* ♿*In-room: Ethernet. In-hotel: bar, spa, public Internet, parking (no fee)* ▭*AE, DC, MC, V.*

$$$–$$$$ 🏨**Great Ponsonby Bed & Breakfast.** Convivial hosts Gerry and Sally will
★ welcome you into their Pacific-theme villa on a quiet street off Ponsonby Road. Rooms are brightened with colorful, locally made tiles and art, and the windows are sandblasted with Pacific designs. The cozy lounge is stocked with music, films, books, and magazines, and

has an honor bar. Five of the rooms have kitchenettes and open off the courtyard. A few minutes' walk puts you in the thick of the Ponsonby cafés. **Pros:** Friendly, relaxed, low-key. **Con:** City almost too far to walk to. ⊠ *30 Ponsonby Terr., Ponsonby* ☎ *09/376–5989* 🖷 *09/376–5527* ⊕ *www.greatpons.co.nz* 🛏 *10 rooms, 1 suite* ♿ *In-room: no a/c, DVD, VCR, Ethernet. In-hotel: public Internet, parking (no fee)* ☰ *AE, MC, V* ⑩*BP.*

DEVONPORT/NORTH SHORE

$$$$ 🏨**Esplanade Hotel.** Commanding the corner opposite the pier, this turn-of-the-20th-century Edwardian baroque-revival hotel is the first thing you see when approaching Devonport by ferry. Upstairs, a wide corridor hung with chandeliers leads to generous rooms with period furnishings and long drapes hanging from high windows. Harbor views come at a slightly higher rate. The elegant two-bedroom, two-bathroom "Penthouse Suite" is ideal for families (at around twice the standard rate). **Pros:** Stunning views, lovely atmosphere. **Con:** Poor car parking. ⊠ *1 Victoria Rd., Devonport* ☎ *09/445–1291* 🖷 *09/445–1999* ⊕ *www.esplanadehotel.co.nz* 🛏 *15 rooms, 2 suites* ♿ *In-room: no a/c, dial-up. In-hotel: restaurant, bar, public Internet* ☰ *AE, DC, MC, V* ⑩*BP.*

$$$$ 🏨**Stafford Villa.** Once a missionary's home, this early-1900s building
★ is now an elegant B&B filled with Asian antiques and other artwork. Each room has a thematic bent, such as butterfly-decorated wallpaper and China Blue's Asian inflection. The latter is a honeymoon favorite, with a four-poster bed and an antique Chinese chest. There are plenty of gracious touches, from chocolates and fresh flowers to sherry in the guest rooms and predinner drinks. The ferry to the city leaves regularly from the bottom of the road—a five-minute walk. **Pros:** Quiet, warm hosts, lovely food. **Cons:** Decor is fussy, very few good restaurants close by. ⊠ *2 Awanui St., Birkenhead Point, North Shore* ☎ *09/418–3022* 🖷 *09/419–8197* ⊕ *www.staffordvilla.co.nz* 🛏 *3 rooms* ♿ *In-room: no a/c, DVD. In-hotel: public Internet* ☰ *AE, MC, V* ⑩*BP.*

$$$ 🏨**Peace and Plenty Inn.** Antiques brought over from England are scat-
★ tered throughout this lovely B&B which is a mix of luxury and also simplicity. The largest room, the Windsor, has a high antique English pine bed and a small but charming bathroom with a Victorian claw-foot tub. Conversely, the smallest room, decorated in blue and white with a brass bed, has a larger bathroom with a full-size claw-foot bath. For a view of the city, ask for the upstairs Waitemata room. Children are welcome with under-five free. **Pros:** Lovely atmosphere, good food, close to Devonport. **Con:** Some may find the antiques too fussy. ⊠ *6 Flagstaff Terr., Devonport* ☎ *09/445–2925* 🖷 *09/445–2901* ⊕ *www.peaceandplenty.co.nz* 🛏 *7 rooms* ♿ *In-room: no a/c, Ethernet. In-hotel: restaurant, public Internet* ☰ *MC, V* ⑩*BP.*

OTHER SUBURBS & AUCKLAND ENVIRONS

$$$$ **Heritage Hotel du Vin and Spa.** For an excellent introduction to rural New Zealand, head south from Auckland to this smart, single-level luxurious hotel, surrounded by native forests, and the grapevines of the hotel's estate, Firstland Vineyards. Standard rooms are very good and the newer rooms at the far end of the resort are the best. If you're so inclined they will organize clay-bird shooting and archery. The restaurant has a strong reputation, though prices are high. If you're not staying overnight, you can still stop over for a wine tasting or dinner—a great way to break the journey between Auckland and the Coromandel region. **Pro:** Lovely, quiet, rural setting. **Con:** A bit far from town. ⊠*Lyons Rd., Mangatawhiri Valley ⊕64 km (40 mi) south of Auckland* ☎*09/233–6314* 🖷*09/233–6215* ⊕*www.hotelduvin.co.nz* ➷*48 rooms* ⚬*In-room: no a/c. In-hotel: restaurant, bar, tennis court, pool, spa, bicycles* ⊟*AE, DC, MC, V.*

$$$–$$$$ **Bethells Beach Cottages.** Surrounded by pohutukawa trees and over-
★ looking one of West Auckland's beautiful rugged beaches, these two cottages plus an apartment offer the opportunity for a true Kiwi *bach* (rustic beach house) experience. From the conservatory in Turehu Cottage—a converted brick farm building that sleeps two and a child—you can watch the sun set over the ocean, or you can wander out onto the patio and fire up the barbecue. Te Koinga, the larger of the two, sleeps two couples or a family, and has a deck furnished with a large driftwood table. The view is good from the long dining table inside, too. Both cottages are self-contained, but owner Trude will prepare meals by arrangement. A short stroll on a track through the dunes leads to the patrolled beach. **Pros:** Relaxed environment, cozy, close to magnificent beach. **Con:** Some may find it too rustic. ⊠*Bethells Rd., Bethells Beach* ☎*09/810–9581* 🖷*09/810–8677* ⊕*www.bethellsbeach.com* ➷*2 cottages* ⚬*In-room: kitchen* ⊟*MC, V.*

$–$$ **Florida Motel.** This motel in a harborside suburb a 15-minute drive east of the city center (and close to a major bus route into the city) has been owned by the same family for 30 years and offers exceptional value in one of Auckland's most exclusive suburbs. Rooms come in three versions: studios or one- or two-bedroom units; the two-bedroom units are particularly good for families, with a lounge room separate from the bedroom. All rooms have separate, fully equipped kitchens, including French-press coffeemakers and they are thinking about installing Internet access. Because the motel is immaculately maintained and extremely popular, particularly with an older set, rooms must be booked several months in advance. Rates do not rise over the busy summer period. **Pros:** Close to the beach; lovely suburb; friendly, knowledgeable hosts. **Cons:** No Internet, very basic. ⊠*11 Speight Rd., Kohimarama* ☎*09/521–4660* 🖷*09/521–4662* ➷*8 rooms* ⚬*In-room: kitchen* ⊟*AE, MC, V.*

NIGHTLIFE & THE ARTS

For the latest information on nightclubs get your hands on *What's On Auckland,* a pocket-size booklet available at all visitor information bureaus. The monthly *Metro* magazine, available at newsstands, has a guide to theater, arts, and music, and can also give you a helpful nightlife scoop. *City Mix* magazine, also published monthly and stocked at newsstands, has a complete guide to what's happening in the city, and the Friday and Saturday editions of the *New Zealand Herald* run a gig guide and full cinema and theater listings.

THE ARTS

The Auckland arts scene is busy, particularly in the area of visual arts, with some 60 dealer galleries operating. Theater is on the rise and more touring exhibitions and performing companies are coming through the city than ever before, and the Auckland Philharmonia Orchestra performs regularly, including at the summer series of free concerts in the park at the Domain, when thousands of music lovers sit with picnics under the stars. The new Vector Arena by the harbor is attracting plenty of rock acts, too.

For tickets, **Ticketek** (☎09/307–5000 ⊕*www.ticketek.com*) is the central agency for all theater, music, and dance performances, as well as for major sporting events.

ART GALLERIES & STUDIOS

An independent contemporary gallery, **Artspace** (✉*300 Karangahape Rd.* ☎09/303–4965) shows both international artists and the best of local artists. A group of 30 artists living and working in Waitakere, west of Auckland, have set up the **Art Out West Trail,** so that visitors can view and purchase art in artists' private studios. Many of the studios require advance notice, and you'll need a car. Brochures are at the Auckland I-SiteVisitor Centre (⇨*Visitor Information in the Planner section, above*).

For a one-stop sample of West Auckland art, visit **Lopdell House Gallery** (✉*Titirangi and S. Titirangi Rds., Titirangi* ☎09/817–8087 ⊕*www. lopdell.org.nz*). The gallery shows local works but also has regular exhibitions by national and international artists. In a restored villa, **Masterworks** (✉*77 Ponsonby Rd., Ponsonby* ☎09/378–1256) exhibits and sells contemporary New Zealand art glass, ceramics, and jewelry.

At the Otara Shopping Centre in Manukau City is the **Fresh Gallery** (✉*5/46 Fairmall, Otara Town Centre, Otara* ☎09/274 6400 ⊕*www. manukau.govt.nz*), an initiative of the Manukau City Council's Art Programme. This gallery space is a little off the beaten art track but worth the visit for the extraordinary work. Here emerging artists, many of whom are Pacific, test boundaries not only in materials used, but also with content and techniques.

MUSIC & OPERA

The **Aotea Centre** (⊠ *Aotea Sq., Queen St., City Center* ☎ *09/309–2677* ⊕ *www.the-edge.co.nz*) is Auckland's main venue for the performing arts. The **New Zealand Opera** company performs three annual main-stage opera seasons at the Aotea Centre, accompanied by either the **Auckland Philharmonia Orchestra** or the **New Zealand Symphony Orchestra**. Both orchestras perform at the Aotea Centre on occasion, but perform more regularly at the **Auckland Town Hall** (⊠ *303 Queen St., City Center* ☎ *09/309–2677* ⊕ *www.the-edge.co.nz*).

The **Civic Theatre** (⊠ *Queen and Wellesley Sts., City Center* ☎ *09/309–2677*) is host to many of the performances by international touring companies or artists. For general inquiries about all three venues check by the information desk on Level Three of the Aotea Centre. If you haven't booked beforehand, hit the Civic and Auckland Town Hall box offices, which open one hour before performance.

THEATER

Theater in Auckland went through a slump in the 1990s when the Mercury Theatre, then the main professional theater, closed down. Aucklanders had to endure accusations of philistinism, mostly from Wellingtonians, for not being able to support even one theater. One of the newly out-of-work actors took up the matter as a personal crusade and formed the **Auckland Theatre Company** (☎ *09/309–0390* ⊕ *www.atc.co.nz*). The ATC has a mixed repertory that includes New Zealand and international contemporary drama and the classics. The company performs at the Herald Theatre at the Aotea Centre, Sky City Theatre, and the Maidment Theatre at the university.

NIGHTLIFE

After sunset the bar action is split across four distinct areas, with the central city a common ground between the largely loyal Parnell and Ponsonby crowds. Parnell has several restaurants and bars frequented by a polished, free-spending crowd. For a more relaxed scene, head to Ponsonby Road, west of the city center, where you'll find street-side dining and packed bars—often at the same establishment. If you prefer to stay in the city center, the place to be for bars is the Viaduct, particularly in summer, or High Street and nearby O'Connell Street, with a sprinkling of bars in between. At the Queen Street end of Karangahape Road (just north of Highway 1) you'll find shops, lively bars, cafés, and nightspots. Nightclubs, meanwhile, are transient animals with names and addresses changing monthly if not weekly.

There is also a growing nightlife scene on the North Shore—particularly in the upmarket seaside suburb of Takapuna. If you make the trip over the bridge, you'll be rewarded by bars and restaurants with a very relaxed atmosphere; it's the sort of place where people spill into the streets.

From Sunday to Tuesday many bars close around midnight, and nightclubs, if open, close about midnight or 1 AM. From Thursday to

Saturday, most bars stay open until 2 or 3 AM. Nightclubs keep rocking until at least 4 AM and some for a couple of hours after that. People dress relatively casually, but that said, some doormen or bouncers can be unreasonable sticklers and may refuse entry if you're wearing jeans and for men jandals or open-toed sandals.

An institution with the central city bar crowd is **the White Lady.** Indecorously towed by a tractor to her permanent spot on the corner of Shortland and Queen streets, this long, slumped trailer is far from genteel. But she beckons those in need of sustenance between bars, serving up burgers crammed with extras such as fried egg, onion, and beetroot that vanquish the appetite of even the hungriest night owls. She's on duty daily from 8 PM to 4 AM. Farther up the street many of the Asian restaurants are open very late, too.

BARS & LOUNGES

At the heart of the city center, the **Civic Tavern** (⊠ *1 Wellesley St., City Center* ☎ *09/373–3684*) houses three bars. The **London Bar** has a vast selection of beer and an impressive variety of Scotch whiskey. The **London Underground Bar** has 8-ball pool tables and casino-style poker machines. For a glass of Irish stout, stay on the ground floor and visit **Murphy's Irish Bar.**

★ You might as well leave your inhibitions at the door when you enter **Lime** (⊠ *167 Ponsonby Rd., Ponsonby* ☎ *09/360–7167*), because everybody else does. People packed in the narrow bar inevitably end up singing their hearts out to classic tunes from the 1960s and '70s. There is always a lively time at the twin bars **Indians and Cowboys** (⊠ *95–97 Customs St. W* ☎ *09/357–0980*) in the Viaduct, where despite the name the crowd is older and upmarket and every so slightly wild. Door policy tries to filter out under-thirties.

Part of the Viaduct Village development, the **Loaded Hog** (⊠ *104 Quay St., City Center* ☎ *09/366–6491*) has a vaguely nautical-cum-farm feel. This popular brewery and bistro has indoor and outdoor dining and drinking and can get crowded late in the week. It is very popular with the young crowd. Tables for two line the curved windows of the retro **Match Lounge Bar** (⊠ *Hopetoun and Pitt Sts., City Center* ☎ *09/379–0110*). The cocktails—concoctions such as a poached-pear martini or the Malagassy, made with vanilla vodka and fig-cardamom syrup—are dangerously tempting, but be careful because the steps back to the street are quite steep.

Sequencing colored lights cast a warm glow over the couches and the bar at **Metropole Lounge** (⊠ *223 Parnell Rd., Parnell* ☎ *09/379–9300*). The swank clientele works its way through an extensive cocktail and wines-by-the-glass list. Vulcan Lane has long been an after-work favorite with the suit-and-tie set of downtown Auckland. The lane has been tidied up in recent years, and the **Occidental Belgian Beer Cafe** (⊠ *6 Vulcan La., City Center* ☎ *09/300–6226*) is one of the places that got a face-lift. Pair a pint of Belgian beer with a deep pot of mussels. A noble aim of the stylish **Orchid Bar** (⊠ *152B Ponsonby Rd., Ponsonby* ☎ *09/378–8186*) is to create a place where women can relax. It's not overtly feminine (men are more than welcome here), but the expertly made cocktails come garnished with an orchid. The bar has its own label of Martinborough Pinot Noir, called RGP. There's some uncertainty about what the acronym stands for, but a good guess is "really good plonk."

An atmospheric brewpub, the **Shakespeare Tavern** (⊠ *Albert and Wyndham Sts., City Center* ☎ *09/373–5396*) has beer with colorful names such as Willpower Stout and Falstaff's Real Ale. This bar is very popular with media types—particularly the journalists who write on New Zealand's largest paper, the *New Zealand Herald,* which is across the road. Locals spill onto the street from early evening at **Mea Culpa** (⊠ *3/175 Ponsonby Rd., Ponsonby* ☎ *09/376–4460*), a small, relaxed bar with equally appealing cocktails and wine selections.

★ **Whiskey** (⊠ *210 Ponsonby Rd., Ponsonby* ☎ *09/361–2666*) has cozy leather banquettes where you can talk without competing with the music. For an even more intimate tête-à-tête, you'll find a smaller room through the curtains off the main-bar area where often the patrons can be seen debating the world issues into the night. Wines seldom available by the glass are at **the Wine Loft** (⊠ *67 Shortland St., City Center* ☎ *09/379–5070*). Jocular lawyers and other suits make up most of the after-work crowd. Quotes from the famous are scrawled on the walls—the whole world could indeed be three drinks behind after you leave here.

GAY & LESBIAN

Not many venues are aimed at the gay and lesbian market in Auckland—that's probably because in Auckland what can be more important is the sort of car you drive rather than your sexual preference. And some joints won't let men in if they are wearing sandals or jandals—go figure. The free fortnightly *Gay and Lesbian Newspaper Express* is your best guide. The men-only bar **Urge** (⊠ *490 Karangahape Rd., City Center* ☎ *09/307–2155*) opens Wednesday through Saturday. It has theme nights from time to time, so it's best to call ahead. It is very popular with men with beards who like to dance to disco music with their shirts off.

Women might prefer **Witch** (⊠ *152 Ponsonby Rd., City Center* ☎ *09/360–1395*), which is not strictly a lesbian bar but has a very friendly atmosphere. **Kamo** (⊠ *386 Karangahape Rd., City Center* ☎ *09/377–2105*) is also very gay- and lesbian-friendly and can be a good place to hang out and ask where the latest joint is.

LIVE MUSIC & NIGHTCLUBS

The live music scene in Auckland is fickle—bands often perform in unexpected locations (a bowling alley isn't unheard of), so keep an eye on the entertainment guides.

Playing strictly disco and with a dance floor lighted in colored squares, **Boogie Wonderland** (⊠ *Customs and Queen Sts., City Center* ☎ *09/361–6093*) is stuck in the 1970s. You're encouraged to dress up, bust out your Travolta moves, and have a laugh. There's a $10 cover charge and the queues outside can be long. **Deschlers** (✉*17 High St., City Center* ☎*09/379–6811*), a 1950s-style cocktail lounge, has live jazz on Thursday and Saturday. Park yourself at the long bar or at a paua shell–top table in one of the booths. Take three flights of stairs or the rickety elevator to **Khuja Lounge** (✉*Level 3, Westpac Bank Bldg., Queen St. and Karangahape Rd., City Center* ☎*09/377–3711*), where you'll find live soul, jazz, funk, hip-hop, samba, bossa nova, or DJs. You can hit the dance floor or sink into a couch and watch the Moroccan-style lamps cast stars on the walls.

Rakinos (✉*35 High St., City Center* ☎*09/358–3535*) hosts live bands and DJs in an easy-to-miss upstairs location. One of Auckland's live music institutions is the **Kings Arms Tavern** (✉*59 France St. Newton, City Center* ☎*09/373–3240*), where you will hear very good local bands plus small international acts starting out. Call for details and often you will need to book as gigs sell out fast. There is an outdoor "beer garden" for when the noise is too much.

SPORTS & THE OUTDOORS

BEACHES

Auckland's beaches are commonly categorized by area—east, west, or north. The eastern beaches, such as those along Tamaki Drive on the south side of the harbor, are closer to the city and don't have heavy surf. They usually have playgrounds and changing facilities. **Judge's Bay** and **Mission Bay** are recommended for their settings. One of Auckland's first churches, St. Stephen's Chapel, overlooks Judge's Bay, a tidal inlet. You'll get a clear view of Rangitoto Island from the beach at Mission Bay or one of the many nearby cafés. Both beaches are close to the city center and can be reached by bus.

West-coast black-sand beaches are popular in summer, but be warned: the black iron-sand can get very hot so you need footwear. The beaches tend to have bare-bones facilities, but many have changing sheds near the parking areas, and you need a car to get to them unless you take a tour. The sea at the western beaches is often rough, and sudden rips and holes can trap the unwary. Lifeguard patrol varies among the beaches; don't be tempted in unless they are on duty. Safe swimming areas are marked with flags.

The most visited of these beaches is **Piha,** some 40 km (25 mi) west of Auckland, which has pounding surf as well as a sheltered lagoon dominated by the reclining mass of Lion Rock. A short, steep climb up the rock rewards you with a dramatic view. **Whatipu,** south of Piha, is a broad sweep of sand offering safe bathing behind the sandbar that guards Manukau Harbour. **Bethells,** to the north, often has heavy surf but is superb to walk on, and often there is a van in the carpark serving coffee.

Fodor's Choice
★

In the same vicinity, Karekare is the beach where the dramatic opening scenes of Jane Campion's *The Piano* were shot. Steep windswept cliffs surround the beach, and the surf is rugged. Again, swim only when lifeguards are on duty. A short walk from the parking lot is a 200-foot waterfall, feeding a lagoon that is good for swimming. Another beach **Muriwai** is about 40 km (25 mi) from Auckland and you have the added bonus of passing vineyards on the way home. It has spectacular cliff walks. To get to the west-coast beaches, head to Titirangi and take the winding road signposted as THE SCENIC DRIVE. Once you are on that road, the turnoffs to individual beaches are well marked—and, as advertised, there are lots of beautiful harbor views. Across Waitemata Harbour from the city, a chain of magnificent beaches stretches north as far as the Whangaparoa Peninsula, 40 km (25 mi) from Auckland. Taking Highway 1 north and keeping an eye peeled for signs, for instance, you'll reach **Cheltenham,** just north of Devonport and then after that **Takapuna** and **Milford.**

BIKING

Auckland can be good for cycling if you stick to certain areas, such as around the waterfront. There are few designated bike lanes, but **Adventure Cycles** (⊠ *2 Commerce St., City Center* ☎ *09/940–2453*) arms you with maps of routes that avoid pitfalls such as traffic. Touring bikes are $15 for a half day, $20 for a full day. Mountain bikes are $25. The rental fee includes helmets. While the company does not organize cycle tours they will provide as much information as needed and can open weekends by arrangement.

If you are traveling with a road bike and want to join some cyclists for a "bunch ride," then there are a number of options. Groups of cyclists leave designated points around the Auckland region most mornings and welcome guests. Just call any cycle shop and they'll point you in the right direction. On weekends the bunch rides can cover up to 150 km (93 mi) and will show you parts of the countryside that most won't get to see plus stop off for a mandatory coffee.

BRIDGE ADVENTURES

AJ Hackett Bungy—Auckland Harbour Bridge (⊠ *Westhaven Reserve, Curran St. Herne Bay* ☎ *09/361–2000* ⊕ *www.ajhackett.com*) is the only bungy (New Zealand spelling for bungee) site in Auckland. The company operates bungy jumping off the Harbour Bridge ($100) year-round. You could also sign up for their **Harbour Bridge Experience,** a 1½-hour bridge climb ($100) with commentary on the history of the bridge and the region. There are three trips a day and booking is recommended. Views from the bridge walk are outstanding.

GOLF

Chamberlain Park Golf Course (⊠*46 Linwood Ave., Western Springs* ☎*09/815–4999*) is an 18-hole public course in a parkland setting a five-minute drive (off Northwestern Motorway, Route 16) from the city. The club shop rents clubs, shoes, and carts. Green fees are $28.

Formosa Golf Resort (⊠*110 Jack Lachland Dr., Beachlands* ☎*09/536–5895* ⊕*www.formosa.co.nz*) is about 45 minutes from the city center. The 18-hole course, designed by New Zealand golfing legend Sir Bob Charles, has views of the Hauraki Gulf from most holes and they offer a range of accommodations. Unfortunately, it has a very poor automated phone system so be patient. Green fees are $65 and cart fees $30.

Gulf Harbour Country Club (⊠*Gulf Harbour Dr., Rodney District* ☎*09/424–0971* ⊕*www.gulfharbourcountryclub.co.nz*) course was designed by Robert Trent Jones Jr., who some say is the world's finest designer of classic golf courses. It is set against the spectacular backdrop of the Hauraki Gulf and is about 40 minutes north of Auckland on the Whangaparoa Peninsula on the East Coast. Clubs can be rented; the green fee is $115 and includes a golf cart.

Muriwai Gold Club (⊠*Coast Rd., Muriwai Beach, Waitakere City* ☎*09/411–8454* ⊕*www.muriwaigolfclub.co.nz*), a 40-minute drive north of the city brings you to this links course near a bird sanctuary. The course offers outstanding views of the coast. Because the links are on sandy soil, even if the rest of Auckland is sodden this course can be played. Clubs and golf carts can be rented; the green fee is $50. The views from the "19th hole" are outstanding.

Titirangi Golf Club (⊠*Links Rd., Waitakere City* ☎*09/827–5749*), a 15-minute drive south of the city and with the course designed by renowned golf architect Alister MacKenzie, is one of the country's finest 18-hole courses. Nonmembers are welcome to play provided they contact the course in advance but, like Formosa, Titirangi has a very painful automated phone system. Once booked in you must show evidence of membership at an overseas club. Clubs and golf carts can be rented; the green fee is $120.

HIKING

The scenic **Waitakere Ranges** west of Auckland are a favorite walking and picnic spot for locals. The bush-clad ranges, rising sharply from the west-coast beaches, are threaded by streams and waterfalls. The 20-minute **Arataki Nature Trail** (☎*09/817–4941*) is a great introduction to kauri and other native trees. The highlight of another great trail, **Auckland City Walk,** is Cascade Falls, just off the main track of this easy hour's walk. The **Arataki Visitor Centre** displays modern Māori carvings and has information on the Waitakeres and other Auckland parks.

To get to the Waitakeres, head along the Northwestern Motorway, Route 16, from central Auckland, take the Waterview turnoff, and keep heading west to the gateway village of Titirangi. A sculpture depicting fungal growths tells you you're heading in the right direction. From here the best route to follow is Scenic Drive, with spectacular views of Auckland and its two harbors. The visitor center is 5 km (3 mi) along the drive.

For a Māori perspective on Auckland, take the **Tāmaki Hikoi** (⊠ *Auckland i-Site Visitor Centre, Princes Wharf, 137 Quay St., Viaduct* ☎*09/307– 0612* ⊠*Atrium, Sky City, Victoria and Federal Sts.* ☎*09/363–7182)*, a walking tour with guides from the local Ngati Whatua tribe who tell ancient stories and recount their history on a trek from Mt. Eden through sacred landmarks to the harbor. The three-hour tour ($80) departs at 9 AM and 1:30 PM from the visitor centers at Princes Wharf and Sky City.

RUNNING

Auckland's favorite public running route is **Tamaki Drive,** a 10-km (6-mi) route that heads east from the city along the south shore of Waitemata Harbour and ends at St. Heliers Bay. The **Auckland Domain** is popular with lunchtime runners. The YMCA runs regular events leaving from a grandstand in the domain.

Another good place to run is **Cornwall Park,** which is about 15 minutes south of the central business district. It offers nice open paddocks, tree-lined avenues, and a fantastic hill climb if you are looking for views with your aerobic workout.

Another fantastic run follows the coast from **Point England** on the Tamaki Estuary. This run isn't well known, despite its following marked trails, and it hugs the coast, passing a bird and nature sanctuary. It's not hard running, and exit points allow you to find a bus stop to take you back to the city. If you are super fit, just keep heading north to the city and you'll eventually meet up with Tamaki Drive.

On the North Shore trying running from **Milford Beach to Takapuna Beach** and on weekends you can join members of the North Harbour Triathlon Club who swim along the beach from the boat ramp at the northern end of the beach. They are very friendly and will keep an eye on you though you will need a wet suit, goggles, and cap.

SAILING & KAYAKING

★ Instead of taking the ferry to Rangitoto, you could paddle. **Ferg's Kayaks** (⊠*12 Tamaki Dr.* ☎*09/529–2230* ⊕*www.fergskayaks.co.nz)*, run by four-time Olympic gold medal winner Ian Ferguson, takes guided trips ($120) to the island twice daily, leaving at 9 and 4. The round-trip takes about five hours—two to paddle each way and one to climb the volcano. On the later trip you paddle back in the dark toward the city lights. Booking is essential.

1

No experience is necessary to sail on America's Cup yachts *NZL 40* and *NZL 41* with **Sail NZ** (⊠ *Viaduct Harbour* ☎*09/359–5987* ⊕*www. sailnz.co.nz*). The yachts are crewed, but you can participate. Two-hour trips cost $140. Or you can take part in a match race between the two yachts; these take about three hours and cost $195. An "Experience Sailing" trip ($48) with **Pride of Auckland** (☎*09/373–4557* ⊕*www. prideofauckland.com*) departs at 2:45 daily. The trip takes about 45 minutes and includes entry to the National Maritime Museum. If you are wanting more than a quick trip, the Pride of Auckland team will also organize longer trips, which can include dinner or lunch, or if you are looking to explore the gulf islands they will sort out a boat, skipper, and crew.

SPECTATOR SPORTS

Eden Park is the city's major stadium for big sporting events. This is the best place in winter to see New Zealand's sporting icon, the rugby team All Blacks, one of the best in the world. More frequently, it sees the Auckland Blues, a Super 12 rugby team that plays professional franchise opponents from Australia, South Africa, and other parts of New Zealand. Cricket teams arrive in summer. For information on sporting events, check out *What's On Auckland,* a monthly guide available from the Auckland i-Site Visitor Centre (⇨ *see Visitor Information at start of chapter).* The big games sell fast and tickets can be booked through **Ticketek** (☎*09/307–5000* ⊕*www.ticketek.co.nz*).

SHOPPING

Ponsonby is known for its design stores and fashion boutiques. Auckland's main shopping precincts for clothes and shoes are Queen Street and Newmarket; Queen Street is particularly good for outdoor gear, duty-free goods, greenstone jewelry, and souvenirs. O'Connell and High streets also have a good smattering of designer boutiques, bookstores, and other specialty shops. There is a growing number of big malls in the suburbs, among the busiest Sylvia Park in Mount Wellington, Westfield Albany in Albany, and Botany Downs Centre in Botany Downs. These malls offer a range of shopping but are more fun for people-watching than purchasing.

DEPARTMENT STORE

Smith and Caughey's Ltd. (⊠ *253–261 Queen St., City Center* ☎*09/377– 4770*) is a good place to see plenty of local brands under one roof coupled with very good service. The clothing runs the gamut from homegrown favorites such as Trelise Cooper to international megabrands such as Armani. The lingerie department is known for its large, plush dressing rooms. You'll also find the largest cosmetics hall in the city and a good selection of conservative but well-made menswear and good quality china.

Rugby Madness

New Zealand is to host the 2011 Rugby World Cup, and Auckland is where many of the games will be played—delighting the city's tourism and business community but presenting local government with a slew of problems. Everything from the region's transport network to the condition of the stadium has become everyday conversation as power brokers discuss funding issues and who should be paying.

Rugby evolved out of soccer in 19th-century Britain. It was born at the elitist English school of Rugby, where in 1823 a schoolboy by the name of William Webb Ellis became bored with kicking a soccer ball and picked it up and ran with it. Rugby developed among the upper classes of Britain, whereas soccer remained a predominantly working-class game.

However, in colonial New Zealand, a country largely free from the rigid class structure of Britain, the game developed as the nation's number-one winter sport. One reason was the success of New Zealand teams in the late 19th and early 20th centuries. This remote outpost of the then British empire, with a population of only 750,000 in 1900, was an impressive force at rugby, and this became a source of great national pride. Today, in a country of 4 plus million, the national sport is played by 250,000 New Zealanders at club level and embraced by many with an almost religious fervor. It's not uncommon for infants to be given tiny rugby jerseys and balls are presents.

The top-class rugby season in the southern hemisphere kicks off in February with the Super 14, which pits professional teams from provincial franchises in New Zealand, South Africa, and Australia against one another. New Zealand's matches are generally held in main cities, and you should be able to get tickets without too much trouble. The international season runs from June to late August. This is your best chance to see the national team, the All Blacks, and the major cities are again the place to be. National provincial championship games hit towns all over the country from late August to mid-October. A winner-takes-all game decides who will attain the domestic rugby Holy Grail, the Ranfurly Shield. If you can't catch a live game, you can always count on a crowd watching the televised match at the local pubs or a sports bar.

The sport is similar to American football, except players are not allowed to pass the ball forward, and they wear no protective gear. There's a World Cup for the sport every four years since 1987, which New Zealand has won once. The New Zealand team's failure to win the trophy in 1999, despite being the favorite, sparked off a huge bout of introspection about what went wrong. More soul-searching followed during the 2002 hosting debacle, after which most of the union board members were replaced. In the end, the 2003 World Cup left the southern hemisphere altogether, crossing the equator for the first time with a British victory. In 2005 the All Blacks won every trophy in the cupboard except the World Cup and in 2007 they once again failed to win, leaving the nation in shock.

SPECIALTY STORES

BOOKS & MAPS

Legendary Hard to Find (but worth the effort) Quality Second-hand Books, Ltd. (✉*171–173 The Mall, Onehunga* ☎*09/634–4340*; **Devonport Vintage Books** ✉*81A Victoria St., Devonport* ☎*09/446–0300*; **Hard to Find Central City** ✉*201 Ponsonby Rd., City Center* ☎*09/360–1741*) are all worth browsing in and a good place to find that book you've always wanted. **Unity Books** (✉*19 High St., City Center* ☎*09/307–0731*) is a general bookstore that specializes in travel, fiction, science, biography, and New Zealand–related books.

CLOTHING & ACCESSORIES

★ Six jewelers started **Fingers** (✉*2 Kitchener St., City Center* ☎*09/373–3974*) in the 1970s as a place to display and sell their work. Now it showcases unique contemporary work by about 45 New Zealand artists, working with fine metals and stones. It's jewelry as art. Look out for works that combine precious metal with more mundane materials like rocks or seashells or even plastic.

Kia Kaha (✉*1/100 Ponsonby Rd., Ponsonby* ☎*09/360–0260* ⊕*www.kiakaha.co.nz*), which means "Be Strong" in Māori, carries distinctive casual and sportswear with Māori designs. It makes beautiful men's shirts and has branched into very wearable dresses. The store also stocks the Cambo line of golf shirts, made by Kia Kaha; Michael Campbell was wearing one when he won the 2005 U.S. Open.

Unique pieces from about 25 small local and international designers sit alongside vintage collectibles at **Superette** (✉*12/14 Nuffield St., Newmarket* ☎*09/913–3664*). You'll find very groovy gear here. For bohemian glamour with a deconstructed and sometimes raggedy edge, go to **Trelise Cooper** (✉*147 Quay St., Viaduct* ☎*09/366–1964* ✉*536 Parnell Rd., Parnell* ☎*09/366–1962* ⊕*www.trelisecooper.com*). Flamboyantly feminine designs popular with older curvy women, plush fabrics, extravagant use of colors that make the wearers look like parrots or other tropical birds, and intricate detailing are the hallmarks of this New Zealand frock designer. Ms. Cooper is also making clothes for children; these have been received to great acclaim by mothers who love to dress up their daughters. Fabulously individual **WORLD** (✉*57 High St., City Center* ☎*09/373–3034* ✉*175 Ponsonby Rd., Ponsonby* ☎*09/360–4544*) is one of New Zealand's groundbreaking fashion labels, making contemporary clothing with attitude. Find its funky street wear for men just up the street at **WORLD Man** (✉*47 High St.* ☎*09/377–8331*). Fashion label **Zambesi** (✉*Vulcan La. and O'Connell St., City Center* ☎*09/303–1701* ✉*169 Ponsonby Rd., Ponsonby* ☎*09/360–7391*) eschews populist trends except that global love of black on black and is always among the top New Zealand designers. The slim wear their garments most successfully.

SOUVENIRS & GIFTS

Follow elephant footprints down an alley in Parnell Village to **Elephant House** (✉*237 Parnell Rd.* ☎*09/309–8740*) for an extensive collection of souvenirs and crafts, many unavailable elsewhere, such as one-off hand-turned bowls, pottery, and glass. The sign hanging above **Pauanesia** (✉*35 High St., City Center* ☎*09/366–7282*) sets the tone for this gift shop—the letters are shaped from paua shell, which resembles abalone. You'll find bags, place mats, picture frames, and many other items.

SPORTS GEAR

Kathmandu (✉*151 Queen St., City Center* ☎*09/309–4615*) stocks New Zealand–made outdoor clothing and equipment, from fleece jackets to sleeping bags to haul-everything packs. The extensive range of gear at **Green Coast** (✉*114 Kitchener Rd., Milford* ☎*09/489–0242*) on the North Shore is made especially for New Zealand conditions and run the shop run by very knowledgeable people.

STREET MARKETS

For many years people from all over Auckland have headed south on a Saturday morning looking for bargains to the sounds of hip-hop beats

★ and island music at **Otara Market** (✉*Newbury St., Otara*), which opens around 6 on Saturday morning. Vegetable stalls groan with produce such as taro, yams, and coconuts. More Asian food stalls are joining the traditional Polynesian tapa cloths, paua-shell jewelry, greenstone, and bone carvings, reflecting the city's increasingly multicultural profile, but unfortunately some junky stuff is creeping in. None the less, look out for T-shirts bearing puns on famous brands, such as "Mikey" or "Cocolicious." The T-shirts designed by the Niuean poet Vela Manusaute are particularly sought by collectors. Stalls come down around midday. Exit the Southern Motorway at the East Tamaki off-ramp, turn left, and take the second left.

The beautiful countryside of the Waitakere Ranges has attracted artists seeking an alternative lifestyle, close to a major population (and customer) base but away from the hustle and bustle. Many of their wares are on sale at the **Titirangi Village Market** (✉*Titirangi Memorial Hall, S. Titirangi Rd.* ☎*09/817–3584*). It's held on the last Sunday of each month, 10–2. Auckland's main bazaar, **Victoria Park Market** (✉*208 Victoria St. W, City Center* ☎*09/309–6911*), consists of 2½ acres of clothing, footwear, sportswear, furniture, souvenirs, and crafts at knockdown prices. Be sure to stop by **From N to Z** (☎*09/377–2447*) for Kiwi icons such as plastic tomato-shaped ketchup dispensers and hand-carved bone and greenstone pendants. The market, housed in the city's former garbage incinerator, is open daily 9–6. On a terrace behind the market, you can recharge your batteries with a coffee at **Caffetteria Allpress** (✉*Adelaide and Drake Sts.* ☎*09/369–5842*), where again sunglasses are worn with aplomb.

Northland & the Bay of Islands

WORD OF MOUTH

Northland consists of some beautiful uncrowded bays/beaches, but you need to seek them out, like Matai Bay.

—tropo

One excursion we enjoyed while staying in Pahia was a day trip up to Cape Reinga and 90 Mile Beach. A full day and worth it.

—BillJ

By Richard
Pamatatau

NORTHLAND IS NOT A SINGLE PLACE, more a series of low-key and often out-of-the way destinations that invite you to place city expectations to the side. You can get good coffee in the north, but you'll be better served if you want inspiring views from winding coastal roads, to read on a quiet beach or buy fruit or fish from owner-operated shops.

After driving for an hour northwards you'll begin to leave the sometimes confusing jumble (both charm and scourge) that makes up Auckland. Once over the hill, with the seaside sprawl of Orewa and Waiwera behind you, the air starts to clear and you can see what some call the Northland light. The smaller population of Northland and subsequently less pollution may account for this because it seems brighter the farther north you go, even on overcast days.

The Tasman Sea on the west and the Pacific Ocean on the east meet at the top of the North Island at Cape Reinga. No matter what route you take you'll pass farms and forests, marvelous beaches, and great open spaces. The East Coast up to the Bay of Islands is Northland's most densely populated, often with refugees from bigger cities looking for a more relaxed life clustered around beautiful beaches.

The first decision on the drive north comes at the foot of the Brynderwyn Hills. There's a café if you need somewhere to stop. Turning left will take you up the West Coast through areas once covered with forests and now used for either agricultural or horticulture.

Driving over "the Brynderwyns," as they are known, takes you to Whangarei, the only city in Northland. If you're in the mood for a diversion, you can slip to the beautiful coastline and take in Waipu Cove, an area settled by Scots, and Laings Beach, where million-dollar homes sit next to small kiwi beach houses.

An hour's drive farther north is the Bay of Islands known all over the world for its beauty. There you will find lush forests, splendid beaches, and shimmering harbors. The Treaty of Waitangi was signed here in 1840 between Māori and the British Crown, establishing the basis for the modern New Zealand state. Every year on February 6, the extremely beautiful Waitangi Treaty Ground (the name means weeping waters) is home to celebration of the treaty and protests by Māori unhappy with it.

Continuing north on the East Coast, the agricultural backbone of the region is even more evident and a series of winding loop roads off the main highway will take you to beaches that are both beautiful and isolated where you can swim, dive, picnic, or just laze.

The West Coast is even less populated, and the coastline is rugged and windswept. In the Waipoua Forest, you will find some of New Zealand's oldest and largest kauri trees and the winding road will take you past mangrove swamps.

Crowning the region is the spiritually significant Cape Reinga, the headland at the top of the vast stretch of 90 Mile Beach, where it's believed Māori souls depart after death. Today Māori make up roughly a quarter of the area's population (compared with the national average of about 15%). The legendary Māori navigator Kupe was said to have landed on the shores of Hokianga Harbour, where the first arrivals made their home. Many different *iwi* (tribes) lived throughout Northland, including Ngapuhi (the largest), Te Roroa, Ngati Wai, Ngati Kuri, Te Aupouri, Ngaitakoto, Ngati Kahu, and Te Rarawa. Many Māori here can trace their ancestry to the earliest inhabitants.

Note: *For information on bicycling, diving, deep-sea fishing, hiking, and sailing in Northland and the Bay of Islands, see Chapter 11.*

ORIENTATION & PLANNING

GETTING ORIENTED

As the map indicates, Northland includes the Bay of Islands, but we've divided this chapter into two sections—Northland and the Bay of Islands. The West Coast, from Dargaville all the way up to Cape Reinga, is by far the least populated and developed; the unassuming little towns along the way and the lumbering *Kohu Ra Tuama* Hokianga Harbour ferry stand out in stark contrast to the luxurious lodges and yachts around the Bay of Islands. With the (no small!) exception of the 144 islands that make up the East Coast's Bay of Islands, the terrain is not so dissimilar; no matter where you are in the north, you're never far from the water and the combination of coast, rolling pastures, and ancient native forest is unlike any other part of the country.

Northland. *Te Tai Tokerau,* or Northland, with its no-frills tiny friendly towns and high rates of unemployment, is very different from the affluent Bay of Islands. However, the scenery is just as stunning. But without the infrastructure that goes along with organized tourism you will feel a little off the beaten track. The best approach is to travel according to Hokianga time: explore Cape Reinga, the tip of the country; take the car ferry out past the mangroves and cruise across Hokianga Harbour. The ferry gets busy over summer but half the fun is seeing who else is on board—this quiet route gets its fair share of movie and music stars. Some visitors will stand in awe at the base of a giant kauri tree; or just eat fish-and-chips on Opononi beach and enjoy the views of the enormous golden sand dunes across the water.

The Bay of Islands. This sweep of coastline is home to a flotilla of islands amid a mild, subtropical climate and excellent game-fishing waters. That combination has endowed the Bay of Islands with natural beauty and a slew of things to do while visiting. You'll feel well catered to, whether your interests lie in the history of Waitangi or the sunken *Rainbow Warrior,* or staying somewhere with your own private beach, or you're simply out to catch the biggest marlin on record.

TOP REASONS TO GO

Boating & Fishing: You can sightsee your way around rock formations, take a cruise to an island, whale-watch, or swim with dolphins. Game fishing is another major draw, with the Bay of Islands as the hub.

Bountiful Beaches: Nearly all Northland beaches are safe for swimming. When driving along the coast, keep an eye out for small signs for beaches tucked away nearby—you could find a gem. On the 90 Mile Beach (it's really 97 km [60 mi]) you can swim in two seas— the Tasman Sea and the Pacific Ocean—in one day. Shipwreck Bay at the southern base of 90 Mile Beach is prone to riptides, but it's highly rated by experienced surfers; some head round the point farther south for even better waves.

Superb Diving: Diving is extremely popular in Northland, with spectacular sites such as the Poor Knights Islands, known for their huge variety of subtropical fish. You can also dive the wreck of the Greenpeace vessel *Rainbow Warrior*, sunk by French agents in 1985, or try the Matai Bay Pinnacle in the Far North.

Walking & Hiking: There is superb bushwalking (hiking) around Northland. The bush is full of ancient kauri trees (a local species of pine) and interesting birds, such as *tūī* (*too-ee*), fantails, and wood pigeons. The flightless kiwi is making a comeback; visitors are reporting flashlight sightings, particularly in the north on the Kauri Coast.

PLANNING

An easy trip from Auckland and with predictably balmy weather in summer, stellar views, and upscale accommodations makes the Bay of Islands popular for many travelers. The main town is Paihia, a strip of motels and restaurants along the waterfront. The town of Russell, a short ferry trip away, is a more attractive base for longer stays with empty beaches within a short drive.

In the Far North, above the Bay of Islands, the population thins out, but the distance between sights is short. Turning south and down the West Coast, the roads wind through the forest, heading for the hamlet of Kohukohu, where you can take the car ferry across the serene Hokianga Harbour to Rawene on the southern side. Rawene is a good stop for fresh-smoked fish or to buy a coffee at the café built out over the harbor. It's also the place to buy a Hokianga hat, exquisite and handmade headwear.

From the sleepy village of Opononi, closer to the harbor's mouth, you can continue down the Kauri Coast to the Waipoua Forest, one of the last virgin kauri forests. Once through the forest, Highway 12 runs parallel with the coast, with the odd spur leading to more rugged West Coast beaches, to the arty town of Dargaville, known also for its kūmara (a local sweet potato), and on to Matakohe, site of the renowned Kauri Museum. Another half-hour's drive takes you to Brynderwyn, where you rejoin State Highway 1 about an hour north of Auckland.

GETTING HERE & AROUND

By far the best way to explore Northland is by car, because there are so many lovely bays, sandy beaches, and worthwhile sights along the way. Northland roads are generally just two lanes wide and in remote parts there are many one-lane bridges. Do take care on the narrow—and often unsealed—roads that thread throughout the region, and resist the temptation to drive along 90 Mile Beach; the quicksand and tides can leave you stuck, and your rental car insurance won't cover any accidents here.

You can follow an easy loop from Auckland, driving up the East Coast on State Highway 1 and returning down the West Coast on Highway 12 (or vice versa). It's worth leaving the main highway and following smaller coastal roads. These winding but easy-to-navigate routes have stunning coastlines and dramatic island vistas, whether around the eastern coast near Tutukaka, or along the short loop past Matauri Bay, north of Kerikeri, to Whangaroa Harbour.

Bus travel is a cheap and easy way to get around the north—buses serve most towns—but you may miss out on some of the more out-of-the way spots. **InterCity** (☎ *09/402 7857—use the Paihia number, which is the best for booking up north* ⊕ *www.intercitycoach.co.nz*), **Newmans** (☎ *09/913–6200* ⊕ *www.newmanscoach.co.nz*), and **Northliner Express** (☎ *09/307–5873* ⊕ *www.northliner.co.nz*) buses run several times daily between Auckland and the Bay of Islands and connect to the other Northland centers at least once a day. The trip from Auckland to Paihia takes about 4½ hours. The Auckland–Kerikeri trip takes about 5½ hours.

Between Russell and Paihia, take the car ferry instead of the long twisty road between the two towns. If you're on the East Coast and would like to head directly to the West Coast, take Highway 12 across the peninsula from Kawakawa, just south of Paihia. If you drive up to Cape Reinga, don't take your car onto 90 Mile Beach—you can be caught by the tides or quicksand *(see the Far North CloseUp box)*.

Taking the ferry is a marvelous way to cut down on driving time. You can take the ferry (with or without your car) from Rawene across the Hokianga Harbour to Kohukohu. In the Bay of Islands, you can ferry from Russell across Wairoa Bay to Paihia (or, with your car, from nearby Okiato to Opua).

Three passenger boats cross between Paihia and Russell, with departures at least once every 20 minutes in each direction from 7:20 AM to 10:30 PM from Paihia, and 7 AM to 10 PM from Russell. The one-way fare is $5. It's also easy to take the short drive to Opua, about 5 km (3 mi) south of Paihia, to join the car ferry. This ferry operates from 6:50 AM to 9:50 PM, with departures at approximately 10-minute intervals from either shore. The last boat leaves from Okiato on the Russell side at 9:50 PM. The one-way fare is $9 for car and driver plus $1 for each adult passenger. Buy your tickets on board (cash only).

TIMING & WEATHER

Snow doesn't fall on this part of New Zealand, known as the winterless north but in winter it can get cool. Mid-November through mid-April are the beautiful months, with December through March being the highest season for tourism. December is the best time to see the "New Zealand Christmas tree," the *pohutukawa*, in bloom. If you visit around the Christmas holidays, reserve well in advance. The accommodations in the Bay of Islands often fill months in advance. July and August can be quite wet, and the area is very quiet. For game fishing, the best months are from February to June.

ABOUT THE RESTAURANTS

Seafood abounds in the north with scallops dredged from the harbors and oysters farmed throughout the region though from time to time sewerage scares mean they are off-limits. Snapper and kingfish are available most of the year, and deep-sea boats supply marlin and broadbill swordfish, particularly between January and June.

The region prides itself on its local produce, and with more skillful chefs moving to the region, the restaurant food is improving.

Kerikeri, once known for its oranges, offers good-value eating, but still caters more to the local population than to tourists.

People eat earlier in Northland than in the cities, with restaurants filling around 7. In keeping with the relaxed air dress is casual—jeans are acceptable in all but the most upscale lodges. From May through September, many restaurants close entirely or reduce their opening hours, some to four nights a week. Most increase their hours again in late October.

WHAT IT COSTS IN NEW ZEALAND DOLLARS					
	¢	$	$$	$$$	$$$$
Restaurants	under $10	$10–$15	$15–$20	$20–$30	over $30

Prices are per person for a main course at dinner, or the equivalent.

ABOUT THE HOTELS

Northland has all kinds of accommodations, from basic motels to luxury lodges. Your hosts, particularly in the bed-and-breakfasts, are generally eager to impart their local knowledge, from tips on restaurants to intriguing area walks—they're a great resource on less-obvious attractions.

Paihia has plenty of vacation apartments and standard motels. The larger towns, especially Russell, have a range of high-end B&Bs. Luxury lodges—some of the most expensive in the country—are dotted throughout Northland, some on large swaths of land with private bays. Internet access is in nearly all lodgings, but high-speed access is not as common. Virtually no lodgings have air-conditioning, but it's usually unnecessary because people sleep with windows wide open.

High season runs from December through March. Some lodges have "shoulder seasons" in April and May, and September and October. Overall, room rates drop between May and October.

WHAT IT COSTS IN NEW ZEALAND DOLLARS				
¢	$	$$	$$$	$$$$
Hotels	under $75	$75–$125	$125–$200	$200–$300	over $300

Prices are for a standard double room in high season, including 12.5% tax.

VISITOR INFORMATION

Local visitor bureaus, many known as i-Sites, have information on the whole region, with more extensive information on their particular environs. In addition, some helpful community Web resources include ⊕*www.russell.net.nz,* ⊕*www.kerikeri.co.nz,* ⊕*www.dargaville.co.nz,* and ⊕*www.paihia.co.nz.* Destination Northland, a regional tourism organization, maintains ⊕*www.northland.org.nz.*

NORTHLAND

The Bay of Islands is the target of most tourists while the rest of Northland has large stretches of green farmland separating the mostly tiny towns. Some areas, particularly in the Far North and Hokianga, have higher-than-average unemployment, and New Zealanders joke that cannabis cultivation fuels a giant hidden economy. Whatever their occupation, Northland residents are generally good-humored and hospitable, proud of their varied lifestyles and exceptional scenery.

Northland today is also home to many wealthy people retreating from the city who may live close by people who have never left the area.

Europeans began settling in Northland in the 18th century, starting with whalers around the Bay of Islands, Scots who settled at Waipu on the East Coast, and Dalmatians who worked the West Coast's kauri-gum fields. Anglican missionaries started arriving in Northland in the early 19th century. The first mission was established at Kerikeri by the Reverend Samuel Marsden of the Church Missionary Society, who went about trying to "civilize" the Māori before conversion. He also planted the first grapevines in New Zealand.

If you're driving up the East Coast toward the Bay of Islands in December, you'll see scarlet blossoms blazing along the roadside. These are *pohutukawa* trees in flower, turning crimson in time for the Kiwi Christmas, hence their *Pākehā* (non-Māori) name: "the New Zealand Christmas tree." To the Māori, the flowers had another meaning: the beginning of shellfish season. Along Northland roads you might also see clumps of spiky-leaf New Zealand flax (the Māori used the fibers of this plant, the raw material for linen, to weave into clothing), huge tree ferns known as *punga, and giant mangrove swamps.*

WARKWORTH

59 km (36 mi) north of Auckland.

A sleepy town on the banks of the Mahurangi River, Warkworth was established in 1853. With lime mined from the local river, it became the first cement-manufacturing site in the southern hemisphere. Today, boatbuilding and refitting are the main industries, and Warkworth also serves as a service town for the surrounding farms and market gardens. It's a convenient stopping point en route to nearby marine reserve Goat Island or the superb vineyards at Matakana.

ESSENTIALS

Visitor Info **Warkworth Visitor Information Centre** ⊠ *1 Baxter St.* ☎ *09/425–9081* 🖶 *09/425–7584* ⊕ *www.warkworth-information.co.nz).*

WHAT TO SEE

Two giants stand in Warkworth, near the Warkworth Museum—two giant kauri trees, that is. The larger one, the **McKinney Kauri,** measures almost 25 feet around its base, yet this 800-year-old colossus is a mere adolescent by kauri standards. Kauri trees were highly prized by Māori canoe builders because a canoe capable of carrying 100 warriors could be made from a single trunk. These same characteristics—strength, size, and durability—made kauri timber ideal for ships, furniture, and housing, and the kauri forests were rapidly depleted by early European settlers. Today the trees are protected by law, and infant kauri are appearing in the forests of the North Island, although their growth rate is painfully slow.

The **Warkworth Museum** contains a collection of Māori artifacts and farming and domestic implements from the pioneering days of the Warkworth district, as well as kauri-digging implements and kauri gum. Rotating textile displays cover clothing dating to the late 1700s. There is also a display of a school dental clinic—what Kiwi children called the "murder house." Outside there is a collection of old buildings, including a bushman's hut and an army hut used by Americans stationed at Warkworth in World War II. ⊠ *Tudor Collins Dr.* ☎ *09/425–7093* ⊕ *www.wwmuseum.orcon.net.nz* 🖂 *$6* ◷ *Oct.–Easter, daily 9–4; Easter–Sept., daily 9–3:30.*

☾ Head for **SheepWorld** for a taste of life on a typical New Zealand sheep farm. You can watch working farm dogs rounding up sheep, sheep shearing, and presentations on the wool industry. An ecotrail takes you through the bush, providing information on native trees, birds (and their birdcalls), and boxes of *weta,* large, ugly—yet impressive—native insects. On the weekends, the farm dogs even herd ducks. Children can take pony rides, and, in August, bottle-feed lambs. ⊠ *324 State Hwy. 1* ☎ *09/425–7444* ⊕ *www.sheepworld.co.nz* 🖂 *$8, $18.50 including sheep-and-dog show (on at 11 and 2)* ◷ *Daily 9–5.*

EN ROUTE

Take a trip to the **Goat Island** marine reserve where fishing is prohibited and marine life has returned in abundance, with prominent species including blue *maomao* fish, snapper, and cod. It does get crowded here and midweek is best. You can put on a snorkel and glide safely

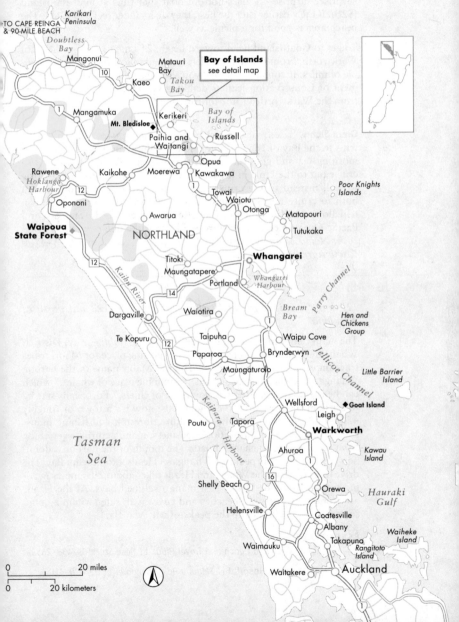

Northland

SOUTH
PACIFIC
OCEAN

Karikari
Peninsula

TO CAPE REINGA
& 90-MILE BEACH

Doubtless
Bay

Mangonui

10

Kaeo

Matauri
Bay

Takou
Bay

Bay of Islands
see detail map

1

Mangamuka

Kerikeri

Bay of
Islands

Mt. Bledisloe

Paihia and
Waitangi

Russell

Rawene

Kaikohe

Moerewa

Opua

Hokianga
Harbour

12

Kawakawa

Opononi

1

Towai

Waiotu

Poor Knights
Islands

Awarua

Otonga

Matapouri

NORTHLAND

Tutukaka

**Waipoua
State Forest**

Titoki

Whangarei

Maungatapere

Kaihu River

Portland

Whangarei
Harbour

Parry Channel

14

Waiotira

Bream
Bay

Hen and
Chickens
Group

Dargaville

Te Kopuru

Taipuha

Waipu Cove

12

Paparoa

Brynderwyn

Jellicoe Channel

Maungaturoto

Little Barrier
Island

Poutu

Tapora

Wellsford

Goat Island

Leigh

Kaipara Harbour

Warkworth

Ahuroa

1

Kawau
Island

Tasman
Sea

16

Shelly Beach

Orewa

Hauraki
Gulf

Helensville

Coatesville

Albany

Waiheke
Island

Waimauku

Takapuna

Rangitoto
Island

Waitakere

Auckland

0   20 miles

0   20 kilometers

1

around the island just a little ways offshore and get up close and personal with a *maomao*. You can rent a mask, snorkel, and flippers ($14)—and a wetsuit if it's too cold for you! ($15)—from **Seafriends** (☎09/422–6212 ⊕*www.seafriends.org.nz*); their sign is about 1 km (½ mi) before the beach on the main road, Goat Island Road. **Glass Bottom Boat** (☎09/422–6334 ⊕*www.glassbottomboat.co.nz*) has—surprise, surprise—a glass-bottom boat that runs around the island ($20). If the weather isn't the best, they do an inner reef trip ($15). The beach area is good for a picnic as well.

To get to Goat Island head toward Leigh, 21 km (13 mi) northeast of Warkworth. From Leigh, take a left turn and follow the signs for a couple of miles. If you arrive by 10, you should avoid the masses. Department of Conservation leaflets detailing Goat Island can be obtained from the Warkworth Visitor Information Centre.

TOURS

Great Sights, based out of Auckland, leads one-, two-, and three-day trips to the Bay of Islands. The one-day tour stops at Warkworth for morning tea and goes on to visit the Waitangi Treaty House and to cruise out to the Hole in the Rock. You can opt for a tour of historic Russell instead of the cruise. Taking the two-day tour allows you both to cruise and visit Russell, and the three-day itinerary adds a trip along 90 Mile Beach to Cape Reinga, where the Tasman Sea and Pacific Ocean meet. Rates start at $199 for the one-day trip. ⊠*Discover New Zealand Centre, 180 Quay St., Auckland* ☎09/375–4700 ⊕*www.greatsights.co.nz*.

WHANGAREI

127 km (79 mi) north of Warkworth, 196 km (123 mi) north of Auckland.

The main center in Northland is the Whangarei (*fahng*-ar-ay) District; Whangarei Harbour was traditionally a meeting place for Māori tribes traveling south by *waka* (canoe). The full Māori name of the harbor, Whangarei Terenga Paraoa, means "swimming place of whales," which can be interpreted as "the meeting place of chiefs." Europeans started to settle in the area from the mid-1800s; now it's a town of roughly 45,000 people, rooted in the agriculture, forestry, and fishing industries. Boatbuilding is a traditional business, manufacturing everything from super-yachts to charter boats. The mouth of the harbor is dominated by the volcanic peaks of Whangarei Heads, atop Bream Bay. The drive from town to the Whangarei Heads takes about 20 minutes heading out on Riverside Drive, past mangrove-lined bays. At the Heads are stunning white-sand beaches and coves with safe swimming, and several hikes, including up the peaks of Mt. Manaia.

ESSENTIALS

Bus Depot (⊠*Northland Coach and Travel Bldg., 11 Rose St.* ☎09/438–2653).

Hospital **Whangarei Hospital** (⊠*Maunu Rd., Whangarei* ☎09/430–4100).

Visitor Info **Whangarei Visitor Information Centre** (⊠ *92 Otaika Rd., Whangarei* ☎ *09/438–1079* 🖷 *09/438–2943* ⊕ *www.whangareinz.com).*

WHAT TO SEE

People often bypass Whangarei on their way to the Bay of Islands. It's easy to see why as the town has a confusing traffic system. but if you can brave that the area known as the **Whangarei Town Basin** is worth a look. The marina is now a haven for traveling yachts, and has cafés, restaurants, galleries, and crafts shops. There's parking behind the Basin off Dent Street.

About every conceivable method of telling time is represented in the Town Basin's **Claphams Clocks—The National Clock Museum.** The quirky collection of more than 1,500 clocks includes primitive water clocks, ships' chronometers, and ornate masterworks from Paris and Vienna. Some of the most intriguing examples were made by the late Mr. Clapham himself, such as his World War II air-force clock. Ironically, the one thing you won't find here is the correct time. If all the bells, chimes, gongs, and cuckoos went off together, the noise would be deafening, so the clocks are set to different times. ⊠*Dent St., Town Basin* ☎🖷*09/438–3993* ⊕*www.claphamsclocks.com* 🖅*$8* ⊗*Daily 9–5.*

The oldest kauri villa in Whangarei, **Historical Reyburn House,** contains the Northland Society of Arts exhibition gallery, which hosts exhibitions from New Zealand artists. The permanent collection focuses on the 1880s to the present. It's separated from the Town Basin by a playground. ⊠*Reyburn House La., Town Basin* ☎*09/438–3074* ⊕*www.reyburnhouse.co.nz* 🖅*Donation* ⊗*Tues.–Fri. 10–4, weekends 1–4.*

A lovely picnic spot is at **Whangarei Falls** on Ngunguru Road, 5 km (3 mi) northeast of town. Viewing platforms are atop the falls, and a short trail runs through the local bush.

Early settlers eager to farm the rich volcanic land around Whangarei found their efforts thwarted by an abundance of rock in the soil. To make use of the stuff they dug up, they built miles of walls. The current settlers at **Greagh,** George and Yvonne Hull, have carried on this tradition, giving their gardens the Celtic name for "land among the stone." The walls form a handsome framework for perennials and roses. ⊠*307 Three Mile Bush Rd.* ☎*09/435–1980* 🖅*$4* ⊗*Oct.–Easter, daily 9–5; Easter–Oct. by appointment.*

Minutes out of town, the 61-acre **Heritage Park Whangarei** is home to a nocturnal kiwi house, several Heritage buildings, and the Whangarei Museum. The museum has fine examples of pre-European Māori cloaks, waka (canoes), and tools. You can also check out Glorat, an original 1886 kauri homestead, and the world's smallest consecrated chapel, built in 1859 from a single kauri tree. On the third Sunday of every month and on selected "Live Days" (call for dates), you can cruise around the park on model reproductions of steam and electric trains, as well as on a full-size diesel train. ⊠*State Hwy. 14, Maunu* ☎*09/438–9630* ⊕*www.whangareimuseum.co.nz* 🖅*Park free, Kiwi House and Whangarei Museum $10* ⊗*Daily 10–4.*

The Treaty of Waitangi

The controversial cornerstone of New Zealand's Māori and Pākehā relations is the 1840 Treaty of Waitangi, the first formal document that bound the Māori to the British crown. This contract became the basis for Britain's claim to the entire country as its colony.

In the mid-1830s, Britain became increasingly concerned about advances by French settlers and the inroads made by the New Zealand Company, a private emigration organization. The British government had an official Resident at Waitangi, James Busby, but no actual means to protect its interests. In 1835, Busby helped orchestrate an alliance between more than 30 North Island Māori chiefs.

In 1840, Captain William Hobson arrived in Waitangi to negotiate a transfer of sovereignty. Hobson and Busby hurriedly drew up a treaty in both English and Māori, and presented it to the Māori confederation on February. On the following day, 43 chiefs signed the treaty.

But there were significant differences between the Māori and English versions. In the first article, the English version said the Māori would cede sovereignty to the Queen of England. But the Māori translation used the word *kāwanatanga* (governorship), which did not mean that the Māori were ceding the right to *mana* (self-determination).

The second article guaranteed the chiefs the "full, exclusive and undisturbed possession of their lands, estates, forests, fisheries and other properties," but granted the right of preemption to the crown. The Māori translation did not convey the crown's exclusive right to buy Māori land, which caused friction over the decades. The third article granted the Māori protection as British citizens—and thus held them accountable to British law.

After the initial wave of signatures at Waitangi, signatures were gathered elsewhere in the North Island and on the South Island. In spring 1840 Hobson claimed all of New Zealand as a British colony. He had not, however, gotten signatures from some of the most powerful Māori chiefs, and this came back to haunt the crown during the Land Wars of 1860.

What wasn't confiscated after the Land Wars was taken by legislation. In 1877 Chief Justice Prendergast ruled that the treaty was "a simple nullity" that lacked legal validity because one could not make a treaty with "barbarians." At first European contact, 66.5 million acres of land was under Māori control, but by 1979 only 3 million remained—of mostly marginal lands.

The battle to have the treaty honored and reinterpreted is ongoing. In 1973, February 6 was proclaimed the official Waitangi Day holiday. From the get-go, the holiday sparked debate, as Māori activists protest the celebration of such a divisive document. The Waitangi Tribunal was established in 1975 to allow Māori to rule on alleged breaches of the treaty, and in 1985 the tribunal's powers were made retrospective to 1840. It has its hands full, as the claims continue to be one of New Zealand's largest sociopolitical issues. The treaty is now in the National Archives in Wellington.

WHERE TO STAY & EAT

$$$–$$$$ ✕Gybe Restaurant and Bar. This octagonal building overlooking the marina may be colonial-style on the outside, but the menu is far from it. Specialty platters focus on fresh seafood; the seafood platter for two brims with grilled garlic black tiger prawns, Pacific oysters, sautéed fish skewers, smoked salmon, green-lipped mussels, seared game-fish salad, spiced oyster shooters, and *kina* ciabatta, all of which go nicely with a glass of Pinot Gris from Northland's Marsden Estate. If you're *still* hungry, the trio dessert platters relieve the stress of choosing between the crème brûlée, tiramisu, and vanilla bean ice cream. Ask for a table on the mezzanine or balcony for the best views. ⊠*Quayside, Town Basin* ☎*09/438–6873* ▭*AE, DC, MC, V.*

$$$ ✕à Deco. In a faithfully restored art deco house, chef Brenton Low has
★ become a regional favorite for his straightforward flavors and inventive twists. He spotlights fresh Northland ingredients, and goes organic whenever possible; for instance, you might find an organic free-range sirloin served with a miso consommé and oxtail, followed by baked chocolate tart with a smoked chocolate fondue. The tasting menu includes seven courses, each matched with local wine. The restaurant is closed for about two weeks over the Christmas break. ⊠*70 Kamo Rd.* ☎*09/459–4957* ▭*AE, MC, V.*

$$$ ✕Tonic. Owner-chef Brad O'Connell's seasonal menu may be French-inspired, but it's flavored with New Zealand; whenever possible he tries to buy local—anything from a lamb to pork—and his wine list has a big selection from the region. Seafood is a favorite and he serves whatever the market offers that day. ⊠*239a Kamo Rd.* ☎*09/437–5558* ▭*AE, DC, MC, V* ⊘*No lunch.*

$$$ ✕Vinyl. A stylishly funky licensed café, Vinyl serves a hip Whangarei crowd. Try the sautéed scallops served on squid ink pasta in a Pernod and garlic sauce. The café is on the opposite side of the marina from the Town Basin, making their alfresco tables the perfect place to enjoy a leisurely brunch of whitebait (a tiny fish) fritters served with grilled lemon and garden greens. There's live entertainment on Thursday from 6 PM. ⊠*Vale Rd. and Riverside Dr.* ☎*09/438–8105* ⊕*www.vinylcafe. co.nz* ▭*AE, DC, MC, V* ⊘*Closed Mon. No lunch Tues.*

¢–$ ✕Soda. This café on the outskirts of town is good for coffee. If you want cake with your coffee, try the pear and ginger, or the apple and walnut. The cabinets are full of freshly made panini and sandwiches. Just off the main road north, Soda is a good place to refuel with a big kiwi fry-up of bacon and eggs, French toast, or corn fritters, before heading to the Bay of Islands. ⊠*505 Kamo Rd.* ☎*09/435–1910* ▭*MC, V* ⊘*Closed Sun. No dinner.*

$$ ⬚Parua House. From this spot on the edge of Parua Bay, you can explore the towering Whangarei Heads. The house dates from 1882 and retains its colonial feel, with antiques brought over from England by the owners, Peter and Pat. You can walk through the nearby bush or even help milk their cow. Three-course dinners with wine are available on request—wholesome New Zealand fare, including vegetables from their garden and their homegrown olives. Pros: Friendly hosts, great location, lovely food. Cons: Decor is a little precious, not close

to town. ⊠*Whangarei Heads Rd., R.D. 4, Parua Bay* ✛*17 km (11 mi) from Whangarei* ☎*09/436–5855 or 021/025– 043892* ⊕*www. paruahomestay.homestead.com* ⌫*3 rooms* ᗐ*In-room: no a/c, no TV. In-hotel: public Internet, no elevator* ⊟*MC, V* ⦿*BP.*

$ 🏠**Graelyn Villa Bed & Breakfast.** This turn-of-the-20th-century villa was once the main homestead in Tikipunga, an outer suburb about 5 km (3 mi) from Whangarei's town center. Urban sprawl has caught up to it, but it still has a large spread of land with mature trees and a cottage garden. Two small but comfortable rooms are in a cottage in front of the villa, with a balcony onto the garden set to catch nearly all-day sun. The third room, in the main villa but with a separate entrance, opens onto an enclosed courtyard with a subtropical garden. The grounds include fruit trees and berry bushes to wander—and munch—among, and you can bring food home to grill on the barbecue. The hosts will cook dinner for you on request. The Whangarei Falls are just a few minutes' walk away. Pros: Friendly hosts, simple rooms. Cons: No in-room Internet, no credit cards. ⊠*166 Kiripaka Rd.* ☎*09/437–7532* 🖶*09/437–7533* ⊕*www.graelynvilla.co.nz* ⌫*3 rooms* ᗐ*In-room: no a/c. In-hotel: public Internet* ⊟*No credit cards* ⦿*CP.*

¢   🏠**Bunkdown Lodge.** A popular backpackers' lodge in a large kauri villa, Bunkdown has clean, bright rooms—two four-bed dorms, one six-bed dorm, two twins, and two doubles. Linen for the dorms is available for a small fee. The lounge has videos, guitars, games, and a piano, as well as a TV; common kitchens are available, too. This isn't a party hostel, but it's very popular with people who want to dive off the Tutukaka coast; dive companies pick up here at 7 am. Friendly hosts Peter and Noell know the area, and are happy to arrange visits to local attractions. Pros: Attracts friendly guests, random open atmosphere, very comfortable for the price. Cons: Can be noisy, very busy, lack of privacy. ⊠*23 Otaika Rd.* ☎*09/438–8886* 🖶*09/438–8826* ⊕*www.bunkdownlodge.co.nz* ⌫*3 dorms, 2 singles, 2 doubles* ᗐ*In-room: no a/c, kitchen, no TV. In-hotel: bar, laundry facilities, no elevator* ⊟*MC, V.*

NIGHTLIFE

Killer Prawn and Killer Pizza (⊠*28 Bank St.* ☎*09/430–3333*) doubles as Whangarei's nightlife hub. It's a good place to start the evening—as the night wears on, just follow the crowd.

SHOPPING

★   Specializing in contemporary fine glass, ceramics, and jewelry, **Burning Issues Gallery** (⊠*8 Quayside, Town Basin* ☎*09/438–3108*) is one of the best places in Northland to buy locally made arts and crafts. Look for beautifully carved *pounamu* (New Zealand greenstone) and bone pendants. A cooperative of local craftspeople, including jewelers, potters, wood turners, and weavers, runs the **Quarry Craft Co-op Shop** (⊠*Selwyn Ave.* ☎*09/438–9884*). You will find unique crafts, including jewelry made from kauri gum. You may run into Sandy Rhynd, an ex-farmer who delights in explaining the venerable craft of stick dressing and showing you his wares, such as musterers' sticks (shepherds in New Zealand are called musterers, and their sticks are something like traditional shepherds' crooks) and walking sticks, many inlaid with stag horn, known as "New Zealand ivory."

HOKIANGA & THE KAURI COAST

85 km (53 mi) west of Paihia.

A peaceful harbor moves inland into the Hokianga region. It's a quiet area with small towns, unspoiled scenery, and proximity to the giant kauri trees on the Kauri Coast, a 20-minute drive south on Highway 12. Here the highway winds through Waipoua State Forest, then stretches south to Kaipara Harbour. Giant golden sand dunes tower over the mouth of Hokianga Harbour, across the water from the twin settlements of Omapere and Opononi. Opononi is the place where Opo, a tame dolphin, came to play with swimmers in the mid-1950s, putting the town on the national map for the first and only time in its history. A statue in front of the pub commemorates the much-loved creature.

ESSENTIALS

Visitor Info Hokianga Visitor Information Centre (⊠*11 State Hwy. 12, Omapere* ☎*09/405-8869*). **Kauri Coast i-Site Visitor Centre** (⊠*69 Normanby St., Dargaville* ☎*09/439-8360* ☐*09/439-8365* ⊕*www.dargaville.co.nz*).

WHAT TO SEE

The 1838 **Mangungu Mission House** is an overlooked stop on the tourist trail. Although Waitangi is the most known site of New Zealand's founding document, this unassuming spot, which looks out over Hokianga Harbour, was the scene of the second signing of the Treaty. Here, on February 12, 1840, the largest gathering of Māori chiefs signed the Treaty of Waitangi (73 chiefs, compared with only 31 in Waitangi's signing). The house is now a museum, furnished with pre-Treaty missionary items, including portraits, photographs, and furniture. ⊠*Motukiore Rd., Hokianga Harbour* ☎*09/401-9640* ☐*$3* ☉*Dec. 26–Jan., daily noon–4; Feb.–Dec., weekends noon–4.*

Fodor'sChoice **Waipoua State Forest** contains the largest remnant of the kauri forests
★ that once covered this region. A short path leads from the parking area on the main road through the forest to **Tane Mahuta,** "Lord of the Forest," standing nearly 173 feet high and measuring 45 feet around its base. The largest tree in New Zealand, it's 1,200 to 2,000-odd years old. The second-largest tree, older by some 800 years, is **Te Matua Ngahere.** It's about a 20-minute walk from the road. Other trees of note are the **Four Sisters,** four kauri trees that have grown together in a circular formation. If you have a couple of hours to spare, head to the Kauri Walks parking lot, about a mile south of the main Tane Mahuta parking lot. From here, you can take the long way through the forest, passing by the **Yakas Tree** (named after an old kauri-gum digger), the **Four Sisters,** and Te Matua Ngahere.

Department of Conservation Visitor Centre (⊠ *Waipoua River Rd., Waipoua Forest* ☎*09/439–3011*). A campground is in the forest—check at the visitor center before you pitch a tent. Facilities include toilets, hot showers, and a communal cookhouse. When it's wet, you

The Poor Knights Islands

Jacques Cousteau once placed the Poor Knights Islands among the world's top 10 dive locations. Underwater archways, tunnels, caves, and rocky cliffs provide endless opportunities for viewing many species of subtropical fish in the warm currents that sweep down from the Coral Sea. On a good day you'll see soft coral, sponge gardens, gorgonian fields, and forests of kelp.

Two large islands and many islets make up the Poor Knights, remnants of an ancient volcanic eruption 12 nautical mi off the stunning Tutukaka coast, a half-hour drive east of Whangarei. The ocean around them is a marine reserve, extending 800 meters (½ mi) from the islands. Indeed the islands themselves are a nature reserve; landing on them is prohibited.

At 7.9 million cubic feet, Rikoriko Cave, on the southern island's northwest side, is one of the world's largest sea caves. It's known for its acoustics. Ferns hang from its roof, and underwater cup coral grows toward the rear of it. (Normally found at depths of 200 meters, the cave light has tricked the coral into thinking it is deeper.) Normal visibility at the Poor Knights is between 20 and 30 meters, but in Rikoriko Cave it goes up to 35 to 45 meters.

A dense canopy of regenerated *pohutukawa* covers the islands, flowering brilliant scarlet around Christmas time. Native Poor Knights lilies cling to cliff faces, producing bright red flowers in October. Rare bellbirds (*koromikos*) and red-crowned parakeets (*kakarikis*), thrive in the predator-free environment. Between October and May, millions of seabirds come to breed, including the Buller's shearwaters that arrive from the Arctic Circle. But possibly the most distinguished resident is the New Zealand native *tuatara*, a reptile species from the dinosaur age that survives only on offshore islands.

New Zealand fur seals bask on the rocks and feed on the abundant fish life, mostly from July to October, and year-round dolphins, whales, and bronze whaler sharks can be seen in the surrounding waters. In summer you can see minke and Brydes whales, too. In March stingrays stack in the hundreds in the archways for their mating season.

Conditions rarely prevent diving, which is good year-round. That said, don't expect the same experience you'll get diving in the Maldives or off Australia's Great Barrier Reef. There aren't as many colorful fish, and the water is cooler. In October, the visibility drops to about 18 to 20 meters because of a spring plankton bloom, though this attracts hungry marine life. The best places for novices are Nursery Cove and shallower parts of the South Harbour.

Dive Tutukaka (⊠ *Poor Knights Dive Centre, Marina Rd., Tutukaka* ☎ *09/434–3867* 🖷 *09/434–3884* ⊕ *www.diving.co.nz*) has trips for $225 with full gear rental (plus $10 for lunch). If you're not a diver, you can see the scenery from *Cave Rider,* a 25-passenger, jet-powered inflatable ($90). You can also sail on *The Perfect Day,* a 70-foot luxury multilevel boat, which includes a half day of sightseeing, with the option to go kayaking, snorkeling, and diving ($130). Free transfers to and from Whangarei are provided.

–Richard Pamatatau & Toni Mason

2

may spot large kauri snails in the forest. Also, the successful eradication of predators such as weasels and stoats has led to a rise in the number of kiwis in the forest. You'll need a flashlight to spot one, because the birds only come out at night.

Sixty-four kilometers (40 mi) south of the Waipoua Forest along the Kaihu River, you'll come to **Dargaville**, once a thriving river port and now a good place to stock up if you're planning to camp in any of the nearby forests. It has some good craft stores, too. The surrounding region is best known for its main cash crop, the purple-skinned sweet potato known as *kūmara*. You'll see field after field dedicated to this root vegetable and shops selling it cheaper than anywhere else.

★ Continuing south of Dargaville, you reach Matakohe, a pocket-size town with an outstanding attraction: the **Matakohe Kauri Museum.** The museum's intriguing collection of artifacts, tools, photographs, documents, and memorabilia traces the story of the pioneers who settled this area in the second half of the 19th century—a story interwoven with the kauri forests. The furniture and a complete kauri house are among the superb examples of craftsmanship. One of the most fascinating displays is of kauri gum, the transparent lumps of resin that form when the sticky sap of the kauri tree hardens. This gum, which was used to make varnish, can be polished to a warm, lustrous finish that looks remarkably like amber—right down to the occasional insects trapped and preserved inside—and this collection is the biggest in the world. **Volunteers Hall** contains a huge kauri slab running from one end of the hall to the other, and there is also a reproduction of a cabinetmaker's shop, and a chain-saw exhibit. The Steam Saw Mill illustrates how the huge kauri logs were cut into timber. Perhaps the best display is the two-story replica of a late-1800s/early-1900s boardinghouse. Rooms are set up as they were over 100 years ago; you can walk down the hallways and peer in at the goings-on of the era. If you like the whirring of engines, the best day to visit is Wednesday, when much of the museum's machinery is started up. ⊠ *Church Rd., Matakohe* 🕾 *09/431–7417* ⊕ *www.kaurimuseum.com* 🖾 *$15* ⊘ *Nov.–Apr., daily 8:30–5:30; May–Oct., daily 9–5.*

WHERE TO EAT

¢–$$$ ✕ **Boatshed Café and Crafts.** This café is also on the waterfront adjacent to the Rawene supermarket, craft shop, and ferry ramp. It's got a lovely outdoor deck and is a good place to take a coffee and piece of pizza while waiting for the ferry. ⊠ *Clendon Esplanade, Rawene* 🕾 *09/405–7728* ▭ *MC, V* ⊘ *No dinner.*

¢–$$$ ✕ **Waterline Cafe.** This café is on the waterfront next to the Kohukohu wharf. On fine days, jump off the dock for a swim before having a pizza, fish-and-chips, or a sandwich under the shade sails, or stop in for coffee and some chocolate macadamia fudge on your way out of town to the Rawene–Kohukohu ferry. ⊠ *2 Beach Rd., Kohukohu* 🕾 *09/405–5552* ▭ *MC, V* ⊘ *No dinner Sun.–Thurs.*

WHERE TO STAY

$$$$
★
╳⊞ **Waipoua Lodge.** Owners Nicole and Chris Donahoe have renovated this 19th-century kauri farmhouse and its buildings into lovely suites. All the rooms are decorated differently, from stylishly modern to more rustic, with plenty of space and natural light, and all have balconies or patios that look out over Waipoua Forest. After dinner, you can toast marshmallows in the central fireplace. Meals, available by arrangement, usually focus on venison, lamb, or beef, garden vegetables, and indigenous seasonings. You can stroll through the native bush on the property, or enjoy a private hot tub by candlelight on a balcony overlooking the forest. At 2 km (1¼ mi) south of Waipoua Forest, the lodge is handy to the legendary kauri Tane Mahuta and one of the few areas where you can take night walks to view kiwi. Pros: Friendly and warm, peaceful, beautiful location. Con: For some, the isolation may be too much. ⊠ *State Hwy. 12, Waipoua* ☎*09/439–0422* 🖷*09/523–8081* ⊕*www.waipoualodge.co.nz* ⟿*4 suites* ♿*In-room: no a/c, kitchen. In-hotel: public Internet, public Wi-Fi, no elevator* ▤*AE, MC, V* ��⎮*BP.*

$$–$$$
⊞ **Copthorne Hotel and Resort Hokianga.** From the deck of this seaside hotel you look straight out to the mouth of Hokianga Harbour, where the Polynesian navigator Kupe first arrived in New Zealand, according to legend, 1,000 years ago. It's safe to say that the view has not changed. The restaurant's specialty is crayfish; choose your live cray from their tank or, as some prefer, meet it for the first time on your plate. The *kaimoana* (seafood) tasting plate for two includes Pacific oysters, seared scallops and calamari, chili mussels, and creamed paua, served with a lime and *horopito* aioli. The hotel is the base for local company Footprints–Waipoua, which takes "Twilight Encounter" tours through the Waipoua Forest to visit New Zealand's largest kauri trees. Pros: Low key, on the beach, family owned. Con: Not what you would call a luxury resort. ⊠*State Hwy. 12, Omapere* ☎*09/405–8737* 🖷*09/405–8801* ⊕*www.omapere.co.nz* ⟿*37 rooms, 9 suites* ♿*In-room: no a/c, kitchen. In-hotel: restaurant, bar, pool* ▤*AE, DC, MC, V.*

¢–$$
★
⊞ **The Tree House.** Amid 15 acres of subtropical jungle, native forest, ponds, fruit trees, and a macadamia orchard, the Tree House is a great reason to stop in Kohukohu. It's aimed at backpackers and cycle tourists on a budget. The little wooden cabins have porches with perfect views of the bush. The two rooms in the main building are simply furnished, with wooden furniture, painted wooden floors, and adobe-painted walls. You can hike through the forest to a lookout for great views of the Hokianga Harbour. All the kitchen and bathroom facilities are in the main house. You can also rent a two-bedroom self-contained cottage in Kohukohu on the harbor. Pros: Inexpensive, simple, friendly. Con: Very basic. ⊠*168 West Coast Rd., R.D. 1, Kohukohu* ☎*09/405–5855* 🖷*09/405–5857* ⊕*www.treehouse.co.nz* ⟿*2 single-bedroom cabins, 1 2-bedroom cabin, 1 housebus, 2 dorm rooms in main house (4 beds and 3 beds, respectively), 3 tent sites, 2 bedroom cottage* ♿*In-hotel: kitchen, laundry facilities* ▤*MC, V.*

¢–$
⊞ **Kauri Coast Top 10 Holiday Park.** With the Trounson Kauri Park marking its northern boundary, owners Herb and Heather Iles can point you in the right direction for several outdoor activities, but perhaps the big-

Twilight Encounter

The night tours to see Tane Mahuta and Te Matua Ngahere are led by **Footprints-Waipoua** (✉ *State Hwy. 12, Omapere* ☎ *09/405–8207* ⊕ *www.footprintswaipoua.com*). Tours are led by local Māori guides, experienced bushmen, who enrich your experience with their knowledge of the forest and wildlife, waiata (traditional Māori song), and tales from Māori legend. The Twilight Encounter is a four-hour night walk ($75); a shortened version, Meet Tane at Night, takes 1½ hours ($50). If you're really pressed for time, but want more than your own self-guided 10-minute jaunt, there is also a 40-minute tour ($15).

The same guides also run **Crossings-Hokianga** (✉ *State Hwy. 12, Omapere* ☎ *09/405–8207* ⊕ *www.crossingshokianga.com*). Centering on a guided boat cruise of the Hokianga Harbour, this day trip begins and ends in the Bay of Islands, with a focus on Hokianga history and the natural environment ($110). The cruise stops at historical spots throughout the harbor, such as Motuti, the Mangungu Mission Station, and Kohukohu. You can also take shorter harbor crossings, skipping the walk. Tours run daily November to April, and Monday, Wednesday, and Saturday, May through October.

gest draw is after-dark exploration. They give guided tours of the kauri park nightly (tours cost $20; reservations essential); guests frequently spot kiwi on the walks. The various lodging configurations—cabins with or without kitchens, and with or without bathrooms, as well as self-contained apartments—are kept spotless, and there's a camp kitchen and barbecue area. If you are traveling from the north, you need to turn left off the state highway and onto Trounson Park Road, 3 km (2 mi) before the small village of Kaihu. The holiday park is clearly signposted. Pros: Good for families, cheap, clean. Cons: Gets crowded, not private. ✉ *Trounson Park Rd., 70 km (43 mi) south of Opononi* ☎🏠 *09/439–0621* ⊕ *www.kauricoasttop10.co.nz* ⇆ *2 motel units, 3 apartments, 8 cabins, 60 campsites* & *In-room: no a/c, kitchen (some), no TV (some). In-hotel: laundry facilities* ▤ *MC, V.*

THE BAY OF ISLANDS

The Bay of Islands was a large Māori settlement when Captain James Cook first anchored off Roberton Island in 1769. He noted that "the inhabitants in this bay are far more numerous than in any other part of the country that we had visited." When the English started a convict settlement in Australia a couple of decades later, many boats stayed in the South Pacific to go whaling and sealing, and the Bay of Islands became a port of call. Consequently, many of the early European arrivals were sailors and whalers, stopping to blow off steam, have a few drinks, and trade with the local Māori. A missionary, Henry Williams, wrote in 1828 that a whaling captain had told him "all the Europeans were in a state of intoxication, except himself and two others."

It took nearly a century for the Bay of Islands to get some positive reviews. American author Zane Grey visited in the 1920s to fish for marlin and was so impressed that he wrote a book about the bay called *Tales of the Angler's Eldorado*. Game fishing remains one of the bay's many draws, with record catches of marlin and mako shark, along with diving, boating, and swimming with dolphins. Many of the 144 islands were farms, but now only one, Motoroa, is still farmed; most others are now used for vacation homes.

PAIHIA & WAITANGI

69 km (43 mi) north of Whangarei.

As the main vacation base for the Bay of Islands, Paihia is an unremarkable stretch of motels at odds with the quiet beauty of the island-studded seascape. With its handful of hostels, plus the long and safe swimming beach, it's popular with a young backpacker crowd. Most of the boat and fishing tours leave from the central wharf, as do the passenger ferries to the historic village of Russell. The nearby suburb of Waitangi, however, is one of the country's most important historic sites. It was near here on the beautiful park that is the Treaty Grounds the Treaty of Waitangi, the founding document for modern New Zealand, was signed.

The main Bay of Islands visitor bureau, in Paihia, is open daily 8 to 5 May through September; 8 to 6 October, November, March, and April; and 8 to 8 December through February. There is a very good toilet facility at the southern end of the strip. **Bay of Islands Visitor Information Centre Paihia** (⊠ *Marsden Rd., Paihia* 🕾 *09/402–7345* ⊕ *www. bayofislands.co.nz*).

ESSENTIALS

Bus Depot **Paihia** (⊠ *Paihia Travel Centre, Maritime Bldg.* 🕾 *09/402–7857*).

WHAT TO SEE

FodorsChoice
★ **Waitangi National Trust Estate** is at the northern end of Paihia. Inside the visitor center a 23-minute video (shown from 9 to 10, noon to 1, and 3 to 6) sketches the events that led to the Treaty of Waitangi. Interspersed between the three rounds of video screenings is a half-hour *kapa haka*, a live Māori cultural performance. The center also displays Māori artifacts and weapons, including a musket that belonged to Hone Heke Pokai, the first Māori chief to sign the treaty. After his initial display of enthusiasm for British rule, Hone Heke was quickly disillusioned, and less than five years later he attacked the British in their stronghold at Russell. From the visitor center, follow a short track (trail) through the forest to **Ngatoki Matawhaorua** (ng-ga-to-ki ma-ta-*fa*-oh-*roo*-ah), a Māori war canoe. This huge kauri canoe, capable of carrying 80 paddlers and 55 passengers, is named after the vessel in which Kupe, the Polynesian navigator, is said to have discovered New Zealand. It was built in 1940 to mark the centennial of the signing of the Treaty of Waitangi.

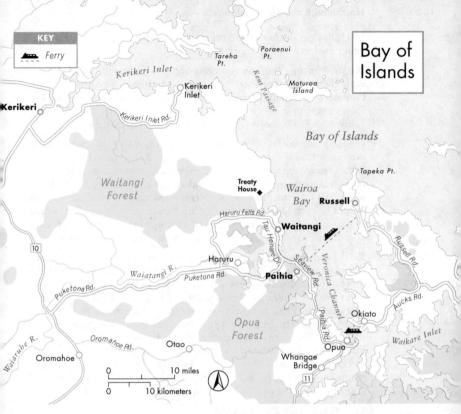

KEY

The **Treaty House** in Waitangi Treaty Grounds is a simple white timber cottage. The interior is fascinating, especially the back, where exposed walls demonstrate the difficulties that early administrators faced—such as an acute shortage of bricks (since an insufficient number had been shipped from New South Wales, as Australia was known at the time) with which to finish the walls.

The Treaty House was prefabricated in New South Wales for British Resident James Busby, who arrived in New Zealand in 1832. Busby had been appointed to protect British commerce and put an end to the brutalities of the whaling captains against the Māori, but he lacked the judicial authority and the force of arms necessary to impose peace. On one occasion, unable to resolve a dispute between Māori tribes, Busby was forced to shelter the wounded of one side in his house. While tattooed warriors screamed war chants outside the windows, one of the Māori sheltered Busby's infant daughter, Sarah, in his cloak.

The real significance of the Treaty House lies in the events that took place here on February 6, 1840, the day the Treaty of Waitangi was signed by Māori chiefs and Captain William Hobson, representing the British crown *(see the Treaty of Waitangi CloseUp box)*. The Treaty House has not always received the care its significance merits. When Lord Bledisloe, New Zealand's governor-general between 1930 and

1935, bought the house and presented it to the nation in 1932, it was being used as a shelter for sheep.

Whare Runanga (fah-ray roo-nang-ah) is a traditional meetinghouse with elaborate Māori carvings inside. The house is on the northern boundary of Waitangi Treaty Grounds. For $10, you can take an hour-long guided tour of the Treaty Grounds. ⊠ *Waitangi Rd., Waitangi* ☎ *09/402–7437* ⊕ *www.waitangi.net.nz* ⊠ *$12* ☉ *Daily 9–5.*

On the National Trust Estate beyond the Treaty Grounds, **Mt. Bledisloe** offers a splendid view across Paihia and the Bay of Islands. The handsome ceramic marker at the top showing the distances to major world cities was made by Doulton in London and presented by Lord Bledisloe in 1934 during his term as governor-general of New Zealand. The mount is 3 km (2 mi) from the Treaty House, on the other side of the Waitangi Golf Course. From a small parking area on the right of Waitangi Road, a short track rises above a pine forest to the summit.

EN ROUTE

The Hundertwasser Public Toilets. On the main street of Kawakawa, a nondescript town just off State Highway 1 south of Paihia, stand surely the most outlandish public toilets in the country—a must-go even if you don't need to. Built by Austrian artist and architect Friedensreich Hundertwasser in 1997, the toilets are fronted by brightly colored ceramic columns supporting an arched portico, which in turn supports a garden of grasses. There are no straight lines in the building, which is furnished inside with mostly white tiles, punctuated with primary colors and set in black grout (something like a Mondrian after a few drinks), and plants sprout from the roof. If you sit in one of the cafés across the road you can watch the tourist buses stop so the visitors take pictures.

SPORTS & THE OUTDOORS

BOATING **Carino NZ Sailing and Dolphin Adventures** (⊡ *Box 286, Paihia* ☎ *09/402–8040* 🖶 *09/402–8661* ⊕ *www.sailinganddolphin.co.nz*) gets close to dolphins (primarily bottlenose) and penguins. Passengers on the 50-foot red catamaran can just relax or pitch in with sailing. This full-day trip ($90) includes a barbecue lunch at one of the islands, weather permitting, and a full bar is on board.

Fodor'sChoice **Dolphin Discoveries** (⊠ *Marsden and Williams Rds., Paihia* ☎ *09/402–8234* ★ 🖶 *09/402–6058* ⊕ *www.dolphinz.co.nz*) offers a range of trips twice a day with an option that allows you to "Swim with the Dolphins."

You might also spot Brydes whales, migrating humpback and orca whales, or groups of tiny blue penguins. Prices begin at $79 with an optional $30 if dolphins are discovered and you wish to swim with them.

★ **Fullers** (⊠ *Maritime Bldg., Marsden Rd., Paihia* ☎ *09/402–7421* ⊕ *www.fboi.co.nz*) runs cruises and sea-based adventure trips departing daily from both Paihia and Russell. The most comprehensive sightseeing trip is the six-hour Best of the Bay Supercruise ($82) aboard a high-speed catamaran. You'll follow about half of what was once called the "Cream Trip" route, but nowadays, instead of picking up cream

2

from farms, the boat delivers mail and supplies to vacation homes. Fullers also visits Urupukapuka Island, once home to a *hapu* (subtribe) of the Ngare Raumati Māori. Little is known about their life, but there are numerous archaeological sites. It's also the only one to go to Otehei Bay, one of the island's most beautiful bays. On this particular trip, the boat stops for an hour and a half on the island, where you can go kayaking, take a short hike, or have lunch at the **Zane Grey Café.** The trip also takes in the Hole in the Rock. A catamaran operated by **Straycat Day Sailing Charters** (*Box 411, Paihia 09/402–6130 or 0800/101–007*) makes one-day sailing trips in the Bay of Islands from Paihia and Russell at $79 per adult and $45 per child, which includes a picnic-style lunch and sake or a kiwi-fruit liqueur, stops at two of the islands, bushwalks, swimming, and snorkeling.

DIVING The Bay of Islands has some of the finest scuba diving in the country, particularly around Cape Brett, where the marine life includes moray eels, stingrays, and grouper. The wreck of the Greenpeace vessel *Rainbow Warrior,* sunk by French agents in 1985, is another Bay of Islands underwater highlight. The wreck was transported to the Cavalli Islands in 1987 and is now covered in soft corals and jewel anemones; it's full of fish life. Water temperature at the surface varies from 16°C (62°F) in July to 22°C (71°F) in January. From September through November, underwater visibility can be affected by a plankton bloom.

Paihia Dive Compass Ltd. (*Box 210, Paihia 09/4343-762 or 0800/107–551 www.divenz.com*) offers complete equipment rental and regular boat trips for accredited divers for $190 per day; they also run dive courses.

FISHING **Marlin Fishing New Zealand** (*Box 285, Paihia 09/402–8189 or 0274/776–604 www.marlinfishing.co.nz*) goes for the big ones off the Northland coast and around Three Kings Islands. The cost is $3,250 per day for a maximum of four, including all tackle and meals. A far less-expensive alternative than pricey marlin fishing is to fish for snapper and kingfish within the bay. **Spot-X** (*Box 361, Kerikeri 09/402–7123 www.fish-spot-x.co.nz*) runs four-hour snapper-fishing trips for about $90 per person and six-hour kingfish trips for $210, including bait and tackle (bring your own lunch).

WHERE TO EAT

$$$–$$$$ ✕ **The Sugar Boat.** High and dry on the banks of the Waitangi River sits this historic kauri sailing vessel, which once carried sugar to a sugar refinery in Auckland. On deck is the Cuban-inspired **Cubar,** serving cocktails and lunch—such as blackened fish tacos and Cuban sandwiches—and providing DJs, live music, and dancing by night; dinner is served below deck on kauri tables inset with relics that the famous New Zealand diver Kelly Tarlton salvaged from wrecks. Dishes might include ostrich fillet served with gnocchi, roasted goat cheese, char-grilled zucchini, and cherry tomatoes in a port and cranberry jus. ⊠ *Waitangi Bridge, Paihia 09/402–7018 www.sugarboat.co.nz* *AE, DC, MC, V.*

$$–$$$ ✕**The Saltwater Café and Bar.** If the sea air's given you an appetite, head to this casual spot, known as The Salty, to grab a steaming pizza. The Salty is the restaurant's signature pizza, brimming with oysters, mussels, baby octopus, shrimp, calamari, and smoked fish, or you could try the Meat Lover's, loaded with salami, ham, bacon, and chicken. The Salty moonlights as one of Paihia's livelier nightspots, with live music and DJs. ⊠*Kings Rd., Paihia* ☎*09/402–6080* ═*AE, DC, MC, V* ⊘*No lunch.*

WHERE TO STAY

$$$$ ⊡**Paihia Beach Resort & Spa.** A large *pohutukawa* tree stands next to the heated saltwater pool in front of this resort overlooking the bay. All the rooms have bay views and a deck or patio plus a large whirlpool tub in the bathroom. You have free use of the sauna or steam room. The state-of-the-art day spa, which is also open to nonguests, has a full range of treatments, including Vichy showers—the mochaccino mud wrap comes highly recommended. Pros: Close to town, stunning views. Con: Road noise can be disturbing. ⊠*116 Marsden Rd., Paihia* ☎*09/402–6140* ≞*09/402–6026* ⊕*www.paihiabeach.co.nz* ↸*19 rooms, 2 suites* ⚐*In-room: kitchen, dial-up, DVD. In-hotel: restaurant, bar, pool, spa, no elevator* ═*AE, DC, MC, V* ⓘⓞⓘ*BP.*

$$$ ⊡**Abri.** These freestanding studio apartments that look like tree houses take advantage of the bush setting just behind the Paihia beachfront, offering lovely sea views. The two units have woodwork with indigenous timber, such as *rimu* flooring and *macrocarpa* walls and jet baths; their large living-room areas open onto outside decks. The apartments have their own kitchen facilities, even a small barbecue on the deck, but most guests take the short walk to the restaurants in town for meals. You'll find fresh cookies and flowers in your room daily. Pros: Close to town, friendly hosts. Con: Entrance up a staircase. ⊠*10–12 Bayview Rd., Paihia* ☎*09/402–8035* ⊕*www.abri-accom.co.nz* ↸*2 studios, 1 suite* ⚐*In-room: kitchen, VCR. In-hotel: no kids under 16, no elevator* ═*MC, V.*

¢–$$$ ⊡**Bay Adventurer.** Accommodations range from dorm rooms for just ★ $20 to studio and one-bedroom apartments, which have kitchens, bathrooms, and TVs. Brightly colored linen is supplied in all rooms, even the dorms (some are women-only). The apartments have two bedrooms sleeping four, a full bathroom (bubble bath supplied), kitchen, lounge, and deck. A subtropical garden surrounds the pool and hot tub, and the beach is a few minutes' walk away, although the hosts will lend you a bicycle or scooter if you feel like taking a ride. Although they offer a Continental breakfast, the hostel also has a deal going with one of the nearby restaurants, and you can have a hot breakfast delivered to your room. Pros: Women-only dorms, fun environment, caters to budget travelers. Cons: Noisy, basic. ⊠*28 Kings Rd., Paihia* ☎*09/402–5162* ≞*09/402–5163* ⊕*www.bayadventurer.co.nz* ↸*14 dorm rooms, 7 doubles, 9 apartments* ⚐*In-hotel: pool, laundry facilities, public Internet, no elevator* ═*MC, V.*

$$ ⊡**Austria Motel.** The large, double-bed rooms are typical of motel accommodations in the area—clean and moderately comfortable but devoid of charm. However, some of the rooms have sea views, and there is covered off-street parking. The shops and waterfront at Paihia are a two-minute walk away. Pros: Friendly; clean; close to town. Con: Very basic. ✉️*36 Selwyn Rd., Paihia* 📞📠*09/402–7480* 🛏️*8 rooms* ⚟*In-room: no a/c, kitchen. In-hotel: no elevator* ⊟*MC, V.*

¢–$
★
🍴 **Saltwater Lodge.** This is one of the best spots in Paihia's Kings Road area (the town's hostel corridor) for cleanliness and comfort. The hostel rooms start at $24 a night, and even the cheapest beds have duvets supplied. Bunk-bed dormitories have en-suite bathrooms with shower, storage facilities, and reading lights over the beds. The second-floor motel units come with king beds and bunks, plus a fridge and a small TV. If you're lucky, you'll nab one of the rooms looking over Paihia beach (don't worry if not; the hostel is a two-minute walk from the beach). The communal kitchen is probably the best equipped in the whole country, with everything from a wok to egg beaters. Even a small gym and bikes can be used at no extra charge. In the garden you'll find barbecues and a wood-fired brazier. Pros: Close to beach, attracts a good crowd, modern architecture. Con: Can be noisy. ✉️*14 Kings Rd., Paihia* 📞*09/402–7075* 📠*09/402–7240* 🌐*www.saltwaterlodge. co.nz* 🛏️*10 double rooms, 9 dorm rooms* ⚟*In-room: no a/c, kitchen, refrigerator (some), no TV (some). In-hotel: restaurant, gym, laundry facilities, public Internet, no elevator* ⊟*MC, V.*

RUSSELL

4 km (2½ mi) east of Paihia by ferry, 13 km (8 mi) by road and car ferry.

Russell is regarded as the "second" town in the Bay of Islands, but it's far more interesting, and pleasant, than Paihia. Hard as it is to believe these days, sleepy little Russell was once dubbed the "Hellhole of the Pacific." In the mid- to late 19th century (when it was still known by its Māori name, Kororareka) it was a swashbuckling frontier town, a haven for sealers and whalers who found the East Coast of New Zealand to be one of the richest whaling grounds on Earth.

Tales of debauchery were probably exaggerated, but British administrators in New South Wales were sufficiently concerned to dispatch a British resident in 1832 to impose law and order. After the Treaty of Waitangi, Russell was the national capital, until in 1844 the Māori chief Hone Heke, disgruntled with recently imposed harbor dues and his loss of authority, cut down the flagstaff flying the Union Jack above the town three times before attacking the British garrison. Most of the town burned to the ground in what is known as the Sacking of Kororareka. Hone Heke was finally defeated in 1846, but Russell never recovered its former prominence, and the seat of government was shifted first to Auckland, then to Wellington.

Today Russell is a delightful town of timber houses and big trees that hang low over the seafront, framing the yachts and game-fishing boats in the harbor. The atmosphere can best be absorbed in a stroll along the Strand, the path along the waterfront. There are several safe swimming beaches, some in secluded bays, as well as the aptly named Long Beach over the hill from the township.

GETTING AROUND

The road between Russell and Paihia is long and tortuous. The best way to travel between the two is by passenger ferry, which leaves from the Russell Wharf, or by car ferry, which departs from Okiato, about 9 km (5½ mi) southwest of town.

ESSENTIALS

Visitor Info **Russell Information Centre** (⊠ *Russell Wharf, Russell* ☎ *09/403–8020*).

WHAT TO SEE

New Zealand's oldest industrial building, the **Pompallier Mission,** at the southern end of the Strand, was named after the first Catholic bishop of the South Pacific. Marist missionaries built the original structure out of rammed earth, because they lacked the funds to buy timber. For several years the priests and brothers operated a press here, printing Bibles in the Māori language. You can try your hand at tanning, printing, and bookbinding, which is still done on-site (although these operations are no longer affiliated with the Church). From December through April you can visit independently, but from May to November the mission organizes tours at set times. ⊠ *The Strand* ☎ *09/403–7861* ⊕ *www. pompallier.co.nz* ⊠ *$7.50* ⊙ *Daily 10–5.*

★ **Christ Church** is the oldest church in the country. One of the donors to its erection in 1835 was Charles Darwin, at that time making his way around the globe on board the HMS *Beagle.* Behind the white picket fence that borders the churchyard, gravestones tell a fascinating and brutal story of life in the colony's early days. Several graves belong to sailors from the HMS *Hazard* who were killed in this churchyard by Hone Heke's warriors in 1845. Another headstone marks the grave of a Nantucket sailor from the whaler *Mohawk.* As you walk around the church, look for the musket holes made when Hone Heke besieged the church. The interior is simple and charming—embroidered cushions on the pews are examples of a folk-art tradition that is still very much alive. ⊠ *Church and Robertson Sts.* ⊙ *Daily 8–5.*

OUTDOOR ACTIVITIES

FISHING **Major Tom Charters** (☎ *09/403–8553* ⊕ *www.majortom.co.nz*) chases game fish such as marlin, kingfish, hapuka, snapper, broadbill, and tuna. A full day, with a maximum of four anglers, is $1,295, which includes lunch. **Triple B Boat Charters** (⊠ *2 Robertson Rd.* ☎ *09/403–7200 or 0274/972–177* 🖷 *09/403–7537* ⊙ *Closed May–Oct.*) runs saltwater fly-fishing and light-tackle trips on a 10-meter boat at $135 per hour (minimum four hours). The extremely affable owner Captain Dudley Smith helms the boat—all tackle is supplied along with tea and coffee but you bring your own lunch.

HIKING There are several pleasant walks around the Russell area; the most challenging—and spectacular—is the **Cape Brett Tramping Track** out to the lighthouse. It takes about eight hours round-trip. It costs $30 to walk the track and you can stay in a hut for $12 per night. It is not for the unfit, and good shoes are a must. Check with the Russell Information Center on the wharf. **Cape Brett Walkways** (☎09/403–8823 ⊕*www. capebrettwalks.co.nz*) has guided walks (lunch is provided) with historical and cultural commentary to Cape Brett lighthouse, via a boat trip to the Hole in the Rock ($175), and to the Whangamumu whaling station ($250). They can also take you out to Moturua Island (one of largest islands in the bay) via Hole in the Rock for a two-hour walk around the island, stopping at four beaches along the way (bathing suit optional), also $175.

For a shorter jaunt on your own (an hour each way), follow the **Whangamumu Walking Track** to the remnants of a whaling station. Many relics such as an old boiler and vats are still left at the station.

WHERE TO EAT

$$$–$$$$ ✕**Gannets.** German chefs Fabian and René combine classic French cui-
★ sine with local flavors. You might find prawns on a kūmara mash, flavored with lime, and served with roast peppers and mesclun greens in a mustard vinaigrette. Seafood is prevalent—try the tuna on red and white jasmine rice or vegetable-filled cannelloni, drizzled with tamarillo sauce. Homemade vodka infusions include a lemongrass version that is particularly refreshing at an outdoor table on a balmy evening. ⊠*York and Chapel Sts.* ☎09/403–7990 ▤*MC, V* ⊙*No lunch.*

$$$–$$$$ ✕**Kamakura.** The prime dining spot in Russell, this waterfront restau-
FodorśChoice rant combines subtly prepared yet flavorsome cuisine with arguably the
★ best restaurant view in town—especially if you nab a table up front. The specialty of the house is the seven-course "Naturally Northland" *degustation* menu, which includes Orongo Bay oysters, and warm quail salad in a lavender vinaigrette. The crab, chili, and lime ravioli on a crayfish bisque with horseradish cream always sells out. If dinner sounds delicious but it's too rich for your wallet, all the lunch dishes are under $20. ⊠*The Strand* ☎09/403–7771 ⊕*www.kamakura.co.nz* ▤*AE, DC, MC, V.*

$$$ ✕**Sally's.** At this restaurant overlooking Kororareka Bay from the Bay
★ of Islands Swordfish Club building, Sally's seafood chowder, packed with fresh mussels, shrimp, and fish, is the most popular dish—despite numerous requests, the chef refuses to divulge his recipe. If you're looking for some local lamb, don't go past the char-grilled lamb rump on roasted kūmara with garlic spinach and a red currant jus. Ask for a window table, or dine outdoors when it's sunny. ⊠*The Strand* ☎09/403–7652 ▤*AE, MC, V* ⑴*Licensed and BYOB.*

WHERE TO STAY

$$$$ ⊡**Flagstaff Lodge and Day Spa.** Photos of this 1912 villa in its original
state line the central kauri hallway. Its outside appearance has changed little, but inside it has been restored with all modern conveniences. The high-ceiling rooms have Italian-tile bathrooms, super-king-size beds, and French doors onto the wraparound veranda from where you can see a peep of the bay, a minute's walk away. Two French bathtubs stand behind a screen off a small courtyard where you can soak in essential oils and rose petals. A separate room houses the spa, offering mas-

sage and beauty treatments. Pros: Good facilities, nicely appointed. Con: No views. ✉17 *Wellington St.* ☎09/403–7117 or 0800/403–711 🖷09/403–7817 ⊕*www.flagstafflodge.co.nz* ➪4 *rooms* ⚏*In-room: no TV, Ethernet. In-hotel: spa* ☰*AE, DC, MC, V* ⍾❙*BP.*

$$$$ 📺**The Homestead at Orongo Bay.** Tucked away in gardens off the road
★   between the car-ferry landing and Russell, this historic lodge, built in 1865, soothes with peace and quiet which is why it's hosted people like Jane Fonda and Jo-Anna Lumley. The two rooms in the main homestead have kauri ceilings and paneling built in a New England colonial style, with large tiled bathrooms. A pair of bi-level barn rooms set back from the main building have angled roofs and skylights. Set on 17 acres of native bush, it's worth bringing your binoculars. The pond hosts a number of endangered birdlife, including the New Zealand native brown teal, the fourth-rarest waterfowl in the world. Sumptuous multicourse dinners are cooked (by prior arrangement) by chef and co-owner Michael Hooper, a food critic, who grows many of his organic ingredients on the property and plucks the oysters out of the bay in front of the house. He's been known to pick the salad while the entrée is being served. Pros: Convivial host, very good food, beautiful garden. Cons: Slightly out of town, small. ✉*Aucks Rd., R.D. 1* ☎09/403–7527 🖷09/403–7675 ⊕*www.thehomestead.co.nz* ➪4 *rooms* ⚏*In-room: DVD, Wi-Fi. In-hotel: public Internet, no elevator* ☰*AE, DC, MC, V* ⍾❙*BP.*

$$$$ 📺**Okiato Lodge.** Okiato is high up on Okiato Point, looking out on Opua, Paihia, and other Bay of Islands locales. Spacious rooms include step-down lounge areas, with high-vaulted ceilings and large windows with great views. With balconies and patios leading out onto the terraced grounds, each room has its own private access to the Point, and a track leads right down to the water. There is also a two-bedroom semi-detached cottage. The high-end rates include drinks and a four-course dinner, which emphasizes New Zealand favorites such as scallops, venison, and lamb. Pros: Lovely grounds, beautiful views. Con: Isolated. ✉*James Clendon Pl., Okiato Point (R.D. 1)* ☎09/403–7948 🖷09/403–7515 ⊕*www.okiato.co.nz* ➪11 *rooms* ⚏*In-room: dial-up, refrigerator. In-hotel: restaurant, bar, pool, no elevator* ☰*AE, MC, V* ⍾❙*MAP.*

$$$$ 📺**Omata Estate.** In a private bay on the end of Omata Estate's penin-
★   sula on 20 acres of vineyard, the main accommodation, a schist (stone) homestead, looks out onto golden sands and over the bay to Paihia. The homestead has four large double bedrooms and a large living area dominated by a kauri-wood bar, with a fireplace to boot. It comes with a fully stocked kitchen and all the fixings for a cooked breakfast feast. Don't miss out on a bath in the tub-for-two, which is surrounded by windows looking out onto subtropical gardens. In the boathouse, there's a beach-style apartment with whitewashed wood and doors opening out onto the bay, and above the garage is a loft apartment. The highly regarded restaurant has spectacular views over the vines to the bay. Seafood platters are lunchtime favorites; try the Best of the Best, a platter for two overflowing with grilled eye fillet, lamb, and chicken, pan-cooked prawns and *hapuka,* oysters from nearby Orongo Bay, and

green-lipped chili-marinated mussels, all served with an antipasto and an assortment of dips, including beet relish and arugula pesto. For dinner try the rack of lamb with five spiced pumpkin on a bed of tabbouleh with a syrah jus. Pros: Beautiful location, private. Con: Pricey. ⊠*Aucks Rd., between car ferry and Russell* ☎*09/403–8007* 🖨*09/403–8005* ⊕*www.omata.co.nz* ⇋*4 rooms, 2 apartments* ⚿*In-room: kitchen, DVD. In-hotel: restaurant, tennis court, public Internet, no elevator* ⊟*AE, DC, V.*

$$$–$$$$ 🏠 **Te Pa Helios.** Leave the drapes open when you go to sleep in this cliff-top B&B so you can wake to the sun rising over the bay. An old Māori *pā* (hilltop fortification) site and a small bay frame a view of islands dotting the clear blue sea. The property evokes Greece with its angular whitewashed buildings. In the main villa are the Island Suite, with a balcony on the cliff edge, and the spacious Russell Room, with a small terrace also set on the cliff. The self-catering Little Villa has two bedrooms. All bedrooms look out onto the ocean. Local art hangs in most of the rooms. Paths lead to the two beaches at the base of the cliff, where there is a three-bedroom bungalow you can stay. There is a two-night minimum. Pros: Relaxed, beautiful views. Con: Russell not within walking distance. ⊠*44 Du Fresne Pl., Tapeka Point* ☎🖨*09/403–7229* ⊕*www.babs.co.nz/helios/index.htm* ⇋*1 room, 1 suite, 1 villa, 1 cottage* ⚿*In-room: no a/c. In-hotel: no elevator* ⊟*MC, V* ⊘*Closed May–Oct.* ❑*CP.*

$$–$$$$ 🏠 **Duke of Marlborough Hotel.** This waterfront hotel with 26 rooms is a no-smoking venue, and with good reason—the previous three incarnations were burnt down (the first by the legendary Māori chief Hone Heke). It's a favorite with the yachting fraternity, for whom ready access to the harbor and the bar downstairs are the most important considerations. Antiques add character and the rooms are bright and cheerful. For more space, opt for one of the waterfront suites with large whirlpool baths, or there's a one-bedroom bungalow right on the waterfront. Pros: Prime waterfront position, busy, lively crowd. Cons: Can be too close to the action, very noisy, no privacy. ⊠*The Strand* ☎*09/403–7829* 🖨*09/403–7828* ⊕*www.theduke.co.nz* ⇋*19 rooms, 6 suites, 1 cottage* ⚿*In-room: no a/c. In-hotel: restaurant, bar, no elevator* ⊟*MC, V* ❑*CP and BP.*

$$–$$$ 🏠 **Arcadia Lodge.** Rumor had it that this gay-friendly bed-and-breakfast, perched over Matauwhi Bay, a few minutes' walk from town, had been supported for more than 100 years by whale vertebrae. Sure enough, when new owners re-piled the foundations of the turn-of-the-20th-century home in 2005, they found that that was virtually the only thing holding it up. One of the "backbones" of the house now sits in the lounge. Two spacious suites off the large guest lounge and dining area both have brass beds, sunrooms, and their own decks. Another three rooms are upstairs. The Tautoru Room has its own entrance, with a deck and a view of the bay where you can watch the boats coming and going from the Russell Boat Club (the club's bar is a good place to meet locals). Wake up with an appetite; breakfast could include fresh asparagus on Kerikeri smoked ham with focaccia and grilled cheese; or slow-roasted tomatoes on pesto bruschetta with pork and

CLOSE UP

The Far North

Above the Bay of Islands Northland are many small communities. For many the big attraction is **90 Mile Beach**, a 100-km (60-mi) or so long clear stretch of golden sand running up North Island's tip. You access it from Kaitaia, a vibrant town with a very good café—Birdies—where the omelets are not only delicious, they will set you up for the day. If you want to travel the beach, take a tour. Don't roll your eyes—a tour is the safest bet. The beach is virtually off-limits to independent travelers, as, thanks to quicksand and incoming tides, rental-car insurance won't cover you here.

Just out of Kaitaia are the beaches at Ahipara and Shipwrecks. Surfers love the long lines and almost perfect waves here. Many surfers head south around the point for even better waves and fewer people.

Cape Reinga, at the peninsula's end, is a sacred Māori area. They believe that spirits depart for the underworld by sliding down the roots of the headland's gnarled *pohutukawa* tree (reputed to be 800 years old) and into the sea. A much-photographed solitary lighthouse stands here.

You can easily drive into the Far North, barring 90 Mile Beach. From the Bay of Islands on State Highway 10 you'll reach Mangonui, a former whaling port on the southeast side of **Doubtless Bay.** Beach lovers should head for the Karikari Peninsula, on Doubtless Bay's northwestern side. From Doubtless Bay it's less than a half-hour's drive west to Awanui, near the service town of Kaitaia. Fill your gas tank in one of these two towns, then head north on Highway 1. The last few miles to Cape Reinga aren't paved. **Kaitaia Visitor Infor-**mation Centre (⊠ *Jaycee Park, South Rd., Kaitaia* ☎ *09/408–0879* 🖷 *09/408–2546*).

WHAT TO DO
The half-moon Matai Bay and Sponge Gardens are good for diving novices: they're safe and go to a depth of 13 meters (43 feet). Experienced divers should try the Matai Bay Pinnacle site, with a 39-meter (130-foot) drop. Odds are good you'll see blue mao-mao, demoiselles, and kingfish. **A to Z Diving** (⊠ *Whatuwhiwhi, Karikari Peninsula* ☎☎ *09/408–7077* ⊕ *www. atozdiving.co.nz*) dives start at around $50 or $135 with gear. **Dune-Rider 4x4 Tours** (⊠ *Maritime Bldg., Marsden Rd., Paihia* ☎ *09/402–8681* ⊕ *www.dunerider.co.nz*) goes to Cape Reinga via 90 Mile Beach. They make special stops, such as a visit to the "world-famous" Mangonui fish-and-chips shop. Trips cost $99. Phil Cross of **Far North Outback Adventures** (☝ *Box 668, Kaitaia* ☎ *09/408–0927* ⊕ *www.farnorthtours.co.nz*) takes groups of up to six in his 4x4 on day trips up 90 Mile Beach to Cape Reinga. He knows a lot of history and gives an excellent commentary. He supplies toboggans for dune sledding, and he visits Māori archaeological sites. He's also the only operator who can take a vehicle to Great Exhibition Bay. Lunch (provided) includes sandwiches, wine, and carrot cake (recipe on request). It costs $550 per trip, but it's worth it.

WHERE TO STAY & EAT
✕ **Waterfront Café** ($$$). Locals favor this relaxed harbor café for its seafood chowder made with fish and oysters. The pizza is also great—try the meat-lover's pie served with Kaitaia Fire, Northland's answer to

Tabasco sauce. ✉ *Beach Rd., Mangonui* ☎ *09/406–0850* 🍴 *AE, MC, V.*

✕🏨 **Carrington Resort** (\$\$\$\$). Carrington overlooks a sweeping white-sand beach. Spacious rooms open onto a wraparound veranda with views of the bay and the par-72 tournament-quality golf course. Chef Mark Oliver puts European and Asian spins on regional produce. The resort also has a vineyard, Karikari Estate. Pros: Beautiful location, golf course, quiet. Con: Lodge capacity may be too much for some. ✉ *Matai Bay Rd., Karikari Peninsula* ☎ *09/408–7222* 🌐 *www.carrington.co.nz* 🛏 *10 rooms, 14 villas* 🔑 *In-room: Ethernet. In-hotel: restaurant, bar, golf course, tennis court, pool, gym, beachfront, public Internet, no elevator* 🍴 *AE, DC, MC, V* 🍴 *BP, MAP.*

🏨 **Cavalli Beach House Retreat** (\$\$\$\$). Curving down a cliff face like a spinnaker in full sail, this retreat overlooks a private horseshoe-shape bay. Rooms are decorated with tapa cloths and local artworks; king-size beds are made up with cream linen and faux fur throws. A path leads up behind the house to a hot tub. Dinners are available on request. Pros: Beautiful architecture, superb location, intimate. Con: Not cheap. ✉ *Mahinepua Rd., Mahinepua* ☎ *09/405–1049* 🌐 *www.cavallibeachhouse.com* 🛏 *1 suite, 2 rooms* 🔑 *In-room: Wi-Fi, DVD. In-hotel: no elevator* 🍴 *AE, MC, V* 🍴 *BP.*

🏨 **Kauri Cliffs Lodge** (\$\$\$\$). Several holes of a par-72 championship golf course sweep past this cliff-top lodge. Ocean views reach to the Cavalli Islands; you also overlook three private beaches—one shimmering pink. The spa specialty is the six-hour "Ultimate Revival" treatment (\$795). Pros:

Absolute luxury, superb environment, sophisticated hospitality. Con: Too slick for some. ✉ *Matauri Bay Rd., Matauri Bay* ☎ *09/407–0010* 🌐 *www.kauricliffs.com* 🛏 *22 suites* 🔑 *In-room: no a/c, refrigerator, DVD. In-hotel: restaurant, golf course, tennis court, pool, gym, spa, beachfront, public Internet, no elevator* 🍴 *AE, DC, MC, V* 🍴 *MAP.*

🏨 **Shipwreck Lodge** (\$\$\$). American owners Roger and Laura Raduenz sailed to New Zealand in the late 1990s, the first stop on a round-the-world voyage, and never left. From the balconies of their contemporary seafront lodge you can look up the sweep of 90 Mile Beach. Three-course dinners are available on request (\$70). Pro: Beautiful beach views. Con: Town is 10 km (6 mi) away. ✉ *70 Foreshore Rd., Ahipara* ☎ *09/409–4929* 🌐 *www.shipwrecklodge.co.nz* 🛏 *3 rooms* 🔑 *In-room: dial-up, refrigerator. In-hotel: laundry facilities, no kids under 16, no-smoking rooms, no elevator* 🍴 *MC, V* 🍴 *BP.*

🏨 **Mangonui Hotel** (¢–\$). This classic wooden two-story pub sits just a few feet from Mangonui's harbor. The upstairs guest rooms are small but fitted in the style of the early-1900s hotel. Pros: Quaint and in town. Con: Very basic. ✉ *Beach Rd., Mangonui* ☎ *09/406–0003* 🌐 *www.mangonuihotel.co.nz* 🛏 *13 rooms* 🔑 *In-hotel: bars, no elevator* 🍴 *AE, MC, V.*

sweet fennel sausage; or zucchini, Parmesan, and mint fritters served with homemade chutneys. All of this comes with organic fruit from the garden, yogurt, granola, and fresh squeezed Kerikeri orange juice, which you can eat on the deck looking over the bay. Pros: Fantastic hosts, lovely rooms, beautiful views. Cons: None, really. ⊠ *10 Florance Ave.* ☎ *09/403–7756* 🖷 *09/403-7657* ⊕ *www.arcadialodge.co.nz* ⟿ *4 rooms, 2 with bath, 2 suites* ⚭ *In-room: no TV. In-hotel: restaurant, no elevator* ⊟ *MC, V* ⊺⊙⏐ *BP.*

¢–$ 🏠 **Sheltered Waters Backpackers.** This small hostel, a leisurely 10-minute walk from town, brings guests back for repeat visits. One dorm room can sleep 10, a double room with a bunk can take 4, and a suite also has beds and bunks. Palms circle the large garden, home to a little aviary (with a resident pair of lovebirds). If you're lucky, you'll stay on one of the nights the hosts cook up a pot of seafood chowder (made with local oysters and mussels). Pros: Affordable, clean, busy. Cons: Dorms can be noisy, lack of privacy. ⊠ *18 Florance Ave.* ☎ *09/403–8818* 🖷 *09/403 8461* ⊕ *www.russellbackpackers.co.nz* ⟿ *1 dorm room, 1 double room, 1 suite* ⚭ *In-room: DVD, kitchen. In-hotel: bicycles, laundry facilities, public Internet, some pets allowed, no elevator* ⊟ *No credit cards.*

TOURS

Fernz EcoTours takes tours in and around Russell. Most popular is the Coast and Kauri tour, which starts with a short excursion around the historic sights of Russell, and a trip to the Orongo Bay oyster farm, followed by a visit to Ngaiotonga Forest for a walk among the kauri. A half-day tour is $125, or you can add a trip to the glowworm caves and the Hundertwasser Public Toilets ($240). ⊠ *Kingfisher Rd., Jack's Bary, Russell* ☎ *09/403–7887 or 027/280–9600* ⊕ *www. fernzecotours.co.nz*

KERIKERI

★   *20 km (12 mi) north of Paihia.*

Kerikeri is often referred to as the cradle of the nation because so much of New Zealand's earliest history, especially interactions between Māori and Europeans, took place here. The main town is small but gaining a reputation for its crafts and specialty shops. A major citrus and kiwifruit growing area, it was once principally a service town for the whole mid-north region. Though newcomers have flocked to Kerikeri for its low-key lifestyle, it still feels like a small town.

The **Kerikeri Proctor Library,** open weekdays 8 to 5, and Saturday from 9:30 to 2, is the only place in Kerikeri that provides visitor information, and it's far less extensive than other bureaus. ⊠ *6 Cobham Rd., Kerikeri* ☎ *09/407–9297.*

WHAT TO SEE

If you happen to be in Kerikeri on a Sunday, head to the **Bay of Islands Farmers' Market,** to sample just about everything the region has to offer, from music to fresh produce, local wines, cheeses, preserves, and oils.

Grab a locally roasted coffee and wander among the stalls. ⊠ *Parking lot, off Hobson Ave., Kerikeri* ⊙ *Sun. 9–noon.*

The **Historic Kerikeri Basin,** just northeast of the modern town on the Kerikeri Inlet, is where most of the interest lies. Anglican missionaries arrived in this area in 1819; they were invited to Kerikeri by its most famous historical figure, the great Māori chief Hongi Hika. The chief visited England in 1820, where he was showered with gifts. On his way back to New Zealand, during a stop in Sydney, he traded many of these presents for muskets. Having the advantage of these prized weapons, he set in motion plans to conquer other Māori tribes, enemies of his own Ngapuhi people. The return of his raiding parties over five years, with many slaves and gruesome trophies of conquest, put considerable strain between Hongi Hika and the missionaries. Eventually his warring ways were Hongi's undoing. He was shot in 1827 and died from complications from the wound a year later.

The **Kerikeri Mission Station,** which includes the 1821 **Kemp/Mission House,** and the **Stone Store** provide a fascinating—and rare—look at pre-treaty New Zealand. **Kemp House,** otherwise known as Mission House, has gone through many changes since 1821, but ironically, a major flood in 1981 inspired its "authentic" restoration. The flood washed away the garden and damaged the lower floor, and during repair much information about the original structure of the house was revealed. Its ground floor and garden have been restored to the style of missionary days, and the upper floor, which remained unharmed by the flood, retains its Victorian decoration.

The **Stone Store** ⊠ *$3.50* ⊙ *Nov.–Apr., daily 10–5; May–Oct., Sat.– Wed. 10–5)* is Kerikeri's most picturesque attraction and the most striking building in the historic basin. Built between 1832 and 1836, it's New Zealand's oldest existing stone building. It held stores for the whole New Zealand mission of the time, and the ground floor is still a working trading store. The upper stories display the goods of a culture trying to establish itself in a new country, such as red Hudson Bay blankets, which were sought after by Māori from the *pā* (hilltop fortification), forged goods, steel tools, an old steel flour mill, and tools and flintlock muskets—also prized by local Māori. Guided tours are available; bookings are essential. ⊠ *Kerikeri Historic Basin, Kerikeri Rd.* ☎ *09/407–9236* ⊠ *$7.50* ⊙ *Daily 10–5.*

Rewa's Village museum re-creates a *kāinga* (unfortified fishing village) where local Māori would have lived in peaceful times. (In times of siege they took refuge in nearby Kororipo Pā.) In the village are reproductions of the chief Hongi Hika's house, the weapons store, and the family enclosure, as well as two original canoes dug up from local swamps and original *hāngi* stones (used to cook traditional Māori feasts) found on-site. A "discoverers garden" takes you on a winding path past indigenous herbs and other plants; information is posted describing the uses of each plant. ⊠ *Kerikeri Historic Basin, Kerikeri Rd.* ☎ *09/407–6454* ⊠ *$5* ⊙ *Nov.–Apr., daily 9:30–5:30; May–Oct., daily 10–4; Jan. and Feb., daily 9–5.*

Across the road from the Basin's Stone Store is a path leading to the historic site of **Kororipo Pā,** the fortified headquarters of chief Hongi Hika. Untrained eyes may have difficulty figuring out exactly where the pā was, as no structures are left. The pā was built on a steep-sided promontory between the Kerikeri River and the Wairoa Stream. There's still a fine view over both.

OUTDOOR ACTIVITIES

FISHING John Gregory of **Primetime Charters & Gamefishing** (✉ *Conifer La., Kerikeri* 📠 *09/407–1299* ⊕ *www.primetimecharters.co.nz*) has more than 25 years' experience at sea. The company, which holds the New Zealand record for most marlin caught, goes after all sport fish, specializing in broadbill swordfish. Prices start at $3,350 per day, with most trips between January and June taking five to seven days.

GOLF The spectacular par-72 championship course at **Kauri Cliffs** (✉ *Matauri Bay Rd., Matauri Bay* 📞 *09/407–0010* ⊕ *www.kauricliffs.com*) has four sets of tees to challenge every skill level. Fifteen holes have views of the Pacific, and six are played alongside the cliffs. You can rent Callaway clubs from the pro shop ($75). Green fees are $400 per person. Kauri Cliffs is approximately 45 minutes' drive from Kerikeri. **Carrington** (✉ *Matai Bay Rd., Karikari Peninsula* 📞 *09/408–1049* ⊕ *www.carrington.co.nz*) has an 18-hole, par 72, tournament quality course, which meanders along 100 acres of coastline. The course shares the land with the Karikari Estate winery, and **Carrington Resort,** a luxury lodge. Green fees are $85 per person, and clubs cost $40 to $65 to rent.

WHERE TO EAT

$$$ ✕**Marsden Estate Winery and Restaurant.** Named after the missionary
★ Samuel Marsden, who planted New Zealand's first grapevines in Kerikeri in 1819, this winery is a popular lunch spot and that's because it is very good. On a fine day ask for a table on the terrace. The seasonal menu is eclectic; try the venison loin on a kūara puree with asparagus, cherry tomatoes in a pomegranate molasses jus, or sample the smoked fish with bacon, potato salad, baby greens, and avocado aioli. Of the winery's small but notable output, the full-bodied Black Rocks Chardonnay has won national and international awards and the 2007 Pinot Gris is worth a try. The winery is open for tastings. ✉ *Wiroa Rd.* 📠 *09/407–9398* ⊕ *www.marsdenestate.co.nz* ▤ *MC, V* ☉ *No dinner Sun.–Thurs.*

¢–$ ✕**Fishbone Café.** The locals come for the great coffee and the thick sandwiches, panini, and frittatas. You'll also join them as they study the extensive blackboard menu, where you'll find the most popular dish of the house, a char-grilled-chicken Caesar salad with garlic aioli dressing. Follow this up with a fresh muffin, or the ever-disappearing caramel slice. Tin fish bones line the walls. ✉ *88 Kerikeri Rd.* 📞 *09/407–6065* ▤ *AE, DC, MC, V* ☉ *No dinner.*

WHERE TO STAY

$$$–$$$$ **The Summer House.** Hosts Christine and Rod Brown come from artistic families, a background that infuses this B&B. The downstairs room, slightly detached from the house, is done in a South Pacific style. It has the most space, a kitchenette, and a higher room rate. The two upstairs rooms in the main house share a guest lounge. One room has an 1860 French bed with furniture to match, and the other has a Victorian brass bedstead. Christine's breakfasts are wonderful, including freshly squeezed juice and fresh or poached fruits—all from the 2½ acres of citrus orchards on the property—Greek yogurt, homemade muesli, jams and marmalade, and free-range eggs cooked as requested. The landscaped subtropical garden surrounding the house attracts native birds, doves, and monarch butterflies. Pros: Lovely environment, friendly hosts. Con: Decor is overstyled. ⊠ *424 Kerikeri Rd.* ☎ *09/407–4294* 🖷 *09/407–4297* ⊕ *www.thesummerhouse.co.nz* 🛏 *3 rooms* ⚲ *In-room: no a/c, no TV, DVD. In-hotel: public Internet, no elevator* ⊟ *MC, V* ⫶⊙⫶ *BP.*

$–$$ **Kauri Park.** This small cluster of chalets is a notch above the usual, with modern decor and a beautiful setting among fruit trees adjacent to farmland. Friendly hosts Dallas and Delphine Eves display the usual Kiwi welcome with a free drink on arrival in the guest lounge. Each unit has a veranda and colorful furnishings. Kauri Park is a little out of town, with a more rural setting, but it's still only a few minutes' drive from the historic sights. Pros: Clean, relaxed, friendly. Con: Not within walking distance of town. ⊠ *512 Kerikeri Rd. (south end)* ☎ *09/407–7629* ⊕ *www.kauripark.co.nz* 🛏 *9 units* ⚲ *In-room: no a/c, dial-up. In-hotel: bar, Wi-Fi, no elevator* ⊟ *AE, DC, MC, V.*

$–$$ **Paheke.** An enormous cedar of Lebanon stands in front of this gracious 1864 kauri homestead; both the tree and the house are listed with the Historic Places Trust. The restored home has one modern wing, but it's designed to blend with the original building. Two rooms with wooden floors and private baths are in the new wing; one has a balcony overlooking the gardens. The rooms in the older wing are smaller but elegantly furnished with antiques. They share a bath. A three-course dinner and picnic lunches are available on request. Paheke is about a 15-minute drive southwest of Kerikeri and Paihia. Pros: Well-priced, relaxing, beautiful grounds. Con: Not close to town. ⊠ *State Hwy. 1, Ohaeawai* ☎ *09/405–9623* 🖷 *09/405–9628* ⊕ *www.paheke.co.nz* 🛏 *4 rooms, 2 with bath* ⚲ *In-hotel: laundry facilities, public Internet, no elevator* ⊟ *MC, V* ⫶⊙⫶ *BP.*

SHOPPING

At **Makana Confections** (⊠ *Kerikeri Rd.* ☎ *09/407–6800*) favorites include the macadamia butter toffee crunch, and it's almost impossible to leave without a bagful of chocolate-coated, locally grown macadamias or liqueur truffles. **Origin Art and Craft Co-op** (⊠ *128 Kerikeri Rd.* ☎ *09/407–1133*), 450 yards south of the Kerikeri turnoff, stocks locally made arts and crafts, such as place mats made from local timber; stained-glass lamp shades and trinket boxes; silver jewelry, textiles and felt work; and beautifully made calfskin and doeskin bags. Andrew and Robyn Leary of **Scopes NZ** (✉ *265 Waipapa Rd.* ☎ *09/407–4415*) produce fabulous kaleidoscopes from kauri wood that was buried in swamps for thousands of years. They also make "bubble scopes" (their own inventions), which view colored liquid in a transparent ball. Prices start at around $45 for small kauri scopes produced with materials such as *paua* (abalone shell), shards of glass, or bits of fishing tackle.

Coromandel Peninsula & the Bay of Plenty

WORD OF MOUTH

The Coromandel Peninsula was our favorite. It was late summer, and we swam each day...Hot Water Beach doesn't always work, you have to be there at the right time, and right tide. The whole Peninsula is worth a few days stay. We particularly liked Hahei Beach. Cormandal Town is a nice town, with quaint shops, and some darn good restaurant/cafes/coffee shops.

—tropo

Cathedral Cove was stunning and I will definitely be returning to do some exploring.

—pykiwi

Updated
by Richard
Pamatatau

THE RUGGED AND EXHILARATING COROMANDEL Peninsula lies some two hours southeast of Auckland. A range of sharp peaks stretches its entire spine with much of the winding coastal road at its base edged by pohutukawa trees clinging tenaciously to precarious walls of crumbling rock. Each curve in the road presents a new vista that varies from tiny islands to sweeping valleys, or beaches literally just off the road. You'll also become familiar with "the one-way bridge"—the road is very narrow in places. You can stop at many spots for a picnic, or a snooze under a tree. As you continue your drive you come to the Bay of Plenty, which—if you love seafood—lives up to its name. (Traffic can build up on this road, particularly in the busy summer months or weekends.)

Beautiful sandy beaches, lush native forests, and some steamy geothermal activity make the Coromandel Peninsula and Bay of Plenty quite a departure from Auckland. Most residents live in fishing villages or small rural towns, with the occasional artsy community or alternative-lifestyle commune thrown in (particularly in the Coromandel). Both areas bask in more than their fair share of sun for much of the year, so avocado, citrus, kiwifruit, nuts, and even subtropical fruits flourish here, and many growers adopt organic practices. Keep an eye out for the ubiquitous unmanned fruit stands and accompanying "honesty boxes."

From the peninsula's East Coast, the road stretches out to the coastal plains and forests of the Bay of Plenty. From the Bay of Plenty's northern gateway of Katikati as far as Whakatane, the coastline consists of huge stretches of sand, interrupted by rivers, estuaries, and sandbars. Inland, the soil is rich and fertile; this is farming territory with sprawling canopies of kiwifruit vines, fields of corn and other produce, and pockets of dense native forest. You'll see people fishing in some of the bays, but others have strict rules; signs in the shape of a fish outline whether or not you can fish.

The Bay of Plenty was one of the country's first areas settled by Māori, and the descendants of these earliest arrivals moved north to the Coromandel Peninsula as well. Although intertribal fighting and European-introduced diseases took a heavy toll on the Coromandel communities, the Bay of Plenty still has a strong Māori presence, particularly around Mount Maunganui.

ORIENTATION & PLANNING

GETTING ORIENTED

The Coromandel and Bay of Plenty region is about two to three hours southeast of Auckland and west of the Waikato farming district and is a mix of rugged and forested hill country and rich plains used for agriculture. It's about a seven-hour drive from Wellington, a few hours from Hamilton and Rotorua. Like many areas with an agricultural base it is dotted with either small rural service towns, or on the coast, by a big port in Tauranga, and then small settlements based on former sites

TOP REASONS TO GO

Beach Bounty. The eastern shores of the Coromandel and Bay of Plenty are major draws for beach-seeking North Islanders. The coastline has so many inlets and coves that it rarely feels overrun, even during the high season—so slather on the sunscreen, swim between the safety flags, and break out the hokey pokey (honeyed-toffee) ice cream.

Volcanoes & Vistas. From the mountainous spine and coastal cliffs of the Coromandel Peninsula to the Bay of Plenty's extinct volcano Mt. Maunganui, this region offers hypnotic views at every turn. The peak of the Pinnacles in Kauaeranga Valley Forest Park is surrounded by sweeping vistas; at White Island, the country's only live marine volcano, the steaming fissures are a dramatic sight by sea, air, or from the deck of a local café.

Walking & Hiking. There is superb bushwalking (hiking) around the Coromandel Peninsula. Inland from Tauranga are stream-side forest walks to McLaren and Kaiate Falls, and the Coromandel bush is full of ancient kauri trees (a local species of pine) and interesting birds, such as *tūī* (*too*-ee), fantails, and wood pigeons.

Watery Wonders. Whether you're in the mood for a day of deep-sea fishing or kayaking, a spot of snorkeling, or a swim with the dolphins, this region delivers. White Island provides some of the richest snorkeling and diving in the region. Surfers come from all over the country to ride the waves at Mount Maunganui, and the underground hot springs at Hot Water Beach are a one-of-a-kind attraction.

that were easily accessible by boats, often used to transport logs from the forestry works.

The Coromandel Peninsula. The Coromandel beckons from the Hauraki Plains like a big lizard lying in the sun—the dark forest on the central mountainous spine promising more than just pretty pictures. When you arrive at the peninsula you'll be surprised how lush the forest growth is, wonder at how the road hugs the coast literally feet above the water, and instantly see why people like living here.

The Bay of Plenty. People refer to the Bay of Plenty as New Zealand's food bowl. Some of the most fertile land for stone fruit and vegetables is found in the region. From the high points on the road you'll notice rolling countryside that's a rich green in winter and a golden sheen in summer as the grasses dry.

PLANNING

Set aside three to four days and get a rental car. The Bay of Plenty and Coromandel need to be approached with a degree of flexibility, rather than a prescriptive list of places to visit. The region has much to offer in a relatively small area, so that five-minute stop at a beach may turn into a long coastal walk. Likewise, the many forest walks can be as challenging as you choose—from an hour to a whole day. You can approach the journey as a loop that begins and ends either in Thames if you are traveling from the north or Whangamata if coming from the south. And be patient—the curvy roads challenge a lot of drivers, especially tourists driving camper vans.

GETTING HERE & AROUND

Although buses connect many of the towns and villages, the best way to explore is by car. Most roads are well maintained and clearly signposted, and a car gives you the freedom to explore hot pools and waterfalls tucked down obscure and winding side roads. The Pacific Coast Highway is popular with cyclists, particularly in summer.

From Auckland take the Southern Motorway, following signs to Hamilton. Just as you get over the Bombay Hills, turn left onto Highway 2; then take the turnoff to State Highway 25, signposted between the small towns of Maramarua and Mangatarata. Follow the signs to Thames. Allow 1½ to 2½ hours for the 118-km (73-mi) journey.

State Highway 25 is the peninsula's main loop, and though winding, the road is in good condition. Highway 25A, to the south, is a quicker way to reach the East Coast from Auckland.

State Highway 30 from Rotorua to Whakatane winds through lush native forest, playing hide-and-seek with the many lakes in the district, then finally reaches the coast. To reach the Bay of Plenty from Auckland, take the Southern Motorway, following signs to Hamilton. Just past the narrowing of the motorway, turn left onto State Highway 2, and travel through Paeroa. Stay on Highway 2 all the way to Tauranga, driving through Waihi and Katikati on the way. The driving time between Auckland and Katikati is around 2 hours, 40 minutes. Between Auckland and Tauranga, it's at least 3 hours, 15 minutes.

There are some tiny airstrips along the Coromandel Peninsula and a commercial airport at Tauranga. A number of scenic flight operators offer trips over the region.

To reach Coromandel from Auckland by boat, a 150-seat catamaran, the *Kawau Kat* (☎ *0800/888–006* ⊕ *www.kawaukat.co.nz*), leaves from Auckland's Pier 3 to Hannaford's Wharf, Coromandel Harbour, in Te Kouma, just outside Coromandel (a waiting shuttle brings you to Coromandel). The two-hour trip costs $49 one-way or $82 round-trip. Departures from Auckland leave Sunday and Tuesday at 9 AM, and Friday at 6 PM; the boat also leaves from Te Kouma on Sunday and Tuesday at 3:30 PM, and on Friday at 8:30 PM.

InterCity Coachlines (☎ *07/868–7251 or 0508/353–947* ⊕ *www.inter citycoach.co.nz*) and **Go Kiwi Shuttles** (☎ *07/866–0336 or 0800/446–549* ⊕ *www.go-kiwi.co.nz*) link Whitianga and Thames with Auckland daily; the trip is just over two hours from Auckland to Thames and just over three hours to Whitianga. Bus travel within the region is reliable, although less frequent in winter. Both InterCity and Go Kiwi travel once daily between Coromandel and Thames. Daily buses connect Coromandel and Whitianga as well.

InterCity and Go Kiwi have special Coromandel passes. Both passes allow you to get on and off at your leisure; the Go Kiwi pass is good for a month, and the InterCity pass is valid for up to three months.

TIMING & WEATHER

These regions are well loved for their beaches and they are crowded between October and February when the weather is mild enough to swim in the ocean, though some locals—often older ladies—swim every day whatever the weather. While the climate is temperate from March through September, over the summer otherwise sleepy seaside towns are filled with citysiders, with a massive tourist surge during the weeks around Christmas and the New Year. But Coromandel has plenty of obscure coves and long sandy stretches to accommodate the masses. Don't overlook the off-season—the weather's usually sunny, prices are lower, and locals have more time to chat.

ABOUT RESTAURANTS & HOTELS

There are many dining options across the Coromandel and Bay of Plenty. You can buy food from roadside seafood shacks and take-out fish-and-chips joints to cafés offering sandwiches and city-style coffee, right through to white-linen affairs. Even when restaurants are formal in appearance, diners and hosts tend toward a relaxed country-casualness. Restaurant owners make a point of using the region's abundant resources: the fish is likely to have been caught that morning from a nearby bay and shellfish are from local mussel and oyster farms. A huge community of artists lives in the region and their work is likely to be for sale even though it adorns restaurant walls.

Dinner service begins about 6 PM in the winter and around 7 PM during the summer months, though many places have "all-day menus." In peak season most places keep serving until at least 9 PM. For many restaurants reservations are a good idea, especially in the summer and particularly in Coromandel. In winter, when it's quiet, phoning ahead means the restaurant will know to stay open.

Like mellow places around the world, you'll find plenty of comfortable bed-and-breakfasts and mom-and-pop motels, but both the Coromandel and the Bay of Plenty also have a sprinkling of luxe boutique lodges tucked away in the forest or along coastal coves. In peak season, from October through February, advance booking is essential across the board and many of the better places have long-term customers who book as much as a year in advance. You'll rarely find air-conditioning in lodgings here, but then you'll rarely need it.

WHAT IT COSTS IN NEW ZEALAND DOLLARS					
	¢	$	$$	$$$	$$$$
Restaurants	under $10	$10–$15	$15–$20	$20–$30	over $30
Hotels	under $75	$75–$125	$125–$200	$200–$300	over $300

Prices are per person for a main course at dinner, or the equivalent. Prices are for a standard double room in high season, including 12.5% tax.

The Coromandel, Katikati, Mt. Maunganui, Tauranga, Thames, Pauanui, Tairua, Waihi, Whakatane, Whangamata, and Whitianga visitor centers are open daily between at least 10 and 4. For tidal information, check the back page of the *New Zealand Herald* newspaper. *Tait's Fun Maps* of Coromandel, Thames, and Whitianga are not drawn to scale, but they clearly mark roads and main attractions. You can pick up a copy at almost any place you overnight, as well as most tour operator offices, and visitor-info centers.

THE COROMANDEL PENINSULA

New Zealand has countless pockets of beauty that escape standard itineraries. As with so many other lands "discovered" by Europeans, the Coromandel Peninsula was looted for its valuable resources: kauri trees, then kauri gum, and finally gold in the 1870s. Relative quiet since the 1930s has allowed the region to recover, and, without question, natural beauty abounds and has attracted many bohemian types.

In the 1960s and '70s, dairy farms and orchards sprang up, as did communes, spiritual retreats, and artists' communities. There is still a strong "alternative" presence (responsible, in part, for the prevalence of organic food on area menus), so it's not uncommon to see people wearing muslin shirts and flowing skirts looking like they just got back from India, but the population increasingly includes Aucklanders looking for a weekend or retirement home.

A craggy spine of peaks rises sharply to almost 3,000 feet and dominates the center of the peninsula. The West Coast cradles the Firth of Thames, which in places is muddy, and along the East Coast the Pacific has carved out a succession of beaches and inlets separated by rearing headlands. Because of its rich soil, the peninsula has many spectacular gardens, and several are open to the public. From the town of Thames, the gateway to the region, State Highway 25 and the 309 Road circle the lower two-thirds of the peninsula—an exhilarating drive with the sea on one side and great forested peaks on the other.

THAMES

120 km (75 mi) southeast of Auckland.

The peninsula's oldest town, Thames has evolved from a gold-mining hotbed in the 1920s to a center for local agriculture. Locals have a saying that when the gold ran out, "Thames went to sleep awaiting the kiss of a golden prince—and instead it awoke to the warm breath of a cow." The main street used to be lined with nearly 100 hotels (bars); gold mining and logging was thirsty work. Only five of these hotels still operate, but the town and environs still offer glimpses of the mining era. Thames today is also the gateway to the Kauaeranga Valley Forest Park, home to waterfalls, ancient kauri groves, and the Pinnacles, the peninsula's highest accessible point.

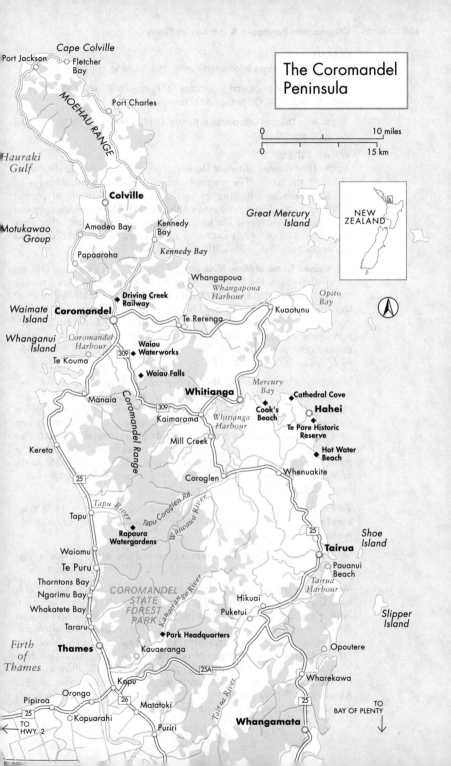

The Coromandel
Peninsula

NEW
ZEALAND

Cape Colville
Port Jackson
Fletcher Bay
Port Charles

MOEHAU RANGE

Hauraki Gulf

Colville

Amodeo Bay
Kennedy Bay

Motukawao Group

Papaaroha

Kennedy Bay

Whangapoua
Whangapoua Harbour

Great Mercury Island

Opito Bay

Driving Creek Railway

Waimate Island

Coromandel

Te Rerenga

Kuaotunu

Whanganui Island

Coromandel Harbour

Te Kouma

309

Waiau Waterworks

Waiau Falls

Whitianga

Mercury Bay

Cathedral Cove

Cook's Beach

Hahei

Manaia

309

Kaimarama

Whitianga Harbour

Te Pare Historic Reserve

Mill Creek

Kereta

25

Coroglen

Hot Water Beach

Whenuakite

Coromandel Range

Tapu River

Tapu

Tapu Coroglen Rd.

Waiwawa River

Rapaura Watergardens

Shoe Island

Waiomu

Te Puru

Tairua

Thorntons Bay

Ngarimu Bay

25

Pauanui Beach

Whakatete Bay

COROMANDEL STATE FOREST PARK

Kauaeranga River

Hikuai

Puketui

Tairua Harbour

Slipper Island

Tararu

Park Headquarters

Thames

Kauaeranga

Firth of Thames

Kopu

25A

Opoutere

Orongo

Pipiroa

26

Matatoki

Tairua River

Wharekawa

25

Kopuarahi

Puriri

Whangamata

25
TO HWY. 2

TO BAY OF PLENTY

0   10 miles
0   15 km

ESSENTIALS

Bus Depot (⊠ *Thames Information Centre, 206 Pollen St.* 📞 *07/868–7284*).

Hospitals **Thames Hospital** (⊠ *Mackay St., Thames* 📞 *07/868–6550*). **Thames Medical Center** (⊠ *817 Rolleston St., Thames* 📞 *07/868–9444*).

Visitor Info **Thames Information Centre** (⊠ *206 Pollen St.* 📞 *07/868–7284* ⊕ *www.thamesinfo.co.nz*).

WHAT TO SEE

At the tiny **Thames Historical Museum,** you can look into earlier ways of life in the town. The museum contains photographic displays of the gold-rush and logging industries, good re-creations of period rooms from the 1800s, and info on the original Māori inhabitants and early European settlers. The garden, with period roses and other flora that settlers commonly planted, is a nice place to rest. ⊠ *Pollen and Cochrane Sts.* 📞 *07/868–8509* 🎫 *$4* 🕐 *Daily 1–4.*

The **Thames School of Mines Mineralogical Museum** gives a geologic take on the area's history. The School of Mines provided practical instruction to the gold miners of the mid-1880s; the museum was established in 1900 to exhibit geological samples. The school closed decades ago, but the museum's still kicking, displaying those turn-of-the-20th-century rock specimens along with scales, models of stamper batteries, and other gold-mining paraphernalia. ⊠ *Brown and Cochrane Sts.* 📞 *07/868–6227* 🎫 *$4* 🕐 *Wed.–Sun. 11–3.*

If you want to learn more about early gold-mining efforts in the Coromandel, stop in at the **Goldmine Experience,** north on the way out of town, and take a 40-minute underground tour of the old Golden Crown Claim, which was first worked in 1868. You'll need sturdy and closed footwear because it can be muddy underground. You can also pan for gold on the surface. Five hundred feet below, the Caledonia strike was one of the richest in the world. ⊠ *State Hwy. 25, north of Waiotahi Creek Rd.* 📞 *07/868–8154* ⊕ *www.goldmine-experience. co.nz* 🎫 *$10* 🕐 *Call to book a tour.*

To soak up a bit of gold-mining atmosphere, head to the 1868 **Brian Boru Hotel.** Stop for a cold drink and check out the mining. ⊠ *200 Richmond St.* 📞 *07/868–6523.*

St. James Anglican Church is worth a look because it is of a similar age and construction. ⊠ *Pahau and Pollen Sts.* 🕐 *Varies day to day.*

Meonstoke is one of New Zealand's most unusual gardens. Since 1954, Pam Gwynne has been working every square inch of her ¼-acre lot. Numerous paths wind through a junglelike space; no lookouts or vistas distract you from the lush surroundings. Pam collects found objects and ingeniously incorporates them into surreal and often humorous tableaux with the plantings. On one path, a row of ceramic pitchers is suspended from a rod. Although the garden is small, allow yourself time to peer at the details. The entry fee goes to local charities. ⊠ *305 Kuranui St.* 📞 *07/868–6560 or 07/868–6850* 🎫 *$4* 🕐 *1st 2 weekends in Oct., 10–4, otherwise by appointment only* 🎫 *$4.*

3

The **Tropical Butterfly Garden** is a few minutes' drive north on the way out of Thames, but it's easy to miss unless you're specifically looking for the signs. It doesn't look impressive when you get there—but don't let that put you off. Roger and Sabine Gass have brought some color to the Coromandel with a flock of butterflies from Australia. Now, up to 20 species and 400 butterflies from all over the world may be on view at any time, including large birdwing butterflies. Birds such as finches, doves, and quails join the butterflies, plus about 100 different plant species. The heliconia and orchids are particularly stunning. ⊠ *Dickson Holiday Park, Victoria St.* ☎ *07/868–8080* ⊕ *www.butterfly.co.nz* ⌨ *$9* ⊘ *Late Aug.–mid-July, daily 10–4.*

The Organic Co-op. This small shop in Thames sells some of the region's best organic produce and you can pick up extra-delicious fruit and vegetables. If you want to try food with flavors that will remind you of how good things can taste, then this is worth a visit. ⊠ *736 Pollen St.* ☎ *07/868–8797* ⊟ *AE, DC, MC, V* ⊘ *Daily 8:30–4.*

Pohutukawa Design. At this tiny gallery you can buy handmade wood bowls and platters, homespun art shawls and scarves, plus paintings, jewelry, and even hand-milled soap. ⊠ *740 Pollen St.* ☎ *07/868–7925* ⊟ *AE, DC, MC, V* ⊘ *Daily 8:30–4.*

OUTDOOR ACTIVITIES

★ **Kauaeranga Valley Forest Park** has 22 walking trails that offer anything from a 30-minute stroll to a three-day trek, overnighting in huts equipped with bunks. The most accessible starting point is the delightful Kauaeranga Valley Road, where the **Department of Conservation Visitors Center** (☎ *07/867–9080* ⊕ *www.doc.govt.nz*) provides maps and information.

The hike to the Pinnacles is the most popular walk on the peninsula; the trek from the trailhead to the Pinnacles hut takes three hours one-way. From the hut you can continue to the peak (another hour one-way) for a view that spans both coasts. An overnight in the Pinnacles hut costs $15; you need to reserve it through the DOC center. You can hike back via the three-hour-long Webb Creek trail or come down the longer (four-hour) alternative route, the Billy Goat track.

Always read the signs at the start of the track to check their state. If you're traveling in the busy season, plan to visit midweek. To reach the Kauaeranga Valley, head south from Thames and on the outskirts of the town turn left on Banks Street, then right on Parawai Road, which becomes Kauaeranga Valley Road.

The DOC Centre provides information on many other walks or tramps to places such as Fantail Bay, Cathedral Cove, or Opera Point. There are numerous places to swim and the beaches are quite safe as you head out along the Coromandel Peninsula. There are not a lot of changing rooms but it's acceptable to change car side with a towel.

WHERE TO EAT

¢–$$ ✗ **Sola Café.** This little self-styled
★ vegetarian health bar is outstand-
ing. The counter displays risotto
cakes, florentines, and apple, pear,
apricot, and fig shortbread; the
berry friand cakes are as good as
any you will find. On the dinner
menu you might find *strozzapriti*
(spinach and Parmesan dump-
lings) or polenta with smoked field
mushrooms and roasted garlic
cream. It's also the hippest place in
Thames for coffee. They also sup-
port local artists and ever-changing
works are for sale on the wall and
on Saturday local cheeses are sold
outside the door. ⊠ *720b Pollen St.*
☎ *07/868–8781* ▤ *AE, DC, MC,*
V ⊖*BYOB.*

NECTAR LOUNGE BAR

Even the most jaded New York
barfly would find it hard to find
fault with this deeply stylish bar
that is only open three nights a
week. It's a tiny bar with room
for 30 people max. With a mix of
recycled and new furniture, fantas-
tic artwork, and the understated
style of the five friends who
opened it so they would have
"somewhere to dance," Nectar is
a drop of sophistication with-
out the conceit of big-city bars.
⊠ *746 Pollen St.* ☎ *07/868–6964*
▤ *AE, DC, MC, V* ⊖ *Thurs.–Sat.*
6 PM*–midnight.*

¢ ✗ **Pipiroa Country Kitchen.** Sweet treats have made this café's reputation.
It's a good stop if you've left Auckland early to avoid the traffic. You'll
be tempted with brownies and lemon cookies, but best of all is the
raspberry tart with a dollop of yogurt. For lunch, try one of the burg-
ers—the most spectacular is the Mountain, topped with cheese, onion,
egg, ham, tomato, apricot, and lettuce. Add to this a sauce of your
choice: peanut, plum, spicy tomato, or just plain ketchup. ▰**TIP→With
outdoor seating on the banks of the Piako River, and a playground that's
easy to see from the tables, this is a particularly good stopover if you're
traveling with kids.** ⊠ *1492 State Hwy. 25, Pipiroa* ✛ *15 km (9 mi)*
southwest of Thames ☎ *07/867–7599* ▤ *MC, V* ⊖ *No dinner Mon.–*
Thurs. and Sat.

WHERE TO STAY

$$ 🛏 **Brunton House.** Built by a local draper in the 1870s and later owned
by three Thames mayors, this two-story colonial villa was built entirely
from kauri wood. All bedrooms but one open out onto the upstairs
wraparound veranda, and although there are only two bathrooms to
share between four bedrooms, the claw-foot bathtub makes up for it.
Breakfast, which is included in the price, is a true Kiwi fry-up of bacon,
eggs, sausages, and hash browns; if you have other requirements, let your
hosts know the night before. **Pros:** Lovely setting; charming hosts; historic building. **Cons:** Jumbled furniture; interior needs refreshing. ⊠ *210*
Parawai Rd. ☎ *07/868–5160* 🖷 *07/868–5160* ⊕ *www.bruntonhouse.*
co.nz ⇆ *4 rooms with shared bath* ⚐ *In-room: no a/c, no phone, no TV.*
In-hotel: tennis court, pool, no elevator ▤ *AE, DC, MC, V* ⊖⎸*BP.*

$–$$ 🛏 **Tuscany on Thames.** The first owners fell in love with Tuscany on a
visit to Italy and brought its style back to their motel. It does look a
little incongruous when you consider the region, but the details—flowers in the rooms, custom-made pottery cups—are nice. For extra space,
ask for Room 1, a two-bedroom suite with access to a small court-

yard. Two rooms have showers only. The hotel is a short walk from town. **Pros:** Comfortable; clean; affordable. **Con:** Proximity to the road means it can be noisy. ✉*Jellicoe Crescent at Bank St.* ☎*07/868–5099* 📠*07/868–5080* ⊕*www.tuscanyonthames.co.nz* 🛏*14 rooms* ♿*In-room: no a/c, dial-up. In-hotel: pool, no elevator* ⊟*AE, DC, MC, V.*

$ 📷 **Brookby Motel.** In this low row of units the off-white brick rooms are small but tidy, with wooden balconies overlooking a tree-lined stream. The best deal is the studio attached to the office/owners' home, a turn-of-the-20th-century pioneer cottage. This studio has wooden floors and furnishings, as well as stained-glass windows, but it costs no more than the standard rooms. The property is close to some easy to moderately challenging walks, and you can explore the road up to the old settlement of Irishtown. **Pros:** Low-key; quiet; clean; close to bush walks. **Con:** Possibly too basic for some. ✉*102 Redwood La.* ☎*07/868–6663* 📠*07/868–6663* ⊕*www.brookbymotel.co.nz* 🛏*4 rooms, 2 studios* ♿*In-room: no a/c, kitchen, refrigerator, dial-up. In-hotel: no-smoking rooms, no elevator* ⊟*AE, DC, MC, V.*

TAPU–COROGLEN ROAD

25 km (16 mi) north of Thames.

The unpaved Tapu–Coroglen Road turns off State Highway 25 in the hamlet of Tapu to wind into the mountains. It's a breathtaking route where massive tree ferns grow out of the roadside hills. But it's not for the faint-hearted as stretches of the road are very narrow with access for only one vehicle. Signs indicate these places. About 6½ km (4 mi) from Tapu you come to the magical or—depending on your frame of mind—silly Rapaura Watergardens. Travel another 3½ km (2 mi) along the road and pull over to climb the 178 steps up to the huge, 1,200-year-old **Square Kauri,** so named for the shape that a cross section of its trunk would have. At 133 feet tall and 30 feet around, this is only the 15th-largest kauri in New Zealand. From a tree-side platform there is a splendid view across the valley to Mau Mau Paki, one of the peaks along the Coromandel Ranges. Continuing east across the peninsula, the road passes through forests and sheep paddocks—a shimmeringly beautiful drive in sun or mist.

Rapaura Watergardens is in a 65-acre sheltered valley in the Coromandel Ranges. Rapaura means "running water" and in the garden's various streams, waterfalls, fountains, and 14 ponds, fish and ducks swim among colorful water lilies while songbirds lilt overhead. Paths wind through collections of grasses, flaxes, gunneras, rhododendrons, and camellias. Giant tree ferns and rimu, *rata* (related to the pohutukawa, it too has bright red flowers), and kauri trees form a lush canopy overhead. You'll find hokey words of wisdom painted on signs around the garden, such as keep your values in balance and you will always find happiness. There is a café on the property, and a wood cottage and a two-story lodge for those who wish to stay longer ($145 and $250 per night, respectively, which includes breakfast). ✉*Tapu–Coroglen Rd., 6 km (4 mi) east of Tapu* ☎*07/868–4821* ⊕*www.rapaurawater gardens.co.nz* 🎫*$10* ⊙*Daily 9–5.*

COROMANDEL

60 km (38 mi) north of Thames, 29 km (18 mi) northwest of Whitianga.

Coromandel became the site of New Zealand's first gold strike in 1852 when sawmill worker Charles Ring found gold-bearing quartz at Driving Creek, just north of town. The find was important for New Zealand, because the country's workforce had been severely depleted by the gold rushes in California and Australia. Ring hurried to Auckland to claim the reward that had been offered to anyone finding "payable" gold. The town's population soared, but the reef gold could be mined only by heavy and expensive machinery. Within a few months Coromandel resumed its former sleepy existence as a timber town—and Charles Ring was refused the reward.

Nowadays, Coromandel is very touristy but manages to retain a low-key charm even when the streets are full of SUVs and camper vans. With 19th-century buildings lining both sides of its single main street, an active artists' collective, and the requisite fish-and-chips shop at either end you could not find a truer example of the relaxed and slightly hippie kiwi town. The local mussel farm means that mussels are served every which way, from smoked-mussel pies to chowder.

ESSENTIALS

Bus Depot (⊠ *Coromandel Visitor Information Centre, 355 Kapanga Rd.* ☎ *07/866–8598)..*

Hospital **Coromandel Medical Center** (⊠ *80 Kapanga Rd., Coromandel* ☎ *07/866–8200)..*

Visitor Info **Coromandel Visitor Information Centre** (⊠ *355 Kapanga Rd., Coromandel* ☎ *07/866–8598* ⊕ *www.coromandeltown.co.nz).*

WHAT TO SEE

☺ **Driving Creek Railway** is one man's magnificent folly and popular with New Zealanders and tourists alike. Barry Brickell is a highly collectible local potter who discovered that clay on his land was perfect for his work. The problem was that the deposit lay in a remote area at the top of a steep slope, so he hacked a path through the forest and built his own miniature railroad to haul the stuff. Visitors to his studio began asking if they could go along for a ride, and Brickell now takes passengers on daily tours aboard his toylike train.

The diesel-powered, narrow-gauge locomotive's route incorporates a double-decker bridge, three tunnels, a spiral, and a switchback through native forest and sculpture gardens, all the way to Barry's "Eyeful Tower," an old-style railway refreshment room and viewing platform. On a clear day you can see all the way to Auckland. The railway also funds a reforestation program; to date more than 15,000 native trees have been planted, and a wildlife sanctuary is also being built. The railway's round-trip takes about 50 minutes. The "station" is 3 km (2 mi) north of Coromandel township. ⊠ *410 Kennedy's Bay Rd.* ☎ *07/866–8703* ⊕ *www.drivingcreekrailway.co.nz*

Taking in the sunset above Franz Josef Glacier, Westland National Park.

(top left) Counting sheep: ewes in pasture, Athol. (top right) Redwood Forest, Rotorua. (below) Kayaking the Marlborough Sounds.

(top) Ski touring, Tasman Glacier, South Island. (bottom) Ngaruawahia *waka* (Maori canoe) regatta, Ngaruawahia.

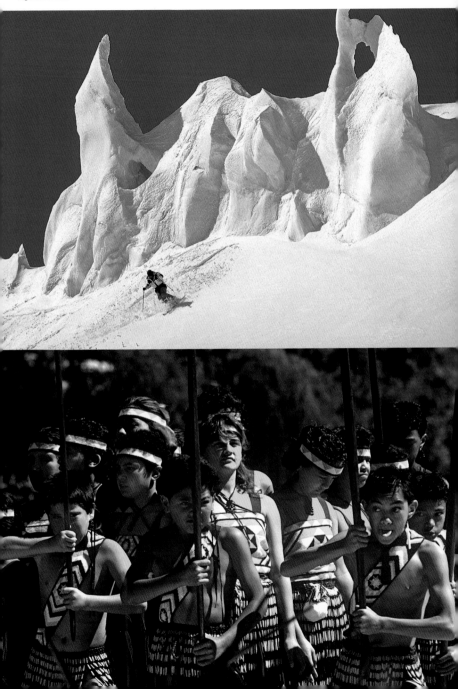

(top left) Tairua, Coromandel, North Island. (top right) Walking through an ice crevasse on the Franz Josef Glacier. (bottom) *Hongi*—saying "hello," Maori-style.

Giant's Gate Falls, Milford Track, Fiordland.

(top left) Hot-air ballooning, Christchurch, South Island. (top right) Vineyard, Blenheim, Marlborough, South Island. (bottom) Horseback riding past Archway Island, Wharariki Beach, Farewell Spit, Golden Bay.

Giant kauri tree aptly named Tāne Mahuta (Lord of the Forest), Waipoua Forest, Northland, North Island.

3

🎟️*$17 ⊙Dec.–Apr., daily 10–evening, with trains running every 1¼ hrs; May–mid-Oct., daily 10–5, with trains at 10:15 and 2.*

Opened around 1900, the **Coromandel Gold Stamper Battery** was New Zealand's last functional gold-processing plant. You can take a guided tour of the old plant, do some gold panning, or stroll through the bush to a lookout. The huge working waterwheel out front claims to be New Zealand's largest. The Stamper Battery is 2 km (1 mi) north of Coromandel township. ✉️*410 Buffalo Rd.* ☎️*07/866–7933* 🎟️*$10 ⊙Daily 10–4; closed Wed. June–Sept.*

🕓 The **Weta Design** gallery is named after the country's largest native insect, which looks like a grasshopper with armor. This gallery has a wide range of items from large and very beautiful glass totems to small finely made tiles, not to mention fabric art, carving, and ceramics. The gallery also has fine New Zealand jewelry. Keep an eye out for the fine silver work by up-and-coming jeweler Anna Hallissey. Her delicate brooches are based on the tiny branches of the manuka tree while a more witty piece is a silver version of the plastic clip used to close bread bags. For a truly unique gift they sell a surprisingly packaged weta. ✉️*46 Kapanga Rd.* ☎️*07/866–8060* ⊕*www.wetadesign. co.nz ⊙Daily 10–4.*

🕓 **The Source** is a gallery that has an outdoor courtyard selling huge ceramic works inspired by native plants. The good thing is that the sculptures (some are over 12 feet tall) can be broken down for shipping overseas. Many of the tall sculptures are based on local plants. The Source also has smaller, well-priced works by local potters and sometimes clothing. ✉️*31 Kapanga Rd.* ☎️*07/866–7345 ⊙Daily 10–4.*

WHERE TO EAT

¢–$$$$ ✕**UMU Café.** The UMU Café does a mean pizza, with asparagus, feta, olives, pepperoni, and anchovies. They also make a delicious club sandwich with pickles, ham, mashed egg, and lettuce. Both the restaurant menu and café counter offer largely organic produce, lots of seafood, and good vegetarian options. Even if you're not planning to eat, stop in to look at the art by Dean Buchanan; he did the locally famous *No Mining* Coromandel protest painting, which you'll see on local postcards or new works by locals. There can be a queue at the restroom, so it's best to use one down the road. ✉️*22 Wharf Rd.* ☎️*07/866–8618* ▤*AE, DC, MC, V.*

$$–$$$ ✕**Pepper Tree Restaurant and Bar.** Coromandel seafood takes precedence on the menu and a giant pepper tree dominates the courtyard. Locally farmed oysters are served on the half shell, and Greenshell mussels are steamed open and piled into bowls, or turned into fritters. Nachos, potato wedges, and other easygoing nibbles dominate the all-day menu, but things get more serious after sundown, with dishes such as raw fish marinated in vodka and citrus with spiced coconut cream, and the restaurant takes on a city feel. ✉️*31 Kapanga Rd.* ☎️*07/866–8211* ▤*AE, DC, MC, V.*

¢–$ ✕**Coromandel Cafe.** Seek out the best breakfast in town at this mainstreet café. The menu may not be extensive or adventurous, and the decor tired, but the substantial servings of tried-and-true choices such as pancakes with maple syrup or bacon and eggs are popular with locals. You won't miss out if you sleep in, as breakfast runs right through the afternoon. ⊠*Kapanga Rd.* ☎*07/866–8495* ▤*AE, MC, V* ⊗*No dinner.*

WHERE TO STAY

$$$ ▦ **Buffalo Lodge.** Perched on a hillside and surrounded by bush just
★ out of Coromandel town, this lodge looks across the Hauraki Gulf toward Auckland. Bedrooms and bathrooms are minimalist in design, with huge windows and balconies with spectacular views of the surrounding native trees and countryside. ■TIP→**The cottage room is a special treat. Its giant tub set beside an enormous window makes you feel as if you're bathing in the middle of the forest.** The restaurant's prix-fixe dinner ($90) has specialties such as king salmon, venison, and locally caught fish. They also roast their own coffee beans. **Pros:** Beautiful setting; private; multi-lingual host. **Cons:** Some might find the decor tired; not suitable for children. ⊠*Buffalo Rd.* ☎☎*07/866–8960* ⊕*www.buffalolodge.co.nz* ⌂*4 rooms* ⌂*In-room: no a/c, no TV. In-hotel: restaurant, no kids under 12, no elevator* ▤*AE, DC, MC, V* ⊗*Closed May–Sept.* ❙⊙❙*BP.*

$$ ▦ **Karamana Homestead.** It's not hard to imagine a distinguished family occupying this 1872 home, built for Jerome Cadman, a prominent Auckland contractor. From the gentlemen's smoking lounge to the huge canopy bed of English oak to the well out back, the house is a well-kept piece of Coromandel history. The adjacent 1850 kauri cottage, with its high-beamed ceilings, wrought-iron bed, and kitchenette, is wonderfully private. Breakfast, included in the price, is a silver-service affair. **Pros:** Historic property; charming hosts; close to town. **Cons:** Basic facilities. ⊠*84 Whangapoua Rd.* ☎☎*07/866–7138* ⊕*www.karamanahomestead.com* ⌂*3 rooms, 1 cottage* ⌂*In-room: no a/c, no phone, no TV. In-hotel: no-smoking rooms, no elevator* ▤*MC, V* ❙⊙❙*BP.*

$–$$ ▦ **Coromandel Colonial Cottages.** These eight immaculate, spacious, and
★ comfortable timber cottages are about the same price as a standard motel room. Six of the units have two bedrooms; a living room with convertible beds; a large, well-equipped kitchen; and a dining area. The other two have only one bedroom. The cottages face one another across a tailored lawn surrounded by green hills on the northern outskirts of Coromandel. For vacation periods book several months in advance. **Pros:** Clean; close to beach; basic; swimming pool. **Con:** Not for those after a luxury lodge. ⊠*Rings Rd.* ☎*07/866–8857* ⊕*www.corocottagesmotel.co.nz* ⌂*8 cottages* ⌂*In-room: no a/c, kitchen (some). In-hotel: pool, no elevator* ▤*AE, DC, MC, V.*

$–$$ ▦ **Coromandel Court Motel.** Tucked behind the Coromandel Information Centre, these down-to-earth units are newer and larger than those of the area's average motel. Rooms are equipped with kitchenettes and dining-room tables. All have showers instead of full baths. **Pros:** In town; clean; basic; friendly; wireless Internet. **Con:** Not for those after a luxury lodge. ⊠*365 Kapanga Rd.* ☎*07/866–8402* ☎*07/866–8403* ⊕*www.coromandelcourtmotel.co.nz* ⌂*9 units* ⌂*In-room: no a/c, kitchen. In-hotel: no elevator* ▤*AE, DC, MC, V.*

3

$ 🏠 **Te Kouma Harbour Farmstay.** A little off the beaten track, these single-story wooden chalets on a deer farm are excellent for families or groups wanting a little rural time. There are plenty of activities to keep you busy: kayaking, soccer, *pétanque* (the French game similar to boccie), and swimming in the pool. Large, bright multiroom cabins have contemporary furniture and kitchen areas. You can arrange for breakfast, but most guests cook for themselves. The cabins are down a long drive that is signposted from State Highway 25 north out of Thames and the hosts Allan and Ritchie are happy to arrange activities. **Pros:** Well-priced rural accommodation; clean; self-contained. **Cons:** A little out of town; basic decor; can be busy at times. ⊠*Te Kouma Harbour* ☎*07/866–8747* ⊕*www.tekouma.co.nz* ⌘*9 cabins* ⌂*In-room: no a/c, kitchen. In-hotel: pool, no elevator* ⊟*No credit cards.*

EN ROUTE
About 2 km (1 mi) out of Coromandel township heading north on the main road to Colville, look for **Taraire Grove Gardens** (⊠*2569 Rings Rd.* ☎*07/866–8053* ⌨*$5* ☉*Daily 10 AM–dusk*). Named for the 13 ancient native taraire trees on the property, the gardens are interspersed with streams, creeks, and water-lily ponds. Once a grassy cow pasture, **Waitati Gardens** (⊠*485 Buffalo Rd.* ☎*07/866–8659* ⌨*$5* ☉*Daily 10 AM–dusk*) now includes a native-plants area and swarms of unusual flowers. Flower-bordered glades and shady spots make for perfect picnic settings.

THE 309 ROAD

The 309 Road is the shortest route between Coromandel and Whitianga; it cuts right across the peninsula. The mostly unpaved road is winding and narrow and takes 35–40 minutes to cross. If you are traveling in a camper van, it's best to leave early in the morning to avoid traffic. If you end up behind one, be patient. The surrounding landscape alternates between farmland, pine trees, and native forest, with numerous reasons to stop along the way.

Five kilometers (3 mi) from Coromandel, the **Waiau Waterworks** is a quirky playground in a series of grassy clearings surrounded by bush, ponds, streams, and a river with a swimming hole. There are sculpture gardens, a number of water-powered artworks, and some unusual takes on playground equipment that invite the inner child to come out and play. ⊠*309 Rd.* ☎*07/866–7191* ⌨*$12* ☉*Daily 9–dusk.*

About 7½ km (4½ mi) from Coromandel, stop for a swim at **Waiau Falls,** a forest-fringed waterfall lagoon that's just a short signposted walk from the road. Additional walking tracks lead farther into the woods. Less than 2 km (1 mi) east of Waiau Falls, a series of easy, clearly marked gravel paths and wooden walkways takes you through lush forest to a protected giant kauri grove. ■TIP➔**The full walk takes about 15 minutes, but the trees are so majestic that you may want to allow a half hour to stroll through this ancient forest.** Continuing along the 309, the road winds through more forest and farmland, past the **309 Manuka Honey Shop,** and eventually comes out on State Highway 25, about 20 minutes south of Whitianga.

COLVILLE & BEYOND

30 km (19 mi) north of Coromandel.

To reach land's end in the wilds of the Coromandel Peninsula—with rugged coastline, beautiful coves, and pastures—take the 30-minute drive from Coromandel up to **Colville.** The town has a grocery store/gas station, post office, hall, and café, and in summer a temporary shop sells items from India and Nepal. There are also a magnificent Buddha shrine or stuppa on the drive in and public toilets with a mosaic worthy of a picture on the outside. Colville is the gateway to some of the peninsula's most untamed landscape, as well as some long-established communes. Maps of the area are available in Coromandel at the Visitor Information Centre and in Colville at the General Store.

Colville's classic counterculture **General Store** (☎07/866–6805) sells foodstuffs (there's a well-stocked organic section), wine, and gasoline. It is the northernmost supplier on the peninsula, so don't forget to fill your tank.

The **Colville Café** (☎07/866–6690), right next door, is open every day for lunch, and Friday for dinner (during December and January it's open for dinner every night). With a focus on locally sourced organic food and fair-trade coffee, this is a good place to pick up fixings for a picnic, or a morning coffee and cake. Beyond Colville, a twisty, gravel (but well-maintained) road continues north, coming to a T-junction about 5 km (3 mi) out of town. It's impossible to fully circumnavigate the peninsula; at the junction, the road to your left follows the West Coast to the stunning sandy beach at Port Jackson. It continues along the cliff top to **Fletcher Bay,** a smaller, sandy cove banked by green pasture rolling down to the beach. Fletcher Bay is the end of the road, at 60 km (38 mi) from Coromandel—a 1¼-hour drive.

From Fletcher Bay, hikers can follow the signposted **Coastal Walkway** to Stony Bay; it's about a three-hour walk each way. If you want to hike the Coastal Walkway but don't fancy driving yourself there, **Strongman Coachlines** (☎07/866–8175 ⊕*www.coromandeldiscoverytours. co.nz*) will pick you up either in Colville or in Coromandel and drive you to Fletcher Bay. From there you can walk to Stony Bay, where you will be driven back to your hotel. The full-day trip ($90) includes stops along the way, including one at Colville's General Store, where you can get lunch for the hike. They also offer a range of other trips in the area.

WHERE TO STAY

$ ⬚ **Anglers Lodge Motel & Holiday Park.** Tucked in a valley off the main road between Coromandel and Colville, these wooden motel units face the Motukawa Islands of Amodeo Bay. The small rooms have 1970s-style plaid upholstery and Formica tabletops, but the owners are very friendly and it's retro without trying to be. If you are traveling with a tent, they have sites. You can head out into the bay for a three-hour fishing trip ($50 per person, $150 minimum). The motel is 7 km (4½ mi) south of Colville. **Pros:** Friendly operators; interesting mix of guests; stunning location. **Cons:** Very basic; focused at budget travelers. ✉*Amodeo Bay, Coromandel* ☎*07/866–8584* 📠*07/866–7352* ⊕*www.anglers.co.nz* 🛏*8 rooms* ⬧*In-room: no a/c, no phone, kitchen, refrigerator. In-hotel: tennis court, pool, laundry facilities, no-smoking rooms, no elevator* ☐*MC, V.*

WHITIANGA

46 km (29 mi) southeast of Coromandel.

As you descend from the hills on the East Coast of the Coromandel, you'll come to the long stretch of Buffalo Beach, lined with motels and hostels. Just past this beach is Whitianga, the main township on this side of the peninsula. Most people use the town as a base for fishing or boating trips, and others stock up for camping at nearby beaches. Over summer it hosts some very good rock music and jazz shows, and people use it as a base for the region's beautiful beaches. Restaurants come and go, but ample choices are on the main streets. If the jazz show is on while you are there—normally the Easter Weekend—check out the lamb pita pockets sold at one of the many food stalls. The Whitianga Information Centre can help you choose an excursion

ESSENTIALS

Bus Depot Whitianga (✉*Whitianga Visitor Information Centre, 66 Albert St.* ☎*07/866–5555*).

Hospital Mercury Bay Medical Center (✉*87 Albert St., Whitianga* ☎*07/866–5911*).

Visitor Info Whitianga Information Centre (✉*66 Albert St., Whitianga* ☎*07/866–5555*).

OUTDOOR ACTIVITIES

BOATING, FISHING & DIVING
You can rent diving and fishing gear from the **Whitianga Sports Center** (✉*32 Albert St., Whitianga* ☎*07/866–5295*). **The Cave Cruzer** (☎*07/866–2574 or 0800/427–893* ⊕*www.cavecruzer.co.nz*) gives you an unusual spin on a boat tour to Cathedral Cove. At one point, you'll head into a sea cave where the guides demonstrate the acoustics by playing a Spanish guitar and African drums. **Blue Boat Cruises** (✉*Whitianga Marina* ☎*027/439–8819* ⊕*www.whitianga.co.nz/blueboat*) leaves Whitianga Marina twice a day for two-hour cruises around Cathedral Cove and Mercury Bay's islands. If you're interested in fishing, contact **Water's Edge Charters** (☎*07/866–5760* ⊕*www.watersedgecharters.co.nz*). **Mercury Bay Seafaris** (✉*Whitianga Visitor Information Centre, Whitianga* ☎*07/866–5555* 📠*07/866–2205*) has a glass-bottom boat trip, which includes a snorkeling option ($65), and a journey around islands in the area ($75). Trips last about 2½ hours; departures from Whitianga Wharf are subject to weather conditions.

WHERE TO STAY & EAT

¢–$ ✕**Café Nina.** Locals gravitate here for breakfast and lunch every day of the week, and it is always busy. Breakfast might bring corn-and-bacon fritters with tamarillo chutney; at lunch you'll find simple dishes such as roasted root vegetables with dips and bread, or seafood chowder, a staple for regulars. Jasmine vines cloak the front porch of this charming 1890 miner's cottage. ⊠*20 Victoria St.* ☎*07/866–5440* ▤*AE, DC, MC, V.*

$$$ 🏠 **Mercury Bay Beachfront Resort.** Step out of this family-run tiny resort's garden and onto a beautiful beach. The downstairs rooms claim the best beach access, but great views and the most sun are upstairs. Either way, seven of the eight rooms have beach views. Sports equipment, including kayaks, fishing gear, and body boards, is available at no extra charge. They have Sky TV and wireless Internet—guests are advised to sit under the pohutukawa tree on the front lawn for best access! Only one room has a full bath; the rest have showers. **Pros:** Stunning location; friendly hosts; good self-contained accommodation. **Con:** Not for those looking for a luxury resort. ⊠*111–113 Buffalo Beach Rd.* ☎*07/866–5637* 🖶*07/866–4524* ⊕*www.beachfrontresort.co.nz* ⇦*8 rooms* ♨*In-room: no a/c. In-hotel: spa, no elevator* ▤*AE, DC, MC, V.*

$–$$$ 🏠 **Oceanside Motel.** The views of Mercury Bay are this motel's best assets. Rooms are small and simply furnished, but each has floor-to-ceiling sliding-glass doors, with unobstructed views of the bay. Many have their own front patio, and you can sleep with the door open and listen to the waves lapping the beach across the street. **Pros:** Excellent location; friendly and down-to-earth hosts; clean and tidy. **Con:** Small rooms. ⊠*32 Buffalo Beach Rd.* ☎*07/866–5766* 🖶*07/866–4803* ⊕*www.oceansidemotel.co.nz* ⇦*12 rooms* ♨*In-room: no a/c, kitchen, refrigerator. In-hotel: room service, laundry facilities, no elevator* ▤*AE, DC, MC, V* ⏍*BP, CP.*

$$ 🏠 **Baytime Bed & Breakfast.** In this blue-and-white two-story house, 2 km (1 mi) from the town marina, you'll have a tight nautical connection: your host Kevin Rintoul is also the skipper of Blue Boat Cruises. As you'd expect from a seafaring man, the home has lots of marine artwork. The high-ceilinged rooms have wicker furnishings and decks overlooking the Whitianga River. **Pros:** Friendly host; clean; nice aspect. **Con:** Basic decor. ⊠*15 Robinson Rd.* ☎*07/866–4904* 🖶*07/866–4990* ⊕*www.baytime.co.nz* ⇦*2 rooms* ♨*In-room: no a/c, no phone, kitchen, refrigerator. In-hotel: pool, bicycles, no-smoking rooms, no elevator* ▤*AE, DC, MC, V* ⏍*BP.*

AROUND HAHEI

57 km (35 mi) southeast of Coromandel, 64 km (40 mi) northeast of Thames.

The beaches, coves, and seaside villages around Hahei make for a great day of exploring—or lounging. If you're day-tripping from Whitianga, take the five-minute ferry ride (which leaves every hour, $4 round-trip) across to Flaxmill Bay and explore by foot. Alternatively, follow State Highway 25 south from Whitianga. The road takes you past the Wilderlands roadside stand (selling organic produce and delicious honey from a local commune) and on to Flaxmill Bay, Cook's Beach, and Hahei. If you're craving a true beach vacation, consider basing yourself in Hahei, rather than in Whitianga. From Hahei, you can easily reach Cathedral Cove, the Purangi Estuary, and Flaxmill Bay; the famous Hot Water Beach is only minutes away.

Past Hahei on Pa Road, **Te Pare Historic Reserve** is the site of a Māori *pā* (fortified village), though no trace remains of the defensive terraces and wooden spikes that ringed the hill. At high tide, the blowhole at the foot of the cliffs adds a booming bass note to the sound of waves and the sighing of the wind in the grass. To reach the actual pā site, follow the red arrow down the hill from the parking area. After some 50 yards, take the right fork through a grove of giant pohutukawa trees, then through a gate and across an open, grassy hillside. The trail is steep and becomes increasingly overgrown as you climb, but persist on to the summit, and then head toward more pohutukawas to your right at the south end of the headland. There's no entry fee.

★ **Cathedral Cove** is a beautiful white-sand crescent with a rock arch. The water is usually calm and clear, good for swimming and snorkeling. The beach is accessible only at low tide, however, about a 45-minute walk each way. To get there, travel along Hahei Beach Road, turn right toward town and the sea, and then, just past the shops, turn left onto Grange Road and follow the signs.

Cook's Beach lies along Mercury Bay, so named for Captain James Cook's observation of the transit of the planet Mercury in November 1769. The beach is notable because of the captain's landfall—it was the first by a European. Because of the surrounding suburban sprawl, the beach is less attractive than its more secluded neighbors.

NEED A BREAK?

Purangi Estate may not make prizewinning wines, but the homemade feijoa liquor is good with club soda over ice, and the café—with its tables made from wine barrels and set under the kiwifruit vines—is worth a stop en route to Cook's Beach. ✉ *501 Purangi Rd., Whitianga* ☎ *07/866–3724* ⊙ *Daily 9–5.*

★ The popular **Hot Water Beach** is a delightful thermal oddity. A warm spring seeps beneath the beach, and by scooping a shallow hole in the sand, you can create a pool of warm water; the deeper you dig, the hotter the water becomes. The phenomenon occurs only at low to mid-tide, so time your trip accordingly. If you are an adventurous sort, it can be fun in winter to sit in warm water while it rains. Hot Water Beach is well signposted off Hahei Beach Road from Whenuakite (fen-oo-ah-*kye*-tee). **Do not swim in the surf at Hot Water Beach; it's notorious for drownings.** However, nearby, at the end of Hahei Beach Road, you'll find one of the finest protected coves on the coast, with sands tinted pink from crushed shells; it's safe to swim here.

NEED A BREAK?

Colenso Country Café & Shop (✉ *Main Rd., Whenuakite* ☎ *07/866–3725*), on State Highway 25 just south of the Hahei turnoff, is a relaxed cottage café named after William Colenso, an early explorer of New Zealand, set in a garden full of lavender and kitchen herbs, and serves fresh juices, soups, focaccia sandwiches, an outstanding vegetable frittata, addictive chocolate fudge biscuits (also called slices), and Devonshire teas. In summer they also make a pavlova stack. A pavlova is a large meringue and they layer three of them into a dish with cream and fresh fruit between each layer! Colenso is open from 10 to 5 daily, September through July.

OUTDOOR ACTIVITIES

BOATING & DIVING You can go on a sea-kayaking tour with **Cathedral Cove Sea Kayaks** (⊠*88 Hahei Beach Rd., Hahei* ☎*07/866–3877* ⊕*www.seakayak tours.co.nz*); prices start at $75 for a half-day trip, and they're happy to work with beginners. You can get a peek of what they do on their Web site video. They take groups of about eight in double kayaks and pride themselves on taking visitors to places they are unlikely to see on foot; **Cathedral Cove Dive & Snorkel Hahei** (⊠*Shop 2, Grange Ct., Hahei* ☎*07/866–3955* ⊕*www.hahei.co.nz/diving*) offers beginner, advanced, and dive-master courses, as well as daily dive trips.

WHERE TO EAT

¢–$$$ ✕**Eggsentric Café.** Energetic owner Dave Fowell (hence the "egg" refer-
★ ences) has created a community hub in his restaurant. It's only open seven months of the year so that he and his better half can travel during the winter months. But while it's open there are live music and jam sessions, poetry and film nights—and that's before you even get to the food. Dave sings most nights and the guest artist lineup can be very impressive. In summer he holds a sculpture symposium where artists get together and create work in public. The menu reaches beyond the standards with dishes such as calamari smoked with tea and *manuka* (a native tree) wood or sticky date pudding with warm caramel sauce. The decor's rough around the edges, but that's part of the Eggsentric charm. To get here, drive just beyond Cook's Beach on Purangi Road or take the ferry from Whitianga to Flaxmill Bay. The café is about 2 km (1 mi) from the ferry landing. ⊠*1049 Purangi Rd., Flaxmill Bay* ☎*07/866–0307* ▤*MC, V* ☉*Call to check opening hrs.*

¢–$$$ ✕**Grange Road Café.** With its roster of seafood and vegetarian dishes paired with New Zealand wines from small boutique vineyards, this restaurant has a big summer draw. However, the potbellied stove brewing complimentary mulled wine and the live music performances are reasons enough to visit in winter. ⊠*7 Grange Rd., Hahei* ☎*07/866–3502* ▤*AE, DC, MC, V* ☉*Closed June and July.*

¢–$$$ ✕**Luna Café.** There's no doubt you're at the beach here: the decor incorporates scallop-shell lei, woven baskets, and cowrie shells, and the walls are lime and blue. The menu sticks to tried-and-true favorites like roast rack of lamb with *kūmara* (native sweet potato) and ginger slice (shortbread with ginger frosting). You can also get muffins or sandwiches, or stop in for brunch. In winter, dinner is served only on Friday and Saturday. ⊠*1 Grange Ct., Grange Rd., Hahei* ☎*07/866–3303* ▤*MC, V* ☉*Closed Tues. and Wed. Apr.–Nov.*

WHERE TO STAY

$–$$ ▥ **The Church.** Originally a 1916 Methodist church, the Church is worth a visit even if you're not staying the night. The church itself, on the main road heading into Hahei, is now a gracious upmarket restaurant ($$–$$$$). Travelers and locals mull over choices such as grilled venison with cherry sauce or house-smoked salmon. Though it's a white-linen place, it maintains a relaxed country atmosphere; you don't have to pull out your Sunday best. Behind the building are wooden studios and cottages connected by winding garden paths, each decorated with stained glass and small arched windows. The rooms are small but bright, and each has a back porch overlooking the gardens. **Pros:** Range of accommodations; lovely garden. **Con:** Very basic furnishings. ⊠ *87 Hahei Beach Rd., Hahei* 🕾 *07/866–3533* 🖷 *07/866–3055* ⊕ *www.thechurchhahei.co.nz* ⌑ *4 studios, 7 cottages* ⌂ *In-room: no a/c, no phone, kitchen (some), refrigerator, no TV (some). In-hotel: restaurant, laundry facilities, no-smoking rooms, no elevator* ⊟ *AE, DC, MC, V* ⊘ *Closed Aug.* ❙⊙❙ *BP.*

$–$$
Fodor's Choice
★

⌱ **Purangi Gardens Accommodation.** As you open the door to your wood cottage nestled in 100 acres of protected park on the shores of the Purangi Estuary, expect to find a loaf of still-warm home-baked bread, a bowl of fruit from the garden, homemade granola and yogurt, and some fresh-laid eggs. Hosts Rod McLaren and Susan Grierson offer homegrown hospitality here. They'll lend you a kayak and send you down the river, but you might prefer lazing on your veranda and enjoying the views. The wood-raftered rooms in the cottages are cozy and compact. If you're traveling *en masse,* or simply wish to spread out, three spacious houses sleep up to 10 people. Set apart from the cottages (two of them are amid orchards), they're fully furnished and have kitchens. **Pros:** Private; beautiful garden; relaxing property. **Cons:** Decor is plain; not for those wanting luxury. ⊠ *321 Lees Rd., Hahei* 🕾 *07/866–4036* 🖷 *07/866–4038* ⊕ *www.purangigarden.co.nz* ⌑ *2 cottages, 3 houses* ⌂ *In-room: no a/c, no phone, kitchen (some), refrigerator, VCR. In-hotel: beachfront, water sports, laundry facilities, public Internet, no-smoking rooms, no elevator* ⊟ *MC, V* ❙⊙❙ *CP.*

¢–$$

⌱ **Tatahi Lodge.** In the center of Hahei and across the street from the beach, this lodge comprises a number of low-lying wooden buildings. Surrounded by trees, accommodations range from doubles and studios to dorms (there's a wide price range, too). **Pros:** Range of accommodation; good for budget travelers. **Con:** Can get crowded with younger travelers. ⊠ *Grange Rd., Hahei* 🕾 *07/866–3992* 🖷 *07/866–3993* ⊕ *www.dreamland.co.nz/tatahilodge* ⌑ *5 double rooms, 2 studios, 1 2-bedroom cottage, 2 6-bed dorms, 1 4-bed dorm* ⌂ *In-room: no a/c, kitchen (some). In-hotel: restaurant, public Internet, no-smoking rooms, no elevator* ⊟ *AE, DC, MC, V.*

TAIRUA

28 km (18 mi) south of Hahei, 37 km (23 mi) north of Whangamata.

A town that you'll actually notice when you pass through it, Tairua is one of the larger communities along the coast. Because State Highway 25 is the town's main road, it's convenient for a bite en route to the prettier seaside spots around Whitianga and Hahei. In Tairua, the twin volcanic peaks of Paku rise up beside the harbor. The short ferry ride from Tairua across the harbor to Pauanui, which is an upmarket area, takes you to the immediate area's best beach; the ferry runs continually October through April, and six times a day during the rest of the year ($4 round-trip). For activities and maps check out the Pauanui and Tairua information centers.

ESSENTIALS

Visitor Information **Pauanui Information Centre** (⊠ *Vista Paku and Shepherd Ave.* ☎ *07/864–7101*). **Tairua Information Centre** (⊠ *Main road, Tairua* ☎ *07/864-7575* ⊕ *www.tairua.info/index.html*).

WHERE TO EAT

¢–$$$ ✕ **Manaia Café & Bar.** This spacious centrally located restaurant is welcoming and it shows—sometimes it can be incredibly busy. You can sit inside or out, depending on your mood and the weather. Try venison served with roast cumin and pumpkin. If you arrive during the day, pop into the adjacent Manaia Gallery, which sells jewelry, art, and crafts. ⊠ *228 Main Rd.* ☎ *07/864–9050* ☰ *MC, V.*

¢–$ ✕ **Surf and Sand.** This is a fantastic place to get a quintessential Kiwi-style beachside lunch of kūmara (native sweet potato) chips, Coromandel mussels, and fresh fish, washed down with a bottle of Lemon & Paeroa (L&P—the iconic Kiwiana soda). The chips are crisp (they're fried in canola vegetable oil). Come early for dinner, they close at 8 PM. ⊠ *Shop 7, Main Rd.* ☎ *07/864–8617.*

WHERE TO STAY

$$–$$$$ ▨ **Pacific Harbour Lodge.** This resort-style property is on the main street in Tairua and looks like it escaped from a tropical island. With a grand Pacific-styled portico, it's a cluster of island-style chalets connected by a white shell path. The units are spacious and quiet with the added bonus of parking outside your door. Furnishings are simple and comfortable, and all the touches expected in an upmarket hotel are present. **Pros:** Tropical feel; good location; well priced. **Cons:** Some may find the woody decor overbearing. ⊠ *223 Main Rd., Tairua* ☎ *07/864–8581* ☐ *07/864–8858* ⊕ *www.pacificharbour.co.nz* ⇄ *48 rooms* ♨ *In-room: no a/c. In-hotel: restaurant, bar, bicycles, Wi-Fi, no elevator* ☰ *AE, DC, MC, V.*

$$–$$$$ ▨ **Puka Park Resort.** This stylish hillside hideaway, which attracts a largely European clientele, lies in native bushland on Pauanui Beach, at the seaward end of Tairua Harbor. Timber chalets are beautifully furnished. Sliding glass doors lead to a balcony perched among the treetops. The restaurant's daily menu merits perusal; keep an eye out for the seafood ragout on braised leeks with kūmara crisps. The turn-off from State Highway 25 is about 6 km (4 mi) south of Tairua. **Pros:** Upmarket and very well appointed; attracts dressy people. **Cons:** None. ⊠ *Mount Ave., Pauanui Beach* ☎ *07/864–8088* ☐ *07/864–8112* ⊕ *www.pukapark.co.nz* ⇄ *48 rooms* ♨ *In-room: no a/c. In-hotel: restaurant, bar, tennis court, pool, spa, bicycles, no elevator* ☰ *AE, DC, MC, V.*

$–$$ ▨ **Blue Water Motel.** These blue-and-white units are at the southern end of Tairua, across the street from a small sandy beach. Each unit mimics a simple beach cottage, with a deck overlooking the harbor. **Pros:** Simple and basic; close to the beach, friendly hosts. **Con:** Underwhelming decor. ✉*213 Main Rd.* ☎🖷*07/864–8537* ⊕*www.coromandelmotel. co.nz* ⊸*8 1-bedroom units, 2 2-bedroom units, 1 3-bedroom house* ⌂*In-room: no a/c, kitchen, refrigerator, dial-up. In-hotel: laundry facilities, no-smoking rooms, no elevator* ⊟*MC, V.*

EN ROUTE

Stop at the beautiful white sand Opoutere Beach and the **Wharekawa Wildlife Refuge** for a 15-minute stroll through the forest to another great stretch of white sand. The long beach is bounded at either end by headlands, and there are stunning views of Slipper Island. An estuary near the parking lot is a breeding ground for shorebirds. A handsome bridge arches over the river to the forest walk. For information and maps about the Wharekawa (fah-ray-*ka*-wa) Wildlife Refuge, ask at the Tairua or Whangamata visitor information centers. Another good info source is the **YHA Opoutere Hostel** (✉*389 Opoutere Rd., Opoutere* ☎*07/865–9072* ⊕*www.stayyha.com*), an exceptional hostel set in 2 acres of native bush, fruit trees, and an herb garden, across the road from the estuary. A notice board marks a number of walking trails, including those to the wildlife refuge, the beach, and a glowworm grotto. Aside from the dormitories in an old schoolhouse, there is a self-contained cabin, and double units are throughout the grounds; costs range from $40 to $66 a night.

WHANGAMATA

37 km (23 mi) south of Tairua, 60 km (38 mi) east of Thames.

The Coromandel Ranges back Whangamata (fahng-a-ma-*ta*), another harborside village. This was once a town of modest houses and with a population of 4,000, but it's been discovered by people wanting a holiday home reasonably close to Auckland. Its harbor, surf beaches, mangroves, and coastal islands are glorious. In summer, the population triples. It's a great spot for deep-sea fishing, and its bar break creates some of the best waves in New Zealand. For classic and muscle car enthusiasts the Whangamata Beach Hop held each year at the end of April is a must-go. You'll see amazing classic cars, and listen to some of the best rock-and-roll bands around.

OUTDOOR ACTIVITIES

A trip to New Zealand really wouldn't be complete without a day or more with Doug Johansen and Jan Poole or one of their expert associate guides from **Kiwi Dundee Adventures** (⎘*Box 198, Whangamata* ☎🖷*07/865–8809* ⊕*www.kiwidundee.co.nz*). Their total enthusiasm for the region rubs off on anyone who takes a Kiwi Dundee tour. There are one- to five-day or longer experiences of Coromandel's majesty, or all of New Zealand if you'd like.

FISHING **Go Deep Sea** (✉*261K Kāitemako Rd., Tauranga* ☎*0800/118–845* ⊕*www.godeepsea.com*) is equipped to fish the deep waters off the coast and around Mayor Island; they'll take you out for a full day of "bottom fishing" for *hapuka, terakihi,* and snapper and pick you up from Whangamata. The minimum trip is a full day, starting at $195 but they have a range of others including a four-day trip from about US$2,000 including transfers from Auckland. **Te Ra** (✉*120 Moana Anu*

Anu Ave., Whangamata ☏*07/865–8681)* is licensed for marine-mammal-watching and can incorporate it into a day's fishing or cruising around the bays. Half-day fishing trips start at $40 on a Wednesday for one person, but groups cost from $400 for up to 10.

SURFING In the center of town, the **Whangamata Surf Shop** (✉*634 Port Rd.* ☏*07/865–8252),* recognized by its bright orange exterior, has surfboards and boogie boards for rent, and wet suits. If you want a surfing lesson, $50 covers surfboard rental and an instructor for an hour.

WHERE TO EAT

$$$–$$$$ ✗**Oceana's Restaurant.** With its white-linen tablecloths, candles, and atmosphere of "fine dining," Oceana's may not be what you'd expect in this small, seaside town. But that hasn't stopped people from flocking to the restaurant for traditional New Zealand cuisine. The restaurant's two signature dishes—the seafood platter for two and the oven-baked lamb loin rubbed with mustard and roasted garlic—are always popular, or you could go easy and have a bowl of seafood chowder and finish up with some old-fashioned bread-and-butter pudding. ✉*328 Ocean Rd.* ☏*07/865–7157* ▭*AE, DC, MC, V* ☾*Closed Mon. Apr.–Nov. No lunch.*

$$–$$$ ✗**Gaga's Restaurant and Cafe.** The kitchen offers a mix of easy food and sophisticated meals using good local ingredients. Its kid's menu has only one deep-fried item, in keeping with the owner's view that young people have to have the best. The wine list offers some superb wines from the country's smaller producers. ✉*501 Port Rd.* ☏*07/865–6999* ▭*AE, MC, V* ☾*Closed Mar.–Nov. No lunch.*

¢–$ ✗**Vibes Café.** This café boasts of being the friendliest place in town,
★ and the daylong crowds support the claim. Paintings by local artists cover the walls (not surprisingly, a beach theme predominates), and magazines and newspapers are on hand for a quick read over your espresso. It's the sort of place surfers might be seated next to older people out for an afternoon coffee. Of the light meals, the vegetarian dishes are the most exciting, with choices such as kūmara (native sweet potato) stuffed with pesto and sun-dried tomatoes, though the menu is often changing. ✉*638 Port Rd.* ☏*07/865–7121* ▭*AE, DC, MC, V* ☾*No dinner.*

WHERE TO STAY

$$$–$$$$ ▦ **Brenton Lodge.** Looking out over Whangamata and the islands in its harbor from your hillside suite, you'll have no trouble settling into a luxurious mood. Fresh flowers and a tray of fruit and muffins greet you on arrival. The lodge's only rooms are two suites on the second floors of attractive outbuildings, plus another in the main house. Stroll around the garden, peep at the birds in the aviary, and in springtime breathe in the scent of orange and jasmine blossoms. **Pros:** Peaceful settings; beautiful views. **Con:** A little to far from town to walk home in the evening. ✉*1 Brenton Pl., Box 216* ☏*07/865– 8400* ⊕*www.brentonlodge.co.nz* ↝*3 suites* ♿*In-room: no a/c, no phone. In-hotel: pool, laundry service, no-smoking rooms, no elevator* ▭*AE, MC, V* ⚹*BP.*

$–$$ **Pipinui Motel.** Just out of town, a two-minute walk to Whangamata harbor and a 10-minute walk to the beach, this motel has simple, modern units, with plain white walls, and dark, stylishly utilitarian furniture. **Pros:** Very cool hosts; simple decor; good location. **Con:** Possibly too plain for some. ✉ *805 Martyn Rd.* 📠 *07/865–6796* 🌐 *www.pipinuimotel.co.nz* 🛏 *4 suites* 🔧 *In-room: no a/c, kitchen (some), refrigerator, dial-up. In-hotel: no-smoking rooms, no elevator* ▭ *AE, DC, MC, V.*

3

THE BAY OF PLENTY

Explorer Captain James Cook gave the Bay of Plenty its name for the abundant sources of food he found here; these days it's best known for its plentiful supply of beaches. Places like Mount Maunganui and Whakatane overflow with sunseekers during peak summer-vacation periods, but even at the busiest times you need to travel only a few miles to find a secluded stretch of beach.

The Bay of Plenty has a strong Māori population; traditional lore (and common belief) has it that this is the first landing place of *Takitimu, Tainui, Arawa,* and *Mataatua,* four of the seven Māori *waka* (canoes) that arrived in New Zealand from Hawaiki. These first arrivals formed the ancestral base for the Māori tribes of the Tauranga region: Ngati Ranginui, Ngai Te Rangi, and Ngati Pukenga.

The gateway to the region is the small country town of Katikati, but the central base is Tauranga, which has retained its relaxed vacation-town atmosphere despite recent development. From Tauranga you can take day trips to beaches, the nearby bush, and offshore attractions such as volcanic White Island.

KATIKATI

62 km (39 mi) southeast of Thames, 35 km (22 mi) northwest of Tauranga.

In its early days, the Katikati area was heavily populated by Māori, and many pā (fortified village) sites have been found—an indication of tribal warfare. These days, fruit growing keeps the economy afloat. Katikati's most noticeable features are the 35 murals around town and good antiques stores. Another unusual attraction is the **Haiku Pathway,** a walking trail studded with haiku-etched boulders. The path starts at the Katikati Bus Company on Katikati's Main Street and leads down to the river. Pick up a map of the route at Katikati Visitor Information.

ESSENTIALS

Visitor Info Katikati Visitor Information (✉ *36 Centre Main Rd.* 📞 *07/549–1658* 🌐 *www.katikati.co.nz*).

The Bay of Plenty

TO WHAKAARI (WHITE) ISLAND ↗

Bay of Plenty

NEW ZEALAND

Waihi
Waihi Beach
Katikati
Matakana Island
Morrinsville
Mount Maunganui
Paparoa Marae
Bethlehem
Tauranga
Kaiate Falls
Maketu
Matamata
Te Puke
McLaren Falls Park
Matata
Whakatane
Ohope
Ngongotaha
Lake Rotoiti
Lake Rotorua
Rotorua
Lake Tarawera

0   20 miles
0   30 km

WHAT TO SEE

Waihi Beach, 19 km (12 mi) north of Katikati, is ideal for swimming and surfing and has access to numerous walkways. At low tide, people dig in the sand looking for *tuatua* and *pipi*—delicious shellfish that you boil until they open. Don't miss the drive to the top of the Bowentown heads at the southern end of Waihi Beach. This is an old Māori pā with stunning views. A short but steep walk from here leads to Cave Bay directly below the view point. Stop by the **Waihi Information Centre** (⊠ *Seddon St., Waihi* ☎ *07/863–6718* ⊕) for maps and tide times.

For great views over the Bay of Plenty go a couple of minutes north of Katikati on State Highway 2 to the **Lindemann Road Lookout.** The only sign to the lookout is right at the turnoff. The road is good but narrow in parts. Once at the lookout (where the road ends) you'll find a map embedded in rock to help orient you. Look for Mayor Island just to the north and Mt. Maunganui to the south.

Just south of Katikati on Highway 2 you'll spot the Cape Dutch design of the **Morton Estate** winery building. Winemaker Evan Ward has won a stack of awards over the years. He also holds some bottles back until he thinks they're at their drinking best, so you'll likely find earlier vintages than at most wineries. The Black Label Chardonnay is particularly good as is the sparkling wine. With views of the vines, **Morton's,**

Whakaari (White) Island

With its billowing plumes of steam, the active volcano of Whakaari (White) Island makes for an awesome geothermal experience. Forty-nine kilometers (29 mi) off the coast of Whakatane, the island is New Zealand's only active marine volcano. Although the last major eruption was in 2000, steam issues continuously from the many fumeroles (vents) and from the central crater, and the area reeks of sulfur. The island itself is eerie but beautiful, with fluorescent sulfuric crystal formations and boiling mud pools.

The least expensive way to see the island is by boat, and, as a bonus, you might see dolphins, seals, and even a whale en route. Peter and Jenny Tait, the official guardians of White Island, operate **White Island Tours** (☎ *0800/733–529* ⊕ *www. whiteisland.co.nz*). Upon arrival, you are issued a hard hat and gas mask and taken for a walk around the volcano and through the remains of a sulfur mine. The cost is $150 and includes lunch. Bring your bathing suit in summer. Alternatively, you can get a bird's-eye view of the steaming hulk. **Vulcan Helicopters** (☎ *0800/804– 354* ⊕ *www.vulcanheli.co.nz*) has a four-seat and a six-seat helicopter; pilot-owner Robert Fleming is also an authority on the island. Two-hour flights cost $395 and include a landing. **Air Discovery** (☎ *07/308–7760*) has a four-seater aircraft that flies over the island's crater; 55-minute trips cost $175.

the winery's on-site restaurant, is a charming place to stop for lunch or dinner. Start off with steamed Coromandel mussels, followed by the pork grilled with fresh ginger and palm sugar—and don't forget to try a glass of the pinot gris. ⊠ *Main Rd., Katikati* ☎ *0800/667–866* ⊕ *www.mortonestatewines.co.nz* ⊙ *Winery, weekdays 10–5; restaurant, no dinner Sun.–Wed.*

WHERE TO EAT

¢–$$$ ✕**The Landing.** You'll find this contemporary restaurant in the 1876 Talisman Hotel. Sit down for a lovely bowl of seafood chowder and a salad, or for something more substantial, try the fillet steak served with scallops in a white-wine-and-cream sauce. ⊠ *7–9 Main Rd., State Hwy. 2* ☎ *07/549–3218* ⊟ *AE, DC, MC, V.*

WHERE TO STAY

$$$$ ⊞ **Fantail Lodge.** This lodge has brought the region some European flair with a Bavarian-style exterior. The lodge owners have good relationships with local landowners, which means you see places (such as a nearby glowworm grotto) not on the tourist route. Rooms in the main lodge are in natural colors with timber ceilings. Fresh fruit and flowers in your room usually come from the lodge's garden—part of 40 acres filled with kiwifruit and citrus orchards, bird-of-paradise flowers, ponds, and courtyards. Breakfast and dinner are included in the price. **Pros:** Charming hosts; lovely grounds; nice rooms. **Con:** Some might find it twee. ⊠ *117 Rea Rd.* ☎ *07/549–1581* ⌨ *07/549–1417* ⊕ *www. fantaillodge.co.nz* ↪ *12 rooms, 2 2-bedroom villas* ₤ *In-room: no a/c,*

kitchen (some). In-hotel: restaurant, bar, tennis court, pool, spa, no elevator ⊟AE, DC, MC, V ⑩MAP.

$$$$ 🏠 **Matahui Lodge.** This lodge is a prime example of the boutique hotels being set up around the area. The harbor views may tempt you to stay on the patio all afternoon, even on cooler days when the outdoor stone fireplace is lit. The bedrooms are spacious and unclut-tered, with simple wooden furniture, olive-and-taupe walls, and wide windows that look out onto the grounds and harbor. Consider staying for dinner—they've stockpiled some excellent New Zealand vintages. **Pros:** Architecturally designed, lovely gardens; good wine list. **Con:** Possibly a little far from town. ⊠*187 Matahui Rd., 9 km (5½ mi) south of Katikati* ☎*07/571–8121* ⊕*www.matahui-lodge.co.nz* ☞*3 suites* ♿*In-room: no a/c, kitchen, dial-up. In-hotel: restaurant, room service, gym, laundry service, no-smoking rooms, no elevator* ⊟*AE, DC, MC, V* ⑩*BP.*

$$–$$$ 🏠 **The Point.** The Point does not take bookings from people who smoke and generally is not interested in guests with children under 18, though babies under one may stay if prior arrangements are made. Built from local river stones and untreated timber, the lodge looks half stone-cottage and half sprawling-barn. The guest rooms have beamed ceilings and four-poster beds; one turreted suite overlooks a small vineyard and the harbor. For an extra charge, hosts Kerry and Anne Guy prepare dinner accompanied by wine from their own vine-yard or a picnic basket to take away. **Pros:** Nice location; nice views. **Cons:** Cheap furniture and bedspreads. ⊠*444 Tuapiro Rd., Tuapiro Point, 8 km (5 mi) north of Katikati* ☎*07/549–3604* 🖷*07/549–3515* ⊕*www.thepointlodge.co.nz* ☞*3 suites* ♿*In-room: no a/c, no phone (some), kitchen (some), refrigerator (some). In-hotel: room service, beachfront, bicycles, laundry service, public Internet, parking (no fee), no-smoking rooms, no kids (children under 1 yr will be accepted), no elevator* ⊟*AE, DC, MC, V* ⑩*BP.*

$ 🏠 **Kaimai View Motel.** The whitewashed rooms in these low green-and-white buildings are simply furnished, but they have views of the Kaimai Ranges. The motel is right on Katikati's main strip, and its proximity to the area's activities makes this a low-key and handy base. **Pros:** Disabled access in one unit; simple decor. **Con:** Basic rooms. ⊠*78 Main Rd. (State Hwy. 2)* ☎*07/549–0398* 🖷*07/549–3684* ⊕*www. kaimaiview.co.nz* ☞*7 rooms, 7 suites* ♿*In-room: no a/c, kitchen (some), refrigerator, dial-up. In-hotel: pool, laundry facilities, parking (no fee), no-smoking rooms, no elevator* ⊟*AE, DC, MC, V.*

TAURANGA

216 km (134 mi) southeast of Auckland.

The population center of the Bay of Plenty, Tauranga is one of New Zealand's fastest-growing cities. Along with its neighbor, Whakatane, this seaside city claims to be one of the country's sunniest towns. Unlike most local towns, Tauranga doesn't grind to a halt in the off-season because it has one of the busiest ports in the country and the excellent waves at neighboring Mount Maunganui always draw surfers. With the addition of an artificial reef, more are sure to come. The Tauranga Visitor Information Centre is open daily from 10 to 4.

GETTING AROUND

To explore the town center, start at the **Strand**, a pretty tree-lined street that separates the shops from the sea. Bars, restaurants, and cafés line the Strand and nearby side streets.

ESSENTIALS

Bus Depot InterCity Tauranga Depot (⊠ *95 Willow St.* ☎ *07/578–8103*).

Hospitals **South City Medical Centre** (⊠ *454 Cameron Rd.,* ☎ *07/578–6808*). **Tauranga Hospital** (⊠ *375 Cameron Rd.* ☎ *07/579–8000*). **Mount Medical Centre** (⊠ *257 Maunganui Rd., Mount Maunganui* ☎ *07/575–3073*).

Pharmacies **John's Photo-Pharmacy** (⊠ *Cameron Rd. and 2nd Ave., Tauranga* ☎ *07/578–3566*). **Dispensary First** (⊠ *Girven Rd. and Grenada St., Mount Maunganui* ☎ *07/574–8645*).

Visitor Info **Tauranga Visitor Information Centre** (⊠ *95 Willow St.* ☎ *07/578–8103* ⊕ *www.bayofplentynz.com*).

WHAT TO SEE

The 1847 **Elms Mission House** was the first Christian missionary station built in the Bay of Plenty. The beautiful late-Georgian house, named for the 50 elms that grew on the property, was home to descendants of pioneer missionaries until the mid-1990s. You can explore the lush grounds, but the real appeal lies in the main house, the small wooden chapel, and the collection of furniture, crockery, and other period items. ⊠ *15 Mission St.* ☎ *07/577–9772* ⊕ *www.theelms.org.nz* ⊿ *$5* ⊙ *House Wed. and weekends 2–4; grounds daily 9–5.*

The **Compass Community Foundation** is an early-1900s cobbled-street village that now houses a couple of crafts shops and a café. It's pleasant to wander among the well-maintained buildings, but visit the **House of Bottles Wood Museum,** where Keith Godwin takes old fence posts originally used in New Zealand's pioneering farms and turns them into handcrafted bottles. ⊠ *17th Ave. W* ☎ *07/571–3700* ⊿ *Free* ⊙ *Daily 10–3.*

One of the quirkier spots in Tauranga is the open-only-occasionally **Mount Surf Museum,** which displays nearly 700 surfboards, some from the beginning of surfing in New Zealand and other surf memorabilia— reportedly the largest collection in New Zealand. ■**TIP**➜**It's best to call before heading over.** ⊠ *139 Totara St., Mount Maunganui* ☎ *07/927–7234* ⊙ *Call for hrs and admission.*

★ The formerly volcanic **Mt. Maunganui** is the region's geological icon, with its conical, rocky outline rising 761 feet above sea level. White-sand beaches with clear water stretch from "the Mount" mile after mile—this is one of New Zealand's best swimming and surfing areas. One of the early Māori canoes, *Takitimu,* landed at the base of the mountain. A system of trails around Mauao—Maunganui's Māori name—includes an easy walk around its base and the more strenuous

Summit Road from the campground by the Pilot Bay boat ramp. The trails are clearly signposted and heavily used, so no bushwhacking is necessary. All roads lead to the Mount, as they say; to get here from Tauranga, follow any road running parallel to the beach. The Mount gets crowded around Christmas and New Year's Eve; to see it at its best, come in November, early December, or between mid-January and late March. On the first weekend in January you watch the Tauranga Half Ironman race while drinking coffee at a sidewalk café, and if keen you can sit on the path around the Mount and cheer runners on. The **Mount Maunganui Visitor Information Centre** is open weekdays only. ⊠ *Salisbury Ave.* ☎ *07/575–5099* ⊕ *www.bayofplentynz.com.*

McLaren Falls Park is a 15-minute drive south of Tauranga off State Highway 29. You can take the 10-minute easy bushwalk to the falls, or tackle the more strenuous walks to Pine Tree Knoll or the Ridge for great vistas across the park. ⊠ *State Hwy. 29* ☎ *07/578–8103.*

Kaiate Falls (Te Rerekawau) is a little off the beaten track but worth the trip. About 15 minutes southeast of Tauranga, just off Welcome Bay Road, the Kaiate Stream drops over bluffs in a series of waterfalls and rocky lagoons, culminating in a deep green lagoon flanked by moss- and fern-fringed cliffs. A 20- to 30-minute loop trail takes you down to the main lagoon and through lush greenery, and the falls' summit (and the parking lot) affords views over Tauranga and the coast. ⊠ *Upper Papamoa Rd.* ☎ *07/578–8103.*

Owner-winemaker Paddy Preston of **Mills Reef Winery** used to make kiwifruit wine, but he hasn't looked back since he turned to the real thing. The lovely 20-acre complex includes pétanque courts, a fancy tasting room, and an underground wine cellar. The restaurant is also worth a visit (it's open for lunch, coffee, and dessert year-round); sautéed black tiger prawns, scallops, and salmon with passion fruit, lemongrass, and pink grapefruit are fabulous with a glass of sauvignon blanc. Although open all year for brunch and lunch, the restaurant is open only occasionally for dinner; it's best to call in advance. ⊠ *143 Moffat Rd., Bethlehem* ⊹ *about 5 km (3 mi) north of Tauranga* ☎ *07/576–8800* ⊕ *www.millsreef.co.nz* ⊙ *Daily 10–5.*

OFF THE BEATEN PATH

Paparoa Marae. The *whanau* (family) of Paparoa Marae offers a marae experience that is very down to earth. It's a working marae so, along with a traditional welcome and cultural performance, Māori elders explain the marae, Māori carvings, and other aspects of Māori history, culture, and protocol. You're invited to share in a *hāngi* (the traditional method of Māori cooking) meal. A marae visit costs around $25–$55, including the hāngi. It's about 20 minutes out of Tauranga, just off State Highway 2 in the village of Te Puna. ⊠ *Paparoa Rd., Te Puna, Tauranga* ☎ *07/552–5904.*

OUTDOOR ACTIVITIES

BOATING & FISHING

Blue Ocean Charters operates three vessels and has half- and full-day trips, plus overnight excursions. A half day of reef fishing costs about $60, but if you want to go for a large hapuka, the cost goes above $100. Equipment is provided and you do need to phone ahead as they get busy. ⊠*Coronation Pier, Wharf St., Box 13–100, Tauranga* ☎*07/578–9685* ⊕*www.blueoceancharters.co.nz.*

SURFING The **New Zealand Surf School, Mount Maunganui** offers lessons mid-November through March at 10, noon, and 2 every day, starting at $80, which includes all the gear. They also rent surfboards and wet suits by the hour or day and have the experience to work with people with a range of special needs. ⊠*Marine Parade and Tay St., Mount Maunganui* ☎*07/825–0064 or 021/477–873* ⊕*www.nzsurfschools.co.nz.*

SWIMMING WITH DOLPHINS Swimming with dolphins is a big summer activity in the Bay of Plenty, especially off Mount Maunganui. The Department of Conservation licenses and regularly inspects operators and sets limits on the number of boats allowed around any pod of dolphins. Touching, handling, and provoking the dolphins are prohibited. Locals say that the dolphins call the shots; if they don't want anyone swimming with them, they'll take off, and no boat has yet managed to catch up with an antisocial dolphin.

Dolphin Seafaris will take you out for a dolphin encounter. Wet suits, dive gear, and towels are included in the $120 price tag for a trip leaving at 8AM and back round 1 PM with breakfast and drinks included. Phone ahead for daily departure times from the Bridge Marina. ⊠*90 Maunganui Rd., Mount Maunganui* ☎*07/575–4620* ⊕*www.nzdolphin.com.*

Graeme Butler of **Butler's Swim with Dolphins** has been running dolphin-swimming and whale-watching voyages on the *Gemini Galaxsea* since the early 1990s. Bring your bathing suit and lunch. Trips leave at 9 AM from Tauranga and 9:30 AM from Mount Maunganui, any day that weather allows. Cost is $125 but you need to bring your lunch with drinks supplied, and if you don't see dolphins you can take another trip for free. ☎*07/578–3197 or 0508/288–537* ⊕*www. swimwithdolphins.co.nz.*

The South Sea Sailing Company will take you out for a full day of sailing on a 60-foot custom-built catamaran around the islands off the coast of Tauranga. With two kayaks on board, as well as snorkels and wet suits, you can jump in for a swim and paddle among the dolphins. You may also see the odd shark or whale——no swimming with those guys advised. Trips are daily (weather-dependent), cost $120, and depart at 10:30 AM (returning around 4:30 PM). Be sure to bring your own lunch; although they will provide it on request. ⊠*Mirrielees Rd. (dock)* ☎*07/579–6376* ⊕*www.southseasailing.com.*

WHERE TO EAT

$$–$$$$ ✕ **Somerset Cottage.** The name says it all—Somerset is a genuine country cottage, and many locals consider it one of the region's best restaurants. The menu is eclectic, with dishes such as panfried squid with tamarind-lime dressing, or roast duck on vanilla-coconut kūmara (native sweet potato) with orange sauce. They also sell some of the products they cook. ⊠*30 Bethlehem Rd., 5 km (3 mi) north of Tauranga center on*

State Hwy. 2 ☎*07/576–6889* ✉*somersetcottage@xtra.co.nz* ☜*Reservations essential* ▱*AE, DC, MC, V* ⊔*Licensed and BYOB* ⊘*No lunch Sat.–Tues.; no dinner Mon.*

$$$ ✕ **The Lobster Club.** This pleasant indoor-outdoor restaurant has great views of Mt. Maunganui and, as the name suggests, specializes in lobster. There are at least three fish-of-the-day options as well. The pan-fried bluenose (that's a fish) with kūmara (native sweet potato) is a popular choice, but you could also go for the apple-and-cinnamon-glazed roast pork. From your table you look across a sea of pleasure craft in one direction and Tauranga township in the other. From Tauranga, head over the Harbour Bridge toward Mount Maunganui and take the first left turn into the marina. ✉*Tauranga Bridge Marina* ☎*07/574–4147* ▱*AE, DC, MC, V.*

¢–$$$ ✕ **Bravo Restaurant Cafe** With jazz and tables spilling out onto the sidewalk patio, this restaurant is most popular during brunch, when you can sip a strong latte and enjoy a dish of smoked salmon with scallion, fried potatoes, poached eggs, and hollandaise sauce. The pizza's a good choice, too, with unusual toppings such as salmon, scallops, capers, and avocado. A range of other dishes changes with the seasons. ✉*Red Sq.* ☎*07/578–4700* ▱*AE, DC, MC, V* ⊘*No dinner Sun. or Mon.*

¢–$ ✕ **Sidetrack Cafe.** At the base of Mt. Maunganui and across the street from the beach, this bustling café is a great place for breakfast or lunch after a climb or swim. Grab a table (there are more outside than in) for a plate of coconut toast, a salad, or a dense chocolate brownie. Or get a huge sandwich and a smoothie to go, and head off to a quiet spot on the trail that rings the Mount. ✉*Shop 3, Marine Parade, Mount Maunganui* ☎*07/575–2145* ▱*DC, MC, V* ⊘*No dinner.*

¢–$ ✕ **Zeytin.** The brightly painted, mismatched wooden chairs bring out the colors from the Turkish tapestries and artifacts on the terra-cotta walls of this Middle Eastern café. The fresh, well-seasoned food arrives in a snap, and portions are generous. The mixed vegetarian pita—falafel, zucchini fritters, marinated red cabbage, tabouleh, and hummus with a garlic sauce, all wrapped in a chewy flatbread—is a highlight. ✉*83 The Strand* ☎*07/579–0099* ▱*No credit cards.*

WHERE TO STAY

$$$$ ⊡ **Ridge Country Retreat.** Set on 35 acres—a short drive from town—the
Fodor'sChoice lodge overlooks a brilliant green valley, all the way to Mt. Maunganui
★ and the ocean. Stellar views are had from the outdoor pool and the in-room hot tubs. Beautifully furnished suites have private balconies and heated bathroom floors, but the best room is the dining room, with its huge stone fireplace, a wall of windows, and a 22-foot-high beamed ceiling. Dinner is a six-course affair, and breakfast is whatever you want it to be; hosts Penny and Joanne pull out all the stops. Some guests like to arrive by helicopter. **Pros:** Sophisticated hosts; beautiful lodge without being overdone; superb location. **Con:** Pricey. ✉*300 Rocky Cutting Rd.* ☎*07/542–1301* 🖷*07/542–2116* ⊕*www.rcr.co.nz* ⇋*11 suites* ⟐*In-room: no a/c, refrigerator, Ethernet, dial-up. In-hotel: restaurant, room service, bar, pool, gym, spa, parking (no fee), no kids under 12, no-smoking rooms, no elevator* ▱*AE, DC, MC, V* ⦿*AI.*

$$-$$$ 🛏 **Hotel on Devonport.** At the most central hotel in Tauranga, each earth-toned room has a balcony looking over the city, the harbor, or the port. It's a groovy little place with a big city feel, especially in terms of design and attitude. In winter, you'll be greeted with a huge fire in the foyer (along with a complimentary drink). **Pros:** Smart; modern; close to town. **Con:** Slightly impersonal feel. ⊠72 Devonport Rd. ☎07/578–2668 🖨07/578–2669 ⊕www.hotelondevonport.net.nz ➷38 suites ⌂In-room: no a/c, safe, kitchen, refrigerator, Ethernet, dial-up. In-hotel: room service, concierge, laundry service, parking (no fee), no-smoking rooms ⊟AE, DC, MC, V ⎮⊙⎮BP.

$$-$$$ 🛏 **Papamoa Beach Top 10 Holiday Resort.** This resort complex has the
★ widest range of accommodations in the area, and they're all on the beach, about five minutes down the road from the madding Mount Maunganui crowd. If you feel like roughing it, campsites begin at $15. There are also Spartan cabins, where you'll need to bring your own bed linens, and bathrooms and kitchen are shared. Or you can stretch out in one of the private rooms, or the spacious, light-filled, cedar-wood suites; the decks are built onto the sand dunes, a couple of feet from the water. This property is popular and the "seaside villas" make a fantastic base for the region. **Pros:** Wide range of accommodations; cheap; on the beach. **Cons:** Gets very busy over summer; can be noisy. ⊠535 Papamoa Beach Rd. ☎07/572–0816 🖨07/572–0816 ⊕www.papamoabeach.co.nz ➷260 campsites, 9 cabins, 13 rooms, 13 suites ⌂In-room: no a/c, no phone, kitchen, refrigerator, no TV (some). In-hotel: tennis courts, beachfront, laundry facilities, public Internet, parking (no fee), no-smoking rooms, some pets allowed, no elevator ⊟MC, V.

$$ 🛏 **Puriri Park Boutique Hotel.** In the mass of Tauranga's central hotels, this Spanish-Revival-influenced property is priced just above the nearby motels but is still less expensive than its location and facilities would suggest. The spacious rooms have private balconies and solid oak work tables. Breakfast can be provided, and for lunch and dinner, guests can walk to a selection of nearby restaurants that have a "charge-back" arrangement with the hotel. **Pros:** Comfortable; clean; close to town. **Con:** Slightly tacky decor. ⊠32 Cameron Rd. ☎07/577–1480 or 0800/478–7474 🖨07/577–1490 ⊕www.puriripark.co.nz ➷21 suites ⌂In-room: no a/c, kitchen, refrigerator, dial-up. In-hotel: restaurant, room service, bar, pool, laundry service, parking (no fee), no elevator ⊟AE, DC, MC, V.

¢   🛏 **Harbourside City Backpackers.** If you're not camping, this is one of Tauranga's cheapest lodging options. The blue-and-white rooms are basic, with shared dorms and a few private twins. The balcony on the third floor overlooking the harbor is a good place for breakfast or a drink at the end of the day and meeting fellow travelers. There is a shared kitchen. **Pros:** Safe; clean; cheap. **Cons:** Can be noisy; not a lot of privacy. ⊠105 The Strand ☎07/579–4066 🖨07/579–4067 ⊕www.backpacktauranga.co.nz ➷6 dorm rooms, 18 suites ⌂In-room: no a/c, no phone, no TV. In-hotel: bar, laundry facilities, no-smoking rooms, no elevator.

WHAKATANE

100 km (62 mi) southeast of Tauranga.

For yet another chance to laze on the beach, Whakatane (fah-kah-*tah*-nee) claims to be the North Island's sunniest town. This was landfall on New Zealand for the first migratory Māori canoes, and the fertile hinterland was the first part of the country to be farmed.

ESSENTIALS

Bus Depot **InterCity Whakatane Depot** (⊠ *The Strand* ☎ *07/308–6058).*

Hospital **Whakatane Hospital** (⊠ *Stewart St., Whakatane* ☎ *07/306–0999).*

Pharmacies **Phoenix Pharmacy** (⊠ *Pyne St., Whakatane* ☎ *07/307–1409).* **Total Health Chemist** (⊠ *252 The Strand, Whakatane* ☎ *07/308–9009).*

Visitor Info **Whakatane Visitor Information Centre** (⊠ *Quay and Kakahoroa Sts., on the Strand* ☎ *07/308–6058* ⊕ *www.whakatane.com).*

WHAT TO SEE

The most popular and safest swimming beach in the area is the 11-km-long (7-mi-long) **Ohope Beach,** in Ohope, a 10-minute drive east of Whakatane. Take the well-signposted Ohope Road out of Whakatane's town center and over the hills to the beach. Pohutukawa Avenue, Ohope's main road, runs parallel to the beach, flanked by lush native forest, citrus trees, and grazing cows, as well as private residences. The beach is far less developed than others along the bay.

NEED A BREAK? Just beyond Ohope, it's not uncommon to see locals out on the Ohiwa Harbor mudflats harvesting dinner. If you don't want to "pick your own," head for **Ohiwa Oyster Farm** (☎ *07/312–4565).* This roadside oyster shack is the place for oysters by the basket, a burger, fish-and-chips, Māori *rewena* (a traditional leavened bread), whitebait fritters, crayfish, and *kina* (akin to a sea urchin).

The native forest reserves around Whakatane provide a range of bushwalks and hiking trails. The 6-km (4-mi) walkway called *Nga Tapuwae o Toi* ("the footprints of Toi") is named for a descendant of Tiwakawaka, one of the first Māori to settle in New Zealand. It's divided into eight shorter walks that take you past historic pā sites, along the coastline and the Whakatane River, around Kohi Point (which separates Whakatane from Ohope), and through the Ohope and Makaroa Bush Scenic Reserves. Walks range from one to three hours. No guide is necessary, and most tourist operators and information centers in Whakatane stock free trail maps. The trailhead is on Canning Place, behind the Whakatane Hotel on the corner of George Street and the Strand. Follow the steps up the cliff and you'll be at the beginning of the trail. ■ TIP➔ **Some trail crossings depend on the tidal schedule, so be sure to check low-tide times.**

OFF THE BEATEN PATH **Maketu.** About halfway between Tauranga and Whakatane is the small seaside village of Maketu, one of the area's least developed places and one of the first points of Māori landfall.

Māori Exhibition. Stop in the Māori Exhibition gallery and shop. It's the first building you see as you come into Maketu, next to the gas station. The shop isn't open often (you might want to call before stopping by), but if you're lucky, you'll find Googie Tapsell, a highly regarded local *kuia* (elder Māori woman), weaving *harekeke* (flax). The store has well-priced Māori art for sale, including *piu piu* (traditional Māori clothing), wooden carvings, jewelry, and *kete* (baskets). If Googie or the other kuia have time to spare, they may teach you to weave a small item, in exchange for *koha* (a donation). ⊠ *Maketu Rd. Village roundabout* ☎ *07/533–2176 or 07/533–2375.*

SPORTS & THE OUTDOORS

Fishing, diving, and swimming with dolphins are popular activities in the Whakatane area. The water surrounding White Island has some extremely warm pockets, with abundant, colorful marine life.

DOLPHIN- & WHALE- WATCHING

For closer aqueous encounters of the mammalian kind, **Dolphins Down Under** (⊠ *2 The Strand E* ☎ *0800/354–7737* ⊕ *www.dolphinswim. co.nz*) has four-hour cruises during which you can swim with or simply view dolphins. Wet suits and snorkels are provided. Cruises leave at 7:30 AM and cost $120. **Whales and Dolphin Watch** (⊠ *The Strand E* ☎ *07/308–2001* 🖷 *07/308–2028* ⊕ *www.whalesanddolphinwatch. co.nz*) has three- to four-hour cruises. Wet suits and snorkels are provided. Cruises leave daily at 8:30 AM year-round, except during the busy summer months, when they leave at 7:30, 9:30, 11:30 AM, and 1 PM. Costs range from $80 to $150.

FISHING & DIVING

John Baker (⊠ *15A James St.* ☎ *07/307–0015* ⊕ *www.divenfish.co.nz*) is one of the area's best-known dive masters. For $1,000, he'll take up to six people out to White Island and some of the smaller nearby islands for a day of fishing and/or diving on his 40-foot boat. Wet-suit and fishing-rod rentals are available, as are $500 half-day trips. A certified diving instructor and local character with stints as a Māori All Black and a radio announcer in his past, **Val Baker** (⊠ *Matata* ☎ *07/322–2340* ✐ *anthea.val@clearnet.co.nz*) has been diving for more than 30 years. He can take you to some of the smaller islands in the bay in his 18-foot "fizzboat." Wet suits and snorkels are provided, and if you want to fish off the boat, he'll provide gear for that, too. ■ TIP→ Ask him to show you the shell of a giant mussel (all that's left of a good meal) he caught in the Cook Strait. Costs begin at around $100 for a half day. He also offers a four-day intensive diving course for beginners.

WHERE TO EAT

$$–$$$ ✕ **The Wharf Shed.** At this restaurant on the Whakatane marina, the dinner menu focuses on seafood, bought that day from the quay outside the kitchen door, but also features local beef and lamb. The "Admiral's Beef" is a tender beef fillet wrapped in smoky bacon, accompanied by whipped sweet potatoes. The marine theme continues in the decor, with models of yachts, maps, and tools of the fishing trade, and large windows look out over the water. There are tables outside on the quay, too—a good spot for a bowl of chowder, or for coffee and dessert. Try the "Berry White Island," their signature

dish, a meringue and custard stack topped by an "eruption" of berries. The kitchen closes at 8:30. ⊠ *Whakatane Wharf, The Strand E* ☎ *07/308–5698* ▤ *AE, DC, MC, V.*

$ ✗ **Peejays Coffee House.** Peejays is filled at lunchtime with Whakatane locals ordering the venison-and-Guinness pie. If you're preparing for a trip out to the island, nab a table on the deck to get an eyeful of your destination, then fuel up with a traditional Kiwi fry-up of sausages, bacon, eggs, and toast. ⊠ *15 The Strand E* ☎ *07/308–9588 or 0800/242–299* ▤ *AE, MC, V* ☉ *No dinner.*

WHERE TO STAY

$$ ▦ **Blue Tides Bed and Breakfast.** At this traditional New Zealand B&B, rooms are modest, but the beds have crisp white cotton sheets and the views from the balcony are terrific, stretching from nearby islands all the way to the Coromandel. The hearty breakfast includes homemade jams and a Kiwi fry-up of fresh fish or bacon and eggs. If you wish, the host will take you flounder fishing at night out on the estuary with spears and lights—guests have even been known to catch a few. It's a private home and it's not set up for children. **Pros:** Homey; low key; restful. **Con:** Lacking in sophistication. ⊠ *7 Awhe Rd., Maketu Beach* ☎ *07/533–2023 or 0800/359–191* ▤ *07/533–2023* ⊕ *www.bluetides. co.nz* ➥ *3 suites, 1 cottage* ⚒ *In-room: no a/c, no phone, no TV. In-hotel: no-smoking rooms, no elevator* ▤ *MC, V* ⦿ *BP.*

$–$$ ▦ **White Island Rendezvous.** Convenient if you're heading out to White Island, this motel run by the owners of White Island Tours is across the road from the marina and within walking distance of town. Rooms have a somewhat nautical cream-and-blue color scheme and fish-theme art on the walls. **Pros:** Friendly hosts; clean and relaxed. **Con:** Basic. ⊠ *15 The Strand E* ☎ *07/308–9500 or 0800/242–299* ▤ *07/308–0303* ⊕ *www.whiteisland.co.nz* ➥ *22 studios, 2 suites* ⚒ *In-room: no a/c, kitchen, refrigerator. In-hotel: restaurant, laundry facilities, no elevator* ▤ *AE, DC, MC, V.*

¢–$ ▦ **Awakeri Hot Springs.** The best reason to stay at this vacation park, about 15 minutes northwest of Whakatane along the Rotorua-Whakatane Highway, is to soak in the hot-spring-fed swimming pool and hot tubs. If you want privacy, you can book a private spa. A steaming stream runs through the property, too, and the forested grounds host an ongoing chorus of birdsong. Rooms are basic but comfortable, and there are also camper-van and tent sites. If you're not staying here, you can still stop for a dip ($4); pool hours are 8 AM–9:30 PM. **Pros:** Cheap and friendly. **Con:** Very basic. ⊠ *Rotorua-Whakatane Hwy. (State Hwy. 30)* ☎ *07/304–9117* ▤ *07/304–9290* ⊕ *www.awakerisprings. co.nz* ➥ *25 rooms* ⚒ *In-room: no a/c, kitchen, refrigerator, no TV (some). In-hotel: pools, laundry facilities, parking (no fee), no-smoking rooms, no elevator* ▤ *AE, MC, V.*

East Coast & the Volcanic Zone

WORD OF MOUTH

"We now had our first real adventure, hiking the crater of Mount Tarawera in the rain. It last erupted in 1886, leaving 150 people dead. Through the rain, the colors of the crater created a painting of soft and subtle pastels. Beautiful! We drove to Rotorua and had dinner at the Fat Dog."

—partypoet

"My friend and I had two very different experiences in Rotorua. I thought the odor was fine, and didn't even notice it after a while, however, my friend is allergic to sulfur, and after our 2 days in Rotorua, she was very sick and couldn't talk for days."

—travelersusan

Updated by
Bob Marriott

WHEN YOU GET TO ROTORUA, the mid-island's major city and a longtime Māori hub, after a trip through the rolling sheep-speckled fields of the Waikato and the wild Mamaku Ranges, the aptly named "Sulphur City," with its mud pots, geysers, and stinky air, comes as a complete surprise. Rotorua has been a tourist magnet since the 19th century, when Europeans first heard of the healing powers of local hot springs.

South of Rotorua is Lake Taupo, the country's largest lake and the geographical bull's-eye of the North Island. From the lake, you'll have a clear shot at Ruapehu, the island's tallest peak and a top ski area, and its symmetrically cone-shaped neighbor, Ngauruhoe. Ruapehu dominates Tongariro National Park, a haunting landscape of craters, volcanoes, and lava flows that ran with molten rock as recently as 1988. As part of the Pacific Ring of Fire (a zone that's earthquake and volcanic eruption prone), the area's thermal features remain an ever-present hazard—and a thrilling attraction.

Southeast of Lake Taupo is the laid-back art deco town of Napier along Hawke's Bay, where you can laze the days away drinking at the local vineyards. To truly get off the beaten path, head to isolated Eastland, the thick thumb of land that's east of Rotorua.

Note: *For more information on bicycling, fishing, hiking, kayaking, and rafting in central North Island, see Chapter 11.*

ORIENTATION & PLANNING

GETTING ORIENTED

This region lies to the northeast of the North Island, and covers some of the most naturally attractive areas in the country. The main towns are busy, despite being connected by isolated roads that wind across mountain ranges through vast areas of bush. Expect steaming thermal regions, rolling farmland, or peaceful sun-drenched vineyards.

The Rotorua Area. Home of geothermal unrest and oddities, Rotorua today is almost entirely a product of the late-19th-century fad for spa towns; its elaborate bathhouses and formal gardens date to this era. You'll find surreal wonders that include limestone caverns, volcanic wastelands, steaming geysers, and bubbling, hissing ponds.

Lake Taupo & Tongariro National Park. Fishing and water sports are popular activities in Lake Taupo, the largest lake in New Zealand, and rivers running into it. The area has its share of geothermal oddities. Tongariro National Park, made up of three volcanic peaks, has some great otherworldly hiking trails.

Napier & Hawke's Bay. On the shores of Hawke Bay, you'll find a fabulous architectural anomaly: the town of Napier, a time capsule of colorful art deco architecture. The Hawke's Bay countryside is thick with vineyards, as this is one of the country's major wine-producing areas.

Gisborne & Eastland. Gisborne, where Captain James Cook first landed in New Zealand, is the area's largest town. Above it juts the largely agricultural East Cape, a sparsely populated area ringed with stunning beaches, and inland lies the haunting beauty of Te Urewera National Park.

PLANNING

GETTING HERE & AROUND

Air New Zealand (☎ *0800/737–000* ⊕ *www.airnewzealand.co.nz*) runs regular flights from Wellington, Auckland, Christchurch, Dunedin, and Queenstown into Napier, Gisborne, and Rotorua. The flights from Napier to Auckland or Wellington take about an hour; the trip to Christchurch lasts roughly two hours.

Start in Rotorua and then head down to Taupo and the National Park region. You'll have to backtrack to Hawke's Bay, but it's all interesting countryside. If fishing is your game, stop over at Turangi. It's a fair trek to Napier and Hastings, but Hawke's Bay is an area not to be missed. Be prepared for a lengthy stretch to Gisborne and the East Cape and if you have the time to take the rugged side road, Lake Waikaremoana is a little piece of heaven.

North Island's East Coast and volcanic zone include some of the country's most popular attractions, so there are plenty of excellent tours and bus routes that hit most highlights. But having your own vehicle gives you the flexibility to seek out an untrammeled scenic spot or that lesser-known but outstanding winery.

Inter-City (☎*09/913–6100 in Auckland, 04/472–5111 in Wellington* ⊕*www.intercitycoach.co.nz*), along with their subsidiary company **Newmans** (⊕*www.newmanscoach.co.nz*), runs regular bus services to cover this entire region. Comfortable, reasonably priced, and efficient, they are particularly useful to backpackers and people who are in no particular hurry.

The Napier-to-Auckland trip takes 8 hours, Napier–Rotorua is 3½ hours, Napier–Taupo is 2¼ hours, and Napier–Wellington is 6 hours. Frequent local services go between Napier and Hastings. There's one bus service a day to Gisborne with Newmans and InterCity from either Auckland, via Rotorua, or from Wellington, via Napier. These trips take a solid day.

The best way to travel in this region is by car. Rotorua is about three hours from Auckland. Take Highway 1 south past Hamilton and Cambridge to Tirau, where Highway 5 breaks off to Rotorua. Roads in this region are generally in good condition. Avis New Zealand has a branch at ther Terminal Building in the Rotorua Airport.

The main route between Napier and the north is Highway 5. Driving time from Taupo is two hours, five hours if you're coming straight

TOP REASONS TO GO

Hiking & Walking: The eastern coast of the North Island has several excellent bushwalking trails, including the Tongariro Crossing, which brings you through the alpine areas in Tongariro National Park. Some of the most rugged bush in the country is in Te Urewera National Park southeast of Rotorua, and hikes abound around Rotorua and Taupo. Just don't tackle the mountain terrain unprepared—the weather changes rapidly.

Māori Ceremonial Feast: Rotorua may be the best place in New Zealand to try the Māori feast known as a *hāngi*. Traditionally, the meal is made by lining a hāngi pit, or earth oven, with heated stones and wet leaves, and then filling it with lamb, pork, chicken, seafood, potatoes, pumpkin, and *kūmara* (sweet potato). Nowadays, the food may be prepared aboveground, but when it's done well, it doesn't lose much in the translation.

Soaking: In Rotorua and Taupo, thermal springs are on tap. You can soak in your own thermal bath in even the cheapest hotels in Rotorua or take advantage of public facilities such as Polynesian Spa. Many Taupo hotels also have their own thermal baths or pools. Lie back and close your eyes.

World-Class Fishing: Central North Island is trout country. You can get out on any of the designated lakes and waterways if you have your own gear and a fishing license—but a local guide can take you to the right spots. Anglers rarely leave Lake Taupo, the lakes around Rotorua, or the rivers farther south around Turangi disappointed.

from Auckland. Highway 2 is the main route heading south; it connects Hastings and Napier. Driving time to Wellington is five hours.

Highway 50, the Napier–Hastings road, can help you steer clear of traffic by avoiding central Hastings; it then joins Highway 2 before Napier. Several wineries are on or near the 50.

The most direct route from the north to Gisborne is to follow State Highway 2 around the Bay of Plenty to Opotiki, Eastland's northern gateway, then continue to Gisborne through the Waioeka Gorge Scenic Reserve. The drive from Auckland to Gisborne takes seven hours. South from Gisborne, continuing on Highway 2, you pass through Wairoa, about 90 minutes away, before passing Napier, Hawke's Bay, and Wairarapa on the way to Wellington, about 7½ hours by car.

Roads can be narrow and winding in places. Remember that driving is on the left and to always keep the tank full, as gas stations can be hard to come by.

WHEN TO GO

Mid-November through mid-April is the best time in central and eastern North Island. The weather is balmy and, apart from Christmas Day, New Year's Day, and Easter, everything is open. This is also the season for vineyard festivals, so keep an eye on the local calendars. Try to avoid the school holidays (from early December to late

January), when the roads and hotels get clogged with Kiwi vacationers. If you'd like to see the gannet colony at Cape Kidnappers, you need to go between October and March, when the birds are nesting and raising their young.

Hawke's Bay and Gisborne can be remarkably mild in winter, but Rotorua and Taupo can get very cold. It's not unusual for the Desert Road—the stretch of State Highway 1 between Waiouru and Turangi—to be closed by snow for short periods. If you want to do some skiing, August is the month to hit the slopes of Tongariro National Park, though the first major snows can fall as early as late June.

ABOUT THE RESTAURANTS

4

Rotorua has the area's most diverse dining scene. You can find anything from Indian to Japanese fare, or try a Māori *hāngi* (meal cooked in an earth oven or over a steam vent). Hawke's Bay is another hot spot; its winery restaurants emphasize sophisticated preparations and food-and-wine pairings. Around Eastland, which is so laid-back it's nearly horizontal, the choices are simpler, but you'll be treated with the area's characteristic friendliness. One thing you won't find on any menu is fresh trout. Laws prohibit selling this fish, but if you catch a trout, chefs at most lodging establishments will cook it for you.

Dressing up for dinner, or any other meal, is a rarity, expected at only the most high-end lodges and restaurants.

WHAT IT COSTS IN NEW ZEALAND DOLLARS					
	¢	$	$$	$$$	$$$$
Restaurants	under $10	$10–$15	$15–$20	$20–$30	over $30

Prices are per person for a main course at dinner, or the equivalent.

ABOUT THE HOTELS

Accommodation ranges from super-expensive lodges to multistory hotels and a great selection and price range of motels. Another excellent option are the bed-and-breakfast establishments in town centers or in the depths of the countryside where you can succumb to the silence, curl up, and read a book, or cast a fly in a quiet stream.

Rotorua has lodgings in all price ranges. If you're willing to stay out of the town center, you can find bargain rates virtually year-round. In both Rotorua and Taupo, many hotels and motels give significant discounts on their standard rates in the off-season, from June through September. For stays during the school holidays in December and January, book well in advance. Also note that peak season in Tongariro National Park and other ski areas is winter (June–September); summer visitors can usually find empty beds and good deals. Many places, even the fanciest lodges, don't have air-conditioning, as the weather doesn't call for it.

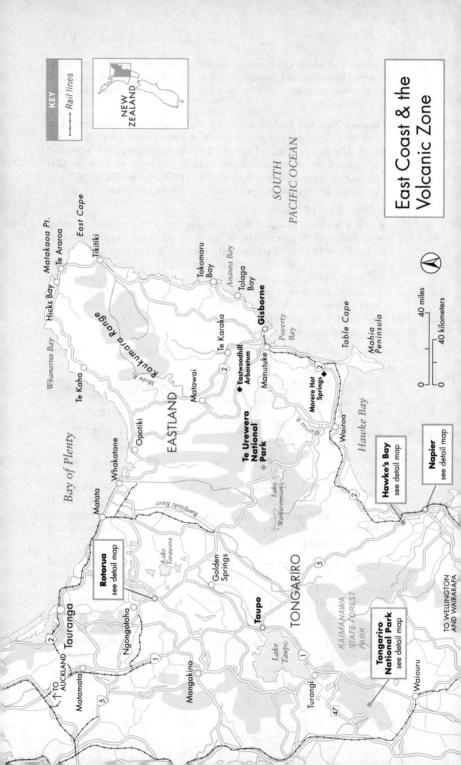

East Coast & the Volcanic Zone

KEY

→← Rail lines

NEW ZEALAND

SOUTH
PACIFIC OCEAN

0   40 miles

0   40 kilometers

Bay of Plenty

TO AUCKLAND

Tauranga

Matamata

Ngongotaha

Rotorua
see detail map

Matata

Whakatane

Opotiki

Te Kaha

Whanarua Bay

Hicks Bay

Whangara Bay

Matakaoa Pt.

Te Araroa

East Cape

Tikitiki

Raukumara Range

Mota R.

Matawai

Te Karaka

Te Araroa

Tokomaru Bay

Anaura Bay

Tolaga Bay

EASTLAND

◆ Eastwoodhill Arboretum

Manutuke

Gisborne

Poverty Bay

Table Cape

Mangakino

Golden Springs

Lake Tarawera

Lake Rotorua

Rangitaiki River

Te Urewera National Park

Lake Waikaremoana

◆ Morere Hot Springs

Wairoa

Wairoa R.

Mahia Peninsula

Hawke Bay

Taupo

Lake Taupo

TONGARIRO

KAIMANAWA STATE FOREST PARK

Turangi

Waiouru

Tongariro National Park
see detail map

TO WELLINGTON
AND WAIRARAPA

Hawke's Bay
see detail map

Napier
see detail map

The Hinemoa Legend

One of the great Māori love stories has a special local connection, because it takes place on Mokoia Island in Lake Rotorua—and it's a true tale at that. Hinemoa, the daughter of an influential chief, lived on the lakeshore. Because of her father's status she was declared *puhi* (singled out to marry into another chief's family), and her tribal elders planned to choose her husband for her when she reached maturity. Although she had many suitors, none gained the approval of her tribe.

Tutanekai was the youngest son of a family who lived on Mokoia Island. Each of his older brothers had sought the hand of Hinemoa, but none had been accepted. Tutanekai knew that because of his lowly rank he would never win approval from her family. But he was handsome and an excel-lent athlete—and eventually Hinemoa noticed him and fell in love.

From the lakeshore, Hinemoa would hear Tutanekai play his flute, his long-ing music drifting across the water. Hinemoa's family, suspicious that their daughter would try to reach the island, beached their canoes so that she could not paddle across to Mokoia. The sound of Tutanekai's flute lured Hinemoa to try to swim to the island. After lashing gourds together to help her float, she slipped into the lake; guided by the music, she reached Mokoia. Cold and naked, she submerged herself in a hot pool, where she was discovered by Tutanekai. Enchanted, he slipped her into his home for the rest of the night. When they were discovered, Tutanekai's family feared an outbreak of war with Hinemoa's tribe, but instead the two tribes were peacefully united.

	¢	$	$$	$$$	$$$$
WHAT IT COSTS IN NEW ZEALAND DOLLARS					
Hotels	under $75	$75–$125	$125–$200	$200–$300	over $300

Prices are for a standard double room in high season, including 12.5% tax.

VISITOR INFORMATION

Information centers known as 'i-Sites' are throughout the region. They supply free information and brochures on where to go and how to get there, available accommodations, car hire, bus services, restaurants, and tourist venues. The centers often serve as bus and tour stops.

THE ROTORUA AREA

One thing that many New Zealanders and visitors share is a love-hate relationship with Rotorua (ro-to-*roo*-ah). It's the spurting geysers, sulfur springs, bubbling mud pools, and other thermal features that set this region apart—but with the sulfurous smell that hangs over the city, some say the farther apart the better. However, this unashamedly touristy town has capitalized on nature's gifts to become one of the country's most famous spots. The "Great South Seas Spa," as Rotorua was known, was among the earliest spa ventures in the country—as far back as the 1860s.

Rotorua sits on top of the most violent segment of the Taupo Volcanic Zone, which runs in a broad belt from White Island in the Bay of Plenty to Tongariro National Park south of Lake Taupo. Wherever you turn in this extraordinary area, the earth bubbles, boils, spits, and oozes. Drainpipes steam, flower beds hiss, jewelry tarnishes, and cars corrode. The rotten-egg smell of hydrogen sulfide hangs in the air, and even the local golf course has its own thermal hot spots where a lost ball stays lost forever.

The city's Māori community traces its ancestry to the great Polynesian migration of the 14th century through the Te Arawa tribe, whose ancestral home is Mokoia Island in Lake Rotorua. The whole area is steeped in Māori history and legend—for hundreds of years, the Māori have settled by the lake and harnessed the geological phenomena, cooking and bathing in the hot pools.

For stunning scenery and picturesque picnic spots, drive around Lake Rotorua. About halfway around the lake look for Hamurana Springs, a large area of land with free public access where crystal-clear water bubbles from springs forming a river that flows into the lake. Walking through this area you will see birdlife and pass through several groves of magnificent redwood trees.

The countryside near Rotorua includes magnificent untamed territory with lakes and rivers full of some of the largest rainbow and brown trout on Earth. Fishing is big business from here down through Taupo and on into Tongariro National Park. If you're dreaming of landing the "big one," this is the place to do it.

GETTING AROUND

Rotorua Airport (airport code ROT) is 10 km (6 mi) from the city center on Highway 33. Taxi fare to the city is about $25. You could also arrange for a ride ($15) with Super Shuttle; call ahead for a reservation.

Rotorua is easy to get around. The streets follow a neat grid pattern, and walking from the lake to the southern end of town takes only a few minutes. Fenton Street, the wide main drag that comes into town from Taupo, starts around the thermal spot of Whakarewarewa. For about 3 km (2 mi), it's lined with motels and hotels until just before it reaches the lakefront, where it becomes more commercial, with shops, restaurants, and the **Tourism Rotorua Visitor Information Centre**, which has a tour-reservation desk, a map shop operated by the Department of Conservation, and a lost-luggage facility.

Most of the sights are outside the city area, and can be reached from State Highway 30, which branches right off Fenton Street at the southern corner of town. Lake Tarawera, the Blue and Green lakes, and the Buried Village are all accessed from Highway 30; farther east, you reach the airport, lakes Rotoiti and Rotoma, and Hell's Gate. Keeping on Fenton Street will lead to Lake Road and back onto Highway 5, which goes to Paradise Valley, Fairy Springs Road, and farther out of town to Ngongataha and the Agrodome.

ESSENTIALS

Airport Transfers **Rotorua Taxis** (☎ 07/348–1111). **Super Shuttle** (☎ 07/349–3444).

Bus Depot **Rotorua** (✉ *Tourism Rotorua Visitor Information Centre, 1167 Fenton St.*).

Car Rentals **Avis New Zealand** (✉ Rotorua Airport ☎ 07/345–6055 ⊕ www.avis.com/nz).

Emergency Services **Fire, police, and ambulance** (☎ 111).

Hospital **Rotorua Hospital** ✉ Pukeroa St. ☎ 06/348–1199).

Pharmacy **Lakes Care Pharmacy** (✉ Arawa St. at Tutanekai St. ☎ 07/348–4385).

Visitor Info **Tourism Rotorua Visitor Information Centre** (☎ 1167 Fenton St. ☎ 07/348–5179 ⊕ www.rotoruanz.com).

WHAT TO SEE IN CENTRAL ROTORUA

Heading south from the lake takes you to the **Government Gardens,** which occupy a small peninsula. The Māori call this area Whanga-piro (fang-ah-*pee*-ro, "evil-smelling place"), an appropriate name for these gardens, where sulfur pits bubble and fume behind manicured rose beds and bowling lawns. The high point is the extraordinary neo-Tudor Bath House. Built as a spa at the turn of the 20th century, it is now the **Rotorua Museum of Art & History.** One room on the ground floor is devoted to the eruption of Mt. Tarawera in 1886. On display are a number of artifacts unearthed from the debris and remarkable photographs of the silica terraces of Rotomahana before the erup-tion. Don't miss the old bath rooms, where some equipment would be right at home in a torture chamber—one soaking tub even adminis-tered electric current to the body. ✉ *Government Gardens, Arawa St.* ☎ 07/349–4350 ⊕ *www.rotoruamuseum.co.nz* 🖃 $11 ⊙ *Oct.–Apr., daily 9–8; May–Sept., daily 9–5.* At the southern end of the gardens, you can soak in the **Blue Baths,** a thermally heated swimming pool built in the 1930s. Open daily 10–7. ✉ *Arawa St.* ☎ 07/350–2119 ⊕ *www.bluebaths.co.nz* 🖃 $9.

Follow pumice paths from the Government Gardens to the naturally heated **Polynesian Spa.** Considered one of the best spas of its kind, there's a wide choice of mineral baths available, from large communal pools to family pools to small, private baths for two. You can also treat yourself to massage or spa treatments, and the Lake Spa has exclusive bathing in shallow rock pools overlooking Lake Rotorua. ✉ *Hinemoa St.* ☎ 07/348–1328 ⊕ *www.polynesianspa.co.nz* 🖃 *Prices range from $12 for freshwater pool to around $170 for lake spa therapies* ⊙ *Daily 8 AM–11 PM.*

A short walk north from the lakefront brings you to the Māori *pā* (fortress) of Ohinemutu, the region's original Māori settlement. It's

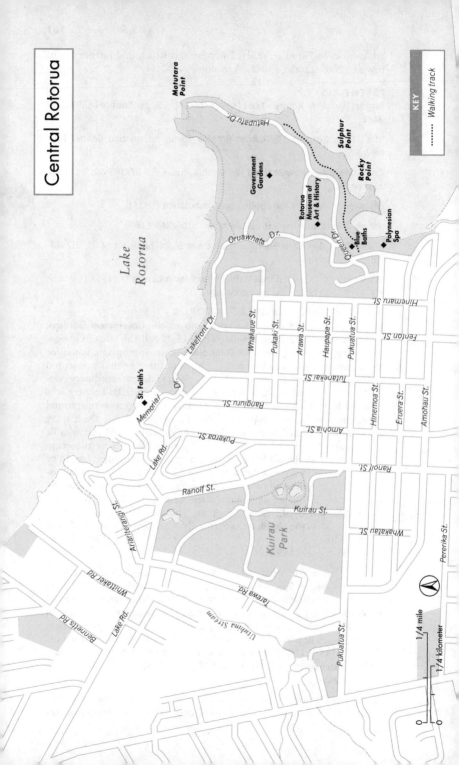

Central Rotorua

Lake Rotorua

Motutara Point

Hatupatu Dr.

Government Gardens

Oruawhata Dr.

Rotorua Museum of Art & History

Sulphur Point

Rocky Point

Queen Dr.

Blue Baths

Polynesian Spa

Lakefront Dr.

St. Faith's

Memorial Dr.

Whakaue St.

Pukaki St.

Arawa St.

Haupapa St.

Pukuatua St.

Hinemaru St.

Fenton St.

Ranginui St.

Tutanekai St.

Amohia St.

Hinemoa St.

Eruera St.

Amohau St.

Pukeroa St.

Lake Rd.

Ranolf St.

Kuirau St.

Ranoff St.

Whakatau St.

Arariterangi St.

Kuirau Park

Tarewa Rd.

Whitaker Rd.

Lake Rd.

Bennetts Rd.

Utuhina Stream

Pukuatua St.

Pererika St.

KEY

······· Walking track

1/4 mile

1/4 kilometer

0

0

Dinner on the Rocks

Rotorua, the cultural home of the Māori, is the best place to experience a *hāngi*, a traditional Māori feast for which the meal-to-be is cooked over steaming vents. Several local organizations offer the chance to try this slow-cooked treat, paired with a concert—an evening that may remind you of a Hawaiian lu'au. Don't pass it up!

As a *manuhiri* (guest), you'll get the full picture, beginning with a *powhiri*, the awe-inspiring Māori welcome that generally includes the *wero* (challenge), the *karanga* (cries of welcome), and the *hongi*, or pressing together of noses, an age-old Māori gesture that shows friendship. If you're not comfortable bouncing noses, a simple handshake will suffice.

While the food cooks, a show begins with haunting harmonious singing, foot stamping, and *poi* twirling (rhyth-mic swinging of balls on strings). The performance might raise the hair on the back of your neck—but this will be assuaged with food, glorious food. The lifting of the hāngi will produce pork, sometimes lamb and chicken, and kūmara (sweet potato), vegetables, and maybe fish and other seafood, followed by dessert.

Matariki Hāngi and Concert. Starting at 6:30 PM in a hall almost alongside the Royal Lakeside Novotel Hotel, the show is informative and enthusiastic, with ample and delicious food. ⊠ *Tutanekai St., lake end* ☎ *0508/442–644* ⊕ *www.novotel. co.nz* ☑ *$60 for food and concert, $28 concert only. There is a free pick-up service from all local hotels.* **The Heritage Hotel** (⊠ *Froude and Tryon Sts.* ☎ *07/348–1189*) also has an excellent cultural show and hāngi for $59.

4

---

a still-thriving community, centered around its *marae* (meetinghouse) and **St. Faith's,** the lakefront Anglican church. The interior of the church is richly decorated with carvings inset with mother-of-pearl. Sunday services feature the sonorous, melodic voices of the Māori choir. The service at 9 AM is in Māori and English. ⊠ *Memorial Dr.*

From St. Faith's it's a short distance to the local hot spot (literally) **Kuirau Park,** a public park that includes an active thermal area. The mud pools and hot springs sit alongside the flower beds, which at times are almost hidden by floating clouds of steam. You can wander around the park or join the locals soaking your weary feet in shallow warm pools. This place is very thermally active and can change overnight, so as you stroll around, stay well outside the fences. ⊠ *Kuirau St., south from Lake Rd.* ☑ *Free.*

WHAT TO SEE AROUND ROTORUA

At the **Agrodome,** a working sheep-and-cattle farm, you can take a guided tour through the farm and the kiwifruit orchard, but the main attraction is the farm show. Well-trained dogs run across the backs of sheep, and there are a shearing demonstration and lots of barking, noise, and farmyard smells. Heads-up to the uninitiated: what the shearer is wearing is *not* an undershirt but a shearing vest, a classic Kiwi item worn at some point by every red-blooded male and, yes, a few women, too! Expect plenty of wisecracks about pulling the wool over your eyes and about Whoopi Goldberg (here, a Lincolnshire sheep with dreadlock-style wool). Sure, it's corny, but it's fun. Shows are at 9:30, 11, and 2:30 daily. ✉ *Western Rd., Ngongataha, 6 km (4 mi) north of Rotorua* ☎ *07/357–1050* ⊕ *www.agrodome.co.nz* ✆ *Farm show $24, farm tour and show $46* ⊙ *Daily 8:30–5.*

Arguably the most active thermal reserve in the Rotorua area, the 50 acres of **Hell's Gate** hiss and bubble with steaming fumaroles and boiling mud pools. Among the attractions here is the Kakahi Falls, reputedly the largest hot waterfall in the southern hemisphere, where, according to legend, Māori warriors bathed their wounds after battle. Warm mud pools are available for public bathing; at the Wai Ora Spa, you can soak in a mud bath or try a *mirimiri*, a traditional Māori massage. Spas and mud treatments cost $70–$230. ✉ *State Hwy. 30, Tikitere, 15 km (9 mi) east of Rotorua* ☎ *07/345–6497* 📠 *07/345–6481* ⊕ *www. hellsgate.co.nz* ✆ *$25* ⊙ *Daily 8:30–8:30.*

⟳ Stroll through the bush at **Rainbow Springs Nature Park** to take a close-up look at native birds such as *tūī*, kea, *kereru*, and *kakariki*. You can also eyeball a tuatara (an endangered lizard) and see skinks, geckos, and some mighty trout. ✉ *Fairy Springs Rd.* ☎ *07/350–0440* ⊕ *www. rainbowsprings.co.nz* ✆ *$25* ⊙ *Daily 8–10 PM.*

⟳ **Kiwi Encounter,** Rainbow Springs' neighbor, works with the Department of Conservation by receiving kiwi eggs, then hatching and rearing these endangered birds before returning them to the wild. From September to April you should see eggs or new chicks, which are high on the cute factor. ✉ *Fairy Springs Rd.* ☎ *07/350–0440* ⊕ *www.kiwiencounter.co.nz* ✆ *$27.50* ⊙ *Daily 10–5.*

Whakarewarewa (*fa*-ka-*ree*-wa-*ree*-wa) is one mouthful of a name—locals call it Whaka. This is the most accessible of the area's thermal spots—it's closest to town—but it's also the most varied, providing insight into Māori culture. The reserve is divided between two different groups; both give you some firsthand exposure to the hot pools, boiling mud, and native culture. **Te Puia** (✉ *Hemo Rd.* ☎ *07/348–9047* ⊕ *www.tepuia.com*) has a carving school that hosts workshops and, on the grounds, the Pohutu Geyser and silica terraces. The Whaka Māori community was founded by people who moved here from around Te Wairoa after the catastrophic eruption in 1886. Don't miss the Nocturnal Kiwi House, where you might spot one of the birds. Open daily October–March 8 AM–6 PM and April–September 8 AM–5 PM. Guided tour and Māori concert costs $50, with cultural show and dinner costing $90. For another introduction to Māori traditions, visit the **Whakarewarewa—The Living Thermal Village** (✉ *Tryon St.* ☎📠 *07/349–3463* ⊕ *www.whakarewarewa.com*), an authentic Māori village set in a landscape of geothermal wonders. On the guided tours you'll see thermal pools where villagers bathe, boiling mineral pools, and natural steam vents where residents cook. Arts and crafts are available at local shops. The village is open to visitors daily from 8:30 to 5, and entry fees are $25 or $55 with cultural show and hāngi. Whakarewarewa is at the southern end of Tryon Street, signposted on Fenton and Sala streets. If you don't have a car, sightseeing shuttle buses leave from the visitor center on Fenton Street.

The **Blue and Green lakes** are on the road to Te Wairoa and Lake Tarawera. The Green Lake is off-limits except for its viewing area, but the Blue Lake is popular for picnics and swimming. The best place to view the lakes' vibrant colors is from the isthmus between the two. Take Highway 30 east (Te Ngae Road) and turn right onto Tarawera Road at the signpost for the lakes and buried village. The road loops through forests and skirts the edge of the lakes.

Skyline Skyrides, which sits alongside the Fairy Springs complex, has a 2,900-foot cable-car system that brings you up to the summit of Mt. Ngongotaha for spectacular views over Lake Rotorua. At the summit, 1,600 feet above sea level, there's a café, a restaurant, a souvenir shop, a shooting gallery, and the Sky Swing, another Kiwi way of triggering a heart attack. Don't miss the luge track, where you can take hair-raisingly fast rides on wheeled bobsled-like luges. (You can also go slowly; a braking system gives you full control of your speed.) The track runs partway down the mountain, winding through the redwood trees; from the bottom, you can return to the summit on a separate chairlift. ⊠*Fairy Springs Rd.* ☎*07/347–0027* 📠*07/348–2163* ⊕*www. skylineskyrides.co.nz* 🎫*$24 cable car, $9 luge.*

At the end of the 19th century, **Te Wairoa** (tay why-*ro*-ah, "the buried village") was the starting point for expeditions to the pink-and-white terraces of Rotomahana, on the slopes of Mt. Tarawera. As mineral-rich geyser water cascaded down the mountainside, it formed a series of baths, which became progressively cool as they neared the lake. In the latter half of the 19th century these fabulous terraces were the country's major attraction, but they were destroyed when Mt. Tarawera erupted in 1886. The explosion, heard as far away as Auckland, killed 153 people and buried the village of Te Wairoa under a sea of mud and hot ash. The village has been excavated, and of special interest is the *whare* (*fah*-ray, "hut") of the *tohunga* (priest) Tuhoto Ariki, who predicted the destruction of the village. Eleven days before the eruption, two separate tourist parties saw a Māori war canoe emerge from the mists of Lake Tarawera and disappear again—a vision the tohunga interpreted as a sign of impending disaster. Four days after the eruption, the 100-year-old tohunga was dug out of his buried whare still alive, only to die a few days later. An interesting museum contains artifacts, photographs, and models re-creating the day of the disaster, and a number of small dwellings remain basically undisturbed beneath mud and ash. A path circles the excavated village, then continues on as a delightful trail to the waterfall, the lower section of which is steep and slippery in places. Te Wairoa is 14 km (9 mi) southeast of Rotorua, a 20-minute drive. ⊠*Tarawera Rd.* ☎📠*07/362–8287* ⊕*www.buriedvillage.co.nz* 🎫*$27* ⊙*Oct.–Apr., daily 9–5; May–Sept., daily 9–4:30.*

From the shores of Lake Tarawera, the **MV *Reremoana III,*** a new lake cruiser, makes regular scenic runs. The three-hour cruise departs daily at 10:30, stopping at Te Ariki, the base of Mt. Tarawera, where you

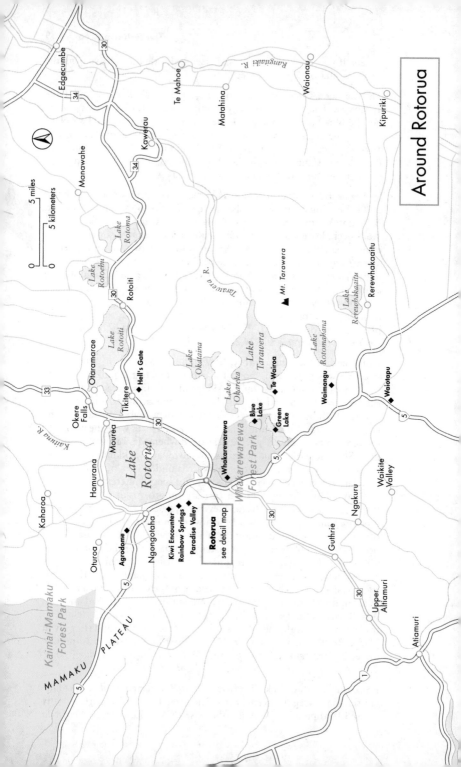

Around Rotorua

0 — 5 miles
0 — 5 kilometers

Edgecumbe
30
34
Te Mahoe
Matahina
Rangitaiki R.
Waionau
Kipuriki

Manawahe
Kawerau
34
Lake Rotoma

Lake Rotoehu
Rotoiti
30
Otaramarae
Lake Rotoiti
Rerewhakaaitu
Lake Rerewhakaaitu

Hell's Gate
Tikitere
Lake Okataina
Lake Okareka
Tarawera R.
Mt. Tarawera
Lake Tarawera
Lake Rotomahana

33
Okere Falls
Mourea
Te Wairoa
Waimangu

Kaituna R.
Hamurana
30
Lake Rotorua
Whakarewarewa
Blue Lake
Green Lake
Whakarewarewa Forest Park
5
Waiotapu
5

Kaharoa
Oturoa
Ngongotaha
Kiwi Encounter
Rainbow Springs
Paradise Valley
Agrodome

Rotorua
see detail map
30
Ngakuru
Waikite Valley

5
Guthrie
30
Kaimai-Mamaku Forest Park
MAMAKU PLATEAU
Upper Atiamuri
5
1
Atiamuri

CLOSE UP

Spellbound in Middle Earth

Some of the most striking elements of the *Lord of the Rings* films weren't created by special-effects—they were the astonishing views of New Zealand's countryside. The film crew traveled all over the country, so there are dozens of locales to tempt you to stop and dream awhile.

On the North Island, you can visit a handful of hobbit homes in rural Matamata (⊕ *www.hobbitontours. com*). The volcanic peaks and blasted terrain of Tongariro National Park provided the setting for Mordor. Tackle one of the park's walking trails to see the otherworldly hot springs, lava rocks, and craggy peaks like Ruapehu, the films' Emyn Muil. Take the spectacular Tongariro Crossing trek to pass Ngauruhoe, the volcano the hobbits Frodo and Sam braved as Mount Doom.

Wellington, the film production's home base, is also the hometown of the director, Peter Jackson. Here the orcs, trolls, and the horrible Balrog all came to life, created by Weta Workshop and the production company Three Foot Six (named for the height of a hobbit). Weta's has had its hands full with other major films, including Jackson's *King Kong*. Local wags dub the capital "Wellywood."

The Hutt Valley, east of Wellington, saw plenty of hobbit action. During filming a huge polystyrene castle towered over a quarry by the Western Hutt road. Unsuspecting drivers would pass by Minas Tirith and the fortress of Isengard, where the wizard Gandalf was betrayed and imprisoned. Stay on Highway 2 to reach the beautiful Kaitoke Regional Park, used for the Elven city of Rivendell and a perfect place to picnic on the riverbank.

On the South Island, Highway 6 unrolls south to glacier country. Stop at Franz Josef and look for Mount Gunn, where the beacon burned. Carving through the magnificent landscape, the road leads on to Wanaka, where the ghastly ringwraiths gave chase to Arwen and Frodo.

The breathtaking White Mountains, or Remarkables, at Queenstown was the background for the Ithilien Camp, the giant statues of the Pillars of Argonath, and other scenes. From nearby Glenorchy, you can hire a horse and ride to Paradise, seen as the Elven Lothlórien forest. Farther south, near Te Anau, the brooding silence of the lake district was shot as the Midgewater Marshes, and is prime trout-fishing territory.

Hungry for more? Then turn to the *"Lord of the Rings" Location Guidebook* by Ian Brodie, which tracks the films up hill and down dale.

–Bob Marriott

4

---

can picnic or swim or walk across the isthmus to Lake Rotomahana. It also includes a stop at Hot Water Beach, a D.O.C. campsite only accessible by boat. The Tarawera landing is on Spencer Road, 2 km (1 mi) beyond the Buried Village. The Landing Café has a small but varied menu and a decent wine list. A sign points to LAUNCH CRUISES and the *Reremoana*'s parking lot. ⊠ *Tarawera Launch Cruises* ☎ *07/362–8595* ⊕ *www.purerotorua.com* ⊠ *3-hr cruise $42.*

★ When Mt. Tarawera erupted in 1886, destroying Rotomahana's terraces, not all was lost. A volcanic valley emerged from the ashes—

Waimangu—extending southwest from Lake Rotomahana. It's consequently one of the world's newest thermal-activity areas, encompassing the boiling water of the massive Inferno Crater, plus steaming cliffs, bubbling springs, and bush-fringed terraces. A path (one–two hours) runs through the valley down to the lake, where a shuttle bus can get you back to the entrance. Or add on a lake cruise as well. Waimangu is 26 km (16 mi) southeast of Rotorua; take Highway 5 south (Taupo direction) and look for the turn after 19 km (12 mi). ⊠ *Waimangu Rd.* ☎ *07/366–6137* ⊕ *www.waimangu.com* ⊠ *$34, including cruise $74* ⊙ *Daily 8:30–5; last entry at least 1 hr prior.*

★ **Waiotapu** (why-oh-*ta*-pu) is a freakish landscape of deep, sulfur-crusted pits, jade-color ponds, silica terraces, and a steaming lake edged with red algae and bubbling with tiny beads of carbon dioxide. The **Lady Knox Geyser** erupts precisely at 10:15 daily and other points of interest include the Devil's Ink Pots, a series of evil-looking, bubbling, plopping mud pools, and the spectacular, gold-edged Champagne Pool, which is 60 meters (195 feet) across and 60 meters deep. Birds nest in holes around the aptly named Birds' Nest Crater—the heat presumably allows the adult birds more time away from the eggs. Waiotapu is 30 km (19 mi) southeast of Rotorua—follow Highway 5 south (Taupo direction) and look for the signs. ⊠ *State Hwy. 5* ☎ *07/366–6333* ⊕ *www.geyserland.co.nz* ⊠ *$28* ⊙ *Daily 8:30–5; last entry at 3:45.*

OUTDOOR ACTIVITIES

BIKING

Planet Bike (⊠ *Waipa Mill Rd.* ☎ *07/346–0717* ⊕ *www.planetbike. co.nz*) runs mountain-bike adventures for everyone from first-timers to experts. You can ride for a couple of hours or several days, and some tours combine biking with rafting, kayaking, indoor climbing, or horseback riding. Prices start at $55 for a full day, or bike the lake for $99, bikes and helmets are provided.

EXTREME ADVENTURE

The folks in Rotorua keep coming up with ever more fearsome ways to part adventurers from their money (and their wits). Try white-water sledging with **Kaitiaki Adventures** (☎ *0800/338–736* ⊕ *www.raft-it. com*). For $120 you get up to two hours shooting rapids on a plastic water raft the size of a Boogie board. You get a wet suit, helmet, fins, and gloves. Outside town and part of the **Agrodome** complex there's the **Agrodome Adventures** (☎ *07/357–4747*), this is also the number of the shuttle service to take you there. Try bungy jumping from a 140-foot-high crane, or **the Swoop** where one, two, or three people are put into a hang-gliding harness and raised 120 feet off the ground before a rip-cord is released. That might be the ground whizzing by at 130 kph (80 mph) as the shrieking fliers swoop overhead but a donkey and a solitary emu graze on nonchalantly. If you're looking for further thrills, try **Freefall Extreme,** where a 180-kph (108-mph) wind from a giant fan lifts you 10 feet into the air…or then again there's The Shweeb, a five-car monorail racetrack using pedal power. Cost of various ways to get you screaming varies from $45 to $95, or choice of any three for $120. Open 9–5 daily.

FISHING

If you want to keep the trout of a lifetime from becoming just another fish story, expect to pay about $80–$90 per hour for a fishing guide and a 20-foot cruiser that takes up to six passengers. The minimum charter period is two hours, and fishing gear and tackle are included in the price. A one-day fishing license costs $18.50 per person and is available on board the boat. (You'll need a special fishing license to fish in the Rotorua area, and also in Taupo.) For general information about local lake and river conditions, check with the Tourism Rotorua Visitor Information.

In Rotorua fishing operators include **Clark Gregor** (☎ *07/347–1123* ⊕ *www.troutnz.co.nz*), who arranges boat fishing and fly-fishing excursions with up to 10 anglers per trip. With **Bryan Colman** (☎ *07/348–7766* ⊕ *www.troutfishingrotorua.com*) you can troll Lake Rotorua or try fly-fishing on the region's many streams, including a private-land source. He takes up to five people at a time. A trip with **Gordon Randle** (☎ *07/349–2555, 027/493–8733 boat*) is about $85 per hour. *See Chapter 11 for more fishing information.*

RAFTING & KAYAKING

The Rotorua region has rivers with Grade III to Grade V rapids that make excellent white-water rafting. For scenic beauty—and best for first-timers—the Rangitaiki River (Grades III–IV) is recommended. For experienced rafters, the Wairoa River has exhilarating Grade V rapids. The climax of a rafting trip on the Kaituna River is the drop over the 21-foot Okere Falls, among the highest to be rafted by a commercial operator anywhere. The various operators offer similar trips on a daily schedule, though different rivers are open at different times of year, depending on water levels. All equipment and instruction are provided, plus transportation to and from the departure points (which can be up to 80 km [50 mi] from Rotorua). Prices start around $72 for the short (one-hour) Kaituna run; a half day on the Rangitaiki costs from $99. Many operators offer combination trips. **Kaituna Cascades** (☎ *07/345–4199 or 0800/524–8862* ⊕ *www.kaitunacascades.co.nz*) organizes one-day or multiday expeditions. **Raftabout** (☎🖻 *07/343–9500* ⊕ *www.raftabout.co.nz*) focuses on day trips, some pairing rafting with jet-boating or bungy jumping. **River Rats** (☎ *07/345–6543 or 0800/333–900* ⊕ *www.riverrats.co.nz*) offers day trips to the main rivers as well as adventure packages. **Wet 'n' Wild Adventure** (☎ *07/348–3191 or 0800/462–7238* ⊕ *www.wetnwildrafting.co.nz*) has multiadventure and double-trip options. One-day itineraries cover the Rangitaiki, Wairoa, and Kaituna rivers. *See Chapter 11 for further rafting information.*

Gentler natures can opt for a serene paddle on one of Rotorua's lakes. **Adventure Kayaking** (☎🖻 *07/348–9451* ⊕ *www.adventurekayaking.co.nz*) has a variety of tours, from half a day spent paddling on Lake Rotorua ($80) to a full day on Lake Tarawera ($110) including a swim in a natural hot pool. Especially magical is the twilight paddle ($80) on Lake Rotoiti that incorporates a dip in the Manupirua hot pools (which you can't otherwise reach) and a BBQ dinner (extra), by arrangement.

WHERE TO STAY & EAT

$$$$ ✗**You and Me.** Chef-owner Hiroyuki Teraoka's cuisine reflects his background: Japanese born and French trained, he gives a mainly French style some Japanese input. The menu takes advantage of seasonal vegetables, but tuna and salmon are standards. Look for dishes such as stuffed rabbit loin with mushroom and spinach duxelles wrapped with filo pastry, green lentil juices, red wine sauce. ⊠*1119 Pukuatua St.* ☎*07/347–6178* ▤*AE, DC, MC, V* ⏏*BYOB* ☉*Closed Sun. No lunch.*

$$$–$$$$ ✗**Herbs Licensed Restaurant & Bar.** The oldest licensed restaurant in New Zealand is a family-run business. Owners Richard and Julie Sewell serve dishes such as pork belly, twice cooked, served on potato kūmara and spiced apple mash, finished with a pear compote and garlic jus and desserts like rich mudcake, chocolate pâté (nuts & dried fruit) with Mövenpick raspberry, and white chocolate ice cream. After this you'll need a walk by the lake. ⊠*Lake End, Tutanekai St.* ☎*07/348–3985* ⚲*Reservations essential* ▤*AE, DC, MC, V* ☉*No dinner Sun. July–Oct.*

$$–$$$$ ✗**Relish.** A boiler-size oven fed on *manuka* wood (a kind of tea tree)
★ is the heart of the kitchen of this busy modern café. Chicken breast wood-oven-roasted on Turkish bread with bacon, Camembert, lettuce, tomato, and avocado relish is delicious, and there is a great selection of pizzas. The wine list is limited but select; the all-day breakfasts are momentous. ⊠*1149 Tutanekai St.* ☎*07/343–9195* ▤*AE, DC, MC, V* ☉*No dinner Sun.–Wed.*

$$–$$$ ✗**Capers Epicurean.** The pleasing scent of spices may entice you into this barnlike restaurant that opens early and closes late. Look for the grilled salmon and Israeli couscous with balsamic baked tomatoes and garnished with egg and capers. Then wander to the dessert cabinet and choose from baked maple fudge cheesecake or lemon citron tart and other goodies. Half of the space is a delicatessen that sells preserves and specialty foods such as chutney made from *kūmara* (a local sweet potato) and *kawa kawa* (a native herb) rub. ⊠*1181 Eruera St.* ☎*07/348–8818* ⊕*www.capers.co.nz* ▤*AE, DC, MC, V* ☉*No dinner Sun. and Mon.*

$$–$$$ ✗**Pig & Whistle.** The name winks at this 1940s city landmark's previ-
★ ous incarnation—a police station. This is pub fare at its very best: fish-and-chips are a favorite or go for prime steak sirloin with Swiss cheese, onion jam, horseradish mayo, and toasted focaccia bread with pigtail fries or salad, followed by a snooze under the enormous elm tree outside. Live music entertains Friday and Saturday nights. ⊠*1182, Tutanekai St.* ☎*07/347–3025* ⊕*www.pigandwhistle.co.nz* ▤*AE, DC, MC, V.*

$–$$$ ✕**The Fat Dog Café and Bar.** The eclectic decor attracts young, old, and everyone in between. A line of paw prints trails along the maroon ceiling. Poetry of somewhat dubious merit also winds along the walls, is painted on the chair backs, and even circles the extremities of plates. On the psychedelic blackboard menu look for Cajun chicken schnitzel on a cheesy veg bake, or pork chops on a two-herb garlic potato mash. ✉*69 Arawa St.* ☎*07/347–7586* ▭*AE, DC, MC, V* 🍴*Licensed and BYOB.*

$$$$ ⬚ **Solitaire Lodge.** High on a peninsula that juts out into Lake Tarawera, this plush retreat is surrounded by lakes, forests, and volcanoes. Check out the volcanoes from the telescopes in the library-bar, or settle down in a shaded garden nook and sip a drink, in surroundings perfect for hiking, boating, and fishing. **Pros:** Quiet, secluded class in superb surroundings, good fishing. **Cons:** When you get the account you'll know you've definitely landed the big one. ✉*Ronald Rd., Lake Tarawera* ☎*07/362–8208* 🖷*07/362–8445* ⊕*www.solitairelodge.com* ⮐*8 suites, 1 villa* ⌖*In-room: DVD. In-hotel: restaurant, bar, spa* ▭*AE, DC, MC, V* ⦿*MAP.*

$$$–$$$$ ⬚ **Cottages at Paradise.** A 20-minute drive from the city center, this cottage stands back from the road on a 12-acre block of rural land (called a "lifestyle block"). With the gin-clear Ngongotaha stream running directly behind the property, it's heaven in a basket for the ardent trout angler. The faux log cabin exterior gives way to a tastefully decorated, contemporary interior, and luxurious self-contained accommodations with gas fire and full kitchen facilities. The cottage is serviced daily and the fridge stocked with breakfast provisions. **Pros:** Far from the maddening crowd, great trout fishing at the doorstep. **Con:** It's a fair drive to town and a decent restaurant or pub. ✉*801 Paradise Valley Rd.* ☎*07/357–5006* ⊕*www.cottagesatparadise.co.nz* ⮐*2 bedrooms* ⌖*In-room: DVD. In-hotel: laundry facilities, public Internet, spa* ▭*MC, V.*

$$$–$$$$ ⬚ **Novotel Lakeside Rotorua.** The Royal Lakeside has the handiest position of any of the large downtown hotels—it overlooks the lake and is a two-minute walk from the restaurants and shops. Guest rooms have sleek furnishings and are decently sized, though you should specify a lake view when booking. At the Atlas Brasserie (**$$$–$$$$**), cervena medallions on a potato rösti (glamorous term for a potato pancake) with ratatouille and red wine jus or Moroccan spiced beef served on vegetable couscous and slow roasted tomato may take your fancy. **Pros:** On the lake and you might snag a room with a view, the Matariki Concert Hall is right alongside. **Con:** They're a bit aloof and you won't get the same friendly service as a bed-and-breakfast. ✉*Tutanekai St.* ☎*07/346–3888* 🖷*07/347–1888* ⊕*www.novotel.co.nz* ⮐*199 rooms* ⌖*In-room: dial-up. In-hotel: restaurant, bar, pool, spa, no-smoking rooms* ▭*AE, DC, MC, V.*

$$–$$$$ ⬚ **Regal Palms 5 Star City Resort.** Well-appointed studio, one-bedroom,
★ and two-bedroom suites are surrounded by spacious grounds. You can also happily lounge on the patio of the outdoor pool, purify in the sauna, or while away the evening in front of the fire in the guest lounge bar. It's 2 km (1 mi) from downtown Rotorua. **Pros:** Good

facilities without leaving the complex, roomy accommodation. **Con:** You'll want to take the car to town. ⊠*350 Fenton St.* ☎*07/350–3232* 🖷*07/350–3233* ⊕*www.regalpalms.co.nz* 🛏*44 suites,* ⚘*In-room: kitchen, Wi-Fi. In-hotel: bar, tennis court, pool, gym, spa, laundry facilities, no-smoking rooms* ▤*AE, DC, MC, V.*

$$$
Fodor$Choice
★

🛏 **Country Villa.** Morning sunshine floods through stained-glass windows in Anneke and John Van der Maat's charming country home, which has scenic views of the lake and Mt. Tarawera. Colored friezes run at ceiling height around every room; as befits two former professional rose growers, the decor emphasizes flowers. Throughout the house are mementos of the hosts' travels—a Buddha figure here, a prayer wheel there, blue-eyed dolls from Europe. An antique chandelier is suspended over the table in the five-sided breakfast room, where the morning meal includes homemade bread. One room is self-contained, with a separate entrance and a small kitchenette. **Pros:** The hosts are welcoming and sincere, the homemade cookies are delicious. **Con:** So, it's a drive to town! But you won't want to leave anyway. ⊠*351 Dalbeth Rd.* ☎🖷*07/357–5893* ⊕*www.countryvilla.biz* 🛏*5 rooms* ⚘*In-room: no a/c, no phone, no TV (some). In-hotel: no-smoking rooms, no elevator, public Internet, public Wi-Fi* ▤*MC, V* ⦿*BP.*

$$$
🛏 **Heritage Hotel.** From the massive but welcoming entrance foyer with its giant stone fireplace, to the thermal and lake views from the tower block, this up-to-the-minute hotel spells class. Next to the Whakarewarewa reserve, it runs a complimentary shuttle service to town. The superb Pohutu Cultural Theatre inside the hotel, with its carvings and giant statue of the Māori deity Maui, is home to a colorful nightly concert and hāngi feast. At Chapmans Restaurant ($$$), you can indulge in the barbecue marinated salmon fillet on a sweet-corn cream and fried potatoes with turmeric oil, or sample the extensive smorgasbord. **Pros:** Top-class accommodation at all levels and a Māori concert and hāngi on the premises. **Con:** It's close enough to Whakarewarewa to get more than a whiff of the local vapor. ⊠*Froude and Tryon Sts.* ☎*07/348–1189* 🖷*07/347–1620* ⊕*www.heritagehotels.co.nz* 🛏*200 rooms, 3 suites* ⚘*In-room: dial-up. In-hotel: restaurant, pool, gym, spa, laundry facilities* ▤*AE, DC, MC, V.*

$$
🛏 **Princes Gate Hotel.** This ornate timber hotel was built in 1897 on the Coromandel Peninsula; it was transported here in 1920. Guest rooms are large and beautifully appointed, and the bathrooms have both tubs and showers. The restaurant has live shows Saturday and Sunday evenings, and there's a deck where you can pull up a chair and gaze across the street at the Government Gardens. **Pros:** Comfortable and stylish accommodation in town, handy to all attractions. **Con:** You'll feel you have to whisper in the lounge. ⊠*1057 Arawa St.* ☎*07/348–1179* 🖷*07/348–6215* ⊕*www.princesgate.co.nz* 🛏*36 rooms, 2 suites, 12 apartments* ⚘*In-room: no a/c, kitchen (some). In-hotel: restaurant, bar, pool, no elevator* ▤*AE, DC, MC, V.*

$–$$
🛏 **Cedar Lodge Motel.** These spacious, modern, two-story units, about 1 km (½ mi) from the city center, are a good value, especially for families. All have a kitchen and lounge on the lower floor, a bedroom on the mezzanine above, and at least one queen-size and one single bed; some

have a queen-size bed and three singles. Every unit has its own hot tub in the private courtyard at the back. Green-flecked carpet, smoked-glass tables, and recessed lighting give a clean, contemporary look. Request a room at the back, away from Fenton Street. **Pro:** Put the kids to bed in the upstairs room and get in the hot tub. **Con:** If you get this the wrong way round you might be in trouble! ✉*296 Fenton St.* ☎*07/349–0300* 🖷*07/349–1115* ⊕*www.cedarlodgerotorua.co.nz* ⇱*15 rooms* ⚿*In-room: no a/c, kitchen. In-hotel: laundry facilities, no elevator* ▤*AE, DC, MC, V.*

$ 🖬 **Ashleigh Court Motel.** Each well-maintained modern room has an individual hot tub, which helps distinguish this place from the many motels on Fenton Street. It's near Whakarewarewa and the golf course, and it's not too far from town, either. **Pros:** Clean, tidy, reasonably priced, close to Whakarewarewa and the golf course. **Con:** The owner is a rugby fanatic: fair enough—but he supports Wales! ✉*337 Fenton St.* ☎🖷*07/348–7456* ⊕*www.ashleighcourtrotorua.co.nz* ⇱*13 rooms* ⚿*In-room: no a/c, kitchen. In-hotel: no-smoking rooms* ▤*AE, DC, MC, V.*

$ 🖬 **Inglenook Cottage.** This modern cottage is set away from the farm-house in a country location surrounded by fields and lovely rural views and is quite safe for children. Breakfast provisions are taken across daily. ✉*149 Hamurana Rd, Rotorua* ☎*07/357–2430* ⊕*www.inglenookcottage.co.nz* ⇱*1 cottage, 2 bedrooms* ⚿*In-room: no a/c* ▤*MC, V*

¢ 🖬 **Base Backpackers.** At this hostel, an easy walk from the visitor center and bus stop, there are 95 beds in a combination of four- to eight-bed dorms, singles, and doubles (including a few with private showers, and four with en suite and TV). Women travelers might want to check out the popular "Sanctuary" floor, where the posh-for-a-hostel amenities include hair dryers in the bathrooms, fluffy towels, and a gift package of hair-care products. There's even a climbing wall if you'd like to get vertical. **Pros:** In the heart of town, TV lounge with games room. **Con:** Some of the rooms are a little cramped. ✉*1140 Hinemoa St.* ☎*07/350–2040* 🖷*07/350–3020* ⊕*www.basebackpackers.com* ⇱*95 beds* ⚿*In-room: no a/c, no phone, no TV. In-hotel: no-smoking rooms, no elevator* ▤*MC, V.*

¢ 🖬 **Base Hot Rock Backpackers.** The dorm rooms sleep anywhere from 4 to 12 people and several doubles and a pair of family rooms have private baths and balconies. If you're sore from hiking or hauling luggage, there are two indoor thermal pools and an outdoor heated pool. A youthful buzz and the on-site Lava Bar give this place a high profile. It's by Kuirau Park, a few minutes' walk from the center of town. **Pros:** Great to soak in the thermal pools, it's very handy to Kuirau Park. **Con:** The disco could keep you awake. ✉*1286 Arawa St.* ☎*07/348–8636* 🖷*07/348–8616* ⊕*www.stayatbase.com* ⇱*13 rooms, 18 dorm rooms* ⚿*In-room: no a/c, no phone, kitchen, no TV. In-hotel: bars, pools, laundry facilities, public Internet, no elevator* ▤*MC, V.*

¢ 🖬 **Kiwi Paka YHA.** This well-maintained lodge overlooking the thermal Kuirau Park is a 10-minute walk out of town. You can take advantage of the area's natural heating by soaking in the thermal pool for free.

Rooms range from shares for four or five people to single rooms for $35. Meals at the café are a steal as well. **Pros:** Nice quiet location, you could snag a chalet with an en-suite. **Con:** It's quite a walk to town. ⊠*60 Tarewa Rd.* ☎*07/347–0931* ⊕*www.kiwipaka-yha.co.nz* ↜*83 rooms* ⌂*In-room: no a/c, no phone, no TV. In-hotel: restaurant, bar, pool* ⊟*MC, V.*

SHOPPING

See jade carvers at work at the **Jade Factory** (⊠*1288 Fenton St.* ☎*07/349–1828*), a bright, spacious shop where handcrafted gifts are for sale.

The **Te Puia** (⊠*Hemo Rd.* ☎*07/348–9047* ⊕*www.tepuia.com*) was established in 1963 to preserve Māori heritage and crafts. At the institute you can watch wood-carvers and flax weavers at work and see New Zealand greenstone (jade) sculpted into jewelry. The gift shop sells fine examples of this work, plus other items, from small wood-carved kiwis to decorative flax skirts worn in the Māori cultural shows.

TOURS

ADVENTURE TOURS

Mount Tarawera 4WD Tours has a sensational half-day, four-wheel-drive trip to the edge of the Mt. Tarawera crater. Departures are at 8 AM and 1 PM; the tour costs $133.

The Waimangu Round Trip is probably the most complete tour of Rotorua. It includes an easy 5-km (3-mi) hike through the Waimangu Thermal Valley to Lake Rotomahana, where a cruiser takes you past steaming cliffs to the narrow isthmus that divides the lake from Lake Tarawera. After crossing the lake, the tour visits the Buried Village and ends with a dip in the Polynesian Pools in Rotorua. The trip costs $280; reserve a place with the Rotorua visitor center.

Contacts **Mount Tarawera 4WD Tours** (☎*07/349–3714* ⎙*07/349–3704* ⊕*www.mt-tarawera.co.nz*). **Waimangu Round Trip** (☎*07/366–6137* ⊕*www. waimangu.com*).

BOAT TOURS

Carrying 130 passengers, the *Lakeland Queen,* a genuine stern-wheel paddle ship, has breakfast, luncheon, and dinner cruises to Mokoia Island. A popular trip includes dinner on the boat and costs $68. *Kawarau Jet,* a speedboat, takes trips on Lake Rotorua; one option is a 1½-hour trip to Mokoia that includes a guided tour of the island and costs $89.

Contacts **Kawarau Jet** (☎*07/343–7600* ⊕*www.nzjetboat.co.nz*). **Lakeland Queen** (☎*07/348–0265* ⊕*www.lakelandqueen.com*).

BUS TOURS

Newmans Coach Lines (working with InterCity) runs a variety of trips around Rotorua. A tour that includes Whakarewarewa Thermal Reserve Te Puia, Rainbow Springs, and the Agrodome is $101, including all entrance fees. Geyser Link runs several local tours that include attractions such as Hells Gate and Waiotapu; prices start at $25.

Contacts **Geyser Link** (☎ 0800/000–4321 or 027/544–8820 ⊕ www.geyserlink. co.nz). **Newmans Coach Lines Rotorua** (☎ 07/348–0366 ⊕ www.newmans coach.co.nz).

HELICOPTER TOURS

Volcanic Air Safaris fly helicopters and floatplanes from their office on the Rotorua Lakefront. Trips include over-city flights, crater-lake flights, and excursions to Orakei Korako and White Island. The floatplane trip over the lakes is superb. Prices run from $60 to $415 per adult.

Contact **Volcanic Air Safaris** (☎ 07/348–9984 ⊕ www.volcanicair.co.nz).

LAKE TAUPO & TONGARIRO NATIONAL PARK

4

The town of Taupo on Lake Taupo's northeastern shore has blossomed into a major outdoor activities center, offering everything from rafting to skydiving. Taupo is also home to geothermal wonders.

Fishing is a major lure, both on Lake Taupo and on the rivers to the south. The lake and backcountry rivers are some of the few places where tales of the "big one" can actually be believed. The Tongariro River is particularly famous as an angler's paradise.

Southwest of Lake Taupo rise the three volcanic peaks that make up Tongariro National Park, New Zealand's first national park. Even if you don't have much time, skirting the peaks provides a rewarding route on your way south to Wanganui or Wellington.

TAUPO

82 km (51 mi) south of Rotorua, 150 km (94 mi) northwest of Napier.

The tidy town of Taupo is the base for exploring Lake Taupo, the country's largest lake. Its placid shores are backed by volcanic mountains, and in the vicinity is more of the geothermal activity that characterizes this zone (and, unlike Rotorua, most of the natural sites are free to visit). Water sports are popular here—notably sailing, cruising, and waterskiing—but Taupo is most known for fishing. The town is the rainbow-trout capital of the universe: the average Taupo trout weighs in around 4 pounds, and the lake is open year-round. Meanwhile, the backpacker crowd converges upon Taupo for its adventure activities. The town has skydiving and bungy-jumping opportunities, and white-water rafting and jet-boating are available on the local rivers.

GETTING HERE & AROUND

Taupo is four hours from Auckland, taking Highway 1 the whole way. It's 70 minutes from Rotorua, also via Highway 1. The streets are laid out in a grid pattern. Lake Terrace runs along the lakefront; it turns into Tongariro Street as it heads north, crossing the Waikato River and the gates that control the flow of water from the lake. Heu Heu Street is the main shopping street and runs from the traffic lights on Tongariro Street.

InterCity buses (☎09/913–6100 ⊕*www.intercitycoach.co.nz*) run five times daily from Auckland to Taupo. The trip takes approximately five hours. From Rotorua to Taupo, four daily buses make the 1-hour-and-20-minute trip.

ESSENTIALS

Bus Depot **Taupo** (✉*Gasgoine St.*).

Pharmacy **Main Street Pharmacy** (✉*Tongariro and Heu Heu Sts., Taupo* ☎*07/378–2636*).

Visitor Info **Taupo Visitor Information Centre** (✉*30 Tongariro St., Taupo* ☎*07/376–0027* ⊕ *www.laketauponz.com*).

WHAT TO SEE

At **Huka Falls,** the Waikato River thunders through a narrow chasm and over a 35-foot rock ledge. The fast-flowing river produces almost 50% of the North Island's required power, and its force is extraordinary, with the falls dropping into a seething, milky-white pool 200 feet across. The view from the footbridge is superb, though for an even more impressive look, both the Huka Falls Jet and the Maid of the Falls (⇨*Outdoor Activities and Taupo & Tongariro National Park Tours, below*) get close to the maelstrom. The falls are 3 km (2 mi) north of town; turn right off Highway 1 onto Huka Falls Road.

The construction of the local geothermal project had an impressive—and unforeseen—effect. Boiling mud pools, steaming vents, and large craters appeared in an area now known as **Craters of the Moon.** A marked walkway snakes for 2.8 km (2 mi) through the belching, sulfurous landscape, past boiling pits and hissing crevices. Entrance (during daylight hours) costs $5. The craters are up Karapiti Road, across from the Huka Falls turnoffs on Highway 1, 3 km (2 mi) north of Taupo.

The Waikato River is dammed along its length; the first construction is the **Aratiatia Dam,** 10 km (6 mi) northeast of Taupo (turn right off Highway 5). The river below the dam is virtually dry most of the time, but three times a day (at 10, noon, and 2), and four times a day in summer (October–March, also at 4), the dam gates are opened and the gorge is dramatically transformed into a raging torrent. Watch the spectacle from the road bridge over the river or from one of two lookout points a 15-minute walk downriver through the bush.

Even if you've seen enough bubbling pools and fuming craters to last a lifetime, the thermal valley of **Orakei Korako** is still likely to captivate you. Geyser-fed streams hiss and steam as they flow into the waters of the lake, and a cream-and-pink silica terrace is believed to be the largest in the world since the volcanic destruction of the terraces of Rotomahana. At the bottom of Aladdin's Cave, the vent of an ancient volcano, a jade-green pool was once used by Māori women as a beauty parlor, which is where the name *Orakei Korako* (a place of adorning) originated. The valley is 37 km (23 mi) north of Taupo (take Highway 1 out of town) and takes about 25 minutes to reach by car; you could always see it en route to or from Rotorua, which lies another 68 km

(43 mi) northeast of the valley. ☏*07/378–3131* ⊕*www.orakeikorako. co.nz* ⊜*$28* ⊙*Oct.–May, daily 8–5:30; June–Sept., daily 8–5.*

OUTDOOR ACTIVITIES

BUNGY JUMPING **Taupo Bungy** (⊠*202 Spa Rd., off Tongariro St., 1 km [½ mi] north of town* ☏*07/377–1135 or 0800/888–408* ⊕*www.taupobungy.com*) provides jumps from a cantilevered platform projecting out from a cliff 150 feet above the Waikato River. You can go for the "water touch" or dry versions. Even if you have no intention of "walking the plank," go and watch the jumpers from the nearby lookout point. The jumps cost from $99 a shot and are available daily from 9 to 5.

FISHING There are great fishing in the Taupo area and an attendant number of guides with local expertise. Guides work the Tongariro River and the lake. The high season runs from October to April. Costs are usually $90 per hour, and include all equipment plus a fishing license (note that you need a special license to fish here and in Rotorua). Book at least a day in advance.

Mark Aspinall (☏*07/378–4453*) leads fly-fishing trips for rainbow and brown trout. Gus Te Moana, who runs **Te Moana Charters** (☏*07/378–4839*), also offers fishing trips on his 24-foot boat and will quote you a price that includes the trip, all equipment, a license, and usually lunch and beer. **Mark Collins** (☏*07/378–1364*) offers fly-fishing with instruction for novices. A luxury cruiser on Lake Taupo costs about $150 per hour; for more information, contact **Chris Jolly Outdoors** (☏*07/378–0623* ⊕*www.chrisjolly.co.nz*). *See Chapter 11 for more fishing information.*

JET-BOATING For high-speed thrills on the Waikato River take a trip on the **Huka Falls Jet** (☏*07/374–8572* ⊕*www.hukafallsjet.com*), which spins and skips its way between the Aratiatia Dam and Huka Falls. Departures are every 30 minutes from Karetoto Road throughout the day; cost is $95 per person.

RAFTING The Grade 5 Wairoa and Mohaka rivers are accessible from Taupo, as are the Rangitaiki and more family-friendly Tongariro. Different rivers are open at different times of year, and operators run similarly priced trips, starting around $95 per person. Call **Rapid Sensations** (☏*07/378–7902 or 0800/353–435* ⊕*www.rapids.co.nz*), which provides transportation, wet suits, equipment, and much-needed hot showers at the end. *See Chapter 11 for more rafting information.*

SKYDIVING On a tandem skydive, you're attached to a professional skydiver for a breathtaking leap. Depending on altitude, free fall can last from a few seconds to close to a minute. **Freefall** (☏*07/378–4662 or 0800/373–335* ⊕*www.freefall.net.nz*) is one local operator. **Taupo Tandem Skydiving** (☏*07/377–0428 or 0800/275–934* ⊕*www.tts.net.nz*) is another option. Call at least one day in advance to arrange your jump—weather permitting—and expect to pay around $219–$314 per jump.

TONGARIRO NATIONAL PARK

Fodor'sChoice
★

110 km (69 mi) southwest of Taupo.

Tongariro is the country's first national park, established on sacred land given by the Ngati Tuwharetoa people in 1887. A trio of active volcanoes dominates the park. Tongariro, the shortest and least active, has a heavily truncated cone; Ngauruhoe, a single-vent volcano, has a distinctively smooth cone shape. Ruapehu is the tallest (and at 9,175 feet, the highest mountain on the whole North Island), with a longer, irregular snow-topped profile and a large crater lake. It's also the most active of the three. Ruapehu erupted in 1995 and 1996, each time giving little warning before spewing forth ash and showers of rocks and unleashing lahars (the water of the crater lake churned with rock). Luckily, no one was hurt, though the eruptions occurred during ski season. When Ruapehu's crater lake fills up, there's a risk that another lahar will burst through the crater walls. A lahar in 1953 killed more than 150 people as the flood destroyed a railway bridge. This phenomena is now intensely monitored and a similar lahar in 2007, though spectacular, passed without danger to human life.

Tongariro's spectacular combination of dense *rimu* pine forests, crater lakes, barren lava fields, and birdlife makes it the most impressive and popular of the island's national parks. It has many hiking trails, the most famous of which is the **Tongariro Alpine Crossing,** a 16-km (10-mi) hike that traverses the mountain, passing craters and brilliantly colored lakes, and is generally considered one of the finest walks in the country. You need to be reasonably fit to tackle it, because there are steep inclines and the volcanic terrain can be punishing on a hot day, also the weather is notoriously fickle. Other hikes in the park range from multiday circuits to short treks of an hour or two *(⇨ Outdoor Activities, below).*

Whakapapa Village, on the north side of Ruapehu, is the only settlement within the national park with services and is the jump-off point for the Whakapapa ski slopes. The second ski area is Turoa, and its closest town is **Ohakune,** which is just beyond the southern boundary of the park—take Highway 49, which runs between Highways 1 and 4. Although ski season is the busiest time of year, these towns keep their doors open for hikers and other travelers when the snow melts.

GETTING HERE & AROUND
The main approach is along Highway 4 on the park's western side; turn off at National Park for Whakapapa and the northern ski slopes, or at Raetihi for Ohakune and the south. From Taupo to the park, follow State Highway 1 south and turn off at Turangi onto State Highway 47. The roads are generally good. Around the national park, snow and ice can be a problem in the winter.

It's difficult to reach Tongariro National Park by public transportation, though there is a daily summer InterCity/Newmans bus service (mid-October–April) between Taupo, Whakapapa Village, and the village of National Park; the trip takes around 1½ hours. *For information on shuttles to trailheads, see Outdoors Activities, below.*

For helpful hiking and skiing advice, stop off at the **Whakapapa Visitor Centre**. This is the best place to buy maps and guides, including the Department of Conservation park map—essential for hikers—and individual local-walk leaflets. Check the seismograph in the office that records the seismic activity from the mountain. If it starts trembling, at least you'll have a head start.

The Department of Conservation's Web site includes a good rundown on Tongariro National Park. There's also a Ruapehu promotion site, with events listings, snow conditions, and more.

For Tongariro National Park, the Tranz Scenic *Overlander*, which connects Auckland and Wellington, stops at National Park village and Ohakune Friday, Saturday, and Sunday from May to December and daily from December to April. N.B. These times can vary and need to be checked locally. The journey from Wellington passes over five high viaducts. The train from Auckland goes around the remarkable Raurimu Spiral, where the track rises 660 feet in a stretch only 6 km (3½ mi) long.

ESSENTIALS

Train Contact **Tranz Scenic Overlander** ☎0800/872–467 ⊕www.tranzscenic. co.nz).

Visitor Info **Department of Conservation** ⊕www.doc.govt.nz)**Ruapehu Promotion Site** ⊕www.ruapehu.co.nz). **Whakapapa Visitor Centre** ✉Hwy. 48, Mt. Ruapehu ☎07/892–3729 ⊕www.doc.govt.nz). ⊗In summer 8–6 daily; in winter, 8–5 daily.

OUTDOOR ACTIVITIES

HIKING
Fodor'sChoice
★
The **Tongariro Alpine Crossing** trail grabs the hiking limelight. A one-way track starting at Mangatepopo, the crossing is a spectacular six- to seven-hour hike that follows an 18.5-km (11-mi) trail up and over the namesake mountain, passing craters, the evocatively named Emerald Lakes, old lava flows, and hot springs. Although children and school groups commonly do the hike, it is not to be taken lightly. Be prepared for rapidly changing weather conditions with warm and waterproof clothing. Wear sturdy footwear, and take food, plenty of water, sunblock, and sunglasses—and don't forget a hat! Also, be careful not to get too close to steam vents; the area around them is scorchingly hot. From late November to May, you'll be sharing the trail with many other hikers. In the colder months, it's really only for experienced winter hikers who can deal with snow and ice; some transport companies will take you only if you have an ice axe and crampons. It is recommended that you get up-to-date track and weather conditions from the D.O.C. Whakapapa Visitor Centre before starting out. A number of track transport operators provide shuttles to and from the Tongariro Alpine Crossing picking up from a number of locations in Whakapapa Village usually around 6, 7, 8, or 9 AM. Bookings can be made at accommodation providers in the area.

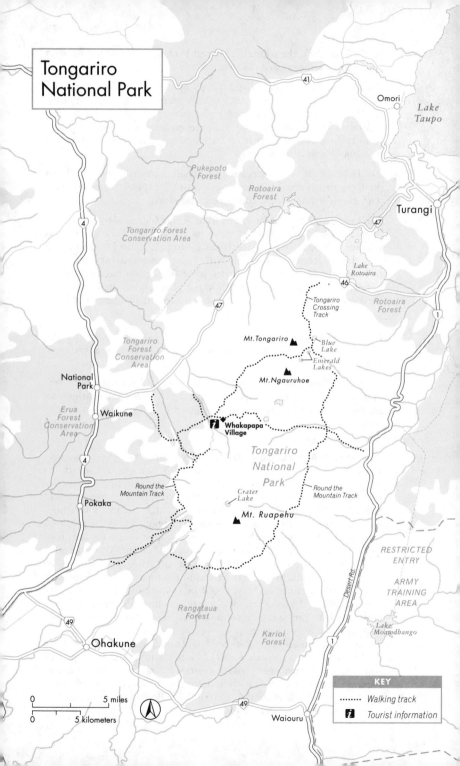

Alpine Scenic Tours (☎0508/468–287 ⊕*www.alpinescenictours.co.nz*) provides transport to the trailhead from the Taupo visitor information office for $45, with returns from Turangi for $35. In addition, many of the motels and lodges in National Park village can arrange transport to the track for about $15. You usually need to make a reservation; they pick you up at the end of the track. The longest hikes in the park are the three-day **Northern Circuit**, which goes over Tongariro and around Ngauruhoe, and the four-day **Round-the-Mountain Track,** which circles Ruapehu. There are trailside huts throughout the park to use on over-night trips. You'll need to buy a hut pass at the visitor center; it costs $20 from October 1 to the first weekend in June and $10 the rest of the year. Reservations cannot be made. Gas cookers are available in the huts. You could also tackle short half-hour to two-hour walks if all you want is a flavor of the region. A 1½-hour round-trip trek to the Tawhai Falls via the **Whakapapanui Track** takes you through the forest, and a two-hour round-trip to Taranaki Falls is in subalpine surroundings.

SKIING   The **Mt. Ruapehu ski slopes** (⊕*www.mtruapehu.com*) add up to New Zealand's most extensive skiing and snowboarding terrain. The **Whakapapa** ski area, on the mountain's north side, has more than 30 groomed trails, including beginners' slopes. **Turoa,** on the south side, has a half-pipe. Ski season generally runs from June through October. Both areas can provide lessons and rental equipment. Lift passes cost around $60–$80 for access to the whole mountain, but a variety of combination tickets are available. The area's Web site includes snow reports, trail maps, and other information.

WHERE TO STAY & EAT

$$$ ✕**The Station Cafe.** Modern prints alight the dusky pink and wood-pan-eled walls of this café/bar where the tracks of the north–south railway are right outside the door. Coffee comes in all shades, and at lunch, the food runs from nachos to ploughman's sarnies (thick sandwiches with meat, cheese, and onion). In the evening, try the venison medallions draped in a vanilla and raspberry glaze served with a potato, pea, and pesto mash, and steamed greens. Finish up with sweet velvet choco-late parfait with espresso jelly. ⊠*Findlay St., National Park Village* ☎07/892–2881 ▤*AE, DC, MC, V.*

$$–$$$ ✕**Eivins Café, Wine Bar, and Restaurant.** This modern diner's trump card is the panoramic mountain views from its front veranda. The scotch fillet salad and potato fries topped with Dijon cream mustard sauce might go cold if you gaze in awe too long. ⊠*State Hwy. 4, National Park Village* ☎07/892–2844 ▤*MC, V* ⊗*No lunch.*

$$–$$$$ ▦ **Bayview Chateau Tongariro.** Built in 1929, this French neo-Georgian style property stands out in Whakapapa Village. Most rooms have views of the surrounding National Park. Meals are taken in the Rua-pehu Restaurant ($$$–$$$$)—serving traditional New Zealand cui-sine with a modern slant—or there's a less formal café. The hotel can arrange guided hikes on all the best-known routes in the park. **Pros:** Classy, restful place, the enormous lounge area has a welcoming open fire and a full-size billiard table. **Con:** When the mist comes down you won't get a view from even the most expensive suite. ⊠*Hwy. 48*

☎07/892–3809 or 0800/242–832 🖷07/892–3704 ⊕*www.chateau. co.nz* ⇨*106 rooms, includes 7 suites and 9 motel units* ♿*In-room: a/c (some). In-hotel: 2 restaurants, bar, golf course, tennis court, pool, gym* ▤*AE, DC, MC, V.*

¢–$$ 🏨 **Discovery Lodge.** The only tourist accommodation in the park to give a panoramic view of three active volcanoes is this friendly complex, only minutes from the ski slopes. Most accommodations are in self-contained motel units and chalets. One-bedroom units sleep up to six people. There are also some doubles priced for backpackers, and powered campsites. The restaurant serves breakfast and dinner, and you can request a packed lunch. The lodge runs its own shuttle to the Tongariro Track (one of the earliest), a 10-minute drive away. **Pros:** Handy to the village, close to the start of the Tongariro Alpine Crossing and their shuttle gets you there very early. **Con:** Bleak in winter. ⊠*State Hwy. 47, Whakapapa Village* ☎07/892–2744 or 0800/122–122 ⊕*www. discovery.net.nz* ⇨*22 rooms* ♿*In-room: no a/c, no phone, no TV (some). In-hotel: restaurant, bar, laundry facilities, public Internet, no-smoking rooms* ▤*AE, DC, MC, V.*

$ 🏨 **Riverstone Back-Packers.** Riverstone is handy to State Highway 1 and the Tonariro River. A large comfortable lounge with an open fire and a sheltered outdoor area make this tidy place with modern facilities a good stopover for fishing or other outdoor activities. ⊠*222 Tautahanga Rd, Turangi* ☎07/386-7004 ⊕*www.riverstonebackpackers.com* ⇨*5 double rooms (2 have en suite), 1 bunk room sleeps 6* ♿*In-room: no a/c, kitchen. In-hotel: laundry, bicycles* ▤*MC, V*

TOURS

BOAT TOURS & LAKE CRUISES   Cruises on Lake Taupo usually involve a couple of hours out on the lake visiting local bays and modern Māori rock carvings. The *Barbary* is a 1920s wooden yacht believed to have once been the property of Errol Flynn. Departures are at 10:30 and 2, and summer evenings at 5 ($40). Huka Falls River Cruise runs trips to the falls on the *Maid of the Falls* leaving from Aratiatia Dam (north of Taupo) at 10:30, 12:30, and 2:30 ($30).

Contacts **Barbary** (☎*07/378-3444* ⊕*www.barbary.co.nz*). **Huka Falls River Cruise** (⊠*Aratiatia Dam Rd.* ☎*0800/278-336* ⊕*hukafallscruise.co.nz*).

BUS TOURS   Within Taupo, the Hot Bus is a hop-on/hop-off service that takes in all the local sights. Although there's no commentary, it is convenient, because it leaves the visitor center daily on the hour 10–3. Each attraction stop costs $10, or you can get an unlimited pass for $25. Paradise Tours also visits the local attractions in Taupo and travels as far afield as Napier and Hawke's Bay. Tours start at $85.

Tongariro Expeditions runs trips to Tongariro National Park from the Taupo visitor information center and serves the Tongariro Alpine Crossing. It costs $49, and equipment can be hired on the bus. It's more of a transport service than a full-blown tour. Winter rates are $99, and staff accompany walkers on the track.

Contacts **Hot Bus** (☎ *0508/468–287*). **Paradise Tours** (☎ *07/378–9955* ⊕ *www. paradisetours.co.nz*). **Tongariro Expeditions** (☎ *07/377–0435* ⊕ *www.the tongarirocrossing.co.nz*).

NAPIER & HAWKE'S BAY

New Zealand prides itself on natural wonders. But Napier (population 50,000) is best known for its architecture. After an earthquake devastated this coastal city in 1931, residents rebuilt it in the art deco style of the day. Its well-kept uniformity of style makes it an exceptional period piece. There's a similar aspect to Napier's less-visited twin city, Hastings, just to the south, which was also remodeled after the earthquake. After stretching your legs in either place, go on a brief wine-tasting tour—the region produces some of New Zealand's best wines. The mild climate and beaches of Hawke Bay make this a popular vacation area. (*Hawke* Bay is the body of water; *Hawke's* Bay is the region.) Make a point of visiting the gannet colony at Cape Kidnappers, which you can see only between October and March.

NAPIER

150 km (94 mi) southeast of Taupo, 345 km (215 mi) northeast of Wellington.

The earthquake that struck Napier at 10:46 AM on February 3, 1931, was—at 7.8 on the Richter scale—the largest quake ever recorded in New Zealand. The coastline was wrenched upward several feet. Almost all the town's brick buildings collapsed; many people were killed on the footpaths as they rushed outside. The quake triggered fires throughout town, and with water mains shattered, little could be done to stop the blazes that devoured the remaining wooden structures. Only a few buildings survived (the Public Service Building with its neoclassical pillars is one), and the death toll was well over 100.

The surviving townspeople set up tents and cookhouses in Nelson Park, and then tackled the city's reconstruction at a remarkable pace. In the rush to rebuild, Napier went mad for art deco, the bold, geometric style that had burst on the global design scene in 1925. Now a walk through the art deco district, concentrated between Emerson, Herschell, Dalton, and Browning streets, is a stylistic immersion. The decorative elements are often found above the ground floors, so keep your eyes up.

ESSENTIALS

Emergencies **Fire, police, and ambulance** (☎ *111*).

Pharmacy **Radius Care Pharmacy** (✉ *32 Munroe St.,* ☎ *06/834–0884*).

Visitor Info **Napier Visitor Information Centre** (✉ *100 Marine Parade* ☎ *06/834–1911*).

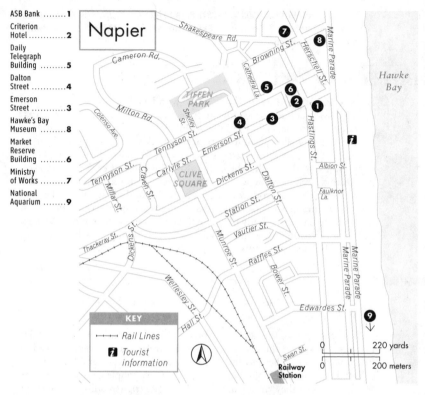

WHAT TO ·SEE

❶ One of Napier's notable buildings is the **ASB Bank,** at the corner of Hastings and Emerson streets. The Māori theme on the lintels is probably the country's finest example of *kowhaiwhai* (rafter) patterns decorating a European building. The traditional red, white, and black pattern is also continued inside around a coffered ceiling.

❷ The **Criterion Hotel** (⊠*48 Emerson St.*) is typical of the Spanish Mission style, which Napier took on because of its success in Santa Barbara, California, where an earthquake had similarly wreaked havoc just a few years before the New Zealand catastrophe. It has smooth plastered concrete walls (in imitation of adobe construction) and tiled parapets. The small square windows and larger round-arched glass doors also reflect features of mud-brick construction.

❺ The **Daily Telegraph Building** (⊠*Tennyson St. and Church La.*) is another Napier classic, now a real-estate office. It has almost all the deco style elements, incorporating zigzags, fountain shapes, ziggurats, and a sunburst.

❹ **Dalton Street** has its treasures, too. South of the intersection with Emerson Street, the pink **Countrywide Bank Building,** with its balcony, is one of Napier's masterpieces. **Hildebrand's,** at Tennyson Street, has an excellent frieze, which is best viewed from across Dalton. Hildebrand was a German who migrated to New Zealand—hence the German flag at one end, the New Zealand at the other; the wavy lines in the middle symbolize the sea passage between the two countries.

❸ Along **Emerson Street** and its pedestrian mall, **Hannahs** and the **Hawke's Bay Chambers** are among the city's finest art deco examples. **Bowmans Building** is a Louis Hay design in brick veneer with the characteristic eyebrow (brick or tiles, often curved, set over a window). Some of Hay's work was influenced by Chicago's Louis Sullivan; his best-known design is the National Tobacco Building in Ahuhiri.

❽ Using newspaper reports, photographs, and audiovisuals, the **Hawke's Bay Museum** re-creates the suffering caused by the earthquake. It also houses a unique display of artifacts of the Ngati Kahungunu Māori people of the East Coast—including vessels, decorative work, and statues. ⊠*65 Marine Parade and 9 Herschell St.* ☏*06/835–7781* ⊕*www.hawkesbaymuseum.co.nz* ⊑*$7.50* ⊘*Daily 10–6.*

❻ If you can turn back the clock in your mind and imagine the city littered with heaps of rubble, you would see the **Market Reserve Building** (⊠*Tennyson and Hastings Sts.*) as the first to rise after the earthquake. Its steel metal frame was riveted, not welded, so that the construction noise would give residents the message that the city was being rebuilt. The bronze storefronts with their "crown of thorns" patterned leaded glass are still original.

❼ The **Ministry of Works** (⊠*Browning St.*), with its decorative lighthouse pillar at the front, takes on the almost Gothic menace that art deco architecture sometimes has (like New York's Chrysler Building).

A little over a kilometer (½ mi) north of the central area stands one of the finest deco buildings, commonly known as the **Rothmans Building** (⊠*Bridge St.*). The magnificent 1932 structure has been totally renovated and its original name reinstated: the National Tobacco Company Building. It has a rose theme on the stained-glass windows and on a magnificent glass dome over the entrance hall.

❾
★
☼
At the **National Aquarium,** you can stand on a moving conveyor that takes you through the world of sharks, rays, and fish. Environmental and ecological displays feature a saltwater crocodile, tropical fish, and other sea creatures. There is also a kiwi enclosure where these birds can be seen in ideal viewing conditions. ⊠*Marine Parade* ☏*06/834–1404* ⊕*www.nationalaquarium.co.nz* ⊑*$15* ⊘*Daily 9–5.*

Ocean Spa. In a resort where the beaches are not really suitable for bathing this spa complex is a delight for the sun- and water-seeking tourist, its open-air pools being right alongside the beach. Sun beds, spa treatments, and massage are also available. ⊠*42 Marine Parade, Napier* ☏*06/835–8553* ⊑*$6.50; treatments run $15–$90* ⊘*Mon.–Sat. 6–10, Sun. 8–10.*

Silky Oak Chocolate Company. This complex comprising factory, museum, shop, and café is a chocoholic's fantasyland. The museum details the story of chocolate through the ages, and the café has a nice selection of goodies. ✉*1131 Links Rd., Napier* ☎*06/845–0908* ⊕*www.silky oakchocs.co.nz* ⊡*Museum-tasting tours $14–$57* ⊙*Mon.–Thurs. 9–5, Fri. 9–4, weekends 10–4.*

WHERE TO STAY & EAT

$$$–$$$$ ✕**Caution.** Massive wood-frame mirrors reflect the candles behind the bar in this northern Napier spot overlooking the boat masts in the basin. Try the aged beef fillet served with light truffle-scented pommes marquise, filled with wild mushroom ragout finished with braised shallots, Parisian potato, and red wine jus. Caution shares ownership with the attached Shed 2, an old wool store that is now a bar. ✉*West Quay, Ahuhiri* ☎*06/835–2202* ⊟*AE, DC.*

$$$–$$$$ ✕**Restaurant Indonesia.** The interior of this tiny Hawke's Bay institution
★   may be a bit gloomy, but the selection of the Dutch-Indonesian food is a revelation. Try sharing a *rijsttafel*, which consists of 13 sampling dishes. Other favorites: Rendang Sapi, slow-cooked beef spiced with galangal, coriander, and lemongrass, and Babi Kecap, pork cubes in sweet soy sauce. ✉*409 Marine Parade* ☎*06/835–8303* ⚔*Reservations essential* ⊟*AE, DC, MC, V* ⊙*Closed Mon. and Tues.; last bookings 8:30* PM.

$$–$$$$ ✕**Pacifica Restaurant.** Watch Jeremy Remeka at work producing your tasty lightly crisped duck breast confit, berri chrome pie, and foie gras sauce. You can follow this with a rhubarb soufflé sorbet trio: kiwifruit, strawberry, and pineapple, before sipping a nightcap in the small bar area overlooking the tree-lined Marine Parade. It's got to be good for you! ✉*209 Marine Parade, Napier* ☎*06/833–6335* ⊟*AE, MC, DC, V* ⊙*Closed Mon. Nov.–Apr.; Sun. and Mon. May–Oct.*

$$$$ ⌂ **The County Hotel.** Built in 1909 as the Hawke's Bay County Coun-
★   cil headquarters, this is one of the few Napier buildings that survived the 1931 earthquake. Wood paneling, chandeliers, and claw-foot bathtubs conjure up a more gracious era. At the Chambers Restaurant ($$$–$$$$) highlights include the herb encrusted rack of lamb, cumin-scented field mushrooms, fondant potato, and the vanilla bean crème brûlée with a poached pear, steeped in cranberry sauce. Churchill's Bar is decorated with quotes from the great man's speeches, and a cellar room is used for evening wine tastings. **Pros:** You'll sleep in a room with a bit of history and dine without leaving the building. **Con:** Wood paneling is not everyone's choice of decor. ✉*12 Browning St.* ☎*06/835–7800* ⊜*06/835–7797* ⊕*www.countyhotel.co.nz* ⇖*18 rooms* ⌂*In-room: dial-up. In-hotel: restaurant, bar, spa, laundry facilities, no-smoking rooms* ⊟*AE, DC, MC, V.*

$$$$ ⌂ **McHardy House.** The gardens at this colonial mansion, high on Napier Hill, have panoramic views of the Pacific Ocean and the beautiful Kaweka Ranges. The rooms have native timber floors, American king-size beds, and elaborate bathrooms. Large verandas open onto landscaped grounds, where you can lounge by the heated swimming pool; there's also a lovely fireplace in the lounge. The four-course set dinners are accompanied by a predinner drink and hors d'oeuvres, but must be booked in advance. **Pros:** A warm welcome from friendly hosts, fabulous views, most of the vegetables are home grown. **Con:** It

would be hard to find on a dark night. ✉*11 Bracken St.* ☎*06/835–0605* 🖷*06/834–0902* 🛏*2 rooms, 4 suites* ⚭*In-room: no a/c, no TV. In-hotel: bar, pool, laundry facilities, no-smoking rooms* ▭*AE, DC, MC, V* ❍*MAP.*

$$–$$$ 🏨 **Pebble Beach Motor Inn.** All the units have balconies facing Marine Parade, overlooking the sea. It's just a short walk to many of the town's sights, restaurants, and cafés. The plush rooms are spacious and finished in soft tones of beige and gray, and all have whirlpool baths. **Pros:** Every suite has an ocean view and balcony, step out of bed into a spa bath, air-conditioning throughout. **Con:** Apartment-style living. ✉*445 Marine Parade* ☎*06/835–7496* 🖷*06/835–2409* ⊕*www.pebblebeach. co.nz* 🛏*25 suites* ⚭*In-room: dial-up. In-hotel: spa, laundry facilities, no-smoking rooms* ▭*AE, DC, MC, V.*

¢–$ 🏨 **Mon Logis.** Built in the 1860s and one of the few houses that escaped destruction in the 1931 earthquake, this splendid mansion–cum–boutique hotel feels like a little piece of France. Its front windows overlook the ocean and distant Cape Kidnappers; in the guest rooms, white match-board ceilings hover above white bedspreads and lace-trimmed pillowcases. Gallic host Gerard Averous is passionate in his desire to ensure his guests are comfortable and enjoy their stay. Breakfast can include freshly baked croissants. **Pros:** A superb breakfast with a genial Gallic host, sea views. **Cons:** His rugby team knocked the All-Blacks out of the world cup, twice! ✉*415 Marine Parade* ☎*06/835–2125* 🖷*06/835–8811* ⊕*www.babs.co.nz/monlogis* 🛏*4 rooms* ⚭*In-room: dial-up. In-hotel: laundry facilities, no elevator* ▭*AE, DC, MC, V* ❍*BP.*

¢ 🏨 **Criterion Art Deco Backpackers.** On the top floor of the old Criterion Hotel, one of Napier's central art deco buildings, this hostel offers well-maintained rooms and secure storage. All rooms have washbasins; a few have bunks, but most have regular beds. There's a roomy lounge and a separate TV room. **Pros:** Bang in the center of town, great value, café on the premises. **Cons:** Basic beds, sometimes bunks. ✉*48 Emerson St.* ☎*06/835–2059* 🖷*06/835–2370* ⊕*www.criterionartdeco. co.nz* 🛏*27 rooms* ⚭*In-room: no a/c, no phone, no TV (some). In-hotel: restaurant, bars, laundry facilities, public Internet, no-smoking rooms, no elevator* ▭*MC, V.*

SHOPPING

Napier's Art Deco Trust maintains an **Art Deco Shop.** This beautifully laid-out shop sells everything from table lamps to tiles to ceramics, as well as hats, jewelry, rugs, and wineglasses. You can also pick up booklets outlining self-guided walks through town. ✉*163 Tennyson St.* ☎*06/835–0022* 🖷*06/835–1912* ⊕*www.artdeconapier.com.*

Opossum World pairs a shop selling opossum fur products with a mini-museum about the opossum's effects on New Zealand's environment. Products made with opossum fur include hats, gloves, and rugs; a soft blend of merino wool and opossum fur is made into sweaters, scarves, and socks. ✉*157 Marine Parade* ☎*06/835–7697* ⊕*www. opossumworld.co.nz.*

TOURS

ARCHITECTURE TOURS
The Art Deco Trust has a couple of excellent guided walking tours of Napier. A one-hour walk starts daily at 10 from the Napier Visitor Information Centre ($14). A two-hour afternoon walk, starting at the Art Deco Shop at 2, includes slide and video presentations ($20). Both walks end with optional free video screenings and refreshments. Or take the trust's self-guided Art Deco Walk; leaflets ($4) are available at its shop or at the visitor center. There's also the Marewa Meander around Napier's art deco suburb, and the Art Deco Tour Map, which plots a self-drive route through Napier and Hastings. To really submerge yourself in the 1930s aesthetic, join Bertie in a 1934 Buick for a drive around Napier ($130 for up to three people; book through the Art Deco Shop). For customized half-hour to half-day private tours, contact Art Deco Tours.

Contacts **Art Deco Trust** (✉ *Art Deco Shop, 163 Tennyson St.* ☎ *06/835–0022* ⊕ *www.artdeconapier.com*). **Deco Affair Tours** (✉ *Box 190, Napier* ☎ *025/241–5279* 🖷 *06/835–4491* ✎ *decoaffair@yahoo.co.nz*).

WINE TOURS
Bay Tours runs a variety of wineries tours, starting around $45, where you can sample some of the boutique wines unavailable to independent travelers. Lunch at one of the winery restaurants is usually available (at your own cost). Vince Picone, at Vince's World of Wine, knows the local wines and vineyards better than most, and is a fun guide. On Yer Bike Winery Tours is a great self-guided wine and cycling experience on flat, scenic terrain with some off-road cycling through the vineyards. Bikes, helmets, and a packed lunch are provided; they'll also lend you a cell phone. Rates start at $50.

Contacts **Bay Tours** (✉ *6 Magdalen Crescent, Napier* ☎ *06/843–2046, 027/449–0778 cell* ⊕ *www.baytours.co.nz*). **On Yer Bike Winery Tours** (✉ *129 Rosser Rd., R.D. 4, Hastings* ☎ *06/879–8735, 025/233–3398 cell* ⊕ *www.onyerbikehb.co.nz*). **Vince's World of Wine** (✉ *9 Thurley Pl., Bay View, Napier* ☎ *06/836–6705, 025/506–658 cell* ⊕ *www.vincestours.co.nz* ✎ *vincetours@hotmail.com*).

HAWKE'S BAY

Not for nothing is Hawke's Bay, bounded by the Kawera and Ruahine ranges, known as the fruit basket of New Zealand. You can't travel far without seeing a vineyard or an orchard, and the region produces some of the country's finest wines. Roughly 20 years ago, a dry, barren area known as the **Gimblett Gravels** was about to be mined for gravel. Then an enterprising vine grower took a gamble and purchased the land. The stony soil turned out to be a boon for grapevines because it retains heat, and now several wineries benefit from its toasty conditions. Chardonnay is the most important white variety here; you'll also find sauvignon blanc, bordeaux varieties, and syrah.

On the coast east of Hawke's Bay is Cape Kidnappers and its colony of gannets, a fascinating area that is home to as many as 15,000 of these large seabirds. To the south, the architecturally notable town of Hastings sits near the charming town of Havelock North, known locally as "the Village," with the Te Mata Peak rising dramatically beyond.

Farther south, a hill near Porangahau is the place with **the longest name in the world.** Take a deep breath and say, "Taumatawhakatangihangakoauauotamateaturipukakapikimaungahoronukupokaiwhehuakitanatahu." Now, that wasn't too hard, was it? Just remember it as "the place where Tamatea, the man with the big knees who slid, climbed, and swallowed mountains, known as landeater, played his flute to his loved one," and it should be no problem at all!

Hawke's Bay Tourism, a regional organization, puts up the ⊕*www. hawkesbaynz.com* Web site for area information. The small Hawke's Bay Airport (NPE) is 5 km (3 mi) north of Napier. Shuttle taxis run into town.

WHAT TO SEE

FodorsChoice **Cape Kidnappers** was named by Captain James Cook after local Māori
★ tried to kidnap the servant of Cook's Tahitian interpreter. The cape is the site of a large **gannet colony.** The gannet is a large white seabird with black-tipped flight feathers, a golden crown, and wingspans that can reach 6 feet. When the birds find a shoal of fish, they fold their wings and plunge straight into the sea at tremendous speed. Their migratory pattern ranges from western Australia to the Chatham Islands, about 800 km (500 mi) east of Christchurch, but they generally nest only on remote islands. The colony at Cape Kidnappers is believed to be the only mainland gannet sanctuary in existence. Between October and March, about 15,000 gannets build their nests here, hatch their young, and prepare them for their long migratory flight.

You can walk to the sanctuary along the beach from Clifton, which is about 24 km (15 mi) south of Napier, but not at high tide. The 8-km (5-mi) walk must begin no earlier than three hours after the high-tide mark, and the return journey must begin no later than four hours before the next high tide. Tidal information is available at Clifton and at Napier Visitor Information Centre. A rest hut with refreshments is near the colony.

One easy way to get to the colony is to take a **Gannet Beach Adventures** (☎06/875–0898 ⊕*www.gannets.com*) tractor-trailer, which is pulled along the beach starting from Clifton Reserve, Clifton Beach. Tractors depart approximately two hours before low tide, and the trip ($33–$50)—with pick-ups from Napier, Hastings, and Havelock North—takes 4–4½ hours. If tides prevent the trip along the beach, the only other access is across private farmland. **Gannet Safaris** (☎06/875–0888) runs a four-wheel-drive bus to Cape Kidnappers from Summerlee Station, just past Te Awanga. A four-person minimum is required for this three-hour tour ($50 each). Advance booking is essential for all gannet colony tours. Both pick up by shuttle at an additional cost.

Wool World at Clifton Station. Capture the rustic charm of life on the farm in an original 1890s woolshed. View century old equipment, learn the history of wool in Hawkes Bay, and watch sheep being shorn daily at 2 PM by hand and machine. This is the real McCoy! ⊠*459 Clifton*

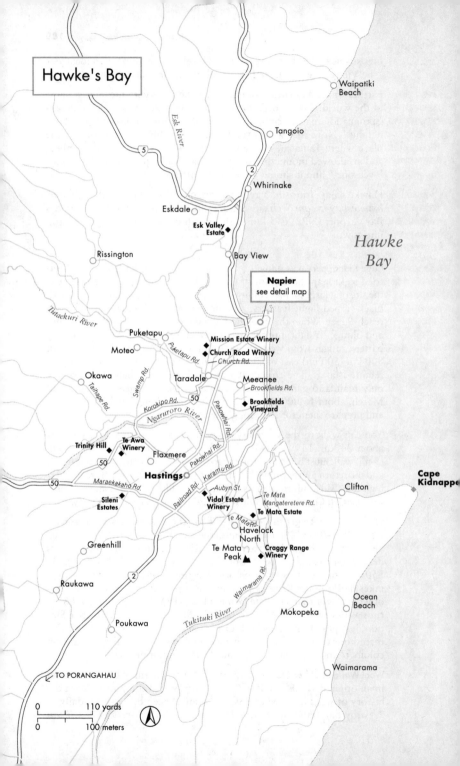

Road, Hawkes Bay ☎*06/875–0611* ⊕*www.cliftonstation.co.nz* ☒*$5 museum; $20 show* ⊙ *Daily 10–4*

Hastings is Napier's twin city in Hawke's Bay, and it's 18 km (11 mi) south of Napier, down Highway 2. The town doesn't have the same concentrated interest of Napier, but buildings in the center exhibit similar art deco flourishes—the 1931 earthquake did a lot of damage here, too. Where Hastings stands out is in its Spanish Mission buildings, a style borrowed from California, which produced such beauties as the **Hawke's Bay Opera House** (☒*Hastings St. and Heretaunga St. E*) and the **Westermans Building** (☒*Russell St. and Heretaunga St. E*). For picnic supplies, visit the **Hawke's Bay Farmers' Market** (☒*Kenilworth Rd.*) at A&P Showgrounds on Sunday from 8:30 to 12:30. Local products include handmade cheese, breads, ice cream, and fruit. The **Hastings Visitor Information Centre** (☒*Russell St. N, Hastings* ☎*06/873–5526*) is open from 8:30 to 5 on weekdays, and from 10 to 4 on weekends. Out of town, 3 km (2 mi) to the southeast, the village of Havelock North provides access to **Te Mata Peak**, a famed local viewpoint where it's possible to gaze across the plains to Napier and the rumpled hills beyond. The summit is a 15-minute (signposted) drive along Te Mata Peak Road from Havelock North.

WINERIES

Esk Valley Estate Winery is on a north-facing hillside, ensuring it full sun. Winemaker Gordon Russell produces chardonnay, sauvignon blanc, merlot, and blends with cabernet sauvignon, merlot, cabernet franc, and malbec in various combinations, including a rare and expensive red simply called the Terraces. White varieties include Riesling, verdelo, chenin blanc, and pinot gris. Look for the reserve versions of chardonnay and merlot-malbec blend to find out what he has done with the best grapes from given years. The winery is 12 km (8 mi) north of Napier, just north of the town of Bay View before Highways 2 and 5 split. ☒*745 Main Rd., Bay View* ☎*06/273–7430* ⊕*www.eskvalley.co.nz* ⊙ *Daily 10–5, tours by appointment.*

★ Gardens surround the former seminary building of the **Mission Estate Winery** in the Taradale hills overlooking Napier. As the country's oldest winery, dating back to 1851, it should be added to your "must-see" list. Award-winning wines, including the Mission Jewelstone range, can be bought or tasted at the cellar door. Join one of the tours for a look at the underground cellar and a discussion of the mission's history. A gallery sells local handmade pottery and crafts. If you stay for a meal, get a seat on the terrace for a terrific view of the vineyard and Napier. To reach the vineyard, leave Napier by Kennedy Road, heading southwest from the city center toward Taradale. Just past Anderson Park, turn right into Avenue Road and continue to its end at Church Road. ☒*198 Church Rd., Taradale* ☎*06/845–9353* ⊕*www.missionestate. co.nz* ⊙ *Mon.–Sat. 9–5, Sun. 10–4:30.*

The **Church Road Winery** is owned by Pernod-Ricard, but it operates pretty much as a separate entity. The wines are labeled Church Road: their chardonnay is a nationwide restaurant staple, and the many variations on the cabernet sauvignon and merlot themes are all worth sampling. A "cuve" series features limited-release wines with styles and varieties unique to this winery. A wine tour of the unique wine museum and beautifully restored cellars (a tasting is included, too) costs $12. Dining can be enjoyed in the indoor-outdoor restaurant. ✉ *150 Church Rd., Taradale* ☎ *06/845–9137* ⊕ *www.churchroad.co.nz* ☉ *Daily 9–5; tours at 10, 11, 2, and 3.*

Brookfields Vineyard is one of the most attractive wineries in the area, with rose gardens and a tasting room that overlooks the vines. The gewürztraminer and pinot gris are usually outstanding, but the showpiece is the reserve cabernet sauvignon–merlot, a powerful red that ages well. Syrah grapes are proving spectacular as is the Brookfields Hillside syrah. The casual winery restaurant is very good, and wine tasting is offered before your meal. From Napier take Marine Parade toward Hastings and turn right on Awatoto Road. Follow it to Brookfields Road and turn left. Signs will point to the winery. ✉ *376 Brookfields Rd., Meeanee* ☎ *06/834–4615* ⊕ *www.brookfieldsvineyards.co.nz* ☉ *Daily 10:30–4:30. Restaurant Wed.–Sun. 11:30–3* PM.

Te Mata Estate is one of New Zealand's top wineries, and Coleraine, a rich but elegant cabernet–merlot blend named after the much-photographed home of the owner, John Buck, is considered the archetypal Hawke's Bay red. Bullnose syrah-Elston Chardonnay and Cape Crest Sauvignon Blanc show similar restraint and balance. If there's any viognier open (it's made only in tiny quantities), try it—it's excellent. From Napier head south on Marine Parade through Clive and turn left at the Mangateretere School. Signs will then lead you to Te Mata Road and the estate. ✉ *349 Te Mata Rd.* ✑ *Box 8335, Havelock North* ☎ *06/877–4399* ⊕ *www.temata.co.nz* ☉ *Weekdays 9–5, Sat. 10–5, Sun. 11–4; tours mid-Dec.–Jan., daily at 10:30.*

★   By a small lake with the towering heights of Te Mata Peak beyond, the **Craggy Range Winery** has a stunning setting for wine making and tasting. The wines include single-varietal chardonnay, merlot, and syrah; a predominantly merlot blend called Sophia; and a cabernet sauvignon blend known as the Quarry. You can sample wines at the cellar, tour the facility by appointment, or enjoy a meal at the Terroir restaurant looking out over the lake. ✉ *253 Waimarama Rd., Havelock North* ☎ *06/873–0141* ⊕ *www.craggyrange.com* ☉ *Daily 10–6.*

Vidal Wines, founded in 1905, is one of Hawke's Bay's oldest boutique wineries and a producer of premium quality wines. Its restaurant is a popular spot to laze away the afternoon with a glass of sauvignon blanc, chardonnay, or syrah. ✉ *913 St. Aubyn St. E, Hastings* ☎ *06/872–7440* ⊕ *www.vidal.co.nz* ☉ *Nov.–Apr., Mon.–Sat. 10–6, Sun. 10–5; May–Oct., daily 10–5.*

Trinity Hill, in the Gimblett Gravels region, produces distinctive wines reflecting the character of the vineyard sites. A diverse range includes chardonnay, viognier, pinot gris, and many others. Wines with the Hawkes Bay White label are suited for early drinking. Have a glass of wine with a cheese or antipasto platter in the landscaped grounds. The winery holds periodic art exhibitions. ✉*2396 State Hwy. 50, Hastings* ☎*06/879–7778* ⊙*Oct.–Easter, daily 10–5; Easter–Oct., daily 11–4* ⊕*www.trinityhill.com.*

WHERE TO STAY & EAT

$$$–$$$$ ✕**Terroir Restaurant.** The massive cedar doors and high circular roof
★ give this well-regarded restaurant at Craggy Range Winery a rustic feel. Although the menu is loosely country French, "rustic" here is far from unsophisticated. The open wood fire turns out dishes such as pepper-encrusted beef fillet with herb hollandaise, and spit-roasted chicken with red wine–radicchio risotto. From the eclectic dessert offerings, thin apple tart with caramel sauce and vanilla ice cream is an appealing choice. On a warm evening, you can dine on the terrace with views of Te Mata Peak. ✉*253 Waimarama Rd., Havelock North* ☎*06/873–0413* ▤*AE, DC, MC, V* ⊙*Closed Mon. Easter–Labour weekend. No dinner Sun.*

$$$–$$$$ ✕**Vidal Wines Restaurant.** Open seven days for lunch and dinner, Vidals is acknowledged as one of Hawke's Bay's finest eating places. A signature dish is the Hawkes Bay natural lamb rack, mushroom and lamb shank filo roll on a warm celeriac slaw, and caramelized onion-filled kūmara finished with vincotta and pomegranate jus. ✉*913 St. Aubyn St. E, Hastings* ☎*06/876–8105* ⊕*www.vidal.co.nz* ▤*AE, DC, MC, V.*

$$$ ✕**Brookfields Vineyard Restaurant.** Open only for lunch, this winery restaurant's menu is not far-reaching—perhaps three first-course choices and four main dishes—but the contemporary fare is first-rate, particularly with a glass of wine. The beef scotch fillet on asparagus with fried spaetzle, baby spinach, and slow-roasted tomato jus is well matched by the cabernet merlot. ✉*Brookfields Rd., Meeanee ✦5 km (3 mi) south of Napier* ☎*06/834–4615* ⊕*www.brookfieldsvineyards.co.nz* ▤*AE, DC, MC, V* ⊙*No dinner.*

$$$ ✕**Corn Exchange.** On sunny days, you can sit outside on the patio; a
★ large fireplace warms you in winter. Either way, the service is swift and friendly. Try the pan-baked lamb rump on roasted vegetables with paprika glaze or the Mediterranean platter—salami, pesto dip, hummus, Brie, croute, roasted capsicum, and sun-dried tomatoes. The lemon and lime tart, homemade with a confit of citrus fruits, is delicious. ✉*118 Maraekakoho Rd., Hastings* ☎*06/870–8333* ▤*AE, DC, MC, V.*

$$$ ✕**Sileni Estates.** More than a simple winery, this property houses a restaurant, gourmet cellar store, Wine Discovery Centre, Culinary Arts Centre, and the Village Press Olive Oil press house. Sileni Estates restaurant, specializing in the finest wines and freshest local produce matched with Sileni's extensive range of wines, is open seven days for lunch and dinner. ✉*2016 Maraekakaho Rd., Bridge Pa, Hastings* ☎*06/879–8768* ▤*AE, DC, MC, V.*

$$–$$$ ✕**Rose & Shamrock.** This lovely old-world pub in the heart of Havelock North village has the largest selection of tap beer in Hawke's Bay. The pints mix with pub fare like grilled beef sirloin and a generous platter of seafood or hearty beef and Guinness pie. ✉*Napier Rd., Havelock North* ☎*06/877–2999* ▤*AE, DC, MC, V.*

4

$$-$$$ ✕**Te Awa Winery.** Profiting from the Gimblett Gravels terrain, this winery produces single-estate wines, which are carefully matched with the restaurant's menu. You might find such pairings such as the Te Awa Chardonnay 2004 or Pinotage 2004 with Ras-el-Hanout dusted Hawke's Bay natural lamb rump, parsnip cordalia, eggplant and roasted pepper stack, poppy-seed lavosh, and porcini jus. ⊠*2375 State Hwy. 50, Hastings* ☎*06/879–7602* ▤*AE, DC, MC, V* ☾*No dinner.*

$$$$ 🏠 **Hawthorne Country House.** The guest rooms at this beautifully reno-
★ vated Edwardian villa have private verandas, from which you look out over 14 acres of lushly landscaped grounds. Each room boasts a high ceiling, antique-style furnishing and fixtures, and embroidered bed linens. There are also tea- and coffee-making facilities, so you can enjoy a morning cup before heading off for a sumptuous cooked breakfast (often with eggs laid by the property's free-range chickens). **Pro:** A quiet place to read and relax. **Cons:** No evening meal available, transport necessary to restaurants and attractions. ⊠*1420 Railway Rd. S, Hastings South* ☎*06/878–0035* 🖷*06/878–0035* ⊕*www. hawthorne.co.nz* ⥹*4 rooms* ♿*In-room: no a/c. In-hotel: no-smoking rooms* ▤*MC, V* ❐*BP.*

$$$$ 🏠 **Mangapapa Petit Hotel.** This restored lodge, built in 1885, stands in 20
★ acres of working orchards. A dozen guest suites are luxuriously furnished and the manicured gardens include a grass tennis court, a heated swimming pool, and a sauna. Local produce features on the five-course dinner menu, with dishes such as fresh whole baby Aoraki salmon in a creamy champagne-and-mushroom sauce, and the wine list includes superb Hawke's Bay wines. **Pros:** A private, quiet setting; luxury to lighten your heart. **Con:** It will also lighten your wallet. ⊠*466 Napier Rd., Havelock North* ☎*06/878–3234* 🖷*06/878–1214* ⊕*www.mangapapa.co.nz* ⥹*12 suites* ♿*In-room: Ethernet. In-hotel: restaurant, bar, tennis court, pool, spa, bicycles* ▤*AE, DC, MC, V* ❐*BP, MAP.*

$$$$ 🏠 **The Masters Lodge.** New Yorkers Joan and Larry Blume fell in love with this art deco masterpiece and are now its gracious hosts. Stunning views from an elevated veranda stretch seaward to Cape Kidnappers, but it's the lovely interior and magnificent stained-glass windows in every room that will keep you entranced. **Pros:** Incredible views, fabulous coffee, and welcoming hosts. **Cons:** Parking is limited, not within walking distance of shops or restaurants. ⊠*10 Elizabeth Rd.,* ☎*06/834–1946* ⊕*www.masterslodge.co.nz* ⥹*2 rooms* ♿*In-hotel: no smoking, public Internet* ▤*AE MC, V.*

$$ 🏠 **Harvest Lodge.** Close to the center of Havelock North, this up-to-the-minute motel has spacious studios with original artwork and comfortable king-size beds. All units have bifold windows that open wide onto the lovely courtyard. **Pro:** It's just a short stagger from the Rose and Shamrock pub. **Con:** Very close to main road, don't stagger off the sidewalk!. ⊠*23 Havelock Rd., Havelock North* ☎*06/877–9500* 🖷*06/877–9800* ⊕*www.harvestlodge.co.nz* ⥹*19 rooms* ♿*In-room: VCR, dial-up. In-hotel: spa, laundry facilities, no-smoking rooms* ▤*AE, DC, MC, V.*

$–$$ 🏠 **Portmans Motor Lodge.** These 20 units surround a spacious courtyard; they're also conveniently near the center of town. Ten rooms have whirlpool baths: the outdoor swimming pool is not heated in winter. **Pros:** Reasonable priced accommodation, very handy to town. **Cons:** The outdoor pool is not heated, some parking a little cramped. ✉*401 Railway Rd., Hastings* ☎*06/878–8332* 🖷*06/878–8620* ⊕*www.portmans.co.nz* ⮐*20 rooms* &*In-room: no a/c, kitchen. In-hotel: pool, spa, laundry facilities, no-smoking* ▤*AE, DC, MC, V.*

GISBORNE & EASTLAND

Traveling to Eastland takes you well away from the tourist track in the North Island. Once here, you will find rugged coastline, beaches, dense forests, gentle nature trails, and small, predominantly Māori communities. Eastland provides one of the closest links with the nation's earliest past. Kaiti Beach, near the city of Gisborne, is where the *waka* (long canoe) *Horouta* landed, and nearby Titirangi was named by the first Māori settlers in remembrance of their mountain in Hawaiki, their Polynesian island of origin. Kaiti Beach is also where Captain Cook set foot in 1769—the first European landing in New Zealand. Cook's initial landing was unsuccessful, for even though the natives were friendly, several were killed because of misunderstandings. When Cook left, he named the place Poverty Bay—"as it afforded us no one thing we wanted." Although Cook's name stuck to the body of water that hugs the eastern shore, the region is now generally known as Eastland.

Gisborne's warm climate and fertile soil produce some of New Zealand's top wines. Often overshadowed by Hawke's Bay (and its PR machine), Gisborne has about 7,000 acres under vine, and it is the country's largest supplier of chardonnay grapes.

The region has some of the finest and often almost deserted surfing beaches in the country; it's also ideal for walking, fishing, horse trekking, and camping. The international spotlight focused briefly on Eastland when scenes for the film *Whale Rider* were shot at Whangara, north of Gisborne, but there have been few changes to what is mainly a quiet, rural place.

GISBORNE

210 km (130 mi) northeast of Napier, 500 km (310 mi) southeast of Auckland.

The Māori name for the Gisborne district is Tairawhiti (tye-ra-*fee*-tee), "the coast upon which the sun shines across the water," and Gisborne is indeed the first city in New Zealand to see sunrise. Although the city (population 30,000) is hardly large, you need a day or so to get around town properly. The landmark Town Clock stands in the middle of Gladstone Road; nearby, in a house on Grey Street, Kiri Te Kanawa, New Zealand's world-famous opera diva, was born in 1944 (the house is no longer there).

Europeans settled the Gisborne area early in the 19th century. A plaque on the waterfront commemorates the first official sale—of an acre of land—on June 30, 1831. On that site, the first European house and store was reportedly erected (it's long gone, too).

GETTING HERE & AROUND

Gisborne is a long way from almost anywhere, though the coastal and bush scenery along the way makes the drive wholly worthwhile. Most of the town's historical sights and other attractions are too spread out to explore them by foot, and a car is needed for the spectacular countryside.

ESSENTIALS

Visitor Info **Gisborne–Eastland Visitor Information Centre** ✉ *209 Grey St., Gisborne* ☎ *06/868–6139* 📠 *06/868–6138* ⊕ *www.gisbornenz.com).*

WHAT TO SEE

The **Tairawhiti Museum,** with its Māori and Pākehā (non-native) artifacts and an extensive photographic collection, provides a good introduction to the region's history. A maritime gallery covers seafaring matters, and there are changing exhibits of local and national artists' work. The Exhibit Café serves excellent light refreshments and the Art Bear Gallery Shop sells locally made artifacts. Outside the museum, the colonial-style **Wyllie Cottage,** built in 1872, is the oldest house in town. ✉ *10 Stout St.* ☎ *06/867–3832* ⊕ *www.tairawhitimuseum.org. nz* 💵 *$5* ⊙ *Mon.–Sat. 10–4, Sun. 1:30–4.*

Cook Landing Site National Historic Reserve has deep historical significance for New Zealanders, but not so much to keep an international visitor amused. A statue of Captain James Cook, who first set foot on New Zealand soil here on October 9, 1769, stands on Kaiti Beach, across the river southeast of the city center. The beach itself, at low tide, attracts interesting birdlife. ✉ *Esplanade on south end of Turanganui River.*

The **Titirangi Domain** on Kaiti Hill has excellent views of Gisborne, Poverty Bay, and the surrounding rural areas. Titirangi was the site of an extensive *pā* (fortified village), which can be traced back at least 24 Māori generations. The **Titirangi Recreational Reserve,** part of the Domain, is a great place for a picnic or a walk. The Domain is south of Turanganui River. Pass the harbor and turn right onto Esplanade, then left onto Crawford Road, then right onto Queens Drive, and follow it to several lookout points in the Domain.

Te Poho o Rawiri Meeting House is one of the largest Māori marae in New Zealand, and the interior has excellent, complex traditional carving. One example is the *tekoteko,* a kneeling human figure with the right hand raised to challenge those who enter the marae. There are also unusual interior alcoves and a stage framed by carvings; it's essentially a meetinghouse within a meetinghouse. Photography is not allowed inside. On the side of the hill stands the 1930s Toko Toro Tapu Church. You'll need permission to explore either site; contact the Gisborne-Eastland Visitor Information Centre *(see above),* and donations are requested.

The Elusive Te Kooti

Of all the Māori leaders who opposed the early Pākehā settlers in New Zealand, Te Kooti was the most elusive and most awe inspiring. He was born at Matawhero, near Gisborne, in the early 19th century. As a young man he fought with government troops in a local uprising, but he was accused of treachery and deported without trial to the remote Chatham Islands in 1866. While detained on the island, he experienced visions and initiated a new creed he called Ringatu ("raised hand," for the practice of raising the right hand after prayer). Ringatu is still practiced by several thousand people in New Zealand.

With his charismatic personality, Te Kooti became the de facto leader of the island's more than 200 prisoners. After two years he engineered their escape by capturing a ship and forcing the crew to sail them back to Poverty Bay. With arms seized from the ship, Te Kooti led his followers to the Urewera mountains, fighting off government troops as they went. In the years that followed, he was relentlessly hunted but continued to carry out vicious raids on coastal settlements. His last stand (and the last major engagement of the New Zealand wars) was at a fortified position at Te Porere, which you can still see near the road between Turangi and Te Urewera National Park. Te Kooti was defeated but escaped yet again. He eluded capture and spent the late 1870s in Te Kuiti, near Waitomo, under the protection of the Māori king. The government formally pardoned him in 1883; he died a decade later.

Lindauer Cellars is Gisborne's largest wine outlet. The cellar has wooden beams and a Nuhaka stone floor, with a large selection of Montana wines available for sale or tasting. Across the courtyard is the dimly lit and cavernous winery museum with *methode traditionelle* wines such as Lindauer, and a history of wine making in the region. The restaurant provides indoor and alfresco dining; lunch is available, as are coffee and light refreshments. ⊠ *11 Solander St.* ☎ *06/868–2757* ⊟ *06/868–2758* ⊕ *www.montanawines.co.nz* ⊘ *Daily 10–5.*

Millton Vineyard has an attractive garden area, where you can sit with a picnic lunch and sip barrel-fermented chardonnay. The Te Arai vineyard chenin blanc and malbec are very good wines, and the award-winning Opou Riesling is also recommended. James and Annie Millton grow their grapes organically and biodynamically, following the precepts of philosopher Rudolf Steiner. The vineyard is signposted off State Highway 2, about 11 km (7 mi) south of Gisborne. ⊠ *Papatu Rd., Manutuke* ☎ *06/862–8680* ⊕ *www.millton.co.nz* ⊘ *Nov.–Mar., Mon.–Sat. 10–5; Apr.–Oct., by appointment.*

OFF THE BEATEN PATH

Eastwoodhill Arboretum. Inspired by the gardens seen on a trip to England in 1910, William Douglas Cook returned home and began planting 160 acres. His brainchild became a stunning collection of more than 600 genera of trees from around the world. In spring and summer daffodils mass yellow, magnolias bloom in clouds of pink and white, and cherries, crab apples, wisteria, and azalea add to the spectacle. The main tracks in the park can be walked in about 45 minutes. Maps and self-guided tour booklets are available. Drive west from Gisborne center on Highway 2 toward Napier, cross the bridge, and turn at the rotary onto the Ngatapa–Rere Road. Follow it 35 km (22 mi) to the arboretum. ✉ *Ngatapa–Rere Rd.* ☎ *06/863–9003* ⊕ *www.eastwood hill.org.nz* ✉ *$10* ⊙ *Daily 9–5.*

Morere Hot Springs. Set in 1,000 acres of native bush, this unique place provides modern bathing facilities in an unusual natural environment. A cold outdoor pool is alongside a warm indoor pool, and in the forest a few minutes' walk away are smaller hot or warm pools with a cold plunge pool. Two private hot pools are also available. Following the walking trails through the forest can take 20 minutes or stretch to two to three hours. Morere is roughly halfway between Wairoa and Gisborne, north of the Mahia turnoff. ✉ *State Hwy. 2, Morere, Gisborne* ☎☎ *06/837–8856* ✉ *morere@xtra.co.nz* ✉ *$5, private pools $8* ⊙ *June–Oct., daily 10–6; Nov.–May, daily 10–9.*

SPORTS & THE OUTDOORS

FISHING   Albacore, yellowfin tuna, mako shark, and marlin along with the yellow-tail kingfish are prized catches off the East Cape from January to April (no fishing licenses needed). Fishing operators include **Dive Tatapouri** (☎ *06/868–5153* ⊕ *www.divetatapouri.com*), 14 km (9 mi) north of the city off State Highway 35. Dean and Chrissie of Dive Tatapouri cater for all types of fishing and diving; if you get to the dive shop at the right time, you might be lucky enough to hand-feed stringrays that swim close in to the nearby rocks. **Surfit Boat Charters** (☎ *06/867–2970 or 027/230–7016* ⊕ *www.surfit.co.nz*) is based in Gisborne. Fishing trips start at $140 per person. If you fancy being lowered in a shark cage to come face-to-face with a white pointer shark, aka a "great white," you can take the plunge for $250.

GOLF   The **Poverty Bay Golf Course** (✉ *Lytton and Awapuni Rds., Gisborne* ☎ *06/867–4402*), an 18-hole championship course, ranks among the top-five courses in the country. The green fee is $35.

SURFING   Gisborne has three good surfing beaches close to town. Waikanae Beach, a short walk from the visitor information center on Grey Street, usually has good learners' surf, and the Pipe and the Island are for the more experienced. The Pipe is just south of Waikanae; the Island fronts the Titirangi Domain. You can arrange for lessons at the **Gisborne Surf School** (☎ *06/868–3484, 027/482–7873 cell* ⊕ *www.gisbornesurf school.co.nz*). Rates start at $45 per person for two hours; a private two-hour session costs $60. Surfboard rentals are $25 for a half day or $40 for a full day.

WHERE TO STAY & EAT

$$$–$$$$ ✕**Wharf Café Bar Restaurant.** At a former storage shed overlooking the Gisborne Wharf, find a seat at a sunny outdoor table for breakfast or go for a lively evening. The fresh market fish of the day comes with a truffle dauphine, summer greens, crispy pancetta, and chorizo oil, and is matched with a Millton Opou Chardonnay. If you have room, try the Kapiti lime sorbet with fresh fruit. The wine list leans to local and

other New Zealand producers. ⊠*60 The Esplanade* ☎*06/868–4876* ⊕*www.wharfbar.co.nz* ▤*AE, DC, MC, V.*

$$$ ✕**The Marina Restaurant & Bar.** In the high-ceiling dining room, light filters through stained glass and floor-length cappuccino-color drapes grace the windows that look out towards the river. An upended wooden rowboat serves as an interesting wine rack. Seafood is the specialty; look for the fish of the day, with lemon and thyme risotto, and spring asparagus with citrus emulsion. ⊠*Marina Park* ☎☎*06/868–5919* ▤*AE, MC, V* ☉*Closed Sun. No lunch.*

$$$ ✕**The Works Café & Winery.** In a building that was once the Gisborne
★   Freezing Works, this restaurant harks back to the industrial past, with a large drive shaft and pulleys on the brick walls. The menu builds on local products, from cheeses to fruit, scallops to calamari. Natural Pacific plate oysters with a soy and chili dip would be a good starter, followed by smoked maple chicken breast stuffed with Camembert cheese and sun-dried tomatoes, sitting on jasmine rice then drizzled with tomato pesto cream. Wrought-iron gates at the back lead to a boutique winery. ⊠*Kaiti Beach Rd.* ☎*06/863–1285* ▤*AE, DC, MC, V.*

$–$$ ✕**The Meetings.** For a casual place to hoist a few while nibbling hearty pub fare, you can't beat an Irish pub, and Gisborne now has one of its own. Stained-glass partitions separate the dining alcoves, which have brass chandeliers, dark woodwork, and green leather upholstery. On a warm evening you can sit outside in the Garden Bar and try the hearty beef and Guinness pie with gravy, washed down with a glass of real ale. ⊠*At Reads Quay and Gladstone St.* ☎*06/863–3733* ▤*MC, V.*

$–$$ ✕**Verve Café.** This funky little midtown coffee bar has an ever-changing display from local artists; the reading matter is interesting, and the food is honest and generous. Ask for the famous chicken sandwich on grilled focaccia with fresh salad greens, roasted peppers, spicy mayo, and blue or Brie cheese—it's superb. Best of all, the coffee is terrific, they say the best in NZ and we didn't argue!. ⊠*121 Gladstone Rd.* ☎*06/868–9095* ▤*AE, DC, MC, V.*

$$$–$$$$ ▦ **Repongaere Estate.** Situated for privacy, these three modern villas stand on separate elevated positions. Each villa has a spacious ultra-modern living area with huge ranch-sliders taking in mind-blowing rural views that extend over the vineyard to Young Nicks Head and Gisborne City. The facilities include two large double bedrooms each with private bathroom and laundry, and full kitchen facilities. Basic breakfast provisions are provided, and with notice meals can be arranged. Olive oil and white wines are produced on the estate and tasting is available on request. **Pros:** The silence is golden, the views outstanding, you can do wine tasting without worrying about driving afterwards. **Con:** It's a good drive to town or beaches. ⊠*30 Repongaere Rd., Box 1073, Gisborne* ☎*06/862–7515* 🖶*06/862–7687* ⊕*www.repongaere.co.nz* ⚐*In-room: Wi-Fi, VCR, no a/c. In-hotel: no smoking* ▤*AE, MC, V.*

$$–$$$ ▦ **Cedar House Bed & Breakfast.** Bay windows overlook the garden at this gracious Edwardian villa with its huge paneled entrance hall, period furniture, and massive rooms. Crisp linen and a guest lounge with outdoor deck and tea/coffee facilities ensure a comfortable stay.

Pro: Nothing has been overlooked for a comfortable stay. **Con:** You have to be keen on that English stately home look. ⊠ *4 Clifford St., Gisborne* ☎*06/868–8583* ⊕*www.cedarhouse.co.nz* 🛏*4 rooms, 2 with bath, 1 self-contained unit.* ⟳*In-room: no a/c. In-hotel: no-smoking, pool, spa* ⊟*AE, MC, V.*

$$–$$$ 🏨 **Portside Hotel.** This modern hotel is a sparkling addition to the local accommodations. Overlooking an outdoor pool, the lofty open foyer is inviting, the contemporary look complimented by dark wood furniture on a tiled floor and quality local paintings. All rooms and suites—one, two, or three bedrooms—are spacious with comfortable furnishings and full kitchen facilities. You pay more for an estuary or sea view. **Pros:** Quiet, comfortable, well-appointed suites; well situated for a quiet stroll by the river, yet handy to all facilities. **Con:** The pool is not heated. ⊠*2 Read Quay,* ☎*06/869–1000* 🖷*06/869–1020* ⊕*www. portsidegisborne.co.nz* 🛏*64 suites* ⟳*In-room: DVD, Ethernet. In-hotel: gym, no-smoking rooms* ⊟*AE, DC, MC, V.*

$$ 🏨 **Captain Cook Motor Lodge.** A stone's throw from Waikanae Beach, all the units are roomy, with clean, modern lines and comfortable furnishings, including king-size beds and kitchen facilities. Three of the rooms have whirlpool tubs. There is a restaurant and bar for in-house guests. **Pros:** Spacious well-furnished units, convenient to the beach and town facilities. **Con:** You might get some early morning traffic noise. ⊠*31 Awapuni Rd., Waikanae Beach* ☎*06/867–7002* 🖷*06/867–7073* ⊕*www.captaincook.co.nz* 🛏*21 rooms* ⟳*In-room: kitchen, VCR, dial-up. In-hotel: restaurant, bar, no-smoking rooms* ⊟*AE, DC, MC, V.*

$$ 🏨 **Tunanui Station Cottages.** For a taste of the real New Zealand relax on the 5,000-acre sheep-and-cattle station of Leslie and Ray Thompson. Among the trees is a fully restored 90-year-old cottage with original rimu flooring, kauri doors, and open fireplace, or a fair way along the track you may prefer the modern spacious comfortably furnished four-bedroom farmhouse. From here views over the Mahia peninsula to the ocean are spectacular. Both houses have great self-catering facilities, ideal for longer stays (bring your own supplies). City dwellers beware, the silence at night has been known to keep folks awake, but only the owls give a hoot! **Pros:** These cottages are full-size houses with excellent facilities, ideal for families and people who want to stay in one place after traveling a while. **Con:** A fair distance from the main road and beaches. ⊠*1001 Tunanui Rd., Opoutama, Mahia* ☎*06/837–5790* 🖷*06/837–5797* ⊕*www.tunanui.co.nz* 🛏*1 cottage, 1 farmhouse* ⟳*In-room: no a/c, kitchen. In-hotel: laundry facilities* ⊟*No credit cards.*

$ 🏨 **Goldspree Kiwi Fruit Orchard Stay.** This large self-contained cottage, with windows overlooking 25 acres of grapevines and kiwifruit orchards, is ideal for a quiet family holiday. There are two bedrooms, a roomy sitting area, a modern bathroom, and a fully equipped kitchen. Yummy breakfast supplies are brought to the door every day by the owners, Mark and Marjorie Hayes, and meals and picnic lunches can be supplied, though a restaurant is only five minutes' drive away. Gisborne Centre and beaches are also close by. **Pros:** Good homey accommodation, quiet setting. **Con:** It's quite a distance from town. ✉*37 Bond Rd., Ormond, Gisborne* ☎🖷*06/862–5688* ⊕*www.kiwifruit orchardstay.co.nz* ⇲*1 cottage* ⌂*In-room: kitchen. In-hotel: pool, no-smoking rooms* ▭*MC, V* †⊙*|BP.*

GISBORNE–OPOTIKI LOOP

Soak in the beauty and remoteness of Eastland driving the Provincial Highway 35 loop between Gisborne and Opotiki, the northwest anchor of the East Cape. Rolling green hills drop into wide crescent beaches or rock-strewn coves. Small towns appear along the route, only to fade into the surrounding landscape. It is one of the country's ultimate roads less traveled. Some scenic highlights are **Anaura Bay,** with rocky headlands, a long beach favored by surfers, and nearby islands; it is between **Tolaga Bay** and **Tokomaru Bay,** two former shipping towns. Tolaga Bay has an incredibly long wharf stretching over a beach into the sea, and Cooks Cove Walkway is a pleasant amble (two-hour round-trip) through the countryside past a rock arch. In **Tikitiki,** farther up the coast, an Anglican church is full of carved Māori panels and beams. Tikitiki has a gas station.

East of the small town of **Te Araroa,** which has the oldest *pohutukawa* (po-hoo-too-*ka*-wa) tree in the country, the coast is about as remote as you could imagine. At the tip of the cape (21 km [13 mi] from Te Araroa), the East Cape Lighthouse and fantastic views are a long, steep climb from the beach. **Hicks Bay** has another long beach. Back toward Opotiki, **Whanarua** (fahn-ah-*roo*-ah) **Bay** is one of the most beautiful on the East Cape, with isolated beaches ideal for a picnic and a swim. Farther on, there is an intricately carved Māori marae (meetinghouse) called Tukaki in **Te Kaha.**

If you plan to take your time along the way, inquire at the **Gisborne–Eastland Visitor Information Centre** (✉*209 Grey St., Gisborne* ☎*06/868–6139* 🖷*06/868–6138* ⊕*www.gisbornenz.com*) about lodging. There are motels at various points on the cape and some superbly sited motor camps and backpackers' lodges, though you'll need to be well stocked with foodstuffs before you set off. Driving time on the loop—about 330 km (205 mi)—is about five hours without stops. You can, of course, drive the loop the other way—from Opotiki around the cape to Gisborne: to get to Opotiki from the north, take Highway 2 from Tauranga and the Bay of Plenty.

GETTING HERE
Air New Zealand Link flies daily to Gisborne from Auckland and Wellington. Flights last about an hour. The small Gisborne Airport (GIS) is about 5 km (3 mi) from town. You can catch a taxi to the city center for $18.

ESSENTIALS
Airport Gisborne Airport (✉*Aerodrome Rd.* ☎*06/867–1608*).

Bus Depot Gisborne ✉*Gisborne–Eastland Visitor Information Centre, Grey St..*

Emergencies **Fire, police & ambulance** (☎111).

Pharmacy **Pharmacy 53 Limited** (✉ *Ballance Street Village, Ballance St., Gisborne* ☎ *06/867–3038*).

TE UREWERA NATIONAL PARK

Fodor's Choice   *163 km (101 mi) west of Gisborne.*
★

Te Urewera National Park is a vast, remote region of forests and lakes straddling the Huiarau Range. The park's outstanding feature is the glorious **Lake Waikaremoana** *("sea of rippling waters")*, a forest-girded lake with good swimming, boating, and fishing. The lake is encircled by a 50-km (31-mi) walking track; the three- to four-day walk is popular, and in the summer months the lakeside hiking huts are heavily used. For information about this route, contact the **Department of Conservation Visitor Centre** (☎ *06/837–3803* ⊕ *www.doc.govt.nz*) at Aniwaniwa, on the eastern arm of Lake Waikaremoana. The visitor center is also the site of a major modern artwork, the *Te Urewera* triptych by New Zealand artist Colin McCahon. The painting, done in 1976, shows a partial cross shape against a dark landscape, superimposed with English and Māori words and a reference to Te Kooti *(see "The Elusive Te Kooti" CloseUp box).* The painting generated controversy, because a Pākehā (non-Māori) artist had incorporated Māori text, and in 1997 it was stolen (or liberated, depending on your point of view) in protest, resurfacing the following year. You can pick up walking leaflets and maps and ask advice about the walks in the park, such as the one to the **Aniwaniwa Falls** (30 minutes round-trip) or to **Lake Waikareiti** (five to six hours round-trip). The motor camp on the lakeshore, not far from the visitor center, has cabins, chalets, and motel units. In summer a launch operates sightseeing and fishing trips from the motor camp. There are areas of private Māori land within the park, so be sure to stay on marked paths. Access to the park is from Wairoa, 100 km (62 mi) southwest of Gisborne down Highway 2. It's then another 63 km (39 mi) from Wairoa along Highway 38 to Lake Waikaremoana.

TOURS

Anne McGuire specializes in guided tours with bicultural perspectives, weaving the past and present in the rich landscape of the Tairawhiti on the East Coast. Tours can be tailored to suit individual preferences. A feature tour for movie enthusiasts is a visit to Whangara Marae, location and set for the film *Whale Rider*. Paradise Leisure Tours offer a variety of small group tours around Gisborne and the East Cape Area.

Contacts **Paradise Leisure Tours** (☎ *027/223–9440, 06/868–6139 Gisborne-Eastland Information Centre booking* ⊕ *www.gisbornenz.com*). **Tipuna Tours** (☎ *06/867–6558 or 027/240–4493*).

North Island's West Coast

WORD OF MOUTH

By all means arrange to go to Waitomo Cave. It's a spectacular sight to see all the glowworms and the boat ride on the underground lake with all of those glowworm lights is magical.

—longhorn55

Our favorite outdoor activities [included] blackwater rafting in Waitomo, and hiking in Egmont National Park.

—ElendilPickle

Updated by
Kathy Ombler

THE NORTH ISLAND'S WEST COAST encompasses a diversity of landscapes; top surfing beaches, world-renowned limestone caves, two national parks, one centered on a volcanic mountain, the other on a wilderness river. The land is generally rural, ranging from tidy thoroughbred horse studs to sheep and cattle farms located on remote, rolling hill country and a jumble of forest-covered mountain ranges. Small cities and rural towns throughout the region offer a high level of sophistication, for their size, of accommodation, food service, and tourism ventures.

The Taranaki region sprang from the ocean floor in a series of volcanic blasts, forming that distinctive curve along the West Coast of the North Island. The symmetrically shaped cone of Mt. Taranaki is the province's dramatic symbol and the setting for climbing routes and hiking tracks (trails). Agriculture thrives in the area's fertile volcanic soil, and the gardens around Taranaki and New Plymouth city are some of the country's most spectacular. The mythology and historical sites relating to the local people are an integral part of Taranaki.

Note: *For more information on hiking, surfing, and kayaking on the North Island's West Coast, see Chapter 11.*

ORIENTATION & PLANNING

GETTING ORIENTED

The region's geography encompasses the majestic, Fuji-like Mt. Taranaki, the gorges and wilderness of the Whanganui River region, the underground wonders of the Waitomo Caves, world-renowned surfing beaches, two national parks, and a host of forest-covered conservation areas, along with highly fertile farmland.

In the north, Cambridge is close to the major city of Hamilton and about a 90-minute drive from Auckland, on the main State Highway 1 (SH1). Surfing town Raglan is off the beaten track in a sparsely populated area of the West Coast, an easy hour's drive from SH1. Continuing south, Waitomo sits on a popular North Island tourist trail linking Rotorua and Tongariro National Park. It's also on the westward route to New Plymouth city and the Taranaki region. While SH1 traverses the center of the North Island, SH3 makes a dogleg to the west and travels through the Taranaki bight to Wanganui, then continues south to meet again with SH1, close to Palmerston North.

The Waikato & Waitomo. Waikato's landscape is a mosaic of fenced dairy farms and thoroughbred horse studs, dotted with rural service towns. In the west, a jumble of forest-covered ranges forms a buffer between the farms and wild West Coast surfing beaches of Raglan. The hilly country continues to the south, where the small Waitomo caves tourist center is surrounded by steep country, a mix of forest reserve and sheep and cattle farms.

New Plymouth & Taranaki. The Taranaki region juts away, westward from the North Island landmass. Dominating the landscape is Mt. Taranaki (Egmont is the mountain's English name). Encircling this Mt. Fuji look-alike volcano are the forests of Egmont National Park, then the landscape turns to farmland, interspersed by outstanding public gardens. Along the coastline are popular surf beaches. Think, then, of this region for climbing, hiking, surfing, fishing, cultural museums, and top music events in the main city, New Plymouth.

Wanganui, the Whanganui River & Palmerston North. The Whanganui River, flowing from the central North Island mountains and cutting a swath through a vast, forest-covered wilderness, is the focus of this region. At its mouth, Wanganui City was established before roads were built and river travel was the main form of transport. Today, visitors traveling by kayak or jet-boat enjoy the scenic, historic, and wilderness experiences of Whanganui National Park. Close by is the university city, Palmerston North, surrounded by fertile plains, and productive farm and horticulture land.

PLANNING

WHEN TO GO

Although the most popular time is from December through mid-April, most attractions can be enjoyed any time. Summer is obviously warmer—great for swimming or surfing, hiking the mountains, and paddling the rivers. However, the weather is often more settled during winter, there are fewer people and, unlike some South Island regions, there are no harsh snow or ice conditions to thwart travel. Throughout the year, the exposed coast gets more than its fair share of rain and southerly winds, so even in summer, be prepared for the odd chilly day. The upper slopes of Mt. Taranaki are steep, snow covered in winter, and especially exposed to sudden changing weather; ask advice from park staff about heading up there. The national summer school holidays run from December to the end of January, so the beach areas will be busy, especially over the Christmas/New Year's period.

GETTING HERE & AROUND

BY AIR

Airports serve the main centers but many areas are quite remote and driving or taking a bus is the best option. **Air New Zealand** (☎0800/737–000 ⊕www.airnewzealand.co.nz) operates flights daily from Auckland and Wellington to Hamilton, New Plymouth, and Palmerston North. It also flies to New Plymouth and Palmerston North from Christchurch. Flights to Australia fly out of Hamilton and Palmerston North.

BY BUS

Intercity (☎09/913–6100 ⊕www.intercitycoach.co.nz) links all cities and towns throughout the region with regular, daily scheduled bus service. Flexible travel passes allow independent travelers the chance to stop off at towns and visitor attractions along the way, and then continue on when it suits. Shuttle transport from nearby towns is available to major visitor attractions, such as, the Waitomo Caves and Egmont National Park.

One **Newmans** (☎09/913–6200 ⊕*www.newmanscoach.co.nz*) bus leaves Auckland daily direct to Waitomo. The **Waitomo Wanderer** (☎07/349–2509 or 0508/926–337 ⊕*www.waitomotours.co.nz*) makes the two-hour trip between Rotorua and Waitomo once (each way) daily. From Otorohanga, the **Waitomo Shuttle** (☎0800/808–279) makes the half-hour trip to Waitomo five times daily, connecting with major bus and train arrivals. ■TIP➔**Book in advance: the shuttle is $7 per person each way, but $30 for those who don't book in advance.**

White Star (☎06/758–338 ⊕*www.yellow.co.nz/site/whitestar/index.html*) provides a daily city-to-city service linking New Plymouth, Wanganui, Palmerston North, and Wellington.

BY CAR

Driving is the most flexible way to travel through this region. Roads are nearly all clearly signposted, and pass through diverse and scenic landscapes of farmland, forest-covered ranges, and rugged coastline.

To reach the Taranaki region, you could travel south from Auckland, explore the surfer's paradise town of Raglan, and continue south along the remote coast road, or detour inland via Cambridge, then Waitomo and on to New Plymouth. This city is an excellent base for exploring Taranaki/Egmont National Park, the gardens of Taranaki, and the surfing beaches. From there, you can continue southward to the Whanganui River region for kayaking, canoeing, or simply exploring this scenic and historic wilderness. En route to Wellington, Palmerston North—one of New Zealand's leading university towns—and its farming surrounds are worth a quick stopover.

Access to the Waikato region is straight down SH1 from Auckland—count on 90 minutes to Hamilton. Cambridge is another 15 minutes southeast on Highway 1. For Raglan, take Highway 23 west, a 40-minute drive. For Waitomo (one hour from Hamilton), take Highway 3 south and turn off onto Highway 37 past Otorohanga.

New Plymouth looks well out of the way on the map, but it is only 5 to 6½ hours from Auckland and 5 hours from Wellington. From the north, head to Te Kuiti near Waitomo Caves, and then simply continue on State Highway 3. Leaving Taranaki heading south, take State Highway 3 to Wanganui. Staying on Highway 3, keep traveling to Sanson, where you have the option of heading east—still on Highway 3—through Palmerston North, the Manawatu Gorge, and on to the Hawke's Bay and Wairarapa regions; or following State Highway 1 south to Wellington.

BY TRAIN

The *Overlander,* the daily 12-hour Auckland/Wellington train service, stops at Hamilton, Te Kuiti (near Waitomo), and Palmerston North. This is the only train service in the region.

TOP REASONS TO GO

Caving: Waitomo has an amazing underground landscape of ancient limestone formations, fossils, passages, shafts, hidden streams, and brilliant galaxies of glowworms. You can explore these stunning cave systems by taking underground walks, boat rides, or adrenaline-pumping "black-water" rafting and abseiling tours.

Hiking & Walking: Explore the steep, rocky alpine terrain, tussock and herb fields, wetlands, and dense lowland rain forest. Multiday and short walks alike provide impressive views. Take a fascinating short (30-minute) walk through the forest-covered limestone formations at Ruakuri Reserve in Waitomo Cave country.

Kayaking & Canoeing: Whanganui River, the longest navigable waterway in the country, is a prime destination for adventurers; it's also an ideal beginner's river. A multiday journey by kayak or canoe is a truly historic, as well as scenic, experience: the lower reaches of the river from Pipiriki to Wanganui pass several small, historic Māori settlements.

Surfing: The black-sand surfing beaches along the North Island West Coast rival any other surfing spots in the world. Manu Bay, near Raglan, is famous for its left-hand break. Just along the road is Whale Bay, another top spot to catch a wave. In Taranaki, "Surf Highway 45" accesses some of New Zealand's premier surfing coastline. Surfing schools, hip cafés, crafts galleries, and a cool laid-back vibe pervade the small surfing communities established near these beaches.

EMERGENCIES

The hospital for the Waikato and Waitomo regions is in Hamilton; Anglesea Accident and Urgent Medical Centre is open 24/7 and serves the region surrounding Hamilton.

Emergency Services Fire, police, and ambulance (☎ 111).

Hospitals & Medical Centers
Anglesea Accident and Urgent Medical Clinic (✉ Anglesea St., Hamilton ☎ 07/858–0800). **Waikato Hospital** (✉ Pembroke St., Hamilton ☎ 07/839–8899).

5

ABOUT THE RESTAURANTS

Throughout western North Island is a mix of city restaurants and small, tourist-town cafés with several things in common: wholesome and hearty, fresh and tasty food; good espresso and loose-leaf teas; wine lists featuring high-quality local wines; and an overall sophistication you might not expect away from major cities. Counter food for lunches and snacks will generally be fresh salads, paninis, focaccia, filled rolls, quiche, pies, and, in winter, hearty homemade soups.

Dinner menus in the higher-end restaurants will be a gourmet list of the chef's latest creations using high-quality New Zealand eye fillet of beef (beef tenderloin), fish, salmon, lamb racks, pork fillets, and chicken. The best local chefs use fresh regional and seasonal ingredients and specialties, and they're not afraid to borrow techniques and flavors from other cuisines, particularly from Asia. You're also likely to find Indian, Thai, Malaysian, Japanese, Mexican, and Italian restaurants, even in smaller provincial centers.

On the other hand, a legacy of the more basic cafés and hotel restaurants lives on, particularly in some smaller towns, where one can still come across instant coffee, tea-bag tea, and lesser-quality fare and service that is less than professional, so check the guidebook, and be as selective as you wish.

Though locals have a high standard for what's on their plates, their habits are pretty relaxed when it comes to dress. "Smart-casual" is about as formal as you have to get.

WHAT IT COSTS IN NEW ZEALAND DOLLARS					
	¢	$	$$	$$$	$$$$
Restaurants	under $10	$10–$15	$15–$20	$20–$30	over $30

Prices are per person for a main course at dinner, or the equivalent.

ABOUT THE HOTELS

Bed-and-breakfasts are often stylishly converted country houses or custom-built to ensure the best views and comfort for guests. Some of New Zealand's finest luxury lodges are found in the region, along with a wonderful range of self-catering villas and cottages, some on working farms, others with spectacular coastal locations, and a few deep in the forest-covered hinterland. There are mountain lodges and river lodges in the national parks and, for hikers, climbers, and canoeists, basic backcountry huts and camping spots managed by the Department of Conservation.

In the small tourist towns and larger cities, there's the full range of boutique hotels (small, personal, and stylish), standard hotels with basic rooms, motels with full kitchen facilities, and backpacker hostels. Although the latter are generally budget options, many with shared facilities, an increasing number of new backpacker properties have private, en-suite rooms and modern facilities.

WHAT IT COSTS IN NEW ZEALAND DOLLARS					
	¢	$	$$	$$$	$$$$
Hotels	under $75	$75–$125	$125–$200	$200–$300	over $300

Prices are for a standard double room in high season, including 12.5% tax.

VISITOR INFORMATION

Tourism Waikato (⊕ *www.waikatonz.co.nz*),online only, is a helpful regional resource. The regional tourism organization in Taranaki maintains a Web site, ⊕ *www.taranakinz.org*, with local listings and event information. The site ⊕ *www.windwand.co.nz* also has good regional listings.

Something to Chew On

A poetic gourmet once called New Zealand "the little green garden at the bottom of the world." It's an apt description, as all kinds of plate-bound treats thrive in the country's temperate climate.

New Zealand first earned international food fame for its butter and its lamb, but today other local staples such as taro, a root vegetable that is a mainstay of Pacific Islanders' diets, are finding their way to restaurant menus. A popular local meat is *cervena* (farmed venison), which is less gamey than its wild counterpart.

Locally reared ostrich and emu, whose flavors are mildly gamey, are also turning up in dining rooms. They are relatively expensive compared with other meats, but are virtually fat-free; they are eaten as steaks, casseroles, burgers, and sausages. Generally, the most popular meats found on a New Zealand restaurant table are locally farmed lamb, chicken, and beef.

Several unique species of shellfish are caught around the coast. *Pipi* and *tuatua* are similar to clams. Greenshell, the succulent and slightly sweet New Zealand farmed mussel, is larger than its North American counterpart. Oysters are available in several species—look for bivalves from Bluff and Nelson bays. Whitebait, the juvenile of several fish species, are eaten whole, usually mixed into an omeletlike fritter. Another local delicacy from the sea is the roe of the *kina*, or sea egg; it's similar to sea urchin, and you might find it in innovative restaurants. Salmon is farmed in several locations and thus a reliable, and very high quality, source of seafood that is frequently found on good restaurant menus.

If you're looking for a good-natured argument with a Kiwi, suggest that it was the Australians who invented that cream-topped, fruit-and-meringue concoction called the pavlova. Though it was certainly named for Russian ballerina Anna Pavlova, the question of where it originated is a source of ongoing trans–Tasman Sea rivalry.

There's a small but quietly growing Māori influence on mainstream New Zealand cuisine. The best-known Māori meal is a *hāngi*, a traditional cooking method that involves cooking food over heated stones buried in the earth. There are opportunities to try the real thing in Māori tourism ventures throughout the country, in particular in Rotorua. One vegetable that is a common sight on most New Zealanders' tables is the *kūmara*, or sweet potato. It's eaten boiled, baked, mashed, or whipped into elaborate concoctions. Look for kūmara *rösti*, a sweet-potato fritter, in top urban restaurants. The use of native herbal plants, for example horopito with its peppery-tasting leaves, and sweet, succulent pikopiko ferns are increasingly being incorporated into and enhancing restaurant dishes.

At the bottom of the South Island and on Stewart Island you might be offered muttonbird, also known as *titi*, eaten by local Māori for centuries and today regarded as a delicacy. It's a young seabird, cured for eating, and is extremely fatty. Kiwi cynics, who quip that the muttonbird tastes like an extremely salty boot sole, remark that the bird is better boiled for several hours with a stone, after which it is a good idea to throw away the bird and suck the stone. As you'll find, the local sense of humor is an essential ingredient in virtually every meal.

5

THE WAIKATO & WAITOMO

Many think of the Waikato region—a fertile, temperate, agricultural district south of Auckland—as the heartland of the North Island. It's home to New Zealand's largest inland city (Hamilton) and some of the most important pre-European sites. Polynesian sailors first landed on the region's West Coast as early as the mid-14th century; by way of contrast, Europeans didn't settle here until the 1830s. In the 1860s, the Waikato's many tribes united to elect a king in an attempt to resist white encroachment. This "King Movement," as it is known, is still a significant cultural and political force within Waikato Māoridom.

Hamilton is a city you can miss if time is tight. Instead, explore and enjoy three nearby attractions: the surfing hot spot of Raglan on the West Coast; attractive Cambridge, an agricultural town renowned as a horse-breeding center; and the extraordinary cave formations at Waitomo.

RAGLAN

176 km (110 mi) south of Auckland, 44 km (27 mi) west of Hamilton.

It's hard to think of a more laid-back town than Raglan. ■**TIP➜On the drive out, tune in to radio station Raglan FM 96.6 to catch the local news and grooves.** On sheltered Raglan Harbour, and in the lee of Mt. Karioi, the tiny town owes its easygoing ways to the legions of young surfers drawn to the legendary breaks at nearby Manu Bay and Whale Bay, both 8 km (5 mi) southwest of town. The Raglan surf was featured in the 1966 film *Endless Summer*. When the surf's up, drive out to the parking areas above the sweeping bays to see scores of surfers tackling what's reputed to be world's longest left-hand break.

Surfers have made this seaside village cool, and along the tree-lined main street, Bow Street, barefoot dudes in designer shades pad in and out of the few hip café-bars or hang in the smattering of crafts and surf-wear shops. Families vacation here, too, staking out their patch of sand on the beaches on either side of the harbor entrance.

Buses for Raglan ($5.50) run from Hamilton three times daily and return from the Hamilton Transport Centre. They stop at several points in Raglan, including the Raglan Library.

ESSENTIALS

Bus Depot Raglan Library (⊠ *Bow St.*).

Visitor Info Raglan Information Centre (⊠ *Bow St.* 🕾 *07/825–0556*).

OFF THE BEATEN PATH

Kawhia. With time on your hands, explore the road from Raglan to this isolated, coastal harbor settlement 55 km (34 mi) to the south. It's a fine route, skirting the eastern flank of Mt. Karioi and passing the turnoff for Bridal Veil Falls, but much of the road is gravel. In 1350 Kawhia was where the Tainui people, the region's earliest Polynesian settlers, first landed after their long sea voyage from Polynesia. Permission is

Western North Island

Tasman Sea

Raglan Harbour

Raglan

Kawhia

Kawhia Harbour

Te Anga

Waitomo Caves

Marokopa

TO AUCKLAND

Hamilton

Cambridge

Te Awamutu

W A I K A T O

Otorohanga

Te Kuiti

Mangakino

Piopio

Mahoenui

Pureora Forest Park

Awakino

Taumarunui

Lake Taupo

Turangi

Whakahoro

North Taranaki Bight

Waitara

New Plymouth

Inglewood

Egmont National Park

Cape Egmont

Mt. Taranaki

Stratford

Eltham

Opunake

Taranaki see detail map

Hawera

South Taranaki Bight

Whangamomona

Whanganui National Park

Raetihi

Tongariro National Park

Ohakune

Waiouru

Pipiriki

Whanganui R.

Whangaehu R.

T A R A N A K I

Wanganui

W A N G A N U I

Taihape

Marton

Bulls

Feilding

Palmerston North

TO WELLINGTON

0   40 miles
0   60 km

KEY

+—+—+ *Rail lines*

sometimes granted (inquire at the harborside museum) to visit the local *marae* (traditional village). What those in the know come for, however, are the Te Puia hot springs at Ocean Beach, east of town. There's road access to the beach (or it's a two-hour walk from Kawhia). You can find the springs only by digging into the sand a couple of hours either side of low tide, so check the tide tables in Raglan before you set off.

SPORTS & THE OUTDOORS

BOATING Local boatman Ian Hardie of **Raglan Harbour Cruises** (☎☎07/825–0300) welcomes you aboard the *Harmony* for a 1½-hour cruise around the tidal inlets and bays of huge Raglan Harbour. See forest reserves, historic habitation sites, isolated beaches, the "pancakes" limestone outcrops, seabirds, and, if your timing is lucky, the pod of orca that occasionally visits the harbor. Ian's been operating these cruises for 15 years, so he knows his way around the harbor. Dinner cruises are available, there's a barbecue on board. Sailings are weather permitting. It's $20 for adults and $10 for children. Advance phone reservations are essential as cruise times change with the tide. Bookings can be made directly with Raglan Harbour Cruises or with the **Raglan Information Centre** (☎07/825–0556).

SURFING If you're itching to hit the waves, stop by **Raglan Surf Co.** (⊠3 *Wainui Rd.* ☎07/825–8988), a top surfing store. It stocks equipment by all the leading brands and rents surfboards, wet suits, and boogie boards. It's open daily, and the staffers pass along helpful local surf tips.

Raglan Surfing School (⊠*Summer: Whaanga Rd., Whale Bay; winter: Karioi Lodge* ☎07/825–7873 ⊕*www.raglansurfingschool.co.nz*) has a variety of options for learning to ride the waves. The school was started by local Tim Duff, who spent years following the best surf around the world only to decide that nowhere could beat his hometown. (Duff has since moved on to become co-owner at Raglan Backpackers & Waterfront Lodge.) The school is now in the capable hands of another hometown boy, Eric (Rock) Milroy, and several present or past national surfing champions work as instructors. A three-hour session (which includes board and wet suit) is around $89, plus a free sauna afterwards! Surf Adventure Packages run two to five days and include transport, daily surfing lessons, and accommodation, as well as other adventures such as abseiling (rappelling), paragliding, and jet-boating. There's also a choice of "surf dames," women's and luxury surfing retreats on offer throughout the year.

Fodor's Choice There's no better way to explore huge Raglan Harbour than on nature's
★ terms, with Steve and Candide Reid and their company **Raglan Kayak** (☎07/825–8862 ⊕*www.raglaneco.co.nz*). Like surfer Tim Duff, local boy Steve searched the world for the perfect place to work on water, then realized it was back home. People of any age and ability are welcome on his shorter kayak trips, where the focus is on paddling with the tide and wind, great scenery, espresso, and home baking. Trips range from two hours ($50) to six hours ($95) and include gorgeous sunset excursions. Kayaks are also available for rent ($15 single, $25 tandem per hour; $35/$55 per half day; $45/$65 per day).

SWIMMING   Although the surf looks inviting at most of the West Coast beaches, there can be dangerous rips and undertows, so be careful where you take a dip. The safest spots around Raglan are Te Aro Bay (Wallis and Puriri streets), Te Kopua, and at Cox and Lorenzen bays at high tide. Call Raglan Information Centre (☎07/825–0556) for tide times. In summer, lifeguards patrol the beach at Ngarunui; to avoid the strong rips, swim between the flags.

WALKING &   From Raglan, a number of walks and hikes give you wonderful views
HIKING   of the coastline and take you through beautiful native bush. **The Department of Conservation** (☎07/838–3363 *Hamilton*) manages these tracks and surrounding conservation land. The Raglan Information Centre (*see above*) can provide maps. Don't leave valuables in your vehicle while you're away walking.

On hot days, the spectacular **Bridal Veil Falls** make an appealing destination. A 10-minute shaded hike from the parking lot leads to a viewing platform above the 150-foot drop; from here, another 10-minute walk down a steep, stepped trail puts you on a wooden platform at the base of the falls. Bring your swimsuit and, if you dare, plunge into the very cold water. (Watch for the resident eels.) The falls are 20 km (12 mi) south of Raglan; take the Kawhia road from town.

A great walk, although somewhat more difficult than the Bridal Veil Falls trail, is up **Mt. Karioi.** Some sections are quite steep, so good walking gear is required, but it's worth the challenge for the fantastic views of the coast. The Te Toto Gorge option is 3½ hours to the summit (one-way); if you leave from Whaanga Road in Kariori, it's 2½ hours to the summit (one-way).

WHERE TO EAT

$$$ ✕**Aqua Velvet Kitchen and Ballroom.** There's no dancing, but this café is plenty big enough to warrant its ballroom moniker, and live music is an occasional treat. Aqua Velvet supports local organic suppliers and carries one of the country's top espresso brands, Havana organic coffee. The food is made in-house; there are fresh baked goods, a salad bar, and dishes such as lentil, chickpea, and fresh-herb fritters with spicy tomato relish, organic salad, and minted yogurt. It's open from 8 to 3 and occasional evenings in summer. ✉*17 Bow St.* ☎*07/825–8588* ▭*AE, DC, MC, V* ⊘*No dinner in winter; evening hrs vary in summer.*

$$–$$$ ✕**Vinnie's World of Eats.** In this historic kauri cottage, you can eat any-
★   thing from Mexican food to gourmet burgers and pizzas to Thai curries. There's also a lot of seafood and a kids' menu. A full breakfast menu, plus lunches, summer salads, and nibbles will keep you fed no matter when you visit. Vinnie's is fully licensed and has a full range of smoothies, fresh juices, and espresso. ✉*7 Wainui Rd.* ☎*07/825–7273* ⊕*www.vinnies.net.nz* ▭*AE, DC, MC, V.*

$–$$$ ✕**Tongue & Groove.** Popular with the locals, this funky corner café has comfy couches and Formica tables; the walls are lined with surfboards and decorated with Raglan beach scenes—there's even a surfboard table. The menu is huge and the meals are hearty, starting at 9 AM with breakfast. Try the stewed fruit and organic yogurt with toasted almonds, or the "hell fry-up in chunky pots, mushies, bacon, sausie, eggs, toast, and caramelized onions." All-day snacks come from around the globe: veggie roti, tofu burgers, chicken kebabs, and miso noodles. Evening main courses include a similarly eclectic range, such as organic ramen noodles or lamb shanks. There's a great selection of beers, wines, espresso, loose-leaf teas, smoothies, and fresh juices. ⊠ *Wainui Rd. and Bow St.* ☎07/825–0027 ▤*AE, DC, MC, V.*

WHERE TO STAY

¢   **Karioi Lodge.** Nestled into the hills above Raglan, this backpackers' lodge and outdoor adventure center is the ultimate off-the-beaten-path place to kick back and unwind—or not. American proprietor Charlie Young and his partner, Erin, may have you "sucking back the fresh air of the native bush" and amped up to ride the waves before you know it. Or, if you'd rather do yoga, meditate in the sun, chill out in the sauna, play pool, or take a *gentle* bushwalk, they'll arrange that, too. Dorm rooms, most with four beds (two bunk beds) per room, are clean and comfy, but they share baths and there are no extras (don't expect plugs for hair dryers, for instance). The staff prepare hearty evening meals, including homemade bread, nachos, burgers, and roasts ($12 per person). **Pros:** Laid back, basic but hearty meals, you could learn to surf! **Con:** You might be sharing with a school group. ⊠ *Whaanga Rd., Whale Bay* ☎07/825–7873 or 0800/867–873 ⇆*5 double rooms with shared bath, 15 dorm rooms (58 beds) with shared bath* ⚐*In-room: no a/c. In-hotel: laundry facilities, public Internet, no elevator* ▤*MC, V.*

¢   **Raglan Backpackers & Waterfront Lodge.** Many rate this supremely
Fodor'sChoice   agreeable, budget-price, harborside lodge the best of its type in the
★   country. An "outdoor living" ideal, rooms open onto a pretty, wood-decked interior courtyard (complete with hammock). From the lounge you can wander onto the lawn and barbecue area. The shared bathroom facilities are spotless, and there's a well-equipped self-catering kitchen. Linen is provided, and rooms are comfortable and clean, with single or double beds, and six have sea views. The rooms sleep between two (for a private room) and eight (in dorm rooms). One self-contained house has two double rooms. If you're feeling adventurous, ask for a surfing lesson ($24; includes board and wet suit), or make use of the kayaks (river kayaks free, sea kayaks $28 single, $35 double half day) and bikes (free). **Pros:** Quiet location, free bike hire, lovely courtyard. **Con:** Not for those seeking resort pampering. ⊠*6 Wi Neera St.* ☎07/825–0515 ⊕*www.raglanbackpackers.co.nz* ⇆*8 rooms with shared bath, 1 dorm (8 beds) with shared bath, 1 2-bedroom house* ⚐*In-room: no a/c. In-hotel: laundry facilities* ▤*No credit cards.*

CAMBRIDGE

53 km (33 mi) east of Raglan.

Because it's on State Highway 1, Cambridge provides a good lunch break on your way elsewhere. But this charming town, with its galleries and cafés and rural English atmosphere, is worth a closer look. In summer evenings or weekends, you're likely to find the locals playing cricket in the park in the center of town. Year-round, trees provide an elegant canopy over streets full of specialty designer shops, art galleries, and cafés.

Cambridge is regarded as New Zealand's Kentucky; the thoroughbred industry has become the most prominent local feature. The surrounding farmland is home to top breeding studs and training stables, including those run by Olympic gold-medal equestrian winner Mark Todd.

GETTING AROUND
The best way to check out Cambridge is to park your car and stroll along Victoria, Empire, and Commerce streets.

ESSENTIALS
Bus Depot **Cambridge Bus Stop** (✉ *Lake St., Cambridge*).

Visitor Info **Cambridge Information Centre** (✉ *Queen and Victoria Sts.* ☎ *07/823–3456*).

WHAT TO SEE
Near the center of the town, the 100-year-old **St. Andrew's Anglican Church** has beautiful stained-glass windows.

Walk among some of the most ancient forests in the region at the small "mountain" called Maungatautari, where the **Maungatautari Ecological Island Trust,** in conjunction with the Department of Conservation, is carrying out one of New Zealand's many successful conservation stories. The trust has built a $14 million, 50-km (31-mi) pest-proof fence around 8,400 acres of native forest on Maungatautari, creating a refuge for some of New Zealand's rarest native species. Interpretive signs at the entrances to the forest describe the conservation project, and you might see or hear a variety of more common native birds, such as the distinctive *tūī* (*too*-ee), with its tuft of white feathers under its chin and resonant song. The closest walk, 14 km (9 mi) from Cambridge, is Te Ara Tirohia Loop Track. ✉ *Hicks Rd.* ☎ *07/823–7455* ⊕ *www. maungatrust.org* ✉ *By donation* ⊙ *Daily dawn–dusk.*

☺ **New Zealand Horse Magic** at Cambridge Thoroughbred Lodge, experienced ringmasters tailor shows for each audience, easily moving from expert-level information to antics for kids. Shows are held every few days, call ahead for times and a reservation. A minimum of 10 people is required; if there are fewer, a more personal guided tour around the stud might be offered. Numerous breeds of horses can be seen, including a Lippizaner, as well as famous racehorses. Kids can go for a short ride on more placid horses, with the guidance of instructors, while you have a cup of coffee and a muffin. The horse auctions can be interesting to drop in on; call for dates. ✉ *State Hwy. 1, 6 km (4 mi) south of Cambridge* ☎ *07/827–8118* ⊕ *www.cambridgethoroughbredlodge. co.nz* ✉ *$12* ⊙ *Stud tours Tues.–Sun. 10–3 (reserve ahead); shows Tues.–Sun. at 10:30* AM *(reserve ahead; minimum 10 people).*

Visit the **Cambridge Country Store,** housed in an old pink church, a historic building not least because this writer was christened here. In its current retail form, the store offers a good selection of New Zealand–made jewelry, clothing, carvings, and wine. Upstairs, the Toccata Café sells muffins, pies, quiche, salads, and sandwiches. ✉ *92 Victoria St.* ☎ *07/827–8715* ⊕ *www.cambridgecountrystore.co.nz.*

WHERE TO EAT

$$$–$$$$ ✕ **GPO Bar & Brasserie.** "Mum used to bring me here to post letters and bank my savings, now I bring my Mum to take her out to dinner." What was the town's post office and savings bank is now one of its most popular eateries, serving contemporary New Zealand dishes with strong Mediterranean, Pacific Rim, and Asian flavors. Choose among a formal dining restaurant, a cozy bar serving top local and New Zealand beers, alfresco street dining, and a covered rear courtyard. The ambience is in keeping with this 1908 Victorian era building, complete with its 53-foot-high clock tower. Open weekdays 10:30 to late, weekends 9:30 to 2 and 5:30 to late. ⊠ *Victoria St, Cambridge* ☎*07/827–5595* ▤*AE, DC, MC, V.*

$$$ ✕**Rosso's.** This stylish restaurant serves homemade Italian pasta dishes such as spaghetti marinara and roast pumpkin and garlic ravioli, along with standard New Zealand fare such as green-lipped mussels, seafood chowder, eye fillet of beef, and salmon dishes. For dessert, try their gelato affogati. Open for lunch and dinner. ⊠*72 Alpha St.* ☎*07/827–6699* ▤*DC, MC, V* ⊘*Closed Mon.*

$–$$ ✕**Rata Café.** Rata Café is a daytime café, with wood floors, redbrick walls, local artwork, and comfy sofas, that serves, arguably, the best coffee in town. Food is made on the premises. The huge breakfast menu (try the organic Greek yogurt-and-berry compote) is available all day, as are tempting pre-made salads and pastas, along with dairy and gluten-free options. Drinks include fresh squeezed juices and berry smoothies. ⊠*64C Victoria St.* ☎*07/823–0999* ▤*AE, DC, MC, V.*

Fodor'sChoice
★

¢–$ ✕**Fran's Café and Continental Cake Kitchen.** Snag a table in the main room, or wander to the courtyard out back. Choose from a big selection of imaginative homemade sandwiches, pasta, quiche, or salads, such as the grilled vegetables with balsamic vinegar. The menu changes regularly. Fran makes her own hummus and falafel. ⊠*62 Victoria St.* ☎*07/827–3946* ⊕*www.franscafe.co.nz* ▤*AE, MC, V* ⌂*BYOB.*

WHERE TO STAY

$$$$ ⊡**Maungatautari Lodge.** In an idyllic country setting overlooking Lake Karapiro, and a 10-minute drive from Cambridge, is one of New Zealand's finest luxury lodges. The suites and villa are luxuriously appointed with private balconies, double whirlpool baths, CD players, Sky television, and in-room wireless broadband. The lodge has a spacious lounge, sitting room, formal dining room, and sunny conservatory ideal for breakfasts. New furnishings, complementary to the arresting yet restful decor, and striking new artwork have been introduced by the new owners in 2008. Outside are grass terraces, formal rose and lavender gardens, and an infinity pool. Rates include dinner, predinner canapés and drinks, and breakfast. Host Donna is also a volunteer worker and keen advocate of the Maungatautari Ecological Island Trust, just up the road. **Pros:** Great outlook, infinity pool, restful ambience. **Con:** Idylls cost. ⊠*844 Maungatautari Rd., Lake Karapiro* ☎*07/827–2220* ⎙*07/827–2221* ⊕*www.malodge.com* ⇆*5 suites, 1 villa* ⚴*In-room: Wi-Fi. In-hotel: restaurant, bar, no elevator* ▤*AE, DC, MC, V* ⎟⚭*MAP.*

$ ⌂**Out in the Styx Cafe and Guesthouse.** As the name suggests, this place
Fodor's Choice is in the country, a 20-minute drive from Cambridge. The delightful
★ rural setting looks out to Maungatautari "mountain" (it's more of a
hill). The rooms are spacious, with super-king beds; three have "tribal"
themes. Smart, tidy, shared bunk rooms (five bunks to a room) are a
budget option. Listen to native birdsong while soaking in one of the two
hot tubs in the garden, catch a quiet moment in one of the two small
guest lounges (with tea and coffee facilities), or join the conviviality in
the restaurant and bar, where hosts Mary and Lance Hodgson (former
local farmers) ply you with wholesome country food and enthuse about
the conservation story of Maungatautari. Amazing value prices include
a cooked breakfast and a four-course dinner. **Pros:** Dinner (four course)
and breakfast included in price, sharing the Maungatautari conservation story, hot tubs. **Con:** Lance might convince you to join the Maungatautari Trust. ✉*2117 Arapuni Rd., Pukeatua* ☎*0800/461–559*
⊕*www.styx.co.nz* ⚅ *In-hotel: public Internet* ▤*AE, MC, V.*

5

WAITOMO

*80 km (50 mi) southwest of Hamilton, 65 km (41 mi) southwest of
Cambridge, 150 km (95 mi) west of Rotorua.*

A short drive from the main highway, Waitomo is a pretty village catering to tourists visiting the region's famous cave systems. The surrounding hills are a mix of native bush and verdant farmland, and everything
is within walking distance of the village center.

ESSENTIALS
Bus Depot **Waitomo depot** (✉ *Waitomo i-Site Visitor Centre, Waitomo Caves Rd.,
Waitomo Caves Village* ☎*07/878–7640).*

Pharmacy **Trevor Walters Pharmacy** (✉*44 Maniapoto St., Otorohanga*
☎*07/873–7294).*

Visitor Info **Waitomo i-Site Visitor Centre** ✉*Waitomo Caves Rd., Waitomo
Caves Village* ☎*07/878–7640).*

WHAT TO SEE
★ The **Waitomo Caves** are part of an ancient seabed that was lifted and
then spectacularly eroded into a surreal underground landscape of
limestone formations, gushing rivers, and contorted caverns. Many of
these amazing subterranean passages are still unexplored, although an
increasing number are accessible on adventurous underground activity
trips involving rafting, caving, and rappelling. But you don't need to
be Indiana Jones to appreciate the magnificent underground structures.
Since 1889, guided tours through the biggest, best-known caves have
been available. The caves can be visited—and are spectacular—at any
time of year.

Four major cave systems are open for guided tours: Ruakuri, Spellbound, Aranui, and Waitomo Glowworm Cave. Each has its own
special characteristics, such as impressive limestone formations, glowworm-lighted "starry skies," spiritual significance for the Māori people,

and stories of discovery and intrigue. You won't be disappointed by any. Your guides are likely to be descendants of local chief Tane Tinorau (who discovered Waitomo Glowworm Cave) or local caving experts who have spent years exploring the amazing network of shafts and passageways around Waitomo.

If adventure is your thing, don a wet suit, helmet, and headlamp and take a tour where you can abseil (rappel) through narrow shafts, leap over a waterfall, and go black-water rafting through the dark caves beneath a twinkling roof of glowworms. Bookings for all cave tours and activities can be made with the individual tour operators, or at the Waitomo i-Site Visitor Centre (⇨ *Sports & the Outdoors, below*).

Waitomo Glowworm Cave takes the first part of its name from the words *wai* (water) and *tomo* (cave), since the Waitomo River vanishes into the hillside here. The second part of the cave's name refers to the larvae of *Arachnocampa luminosa*, measuring between 1 and 2 inches, that live on cave ceilings. They snare prey by dangling sticky filaments, which trap insects attracted to the light the worm emits. A single glowworm produces far less light than any firefly, but when they are massed in great numbers in the dark, their effect is a bit like looking at the night sky in miniature. The Waitomo Glowworm Cave was first officially explored in 1887 by local Chief Tane Tinorau, accompanied by the English surveyor Fred Mace. They built a raft of flax stems and, with candles as their only light source, floated into the cave where the stream goes underground. Chief Tane continued his exploration over the years and, in 1889, began leading tours. Like those first explorers, you traverse the cave by boat; tours are 45 minutes and groups meet at the cave. This is one of the more "genteel" options of all the cave tours at Waitomo. ✉ *Waitomo Caves Rd., entrance to cave about 100 meters (300 feet) beyond Waitomo Caves i-Site Visitor Centre* ☎ *0800/456–922* ⊕ *www.waitomocaves.co.nz* ✉ *Tours $35, $50 combo ticket with Aranui Cave, $69 combo with Ruakuri Cave, $93 for "three of the best" Waitomo, Aranui, and Ruakuri* ☉ *Tours daily every half hr 9–5; bookings not required.*

Ruakuri Cave was discovered several hundred years ago by a Māori hunting party and takes its name from the pack of wild dogs that used to inhabit the cave entrance—*rua* means "den" or "pit," and *kuri* means "dog." The cave's original entrance was an *urupa* (burial site) for Māori and is now left alone by visitors, who enter through a dramatic spiral "drum passage." Narrow passages, hidden streams, ancient rockfalls, glowworms, and an amazing variety of limestone formations feature in Ruakuri. The two-hour tours are limited to 15 people. They are the longest cave walking tours and are easily managed by people of reasonable fitness. ✉ *Tour groups meet at the Legendary Black Water Rafting Company, 585 Waitomo Caves Rd.* ☎ *0800/222–323* ⊕ *www.ruakuri.co.nz* ✉ *Tours $49, for combo options see Waitomo Glowworm Cave* ☉ *Tours daily at 9, 10, 11:30, 12:30, 1:30, 2:30, and 3:30; book in advance.*

On the Spellbound Tour, you visit **Spellbound and Te Ana o te Atua caves.** At Spellbound, a gentle raft ride passes through a magnificent glow-worm chamber, one that has been filmed by the BBC with Sir David Attenborough. Te Ana o te Atua (Cave of the Spirit) has been known to the Ngati Kinohaku people for centuries. On the walking tour, the highlights are limestone formations, fossils, and bones. The 3½-hour tours are limited to 12 people. ✉ *Tours leave from Waitomo Caves i-Site Visitor Centre, Waitomo Village* ☎ *0800/773–552* ⊕ *www. waitomospellbound.co.nz* 🎟 *Tours $55 adult, $20 child* ☉ *Five tours daily; book in advance.*

At **Aranui Cave,** eons of dripping water have sculpted a delicate garden of pink-and-white limestone. Keep an eye out for the resident cave wetas! The cave is named after a local, Te Rutuku Aranui, who discovered the cave in 1910 when his dog disappeared inside in pursuit of a wild pig. Tours (45 minutes) lead along boardwalks into tall, narrow chambers. Tickets must be purchased from the Waitomo Glowworm Cave, before meeting at Aranui. ✉ *Entrance at Ruakuri Reserve, on Tumutumu Rd., 3 km (2 mi) beyond Waitomo Caves Village* ☎ *0800/773–552* ⊕ *www. waitomocaves.co.nz* 🎟 *Tours $32, $50 combo ticket with Waitomo Glowworm Cave* ☉ *Several tours daily; book in advance.*

One of the most interesting short walks in the country is at the **Waitomo Walkway.** The 5-km (3-mi), approximately 2½-hour walk begins across the road from the i-Site and follows the Waitomo River. The relatively easy track passes through forests and impressive limestone outcrops. You walk back to Waitomo Caves Village on the same path, or you can follow the road, a distance of just over 2 km (1 mi). For a shorter alternative, take Te Anga Road from the village, turn left onto Tumutumu Road, park at Ruakuri Reserve, and walk the final section (about 30 minutes) of the track. Two natural rock tunnels are on the way. Many people come after dusk for a free view of the local glowworms; bring a flashlight to find your way.

OFF THE BEATEN PATH

Te Anga–Marokopa Road. This classic backcountry road works its way west out of Waitomo toward the coast. It makes for a spectacular detour—or a long scenic drive to Taranaki—winding past stunning vistas. If the weather is clear, **Haggas Lookout,** 7 km (4 mi) from Waitomo, has an expansive view that extends southward to the volcano mountains of Tongariro National Park. Some 26 km (16 mi) from Waitomo, stop at the **Mangapohue Natural Bridge** (pronounced mang-ah-po-*hoo*-ay). From the parking area, there are two approaches to the bridge. One to the right climbs over a hill, dropping into a valley strewn with boulders embedded with oyster fossils—the remains of a seismic shift that thrust up the seabed millions of years ago. The natural bridge rises off the left of the boulders. The other path follows a stream through a gorge it has carved out. The gorge walls climb ever higher until they meet and form the bridge that closes over the path. The circular walk—going out on one path, returning on the other—takes only 15 to 20 minutes. A note of caution: carry your valuables such as wallet and passport with you, and keep luggage in your vehicle out of sight.

About 5 km (3 mi) farther along the road from the Mangapohue Bridge to Marokopa, **Piripiri Caves** beckon with their interesting fossil legacy—the marks of giant oysters from the area's onetime subaqueous existence. The approach and entrance to the caves are steep and slippery, so wear appropriate shoes or boots, and bring a jacket for the cool air and a powerful flashlight to cut through the gloom. There are no guided tours; just follow the trail markers. A few kilometers farther still, you can view the 120-foot **Marokopa Falls** from a viewpoint reached via a pleasant forest trail (about 15 minutes round-trip).

Just beyond Marokopa Falls, **Te Anga Tavern** is a good place for refreshments and to meet the locals. It's open daily 2–10:30 for drinks, and serves basic dinners—fish-and-chips, steak, and salad—Friday and Saturday nights. Pool tables are only 50¢ a game!

The road splits at Te Anga, heading north to Kawhia or southwest for 14 km (9 mi) to the small hamlet of **Marokopa,** where there's a stupendous lookout point over the coast's black-sand beaches. At Marokopa you are 50 km (31 mi) from Waitomo; time either to turn back or keep on south on a more difficult (mostly gravel) but very scenic route to the Taranaki region. If you're in for the duration, fill up your gas tank before turning off SH1 for Waitomo.

SPORTS & THE OUTDOORS

Several companies offer an initially confusing range of adventures. Each company has its own booking office and base, but activities can also be booked through the **Waitomo i-Site Visitor Information Centre** (⊠ *Waitomo Caves Rd., Waitomo Village* ☎*07/878–7640* ⊕ *www. waitomo-museum.co.nz*). This free service gives unbiased advice and information about which tours are most suitable.

CAVE
ADVENTURES Most of Waitomo's subterranean adventure tours involve black-water rafting—that is, floating through the underground caverns on inflated inner tubes, dressed in wet suits and equipped with cavers' helmets. Be prepared for the pitch-black darkness and freezing cold water. Your reward is an exhilarating trip gliding through vast glowworm-lighted caverns, clambering across rocks, and jumping over waterfalls. Some tours involve steep rappelling and tight underground squeezes.

★ Most adventurous types will handle the basic trip, "Black Labyrinth," offered by **the Legendary Black Water Rafting** (⊠*585 Waitomo Caves Rd.* ☎*07/878–6219 or 0800/228–464* ⊕*www.blackwaterrafting.co.nz*). Trips finish with welcome hot showers and a mug of soup back at base. The cost is $95 per person for three hours, $185 per person for "Black Abyss" (five hours), and includes free admission to the Museum of Caves. Departure times vary, depending on demand. It's a physical and emotional challenge, with great guides and underground scenery. It can also be scary. Thrill seekers might prefer to venture out with **Rap, Raft 'n' Rock** (⊠*95 Waitomo Cave Rd.* ☎*0800/228–372* ⊕*www.caveraft. com*), which has a 4½-hour combo adventure that includes rappelling, black-water rafting, rock climbing, caving, and checking out the glowworms. The trips cost $125 per person.

HORSEBACK RIDING Take a ride by horseback through the limestone and fossilized countryside with **Waitomo Caves Horse Treks** (☎07/878–5065). The price is $60 for two hours, or $150 for a full day (by arrangement).

WHERE TO STAY

$$
Fodor's Choice
★

Abseil Breakfast Inn. When hosts John and Helen say they treat you better than family, they are not joking (though beware their quirky senses of humor). This delightful B&B property overlooks the green Waitomo countryside and resounds with birdsong on the outside and conviviality within. Four rooms, each tastefully decorated to a local theme (Farm, Cave Room, Bush, and Swamp), have super-queen beds and an entrance from the deck; one has a two-person bathtub. Some excellent New Zealand wines are available at reasonable prices in a trusting self-service, pay-later system. The breakfasts are seriously good. The story goes that John bought the inn as a present for Helen. Now he says it was really an excuse for him to augment his beloved wine cellar. A complimentary bottle of wine comes with a stay of two days or longer. **Pros:** Quirky, helpful hosts; John's big breakfasts; comfy themed rooms. **Con:** Not for those who like big impersonal hotels. ⊠ *Waitomo Caves Rd.* ☎*07/878–7815* ⊕*www.abseilinn.co.nz* ⇨*4 rooms* ⚬*In-room: no TV* ☰*MC, V* ☒*Closed June* ⦿*BP.*

¢–$$

Kiwi Paka Youth Hostel. This relaxed hostel is in the heart of Waitomo village—a couple of minutes' walk from the Waitomo Glowworm Caves. Drawing on the area's rural vernacular, the design is a deliberate cross between New Zealand's archetypal red corrugated wool sheds (for shearing sheep) and ski chalets. You can either stay in the communal rooms with shared or private bathrooms or opt for a chalet. The rooms and chalets share a well-equipped kitchen. The staff provides gumboots and flashlights for exploring the caves, and they organize other activities. The decks overlook the bush at the on-site Morepork Pizzeria and Café, which serves breakfast, lunch, and dinner. **Pros:** Great pizzas, spacious bush and rural setting. **Con:** Helps to be a youth. ⊠*School Rd.* ☎*07/878–3395* 🖷*07/878–3396* ⊕*www.kiwipaka-yha. co.nz* ⇨*22 rooms with shared bath, 2 rooms with private bath, 20 chalets* ⚬*In-room: no phone, kitchen, no TV. In-hotel: restaurant, bar, laundry facilities, public Internet, no elevator* ☰*MC, V.*

TOURS

Newmans has a one-way bus tour from Auckland to the Waitomo Caves and on to Rotorua, or from Rotorua to the Waitomo Caves, ending in Auckland, including a brief stop at a historic battle site, a presentation on warriors, and admission to the Waitomo Caves. You'll be picked up at your Auckland accommodation and dropped at your Rotorua accommodation, or vice versa. The cost is $130 per person. You can also do a one-day round-trip from Auckland for $138.

Contact **Newmans** (☎*09/913–6200* ⊕*www.newmanscoach.co.nz*).

NEW PLYMOUTH & TARANAKI

On a clear winter day, with a cover of snow, Mt. Taranaki (officially, Mt. Egmont) towers above its flat rural surroundings and seems to draw the sky right down to the sea. No less astonishing in other seasons, the solitary peak is similar in appearance to Japan's Mt. Fuji. It is the icon of the Taranaki region, and the province has shaped itself around the mountain. Northeast of Taranaki, the provincial seat of New Plymouth huddles between the monolith and a rugged coastline, and smaller towns dot the road that circles the mountain's base.

Taranaki is one of New Zealand's fastest-growing tourism destinations, and for many visitors, Mt. Taranaki and surrounding Egmont National Park are the major draws. You can climb the mountain (a steep and serious challenge in winter, requiring climbing expertise), hike around the lower slopes, enjoy short forest walks to streams and waterfalls, or even spend the night.

The Taranaki region is one of the most successful agricultural areas in the country, because of the layers of volcanic ash that have created superb free-draining topsoil and the mountainous coastal position that ensures abundant rainfall. What serves farmers serves gardeners as well. Some of the country's most magnificent gardens grow in the rich local soil, and the annual Rhododendron Festival, held late in the year, celebrates the area's horticultural excellence.

This festival and other events, such as the Taranaki International Arts Festival, WOMAD (World of Music, Art, and Dance), Parihaka Peace Festival, ITU World Triathlon, and other international sporting competitions, and a regular calendar of top international performers who love appearing in the unique Bowl of Brooklands in Pukekura Park, add immensely to the area's attractions.

Taranaki has plenty of other ground-level delights. By the water's edge—along the so-called Surf Highway (Highway 45)—you can surf, swim, and fish. Several museums delve into Taranaki history, which is particularly rich on the subject of the Māori.

GETTING AROUND

You could take in most of the area in a couple of days, but that will keep you on the run. Just getting from place to place around the mountain takes time. Most people use New Plymouth as a base, though Stratford and south Taranaki also have comfortable accommodations, and there are lodges, B&Bs, motels, backpacker hostels, and holiday parks spread throughout the region. The roads in this region are generally in good condition. If you're traveling west on a sunny afternoon, watch out for strong glare from the setting sun.

Buses arrive at and depart from the New Plymouth Travel Centre on Queen Street. There is no regular public transportation to Mt. Taranaki, though shuttle-bus services are available to destinations such as North Egmont Visitor Centre and Stratford's Mountain House—call the New Plymouth Travel Centre for details. Taranaki Tours has shuttles from New Plymouth to Mt. Taranaki and Egmont National Park, from $40

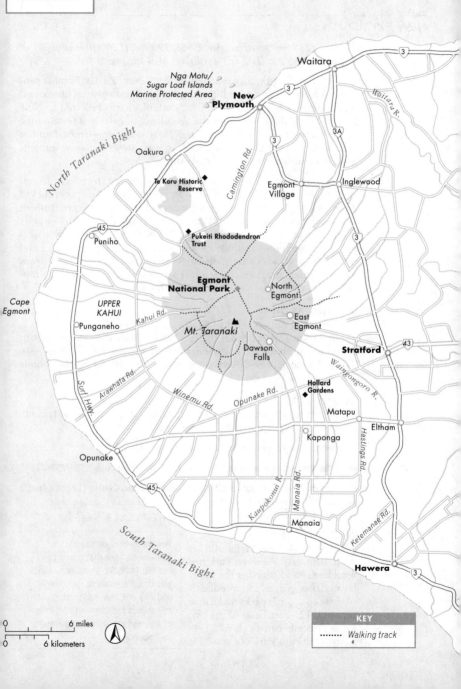

Taranaki

Nga Motu/
Sugar Loaf Islands
Marine Protected Area

New Plymouth

Waitara

3

Oakura

North Taranaki Bight

Camington Rd.

3A

Te Koru Historic
Reserve

Egmont
Village

Inglewood

45

Puniho

Pukeiti Rhododendron
Trust

**Egmont
National Park**

North
Egmont

Cape
Egmont

*UPPER
KAHUI*

Kahui Rd.

East
Egmont

Punganeho

Mt. Taranaki

Dawson
Falls

Stratford

43

Arawhata Rd.

Winemu Rd.

Opunake Rd.

Surf Hwy.

Hollard
Gardens

Waingongoro R.

Matapu

Eltham

Kaponga

Hastings Rd.

Opunake

45

Kaupokonui R.

Manaia Rd.

Ketemarae Rd.

South Taranaki Bight

Manaia

Hawera

3

0   6 miles

0   6 kilometers

KEY
⋯⋯⋯ *Walking track*

round-trip. **Taranaki Tours** (☎06/757–9888 or 0800/886–877 ⊕www.taranakitours.com).

NEW PLYMOUTH

375 km (235 mi) south of Auckland, 190 km (120 mi) southwest of Waitomo, 163 km (102 mi) northwest of Wanganui.

New Plymouth is the city that serves one of New Zealand's most productive dairy regions as well as the gas and oil industries. This natural wealth translates into an optimistic outlook that is reflected in New Plymouth's healthy arts scene, the abundance of cafés and restaurants, and a lifestyle that maximizes the great outdoors—from Egmont National Park, with Mt. Taranaki at its heart, to the extensive gardens and parklands, and the world-class surf beaches.

Before the arrival of Europeans in 1841, several *pā* (fortified villages) were in the vicinity. In the mid-1800s, European land disputes racked Taranaki. An uneasy formal peace was made between the government and local Māori tribes in 1881, and New Plymouth began to form its current identity. On the edge of the Tasman Sea, today's city is second to its surroundings, but its few surviving colonial buildings and extensive parklands merit a half-day's exploration. The cafés and stores along the main drag, Devon Street (East and West), provide as cosmopolitan an experience as you'll find this far west.

GETTING AROUND

New Plymouth Airport (NPL) (⊠192 Airport Dr. ☎06/755–0500) is about 12 km (7½ mi) from the city center. Taxis wait at the airport; expect to pay about $25 to get into town. **Withers Coachlines** (☎06/751–1777) runs a door-to-door shuttle service for $15 per person; phone ahead to book.

ESSENTIALS

Bus Depots **New Plymouth Bus Stop** (⊠19 Ariki St., City Center). **New Plymouth Travel Centre** (⊠32 Queen St. ☎06/759–9039).

Emergencies **Fire, police, and ambulance** (☎111).

Hospital **Taranaki Base Hospital** (⊠David St., New Plymouth ☎06/753–6139).

Visitor Info **New Plymouth i-Site Visitor Information Centre** (⊠Puke Ariki, 1 Ariki St ☎06/759–6060 ☎06/759–6072 ⊕www.newplymouthnz.com).

WHAT TO SEE

The jewels of New Plymouth are most definitely **Pukekura Park and Brooklands Park.** Together the valley lawns, lakes, groves, and woodlands of these connected parks make up a tranquil, 121-acre heart of the city. From December through mid-February, **Pukekura Park** comes to life

---

THE FICKLE SKIES

The weather is constantly in flux—locals joke that if you can't see Mt. Taranaki, it's raining, and if you can, it's going to rain. Day in and day out, this meteorological mix makes for stunning contrasts of sun and clouds on and around the mountain.

at night with the stunning summer Festival of Lights. Special lighting effects transform the gardens and giant trees into children's (and big children's) delight, and there's free entertainment most evenings. Pukekura has water running throughout; hire a rowboat (from near the lakeside café) and explore the small islands and nooks and crannies of the main lake. The park also has a fernery—caverns carved out of the hillside that connect through fern-cloaked tunnels—and botanical display houses.

Brooklands Park, on Brooklands Road, was once a great estate, laid out in 1843 around the house of Captain Henry King, New Plymouth's first magistrate. Today, Brooklands is best known for its amazing variety of trees, mostly planted in the second half of the 19th century. Giant copper beeches, pines, walnuts, and oaks, and the Monterey pine, magnolia *soulangeana*, ginkgo, and native *karaka* and *kohekohe* are all the largest of their kind in New Zealand. Take a walk along the outskirts of the park on tracks leading through native, subtropical bush. This area has been relatively untouched for the last few thousand years, and 1,500-year-old trees are not uncommon. A *puriri* tree near the Somerset Street entrance—one of 20 in the park—is believed to be more than 2,000 years old.

For a reminder of colonial days, visit Brooklands former hospital, the **Gables,** built in 1847, which now serves as an art gallery. Brooklands has a rhododendron dell and the very popular Bowl of Brooklands, a stadium used for a variety of concerts and events. ⊠ *Park entrances on Brooklands Park Dr. and Liardet, Somerset, and Rogan Sts.* ☎ *06/758–9311* 🖼 *Free* ☉ *Daily dawn–dusk; restaurant Wed.–Mon. dawn–dusk; display houses daily 8:30–4.*

To get a feel for the city, take a stroll or rent a bike and ride along the **New Plymouth Coastal Walkway.** This path runs alongside the city for 7 km (4 mi) from Port Taranaki to Lake Rotomanu and leads past four of the city's beaches, three rivers, four playgrounds, the Aquatic Centre, a golf course, a skating park, and numerous food vendors. You also pass under the *Wind Wand,* a sculpture almost as iconic to New Plymouth residents as the *Statue of Liberty* is to New Yorkers. Created by the late New Zealand artist Len Lye, the red carbon fiber tube stands 45 meters (147 feet) high and, like a conductor's baton, dances in the wind as Lye's tribute to what he called "tangible motion."

Across the road from the *Wind Wand* is **Puke Ariki,** the region's heritage, research, and information center. Though not as large as Wellington's Museum of New Zealand, Te Papa Tongarewa, its displays tell compelling stories of the region, from the Land Wars, to the discovery of natural oil and gas in 1959, to today's surfing culture. Interactive science exhibits for children are on the lower level. The café is worth a stop, too, as the presence of many locals will tell you. ⊠ *Puke Ariki Landing, St. Aubyn St.* ☎ *06/759–6060* ⊕ *www.pukeariki.com* 🖼 *Free* ☉ *Mon., Tues., Thurs., and Fri. 9–6, Wed. 9–9, weekends 9–5.*

The **Govett-Brewster Art Gallery** is one of New Zealand's leading modern art museums. The gallery has a strong collection of New Zealand conceptual art produced in the 1970s, abstract art from the '70s and '80s, and contemporary sculpture. It is also the home of the internationally acclaimed Len Lye collection and has visiting exhibitions from abroad. ✉42 Queen St., at King St. ☎06/759–6060 ⊕www.govettbrewster. com ⊠Free ⊙Daily 10:30–5; café daily 8–4.

There are 35 **Gardens of National Significance** in New Zealand, and 9 are in Taranaki. The rainfall and fertile volcanic-ash soils provide excellent growing conditions, in particular for rhododendrons and azaleas, which are celebrated each year during the Taranaki Rhododendron and Garden Festival. During the festival, these splendid gardens and their colorful profusions are open to the public. Some are open throughout the year, such as Pukerua Park, Pukeiti Rhododendron Trust, and **Hollard Gardens** (⇨Stratford, below). Others are open by appointment outside festival time. Most of these gardens are the labors of love of their private owners, whereas the Taranaki Regional Council supports the development of publicly owned gardens. A brochure listing these gardens is available from i-Site visitor centers in New Plymouth, Stratford and Hawera. Or contact the **Taranaki Regional Council** (☎06/765–7127 🖷06/765–5097 ✐regional.gardens@tre.govt.nz).

★ The **Pukeiti Rhododendron Trust** spreads over 900 acres of lush native rain forest, surrounded by rich Taranaki farmland. The Pukeiti (poo-ke-*ee*-tee) collection of 2,500 varieties of rhododendrons is the largest in New Zealand. Many of the varieties were first grown here, such as the giant winter-blooming *R. protistum var. giganteum* Pukeiti, collected from seed in 1953 and now standing 15 feet tall—or the beautiful Lemon Lodge and Spring Honey hybrids that bloom in spring. Kyawi, a large red "rhodo" is the very last to bloom, in April (autumn). Rhododendrons aside, there are many other rare and special plants to enjoy at Pukeiti. All winter long the Himalayan daphnes fragrance the pathways. Spring-to-summer-growing candelabra primroses reach up to 4 feet, and for a month around Christmas, spectacular 8-foot Himalayan *cardiocrinum* lilies bear heavenly scented 12-inch white trumpet flowers. This is also a wonderful bird habitat. Pukeiti is 20 km (12½ mi) southwest of New Plymouth's center. ✉2290 Carrington Rd. ☎06/752–4141 ⊕www.pukeiti.org.nz ⊠$8 ⊙Oct.–Mar., daily 9–5; Apr.–Sept., daily 10–3.

To get a sense of the turbulent history in Taranaki, drive through the countryside inland from Oakura to **Te Koru Historic Reserve**. A Department of Conservation track leads ½ km (about ¼ mi) to the site of the pā (fortified village), a former stronghold of the Nga Mahanga a Tairi *hapū* (subtribe). Regenerating native forest has covered part of the site, but still visible are the main defensive ditch and stone-wall terraces that drop a considerable way from the highest part of the pā to the Oakura River. No facilities are at the reserve, just a pleasant picnic area. Take Highway 45 southwest out of New Plymouth to the beach suburb of Oakura, 17 km (10 mi) away. Just past Oakura turn left onto Wairau Road and follow the signs to the parking lot, which is 3.7 km (2½ mi) from the turnoff. ☎06/759–0350 Department of Conservation ⊠Free ⊙Daily dawn–dusk.

Taranaki–Waitomo. Mt. Taranaki is an ever-receding presence in your rearview mirror as you head northeast up the Taranaki coast from New Plymouth on Highway 3. The highway provides the most direct route to Waitomo Caves and Hamilton, turning inland at Awakino, 90 km (56 mi) from New Plymouth. The Awakino Gorge, between Mahoenui and the coast, is particularly appealing. Forest-filled scenic reserves are interspersed with stark, limestone outcrops and verdant farmland, where sheep have worn trails that hang on the sides of precipitous green hills. At the mouth of the Awakino River, little whitebaiting shacks dot the river's edge. **Awakino** is worth a stop, either at the family-oriented country hotel or for a rest at the river mouth. Turn off the main road by the hotel for a lovely sheltered picnic spot beneath the summer flowering *pohutukawa* trees. A little farther along is **Mokau**, with a couple of little cafés where, if the whitebait are running, delicious whitebait fritters can be on the menu September to November.

From Awakino, you could be in Waitomo within the hour if you stick to the main highway, but if time is not your master a far more adventurous route is to follow the minor road north, at the turnoff just beyond Awakino. This runs for 58 km (36 mi) to Marokopa *(*⇨ *Waitomo Caves in the Waikato and Waitomo, above)*. It's a gravel road for the most part, but a reasonable trip, provided you take care and remember to keep left especially on blind corners. The drive is through attractive sheep country, passing through the Manganui Gorge, and with a possible 4-km (2½-mi) detour down the Waikawau Road to the stunningly isolated Waikawau Beach. The sweep of black sand here, backed by high cliffs, is reached through a hand-dug drover's tunnel. Total driving time from Awakino to Marokopa, including a picnic stop, is about three hours, plus another hour from Marokopa to Waitomo.

OUTDOOR ACTIVITIES

BEACHES Coastal waters can be quite wild, so it's wise to swim at patrolled beaches. The beaches have black sand and rocky outcrops, which make for interesting rock-pool exploring. In summer, *pohutakawa* trees provide shade in some spots; otherwise bring plenty of sunblock. **Fitzroy Beach** has lifeguards in summer and is easily accessible from New Plymouth, just 1½ km (¾ mi) from the city center. The adjoining **East End Beach** also has lifeguards. **Ngamotu Beach,** along Ocean View Parade, is calm and suitable for young children.

BICYCLING Line up a rental bike with **Cycle Inn** (✉ *133 Devon St.* ☎ *06/758–7418*) to ride the New Plymouth Coastal Walkway. They've got touring bikes with helmets at $10 for a half day, $15 for a full day.

BOATING & A launch with **Happy Chaddy's Charters** (✉ *Ocean View Parade*
KAYAKING ☎ *06/758–9133* ⊕ *www.windwand.co.nz/chaddiescharters*) starts with the guide announcing, "Hold on to your knickers, because we're about to take off." Then the old English lifeboat rocks back and forth in its shed (with you on board), slides down its rails, and hits the sea with a spray of water. The trip ($30 adults $10 under 12) lasts an hour, during which you'll see seals, get a close-up view of the Nga Motu/ Sugar Loaf Islands just offshore from New Plymouth, and have a laugh

5

CLOSE UP

Nga Motu & the Sugar Loaf Islands

About 17,000 seabirds nest in the Nga Motu/Sugar Loaf Islands Marine Protected Area. Shearwaters, petrels, terns, penguins, shags, and herons, some of them threatened species (the reef heron is one), nest and feed on and around these little islands. The islands are also a breeding colony and hauling grounds for New Zealand fur seals; in winter more than 400 seals congregate here. Dolphins and orca and pilot whales frequent the waters around the islands, and humpback whales migrate past in August and September.

Beneath the water's surface, caves, crevices, boulder fields, and sand flats, together with the merging of warm and cool sea currents, support a wealth of marine life. More than 80 species of fish have been recorded here, along with jewel and striped anemones, sponges, and rock

lobsters. The diving is fabulous; visibility is best in summer and autumn (up to 20 meters [65 feet]). Contact **New Plymouth Underwater** (✉ *16 Hobson St.* 🕾 *06/758-3348* ⊕ *www. newplymouthunderwater.co.nz*). On land, more than 80 different native plant species survive on the islands. Cook's scurvy grass, almost extinct on the mainland, grows on two of the islands. The palatable species is rich in vitamin C and was sought by early sailors to treat scurvy.

The best way to appreciate these islands is by boat. Landing is restricted, but kayaking and chartered launch trips leave regularly from New Plymouth. Nga Motu/Sugar Loaf Islands are managed by the **Department of Conservation** (✉ *220 Devon St. W, New Plymouth* 🕾 *06/759-0350*).

with skipper and character Happy Chaddy. You can also charter a boat for a fishing trip ($60 per person, minimum six people); these start at 7 AM to avoid choppy water. **Canoe & Kayak Taranaki** (✉ *631 Devon Rd., Waikwakiho* 🕾 *06/769-5506* ⊕ *www.canoeandkayak.co.nz*) has a range of guided trips, lasting from a couple of hours to a couple of days. One popular kayak tour goes to the Sugar Loaf Islands Marine Park ($50 per person [minimum two], three hours).

SURFING Not for nothing is the coastal road between New Plymouth and Hawera known as the **Surf Highway.** Virtually any beach en route has consistently good waves. Fitzroy and East End (⇨ *Beaches, above*) are both popular with surfers, as are **Back Beach** and **Bell Block Beach.** The favored surf beach by those in the know is at **Oakura,** a village 17 km (10 mi) southwest of New Plymouth teeming with cafés and crafts shops as well as good surf.

Beach Street Surf Shop (✉ *30 Beach Rd.* 🕾 *06/758-0400* ⊕ *www. lostinthe60s.com*) is run by local legend Wayne Arthur, who'll give you the lowdown on the hot surf spots in Taranaki. The shop rents equipment and organizes lessons for beginners and advanced surfers. **Taranaki Tours** (🕾 *06/757-9888 or 0800/886-877* ⊕ *www.taranaki tours.com*) takes experienced surfers on half-day trips to the best breaks of the day (and offers various other tours with cultural, scenic, heritage, or garden focus). At Oakura Beach, accredited surf coach and former

American surf team member Heather Dent runs **Surf School Taranaki** (☎06/752–8283). To try riding a wave with a professional surfer on a tandem surfboard ($80), contact **Hang 20—Tandem Surf Taranaki** (✉27 *Mace St., Oakura* ☎06/752–7734).

WHERE TO EAT

$$$–$$$$ ✕**L'Escargot Restaurant and Bar.** New Plymouth's oldest commercial building houses what many consider the town's finest restaurant. The menu updates classic southern French cuisine like French burgundy snails stuffed in button mushrooms with herb butter or blue-cheese sauce; or half-cured beef Provençal, or classic salade niçoise. White linens contrast pleasingly with dark-wood decor. The intimate dining room seats 50, and the mezzanine area 20. Top French, New Zealand, and Australian wines are available. ✉*37–43 Brougham St.* ☎*06/758–4812* ⊟*AE, DC, MC, V* ☉ *Closed Sun. Lunch by arrangement only.*

$$$ ✕**Macfarlanes Cafe.** This lively place energizes the café scene in Inglewood, a town midway between New Plymouth and Stratford. It's the original outlet of the Macfarlanes Group, which operates several small espresso bars, the café at Puke Ariki, and the Ozone coffee roastery in New Plymouth. All-day breakfasts from 9 AM include the hearty Farmer's Breakfast. Lunches feature fresh salads and pastas. The evening dinner menu is international with a New Zealand inflection, and changes with the seasons. A signature dish is Macfarlanes rib eye with gratin potatoes and garlic spinach, smoked mushrooms, sundried tomato pesto, hollandaise, and red wine jus. ✉*Kelly and Matai Sts., Inglewood* ✛*20 km (12½ mi) east of New Plymouth* ☎*06/756–6665* ⊕*www.macfarlanes. co.nz* ⊟*AE, DC, MC, V* ☉*No dinner Sun.–Wed. (closes at 5 PM).*

FodorsChoice ★

$–$$ ✕**Ultra Lounge.** This funky laid-back bar has white leather booths, big windows for street watching, a courtyard and cocktail bar. It's popular with locals for its good coffee, all-day breakfasts, and light meals such as lamb shanks or roast pumpkin with feta cheese. At night, stop in for dinner, cocktails, or dessert and coffee; most weekends a DJ plays downbeat grooves. Open 8:30 AM to 1 AM Tuesday–Sunday. ✉*Devon St. E* ☎*06/758–8444* ⊟*AE, DC, MC, V.*

¢–$ ✕**Empire.** This sedate café serves excellent espressos but is best known for its huge range of loose-leaf teas, a heady selection that includes jasmine, rose, sunflowers, and calendula flowers, and mixes such as "Cooletta," a refreshing and fruity blend of rosehip, hibiscus, papaya, blackberry leaves, and mango. Food includes a full breakfast menu, bagels served all day, filled rolls, crepes, and salads, and the Empire's signature two-in-a-bowl soup, its flavors changing according to the weather. Vegetarian and gluten-free options are available. ✉*112 Devon St. W* ☎*06/758–1148* ⊟*AE, MC, V* ☉*Closed Sun. No dinner.*

WHERE TO STAY

$$$ ⊡ **Nice Hotel & Table.** Local entrepreneur and now attentive host Terry Parkes transformed this 19th-century hospital into an opulent city-center retreat. Modern art, including works by leading Taranaki artists Don Driver, Tom Kriesler, and Michael Smither, lines the walls, and the chic guest rooms and opulent suites come complete with double whirl-pool baths or massage showers. The bistro, Table ($$–$$$), is regarded as one of the city's best, and has been the recipient of many local

FodorsChoice ★

5

restaurant awards. The menu changes seasonally to emphasize fresh, local fare but is likely to feature delicious presentations of salmon, duck, eye fillet of beef, and perhaps ostrich or rabbit. Individual tastes are catered to: vegetarian, gluten-free, dairy free, and so on; current menus are on the hotel's Web site. The wine list features New Zealand's best varieties. But before you drink, Terry might let you take a hotel bike for a spin to drink in the city's shoreline. **Pros:** Small, intimate ambience; artwork; the house restaurant. **Con:** Bookings a must for the hotel and the restaurant. ⊠ *71 Brougham St.* ☎ *06/758–6423* 🖶 *06/758–6433* ⊕ *www.nicehotel.co.nz* 🛏 *7 rooms, 2 suites* ♿ *In-room: Ethernet. In-hotel: restaurant, airport shuttle, no elevator* ▤ *AE, DC, MC, V.*

$$–$$$
Fodor's Choice
★

🔲 **Ahu Ahu Beach Villas.** A magical place to stay, on coastal farmland just above the beach, this property, with five rustic villas (each sleeps four), has magnificent sea views: you can catch the moon rise over the ocean horizon. The villas are made of recycled materials, including 100-year-old French clay tiles and hardwood wharf piles. The latest addition is a spectacular "underground" villa that's built against the bank and has a grassed roof and dramatic view. Inside there are two queen-size double beds and enough space to host a small party. A dial-up Internet connection is shared between villas. The owners can provide breakfast supplies, or you can drive five minutes to Oakura Village, which has a renowned surf beach. The villas are about a 15-minute drive south of New Plymouth. **Pros:** Dramatic coastal outlook; recycled, zany design. **Con:** A drive to town. ⊠ *321 Ahu Ahu Rd., Surf Hwy. 45, Oakura* ☎ *06/752–7370* ⊕ *www.ahu.co.nz* 🛏 *5 villas* ♿ *In-room: no a/c, kitchen. In-hotel: laundry facilities, public Internet* ▤ *MC, V.*

$$

🔲 **The Waterfront.** Stylish and modern, this is New Plymouth's only waterfront lodging. And it's handily next to the Puke Ariki Museum and the information center. Each room has sea or city views. Configurations range from studios with showers (no tubs), to elite studios with individual whirlpool baths, to the Penthouse Suite with separate bedroom, double whirlpool bath, shower, full laundry and kitchen facilities, and other options in between. All rooms have super-king or queen beds. Salt ($$$), the restaurant and bar, feels almost minimalist, all the better to appreciate the beach vista, the walkway, and the 45-meter (148-foot) flexible statue *Wind Wand* by Len Lye across the road. Have a traditional Kiwi breakfast as you read the morning paper. For dinner, seafood features high on the menu; a favorite is the pan-seared scallops with a sweet chili-ginger sauce. **Pros:** The beach, Puke Ariki Museum, city right next door, good restaurant. **Cons:** Can't complain. ⊠ *1 Egmont St.* ☎ *06/769–5301* 🖶 *06/769–5302* ⊕ *www.waterfront.co.nz* 🛏 *42 rooms, 3 suites* ♿ *In-room: no a/c (some), refrigerator, Ethernet* ▤ *AE, DC, MC, V.*

$–$$

🔲 **Devon Hotel.** This hotel is easy to find, just a short drive (or 20-minute walk) north of the city center. The standard rooms have bathrooms with showers (no tubs); they are on the small side, but look out over a pretty internal courtyard. The larger rooms are better equipped (with refrigerators, minibars, and whirlpool baths) and have either sea or mountain views, though those at the front face a busy main road. Marbles, the hotel's Roman-theme restaurant, serves a buffet breakfast and an à la carte dinner. There is a superb heated pool, a hot tub, and a garden, and the hotel has just completed a major refurbishment. **Pro:** Heated pool. **Con:** Beside a busy road. ✉ *390 Devon St. E* ☎ *06/759–9099* 📠 *06/758-2229* ⊕ *www.devonhotel.co.nz* 🛏 *110 rooms* ⚘ *In-room: no a/c, refrigerator (some), dial-up. In-hotel: restaurant, bar, pool, public Internet, no-smoking rooms* ⊟ *AE, DC, MC, V.*

¢ 🏠 **Shoestring Backpackers.** Within walking distance of New Plymouth's main shops and cafés, this lovely old home has spacious rooms and a welcoming staff. Two dorms each sleep four; rooms come with one double bed, two single beds, or one single bed. All rooms share bathrooms, but there are plenty to go around. There's an outdoor veranda, a communal kitchen, and, in winter, a cozy fire in the lounge. A small private lawn out the back is suitable for tents. **Pros:** Cozy lounge, lots of books to read, friendly hosts. **Con:** Shared bathrooms. ✉ *48 Lemon St.* ☎ *06/758-0404* ⊕ *www.shoestring.co.nz* 🛏 *13 rooms, 2 dorms (8 beds) with shared bath* ⚘ *In-room: no a/c, no phone, no TV. In-hotel: laundry facilities, public Internet* ⊟ *AE, MC, V.*

NIGHTLIFE

The younger, louder set will be happiest at **55** (✉ *55a Egmont St.* ☎ *06/759–0997*), open until 5 AM Thursday–Saturday. If you fancy good live music in a full-on Celtic bar, **Peggy Gordon's Celtic Bar** (✉ *Egmont and Devon Sts.* ☎ *06/758–8561*) is the place to go. Wednesday and Thursday are quiz nights; Thursday through Saturday brings live music in a range of genres. Lunch and dinner are served every day: signature dishes are beef-and-Guinness stew with dumplings, Irish seasoned beef, and Flanaghan's fish-and-chips; gourmet pizzas are good, too. It's open seven days a week. If a classy cocktail is more your thing, the modern, minimalist **Powder Room** (✉ *108 Devon St.* ☎ *07/759–2089*) can oblige. It's open Tuesday–Saturday 4 PM–3 AM.

SHOPPING

Devon Street, which runs from Fitzroy in the east to Blagdon in the west, is New Plymouth's main shopping street.

For beautiful locally made arts and crafts with an edge, visit **Kina** (✉ *101 Devon St. W* ☎ *06/759–1201*), which exhibits the works of Taranaki artists and stocks contemporary design pieces, from jewelry to sculpture. **Trade Aid** (✉ *82 Devon St. E* ☎ *06/758–4228*) sells an eclectic mix of gift items from Asia, Africa, South America, and the Pacific. Boutique shop **Meyer & Prichard** (✉ *40 Powderham St.* ☎ *06/759–1360*) has the best selection of designer clothing in town, carrying leading New Zealand labels such as Karen Walker, World, and Yvonne Bennetti, plus exclusively imported shoes, one-off antique pieces, and a superb, in-store French-style café. If you're after some serious outdoor gear, check out **Taranaki Hardcore Surf Shop** (✉ *454 Devon St. E* ☎ *06/758–1757*), which stocks surf and snow wear and gear, plus the stylish "Taranaki" clothing label.

5

EGMONT NATIONAL PARK

Fodor'sChoice
★ *North Egmont Visitor Centre is 26 km (16 mi) south of New Plymouth; Dawson Falls Visitor Centre is 68 km (42 mi) southwest of New Plymouth.*

Mt. Taranaki dominates the landscape and Egmont National Park. The mountain rises 8,309 feet above sea level; it's difficult not to be drawn toward it. The lower reaches are cloaked in dense and mossy rain forests; above the tree line, lower-growing tussocks and subalpine shrubs cling to spectacularly steep slopes. The mountain's European name is Egmont; James Cook named it in 1770 after the Earl of Egmont, who supported his exploration. Both names are used today.

Mt. Taranaki is notorious for its ever-changing weather conditions, and the peak is often surrounded by a cloud. It may be sunny on the mountain one minute, but the next, rain sweeps in off the West Coast (the mountain is in one of the wettest areas in New Zealand). Bring appropriate gear. On a clear day, from even the mountain's lower slopes you can see the three mountains of Tongariro National Park in the central North Island—and sometimes even as far as the South Island. For more information about Egmont National Park, visit the Department of Conservation's site (⊕*www.doc.govt.nz*) and click on "National Parks."

The mountain is surrounded and protected by Egmont National Park. The three main roads to the mountain turn off State Highway 3 and are all well signposted. The first mountain turnoff, as you drive south from New Plymouth, is Egmont Road and leads to the start of many walking trails and the **North Egmont Visitor Centre**. Drop in to peruse the excellent displays and to learn about the mountain's history and the natural features of the park. There's also a café at the visitor center. The second road up the mountain (Pembroke Road) takes you to the Mountain House and, a little farther on, to **Stratford Plateau,** where there are stunning views. The third mountain turnoff (Manaia Road) leads to the southernmost visitor center, the **Dawson Falls Visitor Centre.** *For information on the hiking trails around and up the mountain, see Outdoor Activities, below.*

ESSENTIALS

Visitor Info **Dawson Falls Visitor Centre** (⊠*Manaia Rd. DR29, Kaponga, Hawera* ☏*027/443–0248*). **North Egmont Visitor Centre** (⊠*Egmont Rd.* ☏*06/756–0990*).

OUTDOOR ACTIVITIES

MOUNTAINEERING Mt. Taranaki is a potentially perilous mountain to climb; unpredictable weather and the upper slopes, with their sheer bluffs and winter ice, are an extremely dangerous combination. For more adventurous pursuits on the mountain, or for midwinter summit climbs, use a local guide. To the local Māori people, the mountain is sacred, regarded as an ancestor. They ask that climbers respect the spirituality and not clamber over the summit rocks.

Ross Eden, who has been mountaineering since the 1980s, is the head guide for **Top Guides** (☎ *0800/448–433* ⊕ *www.topguides.co.nz*). His organization guides adventurers in summit climbs, and instructs and guides in everything from abseiling to avalanche awareness, rock climbing, and bush walking. Daily climbing rates start at $250 for one person with one guide (a summit climb can be made in a day trip). Ian MacAlpine of **MacAlpine Guides** (☎ *06/751–3542 or 0274/417–042* ⊕ *www.macalpineguides.com*) has made more than 1,500 ascents of Mt. Taranaki and climbed in Nepal, India, and Antarctica. He guides individual and group climbs, and leads other outdoor pursuits ranging from bushwalking to abseiling to bridge swinging. Summit-climb daily rates are $250.

SKIING **Manganui** is the one small club-owned and -operated ski run on Mt. Taranaki. The club operates for up to 30 days each winter (June–October), and nonmembers can buy tow passes for a day. Facilities are limited, and the terrain is for intermediate and advanced skiers.

WALKING & HIKING **Egmont National Park** has more than 300 km (180 mi) of walking trails that lead around the mountain and across to the adjoining Pouakai Range, through dense forests, across the higher subalpine slopes, past waterfalls, across mountain streams, and beneath massive lava bluffs. There are signposted short walks, suitable for all ages, from each of the three main park access roads. For a taste of the scenery, the best of these are from the Dawson Falls Visitor Centre, where there are five popular options—each taking 1 to 2½ hours—including the easy walk to the 50-foot-high **Dawson Falls** themselves. In late summer, when there is usually no snow on the mountain, **summit ascents** are a popular challenge. The most straightforward route is from the North Egmont Visitor Centre and takes anywhere from 7 to 10 hours round-trip. You must be properly equipped, keeping in mind that the weather conditions change extremely quickly, and inform the visitor center of your plans.

For a multiday hiking trip, consider the **Pouakai Circuit**, which starts from the North Egmont Visitor Centre, climbs above the forest line, and crosses a huge wetland to the Pouakai Range, then returns through the lower, forested slopes of the mountain. The circuit is well signposted, and accommodation huts are at one-day intervals along the way, costing $10 for adults per night ($5 age 11 to 17). There are also budget bunkhouses at Dawson Falls ($20 per person per night) and North Egmont ($28 per person per night including bedding). Advance bookings for all hiking accommodation are essential; contact the park visitor centers.

WHERE TO STAY

$$$ ⬚**Dawson Falls Alpine Lodge.** On the southern slopes of Mt. Taranaki, this lodge has charming views of the coastline and native bush. With down-to-earth, New Zealand country hospitality in an old Swiss-style inn, you can unwind in front of a roaring fire or in the sauna or alpine plunge pool. The rooms, each with unique decoration, have wood paneling and carved and painted headboards. The Chalet bar and restau-

rant is an intimate space for a drink or to enjoy the daily three-course prix-fixe feast ($$$$) of traditional New Zealand country fare: soups, corned silverside, fish, or pork chops, with a host of accompanying vegetables, followed by dessert. Saturday nights are set aside for roast beef and Yorkshire pudding. **Pros:** Bush setting, waterfalls, birdsong. **Con:** Undergoing upgrade. ⊠*Manaia Rd. off Opunake Rd., Dawson Falls* ☎*06/765–5457* ⊕*www.dawson-falls.co.nz* ⬅*12 rooms* ⚘*In-room: no a/c. In-hotel: restaurant, bar, gym, laundry facilities, no elevator* ▭*AE, DC, MC, V* ⦿*BP, MAP.*

$$–$$$ ⊡ **Anderson's Alpine Lodge.** Beside the national park entrance is Berta Anderson's modern, purpose-built Swiss alpine-style B&B. The trio of rooms includes a deluxe Top Room, with glorious mountain views from a separate lounge area. The lodge has a log staircase, wood-burning fire, and wooden deck; the walls are decorated with paintings of Taranaki, talented works by Berta's late husband, Keith Anderson. **Pros:** Mountain view, Swiss-style lodge ambience, proximity to national park walks, hear kiwi calls at night. **Con:** Not for nature-haters. ⊠*922 Pembroke Rd., Stratford* ☎*06/765–6620* ▤*06/765–6100* ⬅*3 rooms* ⚘*In-room: no a/c. In-hotel: no-smoking rooms, no kids under 10, no elevator* ▭*AE, DC, MC, V* ⦿*CP.*

$$ ⊡ **Mountain House Motor Lodge.** High on Mt. Taranaki, this hotel, motel, and restaurant has a long-standing reputation for its dramatic setting and European-style restaurant. Trails from the lodge traverse the lower reaches of the mountain, through a mix of subalpine shrublands and dense forest, and the small ski club is a 10-minute drive and 20-minute walk away. Six rooms stand apart from the main building and are equipped with kitchenettes. The restaurant ($$$) menu has a good selection of vegetarian options, but the signature dishes are roast lamb shank with homemade Swiss spaetzle, and the tarragon-scented rabbit. **Pro:** Dramatic mountain views. **Con:** Undergoing upgrade. ⊠*Pembroke Rd., E. Egmont, Stratford* ☎*06/765–6100* ⬅*10 rooms* ⚘*In-room: no a/c. In-hotel: restaurant, bar, laundry facilities* ▭*AE, DC, MC, V.*

TOURS

FLIGHTSEEING TOURS   Helicopter and fixed-wing flights are a quick but spectacular way to enjoy views of Taranaki. Not surprisingly, the most popular flight is to the Mt. Taranaki summit (snow covered in winter, steep rocky peaks in summer). Heliview Taranaki offer helicopter flights ranging from five-minute scenic city spins to one-hour custom-designed itineraries taking in the charms of Mt. Taranaki, Pouakai Ranges, the surfing coast, plus waterfalls and bush of the Taranaki interior, including off-base stops at cafés, or breweries, or hidden beaches. Costs range from $45/person for five minutes, $120/per person for 15 minutes and summit view, $460/person for one hour (two-person minimum). Costs with Air New Plymouth (fixed-wing plane) are $88/person (three-person minimum). Beck Helicopters charges $225 per person for a 30-minute flight.

Contacts Heliview Taranaki ⊠*Pouakai Heliport, 1291 Carrington Rd.* ☎ *0508/435–484* toll-free ⊕*www.heliview.co.nz).* **Beck Helicopters** (⊠*Mountain Rd.* ☎*0800/336–644).* **Air New Plymouth** (⊠*New Plymouth Airport* ☎*06/755–0500* ⊕*www.airnewplymouth.co.nz).*

SIGHTSEEING
TOURS

Ann Olsen, who runs Just for You Tours, specializes in private guided tours for individuals or small groups. She'll plan an itinerary to suit your interests and budget, and she can take you well off the beaten track.

Taranaki Tours has an Around Mt. Taranaki Tour ($135 per person) that's a splendid introduction to the region. Knowledgeable Māori guides share the history, legend, and culture of Taranaki in this road trip that circumnavigates the mountain. Trips last six to seven hours, lunch included. The company also has garden tours.

Contacts Just for You Tours (☎ 06/751–2198 🖨 06/751–2180 ⊕ www.wind wand.co.nz/tjfu.htm). **Taranaki Tours** (☎ 06/757–9888 or 0800/886–877 ⊕ www. taranakitours.com).

STRATFORD

41 km (27 mi) southeast of New Plymouth.

The town of Stratford sits under the eastern side of Mt. Taranaki, and is a service town for surrounding farms. Its streets are named after characters from Shakespeare's works, and it has the first glockenspiel in New Zealand, which chimes four times a day. Because the town is at the junction of Highways 3 and 43, you'll likely pass through at some stage if exploring Taranaki. In the valley to the east are some of the country's most interesting private gardens.

ESSENTIALS

Visitor Info Stratford i-Site Visitor Information Centre (✉ Prospero Pl. ☎ 06/765–6708 or 0800/765–6708 ⊕ www.stratfordnz.co.nz).

WHAT TO SEE

Fodor$Choice
★

Surrounded by dairy farms, the **Hollard Gardens** were created by dairy farmer Bernard Hollard, who, in 1927, fenced a 14-acre patch of native bush on his farm and started what is now a Garden of National Significance. There are two distinctive sections, one an old woodland garden of mature native and exotic trees, with closely underplanted rhododendrons, azaleas, camellias, and perennials, the other a more recent creation. Broad lawns, paths with mixed borders, and vistas of Mt. Taranaki are features of the new garden, established in 1982. The gardens are particularly colorful during the rhododendron flowering season from September to late November. ✉ Upper Manaia Rd., off Opunake Rd., Kaponga ✛ 8 km (5 mi) south of Dawson Falls ☎ 06/765–7127 Taranaki Regional Council 🎟 Free 🕙 Daily 9–5.

■ OFF THE
BEATEN
PATH

Stratford–Taumarunui. Known as the Forgotten World Highway, Highway 43, heading northeast from Stratford, takes travelers on an intriguing, history-rich tour of Māori and colonial heritage as it winds through rolling farmland and pristine subtropical rain forests to Taumarunui (the northern access point for the Whanganui River region). Highlights on the way include Mt. Damper Falls, the spectacular view from Tahora Saddle, the dramatic Tangarakau Gorge, two road tunnels, and riverboat-landing sites. A must-stop for its fine food and warm, country hospitality is the **Whangamomona Hotel** (✉ 6018 Ohura Rd.

☎🏠06/762–5823). They offer hearty meals, and the kitchen is open from 11 AM until evenings for overnight guests and casual travelers. With 11 double or twin rooms (shared bathrooms) and a family-sized attic, the hotel sleeps up to 28. $100 gives you dinner, bed (with ironed sheets!), and breakfast. The 155-km (96-mi) highway is sealed for all but 11 km (7 mi). Allow three hours and fill your tank before leaving Stratford. For information contact the **Stratford i-Site Visitor Centre** (☎06/765–6708 or 0800/765–6708 ⊕*www.stratfordnz.co.nz*).

WHERE TO STAY

$$ 🏨**Te Popo.** On a back road northeast of Stratford, this peaceful homestead is magnificently set in one of Taranaki's Gardens of National Significance. *Tūī* (a native bird with a unique, melodic song), wood pigeons, bellbirds, and fantails visit the gardens year-round, and glowworms shine at dusk. The spacious guest rooms have wood-burning fireplaces and private garden views. Breakfast is served in a sunny conservatory; dinner can be arranged separately for $45/person, $35/person if you bring your own wine. A kitchen adjacent to the conservatory is for guest use. Te Popo is a 15-minute drive from Stratford on good country roads. You can visit the gardens separately by appointment ($8). **Pros:** Magnificent garden, huge guest library, organic fruit and vegetables from the home garden, conservatory. **Con:** It helps to like gardens. ✉636 Stanley Rd., Stratford ⌨R.D. 24, Stratford ☎🏠06/762–8775 ⊕*www.tepopo.co.nz* ⬙3 rooms, 1 apartment ⚙In-room: no a/c, dial-up. In-hotel: no elevator ▭AE, DC, MC, V ⑩BP.

SHOPPING

Possums were introduced to New Zealand to generate a fur trade but have had a devastating effect on the native forest and birds. Thus they are regarded as an environmental pest. Nevertheless their fur is known for its softness and warmth. **Environmental Products** (✉*1103 Opunake Rd., Mahoe* ☎*06/764–6133* ⊕*www.envirofur.co.nz*), a small but thriving business near Stratford, is turning this local environmental pest into excellent by-products, using all natural tanning processes (no chemicals!) to produce high-quality opossum fur and leather products such as hats, rugs, coats, and scarves. Deerskin products are also available.

HAWERA

29 km (18 mi) south of Stratford.

This quiet country town, a hub for the farming community, can give you a close look at the local history and way of life. For the more adventurous there is the opportunity to "dam-drop" on the Waingongoro River.

ESSENTIALS

Visitor Info **South Taranaki i-Site Visitor Centre** (✉*55 High St., Hawera* ☎*06/278–8599*).

WHAT TO SEE

An unlikely find in Hawera is the **Kevin Wasley Elvis Presley Memorial Room,** a private museum devoted to "The King." The unique collection includes more than 2,000 records and impressive memorabilia. The museum does not keep regular hours; phone well ahead for an appointment (finding Kevin isn't always easy). ✉ *51 Argyle St.* ☎ *0274/982–942* ⊕ *www.digitalus.co.nz/elvis* ☜ *By donation.*

Fodor'sChoice The **Tawhiti Museum** is a labor of love for Nigel Ogle, and an outstand-
★ ing presentation of regional history. The former schoolteacher-cum-
☾ historian bought an old cheese factory in 1975 and proceeded to fill it up with life-size figures from Taranaki's past. He creates the fiberglass figures from molds of local people and sets them in scenes depicting the pioneering days. Nigel is continually adding "stories." The latest dioramas depict huge intertribal wars of the 1830s and European/Māori land wars of the 1860s. More than 800 model warriors, none of them the same, have been created. On the first Sunday of each month, the museum's Tawhiti Bush Railway springs to life, rattling through a variety of outdoor displays that highlight the historical logging operations in Taranaki. **Mr. Badger's Café,** with its delightful *Wind in the Willows* theme, has excellent food and espresso, and is quite simply one of the best cafés in southern Taranaki. To get to the museum, take Tawhiti Road northeast out of Hawera and continue 4 km (2½ mi). ✉ *401 Ohangai Rd.* ☎ *06/278–6837* ⊕ *www.tawhitimuseum.co.nz* ☜ *$10* ☉ *Sept.–May, Fri.–Mon. 10–4; June–Aug., Sun. 10–4; Dec. 26–Jan. 31, daily 10–4.*

OUTDOOR ACTIVITIES

White-water sledging (like sledding, but on water) has become one of New Zealand's many zany adventure sports. You'll have your nose to the water as you maneuver your sledge headfirst down the rapids. **Kaitiaki Adventures** (☎ *021/461–110* ⊕ *www.kaitiaki.co.nz*) runs daily trips on the Waingongoro River, leaving from the Powerco Aquatic Centre on Waihi Road in Hawera. Bring a swimsuit and towel; you'll be outfitted with a padded wet suit, booties, life jacket, helmet, fins, and a sledge (which resembles a small surfboard). The trips take about three hours and include a journey around Okahutiti Pā, an old fortification. The cost is from $100; advance reservations are required. Kaitiaki Adventures also organizes surfing and mountain-biking tours.

WHERE TO STAY

$$ ⬚ **Tairoa Lodge.** The translation for *Tairoa* is "linger, stay longer," and that's what you'll want to do at this relaxing B&B. In this renovated kauri villa, built in 1875, the two spacious guest rooms look out over the woodland garden and swimming pool. Both rooms have fireplaces with carved wooden mantels; one room is done in deep reds, the other in cheery yellows and blues. A separate two-bedroom cottage can accommodate families; it has a full kitchen as well as a home-theater system and veranda overlooking a spacious lawn. To keep busy, you can peruse piles of the latest magazines, play chess or *pétanque* (the French version of boccie), or take a dip in the pool. Since 2007 "The Gatehouse," a 1930s renovated character villa on the property, has

been available for long-term accommodation, with three bedrooms (queen beds), full kitchen, games room, and large garden. **Pros:** Private; spacious; quiet, rural location; swimming pool. **Con:** Not for those who prefer larger hotels. ⊠*3 Puawai St.* ☎*06/278–8603* ⊕*www.tairoa-lodge.co.nz* ⬅*2 rooms (1 queen, 1 queen and single), 1 cottage (with 2 rooms, 1 queen and 2 king singles)* ⌂*In-room: Wi-Fi. In-hotel: restaurant, pool, DVD, laundry facilities, no elevator* ☐*AE, DC, MC, V* ⦿*BP.*

WANGANUI

163 km (102 mi) southeast of New Plymouth, 193 km (121 mi) north of Wellington, 225 km (141 mi) southwest of Taupo.

Wanganui is a river city and the river its raison d'etre. It began as a small port settlement and a transport junction between the sea and the Whanganui River, which is navigable for miles into the forested interior. With trains, roads, and now planes stealing the transportation limelight, Wanganui city sat quietly for some years while other North Island towns flourished. Today there has been a considerable resurgence, Wanganui's compact city center has lively streets with shops and galleries and restored, heritage buildings that hark back to colonial times, and busy trading days. A stroll along Victoria Avenue, with its Victorian gaslights, wrought-iron seats, and avenue of palm and plane trees, reveals the city's style. Majestic Square, just off Victoria Avenue, is surrounded by galleries and crafts shops, and live performances often feature on the square's small stage. In summer (December to March), there's a profusion of hanging baskets and window boxes.

For hundreds of years, the Māori people have lived along the banks of the Whanganui River, a major access route between the coast and interior. In the 1800s, Wanganui township became established as one of New Zealand's most prosperous early European settlements. Local Māori people trace their occupation of the land around the Whanganui River back as far as the 10th century. European settlers started moving to the area in the 1840s. Subsequent appropriation of land caused conflict with local Māori, and a British garrison was temporarily established in the town. From the 1880s the port and riverboat transport that provided a link to the North Island interior led to a prosperous time for trade and tourism, until completion of the main trunk railway line meant that Wanganui was essentially bypassed. Today, Wanganui has evolved into a small but attractive provincial city, serving local industry, tourism, and the region's farming community.

GETTING AROUND

Wanganui is a three-hour drive from Wellington; take State Highway 1 north to Sanson and Highway 3 west from there. The Whanganui River Road is a minor route—expect it to take two hours to drive from Wanganui to Pipiriki. Remember to keep left on the narrow corners. To reach the kayak starting points, take Highway 4 north from Wanganui; it's a three-hour drive to Taumarunui, via Raetihi. A minor road connects Pipiriki to Raetihi, so you could always drive north up the

Whanganui River Road, cut east along the minor road to Raetihi, and then return down Highway 4 to Wanganui, a paved though winding road through steep farmland and forest.

ESSENTIALS

Bus Depot Wanganui Bus Stop (✉ *156 Ridgeway St.*)..

Hospital Wanganui Hospital (✉ *Heads Rd.* ☎ *06/348–1234*).

Visitor Info Wanganui Visitor Information Centre (✉ *101 Guyton St.* ☎ *06/349–0508* ⊕ *www.wanganui.com*).

WHAT TO SEE

Fodor'sChoice ★ For an overview of the region's history, drop into the **Whanganui Regional Museum,** by Queens Park, which contains *taonga* (Māori ancestral treasures) of the River people, and has one of the best collections of Māori treasures in the country. There are some wonderful *waka* (canoes), as well as carvings, decorative ornaments, kiwi-feather cloaks, greenstone clubs, tools, bone flutes, and ceremonial portraits. The museum also re-creates 19th-century pioneer-town Wanganui in a series of traditional shop windows filled with relics and curios. Another treasure in this museum is Te Pataka Whakaahua (the Lindauer Gallery), with 19th-century paintings of Māori leaders by respected artist Gottfried Lindauer. ✉ *Watt St.* ☎ *06/349–1110* ⊕ *www.wanganui-museum.org.nz* ✑ *$5* ⊙ *Daily 10–4:30*.

On a small hill overlooking the town is the domed **Sarjeant Gallery,** one of New Zealand's finest art galleries and most beautiful heritage buildings, renowned for its neoclassical architecture, natural lighting, and magnificent display spaces. The gallery is highly regarded for the quality of its collection and regularly changing exhibitions from local, national, and international artists. With 6,000 works of art in its care, including 19th- and 20th-century international and New Zealand art, photography, and a dynamic collection of contemporary New Zealand art to draw from, visitors are assured of a stimulating art experience. The gallery's shop stocks a quality selection of books, local art, and glasswork. ✉ *Queens Park* ☎ *06/349–0506* ⊕ *www.sarjeant.org.nz* ✑ *Entry by donation* ⊙ *Daily 10:30–4:30, Anzac Day 1–4:30* PM.

For a taste of the old days on the river, catch a ride on the restored paddle steamer, the *Waimarie*, built in 1899 by Yarrow and Company at Poplar London. Two-hour cruises take you up the Whanganui River from Wanganui. The Waimarie worked the river for 50 years before sinking in 1952. Critics said it couldn't even be salvaged, let alone restored to working order but a dedicated volunteer team proved them wrong, and have since continued restoration on two more formerly derelict riverboats. A museum at the River Boat Centre houses a collection of photographs from the days when riverboats were commonplace. Also on view are images of the salvage of the *Waimarie*, a great engineering feat. The salvaged MV *Waiua*, a smaller vessel, can be chartered. ✉ *Whanganui River Boat Centre, 1A Taupo Quay* ☎ *06/347–1863* ⊕ *www.riverboats.co.nz* ✑ *Cruise $33, museum by donation* ⊙ *Cruises Oct. 22 (approximately)–May 1, daily at 2; May*

2–Oct. 21, weekends, school and public holidays at 1. No cruises in Aug. Museum Mon.–Sat. 9–4, Sun. 10–4.

By day, the formal gardens of **Virginia Lake** are a delight, and at night, the trees and lake fountain are softly illuminated. A gentle 25-minute stroll leads around the lake, through woodlands and gardens and past rose and wisteria pergolas. The lake is just north of Wanganui, off State Highway 3.

WHERE TO EAT

$$$ ✕**Vincent's Yellow House Café and Art Gallery.** Spread throughout the veranda, garden, and several cozy, intimate rooms of this old yellow villa is a café showing local art (for sale). Open daily from 7:30 to late, serving breakfast, lunch (fresh-made salads, pastas, pizzas, muffins) and dinner, the menu changes weekly, but expect something nourishing such as seafood chowder chock-full of kingfish, bluenose, mussels, and salmon. The café is across the road from the river and a two-minute drive from the city center. ⊠*Pitt St. at Dublin St.* ☎*06/347–9321* ▤*MC, V.*

$$–$$$ ✕**Stellar.** Giant gourmet pizzas and generic New Zealand food are specialties at this relaxed restaurant and bar that retains the brick-and-stone interior of an 1850s former hotel. There's a strong Kiwi ambience with stained and polished wool presses for bar stands and giant plasma television screens for engaging in that favorite Kiwi pastime, watching sports. More features are the spacious veranda, free wireless Internet for guests, and very stylish bathrooms. There's live music some nights. ⊠*2 Victoria Ave.* ☎*06/345–7278* ▤*AE, MC, V.*

$$–$$$ ✕**Vega.** With its funky, modern interior, this former warehouse is a stylish spot to sample eclectic cuisine with Mediterranean, Middle Eastern, and Pacific influences (the European owner/chef moved here from Samoa). Signature dishes are snapper fillet with tropical coconut cream sauce, or seared tuna fillet with Cajun crust and island-style marmalade sauce. On Friday and Saturday nights there's live music and dancing. ⊠*49 Taupo Quay* ☎*06/345–1082* ▤*AE, MC, V* ☉*No lunch Sun.–Wed.*

$–$$ ✕**Red Eye Café.** This brightly painted, licensed café is a popular haunt
Fodor'sChoice with the town's many art students and folks who appreciate the hearty
★ muffins, cakes, vegetarian food, and renowned Wellington coffee brand Havana. There's a fire in winter, and locals show off their musical talents on open-mike nights. ⊠*96 Guyton St.* ☎*06/345–5646* ▤*AE, MC, V.*

WHERE TO STAY

$$–$$$ ▥**Arlesford House.** This elegant English-style country home, an easy 10-minute drive from Wanganui, is built almost entirely of native timber and surrounded by beautifully landscaped gardens. Hosts June and George prepare delicious breakfasts. Afterward you can relax by the pool or play tennis or pétanque (similar to boccie). Rooms are large and have good light, king-size beds, inviting armchairs, and either have en suite bathrooms (some with a stunning garden outlook from the bath) or private bathrooms across the hall. Also on the property is a self-catering, three-bedroom log cabin, a one-bedroom self-catering

cabin equipped for wheelchair use, and a purpose-built meeting-room. **Pros:** Country peace and quiet, garden views from the bath. **Cons:** Shared bathrooms for some rooms, 10-minute drive from town. ✉*202 State Hwy. 3 ☎R.D. 4, Westmere* ☎*06/347–7751* 🖷*06/347–7561* ⊕*www.arlesfordhouse.co.nz* ⇆*4 rooms, 2 cottages* ♿*In-room: no a/c. In-hotel: tennis court, pool, no elevator* ▤*MC, V* ⦿*BP.*

$$ ⛶**Aotea Motor Lodge.** Opened in 2007, luxury (Qualmark 5 star) self-contained serviced apartments including studio, one bedroom, two bedroom, and some interconnecting rooms. Very much inner-city corporate accommodation but it's modern, spacious, and very comfortable. Locally owned by a Whanganui River family, all apartments are soundproofed. Cooked breakfasts are available. **Pro:** Double spa baths; new. **Con:** Beside busy road. ✉*390 Victoria Ave., Wanganui* ☎*06 345 0303* ⊕*www.aoteamotorlodge.co.nz* ⇆*38* ♿*In-room: Ethernet, DVD, . In-hotel: laundry, parking, executive floor* ▤*AE, DC, MC, V* ⊙.

$–$$ ⛶**Bushy Park Forest Reserve.** This B&B is in a grand old Heritage homestead, surrounded by ancient forest and prolific native birdlife. The remnant forest is administered by a trust and has been surrounded by an animal predator–proof fence to protect endangered native birds, such as the flightless kiwi. Walking tracks meander through the forest; look for the "Ratanui," the world's biggest rata tree. Back at the homestead are six spacious bedrooms, a formal dining room, several lounges, and a television lounge. The homestead's Category One Heritage status restricts significant changes, and the rooms are grand but large and very hard to heat in winter. The café is known for its espresso and Devonshire teas. Backpackers can share a bunkhouse ($20 per person) that sleeps 11; your own bedding is required, and you will need to bring and cook your own meals. There are campsites and a couple of RV sites as well. **Pros:** Outstanding forest reserve location, varied accommodation options. **Con:** Hard to heat in winter. ✉*Rangitautau East Rd., 24 km (15 mi) northwest of Wanganui* ☎*06/342–9879* ⊕*www.bushypark. co.nz* ⇆*6 rooms, 1 bunkhouse; all with shared bath* ♿*In-hotel: 2 restaurants, bars, public Internet* ▤*MC, V* ⦿*BP.*

$–$$ ⛶**Rutland Arms.** This renovated Victorian inn in the center of Wanganui is the top choice in town. The guest rooms have comfortable beds, reproduction period furniture, and bright bathrooms, four with whirlpool baths. Downstairs, the restaurant/bar has traditional-English character: a roaring fire (in winter) and a wide choice of imported beers. You can eat here ($$–$$$), surrounded by the horse brasses, other agricultural paraphernalia, and pictures of Old Wanganui, or in the sunny courtyard. Food is generous, contemporary New Zealand–style cuisine, and the menu changes regularly. **Pros:** CBD location, cozy feel. **Con:** Can be some bar noise. ✉*Ridgeway St.* ☎*06/347–7677* 🖷*06/347– 7345* ⊕*www.rutland-arms.co.nz* ⇆*8 rooms* ♿*In-room: Ethernet. In-hotel: restaurant, bar, no elevator* ▤*AE, DC, MC, V* ⦿*CP.*

¢ ⛶**Tamara Backpackers Lodge.** You can sit on the balcony of this Edwardian homestead and look out over the Whanganui River (and toward Mt. Ruapehu in the distance) or chill out in a hammock in the expansive back garden. Either way, this budget lodge is a relaxed base, a five-minute walk from town. There is a lounge with piano and TV, dining room, and fully equipped shared kitchen. Or you can head for the café next door. The rooms are varied, each has its individual appeal, some have a river view, others are by the garden, and include those with double beds, one or two single beds, and dorms (with four beds each). **Pros:** Riverside location, very clean and tidy, big garden. **Con:** Some shared bathrooms. ⊠*24 Somme Parade* ☎*06/347–6300* 🖷*06/347–6300* ⊕*www.tamaralodge.com* ↩*12 rooms, 3 dorms (12 beds)* ⌂*In-hotel: restaurant, bar, laundry facilities, public Internet, no elevator* ⊟*AE, DC, MC, V.*

THE WHANGANUI RIVER

The city of Wanganui sits near the mouth of the Whanganui River, which flows through the heart of Whanganui National Park and is one of New Zealand's most historic and scenic waterways. The Whanganui begins its journey high on the mountains of Tongariro National Park. In its 329-km (204-mi) journey the river flows through sheer-sided gorges, forested wilderness, and isolated pockets of farmland. For several hundred years the *Te Atihau nui a paparangi* tribe of Māori āāāhas lived along the riverbanks, and they still regard the river as their spiritual ancestor. Most have now left the river *kainga* (villages), though some remain in small communities along the lower reaches. For a brief period around 1900, thousands of tourists were drawn to riverboats and steamers that plied the river as far up as Taumarunui, 170 km (106 mi) north of Wanganui.

Today the river is popular for kayaking and jet-boating, with 239 named rapids—though most of them are shallow and suitable for novice paddlers. The river's wilderness, its rich culture and history, and its relatively easy navigability are its main features. Guided trips *(⇨ Outdoor Activities, below)* generally operate in summer, the most popular time for kayakers; however, a river trip is feasible any time of the year. Winters are mild in the valley, and floods can occur year-round. For information about Whanganui National Park, visit the Department of Conservation's site (⊕*www.doc.govt.nz*) and click on "National Parks."

WHAT TO SEE

An alternative for those without the time or inclination to travel by kayak is to explore the river's lower reaches by following the **Whanganui River Road** from the city of Wanganui. Built in the 1930s to provide access to communities otherwise reliant on the then-less-frequent riverboat services, the road runs for 79 km (49 mi) north, as far as Pipiriki. It's a narrow backcountry road, unpaved in stretches, although current upgrades that include paving the entire length are due for completion by 2012. Paved or not, be sure to keep left and take it slowly.

★ Many choose instead to take the early-morning **Rural Mail Coach Tour** (☎*06/347–7534*), which gets you to Pipiriki and back in a day and includes sightseeing stops and optional extra tours. The tour is $40, given weekdays only, departing Wanganui between 7:15 and 7:30 AM, returning mid-afternoon: times vary depending on how much mail the postman has to deliver, or whether he waits while you enjoy a jet-boat trip on the river. You'll see the remains of giant, fossilized oyster shells at **Oyster Cliffs** (28 km [17 mi] from Wanganui). You'll call at the marae (village) of **Koriniti** (47 km [29 mi]), with its historic (and still much-used) ceremonial buildings and small Anglican church. You're welcome to look around. If there's anything happening just ask the people there whether it's appropriate to visit—unless it's a private funeral you're likely to be made very welcome. The restored **Kawana Flour Mill** (56 km [35 mi]) and colonial miller's cottage are always open, if you'd like a glimpse of bygone pioneer life. At the farming settlement of **Ranana** (60 km [37 mi]), a Roman Catholic church from the 1890s is still used today. And there is the larger St. Joseph's Church and Catholic Mission, established by Home of Compassion founder Mother Aubert, at pretty **Hiruharama** (66 km [41 mi]), better known locally as Jerusalem. Drive up the track to see the carved altar inside the church.

Finally at **Pipiriki** (79 km [49 mi]), the turnaround point, it's possible to arrange a jet-boat tour to the magnificent river gorges farther upriver. A popular trip continues to the Mangapurua Landing, where a short walk leads to the Bridge to Nowhere, a huge concrete bridge in remote forested country that is a remnant of the pioneering Mangapurua farming settlement, abandoned in 1942.

Other things to do along the lower reaches are short **canoe trips,** with Māori cultural experience included, jet boat trips, a bush walk in the national park (a good track is signposted 1 km [½ mi] past Atene), and overnight stays at some of the idiosyncratic lodges and farms in the area. For information about canoe trips, contact the **Wanganui i-Site Visitor Information Centre** (☎ *06/349–0508* ⊕ *www.wanganui.com*).

OUTDOOR ACTIVITIES

CANOEING & KAYAKING

The main season for Whanganui River trips is between October and Easter; the busiest period is during the summer holidays (Christmas–January). Winter trips are doable; the weather will be slightly colder, but you'll probably have the river to yourself. In summer, although there can be several hundred travelers on the river at any one time, they are all moving in one direction and so a group can travel long periods without seeing another soul. The time they do come together is in the evenings, at the huts and campsites.

Transport on the river is generally in open, two-seater, Canadian-style canoes or in kayaks. Tour options range from one-day picnic trips to five-day camping expeditions. Operators can supply all equipment, transfers, and the necessary hut and campsite passes, and trips can either be guided and catered, or independently undertaken (you supply your own food).

Your first call should be to one of the commercial operators or the **Department of Conservation** (☎ *06/348–8475* ⊕ *www.doc.govt.nz*) to discuss itineraries. No experience is necessary; the Whanganui is considered a beginner's river—it's definitely not "white-water" adventure, though the river should be respected and one or two rapids can play nasty tricks on paddlers. Prices vary considerably according to the length and style of the trip, but you can expect to pay from about $55 for a simple one-day trip and in the $500–$600 range for a fully inclusive three-day excursion.

The **Whanganui Journey,** a canoe journey down the Whanganui River, is regarded as one of nine "Great Walks" in New Zealand's national parks and can be paddled independently or with tour operators (⇨ *below).* Park huts and campsites are along the river. Most tours go from Taumarunui to Pipiriki, a four- to five-day trip, or from Whakahoro to Pipiriki (three to four days). Whakahoro to Pipiriki is a true wilderness experience; there is no road access. A lower river trip, from Pipiriki to Wanganui, passes through a mix of native forest, farmland, and several small communities. Tour operators offer anything from five-day wilderness experiences to one-day or overnight trips on the lower reaches.

Fodor's Choice   **Canoe Safaris** (☎06/385–9237 ⊕*www.canoesafaris.co.nz*) leads two-
  ★   to five-day trips on the Whanganui; their "big boats," six-person open canoes, are built on the lines of the Canadian fur-trapper boats. The price, which starts at $320 for a two-day safari, covers all equipment, including a waterproof gear bag.

Waka Tours (⊠*17a Balance St., Raetihi* ☎☎*06/385–4811* ⊕*www. wakatours.net*) runs one-day, overnight, and three-day guided kayak journeys with a Māori cultural element. Traveling on the lower reaches, local Māori guides share their stories, songs, customs, and love of the river. The tours include visits to or overnight stays on marae (traditional Māori settlements).

JET-BOAT   If you fancy a faster-paced river adventure than a canoe or kayak pad-
TOURS   dle, consider a jet-boat tour—you'll skim across the rapids, dodge the rocks, and see fantastic scenery. One of the most popular trips is from Pipirki to the Mangapurua Landing, then a short walk to the Bridge to Nowhere in the Mangapurua Valley, a Whanganui tributary. The Mangapurua Valley was a farming settlement established in 1918 and abandoned by 1942, owing to the impossibly remote and rugged country. The old concrete bridge in the bush is a fascinating reminder. Jet-boat companies also transport hikers to two national park hiking trails: the Matemateonga Track and Mangapurua Track.

Ken and Josephine Haworth grew up on the river, now their company **Whanganui River Adventures** (⊠*R.D. 6 Pipiri* ☎☎*06/385–3246* ⊕*www.whanganuiriveradventures.co.nz*) has a range of tours from Pipiriki to the Bridge to Nowhere, and shorter tours to scenic delights such as the Drop Scene, and Manganui o te ao River. **Bridge to Nowhere Jet-boat Tours** (☎*0800/480–308* ⊕*www.bridgetonoweretours.co.nz*) runs jet-boat trips from Pipiriki to the Bridge to Nowhere (a four-hour trip) and other natural and historic sights.

WHERE TO STAY

$ ⊞**The Flying Fox.** Even the arrival is exceptional at this truly unique
★   lodging. You'll arrive by river (jet boat or kayak) or reach it by its namesake Flying Fox—a simple aerial cable car—which deposits you high

above the west bank of the Whanganui River. There you'll find a pair of cottages, each accommodating two to four people, plus the romantic "Glory Cart" gypsy caravan hideaway. They're distinctly ecofriendly, from their construction (by host John) using recycled materials to their facilities, such as the wood- and gas-fired showers, solar lighting, and outdoor claw-foot tub. Inside, they're warmly comfortable, with rug-covered brick floors, tie-dye throws, carved screens, and wood-burning stoves. Meals by host Annette (arrange in advance; $110–$120 per day) are very generous, country-style, and hinge on mostly organic and homegrown ingredients: avocados from the owner's trees; smoked eel from the river; seasonal produce; homemade ice cream, kūmara bread (a top seller at the Wanganui Farmer's Market), and muffins. Or you can bring your own groceries. Camping in a bush clearing is another "lodging" option ($10 per person). You can get here from Wanganui on the Rural Mail Coach Tour (⇨*above*); for those who are driving, there's secure parking on the road side of the river. **Pros:** River wilderness, ecofriendly and organic, Annette's home cooking, getting there. **Con:** No cell phone reception. ⊠ *Whanganui River Rd., Koriniti* 🖂📠*06/342–8160* ⊕*www.theflyingfox.co.nz* ⤴*2 cottages* ⚷*In-room: no a/c, no phone, kitchen, no TV* ▭*MC, V* 🍴*MAP.*

PALMERSTON NORTH

145 km (87 mi) northeast of Wellington, 72 km (45 mi) southeast of Wanganui.

Palmerston North—or "Palmy" as the locals call it—is home to more than 70 major educational and research institutes, including the Sport and Rugby Institute, where the All Blacks and other national and international elite sportspeople come to train. Thanks to these magnets, one-third of Palmerston North's population is between the ages of 15 and 30. The biggest influence on the city, however, is Massey University, one of the country's leading universities. The Massey campus has two Palmerston North locations: Turitea, set among huge trees and beautiful gardens, and Hokowhitu, on the city side of the Manawatu River, with modern buildings near the lagoon.

A six-hour drive south from Auckland and two hours north of Wellington, Palmerston North is one of New Zealand's largest regional cities, with a population of 79,000.

GETTING AROUND

The Palmerston North International Airport (PMR) is a 10-minute drive from the city center. Currency exchange is available when international flights arrive, and an ATM is by the escalator. The taxi stand is outside the terminal, and shuttle services are available for roughly $15. The airport also has an Internet kiosk.

Activity in Palmerston North is centered around the Square. From there, you can easily explore on foot most of the city's cafés, restaurants, shops, art galleries, and museums. The **i-Site Palmerston North Visitor Centre** (⊠*The Square* 🖀*06/354–6593 or 06/350–1922* ⊕*www. manawatunz.co.nz*) is open weekdays 9–5 and weekends 10–3.

ESSENTIALS

Bus Depot **Palmerston North Travel Centre** (⊠ *Main and Pitt Sts.*).

Emergencies Services **Fire, police, and ambulance** (☎ *111*).

Hospital **Palmerston North Hospital** (⊠ *50 Ruahine St.* ☎ *06/356–9169*).

WHAT TO SEE

☺ The distinctive **Te Manawa** complex is divided into three sections that weave together the region's history, art, and science. There are artworks and natural history displays, and the history of Rangitane, the local Māori people. If traveling with young ones, the Mind Science Centre, with its quirky interactive science exhibits, is entertaining and educational. ⊠ *396 Main St.* ☎ *06/355–5000* ⊕ *www.temanawa. co.nz* ⬚ *Life and Art galleries free; Mind Science Centre starts from $5 depending on current exhibitions* ☉ *Daily 10–5*.

The only one of its kind in New Zealand, the small **New Zealand Rugby Museum** is worth a visit whether or not you're a fan of the sport, for an insight into the tradition surrounding a game that many in New Zealand treat like a religion. The collection of rugby memorabilia dates back to the start of this national game in 1870. Look for the historic whistle that is used to open the World Cup every four years. ⊠ *87 Cuba St.* ☎ *06/358–6947* ⊕ *www.rugbymuseum.co.nz* ⬚ *$5* ☉ *Mon.–Sat. 10–noon and 1:30–4, Sun. 1:30–4*.

Inside the art deco **Square Edge** building is a center for emerging local artists. Its galleries, boutiques, and gift shops stock unique, locally made artworks. ⊠ *Church St. and The Square* ☎ *06/357–7542* ☉ *Weekdays 10–4:30, Sat. 10–3*.

The **Tararua and Apiti Wind Farms,** two of the largest wind farms in the southern hemisphere, make a dramatic sight on the ranges that overlook the city. A drive up Saddle Road to the largest windmills will reward with fantastic views. There is a carpark directly beneath one huge windmill, and the return drive can be a pleasant look via Woodville and the Manawatu Gorge.

⌐
OFF THE
BEATEN
PATH

Feilding. For a taste of authentic, farming New Zealand, take a side trip to the township of Feilding, 20 km (12 mi) northwest of Palmerston North.

The Feilding Saleyards, one of the largest livestock sales in the southern hemisphere, are close to the Edwardian town center. At least twice weekly, sheep and cattle farmers buy and sell more than 15,000 sheep and 1,400 head of cattle. Every Friday at 11 AM the Feilding Saleyards Guided Tour ($5) through the sheep pens and state-of-the-art computerized cattle auction pavilion provides a fascinating glimpse of one of New Zealand's oldest farming traditions. After your tour, visit the rustic Saleyards Café, where the farmers meet for pie and chips, or toasted steak sandwich. If you prefer, more modern cafés are in town. Other Feilding attractions are the farmers' market (Friday mornings), Kowhai Park, the Manawatu Horsedrawn Vehicle Museum, a steam-rail museum, and Manfeild Park (which hosts events from motor sports to the annual garden festival in early May). In the town itself you could putter about for half a day through the bookshops, art galleries, community Arts Centre, and visit the boutique movie theater. From Feilding, Kimbolton Road passes through prime sheep-farming country to Kimbolton Village (28 km [17 mi] from Feilding), where there is a café. Close to the village (within a few minutes' drive) are two outstanding gardens with rhododendrons and myriad other plants: Cross Hills ($8 admission) and Heritage Park Garden ($7 admission, children free). For more information, contact the **Feilding & District Information Centre** (⊠ *10 Manchester Sq.* ☎ *06/323–3318* ⊕ *www.feilding.co.nz*).

WHERE TO EAT

$$$–$$$$ ✕ **Déjeuner.** This well-regarded restaurant in an old character bungalow draws on influences from French to Asian and Pacific. Try the signature Déjeuner lamb shank (slow-cooked lamb atop garlic mashed potatoes) or the Jack Daniels whiskey-barrel house-smoked venison on kūmara (a native sweet potato) mash and port-and-rhubarb coulis. When you phone for your reservation, inquire about the tasting menu, offered occasionally. ⊠ *159 Broadway Ave.* ☎ *06/356–1449* ⊕ *www.dejeuner. co.nz* ▤ *AE, DC, MC, V* ☷ *Licensed and BYOB.*

$$$ ✕ **Bella's Café.** Serving a mix of Italian, Thai, and Pacific Rim dishes,
Fodor'sChoice Bella's has been a city favorite for more than a decade. It's right on the
★ Square, smart and cheerful, with friendly and efficient service. Try the Bella's classic Thai chicken curry, or steamed mussels with Riesling and sweet chili cream sauce. The café's founders also run the Herb Farm café in nearby Ashhurst. ⊠ *2 The Square* ☎ *06/357–8616* ▤ *MC, V.*

$$$ ✕ **Brewer's Apprentice.** Strategically located beside the old brick church just off the Square, Brewer's Apprentice has plenty of character with lots of brick, stone and timber, open fires, flat-screen televisions, a spacious bar, street-front garden bar, and quiet dining alcove. Meals range from tasting plates to brunch of black pudding on potato rosti; lunches of soups, pizzas, roast meats, and Monteith's (a popular Kiwi beer) battered fish-and-chips; dinners with gourmet grill selections; and wild pork sausage on parsnip and Dijon mash. Live music entertains some evenings. Open 11 AM (10 weekends) until late. ⊠ *334 Church St.* ☎ *06/358–8888* ▤ *AE, DC, MC, V.*

$$$ ✕ **Café Cuba.** Just off the Square, this café is a funky and popular local haunt for breakfast, brunch, lunch, and dinner. Laid-back music plays in the background, and there are plenty of magazines to peruse while you enjoy the Cuba Breakfast—a hearty plate of eggs, bacon, mushrooms, and tomatoes—or later in the day perhaps a Cajun chicken "sarnie" (sandwich) with fried banana, salad greens, and *tzatziki* (tangy cucumber-yogurt sauce). Pastas and salads fill the lunch cabinet. The kids' menu is appealing, too. ⊠ *Cuba and George Sts.* ☎ *06/356–5750* ▤ *MC, V.*

WHERE TO STAY

$$$–$$$$ ▦ **Hiwinui Country Estate.** For a luxurious farm stay, do the short (18-km [11-mi]) drive from Palmerston North to this 1,100-acre working sheep and dairy farm, hosted by the family that has farmed this land for generations. The homestead looks across lawns and gardens, beyond farm paddocks to the forest-covered Ruahine Ranges. You can take a

farm tour, walk in nearby Ruahine Forest Park, or try fly-fishing or jet-boating in the dramatic Manawatu River gorge. Less-active pursuits include lounging by the roaring stone fireplaces (outdoors or in), having breakfast delivered to your room, or being treated to a gourmet dinner of fresh, local produce, complemented by New Zealand wine (by advance arrangement only). The three rooms open out to gardens, lawns, and rural views; all have under-floor heating and high-quality linens. One room has a whirlpool bath, and one has a double shower. **Pros:** Luxury on a working farm, jet-boating in the gorge, interesting artwork. **Con:** You might not want luxury on a working farm. ⊠*465 Ashurst–Bunnythorpe Rd.* ☎*06/329–2838* ⊕*www.hiwinui.co.nz* ↩*3 rooms* ⌂*In-room: DVD, dial-up. In-hotel: no kids under 10* ▤*DC, MC, V* ⏐⏐*BP.*

$$ ▢ **Plum Trees Lodge.** A charming inner-city retreat, this lodge was built in 1999 as a coach house in keeping with the style of the 1920s house, the home of hosts Robyn and Robert Anderson. The apartment is spacious but best suited to couples or solo travelers, because it has only one room. It's full of character, with its stained-glass windows and use of aged native timbers; it also has a private balcony. The lounge area centers around a fireplace, and the room is sunny and light all year round. The breakfast basket is stocked with tasty local nibbles and treats. Dial-up Internet is available for those with laptops. **Pros:** Privacy, garden, Robyn's cookies. **Con:** Stairway access only. ⊠*97 Russell St.* ☎*06/358–7813* ⊕*www.plumtreeslodge.com* ↩*1 studio apartment* ⌂*In-room: kitchen, dial-up. In-hotel: no elevator* ▤*MC, V* ⏐⏐*BP.*

Fodor's Choice
★

$$ ▢ **Travelodge Palmerston North.** In a 1927 Heritage building, this city hotel is minutes by foot from shops, theaters, and cafés. The city's only international hotel, it has a restaurant, intimate lounge bar, and sports bar popular with the local after-work crowd. Rooms have extra-long queen-size sofa beds, with feather duvets and pillows. **Pros:** In the city, good facilities. **Cons:** Comfortable but room lack character, traffic noise. ⊠*175 Cuba St.* ☎*06/355–5895* ⊕*www.accorhotels.co.nz* ↩*95 rooms* ⌂*In-room: safe, Ethernet, Wi-Fi* ▤*DC, MC, V.*

NIGHTLIFE & THE ARTS

NIGHTLIFE

The interior is a mix of tapa cloth and warm woods at the **Fish–Pacific Sushi Cocktail Lounge Bar** (⊠*Regents Arcade* ☎*06/359–3474*), open 4 PM to late Wednesday–Saturday. It was voted the region's best bar for 2007 by the local hospitality association, and it's a popular after-theater haunt, along with other cafés, bars, and pubs in this trendy little brick lane beside the city's grand old Regent Theatre.

Grand Wine, Cocktails and Mezé Bar ⊠*Corner of Church and George Sts.* ☎*06/357–7224*) offers intimate space, dark wood, chandeliers, and lounge chairs. It's open Thursday–Saturday 5 PM until late.

THE ARTS

Several theaters in the city center host local and visiting productions. **Centrepoint** (✉*Pitt and Church Sts.* ☎*06/354–5740* ⊕*www.centrepoint.co.nz*) is the only professional theater company outside New Zealand's main cities and has performances Tuesday through Sunday. Ballet, traveling musical productions, opera, and rock groups take the stage at the opulent **Regent on Broadway** (✉*63 Broadway* ☎*06/350–2100* ⊕*www.regent.co.nz*), which was built in 1930.

SHOPPING

Palmerston North's shopping is concentrated around the Square; Broadway Avenue and the Plaza shopping centers are within easy walking distance. George Street, which is also just off the Square, has a number of specialty shops, galleries, and cafés.

Check out **Taylor Jensen Fine Arts** (✉*39 George St.* ☎*06/355–4278*) for contemporary and traditional New Zealand and international art, sculpture, jewelry, crafts, and furniture. If you're looking for a good read, **Bruce McKenzie Booksellers** (✉*51 George St.* ☎*06/356–9922*) is considered among New Zealand's leading independent bookstores. **IHI Aotearoa** (✉*71 George St.* ☎*06/354–0375*) sells high-quality, contemporary art and crafts, jewelry, and streetwear, much of it made by local artists. You can enjoy gourmet breads and pastries, gluten-free if you prefer, plus salamis, pickles, chocolates, and cheeses at **Breadworks Artisan Breads** (✉*85 The Square*). Indulge your sweet tooth at **Munchkins** (✉*61 Broadway Ave.* ☎*06/356–4615*), a child's haven of chocolates and homemade fudge. **Rêve** (✉*The Elm, Fitzherbert Ave.* ☎*06/353–0570*) is a boutique specializing in trousers for women and garments made with locally spun wool.

5

Wellington & the Wairarapa

WORD OF MOUTH

"I loved Wellington. It's compact and easy to get around—it reminds me a bit of San Francisco, one of my other favorite cities. Te Papa is a wonderful museum, too."

—ElendilPickle

Updated by
Bob Marriott

PEOPLE ARE FINDING THEIR WAY to Wellington, and not merely because it's the sailing point for ferries heading south. From the wind-swept green heights overlooking New Zealand's capital, a crystal clear winter morning reveals stunning views over the deceptively quiet waters of Cook Strait stretching to the snowcapped mountains of the South Island; and it's sheer heaven on a mild summer night when a silver medallion of moon tops mysterious, misty hillsides.

Wellington has developed a lively, friendly, and infectious spirit of a city coming into its own. Attractive and compact enough to be a good walking city, you might find yourself content to laze around the harbor, perhaps sipping a chilled glass of chardonnay from a nearby vineyard. The burgeoning film industry—thanks to the *Lord of the Rings* extrav-aganzas—has injected new life into the local arts scene. Ardent film fans can still visit the many *LOTR* sites around the city, but everyone benefits from the lively cafés and the rapidly expanding restaurant cul-ture. On the waterfront the world-class Te Papa Tongarewa–Museum of New Zealand has many hands-on exhibits equally fascinating for children and adults, and the Museum of City and Sea is dedicated to the history of Wellington.

Wellington and the adjacent Hutt Valley are the southern gateway to the Wairarapa, a region whose name has become synonymous with wine. Journey over the hills and meander along quiet byways from vineyard to vineyard for a day—or two, or three—of wine tasting. If wine isn't your thing, the Wairarapa is still worth an excursion for its gardens, fishing, walks, and even hot-air ballooning. Head for the coast, too, where waves crash against craggy, windswept beaches, and the dramatic sunsets intoxicate you with their beauty.

ORIENTATION & PLANNING

GETTING ORIENTED

All main roads from Wellington and the adjacent Wairarapa head north, as the two regions are at the North Island's southern point where the sometimes-stormy waters of Cook Strait divide the country's two main islands. Separated by mountain ranges that virtually tumble into the Strait, road travel between the two regions is via the Hutt Valley and the winding Rimutaka Hill road. Expect peaceful river scenery, a green and pleasant outlook and spectacular views.

Wellington. People are never far from the water; surfers can be happy on beaches that are virtually in the city, and families can take a meal overlooking the harbor. Wellington's also gained a reputation for fos-tering the arts, and it's easily explored on foot.

Wairarapa. In the eastern Wairarapa rugged windswept cliffs form a boundary against the vast Pacific, on the western side the rugged Rimu-taka and Tararua ranges outline a massive division from the capital city and coastal region beyond. Spreading north from the cold, deep waters of Palliser Bay, a rural panorama of fields and quiet vineyards stretches north as far as the eye can see.

PLANNING

Whether you enter Wellington from the coastal State Highway 1 or over the hills from the flat rural plain of the Wairarapa, the majestic Tararua Ranges, a natural barrier separating east from west, stand like a cardboard cutout against the sky. You don't need a car in the city, but to explore the Wairarapa, and its vineyard-rich countryside, it's best to drive. You also need to drive to go north to the long, sweeping beaches of the Kapiti Coast.

GETTING HERE & AROUND

BY AIR

Wellington International Airport (WLG) lies about 8 km (5 mi) from the city. The airport is small and easy to negotiate, but in winter the airport is sometimes closed by fog. Domestic carriers serving Wellington are **Air New Zealand** (☎*0800/737–000 ⊕www.airnewzealand. co.nz*), **Qantas** (☎*0800/808–767 ⊕www.qantas.com.au*), and **Sounds Air** (☎*0800/505–005 ⊕www.soundsair.com*). Air New Zealand connects Wellington to around 20 other New Zealand cities and Qantas connects with Auckland, Christchurch, and Queenstown. Sounds Air has several daily flights to Nelson and Picton.

BY BOAT & FERRY

The **Interisland Line** (☎*0800/802–802 or 04/498–3302 ⊕www.inter islandline.co.nz*) runs a passenger and vehicle ferry service between Wellington and Picton; the Interislander boats take three hours, and fares vary by time of year and range from $52 to $72 one-way per person; for a car and driver, fares are $165–$255. You can book up to six months in advance. The Interislander ferry terminal is about 3 km (2 mi) from the city. A free bus leaves Platform 9 at the Wellington Railway Station for the ferry terminal 40 minutes before sailings.

The **Bluebridge** (☎*0800/844–844 or 04/471–6188 ⊕www.bluebridge. co.nz*) vessels, *Santa Regina and Monte Stello,* sail up to four times per day between Wellington and Picton. Fares are $55 one-way per person, $185 for a driver with car up to 20 feet in length. All fares vary and there are often specials on offer. The ferries leave from the terminal opposite the railway station.

Most car-rental agencies have North Island–South Island transfer programs for their vehicles; you can drop one car off in Wellington and pick up another in Picton on the same contract.

InterCity (☎*04/472–5111 ⊕www.intercitycoach.co.nz*) and **Newmans** (☎*04/499–3261 ⊕www.newmanscoach.co.nz*) buses have daily departures to all major North Island destinations. They also connect with the Interisland Line, which operates the ferries to Picton in the South Island.

6

BY BUS

Buses are the best way to navigate the city, though service outside the city center is sporadic. Taxis are readily available even in outlying areas, and there are numerous car rental agencies. A taxi ride from the airport to central Wellington costs about $25.

In Wellington, buses are operated by several companies; for information on all routes and fares contact **Metlink** (☎ *04/801–7000 or 0800/801–700* ⊕ *www.metlink.org.nz*). The main terminals are at the railway station and from Courtenay Place. For all inner city trips, pay when you board the bus. Bus stops are marked with red-and-white signs. STARpass tickets ($10) allow a day's unlimited travel on all area buses; a $5 ticket gives you a day's bus travel within the city center.

BY CAR

The main access to the city is via the Wellington Urban Motorway, which starts just after the merging of Highways 1 and 2, a few miles north of the city center. The motorway links the city center with all towns and cities to the north.

A car is unnecessary to get around central Wellington, which is compact and its many one-way streets can frustrate drivers. However, a car is convenient for outlying places such as Akatarawa and the coastal region around Paraparaumu and essential for exploring the Wairarapa.

Avis, Budget, and Hertz have offices at Wellington airport. Offices are open 6 AM–1 AM daily.

BY TRAIN

TranzMetro (⊕ *www.tranzmetro.co.nz*)operates suburban trains to Wellington Railway Station from the Hutt Valley, Palmerston North, and Masterton. Cheap day passes are available and it's best to avoid rush hour.

TIMING & WEATHER

November to mid-April is the best time weather-wise in the Wellington area. Most establishments are open (apart from Christmas Day, New Year's Day, and Good Friday). Book well ahead if you're traveling in summer school holidays from mid-December to the end of January. From February to April, you can expect fewer crowds and many brilliant, warm days. Winters bring more rain, but they're rarely bitterly cold. Be prepared for unpredictable weather; rain and southerly gales are possible even during the summer.

ABOUT THE RESTAURANTS

If New Zealand's national sport is rugby, then surely the national pastime must be eating and drinking. In Wellington, restaurants, cafés, and sports bars have been springing up overnight like mushrooms. Although we'll never be without the classic meal of steak, french fries, and cold ale, and while the humble meat pie is still an iconic Kiwi mouthful, Wellington restaurants have embraced more adventurous fare. Chinese, Thai, Japanese, Malaysian, Mexican, and Italian

TOP REASONS TO GO

Arts & Culture. Even before the blockbuster *Lord of the Rings* trilogy infused serious money into the local film industry—earning Wellington the moniker "Wellywood"—the city offered culture vultures plenty of pickings. The national symphony, ballet, and opera are headquartered here. And the biennial New Zealand International Arts Festival celebrates an extensive program of drama, music, dance, and other arts events.

A Wealth of Wineries. Spend a day or two (or three) wine tasting your way through the Wairarapa; this lovely area that only a few years ago was predominantly agri-cultural is now home to more than 30 vineyards.

Eclectic Cuisine. The great variety of Wellington's restaurants allows you to sample foods from dozens of cuisines, while also serving plenty of down-to-earth Kiwi fare. Grabbing a table at an outdoor café and looking out over the beautiful harbor doesn't hurt the taste either.

The Waterfront. Wandering along the Wellington waterfront is one of the most pleasurable ways to spend a day. You can visit (for free!) Te Papa Tongarewa, one of the coun-try's best museums, and the Museum of City and Sea. Or you can walk to Oriental Bay, where you can join the local residents jogging, swimming, riding a bike, or people-watching. In the afternoon, have a seat at one of the many waterfront cafés, order a meal or a glass of local wine, and just quaff the scenery.

6

cuisines are increasingly common, and wine lists are actually being studied (though not with the same intensity as the racing journals and sports pages). Indigenous food, too, is appearing in restaurants around the city—native plants might be paired with traditional seafood or made into sauces to accompany meat or sweet-potato dishes.

In rural areas outside Wellington, the wine industry has revolutionized local tables, with excellent dining and wine-tasting spots proving more than a match for the old-fashioned greasy spoons. In the Wairarapa, restaurants are winning a reputation for creative cuisine.

It's not unusual to see sidewalk tables in the capital or the suburbs occupied on a fine morning by 10 AM, and late-night spots stay open until the wee hours. Generally, lunch runs from noon until 2, and most restaurants close for a few hours before opening for dinner around 6. On Monday, many restaurants are shuttered. Dress codes are still very relaxed; jeans would be frowned upon only in the top restaurants.

	WHAT IT COSTS IN NEW ZEALAND DOLLARS				
	¢	$	$$	$$$	$$$$
Restaurants	under $10	$10–$15	$15–$20	$20–$30	over $30

Prices are per person for a main course at dinner, or the equivalent.

ABOUT THE HOTELS

Accommodations in Wellington range from no-frills backpacker hostels and motel units, to classic bed-and-breakfasts in colonial-era villas, to sleek central hotels. In the suburb of Island Bay, you can stay in a lighthouse or in a castle's tower with magnificent views of Cook Strait and the South Island mountain ranges. For women travelers a central hostel has a women-only floor, and on the sunny slopes of Mt. Victoria a Wellington author has turned her home into a B&B for book lovers.

As more people move into the city, apartments moonlighting as "serviced-apartment" hotels are gaining steam. Rates are significantly more expensive than those of the average motel, but the apartments, such as City Life Wellington, are a good option if you're planning to stay a while. Most of these apartment/hotels have weekend or long-term specials.

Lodgings generally do not have air-conditioning, but the temperate weather in Wellington rarely warrants it.

WHAT IT COSTS IN NEW ZEALAND DOLLARS					
	¢	$	$$	$$$	$$$$
Hotels	under $75	$75–$125	$125–$200	$200–$300	over $300

Prices are for a standard double room in high season, including 12.5% tax.

WELLINGTON

Wellington, the seat of government since 1865, is between the sea and towering hillsides that form a natural arena with the harbor as the stage. The ferries carve patterns on the green water while preening seabirds survey the scene. Houses cascade down the steep hillsides and create a vibrant collage of colorful rooftops against a spectacular green backdrop. An old brick monastery peers down on the marina—a jigsaw of masts and sails bobbing alongside the impressive Te Papa museum. Modern high-rises gaze over Port Nicholson, one of the finest natural anchorages in the world. Known to local Māori as the Great Harbor of Tara, its two massive arms form the "jaws of the fish of Maui" (Maui is the name of a god from Māori legend).

Civic Square represents the heart of town and forms a busy shopping area with Willis and Cuba streets. The entertainment district is centered around Courtenay Place, south of Civic Square. Thorndon, the oldest part of the city, is notable for its many historic wooden houses just north of the Parliamentary district, which includes the distinctive, some might say bizarre, "Beehive" government building.

At the northern end of the waterfront, the Westpac Trust Stadium, home to rugby matches, soccer games, and rock concerts, dominates the skyline, and Lambton Quay is part of a seafront constructed on reclaimed land. At the southern end of the harbor, Norfolk pines line the broad sweep of Oriental Bay, a suburb with a small beach and a wide promenade, backed by art deco buildings and Wellington's most expensive real estate.

GETTING HERE & AROUND

Wellington is a great **walking** city. The compact area around Lambton Quay and on Cuba Street is flat. A stroll along the waterfront around Oriental Bay offers outstanding sea views. If you head for the hills, take the cable car, and see the sights with a walk down.

For cyclers, designated bike lanes in and around Wellington are marked with a continuous white line and a white bike image on the pavement. More details about urban cycling are on the city's Web site, ⊕*www. wcc.govt.nz.* **Penny Farthing Cycles** (⊠*89 Courtenay Pl.* ☎*04/385–2279* ⊕*www.pennyfarthing.co.nz*) rents bikes for $50 per day (includes helmets) for around-town riding, mountain biking, and off-road use.

Bus travel around the city and environs is cheap, and fairly painless providing you avoid the morning and evening rush. A timetable is often attached to a convenient post at the bus stop. On all buses the driver takes the fare; it helps to have some small change though they will normally change small bills. The City Circular Bus departs every 10 minutes on a loop that passes the center's main sights and attractions.

Taxi ride rates are $3 on entry, then $2.50 per 1 km (½ mi). Taxis idle outside the railway station, on Dixon Street, and along Courtenay Place and Lambton Quay.

ESSENTIALS

Airport Wellington Airport (⊠*Stewart Duff Dr., Rongotai* ☎*04/385–5123* ⊕*www.wellington airport.co.nz*).

Airport Transfers Co-operative Shuttle (☎*04/387–8787*). **Stagecoach Flyer** (☎*04/801–7000*).

Bus Services Met link (☎*04/801-7000* ⊕*www.metlink.org.nz*).

Bus Depot Wellington Railway Station (⊠*Bunny St. and Waterloo Quay* ☎*04/498–3000*).

Emergencies Fire, police, and ambulance (☎*111*).

Hospitals After-Hours Medical Centre (⊠*17 Adelaide Rd., Newtown* ☎*04/384–4944*, open 24 hours. **Wellington Hospital** (⊠*Riddiford St., Newtown* ☎*04/385–5999*).

Pharmacy Wellington Urgent Pharmacy (⊠*17 Adelaide Rd.* ☎*04/385–8810*).

Rental Cars Avis (☎*04/801–8108*). **Budget** (☎*04/802–4548*). **Hertz** ☎*04/384–3809*).

Train Lines Met link (☎*04/801–7000* ⊕*www.metlink.org.nz*). **TranzScenic** (☎*0800/872–467 or 04/495–0775* ⊕*www.tranzscenic.co.nz*).

Train Station Wellington Railway Station (⊠*Bunny St. and Waterloo Quay* ☎*04/498–3000*).

Visitor Info **Wellington Visitor Information Centre** (⊠ *Civic Administration Bldg., Victoria and Wakefield Sts.* ☎ *04/802–4860* ⊕ *www.wellingtonnz.com).*

WHAT TO SEE

❽ Archives New Zealand. History buffs should make a beeline here, as these national archives are a treasure trove of documents, photographs, and maps. One highlight, displayed in the Constitution Room, is *Te Tiriti o Waitangi,* the Treaty of Waitangi. This controversial 1840 agreement between the British crown and more than 500 Māori chiefs is considered the founding document of modern New Zealand. *(See the CloseUp box The Treaty of Waitangi in Chapter 2.)* Outside the Constitution Room is a bowl of water called a *wai whakanoa.* Because documents in the Constitution Room are associated with the dead and regarded as *tapu* (taboo), visitors are invited to sprinkle a little of the water over themselves after leaving the room to lift the tapu and return to the land of the living.

The oldest document on display is the Declaration of Independence of the Northern Chiefs, signed by 34 northern Māori chiefs on October 28, 1835, a confederation agreement that led up to the Waitangi treaty. Also on view is the 1893 Women's Suffrage Petition, which led to New Zealand becoming the world's first nation to grant women the vote. ⊠ *10 Mulgrave St., Thorndon* ☎ *04/499–5595* ⊕ *www.archives.govt. nz* ⊠ *Free* ⊙ *Weekdays 9–5, Sat. 9–1 for exhibitions only.*

❹ Ascot Street. Built in the 1870s, the tiny, doll-like cottages along Ascot remain the finest example of a 19th-century streetscape in Wellington. A bench at the top has been thoughtfully provided in the shady courtyard should you need to catch your breath. ⊠ *Off Glenmore St. and Tinakori Rd. northeast of Wellington Botanic Garden, Thorndon.*

⓮ City Gallery Wellington. Whether it's showing the latest exhibition
★ of New Zealand artists or an international collection on tour, City Gallery Wellington is an excellent representation of New Zealand's dynamic modern culture. The gallery has no permanent collection, so exhibits change constantly; you might be in town during a show by a major New Zealand artist such as photographer Laurence Aberhart or Sam Taylor-Wood. Other attractions include the Michael Hirschfeld Gallery, dedicated to showing Wellington artists, and the popular Nikau Café, which serves some of the city's best coffee. In addition to free tours every weekend, City Gallery runs an extensive events program, including talks by local and international artists, films, and dance performances. ⊠ *Civic Sq., Wakefield St.* ☎ *04/801– 3021* ⊕ *www.city-gallery.org.nz* ⊠ *Most exhibitions free; charges for special exhibits vary* ⊙ *Daily 10–5.*

⓭ Civic Square. Wellington's Civic Square is reminiscent of an Italian piazza, its outdoor cafés, benches, lawns, and harbor viewpoints make both a social hub and a delightful sanctuary from the traffic. The **City Gallery** *(see above)*, perhaps the nation's finest art space, the library, and the Town Hall concert venue are just steps apart. Architect Ian Athfield's steel sculptures of *nikau* palms are a marvel, and Māori artist Para Matchitt contributed the impressionistic sculptures flanking the

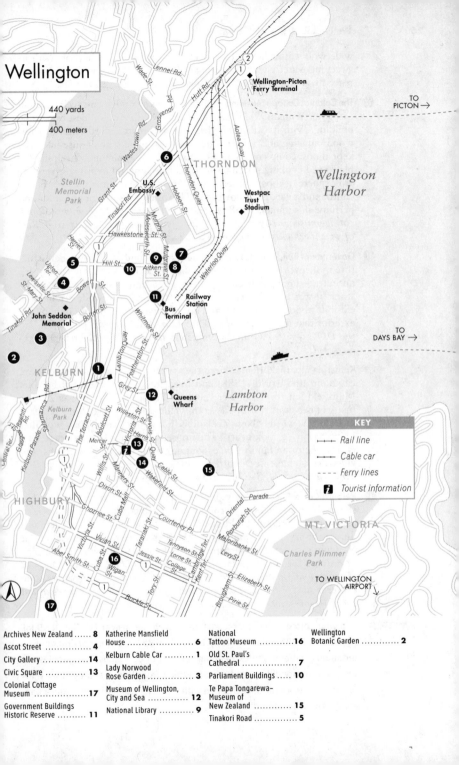

Wellington

440 yards
400 meters

Lennel Rd.

Wellington-Picton
Ferry Terminal

TO
PICTON →

Wellington
Harbor

THORNDON

Stellin
Memorial
Park

U.S.
Embassy

Westpac
Trust
Stadium

Hawkestone St.

Railway
Station

Bus
Terminal

John Seddon
Memorial

KELBURN

Kelburn
Park

Queens
Wharf

Lambton
Harbor

TO
DAYS BAY →

KEY

⊶ Rail line

⊷ Cable car

--- Ferry lines

🛈 Tourist information

Parade

HIGHBURY

MT. VICTORIA

Charles Plimmer
Park

TO WELLINGTON
AIRPORT

wide wooden bridge that connects the square to the harbor. With its sweeping water views, this bridge is a popular spot for picnics or as a place to sit and dream. ⊠ *Wakefield, Victoria, and Harris Sts.*

⑰ The Colonial Cottage Museum. Built in 1858 as a family home by immigrant carpenter William Wallis, this cottage is Wellington's oldest remaining building. With its steep shingled roof and matchboard ceilings, kauri wood paneling and somber Victorian wallpapers, the house has been kept almost completely in its original state. The spinning wheel, smoke-blackened cooking pot, hand-pegged rugs, and oil lamps re-create the atmosphere of those pioneer days. Outside, there's a handmade butter churn, and a garden of flowers and herbs blooms in a riot of color and perfume in summer. ⊠ *68 Nairn St.* ☎ *04/384–9122* ⊕ *www.colonial cottagemuseum.co.nz* ⊒ *$5* ⊙ *Late Dec.– end of Feb., daily 10–4. Rest of year weekends only noon–4.*

⑪ Government Buildings Historic Reserve. This second-largest wooden structure in the world is now home to Victoria University's law faculty. It's an extraordinary conceit—built in 1876 and designed to look like stone, it was entirely fashioned from kauri timber. Inside are historic exhibits about the building and an information center, though it's the exterior that most captivates. ⊠ *15 Lambton Quay* ☎ *04/384–7770, the DOC Visitors Centre administers the building* ⊒ *Free* ⊙ *Weekdays 9–4:30.*

⑥ Katherine Mansfield House. Here the writer, née Kathleen Beauchamp, came into the world (1888) and lived the first five years of her life. Mansfield left to pursue her career in Europe when she was 20, but many of her short stories are set in Wellington. A year before her death in 1923, she wrote, "New Zealand is in my very bones. What wouldn't I give to have a look at it!" The house, which has been restored as a typical Victorian family home, contains furnishings, photographs, and videos that elucidate Mansfield's life and times. ⊠ *25 Tinakori Rd., Thorndon* ☎ *04/473–7268* ⊒ *$5.50* ⊙ *Tues.–Sun. 10–4.*

❶ Kelburn Cable Car. The Swiss-built funicular railway makes a short but sharp climb to Kelburn Terminal, from which there are great views across parks and city buildings to Port Nicholson. Sit on the left side during the six-minute journey for the best scenery. A small Cable Car Museum is situated at the top in the old winding house with a display of restored former cable cars (entry is free). ⊠ *280 Lambton Quay, at Grey St. and Upland Rd.* ☎ *04/472–2199* ⊕ *www.wellingtonnz.com/ cablecar* ⊒ *$ 2.50 each way; $4.50 round-trip* ⊙ *Departures about every 10 mins, weekdays 7 AM–10 PM, weekends 9 AM–10 PM.*

NEED A BREAK?

Sip your coffee at the character-filled **Smith the grocer** (⊠ *The Old Bank Arcade, 233–237, Lambton Quay* ☎ *04/473–8591*). Ornaments range from old radios and beer crates to an ancient set of golf clubs. The goodies are tasty and reasonably priced with anything from bacon and eggs on thick brown toast to warm chicken salad with chicory, mesclun greens, and a Caesar dressing. It's open daily.

❸ Lady Norwood Rose Garden. On a fine summer day you couldn't find a
★ better place to go for a sniff. The rose garden is the most popular part
of the **Wellington Botanic Garden.** Situated on a plateau, the formal
circular layout consists of 106 beds, each planted with a single variety
of modern and traditional shrubs. Climbing roses cover a brick-and-
timber colonnade on the perimeter. Adjacent to the rose beds, the Begonia House conservatory is filled with delicate plants and has a teahouse.
✉ *North end of Wellington Botanic Garden, Tinakori Rd., for parking
lot* ☎ *04/801–3071* 💰 *Donation appreciated* ⊙ *Begonia House daily
10–4, main gardens daily dawn–dusk.*

⓬ Museum of Wellington, City & Sea. You can smell the hessian (burlap)
★ sacks, hear the gulls, and see the (mechanical) rats scuttling around in
this refurbished 1892 bond store, now a museum that portrays the history of the original Māori tribes and the European settlers who arrived
around 1840. Spread over three floors, the displays cover work, leisure,
crime, and education in 19th-century Wellington. Holographic effects
bring to startling life two Māori legends, and in the Wahine Gallery,
exhibits and a short film depict the 1968 *Wahine* ferry sinking that cost
52 lives. The Plimmer's Ark Gallery tells the story of John Plimmer,
known as the "Father of Wellington" for his work in developing the
city. You can see **Plimmer's Ark,** the excavated remains of the ship *Incon-
stant,* wrecked in 1849 on Pencarrow Head, in the Old Bank Arcade,
a shopping center on Lambton Quay. Plimmer bought the damaged
ship in 1850 and used it as a loading dock. Eventually it became land-
locked and later demolished, except that the remains of its hull were
discovered in 1997. ✉ *The Bond Store, Queens Wharf* ☎ *04/472–8904*
🌐 *www.museumofwellington.co.nz* 💰 *Free* ⊙ *Daily 10–5.*

❾ National Library. Opposite the Parliament Buildings is the country's
national library. The Alexander Turnbull Library, a "library within a
library," specializes in documentary materials about New Zealand and
the Pacific. Its books, manuscripts, photographs, newspapers, maps,
and oral history tapes are open for research. Exhibitions are regularly
held in the National Library Gallery. The Gallery has a lively public
events program. ✉ *Molesworth St. at Aitken St., Thorndon* ☎ *04/474–
3000* 🌐 *www.natlib.govt.nz* 💰 *Free* ⊙ *Weekdays 9–5, Sat. 9–1.*

⓰ National Tattoo Museum of New Zealand. This small museum gives a fascinating glimpse of body art, from biceps to buttocks. Tattooing is an
important part of Māori culture; like a coat of arms, a traditional *moko*
(tattoo) demonstrates a person's heritage. The volunteer-run collection
introduces the art with carvings, pictures, and plenty of literature.
One video shows a 74-year-old Māori woman having her chin moko
renewed the traditional way: her skin is carved with a bone chisel...and
she doesn't utter a word of complaint. If you're inspired, you can get
tattooed. ✉ *29 Wigan St. (Underground Arts Bldg.)* ☎ *04/385–2185*
🖶 *04/3852–1812* 🌐 *www.tat2.co.nz* 💰 *$5* ⊙ *Tues.–Sun. noon–5:30.*

❼ Old St. Paul's Cathedral. Consecrated in 1866, the church is a splendid
example of the English Gothic Revival style executed in native timbers.
Even the trusses supporting the roof transcend their mundane function

with splendid craftsmanship. ⊠*Mulgrave St., Thorndon* ☎*04/473–6722* ✆*Free* ⊗*Daily 10–5.*

🔟 **Parliament Buildings** consist of Parliament House with its Debating Chamber, a copy of the one in the British House of Commons in Westminster right down to the Speakers Mace. Here legislation is presented, debated, and voted on. There is fine Māori artwork in the Maori Affairs Select Committee Room. The adjoining building is the Parliamentary Library. The neighboring Executive Wing is known for architectural reasons as The Beehive. Here the Prime Minister and Cabinet Ministers of the elected Government have their offices and Cabinet meetings and press conferences are held. Across the road at the corner of Bowen Street and Lambton Quay, Bowen House is also part of the complex. Tours start in The Beehive, and a guide explains the Parliamentary process in detail. ⊠*Molesworth St.* ☎*04/471–9999, 04/471–9503 tour desk* ⊕*www.ps.parliament.govt.nz* ✆*Free* ⊗*Tours depart on the hr weekdays 10–4, Sat. 10–3, Sun. 11–3.*

Premier House. The official residence of New Zealand's prime minister was a simple cottage when first erected in 1843. It has increased in size and grandeur somewhat since then. Prime ministers remained in residence until 1935, when the new Labour government, caught up in its reforming zeal, turned it into a dental clinic. The house had fallen into disrepair by the early 1990s. Since then it has been restored—and the prime minister has moved back in. The house isn't open to the public. ⊠*260 Tinakori Rd., Thorndon.*

🔟 **Te Papa Tongarewa–Museum of New Zealand.** This museum remains one of New Zealand's major attractions. It provides an essential introduction to the country's people, cultures, landforms, flora, and fauna. Unusual exhibits include a simulated earthquake and a visit to a *marae* (Māori meetinghouse), where a *pōwhiri* (Māori greeting involving song and speeches) welcomes you. You can explore an outdoor forest area with moa (the extinct, ostrichlike native bird) bones and glowworms or delve into the stories of New Zealand's early European migrants. In the Time Warp area, a sort of theme park where most activities have additional fees, you can simulate a bungy jump or leap three generations ahead to Wellington, 2055. Four discovery centers allow children to weave, hear storytelling, and learn a bit of Māori through song. ⊠*Cable St.* ☎*04/381–7000* ⊕*www.tepapa.govt.nz* ✆*Free; some exhibitions cost up to $12* ⊗*Fri.–Wed. 10–6, Thurs. 10–9.*

🔟 **Tinakori Road.** The lack of suitable local stone combined with the collapse of most of Wellington's brick buildings in the earthquake of 1848 ensured the almost exclusive use of timber for building here in the second half of the 19th century. Most carpenters of the period had learned their skills as cabinetmakers and shipwrights in Europe, and the sturdy houses in this street are a tribute to their craftsmanship. Two notables are the tall and narrow No. 306 and **Premier House.**

Fodor's Choice
★
☺

Picnic Botanic Garden Café. Set in a sun-drenched corner of the Botanic Gardens this delightful café is in a large conservatory attached to the Orchid House. From the eggs Florentine breakfast to the chunky steak pie for lunch the menu caters for all tastes. Sit outside, sip a latte, and smell the roses. ⊠ *Tinakori Rd.* ☎ *04/472-6002* ⊙ *8:30 AM–5 PM).*

❷ ★ **Wellington Botanic Garden.** In the hills overlooking downtown is a concentration of beautifully varied terrain. Woodland gardens under native and exotic trees fill the valleys, water-loving plants line a pond and mountain streams, and lawns spread over flatter sections with beds of bright seasonal bulbs and annuals. The lovely **Lady Norwood Rose Garden** is in the northeast part of the garden. **Carter Observatory and Planetarium,** the only one of its kind in New Zealand, has public displays and programs, including evening telescope viewings, which are great opportunities for those from the northern hemisphere to learn about the southern night sky. If you don't want to walk the hill up to the garden, the **Kelburn Cable Car** can take you. Or take the No. 12 bus (direction: Karori) from Lambton Quay to the main (Glenmore Street) entrance. ⊠ *Tinakori Rd. for parking lot; main entrances on Upland Rd. (for cable car) and Glenmore St.* ☎ *04/801–3071 gardens, 04/472–8167 observatory and planetarium* ⊕ *www.carterobs. ac.nz* ⊠ *Main gardens free, Carter Observatory general admission $6, planetarium $12* ⊙ *Main gardens daily sunrise–sunset; observatory May–Oct., Sun.–Thurs. 11–4, Fri. and Sat. 11 AM–late; Nov.–Apr., Sun.–Tues. 10–5, Wed.–Sat. 10 AM–late.*

AROUND WELLINGTON

The Hutt Valley. A 10-minute drive north of Wellington on State Highway 2—with magnificent harbor views all the way—leads you to the Hutt Valley and its namesake river. Attractions in the bustling **Hutt City** include **the New Dowse** (⊠ *45 Laings Rd., Hutt City* ☎ *04/570–6500),* where you will find a changing array of exhibitions showcasing a range of creativity from New Zealand's extraordinary jewelry to fashion, photography, and ceramics to youth culture. Sites such as Māori treasures and Stansborough are adding a new dimension to tourism in the area and the tempting shops and cafés around Jackson Street in Petone make for an interesting morning. Don't miss the small but interesting **Petone Settlers Museum** (⊠ *The Esplanade, Hutt City* ☎ *04/568–8373),* on the waterfront of Wellington Harbour near the landing site of the first organized European settlement in New Zealand. The Petone Esplanade on the eastern side of the harbor, overlooked by houses clinging to steep bush-clad hills, winds about 8 km (5 mi) through the suburb of **Eastbourne.** Stop in the tiny shopping area for an alfresco bite before driving on to where the road eventually transforms into a 4-km (2½-mi) walking track, following the coast to **Pencarrow Head** and its lighthouse, with views across the strait. (There's a kiosk where you can rent a bike if you wish.)

Back in Hutt City, the **Hutt River Trail** starts at Hikoikoi Reserve on Petone Marine Parade near the Hutt River mouth. Specifically for walkers and cyclists, this scenic trail follows the river for more than 32 km (20 mi) between Hutt City and Upper Hutt.

Back on State Highway 2 heading north, enjoy the views of the distant Tararua Ranges, snow covered in winter. If you're a *Lord of the Rings* fan, stop by the **Dry Creek Quarry,** where the scenes of Helms Deep and Minas Tirith were filmed; it's at the bottom of Haywards Hill Road—look for the traffic lights for the turnoff from State Highway 2.

From Upper Hutt, continuing north on State Highway 2 leads to the Wairarapa region, but just beyond Upper Hutt, look for **Kaitoke Regional Park** (⊠ *Waterworks Rd., off State Hwy. 2* ☎ *04/526–7322 for rangers*), a great camping and picnic spot with pleasant walks by the river. In the park, *LOTR* fans can check out the bridge, which stood in for Rivendell, the rallying place for elves. Pause by the crystal-clear river, flanked by towering trees and native bush, and listen to the birdsong.

Karori Wildlife Sanctuary. Minutes from downtown Wellington, 623 acres of regenerating forest have become a sanctuary for some of New Zealand's endangered species. A predator-proof fence surrounds the haven, where rare wildlife like the little spotted kiwi, saddleback, tuatara, and *kaka* (an indigenous parrot) have been introduced, along with stitchbirds. You can walk along bush tracks and stroll around the lakes, or join one of the day or night guided tours. ⊠ *31 Waiapu Rd., Karori* ☎ *04/920–9213* ⊕ *www.sanctuary.org.nz* ⊠ *$12 (self guided walk), tours from $22, 2-hr night tours $45* ☉ *Daily 10–5 all yr, except Christmas Day.*

★ **Māori Treasures.** A visit to this exceptional Māori enterprise gives you a wonderful, firsthand look at Māori arts and culture. Based on the Waiwhetu marae (meetinghouse) about 21 km (13 mi) from Wellington, the complex showcases artisans at work carving, weaving, and fashioning instruments. On the tour you might even hear someone playing the nose flute or get your hands on a woven cloak. A traditionally carved *waka* (war canoe) is on display; other examples of carving and artwork produced in the studio are sold in the gift shop. Guided tours can be arranged through Flat Earth New Zealand Experiences (⇨ *Tours, below).* ⊠ *58 Guthrie St., Hutt City* ☎ *04/939–9630* ☉ *Daily 9–4; tours as arranged.*

★ **Otari-Wilton's Bush.** Devoted to gathering and preserving indigenous plants, Otari's collection is the largest of its kind. With clearly marked bushwalks and landscape demonstration gardens, it aims to educate the public and ensure the survival of New Zealand's unique plant life. While in the garden, you'll learn to identify plant life in the forest, from the various *blechnum* ferns underfoot to the tallest trees overhead. An aerial walkway crosses high above the bush, giving an unusual vantage point over the gardens. Look and listen for the native birds that flock to this haven: the bellbird (*korimako*), gray duck (*parera*), New Zealand wood pigeon (*kereru*), silvereye (*tauhou*), and *tūī,* among others. Take the No. 14 Wilton bus from downtown (20 minutes) and ask the driver

Akatarawa Valley

Winding through the steep bush-clad hills north of Wellington, the narrow road to the Akatarawa Valley (in the Māori language, Akatarawa means "place of tangled vines") requires a degree of driving care, but it leads to a number of hidden gems. About 35 minutes out of Wellington on State Highway 2, turn left at the clearly marked Brown Owl turnoff north of Upper Hutt. About two minutes after the turnoff, look for Harcourt Park, where a number of scenes in the *Lord of the Rings* movies were filmed. Nearby, **Harcourt Holiday Park** (04/526–7400) has motel units, tourist cabins, and tent sites in lovely bush surroundings.

Half a mile farther on, a bridge at the junction of the Hutt and Akatarawa rivers leads into the Akatarawa Valley proper. Drive over the bridge, go past the cemetery, and then on the left, look for **the Blueberry Farm** (04/526–6788), where you can pick your own blueberries (January) or go for a swim in the river. Nearby **Bluebank Blueberry and Emu Farm** (04/526–9540) also grows delicious blueberries and raises the large flightless emus.

Continue on to **Efil Doog Garden of Art** (04/526–7924 www.efildoog-nz.com), where Shirley and Ernest Cosgrove tend a stunning 11-acre garden and sculpture display. They also have an art gallery exhibiting some fine early New Zealand paintings. The grounds are magnificent at rhododendron time, October–early December. The garden's open October through March, Wednesday–Sunday; entry is $12. The winding road crosses some wonderful old trestle bridges over the Akatarawa River before reaching **Staglands**

Wildlife Reserve (04/526–7529 www.staglands.co.nz), filled with friendly animals and birds that will eat out of your hand. As you wander through these peaceful 25 acres, meet the kea, kune-kune pigs (a native variety), deer, and wallabies, and feed trout in the pools. Stop into the falcon aviary before picnicking by the river or stopping by the log-cabin café. The reserve is open daily and costs $16.

Look on the right for the tiny wooden Church of St. Andrews, then turn right almost immediately for the **Reikorangi Potteries** (04/293–5146). Here, Wilf and Jan Wright display local handicrafts and paintings, plus their own pottery. Wander around the small animal park to view rabbits, llamas, wallabies, and a host of different birds, or stroll along the riverbank and take a swim. If you haven't eaten yet, the café is a delightful stop. The potteries are open November through March, Tuesday–Sunday, and April through October, Wednesday–Sunday. Admission is $5. The road continues for about 3 km (2 mi to join State Highway 1 at the Waikanae traffic lights, where you can head back to Wellington; from here, you're about 45 minutes north of the city. You can get more information on the Akatarawa Valley from the **Upper Hutt Information Centre** (84–90 Main St., Upper Hutt 04/527–2141 www.upperhuttcity.com).

6

to let you off at the gardens. ✉ *Wilton Rd., Wilton* ☎*04/475–3245* 🎫*Free* 🕙*Daily dawn–dusk.*

★ **Southward Car Museum.** The largest collection of vintage cars in the southern hemisphere has more than 300 vehicles on display. A Davis three-wheeler, one of only 17 ever made, was used in the inaugural parade of U.S. President Harry Truman. It stands among Cadillacs, Bugattis, and gleaming Rolls-Royces. The motorcycle section is a must for two-wheeler buffs. The museum is just off Highway 1, a 45-minute drive north of Wellington. ✉*Otaihanga Rd., Paraparaumu* ☎*04/297–1221* 🌐*www.southward.org.nz* 🎫*$10* 🕙*Daily 9–5.*

> **AKATARAWA TREK**
>
> Liz and Keith Budd offer two-day walks through the Akatarawa Valley for active groups of up to six. The walks, which take five–six hours, operate from October to April 30 and include all transport, luggage transfer, and comfortable accommodation. Gardens and wildlife park admissions and meals are also included in the cost of $275. Bookings are essential. ☎*04/526–4867* 🖨*04/526–3872* 🌐*www.akatrack.co.nz.*

★ **Stansborough.** Step back to the 1890s to a working mill where wool from an ancient breed of gray sheep, together with alpaca, is woven on 100-year-old looms. Fabric produced here was used for costumes in *The Lord of the Rings, The Lion, the Witch and the Wardrobe,* and other films and it's your opportunity to try to buy the type of cloak worn by Frodo or Sam. Contact info@stansborough.co.nz for guided tour bookings. ✉*100 Hutt Park Rd., Seaview, Hutt City* ☎*04/566–5591* 🖨*04/566–5592* 🎫*$19* 🕙*Weekdays 9:30–4, Sat., 9:30–2.*

OFF THE BEATEN PATH

The Rimutaka Incline. The Rimutaka Incline Railway operated from 1878 until 1955, connecting Wellington and the Wairarapa. Special locomotives known as Fell engines were needed to haul trains up the steepest grade in the country. In 1955, a tunnel superseded the Rimutaka Incline, the tracks were torn up, and the former railway route was converted into a path for walking and cycling. The track runs for about 16 km (10 mi) from Kaitoke, just north of Upper Hutt, to a parking area just beyond Cross Creek near Featherston on the Wairarapa side. It takes about five hours to walk the length. The track passes through two old tunnels, several bridges, and some wild countryside. The track is mostly compacted gravel, but it can get muddy in bad weather. Beware of high winds on the Wairarapa side; a train was once blown off the tracks here!

To arrange transport at both ends of the track, contact Fred Roberts of **Valley Shuttles** (☎*04/973–8150, 027/248–1745 cell).* The only remaining Fell engine is now on display at the Fell Locomotive Museum in the Wairarapa *(⇨ Around Masterton in The Wairarapa, below).*

WHERE TO EAT

$$$$
Fodor'sChoice
★
✕**Logan Brown.** Partners and TV personalities Steve Logan and Al Brown have created a winner in this stylishly renovated 1920s bank building. An aquarium tank is set into the bar top, so that fish swim by under your cocktail. The duck confit with crispy lentil cakes, baby turnips, and peas followed by cinnamon cake with lemon panna cotta and tangelo sorbet makes for a memorable meal. ⊠*Cuba St. at Vivian St.* ☎*04/801–5114* ▤*AE, DC, MC, V* ◯*No lunch Sat.*

$$$$
✕**Shed 5.** Huge windows facing the harbor belie the fact that this historic building on the wharf was once a woolshed. Crisp white tablecloths and sparkling tableware gleam under the dark-wood beams in the spacious dining room. On the broad-ranging, comfort food menu, seafood stands out, especially the steamed sole fillet on soft polenta and potato with brown butter and white balsamic caper dressing. Rich desserts includes pineapple lasagna with piña colada sorbet and spicy caramel. ⊠*Shed 5, Queens Wharf, Jervois Quay* ☎*04/499–9069* ▤*AE, DC, MC, V.*

$$$$
Fodor'sChoice
★
✕**White House.** A Wellington icon that has been serving exceptional food for over 15 years, the menu is driven by seasonal produce and leans to organic wherever possible. Grilled cervena served with mushrooms, truffle foam, and porcini porridge is a good choice, which you might follow with rice pudding and slowly roasted nectarine with raspberry ice-cream and nectarine jelly. Windows on both floors of the namesake house, an early-20th-century beach cottage, give stunning views across Oriental Bay and the harbor. ⊠*232 Oriental Parade* ☎*04/385–8555* ▤*AE, DC, MC, V* ◯*No lunch Sat.–Thurs.*

$$$–$$$$
✕**Boulcott Street Bistro.** A well-respected institution on the Wellington dining scene, this old colonial-style house conveys tradition. Dishes such as pan-seared salmon with sweet pepper, couscous, and Meyer lemon marmalade satisfy the discerning clientele. On the dessert list, keep an eye out for the lemon tart with yogurt sorbet. ⊠*99 Boulcott St.* ☎*04/499–4199* ▤*AE, DC, MC, V* ◯*No lunch weekends.*

$$$–$$$$
✕**Dockside Restaurant & Bar.** A wooden-beam roof and oiled floorboards give this former warehouse on the wharf a nautical feel. You can get close to the water, too, outside on the large harborfront deck. Inside or out, it's a lively spot, particularly on Friday nights, when a DJ spins to a packed house. The menu changes daily but has a seafood bias, including char-grilled Akaroa salmon served with *bocconcini* (small balls of fresh mozzarella). Phone first as this place gets crowded and noisy on weekends. ⊠*Shed 3, Queens Wharf, Jervois Quay* ☎*04/499–9900* ⌂*Reservations essential* ▤*AE, DC, MC, V.*

$$$–$$$$
★
✕**The Green Parrot.** Talk about atmosphere: this stalwart steak-and-seafood joint, which has been serving meals continuously since 1926, has a grill made from melted-down gun barrels. Kosta Sakoufakis, the welcoming chef and co-owner, makes people feel at home and can talk about American Marines visiting the place during World War II. Politicians and celebrities like Peter Jackson gravitate here, and a mural depicts notable clients ranging from famous writers to two former prime ministers. ⊠*16 Taranaki St.* ☎*04/384–6080* ▤*AE, DC, MC, V* ◯*No lunch.*

6

$$$-$$$$ ✗**Herd Street Brasserie.** On the waterfront with a view over a forest of masts in the marina, the food is as good as the outlook. The Waimarino pork loin served with an apricot and cannelloni bean ragout, green beans, and Madeira sauce will leave you smiling. ✉ *Unit 1, Herd La., Chaffers Dock, Waterfront, Wellington* ☎ *04/384–9470* ⚷ *Reservations essential* ▭ *AE, DC, MC, V.*

$$-$$$$ ✗**Great India.** In this award-winning restaurant a lengthy menu packs in dozens of authentic Indian dishes, from curries to vegetarian options to meats cooked in the tandoor oven. Specialties include *rogan gosh* (lamb cooked in a thick tomato gravy) and *samba masala* (venison sauced with coconut cream). Sequined, embroidered tapestries glint in the soft lighting. The service is friendly and helpful. ✉ *141 Manners St.* ☎ *04/384–5755* ▭ *AE, DC, MC, V.*

$$$ ✗**Café Bastille.** This charming French provincial café cheers you with its lemon walls, plum-color ceilings, and "washing line" hung with posters. Huge mirrors make the dining area look extra large, and live jazz is often featured. A stuffed white cockerel stands over the small corner bar emphasizing the French influence. The menu has plenty to recommend, too, including seared rabbit liver, bacon, oyster mushrooms, spinach, and a Dubonnet syrup. The eye fillet of veal with gratin potatoes, forest mushroom cream sauce, and duxelle is superb; so is the Paris bistro–style mousse au chocolat. ✉ *16 Majoribanks St.* ☎ *04/382–9559* ▭ *AE, DC, MC, V* ⊘ *Closed Sun.*

$$$ ✗**Maria Pia's Trattoria.** Patrons relax and laugh a lot in this homey Italian gem. Large potted plants sprawl across window ledges and dark polished wood tables reflect candlelight through glasses of red wine. From the delicious aromas pervading the interior try the artisan pasta from Puglia with tomato, aubergine, and ricotta cheese; for an extra flavor ask for lamb to go with it. Follow with mascarpone chocolate and coffee delight for a superb meal. Wines by the bottle or glass are matched with the menu. Reservations are advisable. ✉ *55 Mulgrave St.* ☎ *04/499–5590* ⊘ *Closed Sun.*

$$$ ✗**The Potters Kiln Café.** If you've got wanderlust and an appetite, drive out to this tiny cottage in the Reikorangi Potteries, 48 km (30 mi) from town. The menu offers mouthwatering creations such as roasted rack of lamb in a spiced plum sauce, and sticky date pudding topped with hot caramel sauce. Pottery and paintings fill the walls, as do interesting curios—an old wooden butter churn stands next to a small accordion. To get here from Wellington, take State Highway 1 north to Waikanae and turn right at the second traffic light. Cross the train tracks, and in about 4½ km (2¾ mi) turn left into the Reikorangi Potteries. Reservations are a good idea. ✉ *27 Ngatiawa Rd., Reikorangi* ☎ *04/293–5146* ▭ *MC, V* ⊘ *Closed Mon. and Tues.*

$$$ ✗**Zibibbo Restaurant & Bar.** From the cozy bar walk upstairs to the restaurant where a large access hatch provides a panoramic view of a spotless white-tiled kitchen with a wood-fired pizza oven. Start with a Zibibbo tapas platter, then go for lemon- and rosemary-rubbed rotisserie chicken with salsa rosso before working your way through the dark chocolate mousse with black cherries. Wow! ✉ *25–29 Taranaki*

Kapiti Coast & Kapiti Island

A drive up the West Coast from Wellington is not to be missed. State Highway 1 takes you north, and about a half hour out of the city you hit the coast at Paremata. From here you can follow South Highway 1 straight up the Kapiti Coast, so called for the view of Kapiti Island. Alternatively, you can take the longer—but infinitely more scenic—drive around the Pauatahanui Inlet and Bird Sanctuary, following the road along the ridge of the rugged, winding, and windy Paekakariki Hill where stunning views of the coastline and Kapiti Island await you. Both routes lead to **Paekakariki** (pie-*kahk*-a-reeky), a small, artsy beach town.

Paekakariki's draw is the shore, but it's also the main entry point of **Queen Elizabeth Park** (⊠ *Entrance on Wellington Rd.* ☎ *04/292–8625*), more than 1,000 acres of fields and sand dunes along the coast. The park has a walking trail, horseback riding, mountain biking, and a playground. A little farther up the coast on State Highway 1 is **Lindale Farm** (☎ *04/297–0916*), which is home to **Kapiti Cheeses and Ice Cream.** Along with terrific locally made cheeses, you can try decadent ice cream with Kiwi flavors, such as feijoa or fig and *manuka* honey (manuka is a kind of tea tree). The farm is just past Paekakariki's neighboring town, Paraparaumu. Paraparaumu is the departure point for one of Wellington's best-kept secrets: **Kapiti Island** (⊠ *Coastlands Parade* ☎ *04/298–8195*). The island has been a protected reserve since 1897 and is a fantastic place to hike. All pests have been eliminated from the island, and birdlife flourishes, including saddlebacks, stitchbirds, and colonies of little spotted and South Island brown kiwi. Don't be surprised if a curious and fearless weka bird investigates your daypack or unties your shoelaces. Climb to the more than 1,700-ft-high Tuteremoana lookout point.

The island's most famous inhabitant was the Ngati Toa chief Te Rauparaha, who took the island by ruse in 1822. From this stronghold, he launched bloodthirsty raids before he was captured in 1846. He died in 1849, but his burial place is a mystery. Old tri-pots (used for melting down whale blubber) on the island bear testimony to the fact that Kapiti was also used as a whaling station in the late 19th century.

The **Department of Conservation** (*DOC* ⊠ *18, Manners St.* ☎ *04/384 7770* ⊕ *www.doc.govt.nz*) oversees the island and restricts visitors to 50 a day. You'll need a permit ($9). Book at least three months in advance. Two tour companies provide transportation to the island: **Kapiti Marine Charter** (☎ *0800/433–779 or 04/297–2585* ⊕ *www.kapitimarinecharter.co.nz*) and **Kapiti Island Tours** (☎ *0800/527–484 or 04/237–7965* ⊕ *www.kapititours.co.nz*). Boats leave from the beach at Paraparaumu; both companies charge $45 round-trip. Once on the island, you're taken to the DOC headquarters, where you can get trail maps. For more information about Kapiti Island, contact the Wellington Visitor Information Centre (⇨ *Visitor Information in Wellington Essentials, above*) or the **Paraparaumu Visitor Information Center** (☎ *04/298–8195* ⊕ *www.naturecoast.co.nz*).

6

St. ☎*04/385–6650* 🖷*04/385–6689* ⊕*www.zibibbo.co.nz* 🖃*AE, DC, MC, V* ⊘*No lunch weekends.*

$$-$$$ ✕**The Back-Bencher Pub & Café.** Right across the way from the Parliament
★ buildings sits "the house that has no peers," a landmark watering hole where politicians grab a cold beer after a hot debate. The walls have become a gallery of political cartoons and puppets tweaking government characters and well-known sports figures. Don't Labour over the prices, it'll be a National disaster if you miss this one. Elect for seared duck breast, Asian spices, noodles, bok choy, with ginger, honey, and soy dressing, but go careful on the chili: you could be breathing fire into the opposition. ⊠*34 Molesworth St.* ☎*04/ 472–3065* 🖃*AE, DC, MC, V.*

$$-$$$ ✕**SOI Café & Bar.** With floor-to-ceiling windows providing sweeping views of Evans Bay, this restaurant feels a bit like a cruise ship. The menu is varied, and the helpings are generous and not too expensive. The char-grilled Hawkes Bay natural lamb, served open on garlic sourdough bread, salad greens, and mint pesto dressing, makes a great main. While watching the white horses (whitecaps) gallop across the bay, finish off with white chocolate and pistachio parfait served with mixed berry compote. ⊠*301 Evans Bay Parade* ☎*04/386–3830* 🖃*DC, MC, V.*

$-$$$ ✕**La Bella Italia.** Within sight of Petone Wharf, an old warehouse has turned into a vital restaurant and delicatessen, the walls alive with in-your-face murals, photographs, and posters with an Italian theme. Savor the atmosphere and fresh food and exotic wines. Enjoy baked fish fillets of the day with broccoli, cauliflower, sun-dried tomatoes, and black olives; warm salad; and a matching pino grigio. It's food for the gods! ⊠*10 Nevis St., Petone* ☎*04/566–9303* ⊕*www.labellaitalia. co.nz* ⌖*Reservations essential* 🖃*AE, MC, V.*

$-$$$ ✕**Vista.** For a breezy meal and some morning sunshine, grab an outdoor table at this busy café with views across Oriental Parade to the bustling harbor. Breakfast is available until 4 PM; try the smoked fish and salmon croquette with sautéed spinach, grilled asparagus, and dill hollandaise. In the evening, you might fancy Moroccan spiced lamb rump with eggplant, capsicum, and tomato ratatouille; fruit and nut couscous; and yogurt chermoula; or try crumbed veal with Parmesan mash and creamed spinach. ⊠*106 Oriental Parade* ☎*04/385–7724* 🖃*AE, DC, MC, V* ⊘*No dinner Sun.–Tues.*

$-$$ ✕**Dixon Street Gourmet Deli.** The owner's grandfather opened this estab-
★ lishment in 1920; the friendly staff and excellent pickings have kept it a local favorite ever since. You could snag provisions for a picnic lunch or get a table inside for a bagel with smoked salmon and cream cheese or a tangy slice of lemon cheesecake. ⊠*45–47 Dixon St.* ☎*04/384–2436* 🖃*AE, MC, V.*

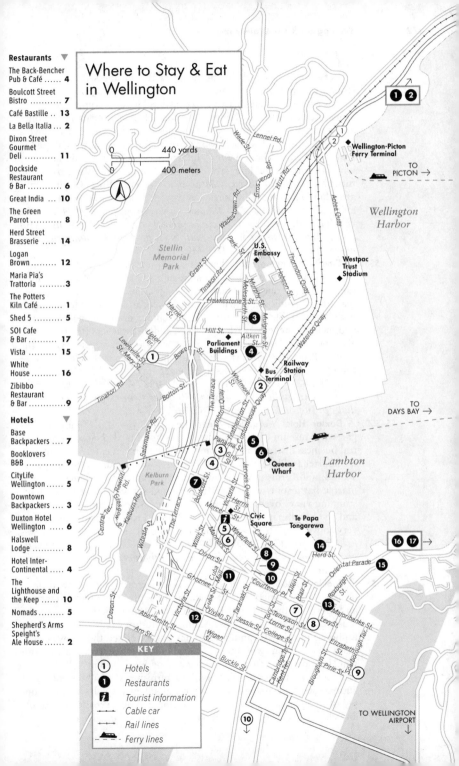

WHERE TO STAY

$$–$$$$

Fodor's Choice

★

🏨**Hotel InterContinental.** In the heart of the business district, and a stone's throw from the waterfront, this landmark high-rise gets the details right. The spacious art deco–inspired foyer is complemented by ferns, orchids, and fruit bowls (help yourself). New Zealand paintings and prints line the hallways and the guest rooms, which also have a faintly deco style. The basic rooms are small but warmly appointed in russet and gold. The top-end "club rooms" are more modern; snowy white duvets on the king-size beds stand out against the dark-wood furnishings. There's even a 24-hour car service. **Pros:** Comfortable, affordable, and on the doorstep of the city happenings. **Cons:** Large and rather soul-less. ⊠*Featherston and Grey Sts.* ☎*04/472–2722* 🖷*04/472–4724* ⊕*www.intercontinental.com* ☞*231 rooms* ⚘*In-room: dial-up. In-hotel: restaurant, bars, pool, gym, laundry service, no-smoking rooms* ⊟*AE, DC, MC, V.*

$$$

🏨**CityLife Wellington.** This all-suites hotel is smack dab in the middle of the city—and if you can snag a suite at a weekend or special summer rate, you've got one of the best-value lodgings in town. You have a wide selection of studios and spacious one-, two-, and three-bedroom suites with comfortable lounge furniture. Facilities are similar in all suites and include kitchens, washers, dryers, and dishwashers (the rooms are also serviced). Despite the location, you don't get street noise in the rooms. **Pros:** In the heart of the city, just an elevator ride to Lambton Quay. **Con:** More suited to a longer stay. ⊠*300 Lambton Quay* ☎*04/922–2800 or 0800/368–888* 🖷*04/922–2803* ⊕ *www.heritage hotels.co.nz/citylife-wellington* ☞*70 suites* ⚘*In-room: kitchen, VCR, dial-up. In-hotel: gym* ⊟*AE, DC, MC, V* ⏃*BP.*

$$–$$$$

🏨**Duxton Hotel Wellington.** Near the waterfront and Te Papa Tongarewa–Museum of New Zealand, this hotel is also close to the central business district and shopping, with the vibrant entertainment area of Courtenay Place at the back door. Rooms are decorated in pastel shades, and furnishings include writing desks, tea/coffeemakers, and marble bathrooms with separate bath and shower. Most rooms have stunning views over the harbor or the city. Valet parking is provided, and the hotel is minutes from the airport. **Pros:** Right by the action, very convenient car parking. **Con:** Some rooms are dated. ⊠*170 Wakefield St.* ☎*04/473–3900 or 0800/655–555* 🖷*04/473–3929* ⊕*www.duxton.com* ☞*192 rooms* ⚘*In-room: Ethernet. In-hotel: restaurant, bar, laundry facilities* ⊟*AE, DC, MC, V.*

$$

★

🏨**Booklovers B&B.** Residents of the Mount Victoria neighborhood claim to live in the sunniest part of town, and the pretty wooden Victorians and views of the city and harbor make Mount Victoria one of the most-painted city landscapes. Wellington author Jane Tolerton has set up house in this villa and, true to her passion, lined the hallways and many of the rooms with books. Some books are free to take away with you (Jane doesn't believe in leaving a good book unfinished). In addition to books, the big, bright rooms are furnished with a hodgepodge of antiques, comfortable sofas, and armchairs. Jane provides a steady supply of homemade oatmeal chocolate-chip cookies. **Pros:** Comfortable and close by the city, a hostess who really cares. **Con:** This district is a little run-down. ⊠*123 Pirie St.* ☎*04/384–2714* ⊕*www.booklovers. co.nz* ⋈*4 rooms, 3 with bath* ♿*In-room: no a/c. In-hotel: no elevator* ▭*MC, V* ⦿*BP.*

$$ 📷**The Lighthouse and the Keep.** These two unique properties—a light-
★ house and a stone tower—have stunning views of Cook Strait and the mountain ranges of the South Island. Each three-story building is primarily a one-bedroom accommodation. The Lighthouse has two wraparound balconies, one at the very top of the building. At the Keep, you can climb through a hatch from the bedroom out onto the roof. The price (on the high end of this category) includes a fully stocked kitchen, with pastries, coffee, and anything you might need to cook your own breakfast. **Pros:** On a good day the views will blow you away, unique places to stay. **Cons:** There's not a lot of spare room, stairs could be a problem for some. ⊠*326 and 116 The Esplanade, Island Bay, 5 km (3 mi) from central Wellington* ☎*04/472–4177* ⊕*www.thelighthouse. net.nz* ⋈*2 suites* ♿*In-room: no a/c, no phone, kitchen, refrigerator, no TV. In-hotel: no-smoking rooms, no elevator* ▭*AE, MC, V.*

$–$$ 📷**Halswell Lodge.** For restaurant, theater, and cinema going, you can't beat this hotel's location, right by the eastern end of Courtenay Place. And you'll find it hard to beat the prices. Standard hotel rooms at the front of the building are small and functional. Motel units are set farther back, each with a kitchenette (two have whirlpool baths). Finally, a restored 1920s villa is at the rear of the property; its six superior rooms come with whirlpool baths, cane chairs, burnished wood decor, antique wardrobes, and restored fireplaces. You can use the villa kitchen to prepare light meals. **Pros:** Reasonably priced accommodation, close by all the action. **Con:** Traffic noise might be a problem. ⊠*21 Kent Terr.* ☎*04/385–0196* 🖷*04/385–0503* ⊕*www.halswell.co.nz* ⋈*25 rooms, 11 motel units* ♿*In-room: no a/c, kitchen (some). In-hotel: laundry facilities* ▭*AE, DC, MC, V.*

$–$$ 📷**Shepherd's Arms Speight's Ale House.** New Zealand's oldest hotel, the Shepherd's Arms, has been refurbished to approximate its original 19th-century state. Two rooms have four-poster beds, all have deep-blue carpets and burgundy curtains, and all are fairly small, especially the three single rooms, which share a bathroom. You can head to the bar and mix with the local after-work crowd; old photos on the wall show Wellington in the hotel's early days. **Pros:** Reasonably priced and fairly close to the city. **Con:** There can be some noise from the bar crowd. ⊠*285 Tinakori Rd., Thorndon* ☎*04/472–1320* 🖷*04/472–0523* ⊕*www.shepherds.co.nz* ⋈*12 rooms, 9 with bath* ♿*In-hotel: restaurant, bar, no-smoking rooms, no elevator* ▭*AE, DC, MC, V.*

¢–$ 📷**Base Backpackers.** This beautiful Heritage building in a great location draws a varied crowd of budget travelers. Rooms are spacious, bedding is provided, and all except the double rooms share bathrooms. The whole establishment is decked out in burgundy and white, with the exception of the Sanctuary floor, a women-only dorm section where, surprise, rooms are pink and white. Sanctuary guests also get some girly perks (full-length mirrors, hair dryers, free Aveda hair products, and feather pillows). The place is kept remarkably clean and the staff are friendly. There is an in-house travel desk and bike-hire is available. **Pros:** Handy to the city, women-only section. **Con:** There might be some traffic noise. ✉ *21–23 Cambridge Terr.* ☎ *04/801–5666* 🖷 *04/801–5668* ⊕ *www.stayatbase.com* 🛏 *10 rooms, 10 dorms* △ *In-room: no a/c, no phone. In-hotel: restaurant, bar, laundry facilities, public Internet, no-smoking rooms* ▤ *AE, DC, MC, V.*

¢–$ 🏨 **Nomads.** This well-kept backpackers place has a prime position in central Wellington across the street from the Michael Fowler Centre and Information Centre. Adjoining and with Internal access is Blend, an excellent bar and café. Private rooms have en suite and towels are supplied. **Pro:** Good location. **Con:** You have to like the backpackers thing. ✉ *126 Wakefield St.* ☎ *04/978–7800* ⊕ *www.nomadscapital. com* 🛏 *36 private rooms with bunk rooms making a total of 188 beds* △ *In-room: no a/c* ▤ *AE, MC, V.*

¢   🏨 **Downtown Backpackers.** Opposite the train station, this hostel stands out by virtue of its amenities and its landmark art deco building. The rooms, which are clean if small and a bit worse for wear, range from singles to six-person shares. The extensive communal areas include a travel desk, a café (serving big and cheap breakfasts), kitchen, bar, and pool room; computers are at the ready. Check out the old Māori carved fireplace in the bar; you won't see anything better in the national museum. **Pro:** Right by the city and the railway, across the road from the ferries. **Con:** Some of the rooms are worn down. ✉ *Bunny St. and Waterloo Quay* ☎ *04/473–8482* 🖷 *04/471–1073* ⊕ *www.downtown backpackers.co.nz* 🛏 *60 rooms, 54 with bath* △ *In-room: no a/c, no phone, kitchen, no TV. In-hotel: restaurant, bar, laundry facilities, public Internet* ▤ *AE, DC, MC, V.*

NIGHTLIFE & THE ARTS

For current event listings in Wellington, check the entertainment section in the *Dominion Post,* Wellington's daily newspaper, or the free weekly entertainment newspaper, *Capital Times.* The free booklet *Wellington What's On,* available from the Wellington i-Site Visitor Centre, has seasonal listings of cultural events. The Wellington City Council puts out the free monthly "Feeling Great" (⊕ *www.feelinggreat.co.nz*) brochure, which lists events, exhibits, lectures, and workshops. The Web site for the **Wellington i-Site Visitor Centre** (⊕ *www.wellingtonnz.com*) also has up-to-date listings, from movies to theater and music. *The Package* (⊕ *www.thepackage.co.nz*), a free palm-size publication, has a weekly event calendar with more alternative and edgy listings; pick up a copy at the Visitor Information Centre or at many cafés, or check it out online. **Ticketek** (☎ *04/384–3840*), between the Michael Fowler Center and the Town Hall, sells tickets for local performances.

THE ARTS

FESTIVALS   The major arts event is the **New Zealand International Arts Festival,** held in March on even-numbered years at venues across the city. A huge array of international talent in music, drama, dance, the visual arts, and media descends upon Wellington. Advance information and a festival program are at the **Festival Office** (☎ *04/473–0149* ⊕ *www.*

nzfestival.telecom.co.nz). Events fill up quickly; book a month in advance if you can.

Wellingtonians turn out in droves for the many free festivals that occur from November to April. One of the largest summer fests is the six-week **Summer City**, which includes more than 70 events throughout the city. At the **Cuba Street Carnival,** which runs on alternative years to the Arts Festival for two days in March, food and crafts stalls, and music and dance performances sweep the length of Cuba Street, culminating in a nighttime parade (a family-friendly show, not a rowdy Mardi Gras-style blowout).

One of the key Māori occasions in Wellington is **Matariki,** the North Island Māori New Year in late May/early June, beginning with the first new moon after the appearance of Matariki (Pleiades). Te Papa Tongarewa–Museum of New Zealand hosts nearly a month of musical, storytelling, and dance performances; the events begin with a ceremony at dawn. Pick up a brochure and calendar of events at the museum. For a unique gift or souvenir, Te Papa Press also publishes a beautifully illustrated Matariki calendar, which runs from June until May and is based on traditional Māori lore of the seasons.

PERFORMING ARTS Wellington is the home of the **Royal New Zealand Ballet,** known as much for contemporary works by New Zealand and international choreographers as for its perennial *Nutcracker* and *Swan Lake* performances. The **NBR New Zealand Opera** and the **New Zealand Symphony Orchestra** mix equal parts "old favorites" with contemporary works. The glass, concrete, and steel Michael Fowler Center and the adjacent, older **Wellington Convention Centre** (✉ *111 Wakefield St.* ☎ *04/801–4231*) jointly operate as the main venue for the symphony and other classical music performances.

The ornate, turn-of-the-20th-century **St. James Theatre** (✉ *77–83 Courtenay Pl.* ☎ *04/802–4060* ⊕ *www.stjames.co.nz*) has dance performances, musicals, and opera. The equally well-preserved **Opera House** (✉ *111–113 Manners St.* ☎ *04/384–3840*), with its plush carpets and tiered seating, has a similar lineup. Because the Opera House and the St. James Theatre are under the same ownership, the NBR New Zealand Opera and the Royal New Zealand Ballet use either venue as schedules allow.

Bats Theatre is Wellington's long-standing source for experimental, sometimes off-the-wall theater. Bats hosts the Fringe Festival during the International Arts Festival, and a range of performances throughout the year. ✉ *1 Kent Terr.* ☎ *04/802–4175* ⊕ *www.bats.co.nz.*

Circa Theatre is a good bet for catching contemporary New Zealand pieces along with established masterworks from Harold Pinter to Oscar Wilde. It's on the wharf next to the Te Papa museum. ✉ *1 Taranaki St.* ☎ *04/801–7992* ⊕ *www.circa.co.nz.*

Downstage Theatre holds performances of stage classics, contemporary drama, comedy, and dance. ✉ *Hannah Playhouse, Courtenay Pl. and Cambridge Terr.* ☎ *04/801–6946* ⊕ *www.downstage.co.nz.*

NIGHTLIFE

Wellington's after-dark scene splits between several main areas. The "alternative" set spends its time at **Cuba Street**'s funky cafés, bars, and clubs, which stay open until around 1 AM during the week and about 3 AM on weekends; cocktails are innovative, and the music is not top 20 radio.

Courtenay Place is home to the traditional drinking action with a selection of brash Irish pubs, sports bars, and a few upscale establishments. It's packed on Friday and Saturday nights, especially when a rugby game is on, and the streets fill with beery couples in their late teens and early twenties (New Zealand's legal drinking age is 18) lining up to get plastered.

In the downtown business district—between Lambton Quay and Manners Street—a couple of brewpubs and a few taverns cater to the after-work mob. Down by the harbor, a flashy corporate crowd hangs out in several warehouse-style bars, sipping martinis on weeknights and filling the dance floor on weekends.

BARS If beer is your thing, head downtown and make an early start at the **Arizona Bar** (⊠ *Grey and Featherston Sts.* ☎*04/495–7867*), a Western-theme bar on the ground floor of the Hotel InterContinental. Modern with polished wood and plate glass aplenty, **Malthouse's** (⊠*48 Courtenay Pl.* ☎*04/802–5484*) long bar with illuminated lettering is a point of interest. Of Courtenay Place's Irish spots, try **Molly Malone's** (⊠*Taranaki St. and Courtenay Pl.* ☎*04/384–2896*), a large, traditional bar with regular live music and a rowdy crowd, particularly on weekends. You can also check out the crowd from **Kitty O'Shea's** (⊠*28 Courtenay Pl.* ☎*04/384–7392*) outside veranda; traditional live music is regularly played. The well-lived-in **Shooters Bar** (⊠*69–71 Courtenay Pl.* ☎*04/801–7800*), once a brewery and then a distillery, has exposed brick walls, timber floors, and four levels with everything from a 400-person main bar to a garden bar to a 10-table poolroom.

Wellington's hipsters gravitate toward **Motel** (⊠ *45 Tory St.* ☎*04/384–9084*), with its dimly lighted booths and the DJ playing funky, downtempo hip-hop. As an added bonus, you can order food at the bar from the adjacent **Chow**, a pan-Asian eatery. Although it's not formal, you'll want to leave the jeans and sneakers behind; legend has it that Motel's bouncers turned away *Lord of the Rings* star Liv Tyler because she wasn't properly attired. Centrally located **Matterhorn** (⊠*106 Cuba St.* ☎*04/384–3359*), which also has a good restaurant, draws a refreshing mix of urban hipsters and after-work corporate crowds with its indoor and outdoor fireplaces, a laid-back DJ, and a list of inventive cocktails—you can blow $100 on the "Bling Bling," a top-shelf Long Island Ice Tea that comes in a trophy with your name engraved on it.

Although it's right on bustling Cuba Street, **Good Luck** (⊠*126 Cuba St.* ☎*04/801–9950*) is a little hard to find. Stairs take you below street level to a club done in the style of a Shanghai opium den, glowing with candles in Chinese teapots. On the waterfront, the two big draws are restaurant bars. **Shed Five** (⊠*Shed 5, Queens Wharf, Jervois Quay*

☎*04/499–9069*) is an airy, high-beamed space, decked out with lilies, stained-glass windows, and gilded mirrors. **Dockside** (✉*Shed 3, Queens Wharf, Jervois Quay* ☎*04/499–9900*), a restaurant and bar with a nautical theme, has antique boats hanging from the ceiling. In good weather, everyone spills outside for the best close-up harbor views in Wellington. Later on, move across to **Chicago** (✉*Jervois Quay* ☎*04/473–4900*) on Queens Wharf, a spacious sports bar that sees boisterous postgame parties.

LIVE MUSIC &
DANCE CLUBS
Valve (✉*154 Vivian St.* ☎*04/385–1630*) is one of the best places to catch live local rock music. It's a classic hole-in-the-wall: small, dark, and a little seedy, with concrete floors. Another good bet for local bands is **Bodega** (✉*103 Ghuznee St.* ☎*04/384–8212*), which pulls in a slightly more wholesome crowd than Valve. It's larger, with couches in the front and a dance floor by the stage. Both spots attract a predominantly university student crowd; the nights with cheap drink specials are packed.

Bigger international stars play at **Westpac Stadium** (✉*1 Waterloo Quay* ☎*04/471–0333*). The **TSB Bank Arena** (✉*Queen's Wharf, Jervois Quay* ☎*04/801–4231 or 04/499–4444* ⊕*www.tsbbankarena.com*) also gets its share of the headlining tours. At the bottom end of Courtney Place, **Sandwiches** (✉*Majoribanks St. and Kent Terr.* ☎*04/385–7698*) has a stylish bar filled with long, black vinyl couches on one side and a dance floor on the other, where international DJs play soul, funk, disco, and jazz. Live jazz is played on Wednesday and on the last Sunday of every month.

6

SHOPPING

The main downtown shopping area, for department stores, clothes, shoes, books, outdoor gear, and souvenirs, is the so-called **Golden Mile—** from Lambton Quay, up Willis, Victoria, and Manners streets. For smaller, funkier boutiques, visit **Cuba Street.**

DEPARTMENT STORE & MALLS

★ ”**Kirkcaldie & Stains** (✉*165–177 Lambton Quay* ☎*04/472–5899*) is Wellington's version of Harrod's. If you appreciate having the door opened by a top-hatted, liveried doorman as you enter a lovely early-19th-century facade, then this is the place for you. The extensive perfume department is a delight to the nose, and you can relax in the modern café and listen to live piano music between browsing.

A couple of indoor malls are on upper Lambton Quay: **Harbour City** and **Capital on the Quay** have a decent range of jewelry, lingerie, housewares, and clothing boutiques. A better mall is the **Old Bank Arcade** (✉*233–237 Lambton Quay, at Customhouse Quay and Willis St.* ☎*04/922–0600*) in the charming former Bank of New Zealand building, which is becoming something of a fashion enclave. The Arcade contains a slew of well-known boutiques, including New Zealand designer Andrea Moore and the tempting Minnie Cooper shoe store.

Napoleon Cosmetics does wonderful makeovers, and for both guys and dolls Rixon Groove are shirt- and tie-makers par excellence.

MARKETS

For a look at the weekly market of a close-knit ethnic community, catch an early train or take a drive north of Wellington on SH1 to Porirua and hit the morning-only **Porirua Market** (✉ *Cobham Ct.*). The stalls sell everything from eggplants and pineapples to colorful clothing to woven basketry and beadwork. Entertainers and hoarse-voiced evangelists play to the crowd. If you get hungry, there are food stalls galore selling curry and roti, chop suey, banana pancakes, and nearly every other treat you can imagine. The stalls open at 5:30 AM but close at 10 AM sharp.

Two **outdoor markets** (✉ *Chaffers St. opposite New World supermarket* ✉ *Willis St. between Vivian and Ghuznee Sts.*) set up every Sunday between dawn and noon in parking lots at either end of the city. These fruit-and-vegetable markets are among the most culturally diverse gathering points in the city. If you're looking to picnic, you can pick up supplies.

SPECIALTY STORES

BOOKS &
MAPS

Parson's Books & Music (✉ *126 Lambton Quay* ☎ *04/472–4587*) is not the largest bookstore in town, but it's one of the most intriguing—strong on New Zealand writing and travel, and featuring extensive classical recordings and a small upper-floor café. **Unity Books** (✉ *57 Willis St.* ☎ *04/499–4245*) stocks a generous supply of New Zealand and Māori literature.

CLOTHING &
ACCESSORIES

The nifty (and free) Wellington **Fashion Map,** which you can pick up at the Visitor Information Centre or any number of stores, divides the city into easily navigable shopping quarters and lists a good cross section of women's and men's designer boutiques throughout the city. Slightly off-the-beaten-track streets such as Woodward Street, Customhouse Quay, Wakefield Street, and upper Willis Street are home to some uniquely New Zealand designers and are well worth exploring.

Area 51 (✉ *Cuba and Dixon Sts.* ☎ *04/385–6590*) stocks street-savvy clothing brands like Diesel, but the real reason to come in is to check out the popular local Huffer label. **Gold Ore Silver Mine** (✉ *Left Bank, Cuba Mall* ☎ *04/801–7019*) has one of the city's largest selections of jewelry made from carved *pounamu* (a green stone similar to jade). Prices are reasonable, starting at around $18 for a pendant. The store also sells gold and silver jewelry, crafted on the premises.

Karen Walker (✉ *126 Wakefield St.* ☎ *04/499–3558*) has made a name for herself overseas. Her Wellington store carries her own designs and also stocks international labels, such as Victor & Rolf. **unity collection** (✉ *101 Customhouse Quay* ☎ *04/471–1008*) carries clothing from a clutch of New Zealand designers, good for a one-stop view of the local talent. Long-standing New Zealand designer Elisabeth Findlay of **Zambesi** (✉ *107 Customhouse Quay* ☎ *04/472–3638*) whips up innovative but extremely wearable clothes.

OUTDOOR EQUIPMENT Wellington is a fine place to stock up on camping supplies before hitting the great outdoors. **Kathmandu** (✉ *57 Willis St.* ☎ *04/472–0113*) carries its house brand of clothing and equipment. **Ski & Snowboard Centre–Gordons** (✉ *Cuba and Wakefield Sts.* ☎ *04/499–8894*) focuses on snow-sport equipment and clothing.

SOUVENIRS **Kura Contemporary Art and Design** (✉ *19 Allen St.* ☎ *04/802–4934*) is part gallery, part gift store, with a strong Māori current running through the work. Some of the smaller, less expensive items make unique souvenirs. **Living Nature** (✉ *195 Lambton Quay* ☎ *04/499–5060*) has a range of beauty, hair, and skin products "made of New Zealand." Most products include *manuka* honey, a richly scented honey from a kind of tea tree native to New Zealand that's known for its health benefits. On Lambton Quay, the best bet for souvenirs is **Sommerfields** (✉ *296 Lambton Quay* ☎ *04/499–4847*). Everything in the store—from jewelry to artwork, scarves, and soaps—has been made in New Zealand.

TOURS

BOAT TOURS **East by West Ferries** runs the *Dominion Post* Ferry, a commuter service between the city and Days Bay, on the east side of Port Nicholson, and it's one of the best-value tours in the city. On the way to Days Bay you can stop at Matiu or Somes Island; this former quarantine station makes an unusual picnic spot on a warm afternoon and you might see a native Tuatara. Days Bay has a seaside village atmosphere, a lovely bathing beach, local craft shops, and great views of Wellington. Weekdays the catamaran departs from Queens Wharf every 25 minutes from 6:25 AM to 8:35, then at 10, noon, and 2:15 and from 4:30 every half hour until 7 PM. The return boats leave Days Bay roughly 30 minutes later. The sailing schedule is cut back on weekends and holidays but additional Harbour Explorer Tours visit Petone Wharf and Seatoun Wharf. The one-way fare to Days Bay is $8.50; the cost if you include a Matiu/Somes Island stop is $18.50 round-trip. You can pick up tickets at the ferry terminal between 8 and 5; otherwise, tickets can be bought on board.

Contact **Dominion Post** Ferry (✉ Queens Wharf ☎ 04/499–1282 or 04/494–3339 ⊕ www.eastbywest.co.nz).

BUS TOURS **Wellington Rover** runs local tours that range from a two-hour overview ($50) to a full-day *Lord of the Rings* sites tour ($150), which includes a picnic lunch. Tours leave from the visitor information center on Wakefield Street. Reservations are essential.

Contact **Wellington Rover** (☎ 021/426–211 cell ⊕ www.wellingtonrover.co.nz).

PRIVATE GUIDES **Wally Hammond,** a tour operator with a great anecdotal knowledge about Wellington, offers a 2½-hour minibus tour of the city. This can be combined with a half-day Kapiti Coast Tour, which includes a Southward Car Museum visit. The city tour costs $50, and the Kapiti Coast tour is $80. A full-day Palliser Bay and *Lord of the Rings* sites tour is $165.

Matiu/Somes Island

A wonderful place to spend a day walking and exploring, the Matiu Island Scientific and Historic Reserve lies in Wellington Harbour approximately 8 km (5 mi) from the city. The island has lots of walking tracks, great beaches for swimming, good picnic spots, and opportunities to see whales, dolphins, penguins, and other birds (sharp eyes may also pick out skinks and other small lizards, and giant weta insects on the paths). Because the boats carry a limited number of passengers to the island at a time, it's never crowded.

Although the 62-acre island was opened as a DOC reserve in 1995, it has an interesting history. From the early 1880s until around 1980, it was used as a quarantine station by early European settlers for both humans and animals—including dogs, cattle, sheep, red deer, llamas, and other livestock—on their way into the country. During the world wars, it was also used as a place of internment for aliens considered a security threat.

In 1981 Matiu became a project of the Royal Forest and Bird Protection

Society. Volunteers began planting trees that year to replace vegetation that had previously been cleared to allow grazing for quarantined animals. Many other native plants that flourished before the arrival of Europeans have also been replanted, and native insects such as wetas reintroduced. The island is now a breeding ground for a variety of seabirds.

The island is strictly a place to enjoy natural beauty for a few hours at a time. The few man-made structures on Matiu today include the old quarantine station, and gun emplacements from World War II—which were never used, and which remain on the southernmost summit of the island. An automated lighthouse built in 1900 to replace the original structure from 1866 also still sends out its southward beacon to ships traveling from Wellington Harbour.

The island can be reached by the Dominion Post East/West ferry service; there are nine round-trip runs made from Wellington Harbour per day. *For more information, see Tours.*

Contact **Wally Hammond** (☎ *04/472–0869* ⊕ *www.wellingtonsightseeing-tours.com*).

SIGHTSEEING TOURS **Flat Earth–New Zealand Experiences** runs a wide range of tours to scenic areas both locally and countrywide.

Contact **Flat Earth–New Zealand Experiences** (☎ *04/977–5805 or 0800/775-805* ⊕ *www.flatearth.co.nz*).

TRAVEL AGENCIES

Local Agents **House of Travel** (✉ *6 Margaret St., Lower Hutt* ☎ *04/569–0950* 🖨 *04/570–2845*). **Lambton Quay Flight Centre** (✉ *182 Lambton Quay* ☎ *04/471–2995 or 0800/354–448*).

THE WAIRARAPA

To cross the Rimutaka Ranges, which form a natural barrier between Wellington and the Wairarapa, you climb a twisting snake of a road known locally as "The Hill." Near a small plateau at the road's peak, at a height of about 1,800 feet, a footpath leads to even higher ground and spectacular views on all sides. Heading down from the summit, the road plunges through a series of hairpin turns to reach the plain that the Māori called "Land of Glistening Water."

For some years, the rather daunting access road gave a sense of isolation to the Wairarapa, which was essentially a farming area. But the emergence of the wine industry has triggered a tourism boom in the region. Red grape varieties flourish in the local soil (the pinot noir is particularly notable), and Wairarapa wines, produced in small quantities, are sought after in New Zealand and overseas. These days, vineyards, wine tasting, olive farms, and the twice-yearly Martinborough Fair are firmly established attractions. Hot-air ballooning, sea and freshwater fishing, walking, and other outdoor activities have also brought visitors over "The Hill."

6

GETTING HERE & AROUND

You need a car. State Highway 2 runs north–south through the region between Napier and Wellington. From Wellington you drive through Upper Hutt (the River Road bypasses the town), over the hills into the gateway town of Featherston. Highway 53 takes you to Martinborough; turn southwest here on Lake Ferry Road for Lake Ferry and Cape Palliser. Masterton is farther north along State Highway 2, roughly a half-hour drive from Martinborough. The journey from Wellington to Martinborough takes 1½ hours; Masterton is another half hour. From Napier, Masterton is about three hours.

MARTINBOROUGH

70 km (44 mi) north of Wellington.

The pleasant town of Martinborough embodies the changes that have taken place in the Wairarapa as a result of the burgeoning wine industry. The town gets its name from its founder, John Martin, who, in 1881, laid out the streets in a Union Jack pattern, radiating from the square that forms the hub. Most restaurants and shops are on or close to the square.

To tap into the Wairarapa wine world, Martinborough is the place to come. More than 20 vineyards are within a few miles of town—an easy drive or horse-drawn-carriage ride away.

ESSENTIALS

Visitor Info **Martinborough Visitor Information Centre** (✉ *18 Kitchener St.* ☎ *06/306–5010).*

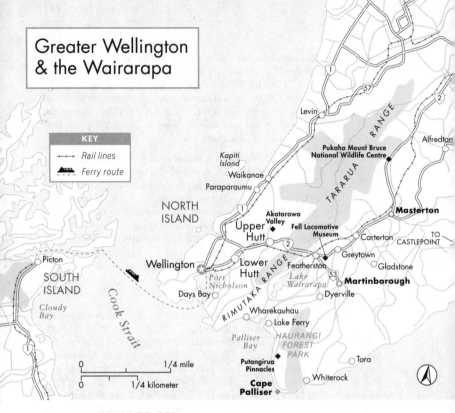

Greater Wellington & the Wairarapa

KEY

⊢—⊢ Rail lines

⛴ Ferry route

NORTH ISLAND

SOUTH ISLAND

Cloudy Bay

Cook Strait

Port Nicholson

Picton

Wellington

Days Bay

Lower Hutt

Upper Hutt

Akatarawa Valley

Fell Locomotive Museum

Featherston

Wharekauhau

Lake Ferry

Lake Wairarapa

Greytown

Gladstone

Martinborough

Dyerville

Carterton

TO CASTLEPOINT

Masterton

Alfredton

Levin

Kapiti Island

Waikanae

Paraparaumu

Pukaha Mount Bruce National Wildlife Centre

TARARUA RANGE

RIMUTAKA RANGE

Palliser Bay

HAURANGI FOREST PARK

Putangirua Pinnacles

Cape Palliser

Whiterock

Tora

0   1/4 mile

0   1/4 kilometer

WHAT TO SEE

The **Toast Martinborough Wine, Food & Music Festival** (☎06/306–9183 ⊕*www.toastmartinborough.co.nz*) occurs on the third Sunday of November; thousands of tickets are typically sold within hours. You can get tickets ($50) through the Web site.

The **Martinborough Fair,** held on the first Saturday of February and March, also draws thousands of people; this free event packs the town with crafts stalls.

For an overview of the area's wines, take an oenophile's shortcut and hit the **Martinborough Wine Centre** (⊠*6 Kitchener St.* ☎*06/306–9040* ⊕*www.martinboroughwinecentre.co.nz*). The shop stocks a thorough selection of local vintages for sipping and purchasing, plus books and wine accessories, and ships wines all over the world. It's open daily 9–5.

The **Horse and Carriage Establishment** (⊠*Martinborough* ☎*021/035–3855* ⊕*www.horseandcarriage.co.nz)*runs tours around the Martinborough-area vineyards. It's $60 per person for a two-hour tour; advance booking is essential. The company has twilight carriage drives, scenic picnic tours, and horse-and-carriage rental for any specific journey..

Olives are another local crop. For a taste-bud-tickling exercise that doesn't involve grapes, head to **Olivo** (✉*Hinakura Rd.* ☎*06/306–9074* ⊕*www.olivo.co.nz*), Helen and John Meehan's olive grove, 3 km (2 mi) north of Martinborough. You can tour the grove and its 5 acres of gardens to learn how their oils are produced. Tastings (and sales) of their extra-virgin and infused olive oils are encouraged. They're open Friday–Monday 10–5 and otherwise by appointment.

WHERE TO STAY & EAT

$$$–$$$$ ✕**The French Bistro.** Like the black-and-white photos of Parisian models that adorn the walls of this compact, trendy bistro, the regional cuisine is done with style. Settle into the modern chrome-and-black room for chef-owner Wendy Campbell's similarly contemporary creations. Critics pour praise on the food. You might enjoy the crusted Normandy-style free-range NZ pork cutlet in calvados apple brandy served with Jersey renne potatoes. There is an excellent selection of local wines. ✉*3 Kitchener St.* ☎*06/306–8862* ⚐*Reservations essential* ▤*AE, DC, MC, V* ⊙*Closed Mon. and Tues. No lunch Wed.–Fri.*

¢–$$$ ✕**The Village Café.** At this rustic café with a sunny outdoor courtyard, all the food is made from local produce. The cooks smoke their own salmon and make their own sausages. Breakfast is served all day, and a typical lunch is chicken braised in sauvignon blanc, served with Mediterranean vegetables. The café shares a building with Martinborough Wine Centre. ✉*6 Kitchener St.* ☎*06/306–8814* ▤*MC, V* ⊙*No dinner.*

$$$ ▦**Peppers Martinborough Hotel.** Sitting on a corner of the Martinbor-
★ ough Square, this 1890s hotel has rooms that open onto either the veranda or the garden. The rooms mix antique and contemporary fittings, such as four-poster beds or writing tables, and the classic decorating styles vary from French provincial to Shaker to comfortable country. In the restaurant ($$$–$$$$), the menu leans toward steak and seafood. The wine list is impressive. Reservations are essential for dinner. **Pros:** Fine accommodation in the town center, handy to everything. **Con:** You'll need your best manners to match the decor. ✉*The Square* ☎*06/306–9350* 🖷*06/306–9345* ⊕*www.peppers.co.nz* ⇲*16 rooms* ⚐*In-room: no a/c, dial-up. In-hotel: restaurant, bar, no elevator* ▤*AE, DC, MC, V.*

$$ ▦**The Claremont.** In a quiet rural area just outside the village center, this motel complex has a variety of stylishly modern, self-contained accommodations to suit a range of budgets. All have decks; the apartments have whirlpool baths. The studios and one- and two-bedroom apartments are in a garden setting with ample parking. **Pros:** Quiet location out of the town center, good modern accommodation. **Cons:** No swimming pool or activities, you need to go into town for a restaurant. ✉*38 Regent St.* ☎*06/306–9162* 🖷*06/306–8289* ⊕*www.the claremont.co.nz* ⇲*16 rooms, 7 apartments* ⚐*In-room: no a/c, kitchen. In-hotel: bicycles, laundry facilities, no-smoking rooms, no elevator* ▤*AE, DC, MC, V.*

Wairarapa's Best Wineries

Pick up a map of the area vineyards at Martinborough's visitor center, then hit the road to sample some of the country's best up-and-coming vineyards. Here are the top local picks.

Ata Rangi Vineyard. This winery makes exceptional chardonnay, pinot noir, and Célèbre (a cabernet-merlot-shiraz blend) in small quantities. ⊠ *Puruatanga Rd.* ☎ *06/306–9570* ⊕ *www.atarangi.co.nz* ☉ *Tastings Oct.–Apr., weekdays 1–3, weekends 11–5.* **Coney Wines.** Have lunch here for a view over the vines that produce a terrific pinot noir and pinot gris plus a rosé you can get only on-site. ⊠ *Dry River Rd.* ☎ *06/306–8345* ☉ *Tastings Fri.–Sun. 11–5.* **Martinborough Vineyard.** This fine regional winery was the first to convince the world of the Wairarapa's pinot noir potential. The chardonnay is also exceptional. ⊠ *Princess St.* ☎ *06/306–9955* ⊕ *www.martinborough-vineyard.*

co.nz ☉ *Tastings daily 11–3.*
Murdoch James Vineyard. This boutique producer of a wide range of Martinborough wines is a 10-minute scenic drive out of town. Try their smooth 2004 Blue Rock pinot noir in the on-site Riverview Café, paired with a pan-seared sirloin with wild mushrooms on soft polenta. The café opens 11:30–3:30 Thursday–Monday December to February, rest of year Friday–Sunday. ⊠ *Dry River Rd.* ☎ *06/306–9165* 🖷 *06/306–9120* ⊕ *www.murdoch james.co.nz* ☉ *Tastings year-round, daily 11–5:30.* **Palliser Estate.** Don't miss the whites here—they're some of the best locally. Of particular note is the sauvignon blanc, which is renowned for its intense, ripe flavors, and the pinot noir, which is made in an elegant, classic style. ⊠ *Kitchener St.* ☎ *06/306–9019* ⊕ *www.palliser. co.nz* ☉ *Tastings daily 10–4.*

PALLISER BAY & CAPE PALLISER

Southwest of Martinborough: 25 km (16 mi) to Lake Ferry, 40 km (25 mi) to Putangirua Pinnacles, 60 km (37 mi) to Cape Palliser.

To witness Wairarapa's most remote, blustery scenery—and to see the North Island's southernmost point, Cape Palliser—drive southwest from Martinborough. It's 25 km (16 mi) through rolling sheep country to the coast at the little settlement of **Lake Ferry** on Palliser Bay. The lake in question, called Onoke, is a salt lagoon formed by the long sandbank here. Vacation homes, fishing spots, and remarkable sunsets bring in the weekend Wellingtonian crowd.

Just before Lake Ferry, turn left (coming from Martinborough) at the sign for Cape Palliser and drive another 15 km (9 mi) around Palliser Bay to Te Kopi, where the **Putangirua Pinnacles Scenic Reserve** is protected from the hordes by its relative isolation. The spectacular rocks have been formed over the last 120,000 years as rains have washed away an ancient gravel deposit, and pinnacles and towers now soar hundreds of feet into the air on both sides of a stony riverbank. An hour-long round-trip walk from the parking area takes you along the riverbank and close to the base of the pinnacles. If you're feeling adventurous, a three- to four-hour bushwalk involves some steep climbs and wonderful vistas of the coast—

as far off as the South Island on a clear day. Stout footwear and warm clothing are essential. The Pinnacles are an hour's drive from Martinborough. The Martinborough visitor bureau is the best place to check for more information.

The road to Cape Palliser deteriorates after the Pinnacles and is unpaved in places. It's a dramatic, bleak ride, though not particularly hard, provided you take care. After 20 km (12 mi), the road ends at **Cape Palliser,** where 250 (sign says 258) wooden steps climb up to the candy-striped lighthouse. The views from here, up and down the wild coastline, are terrific. Below the lighthouse, splashing in the surf and basking on the rocks, are members of the North Island's only resident **fur seal colony.** You'll be able to get pretty close for photos, but not too close—these wild animals are fiercely protective of their young. Don't get between seals and pups, or seals and the ocean.

> **PUB BOAT**
>
> An interesting point with Lake Ferry Hotel, apparently under a very old ruling written into the license, the licensee of the pub must provide a ferry service across the lake if requested. Years ago it would have been a rowboat, today an outboard motor, but the proprietor says he has only been asked for this service once, probably for a joke as there is precious little on the other side, unless you want to travel a novel way to Wharekauhau.

6

WHERE TO STAY

$$$$
Fodor's Choice
★

Wharekauhau. This Edwardian-style lodge is set on a 5,000-acre working sheep station, self-contained guest cottages being scattered around the main lodge each with a king-size bed, a small patio, and an open fireplace. Walks around the gloriously remote coastline are an option plus trout fishing and tours to the seal colony at Palliser Bay. The dining room menu ($$$$) highlights the best of local produce—especially lamb and fish—with fine Martinborough wines. **Pros:** Luxury and privacy far from the madding crowd. **Cons:** You won't want to move far from the open fire in rough weather, don't expect the nightlife to set you alight. ⊠ *Western Lake Rd., Palliser Bay* ⊕ *R.D. 3, Featherston* ☎ *06/307–7581* ☏ *06/307–7799* ⊕ *www.wharekauhau. co.nz* ↪ *12 cottages* ⌂ *In-room: no a/c, no TV, dial-up. In-hotel: restaurant, bar, tennis court, pool, gym, no-smoking rooms* ☐ *AE, DC, MC, V* ⧖ *MAP.*

¢–$

Lake Ferry Hotel. The North Island's southernmost pub sits almost on the beach, with breathtaking views across Cape Palliser to the South Island's Kaikoura Ranges. The rooms are no-frills (in addition to the doubles, there's a 10-bunk dorm), but having a drink on the deck at sunset is an unbeatable experience. The menu ($–$$$) focuses on fish; the local classic whitebait fritters are served on salad greens with tomato salsa. This place is so Kiwi, you get a chocolate fish with your cappuccino. (Chocolate fish are iconic Kiwi candy, chocolate-covered pink marshmallows.) **Pros:** If you like the feeling of being at the end of the earth, this is for you. You'll also love the food and the friendly welcome. **Con:** Not great on comfort. ⊠ *Lake Ferry* ☎ *06/307–7831*

☎06/307–7891 🛏8 rooms, 1 with bath; 1 10-bunk dorm ♿In-room: no a/c, no phone, no TV. In-hotel: restaurant, no-smoking rooms, no elevator ⊟MC, V ⫶◯⫶BP.

AROUND MASTERTON

Masterton is 40 km (25 mi) northeast of Martinborough.

State Highway 2 strings together a handful of eye-catching small towns on its way north past the Rimutakas.

ESSENTIALS

Visitor Info **Featherston Visitor Centre** (⊠ *The Old Courthouse, State Hwy. 2, Featherston* ☎06/308–8051 ⊕ www.wairarapanz.com). **Masterton Visitor Centre** (⊠ *316 Queen St., Masterton* ☎06/370–0900 ⊕ www.wairarapanz.com).

WHAT TO SEE

★ The tiny town of **Featherston** is worth a stop for the **Fell Locomotive Museum** (⊠ *Lyon and Fitzherbert Sts., behind the Information Centre on State Hwy. 2, Featherston* ☎06/308–9379 ✎ *fell.loco.museum@ xtra.co.nz*).

Along with photos, models, and memorabilia, it has the last remaining Fell locomotive in the world; built in 1875 and beautifully restored, the engine is one of only six that clawed their way up the notorious Rimutaka Incline on the way to Wellington. The museum's open weekdays 10–4:30 and weekends 10–4; admission is $5.

Roughly 10 km (6.2 mi) farther up the arrow-straight highway is **Greytown,** where well-preserved Victorian buildings now filled with cafés and boutiques line the main street. After a few miles more you'll reach **Carterton,** another small town with a handful of tempting crafts and antiques stores—especially Paua World (⇨ *Shopping, below*).

Masterton is Wairarapa's major population center, and like Martinborough to the south, it's in a developing wine region. There's not much to do in the town, but it's a handy gateway for hiking in the nearby parks and on the coast. Popular annual events include the Hot Air Balloon Festival in the first few days of April and the Golden Shears sheepshearing competition, usually held the first weekend in March.

★ Nearby **Pukaha Mount Bruce** (⊠ *State Hwy. 2, 30 km [19 mi] north of Masterton* ☎06/375–8004 ⊕ *www.mtbruce.org.nz*) makes a fine introduction to the country's wildlife, particularly its endangered bird species. An easy trail (one hour round-trip) through the bush takes you past aviaries containing rare, endangered, or vulnerable birds, including the *takahē,* a flightless bird thought to be extinct until it was rediscovered in 1948. The real highlight, though, is the nocturnal habitat containing foraging kiwis, the country's symbol, who are endearing little bundles of energy. It takes a while for your eyes to adjust to the artificial gloom, but it's worth the wait. The *kaka* (indigenous parrots) are fed daily at 3. Don't miss the eel feeding at 1:30, when the reserve's stream writhes with long-finned eels. The center is open daily 9–4:30; admission costs $10.

An hour's drive east of Masterton along Te Ore-ore Road (which turns into the Masterton–Castlepoint road), **Castlepoint** is perhaps the most spectacular site on the entire Wairarapa coast. Castle Rock rises a sheer 500 feet out of the sea; below, in **Deliverance Cove,** seals sometimes play. There's a fantastic walk to the peninsula lighthouse, and surfers flock to the beach break at Deliverance Cove.

Enjoyable bushwalks in beautiful forests laced with streams are in **Tara-rua Forest Park** (☎ *06/377–0700 DOC office*), which also has picnic facilities. The Mt. Holdsworth area at the east end of the park is popular for tramping. To get there turn off State Highway 2 onto Norfolk Road, 2 km (1 mi) south of Masterton.

WHERE TO STAY & EAT

$$$–$$$$ ✕**Café Cecille.** Set in Queen Elizabeth Park, this colonial wooden pavilion has a covered veranda and windows overlooking the grounds and lake. The prints on the wall nod to Paris, but the menu sticks to New Zealand strengths, such as the in-house smoked loin of venison with butternut, green bean, feta, and raspberry vinaigrette. For on-site parking drive down the Park Avenue entrance—about 150 yards. ⊠ *Queen Elizabeth Park, Masterton* ☎ *06/370–1166* ▭ *AE, DC, MC, V.*

$$$–$$$$ ✕**Salute.** It's worth a stop at Greytown to eat at this bistro—it's considered by some to be among the best in the country. Chef Travis Clive-Griffin puts a Middle Eastern twist on contemporary Mediterranean dishes. Two dishes not to miss are the char-grilled spring lamb with mandioca chips, spiced figs, wild rocket, and pomegranate seeds, followed by the bitter chocolate tart with almond milk sorbet and orange blossom syrup. Go for it! In summer a large outdoor courtyard with oak trees and a fountain is the perfect place to while away the afternoon. ⊠ *83 Main St., Greytown* ☎ *06/304–9825* ⚞ *Reservations essential* ▭ *AE, MC, V* ⊘ *Closed Mon.*

$$–$$$ ✕**Gladstone Vineyard.** Sip a pinot noir or try your hand at pétanque while you're waiting for feta cheese omelet with smoked mushrooms and fresh herbs and topped with a rocket salad at Stokers the restaurant of this charming little vineyard. The inside dining room has a barnlike ceiling, wine casks, and a display of local art. ⊠ *Gladstone Road, RD2 Carterton* ☎ *06/379–8563* ▭ *AE, MC, V* ⊘ *Closed Mon. –Wed.*

$$–$$$$ ▤**Copthorne Resort Solway Park Wairarapa.** Set in 23 acres of landscaped grounds and gardens on the southern outskirts of Masterton, this is a large complex for a small town. The helpful staff and spacious rooms make this especially good if you're traveling with children. The restaurant has polished floors, an interesting exposed timber ceiling, and leather furniture; folding doors along the front open to a sunny decking. All-day dining and dinner is offered every day. Local produce is popular: the grilled flat point fish served on polenta with sautéed spring onion, bacon, and a lemon chive buerre blanc is a good choice. **Pros:** All single-story accommodation, plenty of in-house activities, good off-road parking. **Cons:** Weekdays popular for corporate conferences, can get crowded on weekends with special family rates. ⊠ *High St. S, Masterton* ☎ *06/370–0500* 🖷 *06/370–0501* ⊕ *www.solway. co.nz* ⚞ *93 rooms, 8 apartments* ⚒ *In-room: no a/c, kitchen (some).*

6

In-hotel: 2 restaurants, bar, tennis court, pools, gym, spa ⊟*AE, DC, MC, V* ⦶*BP.*

BALLOONING

Get a bird's-eye view of the area with **Ballooning New Zealand Ltd.;** a one-hour trip followed by a champagne breakfast costs $290: allow two to three hours for the whole experience. ✉*54b Kent St., next to Paua World, Carterton* ☎*06/379–8223 or 027/2248–696* ✎*ballooning nz@infogen.net.nz.*

SHOPPING

For a unique souvenir, visit **Paua World** (✉*54 Kent St., Carterton* ☎*06/379–6777* ⊕*www.pauaworld.com*). Just off the main highway in the small town of Carterton, Paua World is an interesting and informative diversion. Paua (akin to abalone) has been collected by the Māori since ancient times. The rainbow-color shell interiors are highly prized (used by the Māori to represent eyes in their statues) and are polished and processed, then turned into jewelry and other gifts. Open daily 9–5.

Upper South Island & the West Coast

WORD OF MOUTH

Take the Queens Charlotte route to Picton rather than the Blenheim route (if you have time and are a confident driver on windy, steep roads). The views are just amazing.

—NZSophie

[Picton's] scenery is gorgeous, stay for a few days in Waikawa Bay, fish off the wharf, wind down and relax, take a cruise around the Marlborough Sounds, go for a ride on the mail boat, it is fascinating as it delivers mail and groceries to the people who live in the different bays around the Sounds. Go for a drive through the Grove Track, stop at some of the bays and enjoy the peace and quiet and take in the views.

—nelsonian

Updated by
Sue Farley

SURREAL IS THE IMMEDIATE IMPRESSION upon reaching South Island: the mellow, green beauty of the North Island has been replaced by jagged snowcapped mountains and rivers that sprawl across vast, rocky shingle beds. The South Island has been carved by ice and water, a process still rapidly occurring. Minor earthquakes rattle a number of places on the island every month—and residents are so used to them they often barely notice.

The Marlborough province occupies the northeast corner, where the inlets of the Marlborough Sounds flow around verdant peninsulas and sandy coves. Marlborough is now the largest wine-growing region in New Zealand, with more than 27,000 acres of vineyards. It's a relatively dry and sunny area, and in summer the inland plains look like the American West, with mountains rising out of grassy flats.

The northwest corner of the island, the Nelson region, is a sporting paradise with a relatively mild climate that allows a year-round array of outdoor activities. Sun-drenched Nelson, a lively town with fine restaurants and a vibrant network of artists and craftspeople, is the gateway to an area surrounded by national parks and hiking tracks (trails). Abel Tasman National Park, to the west of the city, is ringed with spectacularly blue waters studded with golden beaches and craggy rocks. To the southwest is Kahurangi National Park, home of the Heaphy Track, one of the world's Great Walks; Nelson Lakes National Park with its alpine lakes and snowcapped peaks lies to the south.

After the gentler climes of Marlborough and Nelson, the wild grandeur of the West Coast comes as a surprise. This is Mother Nature with her hair down, flaying the coastline with huge seas and drenching rains and littering its beaches with acres of bleached driftwood. When it rains, you feel like you're inside a fishbowl; then the sun bursts out, and you swear you're in paradise. (Always check local conditions before heading out for an excursion.) It's a country that has created a special breed of people, and the rough-hewn and powerfully independent locals—known to the rest of the country as Coasters—occupy a special place in New Zealand folklore.

Note: *For more information on bicycling, fishing, hiking, and sea kayaking in Upper South Island, see Chapter 11.*

ORIENTATION & PLANNING

GETTING ORIENTED

A long narrow plain, broken by several mountainous areas, stretches from the Marlborough Sounds down the eastern coast of the upper South Island; State Highway 1 runs along this plain, going through Blenheim and Kaikoura on its way down to Canterbury. To the west, a series of high ranges separates Blenheim and Nelson. The side roads up into the Marlborough Sounds are slow and winding and often unpaved, so the best way to explore is often by boat from either Picton

TOP REASONS TO GO

Mountains & Glaciers. The South Island is piled high with mountains. The massive Southern Alps mountain chain divides the island lengthwise, and many outlying ranges spring up in the north. Extensive parklands make these mountains tantalizingly accessible—walk or ski them, or catch a helicopter to a glacier. In places like Kaikoura, farmers have banded together to create farm-to-farm hiking trails through otherwise inaccessible mountain, bush, and coastal areas.

Pub Life. There's no better place to get time with the locals than in a small-town pub at night, especially on the West Coast. When the wind is howling outside, or the surf is roaring, the pubs feel even cozier. There's often a big fire in a corner fireplace and local farmers, miners, or tour guides standing around the bar, tall stories flowing with the beer. Should you blank on a topic of conversation, you can't go wrong with a rugby question—just don't mention the World Cup.

Wildlife. The upper South Island is the habitat for some very interesting creatures. Tuatara, the last reptiles of their kind, live on the protected Stephens Island in Marlborough Sounds. South by Lake Moeraki, you may see fiordland crested penguins and New Zealand fur seals. On the other side of the island, along the Kaikoura Coast, you can get very close to whales, dolphins, and seals in the wild. In and around the Marlborough Sounds you're likely to see dolphins on a daily basis and killer whales in season. The Abel Tasman coastline is home to several colonies of fur seals.

Wine. It took only a couple of decades for Marlborough to become one of the world's great wine-making regions. The sunny-day–cool-night climate means grapes come off the vines plump with flavor, and that translates into wines with aromas that burst out of the glass. It's an exciting feistiness that some consider too unbridled—but the wine is delicious. At any of the smaller wineries, you'll likely share your first taste with the wine-makers themselves.

or Havelock. South of Nelson and along the West Coast, the country becomes very mountainous. The series of high passes and long river gorges is broken only by small settlements. Much of this area is beautiful parkland, a great buildup to the glaciers and mountains in the South Westland World Heritage Area.

Marlborough & Kaikoura. Marlborough is all about vineyards, wide shingle riverbeds, and the sheltered waterways of the Marlborough Sounds. Kaikoura, meanwhile, is a rocky strip of boisterous Pacific coastline where sperm whales breach just off shore and snowy mountains drop almost to the sea.

Nelson & the Northwest. The area starts with the curving sheltered bays of the Abel Tasman coast and the wide expanse of Tasman Bay. A little inland the economic heart of the region beats with rich farming and the major towns. But from this mellow center the countryside rises into layer after dramatic layer of wild mountains.

The West Coast. It starts in the north around Karamea as a warm, fertile coastal plain where avocados and tamarillos grow alongside the thick native rain forest. Reaching south through Greymouth and Hokitika, the strip of cultivated land narrows. Down south at the glaciers the soaring peaks of the Southern Alps run almost to the sea as the countryside becomes the wilderness of the South Westland World Heritage Area.

PLANNING

Anything less than three or four days through Nelson and Marlborough and an additional two to three days on the West Coast will be too few if you don't want to spend all day in the car. A lot of hills slow down the drive times. Local tourism organizations have developed a driving route called **the Treasured Pathway** that travels across the top of the South Island. A guide to the route, available in local bookshops, details all the significant scenic, cultural, and historic sights along the way.

GETTING HERE & AROUND

BY AIR

Air New Zealand (☎03/547–8721 or 0800/737–000 ⊕*www.airnewzealand.co.nz*) links Nelson with Christchurch, Auckland, Queenstown, Dunedin, the West Coast town of Hokitika, and all major cities on the North Island. **Soundsair** (☎03/520–3080 or 0800/505–005 ⊕*www.soundsair.co.nz*) flies in from Wellington almost daily with a very scenic, low-level flight over the Marlborough Sounds via Blenheim.

Blenheim Airport (BHE) and Picton's Koromiko Airport (PCN) are small regional airports—Picton's Koromiko is little more than a paved runway in farmland. The scenic flight from Wellington to Blenheim takes about a half hour. Air New Zealand Link has at least 10 departures to and from Wellington daily. From Wellington, **Soundsair** (☎03/520–3080 or 0800/505–005 ⊕*www.soundsair.co.nz*) makes the half-hour trip to Picton. They also fly to Nelson (via Blenheim) and Kaikoura from Wellington most days.

BY BUS

InterCity (☎03/365–1113 ⊕*www.intercitycoach.co.nz*) runs between Christchurch and Kaikoura, Picton, Blenheim, and Nelson a couple of times a day. The ride between Christchurch and Blenheim takes about 5 hours, from Christchurch to Picton closer to 6 hours, and from Picton to Nelson, about 2½ hours. A trip between Kaikoura and Christchurch runs 2 hours 40 minutes. At Blenheim, buses stop at the train station; at Picton, they use the ferry terminal. In Kaikoura, southbound buses stop at the parking lot by the Craypot restaurant, northbound buses stop at the Sleepy Whale.

Aside from tour buses, the only reliable local alternatives are **Atomic Shuttles** (☎03/349–0697 ⊕*www.atomictravel.co.nz*) and **Southern Link K Bus** (☎03/358–8355 or 0508/458–835 ⊕*www.southernlinkcoaches.co.nz*). Atomic operates coaches between the most popular tourist spots and shuttle vans on the lower-profile regional runs. Southern Link K Bus also connects from Picton to the West Coast via Nelson Lakes. In the December and January holiday season, book at least a couple of days before you plan to travel, but during the rest of the year a day's advance reservation should do the trick. Bus tickets can also be booked at information centers.

Abel Tasman Coachlines (⊕*www.abeltasmantravel.co.nz*) and Southern Link K Bus run the smaller routes to Motueka, Takaka, and the Abel Tasman and Kahurangi national parks.

Many of the smaller routes cut their service frequency in winter, some stop altogether, and others reduce their destinations, so double-check the schedules.

BY CAR

Roads through the countryside's mountain ranges and deep river gorges can be narrow and winding, and a 160-km (100 mi) drive might take over three hours. However, the roads are generally good and there's always something to look at. There are a number of one-way bridges along the way and several on the West Coast shared with trains. Watch the signposts and road markings for "give way" rules.

Most car rental agencies have North Island–South Island transfer programs for their vehicles: leave one car in Wellington and pick another one up in Picton on the same contract. Some car rental companies are reluctant for their vehicles to leave the sealed roads but Apex Rentals in particular is more lenient about that.

Nelson is about a two-hour drive from Picton. From Nelson, State Highway 6 runs southwest to the West Coast, down the coast to the glaciers, then over the Haast Pass to Wanaka and Queenstown. For the West Coast, allow at least seven hours for the 458-km (284-mi) journey from Nelson to Franz Josef. This route demands frequent scenic stops. The same applies to a drive from Nelson to Christchurch, 424 km (265 mi) to the southeast, whether you go through the mountains of Nelson Lakes National Park or through Blenheim and Kaikoura. Highway 60 splits from State Highway 6 about 13 km (8 mi) out of Nelson near Richmond to reach the Abel Tasman area, Moyueka, and Golden Bay.

The north end of the West Coast is roughly a four-hour trip from Nelson on State Highway 6 or a five- to six-hour drive over Arthur's Pass on Highway 7 from Christchurch. State Highway 7 climbs the steep pass over the backbone of the Southern Alps before winding steeply down through rain forest to the tiny town of Otira and on to the coastal river plains of the mid–West Coast.

It can be a long way between gas stations.

BY FERRY

Many people arrive in the South Island on the ferry from Wellington to Picton, the northern entrance to the South Island. The trip is spectacular in good weather, but Cook Strait between Wellington and Picton can be rough in bad weather. The one-way adult fare ranges from $52 to $72, depending on the time of year, and whether you book from inside New Zealand or not. The fare for a medium-size sedan ranges from $165 to $235, which includes one adult fare. The crossing takes about 3½ hours, but if the weather is bad take sea-sickness medication before boarding. There are several departures in each direction every day, and you should make bookings in advance. Ferries dock in Picton at the town wharf. Often, rental cars and campervans can be left at your departure point, either Wellington or Picton, and a new one picked up on the other side of the strait. **Interislander** (☎ *0800/802–802* ⊕ *www.interislander.co.nz*) runs vehicle and passenger ferries.

BY TRAIN

The West Coast is poorly served by rail, but the exception is the **TranzAlpine Express** (☎ *0800/872–467* ⊕ *www.tranzscenic.co.nz*), which ranks as one of the world's great rail journeys. The train crosses the Southern Alps between Christchurch and Greymouth, winding through beech forests and snow-covered mountains. The train is modern and comfortable, with panoramic windows and a no-frills dining and bar service. The train departs Christchurch daily at 8:15 AM and arrives in Greymouth at 12:45 PM; the return train departs Greymouth at 1:45 PM and arrives at Christchurch at 6:05 PM. The one-way fare is $110–$124, round-trip $182–$235 if returning on the same day.

WHEN TO GO

Nelson and Marlborough are pleasant year-round, but beach activities are best from December to mid-April if you plan to be *in* the water. But December to February is busy with New Zealanders on their own vacations. Snow covers the mountains from June through October. The best time to go whale-watching off Kaikoura is between October and August. The pleasures of winter weather around the West Coast glaciers—clear skies and no snow at sea level—are so far a well-kept local secret. Look into local festival schedules, such as Marlborough's Wine and Food Festival in February, Kaikoura's SeaFest in October, and Hokitika's Wildfoods Festival in March.

ABOUT THE RESTAURANTS

In Marlborough visit a winery restaurant—there's no better way to ensure that your meal suits what you're drinking. Salmon and Greenshell mussels are farmed in the pristine Marlborough Sounds, and local crops—besides grapes—include cherries, wasabi, and garlic. In Kaikoura try crayfish (lobster). The region is named after this delicacy (*kai* means "food" in Māori; *koura* means "lobster"). On the West Coast, try whitebait fritters—a sort of omelet starring masses of baby fish.

Some restaurants close in winter (June through August). Others may open only on weekends, or curtail their weekday hours. In summer, all doors are open and it's best to make reservations. If a restaurant is open on a major holiday, it may add a surcharge to your bill.

Year-round, the restaurants and cafés around the glaciers and other remote spots can be quick to close their doors at night. Arrive by 8:30 (it's sometimes even earlier in winter), or you might go hungry. Some of the smallest towns, including Punakaiki, settlements in the Marlborough Sounds, and parts of Golden Bay, have few cafés and no general stores, so bring your own supplies.

WHAT IT COSTS IN NEW ZEALAND DOLLARS					
	¢	$	$$	$$$	$$$$
Restaurants	under $10	$10–$15	$15–$20	$20–$30	over $30

Prices are per person for a main course at dinner, or the equivalent.

ABOUT THE HOTELS

Bed-and-breakfasts, farm stays, and homestays, all a variation on the same theme, abound in the South Island in some spectacular coastal and mountain settings. Your hosts will feed you great breakfasts and advise on where to eat and what to do locally. Other choices include luxury lodges and hotels, or inexpensive motel rooms and backpacker lodges—which are increasingly becoming more "luxurious," with higher-quality standards and more amenities. Accommodations usually offer your morning coffee in a plunger, which is New Zealand speak for French press.

Locals generally take vacations from Christmas through January, so book early at these times. From March through November everything settles down, and in most towns you can book at short notice. The climate means that although heating is standard in virtually every room, very few places have air-conditioning, or need it.

WHAT IT COSTS IN NEW ZEALAND DOLLARS					
	¢	$	$$	$$$	$$$$
Hotels	under $75	$75–$125	$125–$200	$200–$300	over $300

Prices are for a standard double room in high season including 12.5% tax.

VISITOR INFORMATION

The visitor-information centers in Blenheim, Kaikoura, and Picton are all Destination Marlborough, a regional organization that puts out a nice visitor guide covering local accommodation, cafés, and activities, as well as an events calendar. **The Treasured Pathway** (⊕*www.treasuredpathway.co.nz*) is an excellent joint regional endeavor with the neighboring Nelson area. Its guide outlines the best of the sights in the "Top of the South."

Two regional tourism organizations maintain helpful Web sites: **Tourism West Coast** (⊕*www.west-coast.co.nz*) and **Glacier Country Tourism Group** (⊕*www.glaciercountry.co.nz*). The **Department of Conservation** (⊕*www.doc.govt.nz*) is always a good source for the various national parks.

The Taste Web site (⊕*www.thetaste.co.nz*) is regularly updated, covering the local wine, food, and arts scene in and around the Nelson region.

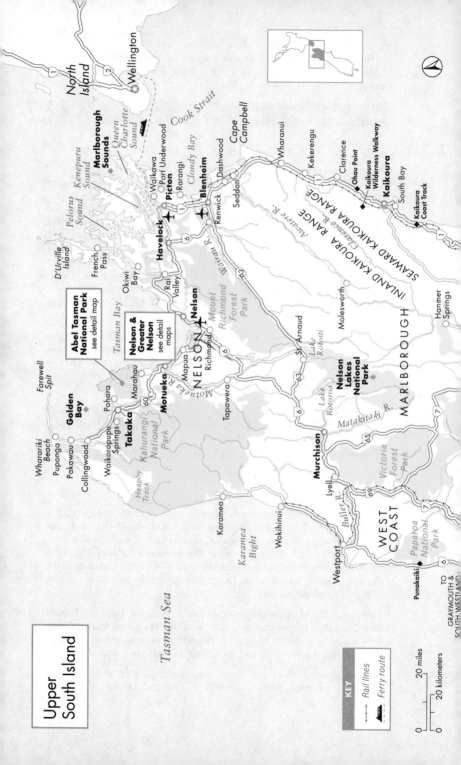

MARLBOROUGH & KAIKOURA

The Marlborough Sounds were originally settled by seafaring Māori people who named the area Te Tau Ihu O Te Waka a Māui ("the prow of Maui's canoe"). As legend has it, the trickster demigod Maui fished up the North Island from his canoe with the jawbone of a whale. Consequently, the North Island is called Te Ika a Māui—"the fish of Maui."

European settlers arrived in the early 1800s to hunt whales and seals. By the 1830s the whale and seal population had dropped drastically, so the settlers looked inland to the fertile river plains of the Wairau Valley, where Blenheim now stands. Surveyors were pressured to open more territory, but local Māori were reluctant to part with more of their land and sabotaged the surveyors' work and equipment.

Outraged European settlers, led by Captain Arthur Wakefield, arrived from Nelson to "talk some sense" into the Māori chiefs. An angry fracas flared up beside the tiny Tuamarina River (now a marked picnic spot on the road between Picton and Blenheim). Captain Wakefield and 21 other Europeans, plus nine Māori, including chief Te Rauparaha's daughter, were killed in what later became known as the "Wairau Incident." Local government officials declared the attack "despicable," and the Nelson settlers were chastised for their actions. The land was later sold reluctantly by the Māori tribes, and by 1850 the Pākehā (non-Māori) began farming.

Thirty years later, the unwittingly prescient Charles Empson and David Herd began planting red muscatel grapes among local sheep and grain farms. Their modest viticultural torch was rekindled in the next century by the Freeth family, and by the 1940s Marlborough wineries were producing port, sherry, and Madeira most successfully. In 1973 New Zealand's largest wine company, Montana, planted vines in Marlborough to increase the supply of New Zealand grapes. Other vintners followed suit, and within a decade today's major players—such as Hunter's—had established the region's international reputation. Marlborough now boasts New Zealand's single largest area under vine, and many local growers sell grapes to winemakers outside the area.

Down the coast from Blenheim, Kaikoura is another area that the Māori settled, the predominant iwi (tribe) being Ngai Tahu. True to their seafaring heritage, they are active in today's whale-watching interests. Ngai Tahu was one of the first major Māori iwi to receive compensation from the New Zealand government—to the tune of $170 million—along with an apology for unjust confiscation of their lands and fishing areas. The iwi today has extensive interests in tourism, fishing, and horticulture.

PICTON

29 km (18 mi) north of Blenheim, 110 km (69 mi) east of Nelson.

The maritime township of Picton (population 4,000) lies at the head of Queen Charlotte Sound and is the arrival point for ferries from the North Island, and a modest number of international cruise ships. It provides services and transport by water taxi to remote communities in the vast area of islands, peninsulas, and waterways that make up the Marlborough Sounds Maritime Park. Picton is a yachting mecca and has two sizable marinas, at Picton Harbour and at the adjacent Waikawa Bay.

There's plenty to do in town, with crafts markets in summer, historical sights, and walking tracks to scenic lookouts over the sounds. The main foreshore is lined by London Quay, which looks up Queen Charlotte Sound to the bays beyond. High Street runs down to London Quay from the hills, and between them these two streets make up the center of town.

ESSENTIALS

Car Rental **Apex** (⊠ *Ferry Terminal* ☎ *03/573–7009 or 0800/939–597* ⊕ *www. apexrentals.co.nz).* **Avis** (⊠ *Ferry Terminal* ☎ *03/520–3156 or 0800/284–722* ⊕ *www.avis.co.nz).* **Budget** (⊠ *Ferry Terminal* ☎ *03/573–6081 or 0800/283–438* ⊕ *www.budget.co.nz).* **Hertz** (⊠ *Ferry Terminal* ☎ *03/520–3044 or 0800/654–321* ⊕ *www.hertz.co.nz).*

Visitor Info **Picton Visitor Information Centre.** (⊠ *Picton Foreshore* ☎ *03/520–3113* 📠 *03/573–5021* ⊕ *www.destinationmarlborough.com* ✉ *picton@i-site.org).*

WHAT TO SEE

The **Picton Museum** (⊠ *London Quay* ☎ *03/573–8283* 💲 *$4* ⊙ *Daily 10–4*) details much of Picton's early seafaring history. The area was first a key Māori settlement called Waitohi, then an important whaling and sealing location for European immigrants in the early 19th century. Until 1860 there was no road access to Picton, so all trade and travel was done by sea.

The preserved hulk of the *Edwin Fox,* now the **Edwin Fox Maritime Museum** (⊠ *Dunbar Wharf* ☎ *03/573–6868*), demonstrates just how young New Zealand's European settlement is. The ship was used in the Crimean War, transported convicts to Australia, and brought settlers to New Zealand. Now dry-docked and preserved, it serves as a museum, bringing to life the conditions the early immigrants faced. The interpretative displays upstairs outline the ship's history and service. Walking through the ship, you can imagine how the settlers felt when shut below decks for months at a time, seasick, homesick, and unsure of what awaited them at landfall. Admission costs $8, and the ship is open daily 9–5 November–March and 9–3 April–October.

Picton is the base for cruising in the **Marlborough Sounds,** the labyrinth of waterways that formed when the rising sea invaded a series of river valleys at the northern tip of the South Island. Backed by forested

A Close Encounter with Dolphins

Near the inner entrance to Tory Channel, Dan, the boatman, skillfully brought the boat around as six of us slid into the water right beside a pod of playful Dusky dolphins. The 15-minute boat ride from Torea Bay had given us time to change, have a quick biology lesson, and learn a bit more about the dolphins. Although not as big as the common bottlenose dolphins, these beautiful silvery creatures were still at least 6 feet long and strongly built. As we lay face down in the water, buoyant in our thick wet suits, the dolphins blasted up from the depths to swim right by us, time and again. Fins, masks, and snorkels made it easier to watch them as they swirled and twirled around us. They never touched us, but wheeled and turned just inches away. As they swam by, they turned on their sides and looked at us with their dark little eyes, their strong tails pushing them through the water. At other times they leaped from the water and came back down with a resounding splash. This was better than any wildlife documentary.

---

hills that rise almost vertically from the water, the sounds are a wild, majestic place edged with tiny beaches and rocky coves and studded with islands where native wildlife remains undisturbed by introduced species. (Operators run tours to several of these special islands.) Māori legend says the sounds were formed when a great warrior and navigator called Kupe fought with a giant octopus. Its thrashings separated the surrounding mountains, and its tentacles became parts of the sunken valleys. These waterways are one of the country's favorite areas for boating.

Much of the area around Picton is untamed, forest-covered country, broken by sheltered bays and deep waterways, and it has changed little since Captain Cook found refuge here in the 1770s. There are rudimentary roads on the long fingers of land jutting into the sounds, but the most convenient access is by water. Many properties only have boat access. Several operators travel the waterways on a daily basis, taking visitors along for the ride as they deliver the mail, groceries, and farming supplies to isolated residents and farms. Both Beachcomber and Cougar Line run from Picton and travel throughout Queen Charlotte Sound; or leave from Havelock aboard the Pelorus mail boat, *Pelorus Express,* which delivers mail and supplies to outlying settlements scattered around Pelorus Sound. To get your feet on the ground in and around the sounds, you can take any number of hikes on the Queen Charlotte Track *(see Outdoor Activities, below).*

OUTDOOR ACTIVITIES

For information on deep-sea fishing out of Picton, see Chapter 11.

DIVING The Marlborough Sounds have an excellent dive site in the *Mikhail Lermontov;* now recognized as one of the world's great wreck dives. In 1986, this massive Russian cruise ship sank on her side in 30 meters (100 feet) of water in Port Gore. (One life was lost.) The 200-meter-long (600-foot-long) ship is now an exciting dive site for anyone with moderate diving skills. Highlights are the swimming pool in its glass veranda room, the bridge, and the huge funnel; and there's some great penetration tech diving if you're competent. September and October generally have the best visibility but the trips run all year.

Dive Marlborough's Brent McFadden takes daily and live-aboard guided trips out to the *Mikhail Lermontov* (as long as at least three people want to go, and the weather cooperates). The $265 day-trip fee includes lunch and all diving gear; it costs a bit less if you have your own kit, and a bit more if you want nitrox. Tech dive gear available as well, but check on booking. Live-aboard trips start from $595 per person for a two-day, one-night adventure. ⊠ *Waikawa Bay Marina* ☎ *03/573–9181 or 0800/463–483* ⊕ *www.godive.co.nz.*

DOLPHIN
ENCOUNTERS
★

Marine biologists Amy and Dan Engelhaupt, who run **Dolphin Watch**, take you on a 15-minute boat ride out of Picton to where you slide into the water and swim with these beautiful creatures ($130), or just watch them from the boat ($80). Dolphin swims aren't available if they are either migrating or breeding, so call ahead. Dan and Amy also run Marine Wildlife and Motuara Island tours, which visit an island wildlife reserve to spy on seals, dolphins, and seabirds. These tours leave at 9 and 1:30, and cost $80–$85. From June through August, daily tours do not run and all tours are by private arrangement only. ⊠ *Picton Harbour* ☎ *03/573–8040 or 0800/9453–5433* 🖷 *03/573–7906* ⊕ *www.dolphinswimming.co.nz.*

HIKING
Fodor'sChoice
★

Starting northwest of Picton, the **Queen Charlotte Track** stretches 67 km (42 mi) south to north, playing hide-and-seek with the Marlborough Sounds along the way. Hike through lush native forests, stopping to swim or to pick up shells on the shore. Unlike other tracks, there are no Department of Conservation huts to stay in, just a few camping areas. Other accommodations are on the walk, however, from backpacking options to lodges, resorts, and homestays. Boats such as the *Cougar Line* can drop you at various places for one- to four-day walks (guided or unguided), or you can kayak or bike parts of it.

Though it's relatively easy to access, the track shouldn't be taken lightly. It has steep inclines and long drop-offs, and the weather can be unpredictable. In particular, Day 3, if you're walking north to south, a 22-km (14-mi) stretch can test even a good hiker's endurance in bad weather.

★

Both the Picton Visitor Information Centre and the local **Department of Conservation–Sounds Area Office** (⊠ *Picton* ☎ *03/520–3002* ✉ *soundsao@doc.govt.nz* ⊕ *www.doc.govt.nz*) are good sources of track information. One way to get the best of the Queen Charlotte Track is a combination trip, with hiking, some arm-flexing in a kayak, and some legwork on a mountain bike. A three-day trip organized by **Marlborough Sounds Adventure Company** (⊠ *The Waterfront, Picton* ☎ *03/573–6078 or 0800/283–283* ⊕ *www.marlboroughsounds.co.nz*) combines these three activities in a fully guided experience with meals and lodging taken care of, and your packs ferried ahead each day. Accommodation is bunk-room standard, and you need to be reasonably fit. The $695 fee includes all water transfers, guide, twin-share accommodation, packed lunches, and equipment. The trip kicks off every Wednesday from November through April. Four- and five-day options can include an ecotour of nearby Motuara Island, dolphin-watching, and resort-style twin-share en suite accommodation. They also have an adventure base at the Portage Resort Hotel (*see* Havelock listing), where you can hire bikes, kayaks, yachts, and scooters to explore around the Kenepuru Sound area.

KAYAKING A great way to experience the Marlborough Sounds is by sea kayak—and the mostly sheltered waters of Queen Charlotte Sound are perfect for it. **Marlborough Sounds Adventure Company** offers guided and self-guided kayak trips, from half-day to three-day tours, in either Queen Charlotte or Kenepuru Sound. The bays are ringed by dense native forest, echoing with the trilling calls of native birds. Costs range from $65 for a half-day guided trip to $495 for a three-day guided trip. Kayak rental is available from $35 a day. Reservations are essential. ✉ *The Waterfront, Picton* ☎ *03/573–6078 or 0800/283–283* ⊕ *www.marlboroughsounds.co.nz.*

You can take a one-day guided kayak trip with **Wilderness Guides** for $95, yummy lunch included. They also do multiday trips beside the Queen Charlotte Track, and kayak rentals if you want to do it on your own (as long as a minimum of two people are paddling together). And there's a special combo day with a guided kayak trip in the morning followed by an independent hike or mountain bike trail along part of the Queen Charlotte Track in the afternoon. Bookings are recommended. ✉ *Picton Railway Station, 3 Auckland St.* ☎ *03/520–3095 or 0800/266–266* 📠 *03/520–3096* ⊕ *www.wildernessguidesnz.com.*

For Boat Tours see Tours, below.

EN ROUTE Heading west out of Picton toward the town of Havelock, **Queen Charlotte Drive** rises spectacularly along the edge of Queen Charlotte Sound. It cuts across the base of the peninsula that separates this waterway from Pelorus Sound, then drops onto a small coastal plain before coming to Havelock. Beyond Havelock the road winds through forested river valleys and over several ranges before it rounds the eastern side of Tasman Bay and reaches Nelson. To start the drive from the InterIslander ferry terminal in Picton, turn right after leaving the parking lot and follow the signs.

About a third of the way to Havelock, Governor's, Momorangi and Ngakuta bays are gorgeous spots for a picnic or a stroll along the forested shore. Cullen Point, at the Havelock end of the drive, is a good vantage point to view the inland end of the Pelorus Sound and across the bay to Havelock. The short walk to the lookout is well worth the effort.

WHERE TO EAT

$$$–$$$$ ✕ **The Chart Room.** True to its name, this smart, central restaurant, hung with copies of Captain Cook's nautical charts and maps, is a cut above the rest in Picton. You can eat out by the pool or on the balcony if the weather is cooperating. The kitchen serves local favorites, such

as green-lipped mussels, scallops, and seafood chowder entrées; lamb, salmon, and eye-fillet beef are typically favorite mains. ✉ *Yacht Club Hotel, Waikawa Rd.* ☎ *03/573–7002 or 0800/991–188* ▭ *AE, DC, MC, V* ⊙ *No lunch Apr.–Dec.*

$$–$$$$ ✕ **Le Café.** Sitting outside Le Café on the waterfront you can look right down Queen Charlotte Sound and watch the local boat traffic and the big InterIslander ferries coming and going. Staff go out of their way to source organic, local, and free-range foods wherever possible—your fish has probably been landed on the wharf at the end of the street. Casual meals are available all day and well into the evening, and as night moves in, the tempo at the bar picks up and live acts appear on a casual basis. ✉ *London Quay* ☎ *03/573–5588* ⊕ *www.lecafepicton.co.nz* ▭ *MC, V.*

¢–$$ ✕ **Seumuss's Irish Nook.** Step inside this super-friendly little pub and you can feel a lilt rise in your throat and your "r"s starting to roll. A main course of curry and gravy starts at $6. The Guinness hot pot and stuffed potatoes is a perennial favorite. Wednesday to Sunday they run a full dinner menu, although Monday and Tuesday has reduced service. The pub is a short walk from the waterfront and it's open daily from midday until 1 AM, making Seumuss's a great spot to wait for the late-night ferry. ✉ *25 Wellington St.* ☎ *03/573–8994* ▭ *MC, V.*

WHERE TO STAY

$$$$ Fodor'sChoice ★ **Bay of Many Coves Resort.** Designed by the architect of the national museum Te Papa in Wellington, this beachfront structure complements its surrounding bush and seascape. The Kumatage lounge and restaurant, and the beautifully furnished units with private verandas, overlook the surrounding bays. The cuisine specializes in fresh, local foods and goodies baked on-site. Bathrooms have open tiled showers, fluffy robes, and locally made herbal toiletries. (There are also six studios, with shared bathroom facilities, that are only available between May and September.) You get here by water taxi from Picton. **Pros:** Idyllic spot in a sheltered, iconic Marlborough Sounds location; cruising, dolphin tours, mountain bikes, bushwalks, kayaking all at your front door. **Con:** Boat or foot access only but there is a helipad if you're in a hurry. ✉ *Bay of Many Coves, Queen Charlotte Sound* ☎ *03/579–9771 or 0800/579–9771* 📠 *03/579–9777* ⊕ *www.bayofmanycovesresort.co.nz* *11 apartments, 6 studios* *In-hotel: 2 restaurants, pool, spa, no elevator* ▭ *AE, DC, MC, V* *EP.*

$$$$ ★ **Sennen House.** Just a 1-km (½-mi) stroll from downtown Picton is this white, peak-roofed 1886 villa. The verandas overlook 5 acres of lush landscaping and bush, and the harbor hints beyond. The suites and apartments are furnished with carved wooden bedsteads and fireplace mantels, stained glass, rich upholstery, and brass fixtures. The spotless bathrooms have heated towel bars and hair dryers, and there's a common high-speed Internet connection for guests. Owners Richard and Imogen Fawcett bring a yummy breakfast hamper to your door each morning. **Pros:** Two apartments have full kitchens and three have kitchenettes. **Con:** Ask for the downstairs rooms if you have limited mobility. ✉ *9 Oxford St.* ☎📠 *03/573–5216* ⊕ *www.sennenhouse.co.nz* *2 suites, 3 apartments* *In-room: kitchen or kitchenette,*

DVD, no a/c. In-hotel: public Internet, no-smoking rooms, no elevator ⊟*AE, MC, V* ⊞*CP.*

$–$$$$ ⊞ **Punga Cove Resort.** Private chalets are tucked into the bush at this Queen Charlotte Track crossroads, with accommodation ranging from a backpacker lodge to luxury suites. The smaller A-frames have balconies. Several larger, more luxurious studio, one-, and two-bedroom chalets have large private decks with vistas of Camp Bay and Endeavour Inlet. You can rent kayaks, dinghies, and mountain bikes on-site, and fishing trips can be arranged. Access is quickest by the water taxi, 60 minutes from Picton. Otherwise, a two-hour-plus drive winds along Queen Charlotte Sound Drive to the turnoff at Linkwater, where you come through the spectacular scenery of the Kenepuru Sound via some 5 km (3 mi) of gravel road. **Pros:** Sitting on the sunny side of Endeavour Inlet, this picturesque place is quite isolated; a favorite overnight stop on the Queen Charlotte Track; at the right end of the sounds if you want to join a dive trip to the Mikhail Lermontov. **Con:** To get the best out of a spot like this plan to stay two nights. ⊠*Punga Cove, Endeavour Inlet, Queen Charlotte Sound, Picton* ☎*03/579–8561* ⊞*03/579–8080* ⊕*www.pungacove.co.nz* ⇆*3 suites, 12 chalets, 4 lodge rooms, 8 backpacker cabins* ⅋*In-room: no a/c (some), kitchen (some), no TV (some). In-hotel: 2 restaurants, bars, pool, spa, no elevator* ⊟*AE, MC, V.*

$$ ⊞ **Jasmine Court Travellers Inn.** A fresh, well-appointed place to stay, this stylish Kiwi-style motel looks down over the town to the main harbor. The guest rooms are well sized and done in soft pastels, with thoughtful touches such as fans, hypoallergenic pillows, and CD and DVD players with a library of discs. Several bathrooms have either a whirlpool tub or a multi-head shower. A supermarket just opposite the motel is handy for stocking up before hitting the remote areas of the Marlborough Sounds. **Pros:** They provide vehicle, bike, and luggage storage if you're off to walk the Queen Charlotte Track. **Cons:** Book ahead in summer as it is often full, kids by arrangement only. ⊠*78 Wellington St.* ☎*03/573–7110 or 0800/421–999* ⊞*03/573–7211* ⊕*www.jasminecourt.co.nz* ⇆*13 rooms, 1 apartment* ⅋*In-room: kitchen, Wi-Fi. In-hotel: laundry service, public Internet, no kids under 14, no-smoking rooms* ⊟*AE, DC, MC, V.*

$$ ⊞ **Whatamonga Homestay.** From the lounge you can watch the ferries and hear fish splash in the water below. Whatamonga is a sheltered bay just a short drive from Picton. Each unit has a kitchenette and balcony overlooking the sea. The water taxi can pick you up from the jetty if you want to do a cruise around the Sounds or get transport to the Queen Charlotte Track. A private jetty, kayaks, a dinghy, and golf clubs are on hand for your use. Kids are welcome by prior arrangement. **Pros:** Option of a guest room in the main house or a private apartment, all have balconies to the sea, beautiful Marlborough Sounds setting with great views. **Cons:** Minimum two-night stay in midsummer, very steep driveway with concealed exit. ⊠*425 Port Underwood Rd., Waikawa Bay* ☎*03/573–7192* ⊕*www.whsl.co.nz* ✎*info@whsl.co.nz* ⇆*2 rooms, 2 units* ⅋*In-room: no a/c, no phone, no TV. In-hotel: no-smoking rooms, no elevator* ⊟*MC, V* ⊞*EP.*

¢   ☐The Villa Backpackers and Lodge. Like a big, happy tribe, Villa guests fill a small, lovely colonial house. The hostel's central courtyard hums day and night with people relaxing after a day on the water, mountain biking, or walking the Queen Charlotte Track. On rainy days you can lie in front of the fire with a book, play guitar, or curl up in a quiet corner to write letters. Pickups and drop-offs, a hot tub, use of the gym, and bike usage are included in the price. New kitchens have space for cooking your own meals. **Pros:** In winter, apple crumble and ice cream for dessert and a Continental breakfast are included; doubles and en suite rooms have own TVs. **Cons:** The cheaper double rooms use shared facilities and have smaller rooms. ☒ *34 Auckland St.* 📞 *03/573–6598* ⊕ *www.thevilla.co.nz* ✎ *stay@thevilla.co.nz* ⇱ *7 double rooms, 2 with en suite, 54 dorm beds* ⚠ *In-room: no phone, no TV (some), no a/c. In-hotel: gym, bicycles, spa, public Internet* ☰ *MC, V.*

TOURS

BOAT TOURS   The Pelorus Sound mail boat, *Pelorus Express*, is a sturdy launch that makes a daylong trip around Pelorus Sound, and is one of the best ways to discover the waterway and meet its residents. Join the mailman as he delivers mail and supplies and checks in with the locals, as it's been done for generations. The boat leaves from Havelock, west of Picton, Tuesday, Thursday, and Friday at 9:30 AM and returns in the late afternoon. The fare is $110 and reservations are advised January through March.

Beachcomber Cruises runs scenic and ecocruises throughout Queen Charlotte Sound, including their well-known Mail Run cruise. Similar to the mail run on the Pelorus Express, but on a completely different waterway, this trip explores the outer reaches of Queen Charlotte Sound. They can also take you to and from any point on the Queen Charlotte Walkway for one-day or longer unguided walks. Boats depart from the Picton waterfront throughout the morning (times vary according to the time of year; check the Web site for options) and cost from $53. The mail boat leaves daily at 1:30 PM and costs $80.

The Cougar Line runs scheduled trips from Picton through the Queen Charlotte Sounds three to four times daily, depending on the time of year, dropping passengers (sightseers included) at accommodations, private homes, or other points. A Queen Charlotte drop-off and pickup service costs $90 for multiday hikes, $63 for day hikes that end at Furneaux Lodge. The twilight Salmon and Sauvignon evening cruise runs through December to February and they have several other scenic cruises varying from their popular three-hour morning and afternoon cruises to shorter ones suitable for passengers waiting for the Inter-Island ferry. Water-taxi service to area lodges costs from $30 to $45, depending on distances and number of people; reservations for all trips are essential at peak times and recommended at others.

Marlborough Sounds Adventure Company has half- to four-day guided kayak tours of the sounds, leaving from Picton, as well as kayak rentals for experienced paddlers. The cost is $65 for a half-day guided tour and $495 for a three-day guided tour, including water transportation, food, and camping equipment. A kayak rental costs $50 per person per day.

★ Green Shell Mussel Cruises will take you into the largely untouched Kenepuru and Pelorus sounds, which are part of the labyrinth of waterways that make up the Marlborough Sounds. The world's largest production of Greenshell mussels is done in the Sounds, and the boat explores the intricate system of waterways of these farms. Try the mussels on board, steamed, with a glass of local sauvignon blanc, while hearing the history of the area. The tour costs $99 per person, and the season runs November through March; you can get more information from Marlborough Travel. They also run winery tours and a combo trip combining a winery tour in the morning and mussel cruise in the afternoon (for $175).

Contacts Beachcomber Cruises (✉ *Beachcomber Pier, Town Wharf, Picton* ☎ *03/573–6175 or 0800/624–526* 🖷 *03/573–6176* ⊕ *www.beachcombercruises. co.nz* ✎ *office@beachcombercruises.co.nz*). **Cougar Line** (✉ *Picton Wharf* ☎ *03/573–7925 or 0800/504–090* 🖷 *03/573–7926* ⊕ *www.cougarline.co.nz or www.queencharlottetrack.co.nz*). **Marlborough Sounds Adventure Company** (✉ *The Waterfront, London Quay, Picton* ☎ *03/573–6078* 🖷 *03/573–8827* ⊕ *www. marlboroughsounds.co.nz* ✎ *walk@marlboroughsounds.co.nz*). **Marlborough Travel** (☎ *03/577–9997* ⊕ *www.marlboroughtravel.co.nz or www.greenshell musselcruise.co.nz* ✎ *info@marlboroughtravel.co.nz*). Pelorus Express (☎ *03/574– 1088* ⊕ *www.mail-boat.co.nz* ✎ *bookings@mail-boat.co.nz*).

FISHING TOURS   The Sounds Connection, a family-run tour company, offers regular half-day fishing trips and full-day trips by request. They leave from Picton; a half day runs at $79. They'll supply all the necessary gear and fillet your catch.

Contact The Sounds Connection (✉ *16 Wellington St., Picton* ☎ *03/573–8843 or 0800/742–866* ⊕ *www.soundsconnection.co.nz* ✎ *tours@soundsconnection.co.nz*).

WALKING & HIKING TOURS   To see the glorious Marlborough Sounds, try a four- or five-day fully catered and guided inn-to-inn walk on the Queen Charlotte Track with Wilderness Guides. The four-day guided gourmet walk includes all land and water transport, as well as overnight stays in three Sounds resorts: Punga Cove Resort, Furneaux Lodge, and the Portage. Experienced guides give talks on the area's natural and human history. Advance bookings are essential; trips cost $1,250 (boutique option available as well). Marlborough Sounds Adventure Company guides hikers on the Queen Charlotte Walkway as well, with four-day ($1,220) or five-day ($1,490) trips.

Contacts Marlborough Sounds Adventure Company (✉ *The Waterfront, London Quay, Picton* ☎ *03/573–6078 or 0800/283–283* 🖷 *03/573–8827* ⊕ *www. marlboroughsounds.co.nz* ✎ *adventure@marlboroughsounds.co.nz*). **Wilderness Guides** (✉ *Railway Station, Picton* ☎ *03/520–3095 or 0800/266–266* 🖷 *03/520– 3096* ⊕ *www.wildernessguidesnz.com* ✎ *info@wildernessguidesnz.com*).

WINERY
TOURS
The Sounds Connection runs full- and half-day tours to a handful of Marlborough's main wineries. Their Gourmet Experience tour (November through May) combines a wine and food appreciation tour with a four-course wine-matched lunch.

Contact The Sounds Connection (✉16 Wellington St., Picton ☎0800/742–866 ⊕ www.soundsconnection.co.nz ✉ tours@soundsconnection.co.nz).

HAVELOCK

35 km (22 mi) west of Picton.

Known as the Greenshell mussel capital of the world (Greenshells are a variety of green-lipped mussels), Havelock is at the head of Pelorus Sound, and trips around the sounds on the Pelorus Sound mail boat, *Pelorus Express*, depart here. Locals will forgive you for thinking you've seen what the Marlborough Sounds are all about after crossing from the North Island to the South Island on the ferry—but that's just a foretaste of better things to come. Small, seaside Havelock (population 400) is a good place to stroll; check out the busy little marina, poke into a few arts and crafts shops, and enjoy those mussels.

WHERE TO STAY & EAT

$$–$$$ ✕**Slip Inn.** Down at the marina, the Slip Inn overlooks the main boat ramp and working port area—it's a sunny spot to stop for a light lunch or dinner. A big outdoor fire keeps it warm even on chilly winter days. The chef favors local mussels; one favorite dish is the Kilpatrick, mussels grilled with bacon and cheese. Or try the bivalves steamed and served with a creamy coriander sauce. If you're not a mussel fan, other options include the panfried fish with a warm zucchini-and-leek salad or a gourmet pizza. ✉*Havelock Marina* ☎*03/574–2345* ▤*MC, V.*

$–$$$ ✕**The Mussel Pot.** Outside, a giant fiberglass mussel pot and some keen little mussels playing on the roof. Inside, the real things are steamed for three minutes in the whole shell or grilled on the half shell. Choose a light sauce for both steaming and topping: white wine, garlic, and fresh herbs or coconut, chili, and coriander. There are also smoked and marinated mussel salads, platters, and their tasty mussel chowder Sauvignon blanc from nearby Marlborough perfectly pairs with almost any dish on the menu. There's a courtyard for those sunny days and choices for those who don't like mussels. ✉*73 Main Rd.* ☎*03/574–2824* ▤*AE, MC, V.*

¢–$ ✕**Pelorus Bridge Café.** Fancy a wild-pork-and-kūmara (native sweet potato) pie, some mussel fritters, or just a nice cup of coffee? One of the better on-the-road cafés in the area, it even has some kid-friendly options. The setting beside the rocky, tree-lined Pelorus River is lovely, especially in summer when you can eat under the trees. The café closes at 5. ✉*State Hwy. 6, by Pelorus Bridge* ☎*03/571–6019* ▤*No credit cards.*

$$$ ☖**Mudbrick Lodge.** The winding road that leads to Mudbrick sets the mood for this charming, welcoming spot. Log fires, excellent meals, and fresh espresso all feed the senses while just out the window the rugged Marlborough landscape seems like the edge of the world.

Experienced hunting and fishing guides can take you to quiet trout pools, deserted islands, and sunny fishing spots and there's horse riding and kayaking nearby. Dinner is available by arrangement. **Pros:** A real rural NZ experience, just over the hill from the magical Marlborough Sounds, take a boat cruise from Tennyson Inlet while you're there. **Con:** A bit off the beaten track. ✉ *Carluke, near Rai Valley* ☎ *03/571–6147* ⊕ *www.mudbricklodge.co.nz* ✎ *tania@mudbrick lodge.co.nz* ➪ *2 self-contained suites* ⌂ *In-room: no a/c, no TV. In-hotel: spa, pool, no elevator* ⊟ *MC, V* ⃝ *BP.*

$–$$$
★ ⊡ **The Portage Resort Hotel.** The remote location doesn't prevent the staff from offering high-quality, even luxurious accommodations. Lodgings range from backpacker beds for hikers straight off the Queen Charlotte Track to very comfortable hotel rooms with private deck sand and fabulous views across Kenepuru Sound. Dining at the Te Weka restaurant ($$$–$$$$) features local seafood and mussels, along with excellent local wines. You can access the Portage by boat (1 minute on a water taxi) or car from Havelock; the drive takes about 1½ hours on a paved but winding road. **Pros:** On-site Portage Adventure Centre rents kayaks, mountain bikes, scooters, yachts, and other toys to explore the area; try the Waterside Bar & Café overlooking the bay. **Con:** Arrive by boat from Picton if you can, as the road is quite demanding. ✉ *Kenepuru Sound, 19 km (12 mi) off Queen Charlotte Dr.* ☎ *03/573–4309* 🖷 *03/573–4362* ⊕ *www.portage.co.nz* ➪ *41 rooms, 8 dorm beds* ⌂ *In-hotel: 2 restaurants, bar, pool* ⊟ *AE, DC, MC, V* ⃝ *EP.*

EN ROUTE The **Pelorus Bridge Scenic Reserve** is about halfway between both Picton and Nelson, and Blenheim and Nelson, on State Highway 6. It's a good example of the native lowland forest—with beech, podocarp, and broadleaf trees—that once covered this whole region. There's a network of easy walking trails through the reserve, and in summer the river is warm enough to jump in (watch out for the sandflies after the sun goes down). **Kahikatea Flat** (☎ *03/571–6019*), a hidden campground, is part of the reserve; it's in a quiet spot where, most of the year, the loudest noises are made by the bellbirds and the nearby river. A $20 fee ($22 with power) gets you a campsite with access to showers. Book ahead over midsummer.

BLENHEIM

29 km (18 mi) south of Picton, 120 km (73 mi) southeast of Nelson, 129 km (80 mi) north of Kaikoura.

People mostly come to Blenheim (pronounced *bleh*-num by the locals) for the wine. There are dozens of wineries in the area, and Blenheim is developing fast, though it still has a small-town veneer, with narrow streets, paved crossings, and low-slung buildings.

In 1973 the Montana (pronounced Mon-taa-na here) company paid two Californian wine authorities to investigate local grape-growing potential. Both were impressed with what they found. It was the locals who were skeptical—until they tasted the first wines produced. After that, Montana opened the first modern winery in Marlborough in

7

1977, although there had been fledgling efforts 100 years earlier by pioneering wine growers. The region now has more than 100 vineyards and wineries.

Marlborough has lots of sunshine, and this daytime warmth combines with crisp, cool nights to give local grapes a long, slow ripening period. The smooth river pebbles that cover the best vineyards reflect heat onto the ripening bunches. All these factors create grapes with audacious flavors. Although Marlborough made its name initially on sauvignon blanc, it's now also known for its excellent Riesling, pinot noir, chardonnay, gewürztraminer, and pinot gris wines. The Marlborough Wine and Food Festival held in mid-February each year celebrates the region's success in suitable style.

Don't bury your nose in a tasting glass entirely, though; the landscape shouldn't be overlooked. The vineyards sprawl across the large alluvial plains around the Wairau River, ringed by high mountains. On clear days you can see Mt. Tapuaenuku, which, at 3,000 meters (10,000 feet), is the tallest South Island mountain outside the Southern Alps.

GETTING HERE & AROUND
The roads to most wineries are arranged more or less in a grid, which makes getting around relatively straightforward. Rapaura Road is the central artery for vineyard visits; wineries also cluster around Jeffries and Jacksons roads, radiating out from Rapaura Road, the area around Renwick village, the lower Wairau Valley, and State Highway 1 south of Blenheim.

Pick up a map of the Marlborough wine region at the **Marlborough Visitor Information Centre** (⊠ *The Old Railway Station, Sinclair St., along State Hwy. 1*).

ESSENTIALS
Hospital **Wairau Hospital** (⊠ *Hospital Rd.* ☎ *03/520–9999*).

Visitor Info **Marlborough Visitor Information Centre** (⊠ *The Old Railway Station, Sinclair St., along State Hwy. 1* ☎ *03/577–8080* 🖶 *03/577–8079* ✉ *blenheim@ i-site.org*).

WINERIES
The wineries described below are among the country's notables, but you won't go wrong at any of the vineyards around Blenheim. Tastings are generally free, although more and more wineries charge a tasting fee, typically around 50¢ per tasting.

★ **Allan Scott Wines.** Allan Scott planted the first grapes in Marlborough in 1973 before planting the family's own vineyard two years later. He helped establish the big-selling Stoneleigh label for Corbans, then the country's second-biggest wine company, before launching his own company in 1990. Now he makes well-respected sauvignon blanc, chardonnay, pinot gris, pinot noir, methode traditionelle, gewürztraminer, and Riesling (the last two are particularly good). Allan's son Joshua is now winemaker and his daughter Sara is viticulturalist. Josh also makes NZ's first methode traditionelle beer—a tasty, rather manly

News from the Grapevine

New Zealand's rugged landscape leads to major differences between the grape-growing regions, even if they're small in scale. This diversity means that most of Europe's great grapes have found a second home somewhere in the country. Pinot noir in particular is benefiting as the hardier European varieties are planted at increasingly higher latitudes, especially in the Otago region. There are currently over 25,000 hectares (61,775 acres) of planted vines producing 76 million liters of wine a year.

Sauvignon blanc, particularly from Marlborough, is the country's most widely planted varietal. It's noted for tropical-fruit characters such as passion fruit and pineapple.

Chardonnay grows well all over the country. Left to its own devices, it has a citric, melonlike flavor, but wood-aging provides spiciness. It's the third-most-planted vine in New Zealand; chardonnays from the Nelson region are very good.

Riesling is a gentle variety, with a floral, lightly scented bouquet and fruity taste. Most local versions have at least a touch of sweetness. Ninety percent of the country's Rieslings are produced in the South Island.

Gewürztraminer is the most distinctive grape variety, with a superspicy bouquet reminiscent of rose petals, lychees, and spices. Many of the best Kiwi examples come from Gisborne,

but a couple of exceptional versions have come out of Hawke's Bay, Marlborough, and Martinborough.

Pinot gris is an up-and-comer in New Zealand. At its best, it produces wine with delightfully grainy character and loads of honest flavor. Marlborough growers see a lot of potential in this thin-skinned variety.

Cabernet sauvignon is suited to warmer parts of New Zealand. Most years, it performs best in Hawke's Bay and on Waiheke Island. It's often blended with merlot and cabernet franc.

Merlot was first used in blends, but more and more Kiwi winemakers are bottling it on its own. It has leather-coffee-tobacco undertones often summed up as "British gentleman's club."

Pinot noir, long considered a stumbling block, has been working well for many winemakers across the country. It's often described in red-fruit terms, with notes of strawberries, cherries, and plums. Central Otago is the top region for this variety, with winemakers rushing to put more acres under vine.

Syrah is an upcoming red known as a food wine. Its complex flavors are floral and spicy with excellent texture. It's a lighter, brighter wine than some of the other reds.

brew called Moa. The tasting room is next to the pleasant indoor-outdoor Twelve Trees restaurant (open for lunch only). ⊠*Jackson's Rd., Blenheim* ☎*03/572–9054* 🖷*03/572–9053* ⊕*www.allanscott. com* ⊙*Daily 9–4:30.*

★ **Cloudy Bay Vineyards.** From the start, Kevin Judd produced first-class sauvignon blanc; an equally impressive chardonnay was added soon afterward. The sauvignon blancs are highly rated for their notes of

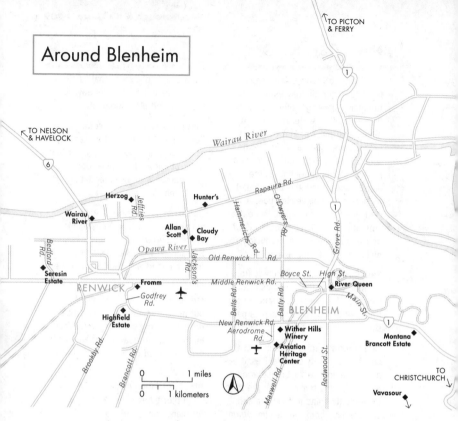

citrus, pear, and passion fruit; these are generally ready for immediate drinking. The chardonnay is more complex and can take medium-term cellaring. ⊠*Jackson's Rd., Blenheim* ☎*03/520–9140* 🖷*03/520–9040* ⊕*www.cloudybay.co.nz* ☉*Daily 10–4:30; tours by appointment.*

Fodor'sChoice
★
Herzog. Therese and Hans Herzog produce a superb range of wines off their pesticide- and chemical-free vineyard. Pinot gris, pinot noir, and what may be the area's only montepulciano are standouts, along with their wonderful merlot-cabernet, aptly named "The Spirit of Marlborough." The tasting area invites you to spend a long sunny afternoon exploring the delights of the cellar. You can enjoy an elegant bistro lunch in the tasting room, or, if you've made reservations, you can have a full meal at the adjoining restaurant—widely considered one of the best in the country (⇨ *Where to Eat, below*). ⊠*81 Jeffries Rd., off Rapaura Rd.* ☎*03/572–8770* ⊕*www.herzog.co.nz* ☉*Daily 9–4; variable hrs in winter.*

★ **Highfield Estate.** This magnificent place sits high on the Brookby Ridge, with spectacular views over the Wairau plains all the way to the North Island. The winery building is signposted by an iconic Tuscan-inspired tower (visitors are welcome to climb). Highfield specializes in sauvignon blanc, with interesting pinot noir, chardonnay, and Rieslings; their best, however, is a sparkling Elstree Cuvée Brut. Their indoor-outdoor lunch restaurant is popular and bookings are recommended in summer, when they also have a brunch menu. ⊠ *Brookby Rd., R.D. 2, Blenheim* ☎ *03/572–9244* 🖷 *03/572–9257* ⊕ *www.highfield.co.nz* ☉ *Daily 10–5.*

★ **Hunter's Wines.** Jane Hunter has been described by the London *Sunday Times* as the "star of New Zealand wine," with a string of successes as long as a row of vines. Building on the success of her late husband and now employing a top-notch winemaker, the wines are impressive; their fume blanc (oak-aged sauvignon blanc) and pinot noir are legendary. ⊠ *Rapaura Rd., Blenheim* ☎ *03/572–8489* 🖷 *03/572–8457* ⊕ *www. hunters.co.nz* ☉ *Daily 9:30–4:30.*

Montana Brancott Winery. This imposing brick structure is not really typical of Marlborough; but it's one of the biggest complexes around. It's worth a visit to sample not only their own wines but also many smaller local labels they stock. The visitor center includes a tasting area, a restaurant, a theater, and of course, retail. Winery tours are given daily from 10 to 3. Their star vintage is sauvignon blanc; their pinot noir is on the rise as well. Tastings cost a few dollars, and if you plan to come in summer, you may need to reserve in advance. ⊠ *State Hwy. 1, 4 km (2½ mi) south of Blenheim* ☎ *03/577–5775* 🖷 *03/579–1067* ⊕ *www.montanawines.co.nz* ☉ *Cellar door daily 10–4:30, restaurant daily 10:30–3.*

Seresin Estate. Named for owner Michael Seresin, a New Zealand filmmaker, this estate stands out by virtue of its meticulous viticulture and subtle wine-making techniques, producing hand-grown, handpicked, and handmade wine. They pursue high standards of environmentally friendly cultivation while using both biodynamic and organic methods to produce the wines. Seresin also produces a Tuscan-style extra-virgin olive oil. ⊠ *Bedford Rd., Blenheim* ☎ *03/572–9408* 🖷 *03/572–9850* ⊕ *www.seresin.co.nz* ☉ *Summer daily 10–4:30, winter closed weekends.*

Vavasour Wines. This winery pioneered grape growing in the Awatere Valley region. As a result a new viticultural subregion of Marlborough was discovered, one that produces wines with distinctive, and much sought after characteristics. Based on the quality of a given year's harvest, grapes are used either for Reserve vintages in limited quantities or the medium-price-range Dashwood label. Sister winery Goldwater also operates from the site. The awards list here is growing annually. ⊠ *Redwood Pass Rd., Awatere Valley* ✛ *20 km (12 mi) south of Blenheim* ☎ *03/575–7481* 🖷 *03/575–7240* ⊕ *www.vavasour.com* ☉ *Weekdays 10–4:30, closed weekends.*

Wairau River Wines. Phil and Chris Rose were the first contract grape growers in Marlborough. Now they produce a very good range of classic Marlborough-grown wines under their own label. The tasting room is made from mud bricks; it also serves as a restaurant concentrating on local produce, which is open noon–3. Try the multi-award-winning sauvignon blanc and other varietals, all from the Wairau River estate vineyards. ✉ *Rapaura Rd. and State Hwy. 6, Blenheim* 🕾 *03/572–9800* 🖶 *03/572–9885* ⊕ *www.wairauriverwines.com* ⊗ *Daily 10–5.*

Wither Hills. Their impressive complex is an architectural delight of river rock, tile, concrete, and wood, fronted by a dramatic tussock planting. The three-story tower offers a commanding view across the middle Wairau Valley and the Wither Hills to the south. Winemaker Ben Glover works with sauvignon blanc, chardonnay, and pinot noir, preferring to specialize with these rather than broaden his focus; there are also limited quantities of pinot gris and noble Riesling at the cellar door. Wither Hills is a quick drive from the Aviation Heritage Centre. ✉ *211 New Renwick Rd.* 🕾 *03/578–4036* ⊕ *www.witherhills.co.nz* ⊗ *Daily 10–4:30.*

WHAT TO SEE

ⓒ The **Omaka Aviation Heritage Centre** features a huge display of World War I–era planes and memorablia in the Knights of the Sky exhibition. Highlights include the world's only Caproni Ca22, a de Havilland DH-4, an Etrich Taube, and a Morane-Saulinier Type BB. New Zealand's movie-making talents have been drawn into constructing the super-realistic displays. The center is backed by the Classic Fighters Charitable Trust, which runs a three-day international air show every two years, alternating with the Wanaka event farther south. The next air show here is April 2009 when vintage and classic aircraft will be on display on the ground and in the sky. ✉ *Omaka Aerodrome, Aerodrome Rd., off New Renwick Rd.* 🕾 *03/579–1305* 🖶 *03/579–1306* ⊕ *www. omaka.org.nz and www.classicfighters.co.nz* 💲 *$18* ⊗ *Daily 10–4.*

Blenheim was established by early settlers at the most inland navigable point on the tiny Opawa River. The *River Queen,* one of the old boats working this picturesque waterway, has now been restored to her former beauty and ambles sedately along the river every day in true country fashion. Unlike the mountainous majesty of the area's braided stone rivers, the Opawa River twists and turns around historic bends and past sun-drenched homes and gardens bordered by weeping willows and lofty poplars. A tasty platter lunch is available on board and the cruise usually takes 2½ hours. ✉ *Riverside Park, under the bridge on SH1* 🕾 *03/577–5510* ⊕ *www.theriverqueen.co.nz* 💲 *Midday cruise $42, with lunch $62* ⊗ *noon and evening cruises.*

WHERE TO EAT

$$$$ ✕ **Gibbs Vineyard Restaurant.** Currently enjoying the reputation of being
★ one of *the* places to eat around Blenheim, this rustic indoor-outdoor restaurant is edged by potted herbs and vineyards, and is shaded by silk trees. Their rack of lamb is always sought after, led by an entrée of delicate homemade ravioli. The dessert cheese platter has an excellent array of local cheeses. ✉ *258 Jacksons Rd., Rapaura* 🕾 *03/572–8048* ⚑ *Reservations essential in summer* ⊗ *Closed July and Sun. and Mon. May–Oct. No lunch.*

$$$$ ✕ **Herzog.** Marlborough's finest dining experience is tucked away along
Fodor'sChoice a short side road leading down to the Wairau River. Superb three- and
★ five-course dinner menus pair Herzog wines with innovative dishes; the

set and à la carte menus might include silky yellowfin tuna carpaccio, seared Nelson scallops with asparagus-ricotta ravioli, or a whole red snapper in a salt crust. The legendary degustation dinners ($185 per person) are booked well in advance, but you can often chance a dinner booking a day or so ahead of your visit. In addition to the wine pairings, you can study the wine list of 500 vintages. Retire to the lounge after dinner for a coffee or a digestif. Herzog runs very popular cooking classes from November to March and has a boutique vineyard cottage for the use of restaurant guests. ⊠*Jeffries Rd. off Rapaura Rd.* ☎*03/572–8770* ⚓*Reservations essential* ▭*AE, DC, MC, V* ⊙*Closed mid-May–mid-Oct.*

$$$–$$$$ ✕**The Vintners Room.** Toward the inland end of the Rapaura Road winery strip this bar and fine dining restaurant enjoys a well-designed Sante Fe–style setting. Stars on the menu include their rack of lamb and a herb-crusted salmon. Their beef fillet is also worth stopping for. Pricing here is very reasonable for the standard of food and service. The courtyard is shaded by spreading cherry trees through summer and there's a small on-site art gallery. ⊠*190 Rapaura Rd.* ☎*03/572–5094* ▭*AE, MC, V* ⊙*No lunch.*

$$$ ✕**Bacchus.** Marcel Rood has cooked at celebrated restaurants in Europe and in New Zealand. Now he's settled in wine country—and loving it. His restaurant has rich burgundy walls and lots of wood. A fountain (in the shape of Bacchus) occupies the small courtyard, and inside an open fire keeps things cozy in winter. Marcel makes good use of New Zealand produce in dishes such as bacon-wrapped beef fillet on *kūmara* (native sweet potato) mash. ⊠*3 Main St.* ☎☎*03/578–8099* ▭*AE, MC, V* ⊙*No lunch.*

$$$ ✕**Bellafico Restaurant & Wine Bar.** Standards are high as the number of
★ full-house nights testifies to. The kitchen serves wild pork and venison whenever it can get it, and if you're a meat lover, you can try the Angus beef served with almond croquettes, potatoes, and balsamic jus. Their field-mushroom pâté is legendary, as is the 16-cm-high (10-inch-high) lemon meringue pie. ⊠*17 Maxwell Rd.* ☎*03/577–6072* ▭*AE, DC, MC, V* ⊙ *Closed Sun. No lunch.*

$$ ✕**Paddy Barry's Bar and Restaurant.** Locals come for a chat and a beer, and the menu is straightforward and well priced. It's a good place to come down from over-enthusiastic gourmandizing—a local peril. Pair a plate of battered and fried seafood with a well-poured Guinness. You'll find Guinness *in* the food, too, in the form of a beef 'n' Guinness hot pot; but try the bangers and mash or the crumbed fish. If they're not busy, the kitchen closes by 8:30. ⊠*51 Scott St.* ☎*03/578–7470* ▭*AE, DC, MC, V.*

¢–$ ✕**CPR.** This small, stylish café in the middle of town has its own roastery (in a separate building) and draws espresso fans from around Marlborough with its excellent coffee and light lunch menu. ⊠*1c Main St.* ☎*03/579–5040* ⊕*www.cprcoffee.co.nz* ▭*DC, MC, V* ⊙*Closed Sun. No dinner.*

¢–$ ✕**Living Room Café and Lounge Bar.** The sunny corner location in the heart of Blenheim's shopping area means this café never lacks for action. Surrounded by glass on two sides, the triangular Living Room serves excellent breakfasts, with choices such as French toast, eggs Benedict, and fruit and muesli. Their breakfast loaf is freshly baked each day. They also do a nice lunch ranging from a lamb and kūmara (sweet potato) pie or a classic Caesar salad, and have a daily blackboard menu for dinner. The walls are lined with deli treats, a hearty fire burns in winter, and they have a wireless hot spot. ⊠*Scott St. at Maxwell Rd.* ☎*03/579–4777.*

WHERE TO STAY

$$$$

Fodor'sChoice
★

Old St. Mary's Convent. This striking turn-of-the-20th-century building was once a convent, beloved by a small group of local nuns who still visit for Christmas cheer. The relocated and refurbished structure hardly evokes a nunnery now with its luxuriously decorated rooms, rambling lawns and gardens, and evening glasses of Marlborough wine. Pétanque, billiards, croquet, and tennis are available to occupy idle moments. The Chapel honeymoon suite is the pick of the rooms, but each has a lovely view. This place books fast every year. **Pros:** Set in 60 acres of vineyard and rambling gardens, in the heart of Rapaura wine country, self-contained vineyard cottage available as well, and a chapel for weddings. **Con:** Book the downstairs room if you have limited mobility. ⊠*Rapaura Rd.* ☎*03/570–5700* 🖨*03/570–5703* ✐*retreat@convent.co.nz* ⊕*www.convent.co.nz* ⇩*5 rooms, 1 cottage* ♿*In-room: refrigerator (some), DVD, Wi-Fi. In-hotel: bar, no-smoking rooms, no elevator* ⊟*AE, MC, V* ♥*Closed June–Aug.* ♦*BP.*

$$$$

Fodor'sChoice
★

Timara Lodge. This 1923 house is one of Marlborough's original homesteads; its craftsmanship, skilled used of native timber, and luxurious decor evoke an elegant past. The gardens extend over 25 acres and include a pool, a tennis court, a private lake, and masses of clipped hedging. Chef Louis Schindler prepares sumptuous four-course table d'hôte dinners based on local ingredients. Wine tours, trout fishing, sea kayaking, golf, skiing, even whale-watching (an hour and a half away in Kaikoura) can be arranged. The owners have their own vineyard and winery, producing the very successful Spy Valley label. **Pros:** Their extensive and beautiful garden is a highlight, the chef is ex-Herzog's and is one of the best around, transfers available from Blenheim airport. **Cons:** Down a narrow country lane, 15-minute drive from Blenheim. ⊠*Dog Point Rd., R.D. 2* ☎*03/572–8276* 🖨*03/572–9191* ⊕*www.timaralodge.co.nz* ✐*timaralodge@xtra.co.nz* ⇩*2 rooms, 2 suites* ♿*In-hotel: tennis court, pool, no-smoking rooms, no kids under 15, no elevator* ⊟*AE, DC, MC, V* ♥*Closed Dec. 22–27, and July and Aug.* ♦*MAP.*

$$$$

Vintners Retreat. At the heart of Marlborough's wine district, this all-villas resort has balconies that overlook six vineyards. As the varieties ripen and are harvested and their leaves turn red, the view changes like a Technicolor quilt. Each villa is a fully equipped home away from home and is well suited for families. **Pros:** All units are beautifully presented, easy access and parking, pricing is for up to four adults. **Cons:** Its size means it loses some intimacy with its setting, busy main road. ⊠*55 Rapaura Rd.* ☎*03/572–5094 or 0800/484-686* 🖨*03/572–5093* ⊕*www.vintnersretreat.co.nz* ⇩*14 1- to 3-bedroom villas* ♿*In-hotel: tennis court, pool, laundry, public Wi-Fi* ⊟*AE, DC, MC, V.*

$$$–$$$$ 🏨 **Straw Lodge.** Down a quiet lane near the Wairau River, Straw Lodge
★ is about as peaceful as it gets, with the choice of self-catering or B&B
accommodation. The buildings are of solid straw bale construction,
making them extra-quiet, warm in winter, and cool in summer. Start
your day with breakfast under the grape-covered pergola overlooking
the lodge's working vineyard (a tasting is included), and end it with
a hot tub soak under the stars, sipping the lodge's own excellent vin-
tage. Self-catering facilities are available if you prefer to DIY. There
is a complimentary platter and wine tasting on arrival. **Pros:** Genuine
vineyard setting with vines running to the house, free use of bikes with
lots of river trails nearby, the owners also have a house in the Marlbor-
ough Sounds. **Con:** A 15-minute drive from town. ⊠ *Fareham La. off
Wairau Valley Rd., Renwick* ☎ *03/572–9767* 🖷 *03/572–9769* ⊕ *www.
strawlodge.co.nz* ✐ *strawlodge@xtra.co.nz* ⇌ *3 suites* ♿ *In-room: no
a/c, refrigerator, DVD. In-hotel: public Wi-Fi, public Internet, bicycles,
no-smoking rooms* ▭ *MC, V* ⓞ *BP.*

$$$ 🏨 **Chateau Marlborough.** Behind its Camelot-esque turret and peaked
gables, this quiet hotel in central Blenheim is a relaxing and conve-
nient place to crash. The good-size rooms have separate kitchen areas;
some have whirlpool baths. Ask for one of the rooms overlooking Sey-
mour Square, with its stone clock tower and memorial gardens. **Pros:**
All super-king beds with quality linens, comfy leather armchairs in the
rooms, good off-street parking. **Con:** Expansion plans afoot. ⊠ *High St.
at Henry St.* ☎ *03/578–0064* 🖷 *03/578–2661* ⊕ *www.marlboroughnz.
co.nz* ⇌ *24 rooms, 6 suites* ♿ *In-room: kitchen or kitchenette, refrigerator, Wi-Fi, no a/c (some). In-hotel: bar, restaurant, pool, laundry,
no-smoking rooms* ▭ *AE, DC, MC, V.*

$$–$$$ 🏨 **Hotel d'Urville.** Every room is unique in this boutique hotel in the
★ well-preserved Art Deco Public Trust building. You could choose the
Raja Room, with its Eastern-inspired decor and carved Javanese day-
bed; the romantic Angel Room; or the sensory trip of the Colours
Room. One room is based on the exploits of Dumont d'Urville, who
made voyages to the Pacific and the Antarctic in the 1820s and '30s.
The excellent restaurant ($$$–$$$$) serves everything from a cup of
coffee to tasty breakfasts and delightful dinners, based on local pro-
duce. Try the lamb, perhaps matched with an offering from Clayridge
or Cloudy Bay vineyards. **Pros:** Fabulous old building right on the main
street, the downstairs bar is a welcoming spot for an evening cocktail.
Con: It's a bit removed from Marlborough's vineyard/winery scene.
⊠ *52 Queen St., Blenheim* ☎ *03/577–9945* 🖷 *03/577–9946* ⊕ *www.
durville.com* ✐ *reservations@durville.com* ⇌ *10 rooms* ♿ *In-room:
refrigerator. In-hotel: restaurant, bar, no elevator, no-smoking rooms,
parking* ▭ *AE, DC, MC, V* ⓞ *CP.*

$ 🏨 **St Leonards Vineyard Cottages.** With five different levels of accommo-
dation dotted around a leafy garden and surrounded by vineyard this
rural retreat has something for everyone. Set around an old farm home-
stead, each accommodation occupies an old farm building, hence names
like the Dairy, the Stable, and the Woolshed. Each is furnished in very
comfortable rural style with private outdoor spaces and verdant views.
This is a great place for kids. **Pros:** The Woolshed has an outdoor bath

7

on a private balcony; lots of sheep, deer, and chickens to amuse the kids; the owners love vintage cars and have a 1930 Chrysler available for transfers and wine tours. **Con:** Kitchens in the cheaper units are fairly basic. ⊠*St Leonards Rd., just off SH6, 3 km (2 mi) from Blenheim* 🕾*03/577–8328* ⊕*www.stleonards.co.nz* 🛏*5 self-contained cottages* ⚷ *In-room: kitchen. In-hotel: pool, tennis court, bicycles, public Wi-Fi, laundry* ⊟*MC, V.*

EN ROUTE

The drive from Blenheim to Kaikoura crosses the dry parched Wither Hills and the rolling farmlands and vineyards of the Awatere Valley. A short distance after the small town of Ward the road drops down to a dramatic coastline, which it follows right through to Kaikoura. This coastal section takes an hour with a few scenery stops. The Tranz-Coastal train also travels this same route. Don't miss the seals at **Ohau Point, south of Kekerengu,** where they can be viewed from the roadside. Don't approach them closely and always maintain at least a 10-meter (30-foot) distance from them—although their pungent smell will help with that. In early summer walk the short track to the nearby waterfall where you may be lucky to see seal pups which have swum up the creek from the sea to play at the base of the falls.

¢–$$ ✕**The Store.** This one-stop store and café is by the rolling surf beach ★ on SH1 heading south, halfway between Blenheim and Kaikoura. On this dramatic perch at the edge of the Pacific, the waves almost reach the open deck. You can choose lunch from either the cabinet or a blackboard menu; try the seafood chowder or a Thai beef salad with a glass of local wine. Dinner bookings are essential in summer (last order taken at 7:30); in winter the Store closes at 7, with the last order taken around 6:30. ⊠*State Hwy. 1, Kekerengu* ⊹*64 km (40 mi) south of Blenheim* 🕾*03/575–8600* 🖶*03/575–8620* ✉*the_store@ xtra.co.nz* ⊟*MC, V.*

KAIKOURA

129 km (81 mi) south of Blenheim, 182 km (114 mi) north of Christchurch.

The town of Kaikoura sits on a rocky protrusion on the East Coast, backed by an impressive mountainous upthrust. View it from the expansive **lookout** up on Scarborough Street. Sperm whales frequent this coast in greater numbers than anywhere else on Earth. The sperm whale, the largest toothed mammal, can reach a length of 60 feet and a weight of 70 tons. The whales concentrate in this area because of the abundance of squid—particularly the giant squid of seafaring lore, which is their main food source. Scientists speculate that the whales use a form of sonar to find the squid, which they then bombard with deep, powerful sound waves generated in the massive cavities in the fronts of their heads. Their hunting is all the more remarkable considering that much of it is done at great depths, in darkness. The whales' food source swims in the trench just off the continental shelf, just kilometers off the Kaikoura Coast. You are most likely to see the whales between October and August, but they are generally there year-round.

Kaikoura's main street straggles along the beach behind a high stony bank, which offers some protection from rough weather. Farther south curves South Bay, the docking point for the whale-watching operators. Kaikoura has undergone a transformation over the past decade as its whale-watching has brought thousands of people to its doorstep.

ESSENTIALS

Hospital **Kaikoura Hospital** (✉ *Deal St.* ☎ *03/319–7760*).

Visitor Info **Kaikoura Information and Tourism Centre** (✉ *West End* ☎ *03/319–5641* 🖷 *03/319–6819* ⊕ *www.kaikoura.co.nz* ✉ *info@kaikoura.co.nz*).

WHAT TO SEE

Fyffe House is Kaikoura's oldest building, erected soon after Robert Fyffe's whaling station was established in 1842. Partly built on whalebone piles on a low rise overlooking the sea, the house provides a look at what life was like when people aimed at whales with harpoons rather than cameras. ✉ *62 Avoca St.* ☎ *03/319–5835* 🖙 *$7, family $15* ⊙ *Oct.–Apr., daily 10–6; May–Sept., Thurs.–Mon. 10–4.*

At **Lavendyl Lavender Farm,** just off the main highway a few minutes' drive north of the town center, rows of lavender stretch out against the stunning backdrop of Mt. Fyffe and the Seaward Kaikouras. Mike and Maureen Morris run a working 5-acre farm; the blooms are harvested in late January and early February. Walk through the heaven-scented gardens, and then head for the shop, where bunches of lavender hang from the ceiling and lavender marmalade, mustards, chutneys, and soap line the shelves. If you can't tear yourself away, stay overnight (⇨ *Dylan's Country Cottages in Where to Stay, below*). ✉ *268 Postmans Rd.* ☎ *03/319–5473* ⊕ *www.lavenderfarm.co.nz* 🖙 *$2* ⊙ *Daily 10–4. Closed July.*

On the first Saturday of October Kaikoura celebrates its annual **Seafest**, during which the best of this coastal area's food, wine, and beer is served while top New Zealand entertainers perform on an outdoor stage. Tickets are available from the town's information center but they do sell out so book ahead.

Seaward Pottery has been running on this dramatic coastal site at Hapuku now since the 1970s, and in that time Juanita Edelmann has refined her ability to catch the colors of the surrounding beach, sea, and snowy mountains in her pottery. ✉ *Just off State Hwy. 1, 15 km (9 mi) north of Kaikoura* ☎ *03/319–5795* ⊙ *Daily dawn–dusk.*

OUTDOOR ACTIVITIES

December and January are the peak months for whale-watching and swimming with dolphins or seals so book well in advance.

BIRD-
WATCHING **Albatross Encounter** (✉ *96 The Esplanade* ☎ *03/319–6777 or 0800/733–365* ⊕ *www.encounterkaikoura.co.nz*) arranges tours by boat to go out and view the large varieties of seabirds off the Kaikoura Coast, including the mighty albatross. Tours operate three times daily in summer and twice daily in winter, and cost $80 for adults and $40 for children.

HIKING   The three-day **Kaikoura Coast Track** walk provides uncrowded, unguided hiking along spectacular coastal farmland south of town for 10 people at a time maximum. Take binoculars to search out whales and dolphins. The first night is at Hawkswood in the historic sheep station setting of the **Staging Post.** A challenging four- to six-hour walk through native bush and down to the coast the next day will take you to **Ngaroma,** a 3,000-acre sheep and cattle farm. The following day's hike is along the beach, passing an ancient buried forest before heading across farmland to an area of regenerating bush to **Medina,** where you'll spend the third night. On the final day, a moderate four- to six-hour walk takes you over the 2,000-foot-plus Mt. Wilson. The total track length is 40 km (25 mi). Bags are transferred to the next night's accommodation daily, so you only need to carry a daypack.

The fee is $170 per person, and a guided walk can be arranged. If you opt to have all meals included and need bedding, the total cost is available on request. Reservations are essential. The start point is a ¾-hour drive south of Kaikoura on State Highway 1. Public transport can drop you at the gate. ⊠ *201 Conway Flat Rd., Cheviot, North Canterbury* ☎ *03/319–2715* 📠 *03/319–2724* ✎ *sally@kaikouratrack.co.nz* ⊕ *www.kaikouratrack.co.nz* 🕐 *Daily Oct.–Apr.*

With the proximity of very high mountains the Kaikoura Wilderness Walkway offers an excellent opportunity to get right up in them. There are two- and three-day guided walks, with overnight accommodation in the very comfy **Shearwater Lodge,** high above the Puhi Puhi Valley in the Seaward Kaikoura Ranges. The walkway crosses through rugged, inspiring terrain where clouds swirl across the tops and giant scree slopes slither down the valleys. Door-to-door pickup can be arranged from Kaikoura, luggage transferred to the lodge, all meals are provided, and you need to be moderately fit and agile. ⊠ *Puhi Puhi Valley* ☎ *03/319–6966 or 0800/945–337* ⊕ *www.kaikourawilderness. co.nz Reservations essential* 🎫 *Tours from $695 per person (4-person minimum)* 🕐 *Oct.–Mar., Sat., Mon., and Thurs. departures.*

The peninsula near town has a much shorter **walking track** that shows off the spectacular coastal scenery and the seal colonies. Consult the town's information center for maps and track information. The walk starts either at the end of Fyffe Quay or round at South Bay. The new entry point at South Bay recognizes the importance of the area to local Māori, whose ancestors lived on this stretch of coast for many generations before Europeans arrived. The first part of the track from South Bay leading to Limestone Bay is wheelchair accessible.

SWIMMING
WITH
DOLPHINS &
SEALS   The dolphin- and seal-spotting opportunities are fantastic. Although operators have led visitors to view and swim with dolphins and seals off the Kaikoura Coast for years, and the animals may be familiar with boats, they are not tame. New Zealand Fur seals are common, and you might spot an octopus or crayfish. Pods of dusky dolphins stay in the area year-round; you may even see them doing aerial jumps and flips.

The offerings vary and operators will explain their expectations before you book. Some boat operators go farther offshore, whereas others hug the coast. If you have any questions about the suitability of a trip, pipe up; these guys are happy to help. Guides can prime you with information on the local species and will be in the water with you. Wet suits and other gear are provided.

But you don't have to join an organized tour to get close to seals. At the **Point Kean** sea colony out on the Kaikoura Peninsula you can see seals in their natural habitat, lying in the sun or playing in the kelp-filled shallows. These are wild animals so don't approach closer than 10 meters (30 feet). With seabirds wheeling above and waves breaking along the shore it's a powerful place just minutes from the main street. Follow Fyffe Quay to the colony at the end of the road.

Dolphin Encounter (✉ *96 The Esplanade* ☎ *03/319–6777 or 0800/733– 365* 🖷 *03/319–6534* ⊕ *www.encounterkaikoura.co.nz* ✍ *info@ dolphin.co.nz*) arranges dolphin watching and swimming. Tours operate three times a day through summer and twice a day in winter, for $150 per person. (It's just $80 to watch them from the boat.) Because they operate in the open ocean, you need to be confident in the water, and it is an advantage to have some snorkeling experience. They also offer "Albatross Encounter" tours that take you out to view the seabirds off the Kaikoura Coast. **Seal Swim Kaikoura** (☎ *03/319–6182 or 0800/732–579* ⊕ *www.sealswimkaikoura. co.nz* ✍ *info@sealswimkaikoura.co.nz*) is New Zealand's original seal-swimming experience and has boat- and shore-based tours running daily from October to May for $90 per person. The swims are easy because they're behind the shelter of the Kaikoura Peninsula, and you're virtually guaranteed to see fur seals.

WHALE-
WATCHING
Fodor$Choice
★

Whale Watch Kaikoura Ltd. Whale Watch is owned by the Ngai Tahu *iwi* (tribe). Since arriving in the Kaikoura area in AD 850, Ngai Tahu, the predominant South Island Māori iwi, claims to have lived and worked based on a philosophy of sustainable management and sensible use of natural resources. Having worked these waters since 1987, Whale Watch skippers can recognize individual whales and adjust operations, such as the boat's proximity to the whale, accordingly. Allow 3½ hours for the whole experience, 2¼ hours on the water. Various dolphins and seals and other species of whales may also be seen on any day.

Book in advance: 7 to 10 days November–April, 3 to 4 days at other times. Their sturdy catamarans are fully enclosed for sea travel, but once the whales are spotted you can go out on the deck for a closer view. Trips depend on the weather, and should your tour miss seeing a whale, which is rare, you will get up to an 80% refund. Take motion-sickness pills if you suspect you'll need them: even in calm weather, the sea around Kaikoura often has a sizable swell. They can't accept children under three on the trip. ⚓ *Whaleway Station, Box 89, Kaikoura* ☎ *03/319–6767 or 0800/655–121* 🖷 *03/319–6545* ✍ *res@ whalewatch.co.nz* ⊕ *www.whalewatch.co.nz* 🖃 *$130* 🖃 *AE, MC, V.*

WHERE TO EAT

For a small place Kaikoura has an excellent choice of restaurants. In addition to the better known spots listed below, the **Pier Brasserie** at the port, the evening dining at **Hapuku Lodge,** and the **Old Convent** are worth trying. There are a number of crayfish stalls along the coast north of town; Nin's Bin has a strong fan base. Crays come cooked or uncooked, or you may prefer to get your crayfish fix at a local café. They are expensive; even a casual place can have main courses over $30. Also try the whitefish like groper (grouper) and terakihi, or the shellfish and crabs.

$$$–$$$$ ✕ **The Craypot.** This casual café relies strongly on the local delicacy. Crayfish isn't cheap, but this kitchen knows how to prepare it. Other seafood also figures large on the menu, and you can choose from several variations on the steak, chicken, and lamb themes. Homemade desserts are worth leaving room for. In summer you can get a table outdoors; in winter an open fire roars at night. ✉ *70 West End Rd.* ☎ *03/319–6027* ▣ *AE, DC, MC, V.*

$$$–$$$$ ✕ **White Morph Restaurant.** Crayfish is always on the menu at this elegant
★ eatery, and options include roasted, in antipasto, or even as a brûlée. Prices vary with availability. Other treats include venison, lamb loin, wild hare, and at least one vegetarian dish. Fish of the Bay is usually a divinely roasted groper fillet, served with walnut-and-parsley pesto and lemon-baked risotto. The desserts are fabulous, too. The best decorations are the seaside views from the front windows; fishing boats, sturdy launches, and the occasional yacht bob at anchor in the rock-strewn bay. ✉ *92–94 The Esplanade* ☎ *03/319–5676* ✍ *camber@ ts.co.nz* ▣ *MC, V* ⊗ *No lunch.*

$$–$$$$ ✕ **Hislops Café.** Wholesome Hislops is a few minutes' walk north of town and worth the trip. In the morning you'll find tasty eggs and bacon, plus freshly baked, genuinely stone-ground whole-grain bread served with marmalade or their own honey. The lunch and dinner menus use organic ingredients, and there are wheat- and gluten-free options. You might choose between a *kūmara* (native sweet potato), bacon, and avocado salad or marinated tofu and falafel. On sunny days, score a table on the veranda. ✉ *33 Beach Rd.* ☎ *03/319–6971* ▣ *AE, DC, MC, V* ⊗ *Reduced hrs in winter; call ahead.*

¢–$$$ ✕ **Café Encounter.** Here's a bright eatery along the Esplanade, sharing space with the Dolphin and Albatross Encounter operations. The partially glassed-in courtyard is sheltered in most winds, and there's plenty of indoor seating. Food is available off the menu or from the cabinet; their range of cakes and slices is quite appealing. But like any outdoor café in Kaikoura, don't leave your food unattended because the seagulls will snatch it quicker than you can say "seagull!" ✉ *96 The Esplanade* ☎ *03/319–6777* ▣ *AE, DC, MC, V* ⊗ *No dinner.*

WHERE TO STAY

Accommodations are a mix of lodges and pubs out in the country and motels and apartments in town. Another option is seaside camping along the coast. Available from Paia Point, south of town, along to Oaro, it's administered by the Kaikoura Coastal Camp at **Goose Bay**

(☎*03/319–5348* ✉*goosebay@ihug.co.nz*), so call before grabbing a site. Powered and tent sites are available.

$$$$ ⊞**Hapuku Lodge and Tree Houses.** This complex has been built by the local Wilson family who have a strong pedigree in New Zealand architecture. Featuring imaginative use of timbers and finishings, the lodge rooms are quietly tasteful. But out in the trees all that changes in the very luxurious but very funky tree houses. Each stands several stories high up into the surrounding cover of native *manuka* and *kowhai* trees and was built with a combination of rough-sawn timber, copper, glass, and steel. Inside, no luxury is spared, with freestanding fireplaces, spa baths, and elegant handmade furniture. Each unit has a wide-reaching view across the coast to the east and the Seaward Kaikoura Ranges to the west, both just a few kilometers away. Dinner is available by arrangement. **Pros:** Specialty breakfasts available on request, surf out the back window and the snow out the front, walking track down to the sea through the olive grove. **Con:** Stay in the main lodge if you're not good with heights. ✉*State Hwy. 1 at Station Rd., 12 km (8 mi) north of Kaikoura* ☎*03/319–6559* 🖷*03/319–6557* ⊕*www.hapuku lodge.com* ↪*6 lodge rooms, 5 1- and 2-bedroom tree houses* ♿*In-room: refrigerator. In-hotel: restaurant, public Internet* ▤*AE, DC, MC, V* ⦿*CP in most rooms.*

$$–$$$ ⊞**White Morph Motor Inn.** A waterfront view is hard to ignore—even
★ more so on the rugged Kaikoura Coast. This hotel is just opposite the beach, a few minutes' walk from the town center. The suites have double whirlpool baths, as do a few of the other rooms; three units are two stories, well suited for families or larger parties. **Pros:** Very comfortable units in a great esplanade location, breakfast served in the neighboring Encounter Café, the White Morph restaurant is worth a visit. **Con:** On the tourist strip. ✉*92–94 The Esplanade* ☎*03/319–5014* 🖷*03/319–5015* ✉*info@whitemorph.co.nz* ⊕*www. whitemorph.co.nz* ↪*31 units (12 with spa baths), 16 studios, 3 self-catering family units* ♿*In-room: no a/c (some), kitchen, DVD (some). In-hotel: no-smoking rooms, no elevator* ▤*AE, DC, MC, V.*

$$ ⊞**Donegal House.** It's surprising what you can find down a quiet country back road. The name here refers to owner Murray Boyd's home county; life-size statues of his ancestors stud the parklike grounds. The units are modern and spacious and a number of the rooms have balconies, but the real attraction is the Irish bar and restaurant ($$$–$$$$), where posters and photographs of "Auld Oireland" and early Kaikoura cover the paneled walls and you almost smell the peat fires burning. Delve into local crayfish with garlic or fresh lime and herb butter, followed by a Guinness or three. Outdoor seating overlooks the pond and garden. Dinner and a cooked breakfast are available. **Pros:** You can come here to stay and go nowhere else, very pretty garden. **Cons:** Can be a bit rowdy when the Irish pub starts to party, 10-minute drive from Kaikoura ✉*School House Rd.* 🖷🖷*03/319–5083* ⊕*www. donegalhouse.co.nz* ↪*30 rooms* ♿*In-room: no a/c, no phone, no TV (some). In-hotel: restaurant, bar, laundry, no-smoking rooms* ▤*AE, MC, V* ⦿*CP.*

7

$$ 🏠**Dylans Country Cottages.** A pair of rustic timber-clad cottages are tucked away in the trees at Lavendyl Lavender Farm. Both make special use of their gardens; Kowhai is the larger one, with a spa bath in the bathroom, and Mahoe has an open-air bath for long steamy evenings (in addition to its standard bath). The cottages' upstairs bedrooms have tiny balconies looking onto the Seaward Kaikoura mountains; living rooms, kitchens, dining areas, and bathrooms are downstairs. Breakfast hampers are delivered to the door each day. **Pros:** Like a Hobbit house, these cute units are tucked into the trees in this extensive garden property; acres of lavender and cottage garden to amble through. **Con:** After a lot of rain the concrete crossings on Postmans Road may be running water. ✉*Postmans Rd., R.D. 1* ☎*03/319–5473* 🖷*03/319–5425* ⊕*www.dylanscottages.co.nz* ⇆*2 cottages* ⚒*In-room: no a/c, no phone, kitchen. In-hotel: no-smoking rooms, no elevator* ▤*MC, V* ☾*Closed July* ⏀*BP.*

$–$$ 🏠**The Old Convent.** It's easy to get into the habit of staying at this oh-so-quiet former convent. Built in 1910 for an order of French nuns, it's now protected by the Historic Places Trust, and the interiors reveal its past. The lounge used to be a chapel and has a cathedral ceiling and an ornate wrought-iron stairwell winding down to a reception area. The Travellers' Bar showcases the owners' souvenirs, and the rooms are colorfully decorated. The lounge is warmed by an open fire, and the Hungry Nun shop sells chocolates and nun-theme items. The kids can swim in the pool or find the friendly pet sheep while you play pétanque or croquet in the grand cottage garden. **Pros:** Leafy country setting a short drive from town, à la carte dinner available through summer, and dinner by arrangement in winter. **Cons:** Big, rambling building with many hallways and mysterious stairways. ✉*Mt. Fyffe and Mill Rds.* ☎*03/319–6603 or 0800/365–603* 🖷*03/319–6660* ⊕*www.theoldconvent.co.nz* ⇆*14 rooms, all en-suite* ⚒*In-room: no a/c, no phone, no TV. In-hotel: restaurant, bar, laundry, pool, bicycles, public Wi-Fi, all no-smoking rooms, no elevator* ▤*DC, MC, V* ⏀*BP (winter), CP (summer).*

¢–$$ 🏠**Alpine-Pacific Holiday Park** A moderate walk from town, this nicely laid-out site has spotless facilities. There are cabins, en suite, studios, and full motel units available; there are also powered campervan sites and campsites. The view of the Seaward Kaikoura mountains is breathtaking. There are two holiday parks on Beach Road—this one is on the inland side of the road. Bookings are essential in summer. **Pros:** Very clean, tidy outfit layered down a terraced slope; trampoline for the kids; bikes for rent. **Con:** Campsites a little cramped if full. ✉*69 Beach Rd.* ☎🖷*03/319–6275* ⊕*www.alpine-pacific.co.nz* ⇆*8 cabins, 4 studio units, 2 2-bedroom units, 50 campsites* ⚒*In-room: no a/c, no phone, kitchen (some), no TV (some). In-hotel: public Wi-Fi, pool, spa, laundry facilities, no-smoking rooms* ▤*MC, V.*

EN ROUTE   When traveling between Christchurch and Kaikoura the **Mainline Station Cafe** at Domett stands out among the slim eating options along the way. Built in the 100-year-old ex-Domett railway station it is a sunny spot with a sheltered area of tables out the back in the middle of rural North Canterbury. There's a good selection of cakes, slices and cabinet food and a small blackboard menu of tasty homemade brunch/ lunch dishes. Sunday in summer is market day with local foods, arts, and crafts available. ⊠ *Corner State Hwy. 1 and Hurunui Mouth Rd., 106 km (71 mi) north of Christchurch, 7 km (5 mi) south of Cheviot* ☎ *03/319–8776* ▤ *MC, V* ⊙ *Daily 9–4, except winter (June–Aug.) 10–4* ⊙ *Closed Tues. in winter.*

NELSON & THE NORTHWEST

On the broad curve of Tasman Bay with views of the Kahurangi mountains on the far side, Nelson is one of the top areas for year-round adventure. To the west beckon the sandy crescents of Abel Tasman National Park and Golden Bay. To the south, mellow river valleys and the peaks and glacial lakes of Nelson Lakes National Park draw hikers, mountaineers, and sightseers. There's a climatic allure as well; Nelson usually has more hours of sunlight than any other city in the country. New Zealanders are well aware of these attractions, and in December and January the city is swamped with vacationers. Apart from this brief burst of activity, you can expect the roads and beaches to be relatively quiet.

Settled by Māori hundreds of years ago, the site, then called Whakatu, was chosen for its extremely sheltered harbor and good climate. These enticements later caught the eye of the New Zealand Company, and Nelson became the second town developed by that organization, with British immigrants arriving in the 1840s. These days Nelson is the country's chief fishing port and a key forestry area, with vineyards and olive groves developing into another major industry. The quiet, beautiful setting has attracted creatively minded people, and there's a significant community of artists, craftspeople, and writers in the countryside around Nelson.

NELSON

116 km (73 mi) west of Blenheim.

Relaxed, hospitable, and easy to explore on foot, Nelson has a way of always making you feel as though you should stay longer. You can make your way around the mostly two-story town in a day, poking into crafts galleries and stopping at cafés, but two days is a practical minimum. Use Nelson as a base for a variety of activities within an hour's drive of the town itself.

GETTING HERE & AROUND

To get your bearings, start at the visitor center on the corner of Trafalgar and Halifax streets. The heart of town is farther up **Trafalgar Street,** between Bridge Street and the cathedral steps, also home to the region's refurbished museum. This area is fringed with shops, and the block between Hardy Street and the cathedral steps is a sunny spot to enjoy a coffee. A weekend crafts market is held at the Montgomery parking lot. There are a few art stores and galleries in Nile Street, too.

French Pass & D'Urville Island

They're not easy to get to, but if you have an adventurous spirit and don't mind a rough road, French Pass and D'Urville Island are two of the best-kept secrets in the whole top of the South Island.

The **road to French Pass** splits off State Highway 6 at Rai Valley, halfway between Havelock and Nelson. It's winding, rough, and steep in places, but quite passable in a regular vehicle if you're a competent driver (check that your rental car can go off the sealed road). The sign at the start says FRENCH PASS 2 HRS, and although it's only 64 km (40 mi) to the pass, this estimate is basically true. The road first climbs over the Rongo Saddle and down to Okiwi Bay through native bush; from here, you'll have spectacular views of D'Urville Island in the distance. Then the road crosses to the Pelorus Sound catchment and climbs along the ridge separating the waters of that sound from Tasman Bay to the west. Small side roads drop precariously to hidden bays such as Te Towaka, Elaine Bay, and Deep Bay.

The last 12 km (7 mi) is a dramatic drop down to sea level, skirting Current Basin before arriving at French Pass, the narrow stretch of water separating Tasman Bay from Cook Strait that moves at up to 9 knots during the tidal run. Both the waterway and the island were named for French explorer Dumont D'Urville, who crossed through the pass in the 1820s when it was uncharted by European navigators. **D'Urville Island** is on the far side of this stretch of water, and it's a fabulous destination to feel what isolated coastal New Zealand is all about. Plan to stay overnight as it's a long drive either way.

Between Okiwi Bay and French Pass there are no facilities—no gas stations, bathrooms, or cafés—so come prepared. Only limited public facilities are at French Pass: a basic toilet, gas pump, and essential supplies during limited hours.

If you want to stay overnight at French Pass, **French Pass Sea Safaris & Beachfront Villas** (☎ 03/576–5204 ⊕ www.seasafaris.co.nz) is on the shores of Admiralty Bay. The property has comfortable, fully self-contained studio apartments and has seal and dolphin swims in season, island walks, kayaking, and wildlife and bird-watching tours. If you're lucky you'll see dolphins from your balcony. Diving and fishing charters can also be arranged. Home-cooked meals, including breakfast, can be arranged but cost extra. It's usually closed June to September, but check the Web site for updates. And if you really want a remote experience, carry on to D'Urville Island, where the best lodging option is the **D'Urville Island Wilderness Resort** (☎ 03/576–5268 ⊕ www.durvilleisland.co.nz), $60–$190. The resort is a 30-minute boat ride across French Pass (a water-taxi service picks you up from the French Pass wharf), and overlooks the sheltered waters of Catherine Cove. You can go hiking, mountain biking, and snorkeling here, or just watch the rosy sunrises and the orca whales passing the end of the bay. The resort has a fully licensed bar and restaurant on-site and accommodation reservations are essential.

For a dose of greenery, the **Queens Gardens** are on Bridge Street between Collingwood and Tasman. The regional arts guide, *Art in Its Own Place,* available at visitor centers and local shops, is a good resource for the area's crafts offerings.

Just a five-minute drive around the waterfront from town, Tahunanui Beach offers some of the safest swimming in the country. This long, open beach is perfect to watch the sunset from and is a favorite spot for kite-boarders with its rollicking summer sea breeze.

Nelson Airport (NSN) is a small regional airport 10 km (6 mi) south of the city center.

ESSENTIALS

Airport **Nelson Airport** (⊠ *Trent Dr.* ☎ *03/547–3199*).

Airport Transfers **Super Shuttle** (☎ *03/547–5782 or 0800/748–885*).

Bus Depot **Nelson** (⊠ *27 Bridge St.* ☎ *03/548–3290*).

Emergencies **Fire, police, and ambulance** (☎ *111*).

Hospital **Nelson Base Hospital** (⊠ *Waimea Rd.* ☎ *03/546–1800*).

Rental Cars **Apex** (⊠ *Nelson Airport, Trent Dr.* ☎ *03/546–9028 or 0800/939–597* ⊕ *www.apexrentals.co.nz*). **Avis** ⊠ *Nelson Airport, Trent Dr.* ☎ *03/547–2727 or 0800/284–722* ⊕ *www.avis.co.nz*). **Hertz** (⊠ *Nelson Airport, Trent Dr.* ☎ *03/547–2299 or 0800/654–321* ⊕ *www.hertz.co.nz*).

Visitor Info **Nelson Visitor Information Centre** (⊠ *Trafalgar and Halifax Sts.* ☎ *03/548–2304* ✎ *vin@nelsonnz.com* ⊕ *www.nelsonnz.com*).

WHAT TO SEE

One of the defining features of the landscape is the **Boulder Bank,** a 13-km (8-mi) natural stone bank, built up by eroding cliff faces farther north along the coast. In creating a sheltered harbor, the bank is essentially the reason Nelson was settled in the first place. You can easily reach it by car, driving 9 km (5½ mi) north of town and turning left into Boulder Bank Drive, then going another mile along a gravel road. The waterfront area along **Wakefield Quay** has been developing steadily for the past few years, and now has several cafés, along with a promenade that incorporates a historic stone seawall built by 19th-century prisoners. A statue commemorates the arrival of the early European pioneers, and Sunderland Quay features a memorial to local fishermen lost at sea (Nelson is New Zealand's chief fishing port). It's also the site of the annual Blessing of the Fleet in October. (Visit ⊕ *www.seafarerstrust. org.nz/fleet* for more information.)

The Suter Te Aratoi o Whakatu exhibits both historical and contemporary art; it's a good place to see a cross section of work from an area that has long attracted painters, potters, woodworkers, and other artists. Many of them come for the scenery, the lifestyle, and the clay, and as a result, Nelson is considered the ceramics center of New Zealand. In recent years the gallery has increased its emphasis on painting and sculpture. National touring exhibits come through regularly. A lunch café in the

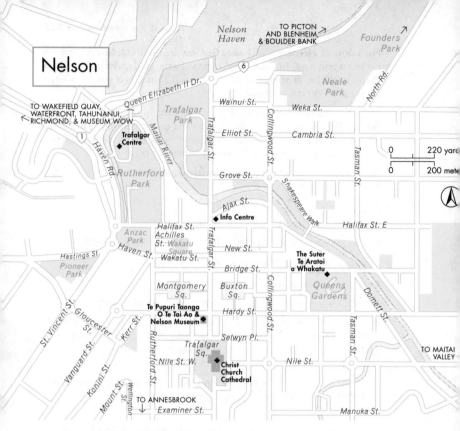

gallery looks out over neighboring Queen's Gardens. ⊠ *Queens Gardens, Bridge St.* ☎ *03/548–4699* ⊕ *www.thesuter.org.nz* ⊠ *$3, Sat. free* ☉ *Daily 10:30–4:30.*

Nelson's regional museum, **Te Pupuri Taonga O Te Taiʾ Ao (Nelson Provincial Museum)**, occupies part of the original site of New Zealand's first museum. It explores the early settlement of the town, its original Māori inhabitants, and the events that shaped the region. Exhibits include a small but outstanding collection of Māori carvings, plus a number of artifacts relating to the so-called Maungatapu murders, grisly goldfields killings committed near Nelson in 1866. The Town Warp is a multimedia wander through the early central-city streets, highlighting local personalities such as Ann Bird the Butcher (a hard-as-nails woman who was one of the town's first European settlers). ⊠ *Hardy St. at Trafalgar St.* ☎ *03/548–9588* ⊕ *www.nelsonmuseum.co.nz* ⊠ *$5 entry and $5 for special seasonal exhibitions* ☉ *Weekdays 10–5, weekends 10–4:30.*

★ Wacky and wonderful, the **World of WearableArt & Classic Car Museum (WOW)** displays garments from the World of WearableArt Awards Show, an event long held in Nelson but now presented in Wellington. The concept of WearableArt is to turn art into garments that adorn the body, something best understood when facing moving mannequins in their inventive ensembles. Imagine brightly colored, hand-painted silks draped into a giant winged headdress. Or papier-mâché fashioned into dramatic body suits, and glittering oceanic creations in the colors of *paua* shells. The elaborate sets, sound, and psychedelic lighting make this gallery a must-see. An adjoining gallery exhibits a superb collection of restored classic cars, ranging from a pink Cadillac to sleek sports tourers. ⊠*95 Quarantine Rd., Annesbrook* ☎*03/547–4573* ⊕*www. wowcars.co.nz* ✐*info@wowcars.co.nz* ⊠*$18* ☉*Daily 10–5.*

On a hilltop surrounded by gardens is **Christ Church Cathedral,** Nelson's boldest architectural "highlight." The site has played an integral part in Nelson's history, first as a Māori *pā* or fortified village, then as the base for the initial city street survey. It housed the immigration barracks when the city was first settled by Europeans. A tent church was first erected in 1842, followed by more permanent ones in 1851 and 1887. Work on the current cathedral began in 1925 and dragged on for 40 years, with middling results. But the steps running down to Trafalgar Street have become a destination in their own right, a social hub in the city center. ⊠*Cathedral Sq.* ⊕*www.nelsoncathedral.org* ⊠*Free*

NEED A BREAK?
Penguino's Cafe (⊠*85 Montgomery Sq.* ☎*03/545–6450*) is a cool source for delicious gelato—particularly their signature creation, the gelato panini. Like a gussied-up version of an ice-cream sandwich, this treat is heated in a panini press and served warm, but with the ice cream still cold inside.

There's fun at **Happy Valley Adventures—4WD Motorbikes and SkyWire,** and lots of it. Hop on a four-wheeled motorbike and go headlong up into the bush before breaking out 14 exciting km (8½ mi) later to see a wide-reaching view across Delaware Bay. If you're not happy driving a quad bike, then hop on as a passenger with someone else or take the 4WD van tour. They also do a Tour of Discovery with a local guide who explains the cultural and historical aspects of the land you cross, and who also demonstrates ancient crafts. There's the world's only Skywire, the longest flying fox in the world—a 10-minute, mile-long high-wire ride that takes you zooming over the surrounding bush and chattering native birds. Or ride an Argo for a thrilling ride through water—and mud!! ⊠*Cable Bay Rd. (15-min drive north of Nelson)* ☎*03/545–0304 or 0800/157–300* ⊕*www. happyvalleyadventures.co.nz.*

WHERE TO STAY & EAT

$$$–$$$$

Fodor'sChoice
★

✕**Hopgoods.** Locally recognized chef Kevin Hopgood dishes up beautifully prepared fresh food at this city restaurant. In the café strip at the top of Trafalgar Street you'll have to book ahead because it's the best spot around. Try the beef, always cooked to perfection with a hint of red, or the fresh fish, battered beautifully and served with a crisp green salad. The food is not overdressed contemporary cuisine but fresh natural ingredients cooked simply, enhanced with tasty dressings and jus. The drinks menu is unashamedly local. ⊠*284 Trafalgar St.* ☎*03/545–7191* ▤*AE, DC, MC, V* ☉*Closed Sun. No lunch Mon.*

$–$$$$

✕**Café Affair.** This busy city restaurant is a favorite with travelers looking for a quick but substantial meal. Options range from a quick muffin or big cooked breakfast to full lunch and dinner menus. The locals go for the stone-grill meals, especially the big chunky fillet steaks and the lamb kebabs. The seafood grill is also a nice option. The central bar has been built from local river rock and big bifold doors open out to the street in summer. ☒ *295 Trafalgar St.,* ☏ *03/548–8295* ♨ *Reservations essential for dinner in summer* ☰ *AE, DC, MC, V.*

$$$ ✕ **Boutereys.** Matt Bouterey brings his reputation with him to this nice
★   new spot in central Richmond. The fresh produce is either picked or dug from the Nelson region. Soft jazz playing and fabric panels to soften the open kitchen noise make for a charming experience. Locals come for the pan-seared scallops with pork belly and avocado salsa. Others come for the aged sirloin with kūmara and parsley flan with a wild mushroom ravioli. The bar opens at 4 PM and dinner is from 6 PM. ☒ *251 Queen St.,, Richmond* ☏ *03/544–1114* ☰ *MC, V* ⊘ *No lunch.*

$–$$$ ✕ **Harry's Bar.** Although there's no sign of Hemingway here, this inti-
★   mate bar and café is hidden down at the river end of Hardy Street. Once inside you'll find the atmosphere upbeat. Asian cuisine is the focus, but the menu also includes Indian dhal and chapatis, and pad thai and green papaya salad (and a not-to-be-missed Kaffir lime tart for dessert). There's a hot selection of cocktails, and on Friday night the bar fills with locals, often overflowing onto the sidewalk on warm evenings. Reservations are essential in summer. ☒ *306 Hardy St.* ☏ *03/539–0905* ✉ *harrysbarnelson@xtra.co.nz* ☰ *AE, DC, MC, V* ⊘ *Closed Sun. and Mon. No lunch.*

$–$$ ✕ **Morrison Street Café.** With its pleasant outdoor terrace and open
★   indoor space, this upbeat café has the best coffee in town. Along with a caffeine fix, come for the bacon and eggs served on fresh *ciabatta* bread with pesto and hollandaise. Local art is on the walls and the menu changes seasonally, as does the wine list. There's a good selection of low-allergy dishes and a healthy kids' menu. ☒ *244 Hardy St.* ☏ *03/548–8110* ☰ *AE, DC, MC, V* ⊘ *No dinner.*

WHERE TO STAY

$$$–$$$$ 🏠 **Wakefield Quay House.** With just the road running between the front
★   door and the sea, Woodi and John Moore's beautiful old villa has one of the best waterfront locations in town. Overlooking Haulashore Island and the harbor entrance, the rooms have dark rimu-wood floors and luxurious furnishings, and are decorated with local artwork and antique maritime memorabilia. Pure wool rugs and carpets warm the floors while heavy feather duvets warm the beds. Silver service breakfast (fresh local eggs, juices, salmon, and freshly ground coffee) is served around the dining table; evening drinks and nibbles on the veranda if the weather is cooperating. Woodi and John's 34-foot yacht is generally on hand for an evening sail. **Pros:** Watch the shipping through the channel from the front door (binoculars in the rooms), easy walk to good waterfront restaurants. **Cons:** Busy road, limited off-street parking, two on-site cats (if that's a problem for you). ☒ *385 Wakefield Quay* ☏ *03/546–7275* ⊕ *www.wakefieldquay.co.nz* ⇦ *2 rooms* ⟁ *In-room: no a/c, no phone, Wi-Fi. In-house: laundry facilities, public Internet, no elevator* ☰ *MC, V* ⦿ *BP.*

$$$ 🏨 **Cambria House.** Built for a sea captain, this 1880s house, now a B&B,
★   mixes old and new, from the original fireplaces and matai and rimu
paneling to the high-speed Internet access. The decor pairs antiques
with modern fabrics and conveniences. Each bedroom has an en-suite
bathroom with shower; three also have a separate bathtub. You can
settle in with coffee or a drink by the wood-burning fireplace or on the
garden deck. The house is near the town center. **Pros:** Elegant old house
in a leafy setting, close to the Maitai River and riverside walkway,
easy walk to town and restaurants. **Con:** On an otherwise quiet subur-
ban street. ✉7 Cambria St. ☎03/548–4681 📠03/546–6649 ⊕www.
cambria.co.nz ✎cambria@cambria.co.nz ➥7 rooms ⚷In-room: no
a/c (some), Wi-Fi. In-hotel: public Internet, no-smoking rooms ▭AE,
MC, V ⓘⓄⓘBP.

$$$ 🏨 **Cathedral Inn.** This beautiful old villa began life in 1856 and was once
the home of prominent Nelsonian Bishop Suter. In turning the house
into a B&B, period details have been matched with modern amenities,
from hair dryers to data ports. You can join the other guests around
the recycled *matai*-wood table for breakfast. The inn is a short walk
through Christ Church Cathedral's garden to city shops and restaurants. **Pros:** A slice of Nelson history in the city, private garden to relax
in, an easy walk to city restaurants. **Con:** Up a steep but sealed driveway. ✉369 Trafalgar St. ☎03/548–7369 or 0800/883–377 ⊕www.
cathedralinn.co.nz ✎info@cathedralinn.co.nz ➥7 rooms ⚷In-room:
no a/c. In-hotel: public Internet, no-smoking rooms, spa, no elevator
▭AE, DC, MC, V ⓘⓄⓘBP.

$$$ 🏨 **The Little Retreat.** Set above a wellness center in the middle of the city,
this stylish retreat is designed to nurture and pamper you. Nelson is
known for its holistic health scene and Angela, the owner of this little
urban hideaway, is closely involved with this. The apartment is yours
for your stay (and some stay for weeks), with a fully equipped kitchen
and laundry, two decks (one with a barbecue) and contemporary fur-
nishings and fabrics. It's a two-minute walk to the Trafalgar Street cafés
and one minute to the cathedral. Angela's health center downstairs can
provide you with various massage techniques, acupuncture, osteopa-
thy, naturopathy, or shiatsu, for an all-round healthy stay. A breakfast
hamper is provided. **Pros:** Balcony overlooking Nile Street, room rate
reduced for multiple nights. **Con:** Busy city location. ✉Level 1, 22 Nile
St. W ☎03/545–1411 📠03/545–1417 ⊕www.nelsongetaways.co.nz
✎the.little.retreat@xtra.co.nz ➥1 apartment ⚷In-hotel: kitchen,
laundry, no elevator ▭AE, DC, MC, V ⓘⓄⓘBP.

$$–$$$ 🏨 **Delorenzo's Studio Apartments.** These reasonably priced self-contained
studio apartments are a short walk from the city center, across the
Maitai River bridge. The decor is bland, but the rooms have plenty
of conveniences, including CD players and washer-dryers. There's
also handy off-street parking. **Pros:** Literally on the main street, these
units are a moment's walk from restaurants, the cinema, and Trafalgar
Park; well-maintained; breakfast is available but not included. **Con:** A
rather busy spot in summer. ✉43–55 Trafalgar St. ☎03/548–9774
📠03/548–9775 ⊕www.delorenzos.co.nz ➥25 suites, 1 family cot-
tage ⚷In-room: kitchen, laundry, Internet. In-hotel: pool, no elevator
▭AE, DC, MC, V ⓘⓄⓘEP.

$–$$ 🖥 **Aloha Lodge.** A stone's throw from Tahunanui Beach, this large bud-
get B&B is a great deal. The design is loosely Asian, even in its garden,
which is landscaped using the principles of the Chinese design philosophy *feng shui*. An ample breakfast is served in the outer courtyard or
the spacious dining room with a cooked option available. Rooms are
very clean and well appointed, many with views of the gardens and
neighboring park. The suites are a special treat, three having a spa bath
and private sauna. You can reach Tahunanui on a five-minute drive
from Nelson via Haven Road. **Pros:** In the center of Tahunanui, a three-
minute walk from the beach and restaurants. **Con:** Can be busy with
bus tours. ⊠*19 Beach Rd., Tahunanui* ☎*03/546–4000* 📠*03/546–
4420* ⊕*www.alohalodgenelson.co.nz* ✉*aloha@ts.co.nz* ↩*17 rooms,
4 suites* ⌂*In-room: no a/c, kitchen, Internet. In-hotel: public Internet,
no-smoking rooms* ▤*AE, DC, MC, V* ⊦⊙⊧*CP.*

¢–$ 🖥 **Accents on the Park.** This guesthouse and backpackers lodge will spoil
★   you for all others. The grand old house in Trafalgar Square, just off the
main street of Nelson, feels more like a boutique hotel than a typical
hostel, with its rich brocade fabrics, soundproof rooms, and immaculate bathrooms with high-pressure showers. Rooms vary from doubles
with private baths to dorm rooms; linen is provided. The balconies
overlook the cathedral and its gardens. **Pros:** Oh so close to town, a
moment's walk to Trafalgar Street; beautiful old Victorian building
with garden walks just across the road, outdoor bar area out the back.
Con: On a narrow street so pull around into the carpark next door to
unload. ⊠*335 Trafalgar Sq.* ☎*03/548–4335* 📠*03/548–4334* ⊕*www.
accentsonthepark.com* ✉*stay@accentsonthepark.com* ↩*18 rooms,
some en suites, 2 with bath, tent sites* ⌂*In-room: no a/c, no phone, no
TV (some). In-hotel: restaurant, bar, kitchen, laundry, public Wi-Fi, no
elevator* ▤*MC, V.*

⚠ Nelson has one of the biggest campgrounds in the country, the
Tahuna Beach Holiday Park (⊠*Beach Rd., Tahunanui* ☎*03/548–5159
or 0800/500–501* ⊕*www.tahunabeach.co.nz*), which fills to capacity
with holiday-makers from down south in the Christmas break. Some of
these families have been coming for generations, and over midsummer
the camp becomes a small city of happy families. It's worth spending a
night here just to experience the atmosphere—if you can get a site.

NIGHTLIFE & THE ARTS

Seventy years ago the first potters were drawn by the abundant clays
in the hills of the hinterlands. Over the decades not only potters, but
painters, ceramists, glass-artists, and mixed-media practitioners have
continued to enjoy the climate, colors, and inspiring light of the region.
Several hundred artists now work in Nelson and Golden Bay and the
locally published **Nelson Guide Book—Art In Its Own Place** is at local visitor centers, bookshops, some hotels and cafés, and online. Check out
⊕*www.nelsonarts.org.nz.*

The **Nelson School of Music** (⊠*48 Nile St.* ☎*03/548–9477* ⊕*www.
nsom.ac.nz*) hosts music performances, mostly local productions (and
surprisingly good ones at that). In July, the school is the site of the
annual **Winter Festival,** which brings in excellent musicians from else-

where in New Zealand. Another top music event is the **Nelson Arts Festival** in October, likewise a magnet for top-notch Kiwi and international acts. Over the Christmas break, the city rocks to the annual **Jazz Festival,** much of which is held in local cafés and parks and in the streets. For the younger set, several late-night clubs and music spots are along **Bridge Street,** which change as venues and acts come and go. Take a wander along the street after 11 PM to check out the options, or grab a copy of the free *Passport* gig guide—it's available in many cafés. Stingray Bar in Church Lane is a haunt for the not quite so young set and the Victorian Rose at the top of Trafalgar Street has live music on Tuesday nights.

SHOPPING

More than 300 artists live around Nelson, working full or part time in various media: ceramics, glassblowing, wood turning, fiber, sculpture, and painting. Not surprisingly there are 16 arts-and-crafts trails to follow, for which there is a brochure at the information center. There is also a colorful Saturday morning crafts market.

Walking through the door of the **Bead Gallery** (✉ *18 Parere St.* 📠 *03/546–7807* ⊕ *www.beads.co.nz*), you may be overwhelmed by the sheer number and range of beads around you. The owner gets his beads from all around the world, with a good selection of Pacific and New Zealand beads and pendants as well. *Paua* shell is big, and there are local greenstone beads and shells from distant islands, not to mention ceramic, wood, bone, porcelain, Swarovski crystal, semiprecious stone, bone, horn, porcelain, and glass beads from far-flung countries. You can put a strand together at a work table or buy separate beads to take with you. They also have a retail gallery at 157 Hardy Street ☎ *03/548–4849*) and another in the Richmond Mall.

The skilled craftspeople of the **Jens Hansen Contemporary Gold & Silversmith** (✉ *320 Trafalgar Sq.* ☎ *03/548–0640 or 021/299–3380* ⊕ *www. jenshansen.com*) create lovely gold and silver jewelry. Contemporary pieces are handmade at the workshop-showroom, and many are set with precious stones or *pounamu* (jade) from the West Coast of the South Island. But they may be best known as the jewelers who made the precious "One Ring" used in the *Lord of the Rings* film trilogy. There's an original prototype on display, and you can order a faithful replica. They will open by appointment outside regular work hours (summer, weekdays 9–5:30, Saturday 9–2, Sunday 10–1; winter, weekdays 9–5, Saturday 9–2, closed Sunday); you can also preview or order merchandise on their Web site.

If you're in Nelson on a Saturday morning, head down to Montgomery Square off Trafalgar Street to the **Nelson Saturday Market,** held from 8 to 1. This market is one of the most successful in the country; it gained its reputation from the wealth of artists and craftspeople who sell their wares here. Now locals and visitors can rely on good bargains while wandering through the maze of stalls, browsing the fresh produce, handmade breads and cheeses, clothing, artwork, flowers, ceramics, and more. The 19th-century, two-story cottage of the **South Street**

Gallery (✉ *10 Nile St. W* ☎ *03/548–8117* ⊕ *www.nelsonpottery.co.nz*) overflows with ceramic art, sculpture, and housewares. The gallery represents 23 Nelson artisans with a national reputation. Upstairs a number of West Coast artists display their work.

TOURS

ACTIVITY Bay Tours Nelson runs daily half- and full-day tours of wine trails,
TOURS arts-and-crafts tours, and scenic adventure tours by arrangement. Trips include the city and its immediate district and also go farther afield to the Marlborough wine region and scenic tours to Motueka and Kaiteriteri Beach and south to Nelson Lakes National Park.

Contact **Bay Tours Nelson** (☎ *03/548-6486 or 0800/229-868* 🖷 *03/548-6481* ⊕ *www.baytoursnelson.co.nz*).

AROUND NELSON

Though Nelson's a bustling city, it retains a rural feel. With Tasman Bay before it and the foothills of the Bryant and Richmond ranges behind, open countryside and vineyards are within easy reach. State Highway 6 south from the city winds through the outlying suburb of Stoke and through to Richmond, a good-size neighboring town. The commercial and civic center of the Tasman District, Richmond has a good library and a modest shopping mall—the only one in the region.

Just south of Richmond, State Highway 60 branches west off State Highway 6, heading toward Mapua, Motueka, and Golden Bay—all friendly rural backwaters. There's a wealth of vineyards along the coastal strip toward Motueka, plus idyllic farms, hop gardens, and craft galleries and serious art studios tucked into the many valleys that run inland. Follow the inland route through **Upper Moutere** on your return. If you carry on south without turning to Motueka look out for the Birth Place of Ernest Rutherford, on the right as you're leaving the small town of Brightwater. Just five minutes south of Richmond the elaborate, atom-shaped monument remembers this local boy's contribution to the world of nuclear science.

WHAT TO SEE

★ One of the best galleries is the **Hoglund Art Glass Studio & Gallery.** From the collectible family of penguins to the bold platters and vases, the Hoglund style is sold internationally. The glass gallery and museum is open year-round. There are also glass-making classes available. ✉ *Lansdowne Rd., Richmond* ☎ *03/544–6500* ⊕ *www.hoglundart glass.com* 🖾 *Gallery free, guided tour $15* ⊗ *Daily 9–5.*

To dip into the local wine scene, drop by the **Grape Escape Complex** for tastings from two top wineries, Te Mania Estate and the organic Richmond Plains. Tastings are free for the wine of the month, and 50¢ for all other wines. The complex also has a crafts gallery, and an indoor-outdoor café. ✉ *State Hwy. 60 and McShanes Rd.* ☎ *03/544–4054* ⊗ *Daily 9–5.*

Greater Nelson

Cape Soucis

TO FRENCH PASS →
& D'URVILLE ISLAND

Rai Valley

6

Pelorus Bridge Reserve

Mount Richmond Forest Park

Pelorus River

Pepin Island

The Glen

6

Atawhai

Boulder Bank

Nelson see detail map

Stoke

Main Rd

6

Richmond

Bryant Range

Tasman Bay

Rabbit Island

Mapua

Ruby Bay

Redwood Rd.

Seifried Estate

Queen St.

Macmillans Gallery

Tasman

60

Moutere Hwy.

Appleby

60

Waimea Estates

Hope

Greenhough Vineyard and Winery

Motueka

TO MARAHAU AND
↑ ABEL TASMAN N.P.

Harakeke

Brightwater

Waimea River

Riwaka

Neudorf Vineyard

Woollaston Estate

Upper Moutere

6

Kaiteriteri

TO
↑ TAKAKA

60

Motueka River

Arthur Range

Kahurangi National Park

6 miles

9 km

0

0

Isel House, in the beautiful tree-filled Isel Park, was built for Thomas Marsden, one of the region's prosperous pioneers. It was Marsden who laid out the magnificent gardens surrounding the house, which include a towering California redwood and a 140-foot Monterey pine. The well-preserved stone house contains stories of Isel and its surroundings, interpreted in part by local artists; also original anecdotal material, family items, and a herbarium. ⊠ *Isel Park, Stoke* ☎ *03/547–1347* ✉ *Donation* ☉ *Sept.–Apr., Tues. –Sun. 11–4; May–Aug., by appointment.*

Broadgreen is a fine example of a Victorian cob house. Cob houses, made from straw and horsehair bonded together with mud and clay, are commonly found in Devon, the southern English home county of many of Nelson's pioneers. The house is furnished as it might have been in the 1850s, with a fine collection of textiles and quilts, including one of the oldest known quilts in New Zealand. The setting of tall trees and large rose gardens completes the scene. ⊠ *276 Nayland Rd., Stoke* ☎ *03/547–0403* ✉ *$3* ☉ *Daily 10:30–4:30.*

Grab a wine trail brochure from the Information Centre in Nelson before heading out to find these wineries. Some are quite difficult to find although they are well signposted from the main roads.

Since 1997, **Waimea Estates** has been creating award-winning wines. The range includes sauvignon blanc, chardonnay, pinot gris, Riesling, rosé, pinot noir, and a cab/merlot blend. The well-crafted dessert wines and a funky "strawberries-and-cream" rosé are also worth trying. Their Café in the Vineyard is open for lunch daily, with a roaring fire in winter and outdoor jazz on sunny summer Sunday afternoons. ⊠ *22 Appleby Hwy., Appleby* ☎ *03/544–4963* ⊕ *www.waimeaestates.co.nz* ☉ *Wine tours and tastings by appointment. Café Oct.–Mar., daily 11–5; Apr.– Sept., Wed.–Sun. 11–4.*

Kahurangi Wine Estate. Beside the main road in the picturesque little village of Upper Moutere this successful winery was first developed by Hermann Seifried (*see* Seifried Estate, *below*) in the 1970s as one of the area's first commercial vineyards. Now owned by Greg and Amanda Day, there is a good range of Rieslings and chardonnays and also a fine gewürztraminer. The cellar door and on-site café/restaurant are open all year. The café runs a tapas menu in summer; otherwise, it's a coffee stop. ⊠ *Cnr Main and Sunrise Rds., Upper Moutere* ☎ *03/543–2980* ⊕ *www.kahurangiwine.com* ☉ *Open 10:30–4:30.*

Seifried Estate is a 20-minute drive from Nelson's main center, on the way to Motueka. Hermann Seifried was one of Nelson's modern-day pioneer winemakers and he has gone on to open this busy complex. The large winery produces fresh, zippy sauvignon blanc, a creamy chardonnay, a very tasty Riesling, and a lush pinot noir. A restaurant next door to the tasting room is open every day for lunch; reservations are recommended. ⊠ *Redwood Rd., Appleby* ☎ *03/544–1555* ⊕ *www. seifried.co.nz* ☉ *Daily 10–5.*

The state-of-the-art, multilevel gravity-fed winery and gallery of **Woollaston Estate** sits on a quiet hillside in Mahana. In an area once known solely for apple production, the wines now being created from this district are maturing superbly. The gallery is part of the tasting area, and features the work of owner Phillip Woollaston's father, Toss, one of the country's best-known artists. Woollaston produces pinot rosé (from 100% pinot noir grapes), sauvignon blanc, Riesling, and pinot gris, and their pinot noir has received special accolades. There's no restaurant, but the extensive views over the mountains and Tasman Bay from the lawn suggest bringing a picnic. It's also a venue for jazz, literature, and other cultural events on the Nelson festival circuit. ⊠*School Rd., Mahana* ⚓ *Turn off coastal State Hwy. 60 at Dominion Rd., turn left into Old Coach Rd., then right into School Rd. The winery is on right opposite school* ☎*03/543–2817* ⊕*www.woollaston.co.nz* ⊙*Late Oct.–Easter, daily 11–4:30 and by arrangement.*

★ Despite its tiny size, **Neudorf Vineyard** has established an international reputation for its pinot noir and chardonnay, but Riesling, pinot gris, and sauvignon blanc are also highly regarded. Owners Tim and Judy Finn will gladly talk at length about local food and wine. The top wines wear the Moutere designation on the label, as the winery is in a valley surrounded by acres of vineyards and hop gardens. ⊠*Neudorf Rd., Upper Moutere* ☎*03/543–2643* ⊕*www.neudorf.co.nz* ⊙*Sept.–May, daily 10:30–4:30.*

OUTDOOR ACTIVITIES

RAFTING **Ultimate Descents New Zealand.** This highly experienced company takes
★ rafting trips on the Maruia (Grade III), Clarence (Grade II), Buller
☾ (Grade III–IV), and Karamea (Grade V) rivers. They also run inflatable kayaking on the easier rivers, half-day kayaking trips suitable for kids ($95), and half-day ($109), full-day ($195), and multiday wilderness trips ($350–$850)—minimum of four. All half-day and day trips have a meal included, and the multiday trips are fully catered. ⊠*51 Fairfax St., Murchison* ☎*03/523–9899 or 0800/748–377* 🖷*03/523–9811* ⊕*www.rivers.co.nz* ✉*ultimate@rivers.co.nz.*

WHERE TO STAY & EAT

The little town of Mapua has retained one nice area to eat; the area down by the wharf, at the far end of Aranui Street, has several small galleries, cafés, foodie stores, and a fish-and-chips shop. Apart from Mapua and a few outlying wineries, though, there are few restaurants in this area. There are, however, a number of B&Bs and boutique lodges for accommodation.

$$$ ✗ **Smokehouse Café.** Don't try to resist stopping here. The menu is
★ based around delicately hot-smoked products, not just fish but lamb and chicken as well. There's also a "smoke-free" seasonal menu. You won't find a better lunch than their specialty platter piled with smoked whitefish, smoked salmon, mussels, and a sweet chili jam and basil pesto dipping sauce, all served with fresh, crusty home-baked bread. There are great views up the estuary from the café and across to the Richmond Ranges, often peaked with snow in winter. You can't miss

the big blue corrugated iron building on the wharf. The café has slightly truncated hours from May through October; reservations are recommended in summer. Last orders are taken around 8:30 PM. They also have a takeout fish-and-chips shop next door where you can buy their smoked products as well. ⊠*Mapua Wharf* ☎*03/540–2280* ⊕*www. smokehouse.co.nz* ⊟*MC, V* ⊗*No dinner Mon. June–Sept.*

$$$$ 🏨 **Bronte Lodge.** Perched on the edge of the Waimea Estuary, this lodge
★ (which is actually a number of villas and suites) gets you right down to the water. At high tide the lawn outside the villas is lapped by the sea, and at low tide you can walk out onto the sandflats. The villas are decorated with original works by well-known local artists. The 2-acre garden, which slopes down to the sea, is draped with flowering wisteria and shaded by tall trees. Should you be feeling competitive, you can play a game of *pétanque* (boccie) or tennis or take a swim in the heated pool. They also have their own small vineyard and winery next door. **Pros:** Also on-site is a two-bedroom luxury villa ($1,000 for two, fully hosted), excellent bird-watching opportunities on the sandflats. **Con:** A 10-minute drive to restaurants in Mapua and Richmond. ⊠*Bronte Rd. E off State Hwy. 60* ☎*03/540–2422* 🖷*03/540–2637* ⊕*www.bronte lodge.co.nz* ⇨*3 villas, 2 suites* ♿*In-room: kitchen. In-hotel: tennis court, pool, bicycles, laundry* ⊟*AE, MC, V* ⊗|*BP.*

SHOPPING

Built in an old apple cool store (where apples were stored at cool temperatures after being picked), the funky **Cool Store Gallery** has reasonably priced art and craftwork. Much of the work has a vibrant Pacific theme, produced by artists from the Nelson and West Coast regions; paintings, sculpture, textiles, *paua*-shell items, ceramics, glasswork, and jewelry line the walls. They have an arrangement with a local shipping company to get hard-to-travel-with purchases home for you in one piece. ⊠*7 Aranui Rd., Mapua* ☎*03/540–3778* ⊕*www.coolstore gallery.co.nz* ⊗*Daily 10–5 in summer, Thurs.–Sun. 11–4 in winter.*

MOTUEKA

50 km (31 mi) west of Nelson.

Motueka (mo-too-*eh*-ka) is an agricultural center—hops, kiwifruit, and apples are among its staples. The town sits at the seaward end of the Motueka Valley, under the ranges of the Kahurangi National Park. Like Golden Bay, Motueka is a stronghold for the "alternative" communities around Nelson, and every byway seems to have a few artisans and erstwhile hippies living side by side with the traditional farming families. The hinterland is now also littered with well-to-do small-holdings, often owned by absentee overseas owners. Most of the good cafés and places to stay are outside the town center, either in the sheltered inland valleys or out along the Abel Tasman coast and nearby bays. South of town, for instance, the Motueka River valley is known for its trout fishing. Motueka's also a good jumping-off point for Abel Tasman National Park, just north of town.

ESSENTIALS

Visitor Info **Motueka Visitor Information Centre** (✉ *Wallace St.* ☎ *03/528–6543* ⊕ *www.abeltasmangreenrush.co.nz* ✎ *info@motuekaisite.co.nz*).

OUTDOOR ACTIVITIES

You won't lack for places to land some whopping brown trout. Fishing season here runs from October to April. Fly-fishing excursions to local rivers and remote backcountry areas, involving hiking or helicopter trips, offer plenty of excitement for visiting anglers. Daily guiding rates are generally around $730 per day and include lunches, drinks, and 4WD transportation. Best areas to base for trout fishing around Nelson Lakes are: St. Arnaud, Motueka, Murchison, and Nelson city itself. Look up **Peter Carty** (✉ *Chalgrave St., Murchison* ☎ *03/523–9525*). Tony Entwistle and Zane Mirfin run **Strike Adventure** (☎ *03/521–0020* 🖷 *03/521–0024* ✎ *fish@strikeadventure.com* ⊕ *www.strikeadventure. com*), the only guiding company in the northern South Island to hold all commercial access permits to crown lands, offering plenty of opportunities in some amazing locations.

WHERE TO STAY & EAT

$–$$$ ✕ **Riverside Café.** Riverside was initially established as a community for conscientious objectors during the 1940s. Its café is now the hot place to eat around Motueka. Set in an old cottage the café is decorated with hand-worked wood, copper and fabric art, and enclosed with a grape-shaded veranda. The menu is built around organic foods from the community's own gardens and nearby suppliers. Choices range from stylish restaurant fare to pizza and fries; desserts often include delights like chocolate and chili ice cream and spicy apple pie. Reservations are recommended. ✉ *Inland Moutere Hwy., 5 mins south of Motueka toward Upper Moutere* ☎ *03/526–7447* ☰ *MC, V* ☉ *Closed Mon. in summer, Mon.–Wed. in winter.*

$–$$ ✕ **Jester House.** This funky place is as much fun as the name suggests,
☺ and is a great spot to bring the kids. The café was rebuilt in 2006 in an ecofriendly timber and light earth style using hand-finished poles and rustic wood, echoing the owners' feelings about a sustainable environment. The food ranges from hearty country fare like soups and quiche to more substantial meals like garlic mussels and panfried fish (their signature dish). In addition to cozy indoor seating, tables are dotted through the garden and on a sunny veranda. For the kids there's a small playground, an enchanted forest, an outdoor chess set, and some very tame eels that they can hand-feed (September–May). Down in the back garden, the Boot B&B has comfy accommodations for couples. ✉ *Coastal Hwy., Tasman* ☎ *03/526–6742* ☰ *MC, V* ☉ *Closed July, and Mon.–Thurs. in winter. No dinner.*

$$$$ 🏠 **Motueka River Lodge.** Tranquillity, marvelous scenery, and a superb
★ standard of comfort are the hallmarks here. The lodge is on 35 acres overlooking the Motueka River, with magnificent mountain views. Its sunny deck, vine-covered archways, and fragrant lavender hedges give the place a Mediterranean feel. The interior of the rustic house is accented with antiques from around the world. You can hike the national parks nearby, but the lodge's specialty is fishing, especially

7

dry fly-fishing for brown trout in the wild river country. Great cuisine is prepared by resident chef Stephen Smith. Bookings are essential during the October to April fishing season. **Pros:** All meals included in the rate including a four-course dinner, fully stocked wine cellar. **Cons:** 25% surcharge on NZ public holidays, 50-minute drive from Nelson airport. ⊠ *Motueka Valley Hwy. (State Hwy. 61), Motueka* ☎ *03/526–8668* ⊟ *03/526–8669* ⊕ *www.motuekalodge. com* ✎ *enquiries@motuekalodge.com* ☞ *5 rooms* ☘ *In-room: no a/c, no phone, Ethernet. In-hotel: restaurant, bar, tennis court, no elevator* ⊟ *AE, DC, MC, V* ⍣ *MAP.*

\$\$–\$\$\$ ▥ **Coastal Palms Apartments.** Just a few minutes' drive from the center of town, these two lovely apartments overlook the sea off Port Motueka. They're a perfect spot to base yourself while exploring the region, especially if you're not necessarily concentrating on the Abel Tasman Park area. A third apartment is under construction as well. **Pros:** Breakfast is on request; both units have fold-out sofa beds to sleep two extra adults; kayaks, bikes, and a dinghy are available for use. **Con:** The seafront along Trewavas Street is mostly tidal sandflats rather than ocean front, but when the tide is in it's beautiful. ⊠ *95 Trewavas St., Motueka* ☎ *03/528–0166* ⊕ *www.coastalpalms.co.nz* ☞ *1 apartments, 1studio* ☘ *In-room: kitchen, , Wi-Fi* ⊟ *MC, V* ⍟ *Closed Oct.–Apr.*

\$\$ ▥ **Doone Cottage.** At this charming 140-year-old cottage, hosts Stan
★ and Glen Davenport have welcomed homestay guests for more than 25 years. The villa sits in a leafy garden overlooking the trout-filled Motueka River; five other trout streams are a short drive away. Guest rooms and the private garden chalet are all done in a low-key, rustic style. Glen spins and weaves wool from her own Suffolk sheep; her on-site studio has sweaters, rugs, and wall hangings for sale. A good selection of local wines is available and they do dinner on request. **Pros:** In the heart of trout-fishing country, a low-key rural setting. **Con:** Quite a drive along the Motueka Valley from town. ⊠ *Motueka Valley Hwy. (SH61), Motueka* ✛ *28 km (17 mi) from Motueka up Motueka Valley Hwy.* ☎☏ *03/526–8740* ✎ *doone-cottage@xtra. co.nz* ⊕ *www.doonecottage.co.nz* ☞ *2 rooms, 1 chalet* ☘ *In-room: no a/c, no phone, no TV (some). In-hotel: no-smoking rooms, no kids under 15* ⊟ *MC, V* ⍣ *BP.*

EN ROUTE

If you are headed for the West Coast from Motueka, turn south onto Highway 61 at the Rothmans Clock Tower in Motueka, following the sign to Murchison. The road snakes through the **Motueka Valley** alongside the Motueka River, with the green valley walls pressing close alongside. If this river could talk, it would probably scream, "Trout!" After the town of Tapawera, turn south on State Highway 6 at Kohatu and continue to the West Coast.

ABEL TASMAN NATIONAL PARK

77 km (48 mi) northwest of Motueka, 110 km (69 mi) northwest of Nelson.

Abel Tasman is a stunning yet accessible swath of national parkland. Its succession of idyllic beaches is backed by a rugged hinterland of native beech forests, granite gorges, and waterfalls. Unlike many of New Zealand's national parks, Abel Tasman has few serious challenges in its climate or terrain, making it a perfect place for an outdoor day trip.

★ The approach is notably lovely. From the town of Motueka, State Highway 60 passes close to Kaiteriteri Beach, then turns inland to skirt Abel Tasman National Park. The road to Kaiteriteri branches off State Highway 60 a few kilometers after the small village of Riwaka; a drive down the narrow, winding route rewards you with **Kaiteriteri Beach,** one of New Zealand's prettiest beaches, with its curve of golden sand, the rocky islets offshore, and deep, clear water. This place is packed in midsummer, but once the six-week Christmas rush is over, the area returns to its usual quiet. (Take care driving on frosty winter mornings, as some corners stay frozen into the day.) Farther on, the small town of **Marahau** is the gateway to the national park. There's an interpretation board posted near the park café, but you may want to stop by the Department of Conservation (DOC) office in Motueka to get maps. (If you're planning to use the DOC huts, you'll need to pick up hut tickets—if you haven't already booked online at ⊕www.doc.govt.nz/explore.) Bookings are essential most of the year. The park has excellent hiking, sailing, and sea-kayaking opportunities—and water taxis service the coves *(see Outdoor Activities, below).* Midsummer, from December to February, is the peak tourist season here, so plan ahead if you'll be visiting then.

OUTDOOR ACTIVITIES

HIKING Abel Tasman has a number of walking trails, with road access from both Totaranui and Wainui at its north end and Marahau in the south. Shuttles and water taxis can take you to the trailheads or pick you up afterward. The tracks and conditions aren't too grueling, but conditions can change quickly, especially in winter. Carry bottled water, as only some sites have treated water available, and bring warm clothing, food, and sun and insect protection. The sandflies can be voracious. The **Department of Conservation offices** provide trail maps. ⊠*King Edward and High Sts., Motueka* ☎*03/528–1810* ⊠*62 Commercial St., Takaka* ☎*03/525–8026* ⊕*www.doc.govt.nz* ✐*greatwalksbooking@doc.govt.nz.*

The most popular hike is the three- to five-day **Abel Tasman Coast Track,** open year-round. Much of the track's popularity is because of its relatively easy terrain and short distances. Launches and water taxis will drop off and pick up hikers from several points along the track, allowing walks from 2½ hours to 5 days. There are 4 huts and 21 campsites along the Coast Track, and spaces in both must be booked year round. Bookings can be made online or through selected DOC offices or agents. For more information contact **Nelson Regional Visitor Centre**

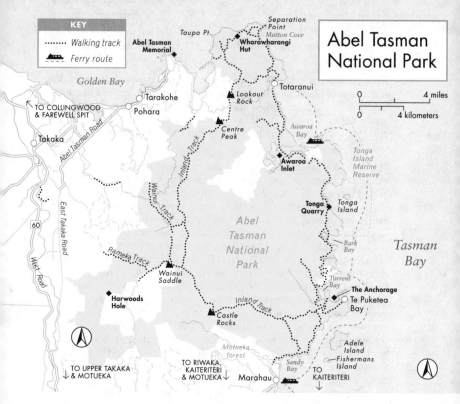

Abel Tasman
National Park

Golden Bay

TO COLLINGWOOD
& FAREWELL SPIT

Takaka

Tarakohe

Pohara

Abel Tasman
Memorial

Abel Tasman Road

East Takaka Road

60

West Road

Rameka Track

Wainui Track

Inland Track

Wainui
Saddle

Harwoods
Hole

Castle
Rocks

Inland Track

Motueka
forest

TO UPPER TAKAKA
↓ & MOTUEKA

TO RIWAKA,
KAITERITERI
& MOTUEKA ↓

Marahau

Taupo Pt.

Separation
Point

Mutton Cove

Wharwharangi
Hut

Lookout
Rock

Centre
Peak

Awaroa
Bay

Awaroa
Inlet

Totaranui

Tonga
Quarry

Tonga
Island

Tonga
Island
Marine
Reserve

Bark
Bay

Torrent
Bay

The Anchorage

Te Puketea
Bay

Adele
Island

Fishermans
Island

Sandy
Bay

TO
KAITERITERI
↓

Tasman
Bay

Abel
Tasman
National
Park

0   4 miles

0   4 kilometers

(⊠ *At Trafalgar and Halifax Sts, Nelson* ☎*03/546–9339*). For help with bookings contact **Great Walks Helpdesk** (☎*03/546–8210* ⊕*www. doc.govt.nz* ✎*greatwalksbooking@doc.govt.nz*).

Remember this area is one of the most highly visited spots in the country and you will rarely find yourselves on that dream deserted beach with nobody else in sight. If you're a die-hard outdoor enthusiast craving peace and quiet and isolation you may want to explore a less busy spot like the Kahurangi or Nelson Lakes national parks. Having said that, Abel Tasman is still an easy, accessible place to wander the coast and paddle through clear, green water for hours at a stretch.

Abel Tasman Wilson's Experiences are the original operators of day excursions to this park. They offer several kinds of bushwalks, trips to beaches, launch cruises, and sea kayaking. They also run one- to five-day hiking or hiking-kayaking treks around the park. ⊠*265 High St., Motueka* ☎*03/528–2027 or 0800/223–582* 🖷*03/528–2029* ⊕*www. abeltasman.co.nz.*

★ If you'd like a day in the park without breaking a sweat, call up **Abel Tasman Sailing.** Their three large catamarans sail daily into the heart of the park from Kaiteriteri Beach. On the way you stop at Split Apple Rock before heading off to swim at a gorgeous beach such as the

Anchorage, where the water is a translucent green. You can also view a colony of fur seals up close. A day trip costs $160, including lunch, hot and cold drinks, and pickup. A range of sail and walk options are available from $80. Advance reservations are not always necessary. It's closed June–August. ☎*03/527–8375 or 0800/467–245* ✐*bookings@ sailingadventures.co.nz* ⊕*www.sailingadventures.co.nz.*

The **Sea Kayak Company** offers a range of guided kayaking options through the pristine waters of the national park to beaches and campsites often inaccessible to hikers. These include the "Ab-Fab" one-day kayak and walk trip ($175), a two-day "More than Beaches" tour ($330), and three- and five-day tours ($410 and $950, respectively). All tours are fully catered and all equipment is supplied. Reservations are recommended at least three weeks in advance. It's closed in September. ⊠*506 High St., Motueka* ☎*03/528–7251 or 0508/252–925* 🖶*03/528–7221* ✐*info@seakayaknz.co.nz* ⊕*www.seakayaknz.co.nz.*

WHERE TO STAY

$$$–$$$$
Fodor'sChoice
★

🏨 **Awaroa Lodge.** Relax in an idyllic part of the spectacular Abel Tasman National Park, surrounded by native bush, two minutes' walk to the beach. You can sea-kayak to the lodge or walk, as the Abel Tasman Track passes right through the property. To reach the lodge by boat, contact **Aqua Taxis** (☎*03/527–8083 or 0800/278–282*), which leaves from Marahau daily, or fly direct from Nelson with **Nelson Helicopters** (☎*03/528–8075*). Choose from luxurious studio, standard, or family rooms. The attached restaurant serves stylish regional cuisine; most of the produce is grown organically on the property. The restaurant is also open to walkers off the park's Coastal Track and visitors arriving by boat, from 8 to 4:30. **Pros:** One of the few lodges in the country surrounded by national park, very special spot well worth the effort to reach it, active management policy for a nearby wetland. **Con:** Tricky to get to but there are options to suit all budgets. ⊠*Awaroa Bay, Abel Tasman National Park, Motueka* ☎*03/528–8758* 🖶*03/528–6561* ✐*stay@awaroalodge.co.nz* ⊕*www.awaroalodge.co.nz* ⇆*26 rooms* ⚘*In-room: no a/c, no TV. In-hotel: restaurant* ☰*AE, MC, V* ⏸*EP.*

$$–$$$
🏨 **Abel Tasman Marahau Lodge.** With Abel Tasman National Park 200 yards in one direction and the Marahau beach 200 yards in the other, this location is hard to resist. The boutique lodge has spacious fully self-contained chalets, clustered in groups of two or four with native gardens between them. Units are finished in natural wood and have high cathedral ceilings, New Zealand wool carpets, queen- or king-size beds, and balconies. Rates do not include breakfast, but room-service breakfasts and a communal kitchen are available, and packed lunches can be prepared. Staff can help make reservations for sea kayaking, water taxis, seal swims, and hiking. **Pros:** Close to everything in Marahau; nice, not-too-flashy accommodation overlooking the bush-covered hills of the Abel Tasman Park. **Con:** No breakfast in the room rate. ⊠*Marahau, R.D. 2, Motueka* ☎*03/527–8250* 🖶*03/527–8258* ✐*robyn@abeltasmanmarahaulodge.co.nz* ⊕*www. abeltasmanmarahaulodge.co.nz* ⇆*12 rooms* ⚘*In-room: no a/c, kitchen (some). In-hotel: spa (closed June and July)* ☰*DC, MC, V.*

7

$$-$$$ ⊡**Kimi Ora Spa Resort.** Kimi Ora means "seek health" in Māori. The developer was set on creating an environmentally friendly resort, including a restaurant (not always open so call first) serving as much organic food as possible, and various activities and therapies relating to holistic health. For all the pampering, the overall vibe is low-key. The guest rooms have cozy wood walls and simple furnishings. **Pros:** Bordered by a mix of exotic forest and regenerating native bush, all the rooms have a distant sea view, as much a health resort as a holiday spot so come for a few days and recharge your batteries, some rooms have a spa bath on the deck. **Con:** 10-minute walk to Kaiteriteri beach. ⊠*Martins Farm Rd., Kaiteriteri* ☎*03/527–8027 or 0508/5464–672* 🖷*03/527–8134* ⊕*www.kimiora.com* ⟋*22 units* ⚲*In-room: no a/c (some), DVD, kitchen (some). In-hotel: pools, gym, spa, bicycles, no-smoking rooms* ⊙*BP* ⊟*MC, V.*

TOURS

WALKING
TOURS

Abel Tasman Wilson's Experiences guides day trips and three- and five-day treks in the beautiful coastal park. Spend nights in comfortable lodges and eat well, without having to carry a big pack. The rates for a five-day kayaking and hiking trip or five-day guided walk are from $1,545, depending on the season; the three-day kayaking and hiking trip or three-day guided walk each start at $1,050.

Contact **Abel Tasman Wilson's Experiences** (⊠ *265 High St., Motueka* ☎*03/528–2027 or 0800/223–582* 🖷*03/528–2029* ✎*info@AbelTasman.co.nz* ⊕*www.abeltasman.co.nz*).

GOLDEN BAY & TAKAKA

55 km (35 mi) northwest of Motueka, 110 km (70 mi) west of Nelson.

From the Motueka–Nelson area, a spectacular hill road, State Highway 60, rises up 2,500 feet before plunging again to sea level to the tiny township of **Takaka**, a jumping-off point for Kahurangi National Park and the Heaphy Track. This road is a 40-minute climb of twisting corners, steep drop-offs, and occasional passing bays. If you don't have your eyes glued to the road, check out the views back across the plains to Nelson, out over the coast along the Abel Tasman National Park, and, toward the end, across the Upper Takaka valley from Harwoods Lookout to the mountains of Kahurangi National Park. **Hawkes Lookout,** on the Nelson side of the hill, and **Harwoods Lookout,** on the Takaka side, make this a lot easier. Golden Bay begs exploring, so if you take the trouble to cross the Takaka hill into this spectacular area, plan to stay at least two nights or you'll spend your whole time driving and none enjoying the rewards of your travels.

The gorgeous stretch of coastline that begins at Separation Point and runs westward past Takaka is known as **Golden Bay,** named for the gold found there in the 1850s. Alternating sandy and rocky shores curve up to the sands of Farewell Spit, the arcing prong that encloses the bay. Other than a 19th-century lighthouse, the spit is pure, raw

Farewell Spit

A 35-km (22-mi) protected sandbar with a 19th-century lighthouse, Farewell Spit is renowned for its tremendous seabird population. A trip with **Farewell Spit Eco Tours** (✉ *Tasman St., Collingwood* ☏ *03/524–8257 or 0800/808–257* ⊕ *www.farewellspit. com*) is a must if you are in Golden Bay. Each of the two tour itineraries takes you out along the Farewell Spit; one tour will take you to a gannet colony. (The company is the only one with a DOC license to visit the gannets.) The other takes you out to the

lighthouse and windswept dunes on the seaward end of the spit. Costs run between $80 and $120; reservations are essential. You could also saddle up with **Cape Farewell Horse Treks** (✉ *Wharariki Beach Rd., Puponga* ☏ *03/524–8031* ⊕ *www.horsetreksnz. com*); this outfit offers some of the best horse trekking in the country, with spectacular beaches and wild views. For the best views, ride the Old Man Range trek ($120) or try the Puponga Beach ride ($60) for something more sedate..

nature. Fault lines slash the cliffs, and the area is a favorite for all kinds of birds. Dutch navigator Abel Tasman anchored here briefly a few days before Christmas 1642. His visit ended abruptly when four of his crew were killed by the then-resident Māori iwi (tribe), Ngāti Tumata Kokiri. Bitterly disappointed, Tasman named the place Moordenaers, or Murderers' Bay, and sailed away without ever setting foot on New Zealand soil. Golden Bay is a delight—a sunny, 40-km (25-mi) crescent with a relaxed crew of locals who firmly believe they live in paradise.

The lifestyle here has always been considered "alternative"—a hideout for hippies, musicians, and artists. But it's also the center of a rich dairy farming area, and its warm, sheltered climate nurtures crops such as citrus, avocados, and kiwifruit that struggle on the colder, Nelson side of "the hill." Overseas buyers have been snapping up Golden Bay properties to get their own little part-time spot of paradise, but local bylaws are changing to encourage full-time residents back to the bay.

ESSENTIALS

Visitor Info Golden Bay Visitor Information Centre (✉ *Willow St., Takaka* ☏ *03/525–9136* ✉ *gb.vin@nelsonnz.com* ⊕ *www.nelsonnz.com*).

WHAT TO SEE

Eight kilometers (5 mi) west of Takaka is Te **Waikoropupu Springs,** known locally as Pupu Springs. This is the largest spring system in the southern hemisphere, and clear, cold water bubbles into the Waikoropupu Valley after traveling underground from its source at the nearby Takaka Hill. The clarity of this water is second only to the Weddell Sea in Antarctica. Swimming is not allowed because of the effect swimmers have on the delicate flora within the springs. In 2006 scuba diving was prohibited due to the risk of spreading didymo, an invasive exotic algae, so leave your swimsuits and dive gear in the car. Instead, grab your shoes and take a leisurely stroll around the valley on the 90-minute Pupu Walkway. Go quietly—the better to spot *tūī*, bellbirds, wood pigeons, and other birdlife. The turnoff from State Highway 60 at the Waitapu River is signposted.

After winding past several small farming districts and beach communities such as Paton's Rock, Onekaka, and Tukurua, State Highway 60 arrives at **Collingwood,** a small seaside village at the mouth of the giant Aorere River, 26 km (16 mi) west of Takaka. The earliest European settlers came here in the 1840s to build small ships from the timber lining the beaches and to farm the fertile river plains that spill out of the surrounding mountains. In the 1850s, gold was discovered nearby and Collingwood became a thriving port-of-entry town; at one time it was even under consideration to be the country's capital.

Collingwood is the northern access point for the Heaphy Track and a good base for trips to Farewell Spit and the West Coast beaches. The old 1910 council office building houses the small **Collingwood Museum,** which has a good photographic record of the area's past. You can make a sweet stop by **Rosy Glow Chocolates** on Beach Road or buy a gift at **Living Light Candles** on Tukurua Road, back toward Takaka a short way.

The wild **Kahurangi National Park** (✉ *62 Commercial St., Takaka* ☎ *03/525–8026* ✐ *GoldenBayAO@doc.govt.nz* ⊕ *www.doc.govt.nz*) covers 1.1 million acres of untamed wilderness, covering fern-clad forests, rocky rivers, rolling tussock-covered hills, rugged snowcapped mountains, and wind-blown beaches pounded by West Coast surf. The park is laced with 570 km (353 mi) of hiking tracks of various levels of difficulty; there are also several rafting and kayaking rivers and some serious caving areas, especially toward the West Coast. Of the various entry points to the park, one of the most convenient is 35 km (21 mi) west of Takaka, south of the town of Collingwood. This is also the northern head of the Heaphy Track *(see Outdoor Activities, below).* The **Department of Conservation Golden Bay Area Office** provides local trail maps.

OFF THE BEATEN PATH

Totaranui. From Takaka the coast road heading east leads around to the northern entry to the Abel Tasman National Park at Totaranui. This very picturesque road passes through Pohara Beach, which has several cafés and a campground, before winding around to Wainui Bay with its alternative Tui community (a onetime commune that welcomes visitors) and cascading waterfall (a slightly rough 75-minute return walk from the road). From Wainui Bay, the road over the Totaranui Hill is a gravel surface and can be treacherous in wet weather. But in good weather, it's a beautiful drive through dense native bush to the coast. Totaranui beach is a long golden-sand beach that is safe for swimming. This area can also be reached by boat from Kaiteriteri and Marahau, on the Motueka side of the Takaka hill. It's a slice of pure beach bliss, and there's an unpowered campground with basic facilities.

OUTDOOR ACTIVITIES

BEACHES　Golden Bay has miles of swimming beaches. **Paton's Rock** is one of the best near Takaka. Check the tides before taking the 10-minute drive from town, as swimming is best at full tide.

★ Out near Farewell Spit and less suitable for swimming, but with spectacular coastal landscapes, is **Wharariki Beach.** Among the massive sand dunes you're likely to come across sunbathing fur seals. If you get too close to them, they might charge or even bite, so keep a 30-foot distance, and never get between a seal and the sea. To get here, drive past Collingwood to Pakawau and follow the signs. Go as far as the road will take you, and then walk over farmland on a well-defined track for 20 minutes. These beaches are quite remote and have no lifeguards.

FISHING   **Note:** *For information on deep-sea fishing in Golden Bay out of Takaka, see Chapter 11.*

★ The most famous walk in Kahurangi National Park is the one-way, 82-km (51-mi), five-day **Heaphy Track.** The track is one of the Great Walks trails, so you need to buy a Great Walks Pass for hut stays and campsites (failure to do incurs a penalty fee). Passes range from $10 to $20 per night, depending on the time of year. It's best to purchase tickets in advance from information centers at Nelson, Motueka, or Takaka or book online at ⊕*www.doc.govt.nz.* Bookings are essential much of the year to avoid having nowhere to sleep. Track-user numbers are limited by the number of beds available on any one night. Tickets in hand, all you really need to do is get to the track and start walking toward Karamea on the West Coast. You need a reasonable level of fitness; conditions can be challenging in poor weather. Huts along the way have water and toilets and some have gas cooking and heating—check before leaving. You need to carry your own food and bedding and may need a small gas stove and canister as well. Be prepared for weather of all kinds all year round—bring rain gear and warm clothing even in summer (and insect repellent for the sandflies. You can get trail maps from the **Department of Conservation Golden Bay Area Office** ⊠ *62 Commercial St., Takaka* ☎*03/525–8026).*

Southern Link K Bus (☎*0508/458–835* ⊕*www.southernlinkcoaches. co.nz*) offers transport to the track from Takaka on demand (drop-off and pickup). It also provides general charter services and scheduled services between Golden Bay, Abel Tasman, and Nelson. From Nelson, **InterCity** (☎*03/548–1538*) runs buses at 6:45 AM each day to the trailhead; the ride costs $30. Some routes do not run year-round, so check when booking. If you'd like some expert company on hikes around the national park, **Kahurangi Guided Walks** (☎*03/525–7177* ✍*john@ kahurangiwalks.co.nz* ⊕*www.kahurangiwalks.co.nz*) runs easy one-day treks on routes known to locals but virtually untouched by visitors. A more strenuous, three-day walk goes to the rarely visited Boulder Lake, and there are also the five-day hike on the Heaphy Track and other hikes as well. Prices vary for each customized trip.

WHERE TO STAY & EAT

$$–$$$ ✕ **Courthouse Cafe.** Set in the old Collingwood Courthouse on the main crossroads into town, this laid-back café makes good use of local foods like smoked Anatoki salmon, organic sausage, and free-range eggs and local wines. The Spanish-style cockle soup infused with saffron and lime is worth stopping for, and the coffee is better than average. There

are indoor and outdoor tables, but it pays to book ahead over summer. ☎ *03/524–8025* ▤ *MC, V* ⊘ *Days vary so call ahead.*

$$–$$$ ✕ **Mussel Inn.** If you want to experience a quintessential slice of Golden Bay life, swing by this place. Locals come for the live music (usually on the weekends, starting around 8:30 pm), a bowl of mussel chowder, and some of the house-brewed beer, including their famous Captain Cooker manuka beer. The decor is self-described as "Kiwi woolshed meets Aussie farmhouse," which seems an apt description. ⊠ *State Hwy. 60, Onekaka* ☎ *03/525–9241* ⚓ *Reservations not accepted* ▤ *MC, V* ⊘ *Closed late July–early Sept.* .

$–$$$ ✕ **Wholemeal Café.** Don't be put off by the laid-back appearance of the staff or the retro-homely decor—the Wholemeal is a long-standing favorite in Takaka. Not only is the food healthy and delicious, but they make excellent coffee. Drop by for a thick slice of pizza or quiche at lunch or dig into one of their curries at dinner. There's also a small list of local wines and a fruit ice-cream counter for hot summer days. ⊠ *60 Commercial St., Takaka* ☎ *03/525–9426* ▤ *MC, V.*

$$$–$$$$ ▦ **Adrift Beachfront Accommodation.** A short walk across soft green grass from your unit gets you to the sea. Sometimes in the evenings sunsets are enhanced with the arrival of little blue penguins, which nest up the creek. Daytimes you can swim, kayak, or wander along the very private beach. Each of the five ecofriendly luxury cottages is self-contained, and there's a studio unit attached to the house; the doors and windows can be left open for the sound of the sea. To get there drive down the signposted driveway and out to the coast. A breakfast hamper is delivered to the units each morning. **Pros:** Just a strip of green grass between your unit and the sea, modern-style units. **Con:** A long drive in through farmland off Tukurua Road. ⊠ *Tukurua Rd, 18 km (11 mi) north of Takaka* ☎🖶 *03/525-8353* ⊕ *www.adrift.co.nz* ✉ *escape@adrift.co.nz* ⌨ *5 cottages, 1 studio unit* ⚏ *In -room: kitchen (some), no a/c (some). In-hotel: public Internet* ▤ *MC, V* �ID *BP.*

$$$ ▦ **Twin Waters Lodge.** Built on the edge of the Pakawau Estuary, this lodge caused a stir when it opened as architecturally it was a few years before its time, especially in Golden Bay. Overlooking the surrounding hills and wetlands, it's a two-minute walk from the sea on the other side of the peninsula. Rooms and shared spaces have sheltered decks, and the themed room decor is enhanced by the leafy views out the windows. The lodge is very close to all the natural wonders of Farewell Spit and its vast coastal wetlands and exceptional birdlife, and it's a short drive to Wharariki and the wild beaches on the West Coast. **Pros:** Interesting wetland setting on the coast, a three-course dinner is available at $50 but book ahead. **Con:** Because of remote setting, plan on two nights minimum. ⊠ *Totara Ave., Pakawau, 9 km (5½ mi) past Collingwood on road to Farewell Spit* ☎🖶 *03/524–8014* ⊕ *www.twinwaters.co.nz* ⌨ *4 rooms* ⚏ *In-room: refrigerator, no phone, no TV, no a/c. In-hotel: public Wi-Fi* ▤ *MC, V* ⊘ *Closed mid-Oct. –Apr.* ID *BP.*

$ ▦ **Anatoki Lodge.** This spacious motel is close to Takaka village center. Owners Gaye and Garth Prince can help point out the main attractions and best places to eat in the area. The lodge has spacious studios and one- and two-bedroom units; each opens out to a private patio and grass courtyard. **Pros:** Cook up a barbecue in the garden, indoor and solar heated pool. **Con:** Although handy to town the motel's semi-urban setting is not typical of Golden Bay. ⊠ *87 Commercial St., Takaka* ☎*03/525–8047* 🖷*03/525–8433* ✐*anatoki@xtra.co.nz* ⇥*5 studios, 6 units* ⚫*In-room: no a/c. In-hotel: pool, no-smoking rooms* ▭*AE, MC, V* ⑩*EP.*

$ 🏠**Sans Souci Inn.** Sans Souci is a mellow, ecofriendly spot with lots of charm a two-minute walk from Pohara Beach. There's a small restaurant, and you can arrange to take breakfast and dinner here, but book this by 4 PM. This hand-built lodge features striking adobe and tile construction and a turf roof; the big communal bathroom is adorned with subtropical plants, and the garden abounds with grape and kiwifruit vines and big leafy shade trees. The rooms are very comfy and all but one (which is self-contained) share a large bathroom complex. **Pros:** Self-contained family unit sleeps up to four, eat in the restaurant or you can cook in the restaurant kitchen for yourself. **Cons:** Restaurant is only open late October to Easter, and is fairly simple. ⊠ *Richmond Rd., Pohara Beach* ☎🖷*03/525–8663* ⊕*www.sanssouciinn.co.nz* ⇥*7 rooms, 1 with bath* ⚫*In-room: no a/c, no phone, kitchen, no TV. In-hotel: restaurant, laundry* ☺*Closed July, Aug., and 1st 2 wks of Sept.* ⑩*EP.*

Golden Bay has a number of highly scenic camp areas. One of the best is the **Golden Bay Holiday Park** at Tukurua Beach which also has good facilities. Tents, powered sites, and cabins are available and you'll sleep to the sound of the sea. ☎*03/525–9742 or 0800/525–972* ✐*golden-bay.holiday@xtra.co.nz.*

NELSON LAKES NATIONAL PARK

100 km (62 mi) south of Nelson.

Spread around two stunningly scenic glacial lakes, Rotoroa and Rotoiti, the Nelson Lakes National Park is an alpine zone of soaring mountains, rocky rivers, and bush-lined trails. The native beech forests pour down to the lakeshore. On cloudy days, mist swirls through the trees, wetting the draping mosses and silencing the birds. On sunny days the intense green comes through and the birds' chorus resumes. Lake Rotoiti is also the site of a kiwi-recovery program; in 2004 several kiwi were released back into the forest after an intense pest-eradication program.

Of the two lakes, Lake Rotoroa is the most pristine, with just a few fishing cottages, a campsite, and a lodge on its shore. The village of St. Arnaud (which is considering changing its name to Rotoiti Village) sits at the northern end of Lake Rotoiti; it's the gateway to the park, with a lodge, a handful of B&Bs, a general store, and the Department of Conservation bureau. The **DOC Headquarters** here is particularly good, with information on the area's geology and ecology. Maps and details on the hiking trails are available, and a mountain weather forecast is issued daily. The DOC office administers two excellent campgrounds around the lake frontage. Call them for details on camp-sites. Bookings can be heavy through midsummer. ⊠ *View Rd., St. Arnaud*

☎03/521–1806 ⊕*www.doc.govt.nz/explore* ⊙*Daily 8–4:30; Christmas–end Jan., daily 8–6.*

Each year in early March the **Antique and Classic Boat Show** is held at the lake with close to 200 antique boats congregating for several days of boat racing and boat talk. Check ⊕*www.nzclassicboats.com* or ✍*pbrain@xtra.co.nz* for details.

OUTDOOR ACTIVITIES

Nelson Lakes park has a number of half-, full-, and multiday trails that can be "freedom walked" (walked without a guide). The **Lake Rotoiti Circuit** gets you around the lake in an easy daylong walk. The rather steep **Mt. Robert Track** zigzags up the face of Mt. Robert, giving you a superb view back across the lake toward St. Arnaud village. The return walk can be done by looping down the face of the mountain to meet up with the Lake Rotoiti Circuit track. Other tracks lead off these into the higher mountain areas. Hut accommodations are available on a "first-in, first-served" basis. Alpine experience and equipment are necessary on the longer tracks.

Nelson Wilderness Guides can take the work out of finding tracks, gear, and accommodation. They have one-, three-, and four-day tours through the park, based at their Golden Downs Lodge, and offer multiday wilderness expeditions into the backcountry. ⊠*Kohatu, Golden Downs* ☎*03/522–4175* ⊕*www.goldendowns.co.nz.*

WHERE TO STAY

$$$$
Fodor's Choice
★

🏨 **Lake Rotoroa Lodge.** Now recognized as one of the best fly-fishing lodges in the world, this truly private haven sheltered beneath tall trees on Lake Rotoroa was built for "gentlemen travelers" in the days when horse and buggy was the local transport. Now it lures anglers with a combination of old-fashioned charm and newfangled luxury, from the brass beds and hunting trophies to the expert fishing guides and outstanding wine list. **Pros:** Old, heritage-style building looks across the lake; some of the best brown trout fishing in the world; beautiful walking tracks through native bush. **Cons:** A very scenic but 90-minute drive from Nelson, use repellent religiously as the sandflies here are legendary, lunch not included in the rate. ⊠*Lake Rotoroa* ☎*03/523–9121* 🖷*03/523–9028* ⊕*www.lakerotoroalodge.com* ⇖*10 rooms* △*In-room: no TV. In-hotel: bar, public Wi-Fi, public Internet, no elevator* ▤*AE, MC, V* ⊙*Closed May–Sept.* ❑*MAP.*

¢–$$
🏨 **Alpine Lodge and Alpine Chalets.** Accommodations run from full suites to backpacker dorms. With the wood paneling and dormer windows, the building may feel somewhat European-alpine, but the view out the window is all Kiwi. Although in the center of the village the lodge is at the national park boundary, a short bushwalk away from Lake Rotoiti. A few two-bedroom apartments are good for families. The lodge has a licensed restaurant and a bar for casual meals. Good meals are also available at Elaine's Café downstairs next door in the Chalets. **Pros:** If you haven't the time for a backcountry lodge then this is a nice substitute, put aside a couple of hours to do a bushwalk. **Cons:** Bring repellent for the sandflies, watch for wasps in midsummer, crowded

midsummer. ✉ *Main Rd., St. Arnaud* ☎*03/521–1869* 🖷*03/521–1868* ⊕*www.alpinelodge.co.nz* 🛏*24 rooms, 4 suites, 4 apartments, 1 dorm* ♨*In-room: no a/c. In-hotel: restaurant, bar, laundry facilities, spa, no-smoking rooms* ▤*AE, DC, MC, V.*

¢–$ 🛏 **Tophouse.** This 120-year-old farm guesthouse just a few kilometers from Rotoiti gives you a chance to kick back and do absolutely nothing. The house has a historic rating so the B&B rooms in the main house are authentic, complete with their original cob walls. The shared bathrooms are just down the hallway. Four self-contained cottages are behind the house. If you just want to stop for lunch ($12) or afternoon tea ($6), there is café service during the day. Dinner is available on request for $35 per person. Tophouse is part of a 700-acre working farm and is close to fishing, skiing, and hiking trails. **Pros:** A hotbed of local history, check out the bullet holes in the veranda wall, choice of modern cottages and lovely old-fashioned rooms in the main house, a short drive from St. Arnaud. **Con:** No en suites in the B&B rooms. ✉*Tophouse Rd, 9 km (5½ mi) from St. Arnaud toward Nelson* ☎*03/521–1848 or 0800/867–468* ⊕*www.tophouse.co.nz* 🛏*5 rooms, 4 cottages* ♨*In-room: no TV, no phone, no a/c. In-hotel: laundry* ▤*AE, MC, V* ﴾Ol*CP, MAP (B&B only).*

MURCHISON

7

125 km (78 mi) south of Nelson, 63 km (40 mi) west of Lake Rotoiti.

Surrounded by high mountains and roaring rivers, this small town is in some very big country. With the Nelson Lakes National Park to the west, the Kahurangi National Park to the north, and the Matakitaki, Buller, Matiri, and Mangles rivers all converging on its doorstep, Murchison has gained the reputation as New Zealand's "white-water capital." There are 13 rivers within 20 km (12½ mi) of town. Fly-fishers, kayakers, hikers, and rafting junkies turn up every year to enjoy the sport. Although most operators now accept credit cards, there is no ATM in the town; so make sure you have some cash on you.

Murchison residents still consider their landmark event "the earthquake," a major quake that hit in June 1929. The epicenter was nearby in the Buller Gorge, and the quake drastically altered the landscape.

The local, very rustic **Murchison District Museum** (✉*60 Fairfax St.* ☎*03/523–9392*) has an excellent exhibit on this disaster. There's also a good collection of farming and agricultural machinery from the town's colonial era, plus displays on a local gold rush.

OUTDOOR ACTIVITIES

Murchison's claim as a white-water destination is not to be ignored. They have some of the best white water anywhere. **Ultimate Descents** *(see Ultimate Descents listing in Around Nelson, above)* runs rafting trips on several local rivers, as does **White Water Action** (☎*0800/100–582*), which operates in the Buller Gorge from both Murchison and Westport. The **New Zealand Kayak School** (☎*03/523–9611*), known to be one of the country's best, offers tuition and training camps based at its Murchison facility.

Murchison is not a gourmet destination, but if you want a decent meal at a good price, there are several options. During the summer **Rivers Café** (⊠ *Fairfax St.* ☎ *03/523–9009*) is open all day every day, serving good food in a funky setting. Hours vary in winter. The **Stables Café** (⊠ *Waller and Fairfax Sts.* ☎ *03/523–9696*) in the Commercial Hotel serves good pub-style food year-round. **Beechwoods Café** (⊠ *Waller St.* ☎ *03/523–9571*) out on the main road heading south through town is a typical roadhouse-style café that is open all day. For the best setting, out on the northern edge of town, try the little **Rock Snot Café** (⊠ *State Hwy. 6* ☎ *03/523–9591*), which fronts the river below the Riverview Motor Camp. Named for an invasive river algae new to the Buller, it's a nice spot to stop if you're traveling with kids. If it's summer they can jump in the river for a swim. The food is simple but tasty; service can be slow, but what's the hurry—this is Murchison after all.

$$$$ 🏚 **Owen River Lodge.** From the dining room you can look across the willow-lined river valley to a large granite escarpment with native forest. Outside, the rush of the river is outdone only by the sometimes-overwhelming chorus of native birds. Host Felix Borenstein is a die-hard fly fisherman who has a strong passion for throwing furry little feathered flies into the beautiful reaches of the area's many trout rivers. He delights in the fact that much of the fishing here is sighted fishing and stalking, but also catch-and-release to preserve the stock. **Pros:** Nicely appointed cottages overlooking the valley and fronted by sheltered verandas; large garden; the fully equipped tackle room has waders, jackets, boots, rods, reels, and everything else a keen angler should desire. **Cons:** The last mile or two to the lodge is gravel but easy to drive, bring repellent for sandflies. ⊠ *Owen Valley E Rd., 15 mins north of Murchison* ☎ *03/523–9075* ⊕ *www.owenriverlodge.co.nz* 🛏 *6 cottage suites* ♿ *In-hotel: restaurant, public Wi-Fi, public Internet, bar, laundry facilities, . In-room: no TV, no phone, safe, refrigerator* ⊟ *D, MC, V* ☉ *Closed Oct.–Apr.*

$$ 🏚 **Murchison Lodge.** Tucked in a tiny back street of Murchison, this rural retreat is within easy walking distance of the mighty Buller River. The guest rooms are comfortably countrified, with strong colors and lots of wood. Breakfast is a big affair with freshly squeezed juices and bread made by Shirley each morning while Merve cooks up bacon and eggs on the barbecue. They can put you in touch with a good local guide for trout fishing. **Pro:** Private access to the Buller River through a grassy field. **Cons:** Hard to find down a long driveway, friendly on-site dog. ⊠ *15 Grey St.* ☎☎ *03/523–9196* ☎ *0800/523–9196* ⊕ *www.murchisonlodge.co.nz* ✉ *info@murchisonlodge.co.nz* 🛏 *4 rooms (3 with en suite)* ♿ *In-room: no a/c, no phone, no TV. In-hotel: bicycles, public Wi-Fi, no-smoking rooms, no elevator* ⊟ *MC, V* ☉ *Closed May–Sept.* ⦿ *BP.*

THE WEST COAST

Southwest of Nelson, the wild West Coast region is a land unto itself. The mystical Pancake Rocks and blowholes around Punakaiki (poon-ah-*kye*-kee) set the scene for the gigantic, rugged, sometimes forlorn landscape. Early *Pākehā* (European) settlers carved out a hardscrabble life during the 1860s, digging for gold and farming where they could, constantly washed by the West Coast rains. After the gold rushes, new waves of settlers arrived to mine the vast coal reserves in the surrounding hills. Farmers and loggers followed; although the gold has gone, the coal mining and farming remain. The towns along this stretch of coastline are generally no-frills rural service centers, but they make good bases for exploring the primeval landscape.

The original Māori inhabitants knew this area to be rich in *kai moana* (seafood), *weka* (bush-hens), and most important, *pounamu* (greenstone or jade). The Māori name for the South Island, Te Wai Pounamu, reflects this treasure. The riverbeds, beaches, and mountains were threaded with walking trails to transport pounamu for intertribal trade, and you'll still hear references to "greenstone trails" throughout the area.

At the glacier towns of Franz Josef and Fox, the unique combination of soaring mountains and voluminous precipitation means that the massive valleys of ice descend straight into rain forests (a combination also found on the southwest coast of South America). South of the glaciers, the road follows the seacoast, where fur seals and fiordland crested penguins inhabit fantastical beaches and forests. On sunny days the Tasman Sea along the stretch between Lake Moeraki and Haast takes on a transcendent shade of blue.

Legal changes in 2000 brought an end to commercial logging of the West Coast's native forests; since then the local communities have been in flux, as residents turn to other jobs and property prices climb surprisingly quickly. But it's the environment that continues to determine the lifestyle here. Locals pride themselves on their ability to coexist with the wild landscape and weather. As a visitor, you may need a sense of adventure—be prepared for rain, swirling mist, and cold winter winds alternating with warm, clear days. "The Barber," Greymouth's infamous winter wind, blasts down the Grey River valley to the sea. The meteorological mix can mean that the glacier flight that you planned at Franz Josef or Fox won't fly that day. Although the coast is well known for its rain, it also has clear, bright days when the mountains shine above the green coastal plains and the surf pounds onto sunny, sandy beaches; often the best weather is in winter.

EN ROUTE If you're driving to the West Coast from Nelson or Motueka, State Highway 6 passes through Murchison before turning right at O'Sullivans Bridge 12 km (7 mi) farther south and heads down through the Buller Gorge toward the West Coast. This twisting, narrow road parallels the tortuous **Buller River** as it carves a deep gorge below the jagged, earthquake-rocked mountain peaks. The upper gorge is tight and hilly but once past Inangahua the lower gorge is easier to negotiate. The Buller once carried a fabulous cargo of gold, but you'll have to use your imagination to reconstruct the days when places such as Lyell, 34 km (21 mi) past Murchison, were bustling mining towns. Not far from here are New Zealand's longest swaying footbridge, the **Buller Gorge Swing Bridge,** and the departure point for the **Buller Experience Jet,** should you want to ride a few rapids. You'll pass high forest-clad mountains, narrow single-lane bridges, and the sleepy little village of Inangahua along the way. **Hawk's Crag and Fern Arch,** where the highway passes beneath rock overhangs with the river wheeling alongside, is another highlight and a low-key café at Berlins offers a pit stop. At the end of the gorge, turn left to continue along State Highway 6 toward Punakaiki, or carry on straight ahead to Westport and Karamea. Although on a map the distances along the West Coast appear small, allow plenty of time to negotiate the hills and to explore the sights. When traveling in midsummer, watch for the giant, spectacular crimson-flowering *rata* trees lighting the forest with their blooms.

WESTPORT

230 km (144 mi) southeast of Nelson.

One of New Zealand's oldest ports, Westport sits at the mouth of the mighty Buller River. Once a boomtown for two separate gold rushes, it's now a quiet little hub (population 3,100) for the local farming and coal industries, plus the rapidly expanding adventure tourism niche. It's a quiet place to stop over before heading south toward Punakaiki and the glaciers or north to Karamea and the Heaphy Track; the best of Westport is out of town, either on the coast or up the rivers. The iconic Westport look is breaking white-capped waves, blue sea, seals, rocky outcrops, and acres of flax and wetlands. Stop by the little **Coaltown Museum** on Queen Street to learn about the port's history and check out an extensive mineral collection. Another museum at **Denniston,** 18 km (11 mi) north of town up a steep mountain range, details life in this lonely outpost from the late 1800s through the early 1900s. Carving a living from the rich seams of coal found in the surrounding tussock-covered hills, the settlers had to struggle with wild weather, isolation, and primitive conditions. A popular historical novel about these pioneers, *The Denniston Rose,* by New Zealand writer Jenny Pattrick, details the area and the early lifestyle.

The **Westport Visitor Centre** can provide information on Karamea and Kahurangi National Park.

ESSENTIALS

Hospital Westland Medical Centre (⊠ *54a Sewell St., Hokitika* ☎ *03/755–8180*).

Visitor Info Westport Visitor Centre (⊠ *1 Brougham St.* ☎ *03/789–6658* ⊕ *www. westport.org.nz*).

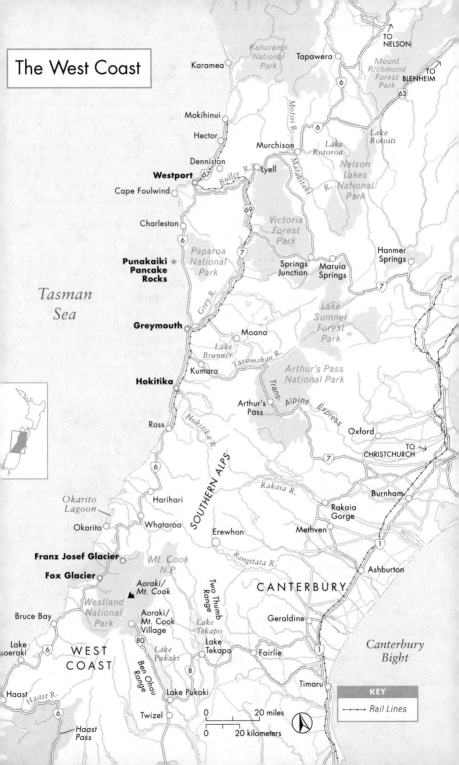

OUTDOOR ACTIVITIES

★ You might actually pray for rain during a tour with **Norwest-Underworld Adventures.** This very popular adventure tour group takes you into the rain forest off the main highway at Charleston. You can sign up for an open-sided bush-train ride through the dense temperate lowland forest, or take a cave walk into one of the giant limestone mountains up the Nile River valley (a glowworm grotto is a highlight). Their most popular trip is a stunning slow drift in a raft through the glowworm caves before breaking out onto the river (four-hour trip). For something more challenging, go for the daylong "Full On" caving adventure with a 47-meter (154-foot) abseil (rappel) down into the mountain, before crawling, swimming, and climbing your way back to the surface. Prices range from $20 for the train ride to $270 for the "Full On" adventure; reservations are essential. ⊠ *Charleston Tavern, Main Rd., Charleston* ☎ *03/788–8168* 🖷 *03/789–5508* ⊕ *www.caverafting.com.*

Buller Adventure Tours at the lower end of the Buller Gorge, before you reach Westport, runs jet-boating and rafting on various parts of the river and horse treks and quad-bike tours in the surrounding bush. Try the Earthquake Slip Rapids section, which includes some Grade IV water, a Grade II swim rapid, and a 9-meter (27-foot) cliff jump. They also run the Earthquake Rapids trip from Murchison (☎ *03/523–9581*). Trips start from $75. ⊠ *State Hwy. 6, Lower Buller Gorge* ☎ *03/789–7286 or 0800/697–286* ⊕ *www.adventuretours.co.nz.*

WHERE TO STAY & EAT

There are several good daytime cafés in Westport. The Bay House, far and away the best, is out of town, but definitely worth the drive. Denniston Dog is a local stalwart for a good down-home West Coast experience. Driving into town from the Buller River **the Yellow House Café** (⊠ *243 Palmerston St.* ☎ *03/789–8765*) has an enclosed sunny back lawn and a bright dining area. They do brunch through dinner every day, have a natural foods menu, BYO and on-site licenses, and a kid's play area. Right in the main street **Dirty Mary's Café and Bar** (⊠ *198 Palmerston St.* ☎ *03/789–6648*) is also open early to late with a daytime and dinner café and late-night bar.

$$$–$$$$ ✕ **The Bay House.** Tucked among flax bushes beside the wild, foaming
FodorsChoice surf beach at Tauranga Bay, this busy little restaurant serves as fine a
★ menu as you'll get anywhere in the South Island. The chef prepares top-quality local beef, lamb, and seafood dishes, and there are specialties like the whitebait (a local fish delicacy). Or try the West Coast beef fillet on a potato rösti, served with a braised beef cheek and mustard ravioli. There's lots of fish; the chowder is recommended, and the kitchen use local touches like *harakeke* seed, *paua,* and *kūmara* (native sweet potato). You'll find an extensive, mainly South Island wine list. It's worth the extra driving and, if you're heading south afterwards, you can follow the signposted shortcut toward Charleston to save going back into Westport. ⊠ *Tauranga Bay, Cape Foulwind, 16 km (10 mi) west of Westport* ☎ *03/789–7133* 🖃 *AE, MC, V.*

$$–$$$ ✕ **Denniston Dog.** This old bank building, complete with a vault, is loaded with local character in its new guise as a cheerful pub and din-

ner spot. They serve good Kiwi tucker here, so order up a fritter with feta cheese and whitebait (tiny fish eaten whole). The meals are big, and it's a very kid-friendly spot. The kitchen is closed mid-afternoon but reopens for dinner. ✉*18 Wakefield St.* ☎*03/789–5030.*

$$$ 🏨 **Riverview Lodge.** Overlooking the lower Buller River, at the seaward end of the Buller Gorge, this B&B gives you a truly rural experience. The house is surrounded by high bush-clad hills and green farmland; each room overlooks the river and has a perfect view of the dramatic sunsets. Owner Noeline Biddulph, a human treasure trove of local lore, keeps a beautiful garden where you can have a stroll after your meal. **Pros:** Very well–maintained property, dinner is available if booked at least a day ahead and BYO allows you to try some of that wine you've picked up on your travels. **Cons:** Slightly out of town on the main highway through to Nelson and the north, on-site dog and cat. ✉*State Hwy. 6, 7 km (4 mi) east of Westport* ☎🖷*03/789–6037* 🌐*www.rurallodge.co.nz* ✉*info@rurallodge.co.nz Reservations essential* 🛏*4 rooms* ♿*In-room: no a/c, no phone. In-hotel: no-smoking rooms, laundry* 🖃*MC, V* 🍴*BP* ☾*Closed June.*

$–$$ 🏨 **Havenlee Homestay.** A homestay in the best sense of the word—truly welcoming—Havenlee exudes comfort without being flashy. The house is near Westport's town center, and owners Jan and Ian Stevenson have a fast-growing, often international clientele. In warm weather, you can hang out in the barbecue area and the lush garden. The simple, bright guest rooms share a bathroom. **Pros:** Close enough in to walk to town, breakfast is Continental plus a few extras added. **Con:** The $160 tariff gives exclusive use of a bathroom. ✉*76 Queen St.* ☎*03/789–8543* 🖷*03/789–8502* 🌐*www.havenlee.co.nz* ✉*info@havenlee.co.nz* 🛏*2 rooms* ♿*In-room: no a/c, no phone, no TV. In-hotel: laundry facilities, no-smoking rooms* 🖃*MC, V* 🍴*CP.*

¢ 🏨 **Trip Inn Hostel.** Backpackers now fill the beds in one of Westport's grandest old 19th-century homes, built as a gentleman's residence in 1863. It's geared for all ages, not just students, and the owners have arranged the rooms for various kinds of travelers, from solos to families. There's a fireplace lounge where people swap stories about their hikes on the Heaphy Track. Lockers and linens are provided. Check out the tall tree ferns on the front lawn. **Pros:** Very relaxed place within walking of the town center, family-style units removed from the main house. **Con:** Lounge areas are dated but comfy. ✉*72 Queen St.* ☎🖷*03/789–7367* 🌐*www.tripinn.co.nz* ✉*tripinn@clear.net.nz* 🛏*16 rooms with changeable single, double, and family room, dorm beds, tent sites* ♿*In-room: no a/c, kitchen, no TV. In-hotel: public Internet, no elevator, no-smoking rooms* 🖃*MC, V* 🍴*EP.*

KARAMEA

98 km (61 mi) north of Westport.

North of Westport, the coastline is squeezed between high mountain ranges and pounding surf. The highlight of the tiny settlements along this stretch is Karamea, known to most people as the southern entry to (or exit from) the renowned Heaphy Track, which starts in Golden

Bay. But Karamea is also a fine trout-fishing destination, the western entry point to the wild ranges of the Kahurangi National Park *(see above)* with its wild rivers and network of hikes, and is home to the **Oparara cave system.** These caves are a series of huge limestone arches (including the largest in the southern hemisphere), passages, and caverns, surrounded by lush forests. One of the best is the Honeycomb Cave, an underground system of roughly 13 km (8 mi) of passages. Bones from the extinct moa bird have been found here, and you'll likely see glowworms. Karamea is also the start for the five- to six-day hikes through the Wangapeka and Karamea-Leslie river systems. These are serious hiking areas through some stunning wilderness area, but the facilities are of a lower standard than the Heaphy Track (which is a Great Walk).

On the drive up to Karamea watch out for **Imagine on the Beach Café** just north of Hector, where you can buy a coffee and a piece of cake from a beachside hut. If you want to stay over stop at the very laid-back **Gentle Annie Coastal Enclave** (⊠*De Malmanche Rd* ⊹ *Turn left directly after crossing Mokihinui River bridge* ☎*03/782–1826* ⊕*www.gentleannie.co.nz*) on the coastline north of the Mokihinui River. Accommodations range from tasteful holiday homes to campsites and they run a morning-only café, all overlooking the coast or the bush. The final hour of the drive crosses the incredibly scenic **Karamea Bluff.** If you prefer you can fly in direct from various places *(see Tours, below).*

Contact the **Karamea Information & Resource Centre** ⊠*Market Cross intersection* ☎*03/782–6652* ⊕*www.karameainfo.co.nz)* for information on cave tours.

WHERE TO STAY & EAT
In addition to the local pub and the café-bar and restaurant at the Last Resort, Saracens Café at Market Cross is a nice daytime café, open for breakfast and lunch. After 4:30 they open their **Bush Lounge** (⊠*99 Bridge St.* ☎*03/782–6711* ⊕*www.kahurangipark.co.nz*), which serves tasty, good-size meals. Check out the boiler-fireplace and the hand-built furniture, and stick around after if it's a live music night.

$$ ⌂**Karamea Lodge.** Overlooking the huge Otumahana Lagoon, this modern, well-priced ecofriendly lodge is the perfect place to watch magnificent sunsets and be soothed to sleep with the ocean's distant roar. They have purposefully not installed TV or air-conditioning so you get to enjoy the quiet. Kayaks are for guests' use and rain-forest bushwalks are just out the door. The rooms are spacious and private balconies overlook the lagoon. A full kitchen and a large dining–lounge area are available if you want to cook. No kids under 12 are allowed. **Pros:** Rooms overlook the lagoon and towards the coast, lodge features lots of natural materials. **Con:** Bring repellent for the outdoor evening biters. ⊠*4589 Karamea Hwy.* ☎*03/782–6033* ⊕*www.karamealodge. co.nz* ✑*info@karamealodge.co.nz* ⇄*3 rooms* ⌕*In-room: kitchen, DVD, no a/c. In-hotel: laundry* ▤*MC, V* ��⚬*CP.*

¢–$ 📺**The Last Resort.** Karamea is one of those deliciously remote places. The Last Resort's glowing hardwood beams, stylish local artwork, and unusual turf roof make it very much at peace with its setting. They can arrange tours, helicopter rides, and shuttles to and from the Heaphy Track, offering a one-stop booking service for the whole experience. Check out the solid 24-meter-long (80-foot-long) hardwood roof beam in the bar area. **Pros:** There are a bar/bistro and a restaurant, helicopters land nearby to whisk you off into the national park, three 2-bedroom cottages are $140 a night. **Con:** In the main street of Karamea village. ✉*71 Waverley St.* ☎*03/782–6617 or 0800/505–042* 🖷*03/782–6820* ⊕*www.lastresort.co.nz* ✎*enquiries@lastresort.co.nz* ⇴*18 rooms (3 self-contained, 13 with kitchenette), 6 lodge rooms (shared bath), 3 cottages, 3 dorm rooms* ♿*In-room: no phone (some), no TV (some), no a/c. In-hotel: restaurant, bar, spa, public Internet, bicycles.*

The **Kohaihai campsite** at the southern end of the Heaphy Track is a stunning spot to camp if you want to experience the pristine setting of this remote spot. It's just a 16-km (10-mi) drive north of Karamea, the last 5 km (3 mi) are gravel, and there are basic facilities only. Inquire at the Karamea Information Centre. As with most of the West Coast, don't swim in the sea here as there are strong rips and undertows. Jump in the river instead.

TOURS

There are fixed-wing and helicopter options for arriving at Karamea and tripping around while you're there, although both are very weather dependent. **HeliCharter Karamea** (☎*03/782–6111* ⊕*www.adventuresnz. co.nz*) specializes in scenic flights but also operates helicopter transfers and day trips to and from Karamea. They provide a shuttle service to the Wangapeka and Heaphy Tracks, hunting and fishing, kayaking and heli-rafting. **Remote Adventures** (☎*0800/150–338* ⊕*www.remotead-ventures.co.nz*) specializes in running Heaphy Track trampers between the Brown Hut, Karamea, Nelson, and Takaka with a fixed-wing small plane service. They also run scenic flights all year, excluding winter.

PUNAKAIKI

269 km (168 mi) southeast of Nelson.

★ At first glance, Punakaiki looks like nothing more than a small cluster of beach houses and shops—a blip on the radar without even a gas station or ATM. It's worth a detour, though, for its nearby maze of limestone stacked high above the sea: the surreal **Pancake Rocks.** The huge swells that batter this coast have eroded the limestone cliffs, carving them into fantastical shapes. A paved walkway leads you through the windswept cover of tenacious New Zealand flax and *nikau* palms to see the most dramatic points, including the boiling cauldron called the Surge Pool and the pumping fissure of the Chimney Pot. At high tide, three blowholes spout a thundering geysers of spray. Aoraki (Mt. Cook) is sometimes visible across the sea to the south. To reach the rocks from the highway, take the easy 10-minute walk from the visitor center. Keep turning left along the path so you don't miss the best bits out around the Surge Pool. High tide on a southwest swell under a full moon at midnight is an outstanding time to visit, if you dare. Otherwise, try for high tide or a big westerly swell. The **Paparoa National Park Visitors Centre** (✉ *Main Rd.* ☎ *03/731–1895* ⊕ *www.doc.govt.nz*), across the road from the main gate, is a handy place to learn more about the formations.

The Pancake Rocks are the star of **Paparoa National Park,** which is based loosely along the Paparoa Range, a long, rugged chain of mountains running parallel to the coast. With craggy summits, serrated ridges, and cirques carved out of ancient granite and gneiss, it's a formidable environment. But its sheer cliffs, flood-prone rivers, dense rain forest, and extensive cave systems spell out paradise for hikers. The major entry points—Bullock Creek, Fox River, and Pororari River—open onto an otherworldly zone of jungly green, striking *nikau* palms, rushing streams, and sweeping coastal views. Much of this area is serious outback country, requiring either a guide or considerable bush experience. There are several short day hikes, canoeing, and horse treks, though; drop by the **Paparoa National Park Visitors Centre** for maps and information.

OUTDOOR ACTIVITIES

☾ **Punakaiki Canoes.** For many, the essence of this gorgeous region can be found in a paddle up the Pororari River, just to the north of the village. Glide silently through the dark, brooding waters between huge limestone cliffs studded with *nikau* and giant *rata* trees. Or head down the estuary toward the coast, where the waterway opens out into a more playful area. Suitable for all abilities and ages, but dependent on the state of the weather and the river. ✉ *State Hwy. 6* ☎ *03/731–1870* ⊕ *www.riverkayaking.co.nz* ✉ *$35 per person for up to 2 hrs, $55 all day. Guided tours from $70. Family rates available.*

WHERE TO STAY

The eating options often fall short, although the new Punakaiki Rocks Hotel with its large oceanfront restaurants and bar has helped that somewhat. Because there are only a couple of places to eat in town, it's best to reserve an evening table in midsummer. There are two small lunch cafés opposite the entry to the Pancake Rocks. If you decide to stay in a self-catering unit, you'll need to bring in all your food, as there are no general stores in town.

$$$ 🏨 **Punakaiki Rocks Hotel & Villas.** The modern beach-house design blends well with the dynamic coastal setting; the front steps of the hotel reach almost onto the beach, and driftwood, flax, sand, and surf are all part of the deal. There's a mix of hotel rooms on the seaward side of the road and eco-rooms and villas just across the road; the villas have a small kitchenette area. The restaurant and bar feature floor-to-ceiling windows and big comfy leather chairs so you can enjoy the setting no matter what the weather. **Pros:** Ask for a hotel room on the seaward side for a really salty taste in your mouth, walk the beach on a windy day with the surf crashing in beside you. **Con:** Ecorooms are across the road from the beach but still have a great coastal views. ✉ *State Hwy.*

6, 2,200 yards of Pancake Rocks ☎*03/731–1168 or 0800/786–2524* 📠*03/731–1163* ⊕*www.punakaiki-resort.co.nz* ⟿*27 rooms, 12 eco-rooms, 24 villas* ⚷*In-room: kitchenette (some), no a/c. In-hotel: bar, restaurant, public Internet, laundries* ▤*AE, DC, MC, V* ⟟⊙⟨*EP.*

$$-$$$ 🖾 **Hydrangea Cottages.** You'll be lulled by the constant roar of the ocean here, ½ km (¼ mi) south of the Pancake Rocks. Three of the apartments—Rata, Mamaku, and Nikau—are brightly colored with recycled native timbers and contemporary furniture. The smaller studio cottage, Rimu, goes rustic with a cute indoor shower built of river rock and corrugated iron. The new two-bedroom Kiwi House is available mid-May to mid-October, with a minimum stay of three nights. All are self-catering. **Pro:** Horse treks available into the national park or along the beach. **Cons:** 600 meters south of Pancake Rocks, reception is not always manned but instructions are left at the door. ⊠*Main Rd.* ☎*03/731–1839* ⊕*www.pancake-rocks.co.nz* ✉*punakaiki@ xtra.co.nz* ⟿*3 suites, 2 cottages* ⚷*In-room: no a/c, no phone, DVD. In-hotel: no-smoking rooms* ▤*MC, V.*

GREYMOUTH

44 km (28 mi) south of Punakaiki.

The town of Greymouth is aptly named—at first take, it's a rather dispirited strip of motels and industrial buildings stretched along a wild beach. It sits, as the name suggests, at the mouth of the Grey River and is thus exposed to a bone-chilling wind in winter. But in warmer weather, its good points come to the fore. Many travelers arrive here on the TranzAlpine train from Christchurch and are plopped into the middle of the West Coast without the stunning drives along either the north or the south coasts to set the scene. If you're arriving and returning by train, take a day or two for a trip up to Punakaiki or down to the glaciers, to grasp the scope of the landscape.

ESSENTIALS

Bus Depot Greymouth (⊠*Railway Station, Mackay St.*).

Hospital Greymouth Base Hospital (⊠*High St.* ☎*03/768–0499*).

Visitor Info Greymouth Visitor Centre (⊠*Herbert and Mackay, Greymouth* ☎*03/768–5101* ⊕*www.greydistrict.co.nz*).

WHAT TO SEE

The land around Greymouth is particularly rich in pounamu, the greenstone highly prized by the Māori. You're in a Ngai Tahu iwi (tribe) area, and as part of the tribe's 1997 Treaty of Waitangi settlement, the government recognized Ngai Tahu as having sole rights to collect and sell the precious jade in its natural form. The **Left Bank Art Gallery** on the corner of Tainui Street and Mawhera Quay is a good place to see some contemporary pounamu carvings.

Better yet, visit the **Jade Boulder Gallery,** which exhibits the work of Ian Boustridge, one of the country's best sculptors of greenstone. The gallery is a great place to pick up a distinctive souvenir; earrings start at about $10, pendants generally cost a couple of hundred, and a sculpture can cost thousands. The gallery's latest addition, the Jade Boulder Trail, is an interpretative walk-through detailing the legends and forms of New Zealand greenstone, with displays of carved and raw jade. ⊠ *1 Guinness St.* ☎ *03/768–0700* ⊕ *www.jadeboulder.com* ☉ *Nov.–Apr., daily 8:30* AM*–9* PM*; May–Oct., daily 8:30–5.*

☖ On the southern outskirts of Greymouth **Shantytown** is a lively reenactment of a gold-mining town of the 1880s. This is how the settlers who stayed on after that gold rush would have lived—but without the electricity, running water, and paved entry road. Except for the church and the town hall, most of the buildings are reproductions, including a jail, a blacksmith shop, a railway station, and a barbershop. The gold-digging displays include a water jet for blasting the gold-bearing quartz from the hillside, water sluices, and a stamper—battery-powered by a 30-foot waterwheel—for crushing the ore. You can pan for gold with a good chance of striking "color," as this was the site of the world's last major gold rush, or catch a steam train ride. ⊠ *Rutherglen* ☎ *03/762–6634* ✎ *shantytown@xtra.co.nz* ⊕ *www.shantytown.co.nz* ▦ *$16* ☉ *Daily 8:30–5; last train leaves at 4* PM.

A few miles south of Greymouth is Kūmara's **Carey Dillon Woodworker.** The namesake artisan's workshop and gallery is devoted to woodturning and landscape photography, and Dillon's work is superb. He turns chunks of aged *rimu,* a native hardwood gathered from fallen logs, into magnificent bowls that glow like amber; each one takes at least a year to create. His large photographs are highly scenic. ⊠ *State Hwy. 73, Main Rd., Kūmara* ☎ *03/736–9741* ⊕ *www.careydillon.com* ☉ *Oct.–Apr., daily.*

WHERE TO STAY & EAT

$$$ ✕ **Bridge Bar & Cafe.** Perched high on the edge of the rugged, wild Taramakau River, this restaurant and bar has blown into the area like a fresh blast off the Southern Ocean, with fresh clean flavors and good service. The menu, like most places on the coast, is based on local foods, but here they spin a contemporary twist. Whitebait is the signature dish but the rack of lamb with creamy minted mash, and the beef fillet with a stuffed wild mushroom also go down a treat. The coffee is probably the best in town. ⊠ *Main Rd. S, 10 km (6 mi) south of Greymouth* ☎ *03/762–6830* ▤ *MC, V.*

$$$ ✕ **Station House Café.** You can come to Lake Brunner on a day drive from Greymouth, as part of a round-the-lake trip, or stop off the TranzAlpine train for lunch while it hops out to the coast and back—about a 90-minute stop. The café is an old railway house, perched on a terrace above the railway station and with a superb view across Lake Brunner and the *kahikatea* forests and wetlands beyond. The menu features venison, lamb, rib-eye steak, and turbot; there's also a small range of salad meals. Mains are served with a healthy side of either cooked greens or root veggies. Reserve ahead in summer. ⊠ *Koe St., Moana* ☎ *03/738–0158* ▤ *AE, DC, MC, V* ☉ *Winter hrs can vary. Call ahead for dinner.*

$$$$ ☷ **Lake Brunner Lodge.** On the southern shore of Lake Brunner, a 40-min-
Fodor'sChoice ute drive southeast of Greymouth, this lodge, first established in 1868, is
★ an enticing retreat at a price that is not as high as most of New Zealand's
elite lodges. Rooms are large and well equipped, with the emphasis on
comfort rather than opulence. The best rooms are at the front of the
villa, overlooking the lake. Brown trout fill the clear waters of the surrounding rivers; fly-fishing is the main sport, but good spin fishing is
also available at certain times of the year. (There's a catch-and-release
policy.) The lodge is surrounded by forest, which you can explore on a
guided environmental tour, and is part of a large working farm, which
you can also explore. The kitchen turns out seasonal dishes with a local
bent, such as roast lamb with ratatouille. Children are welcome only by
advance arrangement. Because of its remote setting, the lodge generates
power with a hydro plant running off a spectacular waterfall behind the
main building. **Pros:** Join a farm tour, go fishing or kayaking, or put on
your walking shoes and climb to the waterfall behind the lodge (you'll
need to be moderately agile), nice decor. **Con:** The road to the lodge is
narrow, winding, and gravel for the last few kilometers. ⊠*Mitchells,
R.D. 1, Kūmara* ☎*03/738–0163* 🖷*03/738–0713* ✒*lodge@brunner.
co.nz* ⊕*www.lakebrunner.com* ↪*11 rooms* ♿*In-room: no a/c, Ethernet, no TV. In-hotel: restaurant, bicycles, no-smoking rooms* ⊟*AE,
DC, MC, V* ⒪|*MAP.*

$$–$$$ ☷ **Rosewood.** Rhonda and Stephan Palten run this B&B in a restored
1920s home close to the town center. Original oak paneling and stained-
glass windows remain, and there are cozy seats in the bay windows.
Some rooms are done in a contemporary look; others have period furniture. Stephan's a chef, so expect a very good breakfast of fresh rolls,
bacon, pancakes, French toast, or eggs any way you want them. Two
rooms share a bathroom. You can get a courtesy pickup at the train
station. **Pros:** Good off-street parking and disabled access, you can
arrange rooms so as not to share a bathroom. **Con:** Busy street. ⊠*20
High St.* ☎*03/768–4674* 🖷*03/768–4694* ✒*stay@rosewoodnz.co.nz*
⊕*www.rosewoodnz.co.nz* ↪*5 rooms, 3 with bath* ♿*In-room: no a/c.
In-hotel: bar, public Internet, no-smoking rooms, no elevator* ⊟*AE,
DC, MC, V* ⒪|*BP.*

$$ ☷ **New River Bluegums.** Looking a bit like the little house on the prairie
this river rock and timber homestay is a delight. There's a B&B room
in the main house and two newly built well-appointed self-contained
cottages out past the barn. With very rural surroundings and a slightly
unkempt acreage this place is full of rustic charm. It's only a 10-minute
walk down to the coast and there's a flood-lighted tennis court for an
evening game (racquets provided). **Pros:** Kids will love the sheep and
pigs and the open spaces; a traditional home-cooked dinner is avail-
able on request, with pavlova for dessert. **Cons:** Big friendly Labrador
on-site, wake to the early morning sounds of roosters and native birds.
⊠*985 Main Rd. S, 9 km (5½ mi) south of Greymouth* ☎*03/762–6678*
⊕*www.bluegumsnz.com* ↪*1 room, 2 cottages* ♿*Phones on demand,
laundry, broadband Internet, kitchens in cottages, no a/c, no elevator,
tennis* ⊟*MC, V* ⒪|*BP.*

7

HOKITIKA

41 km (26 mi) south of Greymouth.

Hokitika is the pick of the towns running down the West Coast, with the pounding ocean before it and the bush-covered hills behind. It's a place of simple pleasures: scouting the crafts boutiques, taking a bush-walk, enjoying the seafood, and looking for evocatively shaped driftwood on the beach. Hokitika is central enough to catch a scenic flight to the glaciers, or take a day trip to Punakaiki or Arthur's Pass.

ESSENTIALS

Bus Depot Hokitika (✉ *Hokitika Travel Centre, 64 Tancred St.*).

Visitor Info Hokitika Visitor Centre (✉ *Hamilton and Tancred, Hokitika* ☎ *03/755–6166*).

WHAT TO SEE

In several places along and just off **Tancred Street,** you can check out the work of local artisans, particularly the pounamu carvings the area's known for. For instance, **Westland Greenstone** (✉ *34 Tancred St.* ☎ *03/755–8713*) has an interesting walk-through workshop where you can watch greenstone being cut, shaped, and polished. At the **Hokitika Craft Gallery Co-operative** (✉ *25 Tancred St.* ☎ *03/755–8802*) greenstone carvings are joined by pottery, woodwork, and textiles. **Ocean Paua** (✉ *25 Weld St.* ☎ *03/755–6128*) has a varied range of *paua* shell, greenstone, and bone artworks, jewelry and a workshop. The larger **Jade Factory** (✉ *41 Weld St.* ☎ *03/755–8007*) also has a greenstone cutting area, stone painting, and a café.

For many Kiwis, Hokitika is on the map purely for its annual **Wildfoods Festival,** which celebrates bush tucker (food from the bush) from the West Coast's natural food sources. Bite into such delectables as *huhu* grubs (they look like large maggots), worm sushi, whitebait patties (far more mainstream), and snail caviar, and follow it all with gorse wine, moonshine, or Monteith's bitter beer. The mid-March fest (book well ahead over this time) attracts crowds of up to 20,000, six times the local population. Go down to the beach later and watch as the bonfires light up and people dig in for the night. Of course, a good dump of West Coast rain quiets things down—until the next year. Take your gumboots. ⊕ *www.wildfoods.co.nz.*

WHERE TO STAY & EAT

$$$–$$$$ ✕ **Café de Paris.** Pronounced *"parr*-iss" in these parts, this spot serves French cuisine with a New Zealand accent. The simple decor is in keeping with owner Pierre Esquilat's straightforward approach: unfussy French cooking with fresh local ingredients. The pork fillet wrapped in pancetta and served on a *kūmara* and pumpkin mash is a delicious example, as is local venison seared and finished with a blueberry and port wine glaze. There's a liquor license, but you're welcome to BYOB. It's open breakfast through dinner, and evening reservations are essential in summer. ✉ *19 Tancred St.* ☎ *03/755–8933* ▭ *AE, DC, MC, V.*

$ ✕**Adz on Tancred.** An enormous collection of teapots marches around the walls here. This isn't the place for dainty finger sandwiches, though; instead, bite into a generous serving of lasagna, homemade fries, or a huge custard square. ✉*39 Tancred St.* ☎*03/755–8379* ▤*MC, V.*

$$$–$$$$ ⊞**Kapitea Ridge Lodge.** This luxurious modern lodge, high on a hill
★ overlooking the coast, has a special connection to its setting; its creek is part of an ancient Māori greenstone trail. The Sunset Room has a sunset color scheme and gazes west to the coast, and the Tasman Room (named for its view of the Tasman Sea) borrows the hues of an opalescent paua shell. Most of the rooms have an ocean view; some have private balconies. You can arrange to go fishing or clay bird shooting, or play pétanque (boccie) before sitting by the outdoor fire in the courtyard for evening drinks. There are beach walks nearby and trout fishing in the Taramakau River (license required). **Pros:** Soothing hot tub in the garden, social lounge area and outdoor courtyard, rooms fitted out with taste. **Con:** Up a short winding gravel road. ✉*Chesterfield Rd. off State Hwy. 6* ✛*Midway between Hokitika and Greymouth* ☎*03/755–6805* 🖷*03/755–6895* ⊕*www.kapitea.co.nz* ➟*6 rooms, some with bath* ♿*In-room: no a/c. In-hotel: no kids under 12, public Internet, no-smoking rooms, no elevator* ▤*AE, DC, MC, V* ☾*Closed May–Aug.* ⏀*BP.*

$$–$$$ ⊞**Teichelmann's Bed & Breakfast.** Named for Dr. Ebenezer Teichelmann, the surgeon-mountaineer-conservationist who built the original part of the house, this is the most comfortable place in the center of town. Its friendly atmosphere has a lot to do with hosts Frances Flanagan and Brian Ward, who are happy to make suggestions for local activities. Furnishings are a combination of antique and country-cottage style, using plenty of native wood. The rimu-wood bookcase is full of literature about the area. **Pros:** One of the West Coast's accommodation icons, for those who enjoy the quieter side of life. **Con:** Opens onto one of Hokitika's main streets. ✉*20 Hamilton St.* ☎*03/755–8232* 🖷*03/755–8239* ✉*teichel@xtra.co.nz* ⊕*www.teichelmanns. co.nz* ➟*5 rooms, 1 cottage* ♿*In-room: no a/c, no phone. In-hotel: public Internet, no kids under 10, no-smoking rooms, no elevator* ▤*MC, V* ⏀*BP.*

¢–$$ ⊞**Shining Star.** These oceanfront chalets are about as close to the
☾ beach as you'll get; the surf rolls in, the air has a salty tang, and the sky is filled with wheeling seabirds. The various units range from basic cabins to chalets with full kitchens and big fluffy duvets; a few have whirlpool baths. There's a menagerie of sorts, too, including sheep, goats, alpaca, and pigs. A Continental breakfast is available on request, and there are powered sites for campervans. **Pro:** Walk out on to the wild surf beach and build a driftwood fire. **Con:** Driveways and park spots are gravel. ✉*11 Richards Dr.* ☎🖷*03/755–8921* ⊕*www. accommodationwestcoast.co.nz* ✉*shining@xtra.co.nz* ➟*12 chalets, 8 cabins, 3 1-bedroom apartments* ♿*In-room: no a/c (some), safe (some), Wi-Fi (some). In-hotel: spa, no-smoking rooms* ▤*AE, DC, MC, V* ⏀*EP.*

WESTLAND NATIONAL PARK

Fodor's Choice
★

North end 146 km (91 mi) south of Hokitika.

Westland National Park joins the Fiordland and Mt. Aspiring national parks to form a sweeping World Heritage Area of more than 5 million acres, including some of the best examples of the plants and animals once found on the ancient Gondwanaland supercontinent. It's a place of extremes, including the extreme precipitation at the top of Westland. Up to 300 inches of snow per annum falls here, feeding Westland's glacier field. The snow is compressed into ice on the névé, or head, of the glaciers (New Zealanders say "glassy-urs"), then flows downhill under its own weight. There are more than 60 glaciers in the park; the most famous and accessible are at Franz Josef and Fox. If you're driving through on a cloudy or wet day you will get no idea of the size of the mountain ranges just a few miles off the road. On a clear day take a moment to stop and admire them disappearing inland, layer after mighty layer. The Harihari, Whataroa, and Fox Glacier valleys are good for this.

The **Fox Glacier** is slightly larger than Franz Josef, but you'll miss nothing important if you see only one. Both glaciers have separate villages, and if you are spending the night, **Franz Josef Glacier** is marginally preferable. (Both towns have solid tourist infrastructures, but the summer tourist rush means you should make reservations in advance for lodgings and restaurants.) There are parking areas outside both towns from which you can walk 20–40 minutes to reach viewing points of the glaciers. Both parking lots are visited by mischievous kea (*kee*-ah)—mountain parrots—that may delight in destroying the rubber molding around car windows and eating left-open lunches. Their beaks are like can openers. *Kea* are harmless to humans, but don't feed them. Trails from the parking lots wind across the rocky valley floor to the glacier faces, where a tormented chorus of squeaks, creaks, groans, and gurgles can be heard as the glacier creeps down the mountainside at an average rate of up to 3 feet per day. Care must be taken because rocks and chunks of ice frequently drop from the melting face.

These being New Zealand glaciers, there is much to do besides admire them. You can fly over them in helicopters or planes and land on the stable névé, or hike on them with guides. Remember that these structures are always in motion—an ice cave that was visible yesterday might today be smashed under tons of ice that used to be just uphill of it. Likewise, some of the fascinating formations that you see on the surface of the glacier were fairly recently at the very bottom of it higher up in the valley. Danger comes with this unstable territory; guides know the hazardous areas to avoid.

For the most part, flights are best early in the morning, when visibility tends to be clearest. Seasonal variables around the glaciers are a surprising thing. Summer may be warmer and by far the busiest season, but there is a lot more rain and fog that can scuttle "flightseeing" and hiking plans. There's a lot to be said for winter visits. In winter, snow doesn't fall at sea level in Franz Josef or Fox; in fact, in winter this area is a lot warmer than the snow towns farther south. Skies are clearer, which means fewer canceled flights and glacier hikes and more spectacular mountains views. Warm clothing is always essential on the glaciers, and evenings can be cold any time of year.

Outside the town of Fox Glacier, **Lake Matheson** has one of the country's most famous views. A walking trail winds along the lakeshore, and the snowcapped peaks of Aoraki/Mt. Cook and Mt. Tasman are reflected in the water. Allow at least three hours for the complete walk from town to the "view of views" and back. The best times are sunrise and sunset, when the mirrorlike reflections are less likely to be fractured by the wind. From town, walk down Cook Flat Road toward the sea where a sign points to Gillespies Beach; turn right to reach the lake.

Lake Moeraki is in the midst of Westland National Park, 90 km (56 mi) south of Fox Glacier. There isn't a town here; it's the site of a thoughtfully designed wilderness lodge (sister lodge to the Arthur's Pass Wilderness Lodge. Access to the coast is easiest at **Monro Beach.** The 45-minute walk to the beach takes you through spectacular, fern-filled native forest to a truly remarkable beach: rock clusters jut out of incredibly blue waters, and rivers and streams flow over the sand into the Tasman Sea. You might arrive at a time when spunky little fiordland crested penguins are in transit from the sea to their stream or hillside nests. Early morning and late afternoon provide the best chance of seeing them.

Two kilometers (1 mi) south of the trail entrance on the beach is a seal colony, which you will smell before you see it. If you venture that way, be sure to keep about 30 feet away from the seals, and don't block their path to the sea. A spooked seal will bowl you over on its lurch for the water. Sculpted dark gray rocks also litter the beach to the south, and seals like to lie behind and among them, so look carefully before you cross in front of these rocks.

Monro Beach is an utter dream, not least if you collect driftwood or rocks. On the road 2 km (1 mi) or so south of it, there is a lookout over the rock stacks at **Knights Point.** Farther south still, between Moeraki and Haast, the walkways and beach at **Ship Creek** are another stop for ferny forests and rugged coastline. Sandflies here can be voracious, so bring insect repellent and hope for a windy day. (There are far fewer sandflies in winter.) For weather conditions and other current information visit the **Fox Glacier Visitor Centre** and the **Franz Josef Glacier Visitor Information Centre** on State Highway 6.

Hukawai Glacier Centre (⌧ *Corner Cron and Cowan Sts., Franz Josef* ☎*03/752–0600 or 0800/485–2921* ⊕*www.hukawai.co.nz* ⌧*$25)* Visit here before you go up on the ice, or if the cloud is down and you're not going to get there anyway. Watch the Māori Creation story, learn how the glaciers are formed, and about the local geology and flora and fauna. If you've got time, and a bit of money, you can have a go on their indoor ice-climbing wall (the only one in the southern hemisphere).

ESSENTIALS

Bus Depot **Franz Josef** (⊠ *Franz Josef Hotel, Main Rd.; Franz Josef YHA, 2–4 Cron St.; Main Rd., opposite Cheeky Kea Bldg.*). **Fox Glacier** (⊠ *Northbound: Alpine Guides, Main Rd.; Southbound: Fox General Store*).

Hospital **Franz Josef Rural Clinic** (⊠ *Main Hwy.* ☎ *03/752–0700*).

Visitor Info **Fox Glacier Visitor Centre** (⊠ *State Hwy. 6, Fox Glacier* ☎ *03/751– 0807* ⊕ *www.glaciercountry.co.nz*). **Franz Josef Glacier Visitor Information Centre** (⊠ *State Hwy. 6, Franz Josef* ☎ *03/752–0796* ⊕ *www.glaciercountry.co.nz*).

OUTDOOR ACTIVITIES

★ Even though the white heron (known to the Māori as *kotuku*) nests
☾ only from October to March, a trip with **White Heron Sanctuary Tours** is worth doing at any time of the year. A rollicking jet-boat ride takes you down the beautiful Waitangiroto River to the sea, passing white-bait fishermen and solitary birds on the swampy banks before winding along a short coastal lagoon and then drifting into a nature reserve. High *kahikatea* and *rimu* trees arch over the river, and flax bushes droop into the dark brooding water. This is the heart of the southern West Coast's coastal rain forest, somber and silent. In season the elegant *kotuku* nest at their only site in the country, and a bird-watching hide has been set up directly opposite. Trip prices start at $95 and reservations are essential. ☎ *03/753–4120 or 0800/523–456* ⊕ *www. whiteherontours.co.nz*.

FISHING   **Note:** *For information on fishing around Franz Josef and Fox, see Chapter 11.*

KAYAKING & RAFTING   Several mirror-still lakes in the area, plus the large Okarito lagoon out on the coast, offer kayaking opportunities in most weather. **Ferg's Kayaks** (☎ *03/752–0230, 0800/423–262 South Island only* ⊕ *www. glacierkayaks.com*) offers guided trips around Lake Mapourika, best paddled in the morning or evening, when the breeze is softer. **Rivers Wild** (☎ *021/748–371 or 0800/469–453, 1877/826–3624 U.S.* ⊕ *www.riverswild.co.nz*) takes adventurers and families on rafting and multisport trips throughout the West Coast, from Grade II to the most extreme Grade V. Popular trips include heli-rafting near Franz Josef Glacier and a multiday wilderness experience on the Landsborough River. Full-day trips start around $195. The rafting season runs November to April; reservations are strongly recommended.

ON & ABOVE THE GLACIERS   The walks to the glacier heads mentioned above are the easiest way of seeing the glaciers. But joining a guided walk and getting up close to the glaciers' ice formations—the shapes created by the glaciers' movement and the streams of water running through them—is unforgettable.

Flying over the glaciers is quite thrilling, and expensive. The ultimate combination is to fly by fixed-wing plane or helicopter to the top or middle of the glacier and get out and walk on it. Fixed-wing landings on the snow atop the ice fields are fabulously scenic, but you have only 10 minutes out of the plane. Heli-hikes give you the most time on the ice, two to three hours of snaking up and down the middle of the glacier.

CLOSE UP

Okarito Town

Back in 1866 Okarito was a thriving town of over 1,200 people, with three theatres and 25 hotels. People came for the gold and for many years there was a working port inside the bar at the entrance to the lagoon. Things have changed dramatically and Okarito is now a nature sanctuary, drawing visitors keen to see kiwi, seabirds, and white herons, and to paddle on the silent lagoon. Its wild black sand surf beach is home to nesting birds and sleeping seals, so watch where you walk. **Okarito Nature Tours** (☎🖶 03/753–4014 ⊕ www.okarito.co.nz) sticks to the lagoon, which is a good spot to see

white herons away from their nesting grounds. Rates start at $35 unguided and $65 for a guided trip (minimum of two people). Ian Cooper's **Okarito Kiwi Tours** (⊠ The Strand, Okarito ☎ 03/753–4330 ⊕ www.okaritokiwi tours.co.nz ⌨ Prices start from $45 ⊙ Evenings only) holds the only concession on the South Island mainland to take visitors to see kiwi in their natural habitat. He'll have you walking softly through the bush, listening for their scuffles and calls, before catching a glimpse of these elusive flightless birds. It's a very rare experience and he gives an 85% chance of seeing one on a night tour.

☼ **Fox Glacier Guiding** has a range of guided walks on Fox Glacier, the only safe way to experience the ethereal beauty of the ice caves, pinnacles, and crevasses on top of the glaciers. There are trips to suit all fitness levels, budgets, and time frames, and even ones that are good for kids (over the age of seven or so). The four-hour walk travels about 2 km (1 mi) up the glacier. The climb requires some fitness; a half day costs $89, a full day $135. Arguably the best option is to heli-hike, combining a helicopter flight onto and off Fox Glacier and walking for 2½ hours on the ice with a guide ($380). Or try the full-day ice-climbing instruction day with mountaineering equipment provided ($225). Half-day tours depart at 9:15 AM and 1:45 PM and advance reservations are recommended for all trips. ⊠ Fox Glacier Guiding Bldg., Main St., Fox Glacier ☎ 03/751–0825 or 0800/111–600 🖶 03/751–0857 ✑ info@ foxguides.co.nz ⊕ www.foxguides.co.nz.

Mt. Cook Ski Planes has fixed-wing ski planes that fly over the glaciers, landing amid craggy peaks in the high-altitude ski slopes at the head of the glaciers. There are 40-minute ($315) and one-hour ($395) flights. Both flights land for 10 minutes and engines are shut down on the snow for complete glacier silence. Departures are from Franz Josef and Fox Glacier villages. ⊠ Main Rd., Franz Josef ☎ 03/752–0714 or 0800/368–000 🖶 03/752–0744 ⊕ www.mtcookskiplanes.com.

Franz Josef Glacier Guides provides a comprehensive guide service with a popular half day walk ($90) for those short on time, a full day trip ($140) or a heli-hike tour ($360). Bookings are essential. ⊠ Main Rd., Franz Josef ☎ 03/752–0763 or 0800/484–337 🖶 03/752–0102 ⊕ www.franzjosefglacier.com.

7

The **Helicopter Line** operates several scenic flights over the glaciers from heliports at Franz Josef Glacier and Fox Glacier. The shortest is the 20-minute flight over Franz Josef Glacier ($185 per person); the longest is a 40-minute flight that includes a landing on the head of the glacier and a circuit of Aoraki and Mt. Tasman ($360). Three-hour heli-hikes are yet another option ($360). Reservations are recommended in summer and essential for the heli-hikes. ⊠ *Main Rd., Franz Josef* ☎ *03/752–0767 or 0800/807–767* 🖷 *03/752–0769* ⊕ *www.helicopter.co.nz.*

WHERE TO STAY & EAT

Both Fox and Franz Josefs are on the backpacker circuit and are well serviced with hostel accommodation, but there is also a good range of hotel lodgings.

$$$–$$$$ ✕ **Blue Ice Café.** The two levels here can carry you from an early dinner through the wee hours. Go downstairs for a fine meal of local stand-bys such as West Coast whitebait, venison, or lamb, with homemade bread. Try the oven-baked fish served on a pumpkin and kūmara mash. Portions are well sized, service is good, and the setting is quieter than upstairs. The Flaming Dessert comes with an absinthe topping, lighted as it's presented at the table. Upstairs there's a bar where you can order a pizza and a beer and rack up at the free pool table. Because it has a 3 AM license and regularly hosts DJs most weekends, this becomes the town's late-night party spot during the tourist season. ⊠ *South end of Main Rd., Franz Josef* ☎ *03/752–0707* ▤ *AE, MC, V* ⊘ *No lunch.*

$$–$$$$ ✕ **Café Neve.** A standout along Fox Glacier's main street, the Neve sparks up no-nonsense options with fresh local flavors, such as the pizza topped with locally made Blackball salami, field mushrooms, spinach, rosemary, and tomato. Beef, lamb, and seafood also feature, and for a tiny place, the wine list of 150 vintages is impressive. The lunch menu is more varied, with choices such as a feta-and-olive salad or a West Coast whitebait omelet, and they're even open for breakfast. ⊠ *Main Rd., Fox Glacier* ☎ *03/751–0110* ⚖ *Reservations not accepted* ▤ *DC, MC, V.*

$–$$$$ ✕ **The Alice May.** This café and bar is one of those cozy, buzzing places so prevalent on the West Coast. After a busy day hiking the glacier, kayaking, or dropping onto the ice by helicopter, it's the perfect place to refuel. The food is good country fare, and lots of it. Favorites are the roast of the day, sticky pork ribs with a barbecue sauce, and the deep sea cod with chips. Desserts are just as wholesome, with apple crumble, a chocolate pavlova, ice-cream sundae, and good ol' banoffie pie. The wine and beer lists are stacked with NZ favorites, and there are sports on-screen, generally muted. ⊠ *Cowan and Cron Sts., Franz Josef* ☎ *03/752–0740* ▤ *AE, MC, V.*

$–$$ ✕ **Matheson Cafe.** Just as the danger of "great view overload" threatens to set in, there's one to beat them all. Lake Matheson is famous for its reflecting view of the country's highest peaks in its still, early morning water. So after the early start, stop at the café for a very good coffee and breakfast. The view from the café is equally stunning in its own way, surrounded by an amphitheater of distant mountains and kahikatea forest. On a cloudy day the view is somewhat diminished but still has that craggy West Coast feel to it. The food is as good as the views, and the sunny terrace is pleasant on a still day. Try the blue cod open sandwich for a tasty lunch. ⊠*Lake Matheson carpark, Fox Glacier* ☎*03/751–0878.*

$$$$ 🛏**Franz Josef Glacier Country Retreat.** Although this grand home was only built in 2006, it evokes a feeling of the past that climbs right out of the landscape. Co-owner Marie Coburn's family has been here for over 100 years and the rooms are all named after early pioneering families in the area. She is happy to share this heritage and folklore with her guests. The lodge is surrounded by a 200-acre working farm and backed by tall snowcapped peaks often shrouded in mist. There are distant views of Lake Mapourika and it's only a five-minute drive into Franz Josef village. The Honeymoon Suite sits in its own turret with commanding views. **Pros:** Farm walks, salmon in the creek, a pet sheep, dinner is available in the restaurant, transfers to Franz Josef village are available on request. **Cons:** Well back from road, up a long driveway, just south of Lake Mapourika. ⊠*State Hwy. 6, Lake Mapourika* ☎*03/752–0021* ⊕*www.glacier-retreat.co.nz* ◄*10 rooms, 2 suites* ⌂*In-room: no a/c, Wi-Fi, refrigerator. In-hotel: restaurant, , public Internet, laundry* ⊟*MC, V* ❢❸*BP.*

$$$$ 🛏**Westwood Lodge.** For unpretentious luxury among the glaciers, turn
★   to this spacious, modern wooden lodge with exceptional alpine views. Rooms have wooden surroundings and a neutral color palette. A huge, open fire warms the lounge, and sunsets turns the snow high above the glaciers a lovely pink. A light dinner is available by arrangement. **Pros:** Mountain views, a big stone fireplace. **Con:** Busy road. ⊠*Main Rd., Franz Josef* ☎*03/752–0112* 🖷*03/752–0111* ⊕*www.westwood-lodge. co.nz* ◄*8 rooms, 1 suite* ⌂*In-room: no a/c, refrigerator, DVD. In-hotel: bar, public Internet, no kids under 12, no-smoking rooms* ❢❸*BP* ⊟*AE, DC, MC, V.*

$$$$ 🛏**Wilderness Lodge Lake Moeraki.** In a World Heritage–listed rain forest on the banks of the Moeraki River and an easy 20-minute bush
★   walk from the Tasman Sea—the superb setting and team of ecoguides make this lodge an ideal place to get absorbed in the environment. On-site naturalists take you along while they feed eels, and show you ancient podocarp trees, orchids, fur seals (year-round), and fiordland crested penguins (June to December). On organized night walks, they'll point out glowworms, freshwater crayfish, and the southern constellations. As well as a full breakfast and four-course dinner, rates include the use of canoes and kayaks, plus two short guided activities daily. Longer guided hikes and canoe safaris, fishing guides, and dinner drinks are extra. **Pros:** All accommodation had a major refurbishing in 2006, an intense ecoexperience with very knowledgeable owners, generate their own hydropower. **Con:** It's a long way from anywhere. ⊠*State Hwy. 6, 90 km (56 mi) south of Fox Glacier* ☎*03/750–0881* 🖷*03/750–0882* ✎*lakemoeraki@wildernesslodge. co.nz* ⊕*www.wildernesslodge.co.nz* ◄*24 rooms, 4 suites* ⌂*In-room: no TV. In-hotel: public Wi-Fi, laundry facilities, all no-smoking rooms* ⊟*MC, V* ❂*Closed June* ❢❸*MAP.*

$$ 🖼 **Glenfern Villas.** A short drive north of the village these tidy villas have a quiet rural setting away from the tourist bustle and helicopters around the village. Built of cedar, in alpine style, and surrounded by thick plantings of natives like punga and tussocks, they have a nice family atmosphere. Eight villas have two bedrooms and each villa has a private park. Kids can run off some energy in the playground while Mum and Dad have a game of pétanque. The cowshed across the road adds a nice rural touch **Pros:** Villas are a real home from home with good-size bathrooms and living areas, a breakfast hamper is available on request. **Con:** You may not be looking for family-friendly. ✉️*State Hwy. 6, Franz Josef* ☎️*03/752–0054* ⊕*www.glenfern.co.nz* ⇆*10 1-bedroom units, 8 2-bedroom units* ⚘*In-room: no a/c, Wi-Fi. In-hotel: public Internet, laundry* ▭*AE, DC, MC, V* ⦿*EP.*

Christchurch & Canterbury

WORD OF MOUTH

"We really enjoyed Christchurch. It is a good size city but very manageable with wonderful parks and playgrounds, and a fascinating artisan district housed at the old university (complete with fantastic fudge shop with tour and lots of samples!)."

—Conny

"[Akaroa is] so different from everywhere else in Aotearoa because it was settled by the French. It still has a lovely French flavor—and French pastries! I stayed there two nights, and bought my special pounamou necklace at a gallery on the main street...One morning I delivered the mail in the mail truck to all of the outlying ranches and villages. Very fun!"

—hikrchick

www.fodors.com/forums

Updated by
Sue Farley

JOHN ROBERT GODLEY, WHOSE BRONZE memorial statue stands in Christchurch's Cathedral Square, would have seen the spectacular views of the Southern Alps when he paused for breath at the top of the Port Hills in 1850. The Canterbury Association, a British organization, had sent him to New Zealand to prepare for the arrival of settlers for a planned Church of England community. That year, four settler ships arrived bearing roughly 800 pioneers, and their new town was named for Godley's college at Oxford.

Built in a Gothic Revival style of dark gray stone, civic buildings such as the Arts Centre and Canterbury Museum give the city an English feel. This style, plus elements such as punting and cricket, often pegs Christchurch as a little slice of England. Though the city may have a conservative exterior, it has been a nursery for social change. It was here that Kate Sheppard, whose portrait is printed on the $10 note, began organizing a campaign that led to New Zealand being the first country in the world to grant women the vote. More recently it has become known as the southern gateway to Antarctica and is developing a keen arts community.

Beyond Christchurch the wide-open Canterbury Plains sweep to the north, west, and south of the city. This is some of New Zealand's finest pastureland, and the higher reaches are sheep station territory, where life and lore mingle in South Island's cowboy country. This is where young Samuel Butler dreamed up the satirical *Erewhon*—the word is an anagram of *nowhere*. But the towns here are no longer considered the back of beyond; communities such as Hanmer Springs, Akaroa, Timaru, and Geraldine are now favorite day-trip destinations. Arthur's Pass, to the west, is probably the best place for a one-day-wonder experience of the Southern Alps while the Waipara Valley to the north of Christchurch is one of the country's developing vineyard areas.

ORIENTATION & PLANNING

GETTING ORIENTED

Canterbury is a roughly rectangular province, with a natural boundary formed by the Main Divide (the peaks of the Southern Alps) in the west and stretching from near Kaikoura in the north down to the Waitaki River in the south. This chapter focuses on the section of Canterbury near the main city of Christchurch, including Banks Peninsula, the Waipara wine country, the ski town of Methven, and the alpine resort town of Hanmer Springs, north and west of the city, plus the towns sprinkled on the plains to the south. The chapter also includes Arthur's Pass National Park, a few hours northwest of Christchurch by car or train and a great mountain day trip from the city.

Christchurch. From the Port Hills the city spreads out below, radiating from the central greenery of Hagley Park. A civic green thumb earned Christchurch the moniker "the Garden City," which it still displays; each spring numerous public and private gardens are open for viewing.

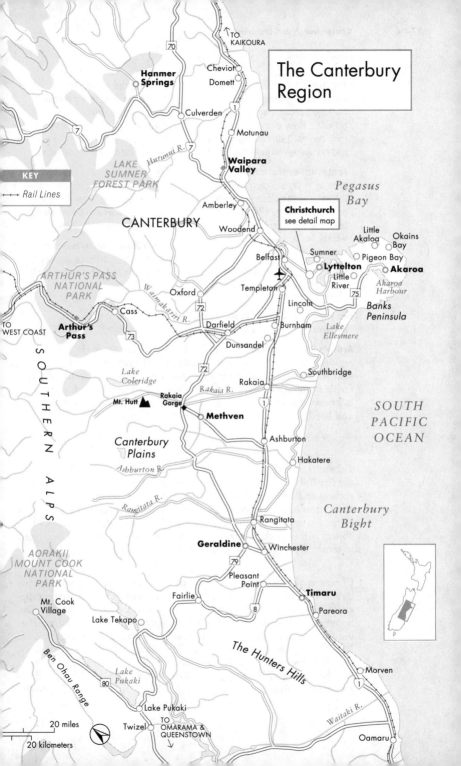

TOP REASONS TO GO

The Arts: Christchurch has a solid collection of galleries, museums, heritage buildings, and cultural activities. Many of these are still in their original 19th-century buildings and occupy key sites in the city.

Fantastic Festivals: Hardly a month goes by in Christchurch without a festival staged by one organization or another. Festivals honor entertainers, children, cuisine, the arts, writers, buskers, and gardens and celebrate seasons and heritage days.

Hiking & Trekking: There are some excellent places in Canterbury to experience the Alps and their foothills. Arthur's Pass and the Rakaia and Rangitata river gorges have walking and hiking trails and boating and picnicking areas. And the gorges make a great backdrop in photos.

Parks & Gardens: The city on the swamp, as it might have been called 150 years ago, blossomed into the Garden City thanks to the foresight of Christchurch's city fathers.

Superb Skiing: Within two hours' drive of Christchurch, Canterbury is a ski mecca from June until September.

But the genteel city is being infused with energy from the arts, technology, and a growing immigrant population.

Arthur's Pass & Canterbury. Arthur's Pass and Hanmer Springs are alpine regions; Akaroa is a seaside village tucked under high hills; and the southern areas around Geraldine and Timaru are the center of large, fertile farming areas. The Waipara Valley, just to the north of the city, is known for its excellent pinot noir, chardonnay, sauvignon blanc, and Rieslings.

PLANNING

Take at least three days to explore the Canterbury region. A full day in the city only skims the surface. An overnight trip to Hanmer for its hot springs and alpine setting, to Arthur's Pass to experience the Southern Alps, or to Akaroa to enjoy a laid-back coastal village gives you a taste of the hinterland. If you're driving farther afield after visiting Christchurch, all of these areas, except Akaroa, may be worked into your itinerary depending on which direction you're heading.

WHEN TO GO

Choosing the best time to come to the Christchurch area depends largely on your tolerance for crowds. In summer, Christchurch is especially busy as its events calendar gets the city buzzing. The Garden City SummerTimes festival runs from New Year's until late February, offering free classical music concerts and other activities in Hagley Park. Mid-January brings the World Buskers Festival with plenty of zany, free acts; the Festival of Flowers is held around February; and there are also the International Jazz & Blues Festival in late March, and the Antarctic Festival in September or October. A list of upcoming events and festivals can be viewed at ⊕*www.bethere.co.nz.*

The song by New Zealand band Crowded House about "four seasons in one day" barely exaggerates the local climate. Summer days can be chilled by a sudden east wind, and the nor'wester can be calm and warm one day and blustery the next. Winter's weather (May–September) is more settled but colder, and though some activities close down, the lack of crowds makes traveling easier. For skiing, snowboarding, and other winter sports, this is *the* time to come. From the first weekend in June through October you can be assured of snow at Mt. Hutt, the first local ski area to open and often the last to close. Snow on the ground in Christchurch is a rarity.

GETTING HERE & AROUND

BY AIR

Direct flights arrive into Christchurch from the major New Zealand cities and regional South Island towns, the larger Australian cities, some parts of Asia, and the Pacific Islands. There are no direct flights in from North America. Air New Zealand (☎03/374–7100 or 0800/737–000 ⊕*www.airnewzealand.co.nz*) Link and the smaller regional airlines connect Christchurch to many South Island centers and the Chatham Islands. Charter helicopters connect to high country and remote lodges.

BY BUS

The nationwide InterCity bus service connects Christchurch with all major towns and cities in the South Island and several smaller shuttle companies also provide a reliable service. Christchurch is serviced by two passenger trains. The Coastal Pacific (☎03/314–8816 ⊕*www. alpinepacifictourism.co.nz*) runs from Picton and Blenheim to the north, climbing through rolling farm and hill country and following the spectacular coastline near Kaikoura. It connects with the Inter-Islander ferry (☎0800/802–802 ⊕*www.interislander.co.nz*)from the North Island. The TranzAlpine is one of the Great Train Journeys of the World, climbing up and over the Southern Alps as it crosses from the East Coast to the West.

Christchurch has a good metropolitan bus service, a rarity in New Zealand. A free shuttle bus service connects points of interest in central Christchurch, and a good network of suburban bus routes links the outer areas of the city.

BY CAR

Outside the city, public transportation relies on daily buses and shuttles, so the best way to explore the region is by car. Roads across the Canterbury Plains tend to be straight and flat—they were often based on old sheep-herding tracks—with good signage and low traffic volume. State Highway 1 runs the length of the region's coast, linking all the major towns. State Highway 72 follows the contours of the hills, farther inland, beneath the Alps. The large braided rivers, such as the Rangitata and Rakaia, can be crossed in only one or two places where they meet state highways. State Highway 7 leaves the main road at Waipara and heads inland to Hanmer Springs before heading north to Nelson.

8

ABOUT THE RESTAURANTS

Christchurch's restaurants are increasingly sophisticated and diverse. There's an established Asian influence, both in restaurants devoted to specific countries' cuisines and in places that fuse Pan-Asian ingredients or techniques with New Zealand cooking. You can also find everything from Cajun to Indian. New Zealand cuisine is now a serious contender in its own right, blending the best fresh and local ingredients with Asian-Pacific tastes. Restaurants in the city are usually open every day; if they do close it is either Sunday or Monday. On Friday and Saturday it's best to reserve; otherwise, you should get a table without trouble. With the exception of the Casino, which has set rules on what not to wear, dress tends to be informal. Outside Christchurch, restaurants are more likely to close on Monday and sometimes Tuesday.

Along with its vineyard boom, the Waipara Valley is seeing a surge in exotic food production. Local food producers are broadening their horizons; for example, North Canterbury is now a key producer in the country's fledgling black truffle industry. Locally sourced saffron, hazelnuts, *manuka* (an indigenous kind of tea tree) honey, olive oil, and ostrich meat are making their way onto area menus in delicious and innovative ways.

WHAT IT COSTS IN NEW ZEALAND DOLLARS					
	¢	$	$$	$$$	$$$$
Restaurants	under $10	$10–$15	$15–$20	$20–$30	over $30

Prices are per person for a main course at dinner, or the equivalent.

ABOUT THE HOTELS

No matter where you stay in Christchurch, you'll find some of the best lodging in New Zealand, from luxury hotels and lodges to fine bed-and-breakfasts to well-maintained, inexpensive hostels. The two main motel strips are along Papanui Road (the end nearest town) and Riccarton Road, both outside the city center. Most of the bigger hotels are in the central city; although the more substantial lodges tend to be out in the hinterland. Many accommodations do not include breakfast in their room rates. Reservations are most necessary in summer (December through March), on public holidays, and during rugby game finals. Christchurch has a healthy festival and conference market so the city can be full at any time of the year.

Outside Christchurch, it can be hard to find a place to stay in summer, especially over the holidays (late December and January). If you're planning on going to Akaroa, Hanmer Springs, or Waipara during this peak season, be sure to reserve well in advance. Bookings can also be heavy in winter around the ski areas and during school holidays.

WHAT IT COSTS IN NEW ZEALAND DOLLARS					
	¢	$	$$	$$$	$$$$
Hotels	under $75	$75–$125	$125–$200	$200–$300	over $300

Prices are for a standard double room in high season, including 12.5% tax.

VISITOR INFORMATION

The **Christchurch–Canterbury i-Site Visitor Information Centre** ✉ *Old Post Office Bldg., Cathedral Sq.* ☎ *03/379–9629* ✍ *info@christchurchnz. net* ⊕ *www.christchurchnz.net)* is open daily from 8:30 to 6. Its Web site is a great resource where you can find out about everything from lodging to bike rentals. The visitor center distributes a monthly brochure called *Canterbury Today & Tonight,* covering sights, events, and more. Another good local Web site is ⊕ *www.localeye.info,* both from a visiting and a local perspective. *Avenues,* a local magazine with events listings and reviews, is also worth a browse.

CHRISTCHURCH

Your initial impression of Christchurch will likely be one of a genteel, green city. But the face of Christchurch is changing, fueled by both internal and international immigration. The Māori community, although still below the national average in size, is growing. Ngai Tahu, the main South Island Māori tribe, settled Treaty of Waitangi claims in 1997 and has been investing in tourism ventures. There is a growing Asian population, reflected in the number of restaurants and stores catering to their preferences. Old wooden bungalows are making way for town houses, the arts scene is flourishing, and the city's university attracts cutting-edge technology companies.

With a population approaching 350,000, Christchurch is the largest South Island city, and the second largest in the country. It is also the forward supply depot for the main U.S. Antarctic base at McMurdo Sound, and if you come in by plane in summer, you are likely to see the giant U.S. Air Force transport planes of Operation Deep Freeze parked on the tarmac at Christchurch International Airport.

GETTING HERE & AROUND

The inner city is compact and easy to explore by foot; the central sights can be reached during an afternoon's walk. Four avenues (Bealey, Fitzgerald, Moorhouse, and Rolleston) define the city center. Beyond this core are a number of special-interest museums and activities, about 20 minutes away by car.

Outside the Four Avenues, the best way to get around the city is to use the network of buses that radiates from the center, or the tram within the city's inner loop. The easiest place to catch a bus is the Bus Exchange, as most buses go through it. Yellow buses and some specially signed red buses are free shuttles that run through the city center, linking the Casino with Moorhouse Avenue. The Red Bus line offers Metrocards, or prepaid travel cards; it also runs the Midnight Express, four routes that run from midnight to 4 AM on Friday and Saturday night.

The Christchurch Best Attractions bus service provides transport (combinable with the entry fees) for several attractions: Willowbank, the Gondola, and the Antarctic Centre at $6 per attraction. Tickets can be booked at the Information Centre or you can pay when you hop on; the bus stop is opposite the main entrance to the visitor bureau.

ESSENTIALS

Airport **Christchurch International Airport** (✉ *Memorial Ave., Harewood* ☎ *03/358–5029* ⊕ *www.christchurch-airport.co.nz*).

Bus Depot **Bus Exchange** (✉ *237–239 Lichfield St.*).

Bus Companies **Best Attractions** (⊕ *www.chchattractions.co.nz*). **InterCity Coachlines** (☎ *03/365–1113 or 0800/222–146* ⊕ *www.intercitycoach.co.nz*).

Medical Assistance **Christchurch Hospital** (✉ *Riccarton and Deans Aves.* ☎ *03/364–0640*). **Fire, police, and ambulance** (☎ *111*). **24 Hour Surgery** (✉ *Bealey Ave. and Colombo St.* ☎ *03/365–7777*). **Urgent Pharmacy** (✉ *Bealey Ave. and Colombo St.* ☎ *03/366–4439*). **Moorhouse Medical Centre** (✉ *3 Pilgrim Pl.* ☎ *03/365–7900*).

Rental Cars **Apex** (✉ *Christchurch International Airport* ☎ *03/357–4536 or 0800/939–597, 011–800/7001–8001 from North America* ⊕ *www.apexrentals. co.nz*). **Avis** (✉ *Christchurch International Airport* ☎ *03/358–9661 or 0800/284–722* ⊕ *www.avis.co.nz*). **Budget** (✉ *15 Lichfield St.* ☎ *03/366–0072 or 0800/283–438* ⊕ *www.budget.co.nz*). **Hertz** (✉ *46 Lichfield St.* ☎ *03/366–0549 or 0800/654–321* ⊕ *www.hertz.co.nz*). **Maui Motorhomes** (✉ *530 Memorial Ave.* ☎ *03/358–4159 or 0800/651–080* ⊕ *www.maui.co.nz*).

Train Information **TranzAlpine and TranzCoastal** (☎ *0800/872–467* ⊕ *www. tranzscenic.co.nz*).

Train Station **Christchurch Railway Station** (✉ *Troup Dr.* ☎ *03/341–2588*).

WHAT TO SEE

❺ **Antigua Boatshed.** Built for the Christchurch Boating Club in 1882, this green-and-white wooden structure is the last shed standing of a half dozen that once lined the Avon. On sunny days, punts and canoes ply the river paddled by visitors and families alike. Join them by renting a boat and taking a champagne picnic into the Botanic Gardens or punting farther up into the woodlands of Hagley Park, spectacular in autumn and spring. Even winter has its own charm. The boat shed has a licensed café (open for breakfast and lunch) with a deck overlooking the Avon. ✉ *2 Cambridge Terr.* ☎ *03/366–5885 boat shed, 03/366–6768 café* ⊕ *www.boatsheds.co.nz* ☎ *Single canoe $8 per hr, double canoe $16 per hr, rowboat $25 per hr (3–4 people), punting $20 per person (minimum 2 people) per ½ hr* ☉ *Dec.–Apr., daily 9–4:30; May–Nov., daily 9–4.*

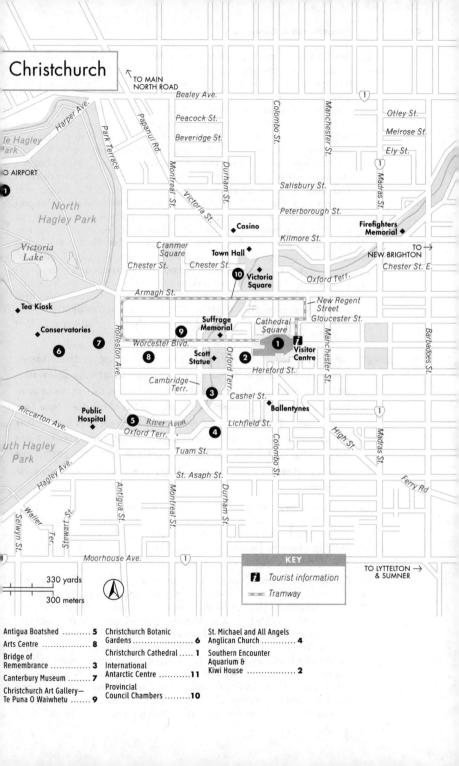

Christchurch

↖ TO MAIN NORTH ROAD

Bealey Ave.

Peacock St.

Beveridge St.

Harper Ave.

Te Hagley Park

O AIRPORT

North Hagley Park

Victoria Lake

Tea Kiosk

Conservatories

Public Hospital

Riccarton Ave.

uth Hagley Park

Hagley Ave.

Park Terrace

Papanui Rd.

Montreal St.

Victoria St.

Durham St.

Colombo St.

Manchester St.

Otley St.

Melrose St.

Ely St.

Salisbury St.

Peterborough St.

Kilmore St.

Casino

Town Hall

Cranmer Square

Chester St.

Chester St.

Victoria Square

Armagh St.

Rolleston Ave.

Worcester Blvd.

Suffrage Memorial

Scott Statue

Cambridge Terr.

Oxford Terr.

Oxford Terr.

Hereford St.

Cashel St.

Lichfield St.

River Avon

Tuam St.

St. Asaph St.

Colombo St.

Cathedral Square

New Regent Street

Gloucester St.

Visitor Centre

Ballentynes

Firefighters Memorial

TO → NEW BRIGHTON

Chester St. E.

Oxford Terr.

Madras St.

Manchester St.

High St.

Madras St.

Barbadoes St.

Antigua St.

Montreal St.

Durham St.

Selwyn St.

Waller Ter.

Stewart St.

Moorhouse Ave.

Ferry Rd

TO LYTTELTON → & SUMNER

330 yards

300 meters

KEY

🅸 Tourist information

Tramway

Antigua Boatshed 5

Arts Centre 8

Bridge of Remembrance 3

Canterbury Museum 7

Christchurch Art Gallery— Te Puna O Waiwhetu 9

Christchurch Botanic Gardens 6

Christchurch Cathedral 1

International Antarctic Centre 11

Provincial Council Chambers 10

St. Michael and All Angels Anglican Church 4

Southern Encounter Aquarium & Kiwi House 2

❽ Arts Centre. By moving to the suburbs in the 1970s, Canterbury University left vacant a fine collection of Gothic Revival stone buildings, which were then transformed into this terrific arts, shopping, and dining complex. Beside the center's information desk in the clock tower you'll find **Rutherford's Den,** where physicist Ernest Rutherford (1871–1937), the university's most illustrious student, conducted early experiments in radioactivity. It was Rutherford who first succeeded in splitting the atom, a crucial step in the harnessing of atomic power. In 1908 Rutherford's work earned him the Nobel Prize—not for physics but for chemistry. Now a dynamic multimedia presentation depicts Rutherford and daily life in the 1890s at Canterbury College, as the campus was known then. The Arts Centre houses more than 40 specialty shops and studios, as well as art galleries, theaters, and art-house cinemas. It's an excellent stop for food, coffee, or a glass of wine—there are several cafés and a wine bar. At the **Saturday and Sunday Market** you'll find jewelry, prints, and handmade clothing and crafts, as well as food stalls. Free live entertainment kicks off at noon on weekends and goes until 3 PM. Stop by the information desk to join one of the free guided tours, offered daily from 10 to 3:30. ⊠ *Worcester Blvd. between Montreal St. and Rolleston Ave.* ☎ *03/363–2836 tours, 03/366–0980* ⊕ *www. artscentre.org.nz* ☉ *Shops and galleries daily 10–5; Rutherford's Den daily 10–5.*

> **NEED A BREAK?**
>
> The Arts Centre has several eateries in its stone buildings and quadrangles. **Dux de Lux** (☎ *03/366–6919*) is a sprawling, upbeat, cafeteria-style restaurant in a mock-Tudor building on the Montreal Street side of the campus. The huge courtyard is a great spot to enjoy a beer from the on-site boutique brewery. The **Backstage Bakery** (☎ *03/377–7948*) turns out specialty breads daily—try their delicious sourdough or ciabatta. It's in the center of the complex. **Annies Wine Bar** (⊠ *41 Hereford St.* ☎ *03/365–0566*) is the most refined option, a pleasant place to taste New Zealand wine alongside bistro fare.

❸ Bridge of Remembrance. Arching over Cashel Street, this Oamaru limestone memorial arch was built in memory of the soldiers who crossed the river here from King Edward Barracks (demolished a few years ago to build a parking lot) on their way to the battlefields of Europe during World War I. ⊠ *Avon River at Cashel St.*

❼ Canterbury Museum. When this museum was founded in 1867, its trading power with national and international museums was in moa bones. These Jurassic birds roamed the plains of Canterbury and are believed to have been hunted to extinction by early Māori. The museum still houses one of the largest collections of artifacts from the moa hunting period. You'll also find a natural-history Discovery center where kids can handle bones and fossils. The Hall of Antarctic Discovery charts the links between the city and Antarctica, from the days when Captain Cook's ship skirted the continent in a small wooden ship. Among the 20th-century explorers celebrated here are the Norwegian Roald Admundsen, who was first to visit the South Pole, and Captain Robert

Falcon Scott, who died returning from the continent. (Follow local tradition and rub the nose of the bronze sculpture of Amundsen's head for good luck.) The café looks out over the Botanic Gardens. ✉️ *Rolleston Ave.* 🕿 *03/366–5000* ⊕ *www.canterburymuseum.com* 🖃 *Free admission, donations appreciated; Discovery exhibition $2* 🕘 *Oct.–Mar., daily 9–5:30; Apr.–Sept., daily 9–5.*

Captain Robert Falcon Scott statue. *Scott of the Antarctic* (1868–1912), who stayed in Christchurch while preparing for his two Antarctic expeditions, is memorialized by this unfinished white marble statue sculpted by his widow, Kathleen. It's inscribed DO NOT REGRET THIS JOURNEY, WHICH SHOWS THAT ENGLISHMEN CAN ENDURE HARDSHIPS, HELP ONE ANOTHER AND MEET DEATH WITH AS GREAT FORTITUDE AS EVER IN THE PAST. Scott wrote these words in his diary as he and his party lay dying in a blizzard on their return journey from the South Pole—a story of endurance taught to all New Zealand schoolkids. ✉️ *Worcester Blvd. and Oxford Terr.*

❾ Christchurch Art Gallery—Te Puna O Waiwhetu. The city's art gallery wows visitors as much for its architecture as for its artwork. Its tall, wavy glass facade was inspired by Christchurch's Avon River and the shape of the native *koru* fern. Outside the building is a growing collection of sculpture, and the downstairs galleries hold special national and international exhibitions. Free guided tours, entertaining events and family activities, and iPod audio tours make the Gallery a must-see. Shop for a great selection of gifts, or relax at Alchemy Cafe and Wine Bar. The museum's Māori name refers to an artesian spring on the site and means "the wellspring of star-reflecting waters." ✉️ *Worcester Blvd. and Montreal St.* 🕿 *03/941–7300* ⊕ *www.christchurchartgallery.org. nz* 🖃 *Free* 🕘 *Daily 10–5, late night Wed. to 9.*

❻ Christchurch Botanic Gardens. One of the largest city parks in the world,
★ these superb gardens are known for the magnificent trees planted here
🕙 in the 19th century. Pick up the Historic Tree Walk brochure from the information center for a self-guided Who's Who tour of the tree world. Spend time in the conservatories to discover tropical plants, cacti, and ferns on days when you'd rather not be outside. Go to the New Zealand plants area at any time of the year. ✉️ *Rolleston Ave.* 🕿 *03/366–1701* 🖃 *Free* 🕘 *Daily 7 AM–dusk, conservatories daily 10:15–4.*

❶ Christchurch Cathedral. The city's dominating landmark was begun in 1864, 14 years after the arrival of the Canterbury Pilgrims, and it wasn't completed until 1904. Carvings inside commemorate the work of the Anglican missionaries, including Tamihana Te Rauparaha, the son of a fierce and, for the settlers, troublesome Māori chief. Free guided tours begin daily at 11 and 2. For a view across the city to the Southern Alps, climb the 133 steps to the top of the bell tower. The cathedral is known for its boys' choir, which sings evensong at 4:30 on Friday; the full choir sings evensong on Tuesday and Wednesday, and the men's evensong is every Thursday at 5:30. **Cathedral Square,** the city's focal point, buzzes with an arts-and-crafts market on Thursday and Friday, complete with food stalls and street musicians. ✉️ *Cathedral Sq.*

8

☎ *03/366–0046*   ⊕ *www.christchurchcathedral.co.nz*   🖾 *Tower $5*
⊙ *Mon.–Sat. 9–5, Sun. 7.30–5* .

★ **Christchurch Tramway.** Jump on the tram for a quick whiz round the central city sights. A ticket gives you 48 hours to hop on and off and visit many of the choice spots—the **Arts Centre** in Worcester Boulevard with its cafés, working artists, and craft markets on weekends; the **Canterbury Museum,** where you can check out the historical development of the region; **Christchurch Cathedral** and **Cathedral Square,** the hub of the city center and where all roads lead. The **Christchurch Art Gallery—Te Puna Wai O Waiwhetu** has some exciting architecture and sculpture on the outside and interesting collections inside; **New Regent Street** is a tiny art deco shopping street; and **Hagley Park** and **Victoria Square** combine leafy green walks with some history along the way. The circuit, without any stops, will only take 20 minutes. ⊠ *Worcester Blvd.*   ☎ *03/366–7830* ⊕ *www.tram.co.nz* 🖾 *$14.*

Firefighters Memorial. Local artist Graham Bennett used crooked girders from the collapsed World Trade Center in this memorial sculpture. The work is dedicated not only to the firefighters who died in New York on September 11, 2001, but also to other firefighters who have died in the course of duty. You can reach the memorial along the riverside path; sit awhile in the small park beside the Avon, not far from the central fire station. ⊠ *Kilmore and Madras Sts.*

♻ **Hagley Park.** Once cultivated Māori land, Hagley Park was developed by Pākehā settlers in the mid-1800s, with imported plants given trial runs in what would become the Botanic Gardens *(⇨ Christchurch Botanic Gardens, above).* Now the park is divided into four sections, which together include walking and jogging tracks, cycling paths, and self-guided historic tours. Hagley Park North draws people to its tennis and *pétanque* (boccie) courts; Little Hagley Park is classified as a Heritage area. ⊠ *Main entrance: Armagh St. at Rolleston Ave.*

⑩ **Provincial Council Chambers.** This complex of Gothic Revival stone buildings beside the Avon River was once the seat of Canterbury's government, which ran from 1853 to 1876. The elaborate decorations include a painted ceiling, stone carvings, and stained-glass windows. It now houses a small museum devoted to the building's history. A large clock intended for the tower proved too big and stands a few blocks away, at the intersection of Victoria, Salisbury, and Montreal streets. ⊠ *Durham St. at Gloucester St.* ☎ *03/941–7680* 🖾 *Free* ⊙ *Mon.–Sat. 10:30–3.*

➍ **St. Michael and All Angels Anglican Church.** One of the bells in this church's belfry came out with the Canterbury Pilgrims on one of the first four ships and was rung hourly to indicate time for early settlers; it is still rung every day. The white-timber church was built in 1872, entirely of matai, a native black pine, and sits on rubble stone foundations. Their original building was the first church to be built in Christchurch. ⊠ *Oxford Terr. at Durham St.* ☎ *03/379–5236* ⊙ *Mon.–Thurs. 8.30–5, Fri. 10–4.*

② **Southern Encounter Aquarium & Kiwi House.** The giant aquarium has an enormous variety of New Zealand fish species—from rocky tidal-pool creatures to those from lakes, rivers, and the briny deep. You can touch some of these critters in the Touch Tank. Watch divers feed giant eels carpet sharks, cod, and skate. ■TIP➔**Try to be there for the salmon and trout feeding at 1** PM. The entrance is through the visitor center or Pathway Shop. ✉*Cathedral Sq.* ☎*03/359–7109* ⊕*www. southernencounter.co.nz* ✉*Adults $15, children $5* ⊙*Daily 9–5, kiwis on display 10:30–4:30; last entry at 4:30.*

> **BOAT TOUR**
>
> Sit back and enjoy the diverse architecture of the central city from water level, framed by weeping willows and ornate bridges. The boat tours leave from the Worcester Street Bridge, near the corner of Oxford Terrace, daily from 9 to 8 in summer and from 10 to 4 the rest of the year. A 30-minute trip costs $20. Call ahead or just stop at the landing. **Punting on the Avon** (✉ *Worcester Blvd. bridge landing* ☎*03/353–5994*).

Suffrage Memorial. Unveiled in 1993, this bronze memorial wall commemorates 100 years of votes for women. New Zealand was the first country in the world to grant women the vote, and Christchurch resident Kate Sheppard played a key role in petitioning Parliament for this essential right. The vote for all women over 21, including Māori women, was granted on September 19, 1893; the work of Sheppard and other activists is celebrated each year on that date at the memorial. ✉*Oxford Terr.*

Victoria Square. This square was named for Queen Victoria in her Jubilee year. On its north side sits the striking Town Hall, with its auditorium, theater, and conference spaces. Nearby stands a *poupou,* a tall carved wood column, acknowledging the site's history as a trading point between Māori and the European settlers. You'll also see Christchurch's oldest iron bridge, a floral clock, two fountains, including one that's illuminated with colored lights at night, and statues of Queen Victoria and Captain Cook. ✉*Armagh and Colombo Sts.*

WHAT TO SEE BEYOND CENTRAL CHRISTCHURCH

★ **Christchurch Gondola.** From high on the Port Hills east of the city, the gondola is the best vantage point to view Christchurch, the Canterbury Plains, and Lyttelton Harbour. At the top, you can journey through the **Time Tunnel** to experience the history and geological evolution of the Canterbury region, and there's a one-hour guided walk that leaves from the Summit Station at 11 AM and 1 PM ($20). Afterward, sit with a glass of local wine at the Summit Café or Pinnacle Restaurant. Ride the gondola with your back to the Port Hills for the best views of the Southern Alps. The adventurous can walk or mountain-bike back down *(Sports & the Outdoors, below).* If you don't have a car, you can hop a number 28 bus from the city center; the Best Attractions Direct bus also includes the gondola. ✉*10 Bridle Path Rd., Heathcote* ☎*03/384–0700* ⊕*www.gondola.co.nz* ✉*$22* ⊙*Daily 10–9.*

8

⑪ **International Antarctic Centre.** Ever since Scott wintered his dogs at nearby
★ Quail Island in preparation for his ill-fated South Pole expedition of
☾ 1912, Christchurch has maintained a close connection with the frozen
continent. You can experience a small taste of the modern polar experience. For instance, bundle up in extra clothing (provided) and brave
a simulated storm in which a bitingly cold wind chills the room to 25
degrees below for a few minutes. Or you could take a ride on the Häg-
glund vehicle used to get around the ice. The audiovisual show of life
at New Zealand's Scott Base is superb, and the new Penguin Encounter
lets you get up close with some blue penguins, the smallest penguin species. It's roughly 20 minutes from central Christchurch by car or on the
Penguin Express shuttle. There's even a free shuttle directly from the
airport. ⊠ *Orchard Rd., Harewood* ☎ *03/353–7798* ⊕ *www.iceberg.
co.nz* ⊠ *$30; including Hägglund tour ride $48* ⊙ *Oct.–Mar., daily
9–7; Apr.–Sept., daily 9–5:30.*

Mona Vale. One of Christchurch's great historic homesteads, the riverside Mona Vale, was built in 1899. The house and garden have been
part of the city since 1967—when the estate was "sold" to individual
Christchurch residents for $10 per square foot. Come for lunch or
Devonshire tea, and you can make believe that you're strolling through
your own grounds along the Avon as you wander under the trees and
through the well-tended perennial gardens. The Fernery sits in the
building used in the 1907 International Exhibition, and the Blue and
White Border garden is worth a look. Pick up their handy map so you
don't miss anything. If the mood really takes you, go for a punt ride.
Catch a number 9 bus from the city; there's a stop outside the front gate
near the gingerbread gatehouse (which is not open to the public). ⊠ *63
Fendalton Rd., Fendalton* ⊕ *2 km (1 mi) from city center* ☎ *03/941–
8999* ⊕ *www.monavale.co.nz* ⊠ *Free* ⊙ *Grounds: daily 7 AM to 1 hr
after dusk; gates open 24 hrs to pedestrians, only vehicle access closes.
Café hs: summer (mid-Sept –mid-Mar.), daily 9:30–5; winter (mid-Mar
–mid-Sept.), Wed.–Sun. 10–3. Closed Mon. and Tues. in winter.*

Ngā Hau e Whā national marae. The "marae of the four winds" is the
largest urban *marae, or* cultural center and meetinghouse, in New Zealand. You can book a tour (tours run 10–noon and 1–3) to see the
striking carvings on the gate, two meetinghouses, and flagpole. Better
yet, sign up for the evening "Night of Māori Magic," starting at 5:45
PM, which includes a tour, cultural performance, and *hāngi* (earth-oven)
dinner. You'll have a chance to see a *powhiri* (welcome ceremony),
action songs, *poi* (balls rhythmically swung on strings), and the *haka*
(war dance). This is not a hands-off experience; you'll be encouraged
to join in and to take photos. The marae is a 10-minute drive northeast
of central Christchurch; to get here by bus take the number 5 bus to
Southshore or New Brighton and ask for the marae stop. All bookings are subject to minimum numbers, and reservations are essential.
⊠ *250 Pages Rd., Aranui* ☎ *03/388–7685* ✉ *nhewmarae@xtra.co.nz*
⊠ *"Night of Māori Magic" $85; tour and concert only $45; daytime
tour $15* ⊙ *Weekdays 9–4:30.* ⊙ *Closed mid-Dec.–mid-Jan.*

☉ **Willowbank.** In addition to familiar farm animals and other zoo regulars, Willowbank has a section devoted to New Zealand wildlife. Here you can have a close encounter with the cheeky mountain parrot, the *kea*. Kiwi can be viewed in an artificially darkened area from 10:30 AM to 10 PM. You can get a special viewing of the native animals on the Māori cultural tour given from **Ko Tane,** a reproduction Māori village. You'll be greeted with a *wero,* a traditional welcome, and you can try your hand at swinging poi, flaxen balls on long strings used in traditional Māori dances (it's not as easy as it looks). The Ko Tane tour starts at $39, with a Kiwi Tour it is $49, and $89 if you include a Taste NZ Buffet Dinner (reservations advised for the dinner). There are guided tours through the "New Zealand Natural Area"—where the native animals are—at 11:30 and 2:30 on request and scheduled tours hourly between 6:30 PM and 9:30 PM in summer. To get here without a car, use the Best Attractions bus. Ko Tane Māori Cultural Performance provides complimentary return transport from the city center. ✉ *60 Hussey Rd., Harewood* ☎ *03/359–6226* ⊕ *www.willowbank.co.nz* ✉ *$21* ☉ *Daily 9:30–dusk.*

SPORTS & THE OUTDOORS

BEACHES

☉ The three main beaches around Christchurch are Sumner Beach, New Brighton Beach, and Taylor's Mistake. **Sumner Beach** is pleasant for the long, relaxing walk between Shag Rock and Scarborough Hill. Walk the first section along the sand to Cave Rock, which you can climb or walk through at low tide; it has wonderful acoustics. Walk the rest of the way along the esplanade, as the beach is fairly rocky. Sumner Village is based around the Cave Rock area, and there are a number of restaurants, including one right on the beach. You can catch a number 30 bus if you don't have a car.

New Brighton Beach, about 8 km (5 mi) from the city center, is popular with surfers and fishers. The long pier that goes well out into the surf is a great place to stroll when the sea is calm, but even better when it's rough. The number 5 bus goes here. Experienced surfers prefer **Taylor's Mistake** because the waves are higher. You can drive there over the Scarborough Hill or walk over a track, but there is no public transport. If you're lucky, you'll see tiny, rare Hector's dolphins playing off Sumner Head on your way out.

BICYCLING

Christchurch's relative flatness makes for easy biking, and the city has cultivated good resources for cyclists. White lines, and sometimes red-color tarmac, denote cycling lanes on city streets, and holding bays are at the ready near intersections. You can pick up a route map from the city council; a particularly nice paved pedestrian and cycling path is along the Avon running from the Bridge of Remembrance. Other popular cycle trails include the Rail Trail at Little River and the spectacular trails around the Port Hills.

Cycles can be rented from **Cyclone Cycles** (✉*245 Colombo St.* ☎*03/332–9588*) for around $30 for half a day, including helmet, and $80 a week. Closed Sunday. **City Cycle Hire** (✉*73 Wrights Rd., Addington* ☎*03/339–4020 or 0800/343–848* ⊕*www.cyclehire-tours.co.nz*) has mountain, touring, and tandem bikes. Rentals include helmets, locks, and cycle map and costs about $25 for a half day and $35 for a full day; they'll deliver your bike to your accommodation. The **Mountain Bike Adventure Company** (✉*73 Wrights Rd., Addington* ☎*03/339–4020 or 0800/424–534*) offers a $60 package including a ride up on the Christchurch Gondola to the summit station. Then there's the choice of either an off-road mountain-bike trail or a scenic road route down to the beach and back to the Gondola base—cycle distance or approximately 16 km (10 mi).

★ **Little River Rail Trail Day Cycle Tour** ☎*03/339–4020* 🎫*$100 per person* ☾*Sept.–May*) follows the new Little River Rail Trail with all off-road flat cycling around Lake Ellesmere. Ideal for a family group with a cycling distance of 19 km (12 mi). Bookings are essential for this full-day trip, and return transfers to Little River are included. Bring insect repellent to stave off the sandflies.

GOLF

With extensive views of Mt. Hutt and Rakaia Gorge, the 18-hole championship course at **Terrace Downs** (✉*Coleridge Rd.* ☎*03/318–6943 or 0800/465–373* ⊕*www.terracedowns.co.nz*) has to be one of the most scenic courses in the South Island. You can rent equipment, and you can even book a villa for the night. The luxurious suites and chalets overlook the golf course and the mighty Southern Alps. Green fees start at $125 per person for 18 holes. The 18-hole championship golf course at the **Clearwater Golf Club** (✉*Clearwater Ave.* ☎*03/360–1103* ⊕*www.clearwaternz.com*) was built on the old Waimakariri riverbed near Christchurch Airport. Home to the NZPGA Championship, it is playable year-round and offers a choice of five tee positions. The green fee is $130; rental equipment is on hand.

HORSE TREKKING

Horse whisperer Kate Tapley and her team guide gentle rides with **Otahuna Horse Riding** (✉*Rhodes Rd., Tai Tapu* ☎*03/329–0160* ⊕*www.otahunariding.co.nz*), set near a historic estate up around the Port Hills. To aid horse/rider connection, each ride begins with a partnering session. You'll have stunning views of the Canterbury Plains and the encircling mountain ranges from your saddle. Guided rides start at $90 for 2½ hours; $200 for a full day. Overnight ride to Governors Bay are available for $300.

RUGBY

Canterbury fans are as rugby-mad as the rest of the country. In fact the first match ever played in New Zealand took place in 1862 in Cranmer Square, in central Christchurch. Every Saturday in winter you can catch little All-Blacks-in-the-making playing games in Hagley Park and suburban parks. Then cheer the Crusaders, the Canterbury rugby team, on their home turf at **Jade Stadium** (✉*30 Stevens St.,*

Phillipstown ☎*03/379–1765* ⊕*www.jadestadium.co.nz).*The season runs from February through September. The stadium also hosts All Blacks games and international cricket matches.

WHERE TO EAT

For bargain eats around Christchurch, look to the simpler restaurants such as Winnie Bagoes on Gloucester Street, a good steak meal from Bealey's Speights Ale House on Bealey Avenue, or pizza or pasta from the Spagalimis chain. For a really cheap take-out meal, you can't beat the price of fish-and-chips or a burger bought at the local take-out store and eaten from the paper wrapping.

$$$$ ⚔**Pescatore.** This second-floor restaurant looking out to Hagley Park
★ is known for creative, Pacific Rim cuisine. Presentation is thoughtful and sometimes spectacular. Seafood dominates the menu, with New Zealand specialties such as roasted Akaroa salmon, char-grilled tuna, or Chatham Island groper and Kaikoura crayfish; there are also a few starters such as scallops and oysters. But for a real treat try the five- or seven-course degustation experience. The "Fang au chocolat" dessert exemplifies the restaurant's theatrical presentations, with its foot-long spikes firing out of a chocolate cylinder filled with two-toned chocolate mousse. There's an extensive wine list. ✉*50 Park Terr.* ☎*03/371–0257* ▱*AE, DC, MC, V* ☾Closed Sun. and Mon. June–Aug.. *No lunch.*

$$$$ ⚔**Saggio di vino.** Wine is the raison d'être for this long-established
★ Christchurch vinotheque on a prominent corner on Victoria Street, but it's also sought out for its truffles in season, from Gisborne and north Canterbury. Truffles are fairly new to New Zealand restaurants, and here you can indulge in a special menu that uses the famous fungi in nearly every dish. The short daily menu can include rack of lamb, fettuccine with pesto, or antipasto, according to season. The wine list has around 300 choices. Book ahead. ✉*185 Victoria St.* ☎*03/379–4006* ▱*AE, DC, MC, V* ☾*No lunch.*

$$$$ ⚔**Sign of the Takahe.** From this spectacular restaurant halfway up the Port Hills, you'll have superb views over Christchurch and the Canterbury Plains to the Southern Alps. The castlelike structure was part of an early-1900s plan to build a series of inns along the Summit Road, all the way to Akaroa. The plan was only partially realized, but the restaurant is a long-standing local favorite for its silver-service style and reinterpretations of classic Kiwi dishes. This imposing place suffers from mixed reviews at times, but new management is turning that around. Try the merino lamb rubbed with peppery horopito and wild briar rose for a distinctly local flavor. ✉*200 Hackthorne Rd., Cashmere* ☎*03/332–4052* ▱*AE, DC, MC, V.*

$$$–$$$$ ⚔**Canterbury Tales.** This fine dining spot is one of three restaurants in
★ the Crowne Plaza Hotel. Service shines, while the lights are low and the music subdued. The menu has local fish, meats, veggies, and seasonal treats like asparagus and truffles. The monkfish wrapped in prosciutto and spinach, with truffle croquets and a saffron mussel fumet, is delicious. The desserts are excellent, and a glossary in the menu helps with the exotic culinary terms. ✉*Kilmore and Durham Sts.* ☎*03/365–7799*

8

Ext. 360 ⊟*AE, DC, MC, V* ⊙*Closed Sun. and Mon. mid-Sept.–mid-Apr.; closed Sun.–Wed. mid-Apr.–mid-Sept. No lunch.*

$$$–$$$$ ✕**Curator's House.** Here you can dine in a 1920s house, looking out on the Botanic Gardens and the Peacock Fountain, or take a garden table and be part of it. The menu has tapas selections and a good variety of seafood, and chef Javier adds Spanish flair with a grand paella. The kitchen garden supplies herbs, berries, and vegetables to the restaurant. ⊠*7 Rolleston Ave.* ☎*03/379–2252* ⊟*AE, MC, V.*

$$$–$$$$ ✕**Sala Sala.** Although the decor is aging, this is generally considered to be Christchurch's top Japanese restaurant. Sala Sala wins praise for its ability to pair wines and sake with its dishes. Diners can choose from sushi, sashimi, teriyaki, tempura, teppanyaki, or traditional kaiseki set meals. The teppanyaki bar gives the chefs the opportunity to demonstrate their considerable skills with flames and flashing utensils. You might not recognize all the ingredients, but they will be fresh and delicious. ⊠*184–186 Oxford Terr.* ☎*03/366–6755* ⊟*AE, DC, MC, V* ⊙*No lunch weekends.*

$$–$$$$ ✕**Cook'n with Gas.** Canterbury foods get the treatment in this charming old house (once the university chaplain's house) with rabbit, lamb, and whitebait on the menu. To go truly local, try some James Cook spruce beer—a modified version of the beer first brewed by the captain in Dusky Sound in 1773, from *rimu* and *manuka* tree twigs—which is reputed to have six times the antioxidants of mere vegetables. It's one of many boutique beers and local wines offered here. Bookings are recommended, and essential Friday and Saturday. You can book up to 10 days ahead online. ⊠*23 Worcester Blvd.* ☎*03/377–9166* ⊕*www.cooknwithgas.co.nz* ⊟*AE, DC, MC, V* ⊙*Closed Sun. and public holidays. No lunch.*

$$–$$$$ ✕**50 on Park.** Don't miss the breakfasts at this restaurant in the George
Fodor'sChoice   Hotel, where you can look out at early-morning joggers in Hagley ★   Park. Start with the likes of homemade baked beans on ciabatta or a smoked groper hash with poached eggs and spinach. Or for something really different try the black rice pudding (this is breakfast, remember) made with coconut milk and toasted coconut. Unusual for New Zealand, there's no eggs Benedict in sight! In the evenings, you can choose from Canterbury lamb, roasted pork roulade, or grilled poussin with a tropical fruit salsa and red curry sauce. ⊠*50 Park Terr.* ☎*03/371–0250* ⊟*AE, DC, MC, V.*

$$–$$$$ ✕**Indochine.** Cross the threshold of this highly rated, mysterious black
Fodor'sChoice   box and you'll be welcomed by a glass bowl of floating yellow chry- ★   santhemums and candles. The space is an intriguing mix of Christchurch and Asia—clearly, the interior designer had fun creating various intimate corners, large group spaces, and a leafy back courtyard. The menu also stretches between the two cultures; nowhere else would you find *sung choi bao* (a dish made with minced pork and finely diced vegetables) done quite like this. Finish with a latte and something unexpected: a little "fullstop," a marble-size orange-and-chocolate candy. ⊠*209 Cambridge Terr.* ☎*03/365–7323* ⌂*Reservations essential* ⊟*AE, MC, V* ⊙*No lunch.*

$-$$$$ ✕**Sticky Fingers.** The Oxford Terrace strip isn't just for evenings. This place is a nice breakfast spot overlooking the Avon River. It was apparently named for its previous life as a pizzeria. Breakfast has standards like eggs a dozen different ways and a big fry-up. But they also have less common breakfasts like sirloin steak with all the trimmings or roasted chorizo sausage with French toast and a mushroom potato cake. You can forget lunch at that point. Both the food and the coffee are good, and the big-screen TVs are thankfully muted. ⊠*Oxford Terr.* ☎*03/366–6452* ⊟*AE, DC, MC, V.*

$$-$$$ ✕**The Cornershop Bistro.** Just a block back from Sumner Beach this urban-style establishment has drummed up a very loyal local clientele. It's a busy café during the day before morphing in to something a little more serious at night. The organic chicken is always popular, either as coq au vin or roasted and served with pancetta, seasonal vegetables, and a lemon butter sauce. Their eggs Benedict and coffee are also predictably good. ⊠*32 Nayland St., Sumner* ☎*03/326–6720* ⊘*Closed Mon. and Tues.*

$$-$$$ ✕**Dux de Lux.** This Arts Centre vegetarian and seafood restaurant inhabits a mock Tudor-style building that was once the university's student center. You'll usually find Akaroa salmon on the menu, along with vegetarian picks such as pasta or quesadillas. The courtyard is popular for dining in summer, particularly on weekends during the market and live music performances. The Dux complex also has a boutique brewery, cocktail lounge, and live bands four nights a week, and was recently voted Pub of the Year. The restaurant has counter service only and can be busy at times, especially Friday evenings. Occasionally reviews are mixed, but the standard is usually very good. ⊠*Hereford and Montreal Sts.* ☎*03/366–6919 or 03/366–6918* ⊟*AE, MC, V.*

$-$$$ ✕**Megawatt–Urban Food Kitchen.** Lighted by early-20th-century street lamps, the Kitchen combines a European-style coffeehouse with an à la carte restaurant featuring seasonal dishes of German and French influence. There are also lots of gluten-free and vegetarian options. ■TIP→**Insider tip: the chef encourages his regular guests to cross the road to the City Seafood Market and pick out fish they'd like cooked.** The desserts are scrumptious—you don't need a food allergy to enjoy the gluten-free dark "chocolate thrill." Megawatt is aptly named, as the meter near the front counter reads how much power the North Canterbury network is using. ⊠*218 Manchester St.* ☎*03/363–9680* ⊟*MC, V* ⊘*Closed early Jan. No dinner Sat.–Tues.*

$-$$$ ✕**Raj Mahal.** The Raj Mahal invites you on a gastronomic tour of India; ★ you can try tandoori from the Punjab, fish masala from Goa, or a vegetarian curry spiced according to your preference. The restaurant uses contemporary as well as traditional Indian methods, so there's no pork, no beef, and no fusion cooking. Of the dozens of Indian restaurants in Christchurch, this is the best for its quality, its sheer variety of dishes, and its uncluttered decor. ⊠*Manchester St. at Worcester Blvd.* ☎*03/366–0521* ⊟*D, MC, V* ⊘*Closed Mon. No lunch.*

8

Where to Stay & Eat in Christchurch

TO MAIN NORTH ROAD

TO AIRPORT

TO AKAROA

Little Hagley Park

North Hagley Park

Victoria Lake

Tea Kiosk

Conservatories

Christchurch Botanic Gardens

South Hagley Park

Arts Centre

Victoria Square

New Regent Street

Cathedral Square

Christchurch Cathedral

River Avon

Bealey Ave.

Peacock St.

Beveridge St.

Salisbury St.

Peterborough St.

Kilmore St.

Armagh St.

Gloucester St.

Hereford St.

Cashel St.

Lichfield St.

Tuam St.

St. Asaph St.

Moorhouse Ave.

Harper Ave.

Park Terrace

Montreal St.

Victoria St.

Durham St.

Colombo St.

Manchester St.

Madras St.

Chester St.

Cambridge Terr.

Oxford Terr.

Otley St.

Melrose St.

Ely St.

Chester St

Cambridge Terr.

Oxford Terr.

Rolleston Ave.

Chester St. W.

Cramer

Square

Worcester Blvd.

Durham St. (The Strip)

Oxford Terr.

Cambridge Terr.

Oxford Terr.

Riccarton Ave.

Hagley Ave.

Antigua St.

Montreal St.

Durham St.

Colombo St.

High St.

Madras St.

Ferry R

Selwyn St.

Waller Terr.

Stewart St.

| 0 | 330 yards |
| 0 | 300 meters |

KEY

① Hotels

❶ Restaurants

🛈 Tourist information

WHERE TO STAY

$$$$
Fodor's Choice
★

🏨 **Charlotte Jane.** Once a girls' school, this 1891 villa now sees pampered guests instead of disciplined students, and its luxurious Victorian style introduces guests to the very English heritage of Christchurch. The centrally located house brims with beautiful elements: the Victorian veranda, a stained-glassed window above the entrance depicting the *Charlotte Jane* (one of the first four ships to bring settlers to Christchurch), a native kauri- and rimu-wood staircase, a rimu-paneled dining room, and period furniture throughout the 10 beautiful guest rooms. **Pros:** Breakfast served in the conservatory restaurant until 10 AM; private, luxury two-bedroom cottage in the garden; on-site restaurant open for dinner Tuesday to Saturday. **Con:** Busy main road location. ⊠ *110 Papanui Rd., Merivale* ☎ *03/355–1028* 🖷 *03/355–8882* ⊕ *www.charlotte-jane.co.nz* 🛏 *12 rooms, 1 cottage* ♨ *In-room: no a/c, VCR. In-hotel: restaurant, bar, laundry service, no elevator, public Internet, no-smoking rooms* ⊟ *AE, MC, V* ⚟ *BP.*

$$$$

🏨 **Elm Tree House.** If you'd prefer a friendly experience away from the city center, this B&B should fit the bill. The 1920s historic house takes its name from the large tree in the front garden. Most of the rooms are upstairs, and each has a distinctive look, from the wood-paneled honeymoon suite to the ground-floor room with French doors that open onto the garden. Papanui sun streams into the enormous lounge through leaded-glass windows, and you can pop an old favorite on the Wurlitzer jukebox. **Pros:** On the main road north from the city, comfy colonial elegance. **Con:** Papanui Road can be noisy with heavy traffic. ⊠ *236 Papanui Rd., Merivale* ☎ *03/355–9731* 🖷 *03/355–9753* ⊕ *www.elmtreehouse.co.nz* 🛏 *6 rooms* ♨ *In-room: Ethernet. In-hotel: laundry service, no elevator* ⊟ *AE, MC, V* ⚟ *BP, CP.*

$$$$
★

🏨 **The George.** In the spacious, modern guest rooms, a crisp, monochromatic color scheme weaves through everything, from the bedside notepads to the luxe bathroom products. Lovely details continually crop up, such as the magnificent brass handles on the entrance door and the verdigris brass banister. It's just a short walk from the Arts Centre and downtown shopping, and the two on-site restaurants, Pescatore and 50 On Park, are top-notch. **Pros:** Consistently voted one of the country's best small hotels, right next to the Avon River and Hagley Park. **Con:** Can be very busy in the public areas with local functions and casual visitors. ⊠ *50 Park Terr.* ☎ *03/379–4560* 🖷 *03/366–6747* ⊕ *www.thegeorge.com* 🛏 *41 rooms, 12 suites* ♨ *In-room: refrigerator, Wi-Fi. In-hotel: 2 restaurants, off-premises gym, laundry facilities, laundry service, parking (no fee)* ⊟ *AE, DC, MC, V*

$$$$

🏨 **Heritage Christchurch.** The Tower Building's rooms are contemporary, whereas the adjacent Old Government Building has suites in an Italian Renaissance style, complete with stained glass and dark-wood paneling. The OGB also has the sports facilities, full gymnasium, heated pool, spa, and sauna in the basement, and Maddison's restaurant is on the ground floor. Watch out for international rugby players, as this is where some of them stay when there's an All Blacks match on at Jade Stadium. **Pros:** Centrally located, a good spa and lap pool help shed some calories. **Con:** Short-term parking can be difficult. ⊠ *28–30 Cathedral Sq.*

8

☎*03/377–9722 or 0800/936–936*
🖷*03/377–9881* ⊕*www.heritage hotels.co.nz* ⊃*135 rooms, 40 suites* ⟳*In-hotel: restaurant, bar, pool, gym, spa* ⊟*AE, DC, MC, V.*

$$$$ 🏠**Otahuna Lodge.** Just 20 minutes from Christchurch and almost hidden by glorious century-old gardens is one of New Zealand's most important historic homes. Built in 1895 for Sir Heaton Rhodes, the three-story homestead has been lovingly restored to its former grandeur, yet has all the modern amenities you would expect in an exclusive luxury lodge. Each of Otahuna's seven suites has a distinctive character and reveals a different element of the Otahuna story. Original fireplaces complement the rooms. Be sure to wander the 30 acres of gardens and take a dip in the heated pool. **Pros:** Country setting on the Canterbury Plains, five-course degustation dinner included, lots of fresh homegrown fruits and vegetables. **Cons:** Not for the budget-minded, a bit out of town. ⊠*224 Rhodes Rd., 17 km (10 mi) from Christchurch, Tai Tapu* ☎*03/329–6333* 🖷*03/329–6336* ⊕*www.otahuna.co.nz* ⊃*7 suites* ⟳*In-room: no a/c. In-hotel: restaurant, gym, tennis court, pool, spa, public Wi-Fi, bicycles, no elevator, no kids under 13* ⊟*AE, MC, V* ⦿*MAP.*

$$$$ 🏠**The Weston House.** Paintings, books, prints, flowers, and objets d'art decorate this carefully restored redbrick Georgian-style house opposite Hagley Park. The pair of spacious suites has private access. You can take breakfast or just relax in the guest lounge, dining area, or secluded garden. The city center is within a 10-minute walk. **Pros:** Beautifully presented property; intimate company with just two guest rooms. **Con:** Only two suites, so book ahead. ⊠*62 Park Terr.* ☎*03/366–0234* 🖷*03/366–5454* ⊕*www.westonhouse.co.nz* ⊃*2 suites* ⟳*In-room: no a/c, Ethernet. In-hotel: bar, laundry service, airport shuttle, no elevator* ⊟*AE, DC, MC, V* ⦿*BP.*

$$$–$$$$ 🏠**The Classic Villa.** What Christchurch has been lacking is a funky, con-
★ temporary style luxury hotel—until now. This bright pink Italian-style villa is directly opposite the Arts Centre. Rooms are beautifully decorated and the amenities and services are tops. Breakfast is Mediterranean style with lots of fruit, cheeses, and cold meats, and is served at the big kitchen table downstairs. The sheltered courtyard is a wonderfully private spot for an evening drink. Children are not allowed, but exceptions are made for small babies. **Pros:** A moment's walk from the city center, fabulous linen and duvets, freshly made gourmet pizza and espresso for breakfast. **Con:** Small off-street parking. ⊠*17 Worcester Blvd.* ☎*03/377–7905* 🖷*03/377–0210* ⊕*www.theclassicvilla.co.nz* ⊃*11 rooms, 1 suite* ⟳*In-room: no a/c, Wi-Fi. In-hotel: no elevator, laundry service* ⊟*AE, DC, MC, V* ⦿*CP.*

$$–$$$$ 🏠**Crowne Plaza.** This plush hotel has a prime location overlooking
★ Victoria Square and the Avon River. You get a good sense of the city from the park-view rooms overlooking Victoria Square, but in winter popularity switches to rooms with views of the snowcapped Alps to the

west. The hotel is especially well equipped with restaurants, including Yamagen for Japanese teppanyaki restaurant and Canterbury Tales for fine dining. A pianist plays in the four-story-high glass-roof atrium at lunch and in the evening. Breakfasts are definitely worth getting out of bed for. **Pros:** In the heart of the city, park view rooms have an enticing view. **Con:** On the city one-way system, so, if driving, your approach for check-in needs to be made from Kilmore Street. ⊠*Kilmore and Durham Sts.* ☎*03/365–7799* 📠*03/365–0082* ⊕*www.crowneplaza. co.nz* ⥥*298 rooms* ⚘*In-room: refrigerator, Ethernet. In-hotel: 3 restaurants, bars, gym, bicycles* ▤*AE, DC, MC, V.*

\$\$–\$\$\$ 🏨 **Riverview Lodge.** This grand Edwardian house overlooking the Avon
★ is one of the finest mid-range B&Bs in Christchurch and is an easy 15-minute walk from the Square. Native timber is used throughout the house. All three guest rooms are upstairs with great balcony views, and breakfast is served in the Turret Room overlooking the garden. **Pros:** Easy access to the city, tram, and Hagley Park; gluten-free breakfast options are available. **Con:** Moderate walk back from town after a night out. ⊠*361 Cambridge Terr.* ☎*03/365–2860* 📠*03/365–2845* ⊕*www.riverview.net.nz* ⥥*3 rooms,* ⚘*In-room: no a/c. In-hotel: bicycles, no elevator* ▤*MC, V* ⭘|*BP*

\$\$ 🏨 **The Chateau on the Park.** Surrounded by 5 acres of landscaped gardens, this Kiwi take on a French château even has its own boutique vineyard that will soon produce its own wine. The main building, with its glass walls and heavy dark wooden beams, has an indoor water garden that wraps around the main entrance and foyer. Rooms are spacious, and all have a view of part of the greenery. **Pros:** Near Hagley Park and a pleasant walk to town, long glass-walled corridors with pleasant garden views, free golf rounds at the Hagley Park golf course. **Con:** In a high-traffic area, so watch when arriving or leaving by car. ⊠*189 Deans Ave.* ☎*03/348–8999 or 0800/808–999* 📠*03/348–8990* ⊕*www. chateau-park.co.nz* ⥥*190 rooms, 6 suites* ⚘*In-room: Ethernet. In-hotel: restaurant, bar, pool, laundry service* ▤*AE, DC, MC, V.*

¢–\$ 🏨 **Base Christchurch.** You can't get any closer to the city center than this upmarket hostel—it's right in Cathedral Square in the former *Christchurch Star* newspaper building. There's an en suite dorm room penthouse with a PS2, Sky TV, private kitchen, and lounge. They keep the fun in-house with the Saints and Sinners bar. On-site breakfast is available for \$7. **Pros:** Women's-only Sanctuary with fluffy pillows, hair-care products, and hair dryers; on the Square in the city. **Con:** A bit hard to "get away from it all" in this busy spot. ⊠*56 Cathedral Sq.* ☎*03/982–2225 or 0800/227–369* 📠*03/982–2226* ⊕*www.stayatbase.com* ⥥*7 rooms (some en suite), 45 dorm rooms* ⚘*In-room: kitchen, no TV (some). In-hotel: bar, public Internet* ▤*AE, MC, V .*

¢–\$ 🏨 **The Old Countryhouse.** This old house is actually two colorful restored villas, both with polished wooden floors and handmade, native-wood furniture. You can whip up breakfast in one of the two large, cheery communal kitchens. The dorm rooms have three to seven beds apiece. It's a 15-minute walk from town but on a bus route, and shops are close by. **Pros:** Pleasant garden to relax in, well heated in winter. **Cons:** Check-in only between 8 AM and 8 PM, no kids under 14, minimum

8

stay requirements in December and January. ⊠*437 Gloucester St.* ☎*03/381–5504* ⊕*www.oldcountryhousenz.com* ⤳*12 private rooms (some en suite), 4 dorm rooms* ⚐*In-room: no phone, no TV, no a/c. In-hotel: kitchen, bar, public Internet, laundry, parking, no kids under 14* ▤*MC, V.*

¢–$ 🏠**Stonehurst Accommodation.** Two blocks from the city center, this
★   cluster of eight bright yellow buildings offers various options, from powered campervan sites and backpacker rooms to well-appointed apartments that can sleep up to six, with two bathrooms, dishwasher, private balcony, and full laundry. **Pros:** Close to the city center and nightspots, good public spaces with nice atmosphere. **Con:** A big complex that can feel like a small village of its own. ⊠*241 Gloucester St.* ☎*03/379–4620 or 0508/786–633* 🖷*03/379–4647* ⊕*www. stonehurst.co.nz* ✉*accom@stonehurst.co.nz* ⤳*46 rooms, 20 motel rooms, 14 apartments, 78 dorm beds* ⚐*In-room: Ethernet, refrigerator, safe (some). In-hotel: bars, pool, parking (no fee), no elevator* ▤*AE, DC, MC, V.*

NIGHTLIFE & THE ARTS

The *Christchurch Press* is a reliable source on the city's arts and entertainment scenes. The Wednesday edition's special arts section lists events and venues, and Thursday's edition has a gig guide on shows and more. You could also check out the Web sites ⊕*www.bethere.org. nz* for arts and entertainment listings and ⊕*www.jagg.co.nz* for information on live music, though it can be a little slow to be updated.

Tickets for many performance venues and concerts are sold through **Ticketek** (☎*03/377–8899* ⊕*http://premier.ticketek.co.nz*). You can find Ticketek outlets in shopping malls or online. If you're out late on a weekend and looking for a cheap way back to your room, try the $5 Midnight Express bus *(see Bus Travel in Christchurch Essentials, above)*, which runs until 4 AM.

THE ARTS

Christchurch has a strong arts scene, with choirs, orchestras, and theater, not to mention dozens of art galleries. Every two years the city hosts a midwinter **Arts Festival** (⊕*www.artsfestival.co.nz*). In alternate years, another biennial arts festival called **SCAPE** (⊕*www.artandindustry.org. nz*) focuses on urban and alternative arts. The next Arts Festival will be in July–August 2009; the next SCAPE will be in spring 2010.

ART GALLERIES   Although the Christchurch Art Gallery Te Puna O Waiwhetu is the mothership of the city's visual arts, there many smaller galleries to check out. For more information, pick up the annually published *Canterbury Arts Trail* booklet at the visitor bureau.

Centre of Contemporary Art (COCA). This gallery actually has a long history of showing contemporary works by Canterbury artists—in fact, it was founded as the Canterbury Society of Arts back in 1880. Now their shows mix established names with up-and-coming, mainly Kiwi artists. One gallery, Artzone, exhibits work by children and runs art classes.

✉*66 Gloucester St.* ☎*03/366–7261* ⊕*www.coca.org.nz* ✉*Donation requested* ⊙ *Weekdays 10–5, weekends noon–4.*

Physics Room. In rooms high above the old High Street Post Office building, the nonprofit Physics Room shows contemporary art (video works, installations, and so on) and occasionally puts on performances, talks, and other public programs. ✉*209 Tuam St., 2nd fl.* ☎*03/379–5583* ⊕*www.physicsroom.org.nz* ⊙*Tues.–Fri. 10–5, Sat. 11–4.*

Te Toi Mana. Māori artist Riki Manuel often carves in this Arts Centre space. The gallery focuses on traditional and contemporary Māori art and is a good place to find creative souvenirs and travel mementos. ✉*Next to the Dux de Lux at the Arts Centre, Hereford St.* ☎*03/366–4943* ⊙*Daily 10–5.*

FILMS   Short film festivals have become popular, particularly in the Christchurch Art Gallery auditorium. Each year in late July or early August there is an international film festival with showings at the Rialto cinema, and it often includes a homegrown section. The independent **Academy Theatre** and **Cloisters Film House** (✉*25 Hereford St.* ☎*03/366–0167* ⊕*www.artfilms.co.nz*) are both in the Arts Centre and are the places to hit for indie and foreign flicks.

MUSIC   If you're here in summer, be sure to check out the **SummerTimes Festival** (⊕*www.summertimes.org.nz*), which includes several free concerts in Hagley Park. The festival kicks off with a New Year's Eve party in Cathedral Square and includes "Classical Sparks," music punctuated with fireworks, usually held in late February or early March. **Town Hall** (✉*86 Kilmore St.*) is host to many performances of the classical persuasion, including those by the **Southern Opera** (☎*03/363–3131*), the **Christchurch City Choir** (☎*03/366–6927* ⊕*www.christchurchcitychoir.co.nz*) whose Christmas "Messiah" always packs the house, and the **Christchurch Symphony Orchestra** (☎*03/379–3886* ⊕*www.chsymph.co.nz*).

THEATER   The **Court Theatre** (✉*Arts Centre, 20 Worcester Blvd.* ☎*03/963–0870, 0800/333–100 bookings* ⊕*www.courttheatre.org.nz*) is New Zealand's leading theater company. In its two auditoriums the company performs everything from Shakespeare to contemporary plays by New Zealand playwrights. The Court also offers children's plays during the holidays; the Court Jesters run the hilarious Scared Scriptless improv-comedy sessions on Friday night (10 to 11:30 PM, $15).

NIGHTLIFE

For concentrated action, one good option is to head to the bars and cafés along the area known as **the Strip.** This is a small section of Oxford Terrace, one of the streets that follow the curves of the Avon River, between Cashel Street and Worcester Boulevard. The end of the Strip near the Bridge of Remembrance has the younger, rowdier crowds. People often spill out onto the footpath, but do all of your drinking in the bars; drinking in public places is banned in parts of the city. The other is the club scene along the area known as South of

8

Lichfield (SOL), with some of the city's most popular dance clubs and late night restaurants.

The **Coyote** (✉ *126 Oxford Terr.* ☎ *03/366–6055*) serves good food during the day and then transforms into a popular bar, with live music on Wednesday evenings. The **Viaduct** (✉ *136 Oxford Terr.* ☎ *03/377–9968*), with its ancient Greek columns and mosaic-tiled counterfront, alludes to a more hedonistic time. But it's an easy place to kick back if you like the music a bit quieter or if you want to enjoy good food with your drinks.**The Base**(✉ *92 Struthers La.* ☎ *03/377–7149* ⊕ *www.thebase.co.nz)* along SOL stays open until morning three nights a week and has a good selection of visiting DJs and House sounds.Head to **Minx** (✉ *96 Lichfield St.* ☎ *03/374–9944* ⊕ *www.minxbar.co.nz)* for cocktails or an excellent meal. Their Rootes Bar is a colorful, eye-catching experience.

For some natural suds in the city center try the **Loaded Hog Bar & Restaurant** (✉ *Manchester and Cashel Sts.* ☎ *03/366–6674*). This brewery produces excellent beers such as Hog Dark and Hog Gold and the food's pretty good, too. The **Victoria Street Cafe** (✉ *Kilmore and Durham Sts.* ☎ *03/365–7799 Ext. 363)* in the imposing atrium of the Crowne Plaza Hotel is a good spot to unwind with a wine or coffee.

For live music head over from the Arts Centre to **Dux de Lux** (✉ *Hereford and Montreal Sts.* ☎ *03/366–6919*), a standby on the local-band circuit. Sometimes there's a cover charge.

Blue Note Piano Bar & Restaurant ✉ *20 Regent St.* ☎ *03/379–9674)* has live music on Wednesday and Thursday evenings 7:30–9:30, and on Friday and Saturday 8–11. Their food is excellent. Live jazz starts at 7:30 Tuesday to Saturday at **Sammy's Jazz Review** (✉ *14 Bedford Row* ☎ *03/377–8618* ⊕ *www.sammys.co.nz)*. When all else has closed, make your way to the 24-hour **Christchurch Casino** (✉ *30 Victoria St.* ☎ *03/365–9999*) for blackjack, American roulette, baccarat, and gaming machines. Dress is smart-casual or better; you will be turned away if you arrive in jeans. Free shuttles go to and from local hotels and motels.

SHOPPING

SHOPPING STREETS

Parts of the **City Mall** area around Cashel and High streets are out of bounds to cars. Major branches of music and clothing chains make up most of the frontage, but there are some one-offs worth stopping like the Vault craft and design boutique and Wild Places for souvenirs, both in the Cashel Mall. Ballantynes, on the corner of Cashel and Colombo streets, is one of the country's better-known department stores.

Graduates from the polytech fashion school only have to cross the road to show their wares on **High Street,** where places such as d'Orsay, Plush, Storm, and Victoria Black display cutting-edge clothes. More daring shoppers seeking amazing jewelry should visit Mask in **Tuam Street.** Secondhand booksellers, antiques and decor stores, and the overflowing Globe café keep things busy. Distinctive and colorful art deco facades line the pedestrian zone of **New Regent Street** between Gloucester and Armagh streets. The buildings are filled with cafés, restaurants, and boutiques. Try Tolaga Bay for cashmere, Boxes for jewelry and floaty scarves, and Cubana for Cuban cigars and coffee. Shoezies stocks embroidered boots. Do watch out for traffic, though; the tram runs right through the sidewalk cafés on its way to the city's newest shopping center, Cathedral Junction.

Victoria Street, which cuts diagonally across the city center's grid pattern out from Bealey Avenue, has a good mix of clothing and decor shops interspersed with cafés. If you need a hat for a wedding or the horse races in November, the Hat Shop has a good range, even for men.

SPECIALTY SHOPS

de Spa Chocolatier's ⊠*663 Colombo St.* ☎*03/379–2203*) delicious sweets pair Belgian chocolate with Kiwi ingredients (fruit for certain fillings, for instance). For a behind-the-scenes look, visit the factory at Ferrymead Heritage Park. **Kathmandu** ⊠*40 Lichfield St.* ☎*03/366–7148*)sells a colorful range of well-priced outdoor clothing, backpacks, accessories, and tents. Base camp for the whole global operation is in Christchurch. There's another branch at 124 Riccarton Road and a Clearance Store at the Tower Junction Mega Centre in Blenheim Road.

Untouched World. All things hip and natural in New Zealand meet up here. While some labels appeal to the backpacker end of the market, Untouched World has much more of a designer edge. Apart from the store's own line of stylish, lifestyle clothing made from Merinomink (a mixture of possum fur and merino wool), organic cotton, and a silky-fine machine-washable organic merino, you'll find New Zealand handcrafted jewelry, natural skin-care products, and great gift ideas. The attached licensed café serves fresh food in its native garden setting. There's also a branch in the Arts Centre in the central city. Both are open dail. ⊠*155 Roydvale Ave., Burnside* ☎*03/357–9399.*

TOURS

BICYCLE
TOURS **Christchurch Bike Tours** (☎*03/366–0337* ⊕*www.chchbiketours.co.nz*) organizes city bicycle tours ($30 per person, limit of 10 people so book ahead), offered daily from November to March. The two-hour route follows the Avon River through the city's parks and gardens before heading back into the city center. Bikes are retro-style with a basket for your goodies, and helmets are provided. Meet at the bike sign outside the visitor center for a 2 PM start.

PRIVATE
GUIDES Descendant of a pre-Adamite (pre-1850) settler, **Jack Tregear** (☎*03/344–5588 or 0800/344–5588* ⊕*www.jtnztours.co.nz*) provides a personal historic tour of Christchurch, covering Lyttelton, Sumner, and the Canterbury Provincial Council buildings. The tour takes just over three hours and includes an elegant morning tea. Jack also takes trips to

Akaroa, the West Coast, and around the South Island and is happy to put a trip together at your request.

SIGHTSEEING TOURS
Christchurch Sightseeing Tours (☎*03/366–9660 or 0508/669–660* ⊕*www. christchurchtours.co.nz*) has three routes: major town sights plus the beaches at Sumner and the Lyttelton Harbour, Heritage homes, and private gardens. Each costs between $40 and $46; book the City tour with one of the others for $75 or all three for $110.

WALKING TOURS
Two-hour guided daily walking tours ($10) of the city led by members of the **Christchurch Personal Guiding Service** (☎*03/379–9679* ✐*chchpgs@ xtra.co.nz*) depart daily at 10 and 1 from the red-and-black kiosk in Cathedral Square. (There is no morning walk from May to September.)

EN ROUTE
If you've left Christchurch a bit late for breakfast, about 30 minutes south stop at the **Dunsandel Store** (✉*Main South Rd., Dunsandel* ☎*03/325–4037* ⊙*Mon.–Thurs. 7–6, Fri–Sun 7*AM*–7:30* PM). It's a fascinating mix of local store, deli, and café, where they sell their own juices, local wines, and excellent food. The cabinets are stuffed with tasty quiches, panini, and baked goods. For an afternoon treat try the old-fashioned, Victorian sponge cake served with lashings of cream and strawberries. There are tables indoors and out, surrounded by a courtyard full of fruit trees and vegetables.

ARTHUR'S PASS & CANTERBURY

East of the city, you can explore the wonderful coastline of Banks Peninsula. The peninsula's two harbors, Lyttelton and Akaroa, were formed from the remnants of two ancient volcanoes; their steep, grassy walls drop dramatically to the sea. Looking north, consider stopping in Waipara and its wineries if you're en route to or from Kaikoura or Hanmer Springs. Hanmer Springs' thermal baths are good for a relaxing soak, or you can ride the white water on the river, ski, or mountain bike. Head south or west of town into the Canterbury Plains countryside, and you can ski at Mt. Hutt or drive the scenic inland highway to Geraldine and Timaru. Where once only sheep and cattle grazed, you're now just as likely to spot deer and ostriches. If you're heading to the West Coast by road or rail, then Arthur's Pass is worth investigating. You should set an entire day aside for any of these side trips, or, better still, stay overnight.

ARTHUR'S PASS

153 km (96 mi) northwest of Christchurch.

Arthur's Pass straddles the Main Divide (the midline of the Alps) and is the major mid-island corridor to the West Coast. The route was first surveyed by Arthur Dudley Dobson during the 1860s as European settlers looked for a quick way through the mountains. The discovery of gold on the West Coast spurred the construction of a road, which was started in 1865. The coach trip from Christchurch was initially a 36-

hour haul over a rough track, through rocky riverbeds and where the travelers had to get out and walk the steepest bits. When the railway arrived, in 1923, the pass's skiing and hiking opportunities came to the fore, and the TranzAlpine train service now offers a supreme way to see this rugged area without getting your shoes dirty.

GETTING HERE & AROUND

For any confident driver the road through Arthur's Pass is a beautiful drive—sealed all the way, but with a few steep, gnarly sections in the middle. The train and bus tours (*see Tours at the end of this chapter*) are good options, but you lose the flexibility to stop and do a walk or follow a waterfall track, or just admire the breathtaking scenery if you're stuck on a tour.

To drive there from Christchurch head out on the West Coast Road—it is very well signposted from town. The turnoff is near the airport. There is only one road over the Alps within 100 km (62 mi) either way so you can't go wrong. The road heads out through the small town of Springfield then heads up towards Porter's Pass and Cass before hitting the real stuff at Arthur's Pass.

ESSENTIALS

Visitor Information Arthur's Pass Visitor Centre (⊠*SH 73, Arthur's Pass* ☎*03/318–9211*). Department of Conservation's Web site (⊕ *www.doc.govt.nz*).

WHAT TO SEE

Arthur's Pass National Park, a spectacular alpine region, is a favorite hiking destination. On the way to the pass, along State Highway 73 from Christchurch, you'll pass the **Castle Hill Conservation Area,** which is filled with interesting rock formations. The gray limestone rocks range in height from 3 to 164 feet and in spring and fall they're tackled by climbers keen to go bouldering. Nearby **Craigieburn Conservation Park** has wonderful beech and fern forests and some great mountain biking trails. Sheltered as they are by the Southern Alps, these parklands get far less precipitation than the western side of the mountains. Still, the area is subject to heavy snowfalls in winter.

The setting is undeniably gorgeous: waterfalls, gorges, alpine herbs and flowers, grasslands, and stunning snowcapped peaks. The landscape and vegetation change dramatically according to the altitude and rainfall, from the drier beech forests and tussock grasslands on the eastern side to the dense forestation on the steep western slopes, which get five times more rain. Above the tree line you'll find snowfields and, between November and March, masses of wildflowers, including giant buttercups. Around the summit you'll also have a good chance of seeing *kea,* the South Island's particularly intelligent and curious mountain parrots.

The west side of the pass has had a bad reputation for its steep, winding, narrow road. The good news is that the highway has been upgraded and a viaduct now eliminates the need to drive through the main slip-prone area. **Arthur's Pass Village,** at 737 meters (2,395 feet), isn't much to speak of, and in bad weather it looks rather forlorn. A couple of

8

restaurants and a store provide basic food supplies, and there are several places to stay, including an excellent wilderness lodge at nearby Cass. There's also a Department of Conservation visitor center to help with enjoying the vast selection of mountains and rivers in the area. Both the Devil's Punchbowl and Bridal Veil Falls are worth the short walk. The tracks are in good condition and, although they're a bit steep and rocky in places, no serious hiking experience is required.

More information on the park is available on the **Department of Conservation's Web site** (⊕*www.doc.govt.nz*) and at the **Arthur's Pass Visitor Centre** (⊠*SH 73, Arthur's Pass* ☎*03/318–9211*).

SPORTS & THE OUTDOORS

Arthur's Pass National Park has plenty of half- and full-day hikes and 11 backcountry trails with overnight huts for backpacking. A popular walk near Arthur's Pass Village is the short Dobson Walk, which crosses the summit. It's a good introduction to subalpine and alpine plants; the alpine flowers are in bloom from November to February. It takes roughly 1½ hours to do the circuit. For a full-day hike, trails leading to the summits of various mountains are found all along State Highway 73. Be prepared for variable weather conditions. Two of the most popular and challenging overnight treks are the Cass Saddle trip and the Minga/Deception route over Goat Pass. For these, you'll need an experienced leader and full gear. The **Department of Conservation Visitor Centre** (☎*03/318–9211* ⊕*www.doc.govt.nz*) has up-to-date information on weather and trail conditions. Fill out an intention form, and remember to let them know when you have completed your trip. The site ⊕*www.softrock.co.nz* is another good source for information on local mountaineering conditions.

WHERE TO STAY & EAT

$–$$$ ✕ **The Wobbly Kea Café and Bar.** This surprisingly pleasant place is named for the cheeky mountain parrots that circle above it day after day. It's open from early in the morning until well into the evening—presuming people are around. The two most popular dishes are their lamb rump salad and the fresh beer-battered fish; both have people asking for more. ⊠*Main Rd.* ☎*03/318–9101.*

$$$$ ☷ **Wilderness Lodge Arthur's Pass.** Surrounded by spectacular peaks,
Fodor'sChoice   beech forests, and serene lakes, this sophisticated (and pricey) back-to-
★   nature lodge shares 6,000 acres with its own working 5,000-sheep farm and nature reserve in a valley called Te Ko Awa a Aniwaniwa (Valley of the Mother of Rainbows) by its first Māori visitors. From a hillside perch it overlooks the Waimakariri River, which has carved a gaping swath through the pass. Rooms have balcony views of this incredible area. By taking advantage of the walks and guided nature day trips with resident biologists (included in the rate), you also get an education in rare high-country ecology. Full-day guided trips in the region can take you to limestone caves, a tranquil lake, a glacier basin, or to spots where you can glimpse rare alpine plants and cheeky kea (the native mountain parrot). There is a sister lodge at Lake Moeraki on the West Coast. **Pros:** On alternate days, guests can muster sheep with border collies and help blade-shear sheep the old-fashioned way; the owners

are committed to preserving the alpine environment. **Cons:** Make sure you're there for a sheep tour, a one-night stop is not enough to experience the activities and environment here. ✉*130 km (81 mi) west of Christchurch on State Hwy. 73, Arthur's Pass* ☎*03/318–9246* ⊕*www. wildernesslodge.co.nz* ⏪*20 rooms, 4 suites* ⌂*In-room: refrigerator, Ethernet, no TV, no a/c. In-hotel: bar, restaurant, laundry service, no elevator* ▭*MC, V* ⊗*Closed June and July* ⏏*MAP.*

¢–$ 🏠**Mountain House Backpackers and Cottages.** Having bought out the neighboring hostels this is now the biggest spot in town. You can sign up for one of the bedrooms in the cottages, reserve an entire cottage, or choose a bed in the four- or eight-person dorm rooms in the main lodge. The decor may be homely, but you can't argue with the impressive peaks right outside your window. **Pros:** A wing of new facilities and private rooms is the pick for clean and tidy; two buildings have Internet kiosks, memory card readers, CD burners, Wi-Fi, and Skype. **Con:** The whole complex is spread out over about a kilometer. ✉*State Hwy. 73* ☎*03/318–9258* ⎙*03/318–9058* ⊕*www.trampers.co.nz* ⏪*12 double rooms* ⏪*4 cottages (3–4 bedrooms), 11 share rooms* ⌂*In-room: kitchen (some). In-hotel: laundry facilities, public Internet, no elevator* ▭*MC, V.*

LYTTELTON

12 km (7½ mi) east of Christchurch.

Lyttelton, a busy port town, was the arrival point for many of the early Canterbury settlers. The Canterbury Pilgrims' landing place is marked by a rock near the road entrance to the port. Those who came off the ships in the early 1850s walked over the Port Hills by the Bridle Path to Ferrymead while their belongings were brought around Godley Heads and across the Sumner Bar by boat, a perilous journey. A mix of renovated wooden villas and contemporary homes now rises halfway up what was once a volcanic crater. Today, because of its relative isolation from Christchurch, Lyttelton has developed its own distinctive feel, attracting creative types who like the small-town atmosphere.

GETTING HERE & AROUND

Lyttelton can be reached by driving down Ferry Road from Christchurch, heading toward Sumner and then taking the road tunnel. Although the tunnel road is convenient, the best way to explore the area is to drive head over Evans Pass from Sumner—stopping to walk on the beach there—and down into Lyttelton. Another scenic route is to follow the main street, Colombo, east out of the city, up the Port Hills, and over Dyers Pass to Governors Bay. Then turn left and head back along the harbor edge to Lyttelton.

ESSENTIALS

Visitor Info Lyttelton i-Site Information Centre (✉*34 London St.* ☎*03/328–9093* ⊕*www.lytteltonharbour.co.nz*)

Thematic Trails

Enterprising local tourist offices have sketched out thematically linked self-guided sightseeing routes throughout the region. You can pick up pamphlets at the pertinent visitor bureaus. The following are the best of the bunch:

Alpine Pacific Triangle. This links three of the most popular getaways in Canterbury: Waipara, Hanmer Springs, and Kaikoura.

The Peninsula Pioneers. Pick up a brochure from the Akaroa visitor center for information on five different routes through the Banks Peninsula

bays. Keep in mind that some of the bay roads are unpaved and steep.

Pioneer Trail. Connecting several historic sights between Timaru and Geraldine, this route includes the Richard Pearse Memorial, dedicated to a local aviation innovator.

Scenic Highway 72. Scenic Highway 72 runs from Amberley, north of Christchurch, along the foothills of the Southern Alps through two spectacular gorges, past Geraldine to Winchester. You can join up with it at various points along the way.

WHAT TO SEE

There's a small maritime museum on Gladstone Quay, but the main local nautical sight is the castlelike **Timeball Station.** In the days before GPS and atomic clocks, ships would make sure their chronometers were accurate by checking them when the large ball at the Timeball Station was lowered. (Clocks were used to calculate longitude while ships were at sea.) Though it's no longer needed, the Historic Places Trust maintains the station and keeps the ball dropping. The ball is raised above the tower five minutes before 1 and then dropped exactly on the hour. ⊠ *2 Reserve Terr.* ☎ *03/328–7311* ☞ *$7* ☉ *Daily 10–5.*

Fodor'sChoice ★ **Ohinetahi.** Sir Miles Warren is one of New Zealand's foremost architects with a pedigree as large as his garden. Ohinetahi, which is also the Māori name for the area, features not only his large stone colonial villa, but also his immaculate garden—considered one of the best formal gardens in the country. Blending Sir Miles's eye for detail and design with a stunning situation this garden maximizes the use of "garden rooms"—the red room being particularly memorable—hedging, and color. ⊠ *Governors Bay/Teddington Rd.* ☎ *03/329–9852* ☞ *$10* ☉ *Mid-Sept.–Dec. 23, weekdays 10–4;; Jan. 7–end of Mar., weekends by appointment.*

Out in Lyttelton Harbour sits **Quail Island,** which was used by the early European settlers as a quarantine zone and leper colony and was named after the now-extinct native quail. It was once a significant area for collecting birds eggs by local Māori. To protect the new community from disease, later settlers could find themselves quarantined on this island if there was an outbreak of cholera or other disease on their ships. Animals were quarantined here, too; Antarctic explorer Robert Falcon Scott's dogs and donkeys ended up wintering on the island. These days Quail Island, also known as Otamahua, is being restored as an ecological reserve. The *Black Cat* ferry from Lyttelton can zip you out here for a hike; stop by the interpretive center near the wharf. Allow for at least three hours on the island. Reservations are recommended. ⊠*Jetty B, 17 Norwich Quay* ☎*03/328–9078* 🎫*$15* ☿*Sept.–Apr., daily 12:30; Dec.–Mar., extra sailing daily at 10:20; May–Aug., by charter only.*

SPORTS & THE OUTDOORS

Diamond Harbour. Diamond Harbour is the largest township on the far side of Lyttelton Harbour. Its main feature is Godley House (☎*03/329–4880* 🌐*www.godleyhouse.co.nz*), a large house with a restaurant, bar, and accommodations. You can drive to Diamond Harbour or take a 10-minute journey on the Black Diamond ferry from Jetty B at Norwich Quay ($10 return). Sailings are frequent.

DOLPHIN-WATCHING

To see some of the small, endangered Hector's dolphins, do the **Christchurch Wildlife Cruise** on the *Canterbury Cat*. During a tour of the outer harbor you'll likely see these playful dolphins; the staff will also point out old shipwrecks, defensive fortifications, and the seabirds that nest in the cliffs. The boat leaves at 1:30 daily. ⊠*Jetty B, 17 Norwich Quay* ☎*03/328–9078 or 0800/436–574* 🌐*www.blackcat.co.nz* 🎫*$55.*

HIKING

Quail Island *(see above)* is a good option, but if you'd rather stay on the mainland, you could instead follow in the trail of the early settlers by taking the **Bridle Path.** The steep zigzag track goes from Cunningham Street up to the crater rim. You can walk to the Gondola Summit Station, a few minutes' farther, to see the Canterbury Plains from the site of the memorial to the pioneer women, or walk down the rest of the trail to finish near the Christchurch Gondola base station. A number 28 bus will take you to Lyttelton, and the same bus will pick you up on the other side. Allow an hour and a half for the walk (some of which is quite steep).

WHERE TO EAT

$$$–$$$$

✗**Volcano Café and Lava Bar.** The Lyttelton volcano is long since extinct, but this long-standing bright-yellow restaurant and its bright-blue neighbor, the Lava Bar, are very much alive. Toys, rainbow-color lamp shades, streamers, Frida Kahlo posters, and Kiwi paintings decorate the former grocery store. Nab one of the 1960s Formica tables and order a great big steak, fresh fish, spicy enchiladas, nachos, or a curry. A good range of wines and beers is available, as are margaritas by the pitcher. If the selection doesn't suit your tastes, you're also welcome to bring your own bottle of wine here. ⊠*42 London St.* ☎*03/328–7077* 🖃*AE, DC, MC, V* ☿*No lunch.*

$$$

✗**London Street Restaurant.** Started by the guys who run the local farmers' market, this place features what the owners call "Local Ingredients, Global Flavours." Try their Farmers Market Brunch on Saturday. The central bar, brick walls, polished wood floors, and coffee-color interior project a degree of urban cool, which is rather out of character for Lyttelton, although not unwelcome. There's a huge wine list and hearty dishes like the wood-grilled hanger steak on a potato gratin and pan-seared groper on lemon-tomato couscous; and an interesting Wee Plates, or tapas, menu. There's a Saturday brunch 10–4. ⊠*2 London St.* ☎*03/328–7171* ☿*No lunch Wed.–Fri. and Sun.* 🖃*AE, MC, V.*

8

AKAROA & THE BANKS PENINSULA

82 km (50 mi) east of Christchurch.

Sheep graze almost to the water's edge in the many small bays indenting the coastline of Banks Peninsula, the nub that juts into the Pacific east of Christchurch. On the southern side of the peninsula, in a harbor created when the crater wall of an extinct volcano collapsed into the sea, nestles the fishing village of Akaroa (Māori for "long harbor"). The port is a favorite day trip for Christchurch residents on Sunday drives, and on weekends and over the summer holidays (December to February) it can be very busy. If you're planning to stay the night during the busy times (summer and weekends), book a room and dinner before you leave Christchurch.

> **BASTILLE DAY IN AKAROA**
>
> July 14 in Akaroa is Bastille Day, as it is in France. In recognition of how close the tiny town came to being the seat of a French government in New Zealand, the buildings are decorated with the red, white, and blue of the tricolor flag. A gala evening in the Gaiety Hall is always booked, and the theme is, of course, le Français. There is also a French Festival in late April.

GETTING HERE & AROUND

The main route to Akaroa is State Highway 75, which leaves the southwest corner of Christchurch as Lincoln Road. The 82-km (50-mi) drive takes about 90 minutes. You can also head out through Lyttelton and Teddington, then over the hill to Little River for a very scenic but slightly longer trip.

If you'd rather not drive, the Akaroa Shuttle has daily service between Christchurch and Akaroa: three trips a day in high season (December–April) ranging from a direct shuttle to a scenic tour, but only once a day otherwise. Direct shuttles run twice a day in summer from Christchurch, with an extra run on Friday night, and there are three runs a day from Akaroa. InterCity Coachlines also runs between Christchurch and Akaroa.

ESSENTIALS

Bus Companies Akaroa Shuttle (☎0800/500–929 ⊕ www.akaroashuttle.co.nz). **Hanmer Shuttle** (☎0800/800–575). **InterCity Coachlines** (☎03/365–1113 or 0800/222–146 ⊕ www.intercitycoach.co.nz).

Medical Assistance Akaroa Hospital (⊠Onuku Rd. ☎03/304–7023). **Akaroa Health Centre** (⊠Aylmers Valley Rd. ☎03/304–7004).

Visitor Info Akaroa Information Centre (⊠80 Rue Lavaud ☎03/304–8600).

WHAT TO SEE

Although **Akaroa** was chosen as the site for a French colony in 1838, the first French settlers arrived in 1840 only to find that the British had already established sovereignty over New Zealand by the Treaty of Waitangi. Less than 10 years later, the French abandoned their attempt at colonization, but the settlers remained and gradually intermarried with the local English community. Apart from the *rue* (street) names, a few family surnames, and architectural touches, there is little sign of a French connection anymore, but the village has a splendid setting. A day trip will get you to and from Akaroa, including a drive along the Summit Road on the edge of the former volcanic dome, but take an overnight trip if you want to explore the peninsula bays as well as the town. It's an easy drive most of the way but the last hill over to Akaroa is narrow and winding with few passing areas. By the time you've checked out a winery, taken a harbor cruise, driven around a few bays, and stopped for a meal, you'll be right in the mood to kick back overnight in this quiet spot.

EN ROUTE

State Highway 75 leads from Christchurch out onto the peninsula, curving along the southern portion past Lake Ellesmere. There are interesting stops on your way out to Akaroa. The small town of **Little River** used to be the end of the line for a now-defunct railway line from Christchurch; the route is now a walkway and bicycle trail. The old wooden train station houses a crafts gallery and information office, and a café is next door in the grocery store. Pick up the *Peninsula Pioneers* brochure of the area, which details the Heritage drive from Little River to Akaroa. When you reach **Hilltop,** pause for your first glimpse of Akaroa Harbour; on a sunny day it's magnificent. (At Hilltop the highway crosses the Summit Road, the other major route through the peninsula.) And if you're hungry after the drive over the hill, swing by **Barry's Bay Cheese Factory** (☎03/304–5809) and taste the local product, one of Akaroa's earliest exports. It's only made every second day and if you're there before about 2, you can watch the day's cheese being manufactured.

The Akaroa Historic Area Walk ambles along the narrow streets past quaint little cottages and historic buildings which reflect the area's multicultural background. A free map that outlines the walk and points of interest is available from the information center. You can start this easy two-hour walk at the **Akaroa Information Centre** (⊠*80 Rue Lavaud* ☎*03/304–8600*).

Along the waterfront from the Garden of Tane to Jubilee Park, the focus of historic interest is the **Akaroa Museum,** which has a display of Māori *pounamu* (greenstone) as well as alternating exhibits on the area's multicultural past. The museum complex includes the Old Courthouse and Langlois-Eteveneaux House, the two-room cottage of an early French settler. ⊠*Rue Lavaud at Rue Balguerie* ☎*03/304–1013* 🎫*$4* ⊙*Daily 10:30–4:30; closes at 4 in winter.*

★ The **French Farm Winery,** the only winery on Banks Peninsula, occupies a stunning site overlooking Akaroa Harbour. The 20-acre vineyard produces sauvignon blanc, Riesling, pinot gris, chardonnay, and pinot noir. The cellar door also has Akaroa Harbour merlot, Riesling, and rosé and Kaituna Valley pinot gris, so there's something for everyone. The onsite restaurant is hailed for its rack of lamb and Akaroa salmon—main courses cost $10 to $29—and the massive indoor fireplace makes it a cozy spot in winter. Bookings are advised and there's an alfresco Pizza

8

Bar out back through the summer. ✉*Just off Wainui Bay Rd., turn off toward the coast at Barry's Bay Cheeses* ☎*03/304–5784* ⊕*www. frenchfarm.co.nz.*

The contrast of the rim of the old volcanic cone and the coves below is striking—and when you drop into one of the coves, you'll likely feel like you've found your own little corner of the world. One of the easiest bays to access is **Okains Bay.** Take the Summit Road at Hilltop if approaching from Christchurch, or Ngaio Point Road behind Duvauchelles if approaching from Akaroa. It's about 24 km (15 mi) from Akaroa and takes about a half hour to drive. The small settlement lies at the bottom of Okains Bay Road, which ends at a beach sheltered by tall headlands.

The **Okains Bay Māori and Colonial Museum** is a collection of buildings containing 20,000 Māori and 19th-century colonial artifacts, including *waka* (canoes) used in Waitangi Day celebrations and displays such as a smithy and print shop. There are also a *wharenui* (Māori meetinghouse), colonial homes, including a totara slab cottage, and a saddlery and harness shop. ✉*Main Rd.* ☎*03/304–8611* 🖃*$6* ⊗*Daily 10–5.*

OFF THE BEATEN PATH

Eastern Bays Scenic Mail Run. For a quirky way of seeing nearly a dozen hideaway bays, sign up to ride with the mailman while he delivers the rural mail on the remote Eastern Bays Mail Run. This highly scenic trip covers the more remote areas and starts from Akaroa at 9, finishing its circuit around 2. The van stops for a tasty homemade morning tea by the beach. Reservations are essential, and it's not suitable for young children. Make reservations at the Akaroa Information Centre. ✉*80 Rue Lavaud* ☎*03/304–8600* 🖃*$50* ⊗*Runs Mon.–Sat.*

Another option is the **Akaroa Harbour Scenic Mail Run,** which travels over 100 km (60 mi) through some of the most beautiful Banks Peninsula scenery, visiting the Māori Marae of Onuku, Robinsons Bay sawmill, Onawe Peninsula (historic pā site), Duvauchelle Hotel, and Barry's Bay Cheese factory (with the promise of tastings and purchases), as well as delivering the mail. This trip stays closer to town than the Eastern Bays run. There's no Sunday run, and reservations are recommended through summer. ☎*027/487–6791* ⊗*Runs Mon.–Sat.*

SPORTS & THE OUTDOORS

The 35-km (22-mi) **Banks Peninsula Track** crosses beautiful coastal terrain. From Akaroa you hike over headlands and past several bays, waterfalls, and seal and penguin colonies, and you might see Hector's dolphins at sea. Two-day ($150) and four-day ($225) hikes are available from October to April. Overnight in cabins with fully equipped kitchens, which you might share with other hikers. Rates include lodging, transport from Akaroa to the first hut, landowners' fees, and a booklet describing the features of the trail. No fear of overcrowding here—the track is limited to 16 people at a time. ☎*03/304–7612* ⊕*www.bankstrack.co.nz* ⊗*Closed May–Sept.*

The *Black Cat* catamaran runs two **Akaroa Harbour Nature Cruises.** You'll pull in beside huge volcanic cliffs and caves and bob around in the harbor entrance while tiny Hector's dolphins—an endangered and adorable species of dolphin with rounded dorsal fins that look like Mickey Mouse ears stuck on their backs—play in the wake of the boat. On some cruises you can swim with them. Trips leave daily at 1:30 PM all year round, plus 11 AM December to March, and cost $55. Dolphin swim trips leave daily at 11:30 AM, $110. Advance reservations are essential. ⊠ *Main Wharf* ☏ *03/304–7641 or 0800/436–574* ⊕ *www.blackcat.co.nz.*

★ **Pohatu Penguins and Marine Reserve.** You won't need your telephoto lens because you'll get almost close enough to touch these rare little birds. Pohatu is a key breeding area for the white-flippered penguin (Korora), which are endemic to the Canterbury region. You may also see the yellow-eyed penguin (Hoiho). Options range from day and evening penguin or nature tours (from $55 per person) and sea-kayaking trips (from $70 from Akaroa). Price includes a scenic drive to Pohatu with photo stops along the way. ⊠ *Akaroa Info Centre* ☏ *03/304–8600* ⊕ *www.pohatu.co.nz* ☉ *Subject to penguin breeding season.*

WHERE TO EAT

$$$$
★ ✕ **Harbour 71.** Eclectic spins on New Zealand produce, meat, and seafood, along with a seaside location, make for sought-after reservations here. Dark wooden floors, provincial-style drapes, and leather chairs lend a country chic feel. Seafood is the highlight, and the grouper comes straight from the fishing boat. Try the Trio of Seafood—a flavorsome mix of squid, salmon, and oysters. The New Zealand wines on the list include Canterbury labels such as Akaroa Harbour and Pegasus Bay. ⊠ *71 Beach Rd.* ☏ *03/304–7656* ▭ *AE, MC, V* ☉ *Closed Tues. and Wed. and July and Aug. No lunch Mon.–Sat.*

$$$–$$$$ ✕ **C'est la vie.** Loitering with intent on the steps of this little wooden bungalow "at the end of the world" is encouraged, because it's the only way to study the blackboard menu. There are only a handful of tables, and sharing space is encouraged. Two sittings, at 6 and 8:30, help get around this. The walls, the window frames, and even the ceiling are covered in graffiti left by happy diners. Your meal—whether it's venison à la Diana, a salmon steak, the filet de boeuf served with blue-vein cheese and blueberries, or the ever-popular escargots—will come to the table in copper dishes for serving yourself. Don't miss the crème caramel or the dame blanche, homemade ice cream served with a hot chocolate sauce. ⊠ *33 Rue Lavaud, Akaroa* ☏ *03/304–7314* ▭ *MC, V* ☉ *Closed June–Aug.*

$$–$$$$
★ ✕ **Bully Hayes.** If you don't feel like fine dining or sharing a table, then sit outside on the deck, overlooking the sea, and enjoy a laid-back meal in the evening sun watching the yachts moored in the harbor. Seafood is a highlight, and why not in a place like Akaroa? There are light and full-size main courses, and other options include lamb, venison, and beef fillet. ⊠ *57 Beach Rd.* ☏ *03/304–5573* ▭ *AE, DC, MC, V.*

¢–$ ✕ **Akaroa Fish and Chips.** Acclaimed around the country as having some of the best fish-and-chips available, this takeaway-style eatery often has queues out the door. Buy deep-fried fish, fresh off the boat, served with a big side of perfectly cooked chips and a big chunk of lemon,

8

and eat them out of the paper at one of the outdoor tables. You'll never want to eat fish-and-chips with a knife and fork again. ✉ *59 Beach Rd* ☎ *03/304–7464.*

WHERE TO STAY

$$$–$$$$ ☐ **Linton.** Nicknamed the Giant's House, because it looked like one to
★ a visiting child, Linton is full of art in unexpected places. Up the steep driveway hides a large garden crisscrossed by paths, larger-than-life mosaics, and colorful, welded sculptures. One of the guest rooms has a boat-shaped bed, another opens to a mosaic rose garden and conservatory. The 1880 house and garden are open for tours from 2 to 4 daily, April to Christmas and noon to 4 through summer ($12). **Pros:** Fabulous, crazy mosaic artwork; beautiful garden and leafy outlook. **Cons:** Very steep driveway, garden tour visitors wander through in the afternoon. ✉ *68 Rue Balguerie, Akaroa* ☎ *03/304–7501* ⊕ *www. linton.co.nz* ⇴ *3 rooms* ⌂ *In-room: no TV. In-hotel: bar, no elevator* ☰ *MC, V* ⊘ *Closed mid-June–Sept.* ⫯⊙⫯ *CP.*

$$$ ☐ **Oinako Lodge.** Surrounded by a tranquil garden, and just a two-
★ minute walk from the town and harbor of Akaroa, this charming Victorian manor house has its original ornate plaster ceilings and marble fireplaces. You'll also find fresh flowers in the spacious and pleasantly decorated rooms; four have whirlpool baths. **Pros:** Old-fashioned leafy garden overlooking the harbor; chocolates, feather pillows, and duvets add a luxurious touch. **Con:** The road runs on to what looks like private driveway shared by a number of properties. Just follow that road a little farther to Oinako, which is signed. ✉ *99 Beach Rd.* ☎☎ *03/304– 8787* ⊕ *www.oinako.co.nz* ⇴ *6 rooms* ⌂ *In-room: no a/c, no TV. In- hotel: no elevator* ☰ *AE, DC, MC, V* ⫯⊙⫯ *BP, CP.*

$$ ☐ **Akaroa Village Inn.** In the heart of Akaroa is this excellent mid-range accommodation overlooking the harbor. Walk out the door to any of the good eateries in town, or across to the wharf for a boat trip. Accommodation ranges from nice two-story apartment-style units to cottages and family units. Pros: Variety of accommodation to suit all tastes and budgets, in the center of town, independent restaurant on-site. Con: Bigger complex that may lose its personal appeal in busy times. ✉ *81 Beach Rd.* ☎ *03/304–7421 or 0800/695–2000* ☎ *03/304–7423* ⊕ *www.akaroavillageinn.co.nz* ✉ *akaroa@clear.net. nz* ⇴ *40 units* ⌂ *In-room: no a/c (some), kitchen. In-hotel: laundry, pool* ☰ *MC, V* ⫯⊙⫯ *EP.*

¢–$ ☐ **Chez la Mer.** This comfortable hostel fills a quaint but charming 1871 building. There's no TV; the preferred form of entertainment is sharing travelers' tales in the kitchen or over the BBQ in the sunny courtyard garden. The hosts share travel advice and free bicycles for exploring Akaroa. Pros: On the main street; feels just like home, only older. Cons: No credit or debit cards accepted, no breakfast. ✉ *50 Rue Lavaud, Akaroa* ☎ *03/304–7024* ⊕ *www.chezlamer.co.nz* ⇴ *5 rooms, 2 with en suite, 3 dorm rooms* ⌂ *In-hotel: bicycles, laundry facilities* ☰ *No credit cards.*

WAIPARA VALLEY

65 km (40 mi) north of Christchurch.

Once known for its hot, dry summers and sheep ranches, the Waipara Valley is now an established vineyard area. The local Riesling, chardonnay, and sauvignon blanc are particularly good. Sheltered from the cool easterly wind by the Teviotdale hills, the valley records hotter temperatures than the rest of Canterbury, and warm, dry autumns ensure a longer time for the grapes to mature. Winemakers are also exploiting the area's limestone soil to grow pinots—pinot noir, pinot gris, and pinotage. Two dozen labels have sprouted up, with more to come, and the area produces more than 200,000 cases of wine a year.

GETTING HERE & AROUND

To reach Waipara from Christchurch, take State Highway 1 north. Waipara's about 45 minutes away, where State Highway 7 turns left off the main road. You can head from here to Hanmer Springs and other northern towns from here. The Hanmer Shuttle runs a daily service between Hanmer Springs and Christchurch that stop in Waipara and elsewhere en route in the Waipara Valley.

ESSENTIALS

Bus Company **Hanmer Shuttle** (☎ *0800/800–575*)

WINERIES

Waipara's wines are celebrated each year at the Waipara Wine and Food Celebration. Held in late March, it fills (ironically enough) the grounds of the local Glenmark Church. Alongside the larger wineries listed below other local high-fliers include Fiddlers Green, Muddy Water, and Torlesse Wines, made by legendary winemaker, Kim Rayner. Athena Olives are also big locally.

There is no specified wine trail or information center in the valley, but a good place to start your visit is the **Pukeko Junction Regional Wine Centre** at Leithfield, 10 km (6 mi) south of Waipara. The center is a café, wineshop, information bureau, and gallery rolled into one. There's a solid range of local wines, often at very good prices, many from smaller wineries not open to the public. The café is famous for its caramel oat slice. ⊠ *458 Ashworths Rd., SH1, Leithfield* ☎ *03/314–8834* ⊙ *Daily 10:30–5:30.*

Although Waipara's vineyards are reasonably close together, they can be hard to find. **Waipara Wine Tours** offers a four-hour tour for $65 and visit three of the area's excellent options or a full-day tour of five wineries for $95 (includes lunch). There are transfers from your Christchurch accommodation. ☎ *0800/081–155 or 03/335–0866* ⊕ *www.waiparavalley.co.nz.*

The huge, cathedral-like limestone and timber building at **Mud House Wine Estate,** although only 10 years old, looks somewhat medieval. Try the sauvignon blanc and pinot gris; their pinot noir is also highly regarded, and they now sell Mud House wines from Marlborough as well. It's open for brunch, lunch and tastings. ⊠ *780 Glasnevin Rd.*

(part of State Hwy. 1), Waipara ☏*03/314–6900* ⊕*www.mudhouse. co.nz* ⊙*Daily 9–5*

★ Family-run **Pegasus Bay** has one of the region's best reputations for wine and food in Canterbury, and the helicopters lined up on the lawn at lunchtime will confirm that. Taste their award-winning Rieslings, chardonnay, and pinot noir while you look through a window at floor-to-ceiling stacks of oak aging casks. In good weather, dine outdoors in the garden or picnic in a natural auditorium by a small man-made lake. Best to book if visiting for a meal or large group tastings. ⊠*Stockgrove Rd., Waipara* ☏*03/314–6869* 🖷*03/314–6861* ⊕*www.pegasus.com* ⊙*Tasting room 10:30–5, restaurant noon–4.*

Daniel Schuster is one of Canterbury's pioneering winemakers. His vines are grown in a traditional manner, without irrigation, and his wines are crafted by hand—a little from this barrel and a little from that. He is a master at work, and his wines are some of the best coming out of Canterbury. Tastings cost $3 (refunded on a wine purchase) and the tasting room is open from 10 to 5 every day. Tea and coffee are served out on the deck, and cellar tours are by appointment. Parking is limited; if they're busy there's a short walk up the hill from the lower parking lot. ⊠*Reeces Rd., Omihi, Waipara* ☏*03/314–5901* ⊕*www. danielschusterwines.com.*

Waipara Springs Winery is one of the valley's oldest wineries; you can stop for lunch along with a wine tasting ($3). The café, in converted farm buildings, serves tasty dishes made with local foods such as olives, goat cheese, asparagus, and bacon. Try their antipasto platter for some of each. These match well with the vineyard's sauvignon blanc, pinot noir, botrytized Riesling, gewürtztraminer, and barrique chardonnay. ⊠*State Hwy. 1* ☏*03/314–6777* ⊕*www.waiparasprings.co.nz* ▭ *AE, DC, MC, V.*

HIKING

Mt. Cass Walkway. Here's a moderately strenuous way to wear off some of those wine- and lunch–induced calories. This two- to three-hour climb up Mt. Cass ends with a spectacular view over the surrounding countryside of the Waipara Valley. As it crosses through working farmland on the Tiromoana Station, be careful to leave gates and marker posts as you find them. Use the stiles provided for crossing fence lines and wear strong walking shoes. The track is closed each year while the sheep are lambing. ⊠*Mt. Cass Rd.* ⊙*Approx. Aug.–Sept.*

WHERE TO STAY & EAT

$$$–$$$$ ✕ **Nor'Wester Café & Bar.** Sophisticated dining in rural places is one
★ of life's great pleasures. Here you can enjoy a meal inside the mellow 1928 bungalow with its fireplace or outside on the palm-shaded veranda. While their most popular dish is the salt-and-pepper squid on Asian salad, there is also a good selection of tapas like oysters, smoked salmon, Parmesan dumplings, and veggie spring rolls. There are locally made breads to take home and a good range of gluten-free dishes. The espresso is superb, and you can complement your meal with a fabulous local wine. Book ahead if it's a weekend. ⊠*95 Main North Rd.,*

Amberley ✢*7 km (4½ mi) south of Waipara* ☎*03/314–9411* ▤*AE, DC, MC, V* ☾*May close some weeknights in winter.*

$$$$

Fodor'sChoice
★

⬚**Claremont Country Estate.** Watch where you walk—that white stone you see might turn out to be a marine dinosaur fossil. This spectacular deer and sheep station is up the Waipara Gorge, a 10-minute drive inland from Amberley; its luxurious homestead was built from limestone quarried on the property in the late 1860s. The five lodge rooms are elegantly furnished with antiques, so families with children under 14 are encouraged to stay in the on-site self-contained cottage. A rugged four-wheel-drive tour is thrown in if you stay two or more nights. You can wander about their 2,400-acre farm, extensive gardens, and private nature reserve as well. Pros: Superb colonial homestead reminiscent of earlier days; options include a full lodge stay, including four-course dinner, or a cheaper B&B accommodations; a winner in Andrew Harper's Hideaway report. Cons: Last part of the drive in is narrow and winding; can be a chilly spot in spring and autumn, but the house is heated. ⊠*828 Ram Paddock Rd.* ☎*03/314–7557* ⊕*www.claremont-estate. com* ⇱*1 room, 4 suites, 3-bedroom cottage* ⚑*In-room: no a/c (some). In-hotel: restaurant, bar, tennis court, pool, spa, no elevator* ▤*AE, MC, V* ☾*Closed July–Sept.* ⎟⚐*MAP, BP.*

$$

⬚**Old Glenmark Vicarage.** The Wicked Vicar, the Vicar's Mistress, and the Divine Daughter are not members of the staff at this pleasant Victorian homestay, but wines produced from their small vineyard. Once a real vicarage, it now provides a very comfortable base while touring the area. The Vicarage Barn has an outdoor fire pit and private spa. Pros: Central to most Waipara wineries and restaurants; on-site boutique vineyard; real farm breakfast with homemade bread, free-range eggs, and butcher's bacon. Cons: Close to busy SH1; only two units, so book ahead. ⊠*161 Church Rd, Waipara* ☎☎*03/314–6775* ⊕*www.glenmarkvicarage.co.nz* ⇱*1 room, 1 unit* ⚑*In-hotel: guest lounge/library, Wi-Fi, pool, spa (for Barn guests only)* ▤*MC, V* ⎟⚐*BP .*

¢

⬚**Waipara Sleepers.** Wake up to fresh-baked bread and newly laid eggs every morning at this very basic but rather quirky backpackers lodge housed in old railway carriages and huts. It's first-come, first-served for breakfast in the station waiting room (now a basic, communal kitchen). Some of the carriages retain old leather seating and travel posters. There are also powered campervan sites and a number of tent sites. Pros: Very rustic and rural, complete with all the sounds and smells of the country; a good stop for anyone cycle-touring. Cons: Some of the accommodations and services are very basic, but so is the price. ⊠*10–12 Glenmark Dr.* ☎☎*03/314–6003* ⊕*www.inet.net. nz/~waipara.sleepers* ⇱*4 rooms, 2 dorms* ⚑*In-room: no TV (some). In-hotel: bar, laundry facilities* ▤*MC, V.*

EN ROUTE

Built from limestone blocks, the **Hurunui Hotel,** New Zealand's oldest continually licensed hotel (since 1860), refreshed weary drovers bringing sheep down from Marlborough. A bed for the night is relatively cheap ($40 per person, including a cooked breakfast), and the restaurant with its old-fashioned pub serves à la carte dinners from $17 and an all-day menu from $15. Repeat visitors come for the tasty game pies—local rabbit with lemon and bacon, ostrich with blue cheese, or

8

venison and red currant. ⊠*State Hwy. 7, about 20-min drive from Waipara turnoff* ☎*03/314–4207.*

HANMER SPRINGS

120 km (75 mi) northwest of Christchurch.

People used to come to Hanmer Springs to chill out with quiet soaks in the hot pools and to take gentle forest walks; but things have been changing fast. The number of boutiques and restaurants has doubled, and an increasing number of off-road and backcountry activities are turning Hanmer Springs into Canterbury's adventure sports hub. On holidays and weekends the springs can be very busy. The Amuri Ski Field, a small ski area in the mountains behind town, attracts a dedicated following of local skiers in winter. Mountain biking is especially big, and Hanmer Springs is now the end point for several long-distance mountain-bike and endurance races through the backcountry. During the summer months Hanmer Springs is also the southern terminus of the drive along the Acheron road through the Molesworth Station, which runs through from the Awatere Valley in Marlborough and is the country's highest public road. This backcountry trail is open for only a few months a year and is a solid six-hour drive on an unpaved road through some spectacular country. Check out ⊕*www.doc.govt.nz* and search for Molesworth.

For additional information, maps, and as a meeting point, go to the **Hurunui Visitor Information Centre.**

GETTING HERE & AROUND

The Hanmer Shuttle runs a daily service between Hanmer Springs and Christchurch. Service goes through Waipara on the way. By car, take State Highway 1 north out of Christchurch. About 45 minutes away, State Highway 7 turns left off the main road. From here drive through the small town of Culverden and the foothills for another 45 minutes on State Highway 7, before turning onto Highway 7A toward Hanmer Springs (this is well signposted).

ESSENTIALS

Bus Company **Hanmer Shuttle** (☎*0800/800–575*).

Medical Assistance **Hanmer Health Centre** (⊠*Amuri Ave.* ☎*03/315–7503*).

Visitor Info **Hurunui Visitor Information Centre** (⊠*42 Amuri Ave., Hanmer Springs* ☎*03/315–7128 or 0800/442–663* ⊕*www.hurunui.com*).

WHAT TO SEE

The scenic gravel drive along **Jacks Pass,** to the north of the village, crosses the lower slopes of Mt. Isobel before dropping into the upper Clarence River valley, an alpine area 10 minutes from Hanmer Springs. This is the beginning of some serious backcountry. The tiny stream trickling past the road at the end of the pass eventually reaches the coast north of Kaikoura as the rough and rumbling Clarence River—a favorite for rafters and kayakers. This is also the southern end of the

Acheron Road through the Molesworth Station *(see above)*. To see some Māori rock drawings, take the **Weka Pass Walkway** from behind the Star and Garter hotel along a disused railway line before turning away and following the fence line. The drawings are under limestone overhangs. It is also limestone that creates the strange formations in Weka Pass, including Frog Rock, so named for its shape.

The **Hanmer Springs Thermal Reserve** consists of 12 outdoor thermal pools of varying temperatures, one freshwater pool, a family activity pool, and two waterslides. There are also six private thermal pools, as well as private sauna and steam rooms. Massage and beauty treatments are available at the on-site spa. ⊠*Amuri Ave.* ☎*03/315–0000* ⊕*www. hanmersprings.co.nz* ⊠*$12; private pool, steam, or sauna $22 per ½ hr (minimum 2 people), waterslide $5* ⊙*Daily 10–9.*

The **Wisteria Cottage Day Spa** is one of the newest day spas in Hanmer, catering to those who don't want or need to soak in a hot pool for their entire stay. Specialty treatments are available, including hot-stone massage, Vichy showers, holistic facials, and massage. ⊠*34 Conical Hill Rd.* ☎*03/315–7026* ⊕*www.nzhotsprings.com/dayspa.*

SPORTS & THE OUTDOORS

ADVENTURE SPORTS With **Alpine Pacific Adventures,** you can kayak on a lake with snow down to the water's edge, or you can go fly-fishing or hunting in the hills. A half-day guided fishing trip starts at $235, plus a license if you don't already have one. All equipment is supplied and they will pick you up from your hotel. ☎*03/315–7387*

Hanmer Springs Adventure Centre runs quad-bike tours, horse trekking, mountain biking, and archery into the hinterlands behind Hanmer Springs. Quad-bike tours leave at 10, 1:30, and 4 each day, bouncing through some spectacular hill country, native bush, river crossings, hill climbs, and stunning scenery on the two-hour trip (costs $129). ⊠*20 Conical Hill Rd.* ☎*03/315–7233* ⊕*www.hanmeradventure.co.nz.*

Thrillseekers Canyon Adventure Centre organizes 35-meter (115-foot) bungy jumps off the 19th-century Waiau Ferry Bridge ($135). You can also choose to raft or ride on a jet-boat through the Waiau Gorge, let the kids do a kart or quad-bike safari, or take a ride in an ATV. Try clay-bird shooting or just peer off the 30-meter-high (100-foot-high) balcony and watch the bungy jumpers and jet-boats in the canyon below. Book at least one day in advance. ⊠*839 Hanmer Springs Rd.* ☎*03/315–7046 or 0800/661–538* ⊕*www.thrillseekerscanyon.co.nz.*

HORSE TREKKING **Hanmer Horse Trekking** takes beginner and advanced riders on guided rides through forest, farmland, and native bush. Be prepared for river crossings and spectacular views. Rides last from 1 to 2½ hours, prices range from $45 to $90. ⊠*187 Rogerson Track* ☎*03/315–7444 or 0800/873–546* ⊕*www.hanmerhorses.co.nz* ⊙*Sept.–Apr. rides leave at 10, noon, 2, and 4; May–Aug. rides leave at 11, 1, and 3.*

8

WHERE TO EAT

$$$–$$$$
★
✕ **The Laurels.** In a renovated villa on the main road into Hanmer, the Laurels maintains high standards of cuisine and service. Their focus has changed from a strong Latin American flavor to a more eclectic style. The chili salt-rubbed beef fillet is a top seller as are the king prawns in a rich red tomato sauce. Venison and pork belly arrangements also have a strong following. It's recommended by locals as the best in town. ✉ *31 Amuri Ave.* ☎ *03/315–7788* ⊙ *Closed in winter. No dinner Tues.; no lunch some days.*

$$$–$$$$
✕ **Malabar Restaurant.** Looking out toward Conical Hill, this restaurant has a fine reputation for its Indian and Asian fusion food presented with a Kiwi flair. The "Four Curries" meal on a traditional thali is a favorite, as is the grilled rack of New Zealand lamb on cumin-crusted potatoes and the barbecued belly of pork with roasted ginger kumara (native sweet potatoes). Their lemongrass and coconut ice cream is a treat. Reservations are essential in summer and they offer a takeaway service. ✉ *Alpine Pacific Centre, 5 Conical Hill Rd.* ☎ *03/315–7745* ⊟ *AE, DC, MC, V.*

$$$–$$$$
✕ **The Old Post Office.** Any message posted here will make it only as far as the kitchen. This old wooden building specializes in lamb and beef and serves elegant meals such as seared venison with kūmara-and-walnut mash. In winter a fireplace keeps the L-shape dining room warm; on a warm evening, ask for a terrace table or a courtyard table. Although service can vary a bit, the food is always excellent. ✉ *2 Jacks Pass Rd.* ☎ *03/315–7461* ⊟ *AE, DC, MC, V* ⊙ *No lunch.*

¢–$$
✕ **Springs Deli Cafe.** For either breakfast or lunch this place has all the comforts of home—tasty café-style food, good coffee, and either a roaring log fire when its cold, or balmy outdoor eating when it's not. There's a solid breakfast menu with all the usuals and a cabinet stuffed full of tasty lunch or coffee treats like generously filled panini, quiches, bagels, croissants, and pastries. They also have a retail shelf with local wines, honey, oils, and preserves. ✉ *Amuri Ave.* ☎ *03/315–7430.*

WHERE TO STAY

$$$$
🏠 **Fontainebleau.** You can see attention to detail in every aspect of this luxurious home which hosts Virginia, John, and their friendly Labrador (he lives outside) share with their guests. Rooms have a variety of views—over surrounding hills, the garden, or the pond—and the furnishings reflect the owners' European heritage. Right down to the lavender toiletries, de-misting mirrors, and the candlelit turndown, Fontainebleau makes you feel special. It's close enough to walk to restaurants in the evening and to stroll up nearby Conical Hill during the day. Pros: Big bathrooms with double showers, some with spa baths; forest walks from the gate; complimentary wines and nightcap. Con: Tucked away at the end of a suburban street. ✉ *6 Lakewood La., Forest View* ☎ *03/315–5189* ⊕ *www.fontainebleau.co.nz* ➵ *3 rooms* ♿ *In-room: Ethernet, DVD, safe, no phone. In-hotel: gym, no elevator* ⊟ *MC, V* ⊙ *Closed May* ⭕ *BP.*

$$–$$$$
🏠 **Settlers Inn Motel.** This property has peaceful apartments and studios set off Amuri Avenue, the main street into Hanmer. Upstairs rooms have balconies with views of Mt. Isobel, and two apartments have

private courtyards. Handcrafted slat beds and furniture have been installed in all the rooms, and each unit has either a full kitchen or kitchenette. A cooked breakfast is available on request. Pros: Quiet, friendly motel-style establishment; short walk to town; flexible check-in and check-out times. Con: Units all open onto central courtyard and parking lot. ⊠6 *Leamington St.* ☎*03/315–7343 or 0800/587–873* 🖷*03/315–7071* ⊕*www.settlersinnmotel.co.nz* ♨*In-room: kitchen, Ethernet. In-hotel: laundry facilities, public Internet, no elevator* ⊟*AE, DC, MC, V* ⊙|*EP.*

$$–$$$ 🏨**Albergo Hanmer Lodge and Alpine Villas.** Experience mountain views
★ even from the showers. The arty-chic interior design has handcrafted touches like textured fabrics, unusual artworks, quirky colors, and many seahorses dotted throughout. Stay in the alpine villa with its private Jacuzzi, or in the lodge. The three-course breakfast is delicious, with 10 meal choices, homemade Swiss miniloaves, and fresh Italian coffee, and is served at your convenience, any time of the day. They can arrange spa treatment and cuisine packages; Swiss-Kiwi cuisine is a specialty, including warming winter fondues and the Albergo Egg Nests, which keep people coming back for more. Pros: Funky but tasteful decor high on visual stimulation, outdoor courtyard overlooked by surrounding mountains. Con: Slightly out of town. ⊠*88 Rippingale Rd.* ☎*03/315–7428 or 0800/342–313* ⊕*www.albergohanmer.com* ⤳*5 suites* ♨*In-room: DVD. In-hotel: bar, public Wi-Fi, public Internet* ⊟*AE, DC, MC, V* ⊙|*BP.*

$$–$$$ 🏨**Heritage Hanmer Springs.** This getaway opened in 1932 as the Han-
★ mer Lodge, when it was the largest hotel in Australasia. Stay in rooms inside the hotel or take a garden suite in among the pine trees on Jollies Pass Road; there are also villas on the rise above the hotel, around a man-made pond. Hotel decor reflects its country heritage, with the public spaces remaining much as they have for years. The rooms, however, are comfortable and more contemporary in finish. The thermal springs are a short walk away. Breakfast is served in the front courtyard. Pros: Lovely old Spanish Mission, set in the middle of town within easy walk of most things. Con: Public areas have not really been modernized. ⊠*1 Conical Hill Rd.* ☎*03/315–7021* 🖷*03/315–7023* ⊕*www.heritagehanmer.nz-hotels.com* ⤳*38 rooms, 11 villas, 16 singles* ♨*In-hotel: restaurant, bar, tennis court, pool, no elevator* ⊟*AE, DC, MC, V* ⊙|*EP.*

¢–$ 🏨**Kakapo Lodge.** You reach this lodge where State Highway 7 ends and the tree-divided Amuri Avenue begins. A short walk from the hot pools, this large two-story building has under-floor heating and comfy wooden slat beds, and offers various options to the budget conscious, from dorm rooms and double rooms to motel accommodation. The sunny hostel is kept very clean and tidy, with views over the mountains and surrounding park. It also doubles as the Hanmer YHA. Pros: Nice public areas with plenty of seating and relaxing spaces, right at the end of the main street and close to everything. Con: Only a few en-suite rooms. ⊠*14 Amuri Ave.* ☎🖷*03/315–7472* ⊕*www.kakapolodge. co.nz* ⤳*10 rooms (2 with en suite), 2 units, 5 dorm rooms* ♨*In-room: kitchen. In-hotel: public Internet, bar, no elevator* ⊟*MC, V.*

NIGHTLIFE

Saints Pizzeria and Bar can claim to be Hanmer Spring's first nightclub. It's open until 1 AM Friday and Saturday, but closes around 11 on other nights. It has a dance floor and pool table and features a DJ most Saturday nights. There's no lunch during the week. ⊠*6 Jacks Pass Rd.* ☎*03/315–5262.*

METHVEN

95 km (59 mi) southwest of Christchurch.

Methven's main claim to fame is as a ski town—it's the closest town to Mt. Hutt, which does not allow accommodation on its slopes. If you happen to be here in summer, don't be put off by the empty streets. There are some bargains to be had, and you can take advantage of walking, salmon fishing, jet-boating, and hot-air ballooning.

GETTING HERE & AROUND

The best way to get to Methven by car is the underused Scenic Highway 72, which you can join near Darfield, or via Hororata (but be wary of icy spots in the shade and hidden speed cameras on these straight roads). You could also travel down the busy State Highway 1 to Rakaia and take Thompson's Track (clearly signposted and paved) to Methven. This Inland Scenic Route makes a nice day drive from Christchurch, taking in the upper Rakaia and Rangitata River gorges, the small towns of Darfield, Methven, and Geraldine, scenic views of the Southern Alps, and the wide open farmlands of the plains.

There are plenty of buses from Christchurch to Methven and Mt. Hutt in ski season, but the options drop off in summer. Newmans also run through Methven daily on their way north and south.

ESSENTIALS

Bus Company Newmans Coachlines (☎*03/365–1114* ⊕ *www.newmans coach.co.nz*).

Medical Assistance Methven Medical Centre (⊠*The Square* ☎*03/302–8105*).

Visitor Info Methven Visitor Centre (⊠*93 Main St.* ☎*03/302–8955* ⊕*www. methveninfo.co.nz*).

SPORTS & THE OUTDOORS

BALLOONING On a clear morning you might catch a glimpse of a rainbow-striped balloon floating high above Methven—chances are it's **Aoraki Balloon Safaris.** From their balloons, you get an incredible view of the patchwork pattern of farm paddocks, the braided systems of the Rakaia and Ashburton rivers, and a full 300-km (190-mi) panorama of the Canterbury Plains and Aoraki/Mt. Cook, the "Cloud Piercer." On landing, you'll be served a buffet breakfast. Flights start at daybreak, and you'll be pitching in to help with the launch. The actual time in the air is about one hour, but the whole experience takes at least four hours, starting at daybreak. Rates for Premier flights—which include breakfast in a meadow after landing—go up to $345 per adult. ☎03/302–8172, 0800/256–837 NZ only ⓕ03/302–8162 ⓦwww.nzballooning.com ✎aoraki@nzballooning.com.

HIKING One of New Zealand's top 10 walkways, the **Mt. Somers Track** is a great way to get a taste of the subalpine New Zealand bush. Start at the Mt. Somers-Woolshed Creek end and hike downhill to the Staveley end and Sharplin Falls. The walk will take one to two days, and there are two huts to stay in along the way—or do it in reverse. Call the Staveley Store (☎03/303–0859) for information on transport to the end of the trail; there are a number of small guiding companies. Leaving from just below the Rakaia River Gorge bridge, the **Rakaia Gorge Walkway** provides upstream access to the northern bank of the river and offers easy walking. You can also take a jet boat upriver and walk back—just name your distance. Rakaia Gorge Scenic Jet *(see below)* also does a guided trip on the trail.

JET-BOATING Zoom along the glacier-fed Rakaia River with **Rakaia Gorge Scenic Jet**; the walkway trip costs $25 and the 40-minute jet-boat ride costs $65. Salmon fishing is available and rafting/jet or heli/jet combos are an excellent option, subject to minimum numbers. The Rakaia's jewel-like aqua water contrasts beautifully with the white limestone cliffs. You'll usually find the jet boat down at the river's edge, just below the Rakaia Gorge bridge on State Highway 72. But call first in case the river is in flood or the boat is busy. ☎03/318–6515 or 0800/435–453 ⓦwww. rakaiagorgescenicjet.co.nz.

SKIING Methven is the gateway to a number of ski slopes (Kiwis say ski fields). Thanks to its altitude (6,780 feet) and snowmaking machines, **Mt. Hutt's** access begins in early June. Its wide basin and a vertical drop of 655 meters (2,148 feet) ensure a 2-km (1-mi) run, with some of the best powder in Australasia. From the chairlifts you'll have terrific views of the mountains and the Canterbury Plains below. Shuttles to the slopes run from Methven and Christchurch, often as part of a package offer including lift fees and equipment rental. You can drive if you've got tire chains, but the road isn't paved and it has a number of hairpin turns. Lift tickets start at $74. Rental equipment is available, and the area is family- and beginner-friendly. There's a ski school and crèche (kids under seven ski for free). Mt. Hutt is occasionally closed by high winds; beginning daily at 7 AM, up-to-date ski conditions are available by phone or on the Web site ☎03/302–8811 ⓦwww.nzski.com). Intermediate and advanced skiers can sign up for **heliskiing** on Mt. Hutt, flying into slopes where no one else may have skied that day. North Peak Run, the most popular, offers an 800-vertical-meter run (2,600 vertical feet). Costs start at roughly $155 for one run; other options include a full day to the Arrowsmiths Range for $795, with gourmet lunch provided. Scenic flights are available in summer. ☎03/302–8401 or 0800/443–547 ⓦwww.mthutthelicopters.co.nz ✎info@mthuttheli.co.nz.

8

WHERE TO STAY & EAT

Methven isn't a culinary hotbed, but it has several good casual places. The Blue Pub on Main Street in the middle of town does has reasonably priced bistro-style meals and a courtyard where you can sit and have a beer. For something more sophisticated head to Arabica on the corner of MacMillan Street and the Mall for good food any time of the day, or Lisah's, also on Main Street, for an evening meal.

$$$$ 🏨 **Terrace Downs.** Although not strictly in Methven, Terrace Downs is a
★   20-minute drive away, with spectacular views of the Rakaia Gorge and the looming presence of Mt. Hutt. Set on one of the country's better golf courses, this resort is a good place to base yourself for a vacation away from the crowds. Accommodation is in a series of contemporary timber-and-stone villas perched on a ridge above the clubhouse and restaurant, with views over the golf course and the mountains from their balconies. Pros: Impressive use of river stone on the exterior and in the public areas, 18-hole championship golf course on-site. Con: You'll need two nights if you want to really appreciate the setting and venue. ⊠*Coleridge Rd., Rakaia Gorge* ☎*03/318–6943 or 0800/465–373* 🖷*03/317–9372* ⊕*www.terracedowns.co.nz* 🛏*50 suites* ♿*In-room: Ethernet, refrigerator. In-hotel: restaurant, golf course, tennis courts, spa, pools, no elevator* ☰*AE, MC, V* ❘⌷❘*BP.*

$$ 🏨 **Mt. Hutt Lodge.** With its stunning setting overlooking the Rakaia River and bridge, this low-key lodge offers a well-priced alternative to other accommodations in the area. The well-appointed rooms have electric blankets, a dishwasher, and, in two units, a spa bath. Pros: Stunning river views; on the Inland Scenic Route to Geraldine; close to jet-boating, hiking, and salmon fishing. Con: Simple decor and furnishings in the public areas. ⊠*Zigzag Rd., just off SH 72 at Rakaia Gorge Bridge, Windwhistle* ☎*03/318–6898* 🖷*03/318–6812* ⊕*www.mthutt lodge.co.nz* 🛏*6 1- to 3-bedroom units* ♿*In-room: kitchen. In-hotel: bar, restaurant, pool* ☰*AE, DC, MC, V* ❘⌷❘*EP.*

¢–$ 🏨 **Alpenhorn Chalet.** The house is an old wooden villa from the early
★   1900s, very typical of small-town Victorian architecture in New Zealand at the time. A log fire in the huge kitchen helps keep the place warm; the bedrooms are centrally heated. At the end of the day, relax in the hot tub or simply sit in the sun (even in winter it can be intense) to bask and read. Pros: Popular with skiers, fishers, and "flashpackers" (well-off travelers who choose backpacker hostels). Con: A short walk from the center of Methven. ⊠*44 Allen St.* ☎*03/302–8779* 🛏*4 rooms with shared bathroom, 1 room with en suite, 2 dorm rooms* ♿*In-hotel: kitchen, spa, laundry facilities, public Internet* ☰*No credit cards.*

GERALDINE

138 km (85½ mi) southwest of Christchurch.

For years, this pretty town has been a favorite stop on the road to Aoraki/Mt. Cook; these days, it's becoming a magnet in southern Canterbury for art mavens and foodies.

GETTING HERE & AROUND

State Highway 1 is the fastest route there from Christchurch; just after crossing the Rangitata River, turn inland for about 10 minutes on State Highway 79. State Highway 72—known as the Inland Scenic Route—gives you closer views of the mountains and river gorges but takes a bit longer. The rolling downs around Geraldine are especially beautiful in the late afternoon, when the sun turns them golden.

Because Geraldine is between Christchurch and the popular draws of Aoraki/Mt. Cook and Queenstown, it's served by several bus companies, including InterCity and Newmans.

ESSENTIALS

Bus Companies **InterCity Coachlines** (☎ *03/365–1113 or 0800/222–146* ⊕ *www.intercitycoach.co.nz*). **Newmans Coachlines** (☎ *03/365–1114* ⊕ *www. newmanscoach.co.nz*).

WHAT TO SEE

You know you're in small-town New Zealand when the biggest store on the main street is the rural merchandiser. Luckily, along Geraldine's main drag, **Talbot Street,** you'll find other stores and galleries to browse as well. Check out Māori portraits and carvings in the **Peter Caley Art Gallery** (⊠ *3 Talbot St.* ☎ *03/693–7278*). Chocaholics may find it difficult to pass by the pralines in **Chocolate Brown** (⊠ *10 Talbot St.* ☎ *03/693–9982*), a small shop run by Swiss chocolatiers. For more foodie treats, stop by **Barker's** in Four Peaks Plaza (⊠ *76 Talbot St.* ☎ *0800/227–537*) to try fruit chutneys, juices and cordials, sauces, and Glory (an intense spread, better than jam, and often made with black currants). Or stop in at Talbot Forest Cheese At the **Geraldine Vintage Car and Machinery Museum** (⊠ *178 Talbot St.* ☎ *03/693-8756*), there's some good rural stuff with more than 100 tractors (some dating back to 1912) and other farm machinery sharing space with vintage cars. Admission is $7 and the museum is open daily 10–4 between early October and late May, weekends only in winter.

★ Looking more like a shearing shed than a store, the **Tin Shed** is exactly that. Surrounded by farmland and animals it is an authentic piece of rural New Zealand architecture being put to good use. Inside is one of the country's largest selections of lifestyle and handmade clothing. There's a good range of merino and possum fur knits and shawls, knitwear, and thermals, oilskins, sheepskin footwear, and locally produced skin-care items. This is a great spot to stock up with gifts before leaving the country, and they can arrange postage. Open daily 8 AM–5 PM September to May; 8:30 AM–5 PM June to August. ⊠ *SH 79, just off SH 1 at Rangitata* ☎ *03/693–9416* ⊕ *www.thetinshed.co.nz.*

SPORTS & THE OUTDOORS

The Unimog vehicles used by **Wilderness Adventures 4X4 New Zealand** go just about anywhere, including riverbeds, through the backcountry of South Canterbury. You can get to the upper reaches of the Rangitata River, seen in the *Lord of the Rings* films. Trips range from half a day to more than a week long; rates start at $120 for the half-day trip. Reservations are essential. ☎ *03/693-7254* ⊕ *www.4x4newzealand.co.nz.*

Rangitata Rafts runs white-water rafting trips on the Grade V Rangitata River from September through May. If you can't face the Grade V section (the last part of the trip), you can walk around with the photographer. The $195 price includes pick up from Geraldine or Christchurch and lunch, hot showers, spectacular scenery, and an evening barbecue. Reservations are essential. ☎ *03/696–3534 or 0800/251–251* 🌐 *www.rafts.co.nz.*

WHERE TO STAY

$$$–$$$$ **Kavanagh House.** Less than 10 minutes' drive from Geraldine, Kavanagh House makes a good base from which to explore South Canterbury. It's a quaint old neo-Tudor brick-and-stucco mansion. One of the upstairs bedrooms has a bath in the middle of the polished floor of the bedroom, where you might expect an armchair. Enjoy lunch or afternoon tea in the garden on a summer's day or in front of a fire in winter. A glass of bubbly and a fruit platter await you upon arrival. Pros: Right on SH1 if you're heading south to Timaru or Dunedin, set in the small village of Winchester, rooms are big with an almost theatrical feel. Con: There's an element of shabby chic in the decor. ✉ *State Hwy. 1, 5-min drive north of Temuka, Winchester* ☎ *03/615–6150* 📠 *03/615–9694* 🌐 *www.kavanaghhouse.co.nz* ✉ *info@kavanaghhouse.co.nz* *3 rooms* *In-hotel: restaurant, bar, no elevator* 💳 *AE, DC, MC, V* 🍽 *BP.*

$$–$$$ **The Downs B&B.** Spread across a large hilltop section in the outskirts of Geraldine this tidy place offers a homey place to stay, with lots of room to spread out and enjoy the rural and garden views. The Geraldine room is the one to book with its huge corner window and giant dressing room. If that's full, ask for the Fitzgerald room as it's not a lot smaller. The third room also has a smaller room for children if you're traveling as a family. Pros: Quiet rural setting close to town, nice family spot with loads of room and a big garden, free bar open 24/7, very clean and tidy. Cons: Quite conservative decor, slightly out of the way if traveling without a vehicle. ✉ *5 Ribbonwood Rd.* ☎📠 *03/693–7388* 🌐 *www.thedowns.co.nz* *3 rooms* *In-hotel: laundry, public Internet, gym* 💳 *AE, DC, MC, V* 🍽 *BP, CP.*

TIMARU

162 km (101 mi) south of Christchurch.

Timaru, whose name comes from the Māori Te Maru (shelter), began life as two towns, one called Government Town and the other Rhodestown. The two towns met at George Street and merged in 1868. As Timaru's harbor was developed and its foreshore reclaimed, the Caroline Bay beach took shape and became a popular summer venue for its concerts and sideshows. These days, Timaru is the urban hub for South Canterbury and is a two-hour drive south of Christchurch—close enough for a weekend trip but far enough away to have its own strong identity.

GETTING HERE & AROUND

State Highway 1 will take you points south from Christchurch, including Timaru. The town is about a half hour south and east from Geraldine on the coast. If you take State Highway 1, be prepared to share the lanes with long-haul trucks, sheep trucks, and logging vehicles. Buses to Dunedin and Invercargill pass through Timaru on the coast.

ESSENTIALS

Bus Company **InterCity Coachlines** (☎ 03/365–1113 or 0800/222–146 ⊕ www.intercitycoach.co.nz).

Medical Assistance **Timaru Hospital** (✉ Queen St. ☎ 03/684–4000). **Timaru Medical Centre** (✉ 46a Harper St. ☎ 03/684–7533).

Visitor Info **Timaru Visitor Centre** (✉ 2 George St. ☎ 03/688–6163 ⊕ www.southisland.org.nz).

WHAT TO SEE

Once a harborside office, the **Landing Service Building** is now set back from the port because of the foreshore's land reclamation. The restored bluestone building houses the information center, a restaurant, and a small maritime display. A significant Māori rock art exhibition is currently under construction. Just outside the building sits *Captain Cain*, cast in bronze. This harbormaster was at the center of a 19th-century scandal when it was revealed that he had been poisoned by his son-in-law. ✉ 2 George St. ✎ timaru@i-site.org ☎ 03/688–6163.

Pronounced "egg and tie," the **Aigantighe Art Gallery** is one of the largest art museums in the South Island. It has special regional, New Zealand, and international exhibitions and rotates the extensive permanent collection, including works by painter Colin McCahon (a Timaru native). Out in the gardens of the historic mansion are sculptures carved by African, Japanese, and New Zealand artists. ✉ 49 Wai-iti Rd. ☎ 03/688–4424 ⊕ www.timaru.govt.nz/artgallery.html ✎ gallery@timdc.govt.nz ⌨ Free ⊙ Tues.–Fri. 10–4, weekends noon–4.

Anything to do with South Canterbury's past gets covered in the **South Canterbury Museum,** from fossils to fashions, Māori artifacts to 19th-century shipwrecks, and Richard Pearse's aviation antics, which predate the Wright Brothers. ✉ Perth St. ☎ 03/687–7212 ⊕ www.timaru.govt.nz/museum ✎ museum@timdc.govt.nz ⌨ Free ⊙ Tues.–Fri. 10–4:30, weekends 1:30–4:30.

A 20-minute drive northwest from Timaru is Pleasant Point, an area known for its role in aviation history. Some months before the Wright brothers took flight in America, a local farmer nicknamed "Bamboo Dick" took bicycle wheels somewhere they'd never been before, launching New Zealand's first powered flight out in the fields a few miles outside town. The **Richard Pearse Memorial,** a reproduction of his plane, marks the spot where Pearse crashed into a hedge on March 31, 1903. To get here, take the Waitohi–Pleasant Point Road, then take a left on Opihi Terrace Road, and another left onto Main Waitohi Road. ✉ Main Waitohi Rd.

8

Māori rock art can be seen at the **Raincliff Historical Reserve.** South Canterbury has one of the country's highest concentrations of Māori rock art paintings, which are documented by the Ngai Tahu Māori Rock Art Trust. Six hundred years ago or more, Māori moa hunters made drawings of animals, birds, and people in black charcoal or red ocher on stone walls created by limestone overhangs. Although many works are on private land, the Raincliff reserve is open to the public. Faint drawings are visible here, particularly on the small overhang. To reach the reserve, follow the signpost in Pleasant Point that points to Raincliff bridge. Allow an hour for the trip. ⊠*Middle Valley Rd. off State Hwy. 79* ☜*Free.*

If you want to look like a real "Kiwi," you'll need to make sure you have a "Swannie," or Swanndri bush shirt. This item, as iconic to Kiwis as the Akubra hat is to Australians, is found in many versions at the **Swanndri Factory Store,** along with other accessories like merino wool thermals, designer knitwear, and woolly blankets. ⊠*24a Church St.* ☎*03/684–9037* ⊕*www.swanndri.co.nz* ☉*Weekdays 10– 5:30, Sat. 10–4.*

Since the 1930s **Temuka Homeware** has been the training ground for some of New Zealand's best commercial potters. Their outlet store in a rambling brick building in central Temuka is a culmination of many years of talented artisans developing their skills. Initially known for their stoneware they now sell a large range of pottery, ceramics, and generic kitchenware. ⊠*Vine St., Temuka* ☎*03/615–7719* ⊕*www. temukahomeware.co.nz* ☉*Weekdays 9–5, weekends 9:30–4.*

WHERE TO STAY & EAT

$$$–$$$$ ✕**Ginger & Garlic Café.** In winter, a big fire warms you up, and, in summer, fabulous sunsets can be seen from a window table. Set in a bold
★   three-sided building at the top of the main street the restaurant, one of Timaru's best eateries, overlooks Caroline Bay and the port—where the head chef, Kerina, gets her seafood fresh each day. The Angus beef with soft-shell crab is popular. ⊠*335 Stafford St.* ☎*03/688–3981* ▤*AE, DC, MC, V* ☉*Closed Sun. and 1st 2 wks of Jan. No lunch weekends.*

$–$$$ ✕**Blue Bay Cafe.** Perched above Caroline Bay, along Timaru's tiny café strip, this fresh clean place has indoor and outdoor tables. There's an all-day breakfast, a full cabinet, and a large blackboard menu, and they have a solid range of espresso options. Their coffee is good. ⊠*68 The Bay Hill,* ☎*03/688-0561* ▤*AE, DC, MC, V* ☉*No dinner.*

$$$$ ▥**Tighnafeile House.** Gaelic for "house of welcome," Tighnafeile (*tyne-*
★   *a-faylee*) was built in 1911. The rooms have antiques, navy fleur-de-lis carpet, and honey-color timbered fireplaces (mostly for show). The house, which has a large garden, is almost opposite the Aigantighe Art Gallery. Pros: Very stately manor house, short drive to town, good off-street parking, the owners love vintage cars and have a courtesy Rolls Royce available. Con: Just a bit far from town to walk home after dinner. ⊠*62 Wai-iti Rd.* ☎*03/684–3333* ☎*03/684–3328* ⊕*www.tighnafeile.com* ✑*tighnafeile-house@timaru.com* ☜*4 rooms* ☖*In-room: Ethernet. In-hotel: restaurant, bar, no elevator, no kids under 12* ▤*DC, MC, V* ☉*BP, CP.*

The Chatham Islands

Although officially part of New Zealand, the Chatham Islands, 800 km (500 mi) east of the South Island, are a land apart. Bearing the full force of the open Southern Ocean, the islands are wild and weather-beaten. The air has a salty taste to it, the colors of the landscapes are more muted, and the vegetation is stunted and gnarly. Many unusual plants and birds are about—including the very rare black robin—and the empty beaches invite fishing and diving (although the presence of sharks makes the latter unadvisable).

Locals here refer to the mainland as New Zealand, as though it were an entirely separate country. Just 2 of the 10 islands are inhabited—the main island and tiny, neighboring Pitt Island. Most residents are either farmers or fishermen, but tourism is increasing. The Chathams were first settled by the Moriori, a race of Polynesian descent, about 800–1,000 years ago, although there are now no full-blooded Moriori left. Māori and

Europeans followed, and conflicts broke out between the separate populations throughout the 1800s. By the end of the 19th century, however, tensions had died down after the Native Land Court intervened in key disputes, and the new settlers established the strong maritime culture that still prevails on the islands.

When booking to fly to the Chathams it's imperative that you make lodging reservations in advance. There is only one round-trip flight a week from Christchurch but you can return earlier through Auckland or Wellington, and Air Chathams (⊕ *www.air chathams.co.nz*) is the only carrier. The islands are 45 minutes ahead of NZ time and therefore the first place on Earth to see the sun each day. Check out ⊕ *www.newzealand nz.co.nz/chatham-islands* for more details. Allow at least four days—you'll rarely get the chance to visit anywhere this remote. And don't forget to try the crayfish (lobsters).

$–$$ 🏨**Panorama Motor Lodge.** Sitting back a bit on the Bay Hill, the Panorama has views of the Pacific Ocean from the front units on the Bay Wing, and smaller views of Mt. Cook from the Alpine Wing units. It's a family-style accommodation ranging from studios to two-bedroom units (ideal if you're traveling with a few others). Each modestly furnished self-contained unit has a kitchen or kitchenette. Pros: Walk to anywhere in town from here, spa and sauna available, breakfast service is available. Con: Off-street parking is a bit cramped, especially if you're driving a camper. ⊠ *52 The Bay Hill* 🕾*03/688–0097* 🖨*03/688–0096* ⊕*www.panorama.net.nz* ✉*lets-stay@panorama. net.nz* ⬚*20 units* ♿*In-room: Ethernet, kitchen, no a/c. In-hotel: spa, laundry.* ▤*AE, MC, V* ⦿*EP.*

TOURS

Taking the **TranzAlpine & High Country Explorer** (🕾*03/377–1391 or 0800/863–975* 🖨*03/313–6494* ⊕*www.high-country.co.nz* ✉*info@ high-country.co.nz*) is definitely one of the best and most action-packed ways of getting into the Canterbury Plains and the Southern Alps, and experiencing the world-famous TranzAlpine train journey. The full-day trip starts with a hotel pickup for a two-hour trip on the TranzAlpine train, then a 65-km (40-mi) four-wheel-drive safari through the vast 35,000-acre Flock Hill sheep station (filming location for *The Lion, The Witch and the Wardrobe*), a 15-km (9-mi) jet-boat cruise, and a one-hour bus trip back to your Christchurch hotel. The scenery is spectacular, the boat ride a thrill, and your safari guide will discuss the region's human and natural history. A full-day trip is $350 per person, bookings recommended and three-course lunch included.

Canterbury Leisure Tours (☎ *03/384–0999 or 0800/484–485* ⊕ *www.leisuretours.co.nz*) runs day trips to Hanmer Springs and Akaroa. In addition to its Christchurch tours, it also offers half-day, full-day, and overnight tours and activities, including wine trails, horse trekking, night tours, sheep-farm visits, dolphin swimming, and a cheese factory visit. Bookings are essential.

Using four-wheel-drive minicoaches, **Canterbury Trails, Ltd.** (☎ *03/337–1185* 🖷 *03/337–5085* ⊕ *www.canterburytrails.co.nz*) can go off the beaten track on its personally guided tours. Among its itineraries is a full-day tour to Akaroa and the Banks Peninsula, which includes a dolphin-sighting cruise. Other day trips visit Arthur's Pass, Kaikoura, and Hanmer and reservations are essential.

On **Diana's Garden Tours** (☎ *03/385–3559*), local garden writer Diana Madgin takes you around some of Christchurch's and Canterbury's beautiful gardens.

Discovery Travel (☎ *03/357–8262* ⊕ *www.discoverytravel.co.nz*) runs day tours to the Waipara wine district, Akaroa, Hanmer and Arthur's Pass; it also organizes tours of some of the area's exceptional private gardens.

New Zealand food writer Mavis Airey of **Taste Canterbury** (☎ *03/326–6753* ⊕ *www.goodthings.co.nz*Imavis.airey@xtra.co.nz*) will guide you through the Canterbury hinterlands, Waipara, and Akaroa, checking out the producers of some of Canterbury's finest wines and food along the way. Runs all year and bookings are essential.

The Southern Alps & Fiordland

WORD OF MOUTH

"During our cruise on Lake Manapouri the guide turned the boat engines off and we stood in silence listening to waterfalls and birdsong. The guide said, 'Many of you are thinking that you'll have to return to reality: your office, your city, your apartment.' I sighed. Then he said: 'I want you all to remember something. This is reality.'"

—Liza Smith, Savannah

Updated by
Jessica Kany

AS MANY AS 60 GLACIERS are locked in the Southern Alps, slowly grinding their way down to lower altitudes, where they melt into running rivers of uncanny blue-green hues. Aoraki, or Mt. Cook, at 12,283 feet, is New Zealand's highest mountain, and 27 other peaks in this alpine chain are higher than 9,750 feet. Aoraki/Mount Cook National Park is a UNESCO World Heritage Area, and the alpine region around it contains the Tasman Glacier, at 27 km (17 mi), New Zealand's longest.

The Southern Alps region is great for hiking. Terrain varies from high alpine tundra to snow-covered peaks, heavily forested mountains, and wide, braided river valleys. A good network of trails and marked routes are throughout the mountains, but be well informed before venturing into them. Always make your intentions known to the local Department of Conservation (DOC) sign-in office before leaving, and check in with them after returning.

There are many easier options for exploring the foothills and less arduous parts of the Southern Alps. On the southwest corner of the island, glaciers over millennia have cut the Alps into stone walls dropping into fjords, and walking trails take you into the heart of wild Fiordland National Park. The Milford Track is the best known—it has been called the finest walk in the world since a headline to that effect appeared in the London *Spectator* in 1908. If you're not keen on walking to Milford Sound, hop on a boat and take in the sights from on deck. Most river valleys with road access have well-marked walking trails leading to scenic waterfalls, gorges, and lookout points.

Floods of tourists have come to see the otherworldly landscape used in shooting the *Lord of the Rings* film trilogy. The vastness of the region keeps it from feeling crowded, even with all the new visitors. Queenstown, often billed as an adventure-sports hot spot, is perhaps the best-known destination in the Southern Lakes district. It, and the nearby town of Wanaka, are steeped in gold-rush history and surrounded by stunning mountain scenery.

Note: *For more information on outdoor activities in lower South Island, see Chapter 11.*

ORIENTATION & PLANNING

GETTING ORIENTED

The Southern Alps start in the northern end of the South Island around Kaikoura and stretch through the provinces of Canterbury, inland Otago, Westland, and Southland. These are serious mountains, with jagged 9,000-plus feet peaks. The Mt. Cook area is the center of Kiwi mountaineering. These majestic formations take center stage, and beautiful landscape unfurls at their feet—green rivers braided with white stone banks, acres of lupines, and lakes hued with indescribable blues. From Lake Tekapo, you finally come to "rest" at the adventure-friendly cities of Queenstown and Wanaka, historic Arrowtown, and the truly restful ambience of the Otago vineyards. To the west, magnificent Milford Sound dominates Fiordland.

The Southern Alps. In Mount Cook National Park, activities naturally revolve around the mountain—climbing, hiking, skiing, and scenic flights. But as you travel down into the foothills and valleys, the choices for adventure multiply. Stargaze at Lake Tekapo, or go gliding at Omarama, "the place of light." Enjoy the miles of hills and farmland as you travel through Lindis Pass, soon the uninhabited country will give way to Wanaka and the bustle of Queenstown.

Fiordland. Te Anau is often referred to as a "jumping off" point to explore Milford Sound. But the town, on the country's second-largest lake, is worth a stay to see the glowworms in Te Anau Caves. Milford has two strikes against it: lots of sandflies and busloads of tourists. However, it's a truly wondrous place, and the enormous beauty makes mere humans and insects—even busloads of them—seem insignificant.

THE SOUTHERN ALPS & FIORDLAND PLANNER

GETTING HERE & AROUND

BY AIR

Qantas and Air New Zealand fly from Auckland and Christchurch into Queenstown, the main hub. Air New Zealand also serves Wanaka Airport. Tourist enterprises operate helicopters and fixed-wing planes which buzz between Queenstown, Wanaka, Milford Sound, Franz Josef, and Mount Cook. You can do fly-cruise-fly packages from Queenstown to Milford, although the flight from Wanaka to Milford is the most spectacular. It may take a full day, but you can take buses to and from the major towns in the Southern Alps and Fiordland area.

BY BUS

InterCity operates a daily bus service between Christchurch and Queenstown via Mount Cook Village, with a one-hour stop at the Hermitage Hotel for lunch. Their coaches also make daily trips from the Franz Josef and Fox glaciers through Wanaka to Queenstown. InterCity also goes down the South Island's eastern flank from Christchurch to Queenstown via Dunedin. Newmans, meanwhile, runs a daily bus service from Christchurch through Mount Cook to Queenstown and a daily bus round-trip route from Queenstown to Milford Sound and Te Anau to Milford Sound. Wanaka Connections sends buses between Wanaka and Queenstown several times a day. They also run to Christchurch, Te Anau, Dunedin, and Invercargill.

BY CAR

Exploring is best done by car on the state highways that weave their way through the vast mountain ranges, skirting several major lakes and rivers. Be prepared for rugged, quickly changing terrain, ice in winter, and frequent downpours, particularly around Milford Sound. Rental-car companies may discourage driving on some of the smaller, unpaved roads, so it is best to avoid them unless you're experienced in

9

TOP REASONS TO GO

Bungy Jumping: Don't worry, New Zealanders aren't going to pressure you into jumping off a bridge with an elastic cord tied to your ankles. But if you have an overwhelming desire to bungy (Kiwi for "bungee"), this is where to do it.

Fly-Fishing: The lakes and rivers of the Southern Alps are some of the world's best fly-fishing spots. The waters are so clear half the challenge is hiding from your target. Most guides follow the catch-and-release policy.

Hiking: South Island's southwestern wilderness areas are the stuff of legendary tramping. It doesn't get any better than the Milford Track, the Kepler, the Routeburn, and the Hollyford. You'll see mountains, fjords, waterfalls, and rain forests, and because the DOC keeps a close eye on trail traffic, you'll have the exhilarating sense of being alone in the wilderness.

Scenic Flights: With high mountain peaks, deep fiords, rambling glaciers, thick forest, and open tussock lands all in close proximity, a scenic flight in either a fixed-wing plane or helicopter is money well spent. If you think the Southern Alps are spectacular from the ground, wait until you see them from above!

driving on gravel roads. That said, an ideal way to see the Alps is to "tiki-tour" (wander around) by car, as the main network of roads is paved and easy to negotiate.

WHEN TO GO

Although the Southern Alps and Fiordland have four distinct seasons, it's not unusual for the mountains to get snow even in summer. If you're traveling in winter, check the weather forecasts and road conditions regularly. Mountain passes can close for short periods because of snow and ice and, even when they are open, can be very dangerous. The road into Milford Sound can close for days at a time because of snow or avalanche risk.

For skiing, snowboarding, and other winter sports, from July through September you can be assured of snow around Queenstown and Wanaka, where the ski scene is ushered in by the Queenstown Winter Festival. In the height of summer—from January to March—both resort towns are crowded with Kiwi holiday makers. To avoid the crowds, hold off until March or April, when the leaves start turning. If you're planning on hiking one of the major trails, such as the Milford Track, summer or early autumn are the best times, but you'll need to book ahead. This is also the best time to visit Fiordland National Park. Fiordland is soaked with rain year-round (it's the wettest place in the country), so there's little use trying to avoid the rainy season.

ABOUT THE RESTAURANTS & HOTELS

Queenstown, as the main regional resort, has the widest range of restaurants. Throughout the area menus focus on local produce, seafood, lamb, and venison. Wine lists often highlight South Island wines, especially those from central Otago and Gibbston Valley. Cafés and restaurants driven by the summer tourist trade shorten their hours in winter. Dress standards are generally relaxed, with jeans or khakis acceptable almost everywhere. At high-end places, particularly in Queenstown, you'll need to reserve a table at least a day in advance.

Outside of Queenstown and Wanaka dining options can be limited. In summer, meals of some sort are available almost everywhere, but outside the high season, options in the smaller settlements can be minimal.

Lodgings in the Southern Alps and Fiordland milk the fantastic views for all they're worth. You can almost always find a room that looks out on a lake, river, or rugged mountain range. Queenstown and Wanaka are busy in the summer (January through March) and winter (July through September), so you should reserve in advance. Award-winning luxury options are plentiful in Queenstown, and costs are correspondingly high. Other towns, such as Aoraki/Mount Cook Village, have very limited options, so you should plan ahead there, too. Air-conditioning is rare since it's rarely needed. Heating, though, is standard, and essential in winter.

WHAT IT COSTS IN NEW ZEALAND DOLLARS					
	¢	$	$$	$$$	$$$$
Hotels	under $75	$75–$125	$125–$200	$200–$300	over $300
Restaurants	under $10	$10–$15	$15–$20	$20–$30	over $30

Prices are for a standard double room in high season, including 12.5% tax.

VISITOR INFORMATION

The regional visitor bureaus are open daily year-round, with slightly longer hours in summer. These local tourism organizations have helpful Web sites, including Destination Fiordland (⊕*www.fiordland.org.nz*) and Mackenzie Winter (⊕*www.mackenziewinter.co.nz)*.

THE SOUTHERN ALPS

The Canterbury Plains ring Christchurch and act as a brief transition between the South Pacific and the soaring New Zealand Alps. The drive south along the plain is mundane by New Zealand standards until you leave State Highway 1 and head toward the Southern Alps.

Then the route south, along the eastern flank of the Alps, can leave you breathless. The mountain ranges reflect in the many lakes and rivers that shimmer among the peaks. No matter how absorbing your activities may be—fishing, hiking, or skiing—take some time to just sit back and gaze at this astonishing landscape. Head through Lindis Pass by traveling inland to Fairlie and Tekapo, then south to Omarama; you'll be entering the country's adventure-sports playground, where Wanaka and Queenstown offer at least a dozen ways to get your adrenaline pumping. A handful of notable vineyards is icing on the cake.

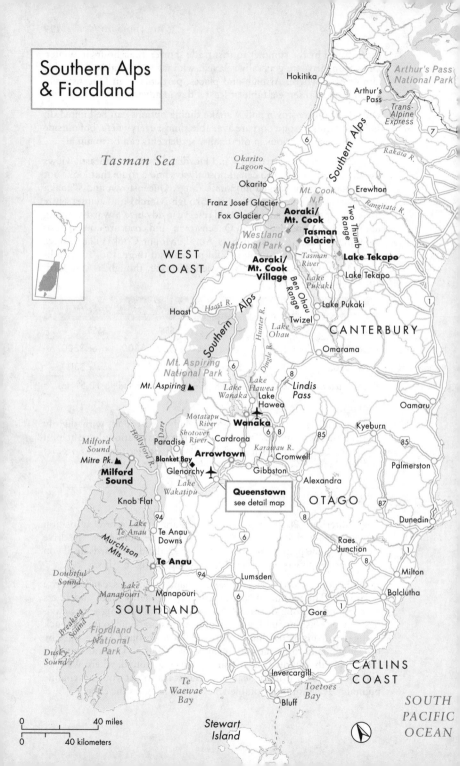

MACKENZIE COUNTRY & LAKE TEKAPO

227 km (141 mi) west of Christchurch.

You will know you have reached the **Mackenzie Country** after you cross Burkes Pass and the woodland is suddenly replaced by high-country tussock grassland, which is dotted with lupines in the summer months. The area is named for James ("Jock") McKenzie, one of the most intriguing and enigmatic figures in New Zealand history. McKenzie was a Scot who may or may not have stolen the thousand sheep found with him in these secluded upland pastures in 1855. Arrested, tried, and convicted, he made several escapes from jail before he was granted a pardon nine months after his trial—and disappeared from the pages of history. Regardless of his innocence or guilt, McKenzie was a master bushman and herdsman. A commemorative obelisk marks Mackenzie Pass, 30 km (18 mi) off the main highway if you turn off at Burkes Pass.

GETTING HERE & AROUND

From Christchurch take Highway 1 south. At the tiny town of Rangitata turn right onto Highway 79 to Lake Tekapo.

ESSENTIALS

Visitor Info **Lake Tekapo Information** (✉ *Main Rd., Lake Tekapo* ☎ *03/680–6686*). **The Resource Centre** (✉ *64 Main St., Fairlie* ☎ *03/685-8496* ⊕ *www.southisland.org.nz/heritagetrails/bullockwagon.html*).

WHAT TO SEE

The long, narrow expanse of **Lake Tekapo,** one of the most photographed sights in New Zealand, anchors the area. Its extraordinary milky-turquoise color comes from rock flour, rock ground by glacial action and held in a soupy suspension. The only thing making the hue more spectacular is a pair of polarized sunglasses. Tekapo, the country's highest large lake, has good fly-fishing in the lake and in the surrounding rivers and canals.

On the east side of the lakeside power station is the tiny **Church of the Good Shepherd.** The simple stone structure doesn't need stained glass; the view through the window is the lake's brilliant blue. A nearby memorial commemorates the sheepdogs of the area. As you drive into the small town, you'll notice a knot of restaurants with tour buses parked outside. It's rather an off-putting image, but it's relatively easy to keep the township at your back and your eyes on the lake and mountains—and get a tasty meal. If you're not planning to stay at Mt. Cook, then Tekapo is the best place in the Mackenzie Basin to stop for the night. And once the buses have passed through for the day, it's a quiet spot—at least until the hordes of Cantabrians arrive for the summer break. A pleasant lakefront recreation area separates the town retail area from the lakeshore.

OFF THE BEATEN PATH

Bullock Wagon Trail. This 268-km (167-mi) heritage highway, which stretches from Timaru to Twizel via Mt. Cook, recognizes the long, arduous journeys early settlers in the region made by bullock wagon.

Leaving the Canterbury Plains at Geraldine or Pleasant Point (depending on whether you are coming directly from Christchurch or through from Timaru), the highways join at Fairlie and quickly climb toward the first of the alpine passes—Burkes Pass—along the Bullock Wagon Trail. The Burkes Pass monument marks the division between the high and low country, and from there the country immediately dries out and takes on the look of high-country tussocklands. To learn more about the trail and the history of the region, stop in at one of two information centers along the way: **Lake Tekapo Information** (✉*Main Rd., Lake Tekapo* ☎☎*03/680–6686*) **The Resource Centre** (✉*64 Main St., Fairlie* ☎☎*03/685–8496* ⊕*www.southisland.org. nz/heritagetrails/bullockwagon.html*).

SPORTS & THE OUTDOORS

FISHING   **Barry Clark Fly-Fishing & Small Game Hunting Guide** (✉*1 Esther-Hope St., Lake Tekapo* ☎*03/680–6513* ⊕*www.fredadufaur.co.nz*) will take you fly-fishing or spinning, whatever your preference, to the most suitable lake or river spot of the day. Barry's knowledge of the local spots is exhaustive.

HIKING   At the Tekapo Information Centre you can pick up a walking-trail map and then take off to hike the **Domain to Mt. John Lookout track.** In a couple of hours you can be well above the township, enjoying extensive views of the Mackenzie Basin, Southern Alps, and Lake Tekapo.

STARGAZING   If you're extremely lucky, you'll see the southern lights! **Earth and Sky** (✉*Main St., State Hwy. 8, Lake Tekapo* ☎*03/680–6960* ⊕*www. earthandsky.co.nz*) operates from the Mt. John Observatory and studies the skies above Lake Tekapo. A sign asks you to dim your headlights on approach; the galaxy is considered part of the park and nobody wants you to outshine the stars. The Astro Café features ham-off-the-bone sandwiches, telescopes, and dizzying views. Stargazing trips leave from the town office at 8 PM in the winter and 10 PM in the summer; they cost $48 per adult ($24 per child), and reservations are essential. Daytime tours of the facility cost $20 ($5 per child) and can be booked at the café.

WHERE TO EAT

$$$–$$$$ ✕**Reflections Café.** Great views of the lake are seen from almost every table at this rustically decorated restaurant. Reflections consistently wins awards for its beef and lamb dishes, and salmon from a nearby hatchery is also delicious. As many ingredients as possible are obtained locally to maintain freshness in the meals. ✉*Lake Tekapo Scenic Resort, State Hwy. 8* ☎☎*03/680–6234* ▤*MC, V.*

$$–$$$$ ✕**The Garden Courtyard.** An impressive buffet appears three times a day in this pleasant dining room. Lunch and dinner selections always include six entrées and another half dozen vegetable dishes, as well as soups, salads, and several desserts. The salmon is reliably good, and if you've caught your own, the restaurant kitchen will cook it for you. Between lunch and dinner, a snack menu offers panini, soup, mussels, warm chicken salad, and the like, all for less than $12. ✉*The Godley Hotel, State Hwy. 8* ☎*03/680–6848* ▤*AE, MC, V.*

¢–$$$$ ✕**Kohan Japanese Restaurant.** Masato Itoh runs the only Japanese restaurant in town, which gives him guaranteed access to busloads of tourists from his home country. Sushi, sashimi, and tempura are all on the menu. The restaurant has some of the best views over Lake Tekapo, but unfortunately it lacks atmosphere. The food, however, is a refreshing change from the more traditional lunch options in town. It's open for lunch from 11 to 2 and for dinner from 6 PM on. ⊠*State Hwy. 8* ☎*03/680–6688* ▤*AE, DC, MC, V* ⊘*No dinner Sun.*

¢–$$ ✕**Jade Palace.** You might pat the big Buddha's tummy on the way into this restaurant, but you will soon be patting your own as it is hard to give the chopsticks a rest here. There is nothing fancy on this menu, just straightforward very good Chinese food in a spacious dining room. At busy times service can be brusque. Open seven days for lunch and dinner. ⊠*State Hwy. 8* ☎*03/680–6828* ▤*AE, MC, V.*

¢–$ ✕**Doughboys.** In a town where most of the dining options are along the main drag of souvenir shops and cafés, it's nice to escape with a sandwich, a pastry, or a pie and eat down at the lakefront. Doughboys bakes several different breads, croissants, and 10 different pies. Sandwiches have yummy fillings such as seafood, chicken, or bacon and eggs, and the scones are legendary. In case that's not enough, you can grab a sit-down breakfast (bacon, two eggs, tomato), for about $12. ⊠*State Hwy. 8* ☎*03/680–6655* ▤*No credit cards* ⊘*No dinner.*

WHERE TO STAY

$$$ ★ ▥**Aldourie Lodge.** With a fireplace, claw-foot bathtub, lake views, and library, this charming house is the perfect place to unwind. The owners Graeme Murray and his wife saved this historic building from being torn down and renovated it, retaining the character while adding modern luxuries. The view is superb. The price is for two people; each additional guest is $35. Inquire about the Murrays' other properties, which are just as beautiful and cozy. (**The Garden Cottage,** across the street, has the Prime Minister in its guest book!) **Pros:** All properties are cozy and thoughtfully decorated. **Con:** It books quickly, so try to reserve well in advance. ⊠*3 Sealy St.* ☎*03/680–6709* ▤*03/680–6709* ⊕*www.parkbrae.co.nz* ➫*3 rooms* ♿*In-room: DVD. In-hotel: kitchen, laundry* ▤*AE, DC, MC, V.*

$$–$$$ ▥**The Chalet.** The Chalet's six fully-self-contained apartments stretch beside the turquoise waters of Lake Tekapo. Units range from studio size to a two-bedroom cottage apartment. The best have spacious living rooms and lake views; two of the rooms open onto a small patio area and lovely alpine gardens. You can arrange a customized local expedition with the host, an experienced hunting, fishing, and nature guide. Tekapo Township is a scenic five-minute walk away. **Pro:** Superb views. **Con:** Decor a bit dated. ⊠*14 Pioneer Dr.* ☎*03/680–6774* ▤*03/680–6713* ⊕*www.thechalet.co.nz* ➫*6 units* ♿*In-room: no a/c. In-hotel: laundry service* ▤*AE, MC, V.*

$$–$$$ ▥**Lake Tekapo Scenic Resort.** A nice mid-range alternative with good family-style facilities, this resort is in the center of town. Still, it opens out to the lakefront area, and many units have lake views. A big three-bedroom upstairs apartment is available if you're traveling with the family. Meals at Reflections restaurant next door are on a charge-back

9

basis. **Pros:** Good value, friendly management, minigolf with lake view. **Cons:** Very basic rooms: no frills. ⊠ *State Hwy. 8* ☎ *03/680–6808 or 0800/118–666* 🖷 *03/680–6806* ⊕ *www.laketekapo.com* 🔧 *6 family units, 12 studios, 1 3-bedroom apartment* 🕭 *In-hotel: laundry facilities* ⊟ *DC, MC, V.*

¢ 🔠 **Tailor-Made-Tekapo Backpackers.** The beautiful garden is made for sunbathing in warm weather. In winter, there's a cozy lounge with a fireplace to curl up in front of. There are various room arrangements, from singles to four- and six-bed dorm rooms; all, including the dorms, have regular beds (no bunks). It's a very kid-friendly spot. Bring your BBH card if you have one. **Pro:** As nice as a backpackers can be. **Con:** Located in residential neighborhood back from the lake. ⊠ *9–11 Aorangi Crescent* ☎ *03/680–6700* ⊕ *www.tailor-made-backpackers.co.nz* 🔧 *13 rooms, 10 with shared bath, 3 dorms* 🕭 *In-room: no TV. In-hotel: tennis court, bicycles* ⊟ *MC, V.*

AORAKI (MT. COOK)

99 km (62 mi) from Lake Tekapo.

GETTING HERE & AROUND

The 330-km (205-mi) drive from Christchurch straight through to Aoraki/Mount Cook Village takes four hours. Take Highway 1 south out of Christchurch. At the tiny town of Rangitata turn right onto Highway 79 to Lake Tekapo. Pass through Lake Tekapo and look on the right for Highway 80 to Aoraki/Mount Cook Village. InterCity buses make daily stops at Mount Cook Village.

ESSENTIALS

Bus Company **InterCity** (☎ *03/443–7885 in Wanaka, 03/249–7559 in Te Anau, 03/442–8238 in Queenstown* ⊕ *www.intercitycoach.co.nz*).

Visitor Info Contact the **Aoraki/Mount Cook National Park Visitor Centre** (⊠ *Aoraki/Mount Cook Village* ☎ *03/435–1186* ⊕ *www.doc.govt.nz* ☎ *03/435–1186*).

Fodor's Choice
★
Above the grassy Mackenzie Basin towers **Aoraki (Mt. Cook)**, at approximately 12,283 feet the tallest of the 22 peaks over 10,000 feet in **Aoraki/Mount Cook National Park.** The mountain's Māori name is Aoraki (Aorangi to North Island Māori), after one of three brothers who were the sons of Rakinui, the sky father. Legend has it that their canoe was caught on a reef and frozen, forming the South Island. In these parts, South Island's oldest Māori name is Te Waka O Aoraki (Aoraki's canoe) and the highest peak is Aoraki, himself frozen by the south wind, then turned to stone. Māori see these mountains as their ancestors. The officially recognized names of this mountain, the national park, and many other South Island places have been changed to their original Māori names as part of a 1998 settlement between the government and the major South Island Māori tribe, Ngai Tahu.

Aoraki was dramatically first scaled in 1894 by three New Zealanders—Tom Fyfe, George Graham, and Jack Clarke—just after it was announced that an English climber and an Italian mountain guide were about to attempt the summit. In a frantic surge of national pride, the New Zealand trio resolved to beat them to it, which they did on Christmas Day. In the summer of 1991 a chunk of it broke away, but fortunately there were no climbers in the path of the massive avalanches. High Peak, the summit, is now about 66 feet lower, but its altered form makes for a much more difficult ascent.

At 439 square km (270 square mi), the park is a formidable area of ice and rock, with glaciers covering 40% of the land and little forest cover. Unfortunately, the high altitude attracts its share of bad weather. Visitors can often stand at the end of Lake Tekapo or Lake Pukaki, looking westward, and not know that the country's highest mountain is just a few miles away. But that shouldn't prevent you from taking the 40-km (25-mi) paved road up to Mount Cook village. And stay the night while you're there—nowhere else in the region compares for a true alpine experience. Accommodation and food options range from luxury rooms to backpackers' lodges and campsites. If the clouds lift, you'll be glad you stayed: the vistas are beyond spectacular.

The national park surrounds **Aoraki/Mount Cook Village** (population 300), which consists of a visitor center, a grocery store, an airfield, a pub, a little school, a hotel/motel complex, and several hostels. Walking is always an option, and in winter there's heli-skiing. If the weather is clear, a scenic flight around the Mt. Cook area and across to the West Coast can be the highlight of your stay in New Zealand. Contact the **Aoraki/Mount Cook National Park Visitor Centre** or the **weather phone** (☎*03/435–1171*) to check conditions before setting out on an unguided excursion. A network of hiking trails radiates from the Aoraki/Mount Cook National Park Visitor Centre, offering everything from easy walking paths to full-day challenges. There are some especially lovely wildflowers to search out, such as the Mount Cook lily, really the world's largest buttercup. A cairn just a few minutes along the track up the Hooker Valley remembers 40 of the more than 180 people who have died in the park since climbing began there. Be sure to fill your car's gas tank before leaving Twizel or Tekapo; although fuel is available at the Hermitage hotel, there are no credit card facilities at the pumps and the hours are limited.

For a unique hands-on educational experience take a half-hour hike to the fast-growing 2-square-km (1-square-mi) **Terminus Lake of the Tasman Glacier.** Fed by the glacier and the Murchison River, the lake was formed only in the past couple of decades, because of the glacier's retreat. Rock flour, a powdery white residue, gives the water a milky color (farther downstream, it also creates the unusual turquoise-blue color of Lake Pukaki). From Terminus Lake, which is officially growing by a foot a week, you can examine up close the terminal face of the glacier, which is 3 km (2 mi) wide. A trip with Glacier Explorers (⇨ *Tours at the end of this chapter*) can take you by boat to explore some of the large floating icebergs that have calved (fallen away) from the Tasman Glacier. It's an eerie experience skimming across the milky-

Safety in the High Country

The Fiordland region's remoteness and changeable weather make it necessary to take some sensible precautions. So, before you head out on that trek or boat trip, keep the following in mind:

Be sure to wear the right protective clothing: sturdy hiking boots, a waterproof jacket, and a warm layer such as a fleece or wool pullover. Weather in this region, especially at high altitude, can change dramatically in a short time.

Watch out for sunburn—take sunscreen and a hat with you. Also bring bug repellent for sandflies, which are impossible to avoid in this region unless you're traveling offshore by boat.

If you're heading off without a guide for more than an hour or

two, let someone know where and when you're going and when you've returned. DOC visitor centers have sign-in books and issue regular weather and trail updates.

Use extreme caution when crossing rivers. Especially after rain, mountain runoff can quickly turn a gentle stream into an angry torrent, and drowning is a major hazard. If you do get trapped on one side of a quickly rising river, wait for the water to recede rather than risk crossing.

For longer treks into serious country always carry a map and compass, first-aid gear, bottled water, high-energy foods, warm clothes and tent, and a mountain radio or EPIRB (locator beacon—these can be rented locally). Cell phones don't work in the mountains.

white water and closing in on icebergs—even riding *through* where they have melted—to touch rocks caught in the ice.

Another main activity is "flightseeing." From the airfield at Mount Cook Village, helicopters and fixed-wing aircraft make spectacular scenic flights across the Southern Alps. One of the most exciting is the one-hour trip aboard the ski planes that touch down on the **Tasman Glacier** after a gorgeous scenic flight. The 10-minute stop on the glacier doesn't allow time for much more than a snapshot, but the sensation is tremendous. The moving tongue of ice beneath your feet—one of the largest glaciers outside the Himalayas—is 27 km (17 mi) long and up to 2,000 feet thick in places. The intensity of light on the glacier can be dazzling, and sunglasses are a must. In winter the planes drop skiers on the glacier at 10,000 feet, and they ski down through 13 km (8 mi) of powder snow and fantastic ice formations. With guides, this run is suitable even for intermediate skiers.

SPORTS & THE OUTDOORS

CLIMBING &
MOUNTAINEERING
Summer is the best climbing season in the Aoraki/Mount Cook National Park area. **Adventure Consultants** (☎ 03/443–8711 ⊕ www. adventure.co.nz), a group specializing in the world's top peaks, guides ascents of Aoraki and Mt. Tasman. They also give multiday mountaineering, alpine-climbing, and ice-climbing courses. Because the company is based in Wanaka, they work Mt. Cook only in good weather, so call and reserve ahead. Experienced climbers or beginners can sign

up for the appropriate level of **Alpine Guides'** (✉ *Bowen Dr., Mount Cook Village* ☎ *03/435–1834* ⊕ *www.alpineguides.co.nz*) 6- to 10-day mountaineering courses, which begin around $2,350. They offer half-day rock-climbing trips costing $150, including equipment. From July to September they also run heli-ski trips, ski tours, ice climbing, and ski mountaineering.

FLIGHTSEEING Flightseeing gives you an unparalleled view of the mountains, with the added thrill of landing on a glacier for a short walk. The light can be intensely bright in such dazzlingly white surroundings, so be sure to bring sunglasses. Generally, the best time for flights is early morning. **Mount Cook Ski Planes** (☎ *03/430–8034 or 0800/800–702* ⊕ *www. mtcookskiplanes.com*) has four options, including a 25-minute flight over two glaciers ($220) or a 55-minute flight with a glacier landing ($430). Or take a breathtaking 50-minute scenic flight to see Aoraki, the Tasman, Murchison, Fox, and Franz Josef glaciers, and the rain forests on the west side of the Main Divide with **Air Safaris** (☎ *03/680– 6545* ⊕ *www.airsafaris.co.nz*). Flights start at $260 per adult. **The Helicopter Line** (✉ *Glentanner Station, State Hwy. 80* ☎ *03/435–1801 or 0800/650–651* ⊕ *www.helicopter.co.nz*) runs 20-minute and 45-minute flights from Glentanner Station, about 20 km (12 mi) toward Pukaki from the Hermitage. You can land on the glaciers or high snowfields, depending on the weather.

HIKING The hiking trails spooling out from the visitor center range in difficulty and length, from the 10-minute Bowen Track to the 5½-hour climb to the 4,818-foot summit of Mt. Sebastopol. Seven tracks can be done in running shoes and don't require hiking experience; the rest of the park's trails require some hiking experience, and the higher routes require serious mountaineering experience. The Mueller Hut route is a popular climb, taking about three hours; a new 30-bed hut provides overnight accommodation. The rewarding Hooker Valley walk, a four-hour round-trip, will take you across a couple of swing bridges to the Hooker Glacier terminus lake, and the Tasman Glacier Lake walk gives an intimate view of New Zealand's longest glacier.

WHERE TO STAY & EAT

The Hermitage Hotel houses two excellent restaurants. As the name suggests, the Panorama Room ($$$–$$$$) restaurant takes in the scenery, too. Its menu leans toward both the Pacific Rim and Europe; you could try panfried monkfish or a char-grilled beef tenderloin. The Alpine Restaurant ($$$–$$$$) serves a huge buffet-style meal for lunch and dinner.

$$$–$$$$ **The Hermitage Hotel.** Famed for its stupendous mountain vistas, this rambling hotel has been substantially revamped over the past few years. The improved layout now gives most of the rooms, as well as the lobby, terrific views over Aoraki and Mt. Sefton. Some accommodations, such as the motel rooms and self-contained chalets, are separate from the main lodge, and the views aren't as spectacular; but the prices and space are good for families. Room rates include breakfast. If you're traveling out of the high season, excellent discounts are available on

room rates. Be sure to keep your car in the hotel's parking, safe from the beaks of the cheeky local keas. **Pros:** Spectacular views, efficiently run establishment. **Cons:** Rooms with views are quite pricey, remember there are no guaranteed views of the mountains as there's often cloud cover. ⊠ *Aoraki/Mount Cook Village* ☎*03/435–1809 or 0800/686–800* 🖷*03/435–1879* ⊕*www.mount-cook.com* ⟲*214 rooms, 19 chalets, 32 motel units* ⟐*In-room: no a/c (some). In-hotel: 2 restaurants, bar, public Internet* ▤*AE, DC, MC, V* ⎮◎⎮*BP, CP.*

$$$ ⌧ **Lake View Homestay.** In addition to views of Lake Pukaki, you'll spy Aoraki/Mt. Cook and the Ben Ohau mountains through the floor-to-ceiling windows or from the porch. The peaks of the roofline mirror the toothy ranges beyond; timber walls inside are comforting. If you'd like to see a working shepherd-dog demonstration, go fishing, or take a helicopter trip, just say the word to your hosts. Breakfast is included. **Pros:** Breathtaking location and views. **Con:** Half-hour drive to Mt. Cook. ⊠ *Mt. Cook Rd., State Hwy. 80, Lake Pukaki* ☎*03/435–0567* 🖷*03/435–0568* ⊕*www.lakeviewhomestay.co.nz* ⟲*4 rooms, 3 with bath* ⟐*In-room: no a/c, no TV. In-hotel: no kids under 12* ▤*No credit cards* ⎮◎⎮*BP, CP.*

$$ ⌧ **Aoraki/Mt. Cook Alpine Lodge.** This lodge, run by a young local family, has dorm rooms, twin, triple, and family rooms, many with private bathrooms. All rooms have mountain views (some are greater than others). The alpine-style decor uses lots of native timber and glass, and a huge stone fireplace is in the lobby. **Pro:** Great guest lounge. **Con:** Not a lot of meal options, so be prepared to buy groceries and cook. ⊠ *Bowen Dr., Mount Cook Village* ☎*03/435–1860 or 0800/680–680* ⊕*www.aorakialpinelodge.co.nz* ⟲*15 rooms* ⟐*In-hotel: kitchen, laundry facilities, public Internet* ▤*MC, V.*

¢   △ **White Horse Hill Campground.** Although this DOC-managed campsite is really just a grassy basin surrounded by massive mountains and a rumbling glacier, its basic facilities and closeness to trails make it ideal to park a camper or pitch a tent in. (Once again, make sure those keas don't steal your lunch or rip the rubber parts off your cars!) You can pay at the DOC Visitors Centre before setting up camp or in the honesty box down at the campsite. The running water needs to be boiled for three minutes before you drink it; you can grab a shower back at the Day Shelter in the village for $1. No reservations are taken; it's first-come, first-served. ⊠ *Hooker Valley Rd., end of road* ☎*03/435–1186* 🖷*03/435–1080* ⊕*www.doc.govt.nz.*

TWIZEL

65 km (40 mi) from Lake Tekapo, 40 km (25 mi) from Aoraki/Mt. Cook.

A service town to its core, Twizel was built in 1968 as a base for workers constructing a major hydroelectric power plant. When the hydroelectric scheme wrapped up, the residents fought to keep their town intact. Now it's a handy place for tourist overflow in the Aoraki/Mt. Cook area. Birders should check with the visitor center about tours to the *kaki* aviary to see these striking, endangered, red-legged birds.

Twizel is close to five good-size boating and leisure lakes and has a great place to eat called Poppies. Having already passed Tekapo and Pukaki, you'll find Lake Ruataniwha a little tame. Lake Ohau is a little off the main road, but is another high-country fishing gem. A ski slope, Ohau Snow Fields, opens in July each winter, and a number of walks are in the nearby Ohau Forest Range. For area information stop by the **Twizel Information Centre** (⊠ *61 Mackenzie Dr.* ☎ *03/435–3124* ⊕ *www. twizel.com*) and the **Lake Pukaki Visitor Information Centre** (⊠ *State Hwy. 8, Twizel* ☎ *03/435–3280* ⊕ *www.mtcook.org.nz*).

WHERE TO STAY & EAT

$–$$$ ✕ **Poppies Cafe.** This is the best place to eat in town. Meat, seafood, pizza, and pasta are complimented by organic produce from the garden, fresh-baked bread and pizza bases, homemade sausage, and a terrific wine list. On hot days Poppies opens up into a garden with long tables: it's a great place to eat, drink, socialize, and bask in the sun. Offering breakfast, lunch, and dinner daily, Poppies is open from 9 AM weekdays and 8 AM weekends. ⊠ *Benmore Pl.* ☎ *03/435–0848* 🖨 *03/435–0324* ⊕ *www.poppiescafe.com* ⊟ *AE, MC, V.*

$$$$ 🏠 **Matuka Lodge.** If fly-fishing's your game, this lodge is ideal. You can arrange for a guide to the nearby rivers to go after rainbow and brown trout, or do a bit of angling on the lodge's private pond. Each room has a veranda with mountain views. The less expensive rate is a room with a shower and no bathtub. Your room rate includes breakfast and predinner drink. **Pro:** Charming hosts. **Con:** Forty-minute drive to Mt. Cook. ⊠ *Old Station Rd.* ☎ *03/435–0144* ⊕ *www.matukalodge.co.nz* ⇖ *3 suites* ♨ *In-room: no TV. In-hotel: restaurant, public Internet, no kids under 12* ⊟ *AE, DC, MC, V* ⭐ *MAP.*

$$ 🏠 **MacKenzie Country Inn.** Its imposing stone-and-timber buildings make an impression in this otherwise nondescript town. Filled mainly by busloads of package tourists, its comfortable rooms and large lounges, complete with welcoming fires, are often full to capacity. Rooms range from standard to deluxe, and the prices are reasonable. **Pro:** Reasonably priced. **Con:** Food isn't great—check out Poppies across the street. ⊠ *Ostler Rd. at Wairepo Rd.* ☎ *03/435–0869 or 0800/500–869* 🖨 *03/435–0857* ⊕ *www.mackenzie.co.nz* ⇖ *108 rooms* ♨ *In-hotel: restaurant, bar* ⊟ *AE, DC, MC, V.*

WANAKA

70 km (44 mi) northeast of Queenstown, 140 km (87 mi) southwest of Twizel.

On the southern shore of Lake Wanaka, with some of New Zealand's most striking mountains behind it, Wanaka is the welcome mat for Mt. Aspiring National Park. It's a favorite of Kiwis on vacation, an alternative of sorts to Queenstown. The region has numerous trekking and river-sports opportunities, and if you arrive on a rainy day, you can hit a couple of unusual cultural attractions. These good points have not gone unnoticed, and Wanaka is one of the fastest-growing towns in New Zealand, with new housing popping up in record time.

A short but pleasant drive to the western side of the lake brings you to Glendhu Bay. With nothing here but a campground and fabulous mountain and lake views, the real charm in this drive lies in the unspoiled atmosphere and surreal quiet (except in midsummer, when it is packed full of vacationing locals). This road also leads to the Aspiring region and the Treble Cone ski area.

Up in the Crown Range, the Snow Park in the Cardrona Valley is the country's only dedicated snowboard park. The 60-acre property has more than 30 rails and kickers, a super-pipe, a half-pipe, and a quarter pipe as well as a bar and restaurant. In summer it becomes the Dirt Park and is a hot spot for mountain bike enthusiasts.

ESSENTIALS

Bus Companies **InterCity** (☎ *03/443–7885 in Wanaka, 03/249–7559 in Te Anau, 03/442–8238 in Queenstown ⊕ www.intercitycoach.co.nz*). **Wanaka Connexions** (☎ *03/443–9122 ⊕ www.time2.co.nz/transport/wanaka_connexions*).

Bus Depot **Wanaka** (⊠ *Edgewater Adventures, 59a Brownston St.*).

Internet Café **Bits N Bytes** (⊠ *46 Helwick St., Wanaka ☎ 03/443–7078*).

Mail **Wanaka** (⊠ *39 Ardmore St. ☎ 03/443–8211*).

Visitor Info **Wanaka Visitor Information Centre** (⊠ *The Log Cabin, Ardmore St. ☎ 03/443–1233 🖷 03/443–1290*).

WHAT TO SEE

Lying spectacularly by the shores of Lake Wanaka, **Rippon Vineyard** is one of the most photographed in the country. The vineyard's portfolio includes sparkling wine, Riesling, gewürztraminer, chardonnay, sauvignon blanc, and fine (but expensive) pinot noir. Every other year, it's the venue for the Rippon Open Air Festival one of the country's most popular music festivals; the next one is scheduled for February 2010. Head west from Wanaka along the lake on Mt. Aspiring Road for 4 km (2½ mi). ⊠ *Mt. Aspiring Rd. ☎ 03/443–8084 ⊕ www.rippon.co.nz ⊙ Dec.–Apr., daily 11–5; July–Nov., daily 1:30–4:30.*

On your way into town on State Highway 6, you'll pass the **New Zealand Fighter Pilots Museum.** The museum is a tribute to New Zealand fighter pilots. The collection of planes includes aircraft used during the two world wars, such as the British Spitfire and rarities like the Russian Polikarpov I-16. Check out the biennial international air show Warbirds over Wanaka, where you can see some of these magnificent aircraft in flight. ⊠ *State Hwy. 6 ☎ 03/443–7010 ⊕ www.nzfpm.co.nz 🖅 $8 ⊙ Daily 9–4.*

☾ **Stuart Landsborough's Puzzling World** features a number of puzzling life-size brainteasers, including the amazing Tumbling Towers and the Tilted House, which is on a 15-degree angle (is the water really running uphill?), as well as the Leaning Tower of Wanaka. The Great Maze can be as demanding as you want to make it by setting individual challenges. In the Following Faces room it's an eerie feeling to have so many famous people watch your every move, and the bathroom is full of bizarre surprises. But the place to really take your time is the popular Puzzle Centre. Just take on the puzzle of your choice, order a cup of coffee, and work yourself into a puzzled frenzy. The place is 2 km (1 mi) east of town—just look for the cartoonlike houses built at funny angles. ⊠*Hwy. 84* ☎*03/443–7489* ⊕*www.puzzlingworld. co.nz* ⊡*$10* ☾*Nov.–Apr., daily 8:30–5:30; May–Oct., daily 8:30–5.*

☼ **Have a Shot.** Pretend you're Tiger Woods or Robin Hood at this excellent rainy-day facility, where you can have a hand at clay bird shooting, archery, or rifle shooting, or get a basket of golf balls and chip away. Prices start at $4 and there's an activity for everyone. ⊠*Mt. Barker Rd. opposite Wanaka Airport* ☎*03/443–6656* ⊕*www.haveashot. co.nz* ☾*Daily 9–5:30.*

SPORTS & THE OUTDOORS

BICYCLING Rent a bicycle and explore along the shores of Lake Wanaka, and out along the Clutha River toward Albert Town. There are many places to rent bikes including Good Sports or Thunderbikes, for hard-core mountain bikes. For three weeks in January, Treble Cone (⊕*www. treblecone.co.nz*) opens intermediate and expert trails to mountain bikers. The Sticky Forest and Dirt Park NZ (the Snow Park in winter) both boast a network of trails for mountain biking. Treble Cone and Dirt Park offer a joint 10-day pass.

CANYONING With the steep rugged waterways of the Matukituki and Wilkin valleys within easy reach, Wanaka is a key spot in the country for canyoning. **Deep Canyon** leads expeditions down the Niger Stream, Wai Rata Canyon, and the Leaping Burn; trips start at $215 for a full day. ☎*03/443–7922* ⊕*www.deepcanyon.co.nz* ☾*Nov.–Mar. or Apr.*

FISHING Locals will tell you that fishing on Lake Wanaka and nearby Lake Hawea is better than at the more famed Taupo area. You won't want to enter that argument, but chances are good you'll catch fish if you have the right guide. Fishing is year-round. **Harry Urquhart** (☎*03/443–1535*) has trolling excursions for rainbow trout, brown trout, and quinnat salmon on Lake Hawea. **Gerald Telford** (☎*03/443–9257* ⊕*www.flyfishhunt.co.nz*) will take you fly-fishing, including night-fishing and multiday Otago/Southland fishing expeditions.

Wanaka Fly Fishing (☎*03/443–9072* ⊕*www.fly-fishing-guide-wanaka-new-zealand.co.nz*) provides instruction, guided trips, and wilderness fishing safaris, including a heli-fishing option. Craig Smith at **Hatch Fishing** (☎*03/443–8446* ⊕*www.hatchfishing.co.nz*) is a superb guide and a really nice bloke who offers several fishing packages. If you're not keen on hiring a guide, you can rent fly fishing gear at **Wanaka Sports** at 8 Helwick Street or **Lakeland Adventures** in the Log Cabin on Ardmore Street.

Note: *For more information on trout fishing around Wanaka, see Chapter 11.*

RAFTING & KAYAKING At **Pioneer Rafting** ☎*03/443–1246 or 027/295–0418)* you can finally do some white-water rafting at a calm pace. Lewis Verduyn is New Zealand's leading ecorafting specialist, with many years' experience as a white-water rafter. Lewis had his share of adrenaline-pumping high-

9

grade trips and then got tired of missing out on what he sees as the real adventure: the environment he was tearing past. His highly informative ecorafting adventure, suitable for most ages, retraces a historic pioneer log-raft route. Both full-day ($165) and half-day ($115) trips are available, and leave from the Visitor Information Centre in Wanaka.

Exploring this beautiful region's rivers with **Alpine Kayak Guides'** ✉ *70 Main Rd., Luggate* ☎ *03/443–9023* ⊕ *www.alpinekayaks.co.nz)* Geoff Deacon is a must while in Wanaka. This company caters to smaller groups, which means a lot of attention for beginners. You'll learn how to glide into a calm eddy, to wave surf, and to safely charge down the center of the white water. You *will* spill, and for this reason all your gear, right down to the polypropylene underwear, is provided. The full-day trip costs $200 per person and a half day is $125. If you're looking for something mellower, sign up for the half-day "relaxed" float, which is rapids-free ($75).

SCENIC FLIGHTS The weather around Wanaka is clear much of the time, which has allowed it to become a scenic-flight base for fixed-wing planes and helicopters. Flights take in Mt. Cook and the West Coast glaciers, the Mt. Aspiring area, Queenstown, and Fiordland. **Wanaka Flightseeing** ✉ *Wanaka Airport* ☎ *03/443–8787 or 0800/105–105* ⊕ *www.flight seeing.co.nz)* runs small Cessna aircraft to all the hot spots.

Aspiring Helicopters ☎ *03/443–1454 or 027/432–3121* ⊕ *www.aspiring-helicopters.co.nz)* does trips ranging from a 25-minute local flight for $155 to a half-day trip to Milford Sound, where you join a boat cruise on the fjord before heading back to Wanaka (from $770). A Mt. Aspiring trip lands on the snowfields (for $375 per person). **Alpine Helicopters** ☎ *03/443–4000* ⊕ *www.alpineheli.co.nz* has heli-skiing options in season, as well as heli-fishing excursions in Fiordland.

SKIING With reliable snow and dry powder, Wanaka offers some of the best skiing and snowboarding in New Zealand. Cardrona and Treble Cone are the two biggest winter-sports resorts. **Cardrona** (☎ *03/443–7341* ⊕ *www.cardrona.com*), 34 km (21 mi) southwest of Wanaka, has a kids' ski school and activity center, plus three kid- and beginner-friendly "Magic Carpet" lifts, and five food outlets. A special "heavy metal" trail pours on the rails and jumps. Two quad chairlifts and a detachable high-speed lift are available. The season is roughly June–October, and a day's lift pass costs $71. A bonus at Cardrona is the 12 apartments up on the mountain (rates range from $180 to $475 a night).

Treble Cone (☎ *03/443–7443* ⊕ *www.treblecone.com*), 19 km (11.5 mi) west of Wanaka, is the South Island's largest ski area, with lots of advanced trails and off-piste skiing. A new quad lift and expanded trails have recently been completed. A day's lift pass costs $89. For snowboarders, the **Snow Park** ✉ *Cardrona Valley, 20 km [12 mi] southwest of Wanaka* ☎ *03/443–9991* ⊕ *www.snowparknz.com)* supplies a huge selection of rails, jumps, pipes, and terrain features. For more information about skiing and snowboarding in the area, check out ⊕ *www.skilakewanaka.com.*

SKYDIVING New Zealand is definitely the place to experiment with wild adventures, and with **Skydive Lake Wanaka** (✉ *Wanaka Airport, Hwy. 6, Wanaka* ☎ *03/443–7207 or 0800/786–877* ⊕ *www.skydivenz.com*) you're in capable hands (staff refer to their boss as "Captain Safety"). You can jump from 12,000 and 15,000 feet ($295 and $395, respectively) with photos or a DVD of your exploit for an extra fee.

WALKING & TREKKING
You could stay for a week in Wanaka, take a different walk into the bush and mountains each day, and still come nowhere near exhausting your options. If you have time for only one walk, **Mt. Iron**, rising 780 feet above the lake, is relatively short and rewarding. A rocky hump carved by glaciers, its summit provides panoramic views of Lakes Wanaka and Hawea, plus the peaks of the Harris Mountains and Mt. Aspiring National Park. The access track begins 2 km (1 mi) from Wanaka, and the walk to the top takes 45 minutes. You can descend on the alternative route down the steep eastern face. You get maximum views for minimal challenge on one of the prettiest local trails, which meanders along the Clutha River from the **Lake Wanaka Outlet** to Albert Town. This is a kid-friendly route, and also fly-fisherman, bicyclist-, and picnicker- friendly. The complete **Diamond Lake Track** takes three hours and starts 25 km (15.5 mi) west of Wanaka, also on the Glendhu Bay/Mt. Aspiring road. The track rises to 2,518 feet at Rocky Peak, passing Diamond Lake along the way. If you've got time for only a short walk, take the one that heads to the lake; it takes only 20 minutes. The Diamond Lake area is also popular with mountain bikers and rock climbers. The Mt. Aspiring National Park offers far more serious hiking and mountaineering opportunities, including Wilkins Valley, Makarora River, and Mt. Aspiring tracks and trails. Many of these require previous experience and excellent fitness and should be done either as guided walks or in full communication with the local DOC office.

★ **Siberia Experience** (☎ *0800/345–666* ⊕ *www.siberiaexperience.co.nz*) offers one of the best adventure packages. For $280, the journey begins with a funky little yellow plane in a paddock-cum-airstrip. After a breathtaking 25-minute journey from Makarora, the pilot drops you off in the pristine wilderness of Mt. Aspiring National Park's Siberia Valley, and points you to a trailhead. From there, embark on a beautiful three-hour hike on a well-marked, relatively easy trail. Finally, a jet-boat meets you at the Wilkin River and returns you to Makarora. There is a hut out there if you'd like to arrange overnight stays. **Wild Walks** (☎ *03/443–4476* ⊕ *www.wildwalks.co.nz*) also leads treks through Mt. Aspiring National Park, including Rabbit Pass, considered one of the most strenuous trails in the country. For maps and information on these and other local walks, contact the **Department of Conservation** (✉ *Ardmore St.* ☎ *03/477–0677*).

9

WHERE TO EAT

$–$$$$ ✕**Missy's Kitchen.** A local favorite, Missy's pulls in a ski crowd to its bar and its dining room. They've got a fun cocktail list including a Kiwi Lush, and dozens of beers and wines. In summer the balcony is a favored spot for dinner or for a glass of wine, and a fireplace warms diners in winter. If the Lake Wanaka view has you thinking of shellfish, lap up some Marlborough mussels flavored with lemongrass, lime, and chili jam. You can also try the rib-eye steak or the escalope of salmon and choose from a list of yummy desserts. The venison is excellent. ⊠ *Ardmore St. and Lakefront Dr.* ☎ *03/443–5099* ⊕ *www. missyskitchen.com* ⊟ *AE, DC, MC, V* ⊘ *No lunch.*

$–$$$ ✕ **Kai Whaka Pai.** There's no better place to stop for breakfast on a crisp, sunny morning than this café, which has more tables outside than in. It's just across the road from the lake, so the views range from pretty nice on a cloudy day to fantastic on a fine one. Meanwhile, the menu ranges from simple breakfast and lunch choices (coffee and croissants, salads, nachos, and kebabs), to beef ribs or rump roast for dinner. Reservations aren't mandatory, but they're a good idea. In addition to consistently good meals, "The Kai" has local beers on tap, fresh bread, and banana cream pies. ⊠ *Helwick and Ardmore Sts.* ☎ *03/443–7795* ⊟ *AE, DC, MC, V.*

$$ ✕ **Thai Siam.** Directly under Missy's Kitchen, this Thai restaurant has interesting alternatives if you prefer a vegetarian cuisine—although they also run the full range of local salmon, steak, and Nelson Bay scallops. Using Thai methods, they incorporate South Island vegetables into their dishes. ⊠ *Ardmore St. and Lakefront Dr.* ☎ *03/443–5010* ⊟ *AE, DC, MC, V* ⊘ *No lunch.*

$–$$ ✕ **Ardmore Street Food Company.** The owners of this fully licensed café have a breakfast menu as sophisticated and extensive as their dinner menu: try the salmon and kumara cakes with wasabi hollandaise, or the Green Eggs and Ham (with basil pesto). Plenty of Kiwi flavors infuse selection like green-lipped mussels with manuka honey, and duck confit with roasted tamarillo, and not many places offer *rewana* (Māori bread) filled with chicken livers! This place is busy, lively, and warm. Visit the on-site deli and bakery, which offer perfect ski-day takeouts like breakfast wraps and spiced omelet sandwiches. ⊠ *155 Ardmore St., beneath Speight's Ale House, on lakefront* ☎ *03/443–2230* ⊟ *AE, DC, MC, V.*

¢–$$ ✕ **Relishes Cafe.** You could hit this lakeside spot for every meal of the day, starting with breakfast—perhaps some homemade muesli with a side of toast and jam (Vegemite for homesick Aussies), or the bacon or salmon eggs Benedict. At lunch and dinner, you'll find ever-changing blackboard specials and good service. ⊠ *99 Ardmore St.* ☎ *03/443–9018* ⊟ *AE, DC, MC, V* ⊘ *Closed 1 wk in June..*

¢–$ ✕ **Café Fe.** Located a short drive up the Cardrona Valley Road, Café Fe (Fe as in Mt. Iron) has great views, comfortable seating inside and out (including a sandbox for the wee ones), and good simple meals for breakfast and lunch. The menu features a twice-baked soufflé du jour, and a great selection of salads and sandwiches. ⊠ *Corner of Cardrona and Orchard Rds.* ☎ *03/443–4683* ⊟ *AE, DC, MC, V* ⊘ *Closed Sun. No dinner.*

¢–$ ✕ **Hammer & Nail.** "Someone must have been in a really good mood when they made this." So a consumer once described a generously cream-filled donut from this popular bakery. Regardless the mood of the kitchen staff, customers are happy enough to regularly flock to Hammer & Nail for breakfast goodies, coffee, and lunch. There's indoor and patio seating, but if you prefer Lake Wanaka to Mitre 10 for views, take your sandwich or square of perfect bacon-egg pie down the hill. ⊠ *3 Cliff Wilson St., opposite Mitre 10 Garden Centre* ☎ *03/443–8500* ⊟ *AE, DC, MC, V* ⊘ *Closed Sun. No dinner.*

WHERE TO STAY

$$$$ 📷 **Minaret Lodge.** A 10-minute walk from town, this luxury retreat has ecofriendly accommodations, from the natural materials used in the rooms to organic coffee and cuisine. It's also hobbit-friendly: they offer a themed *Lord of the Rings* room. The rooms have mountain views and are surrounded by trees and gardens (where there's an outdoor chess board). Rates include regional wine tastings and hors d'oeuvres; you can also arrange for dinner. **Pros:** Stay in a hobbit room and dine from a hobbit menu. **Con:** You'll gain weight from your hosts' gourmet cooking. ⊠ *34 Eely Point Rd.* ☎ *03/443–1856* 🖷 *03/443–1846* ⊕ *www.minaretlodge.co.nz* 🛏 *5 rooms* ⚎ *In-room: refrigerator, dial-up. In-hotel: bar, tennis court, bicycles, no kids under 10, no-smoking rooms* ⊟ *AE, MC, V* ⦿*BP.*

$$$$ 📷 **Wanaka Homestead Lodge and Cottages.** Roger and Shonagh North used local schist and timber from the farm buildings that once stood here to build their solar-powered lakeshore lodge. In the evening, central Otago wines and snacks are served in the lounge. Cottages have extras such as DVD players and kitchens. Children are accepted for cottage stays but not always in the main lodge. **Pros:** Outdoor fireplace and hot tub. **Con:** Occasional noise from the road disrupts tranquility. ⊠ *1 Homestead Close* ☎ *03/443–5022* 🖷 *03/443–5023* ⊕ *www.wanakahomestead.co.nz* 🛏 *5 rooms, 2 cottages* ⚎ *In-room: Ethernet. In-hotel: bar, bicycles, laundry facilities, public Internet, no-smoking rooms* ⊟ *AE, MC, V* ⦿*BP.*

$$$–$$$$ 📷 **Mountain Range Lodge.** Travelers hell-bent on a lake view in Wanaka might stay at a property half as luxurious as this and for twice the coin. Owners Melanie and Stuart have thought of everything here to make their guests feel pampered, relaxed, and happy. Amenities include ski storage, a library, complimentary predinner drinks and fresh baked goodies, hammock, putting green, hot tub, DVDs, a computer and printer, and more. The luxurious rooms and mountain views easily make up for the lack of lake views. **Pros:** One of the nicest B&Bs in the area, reasonable rate. **Con:** You'll need a vehicle to get to town. ⊠ *Heritage Park, Cardrona Valley Rd. (2 km [1 mi] from Wanaka)* ☎ *03/443–7400* 🖷 *03/443–7450* ⊕ *www.mountainrange.co.nz* 🛏 *7 rooms* ⚎ *In-hotel: restaurant, bar,* ⊟ *MC, V* ⦿*CP, BP*

$$$ 📷 **Renmore House.** This cheerful B&B has trellises of flowers at its entrance and the spring-fed Bullock Creek burbling by the back door. Hosts Rosie and Blair understand the traveler's desire to eat in sometimes, so they have provided a kitchenette and a barbecue area in the garden. Afternoon tea and predinner drinks are complimentary; ditto your hosts' extensive knowledge of the area. Bicycles, maps, and a "wee library" are on hand. **Pros:** Hosts are very friendly and the place is clean and cheerful. **Con:** Located on a nondescript residential street.

9

⊠*44 Upton St.* ☎*03/443–6566* 🖷*03/443–6567* ⊕*www.renmore-house.co.nz* ⇙*3 rooms* ⊟*MC, V* ⑩*BP.*

$$–$$$ 🏨**Oakridge Pool & Spa Resort.** With its refreshing, contemporary design, this rather expansive resort is a departure from the usual alpine stone-and-timber lodgings in the region. Oakridge looks across an open valley to the peaks of Aspiring National Park. Four heated swimming pools—two just built last year—and a series of warm spas are set in a rock-lined amphitheater, overlooked by the resort restaurant. Enjoy a glass of local wine while soaking in the spa after a day on the road. **Pros:** The warm outdoor spas and pools. **Con:** In the busy season the pools are sometimes swamped with kids. ⊠*Cardrona Valley Rd. at Studholme Rd.* ☎*03/443–7707 or 0800/869–262* 🖷*03/443–7750* ⊕*www.oakridge.co.nz* ⇙*46 rooms, 19 studios, 27 1- and 2-bedroom apartments* ⚒*In-hotel: restaurant, bar, pools, spa* ⊟*AE, DC, MC, V.*

$$ 🏨**Cardrona Hotel.** The recipe for their famous mulled wine is a secret, ★ but the ingredients that make this place so special are evident. This classic old country hotel and pub, 20 minutes from Wanaka on the Crown Range Road, is the Cardrona après-ski spot for mulled wine in front of the outdoor fireplace. Another fireplace roars inside the spacious bar and restaurant. In the summertime, the outdoor beer garden is a great place to relax after a day spent in Wanaka. The hotel was featured in a well-known Speights ad depicting hundreds of sheep "parked" outside the pub. **Pro:** Stay in a genuinely historic property. **Con:** Historic properties mean squeaky floorboards and hinges. ⊠*9 Lakeside Rd.* ☎*03/443–8153* 🖷*03/443–8163* ⊕*www.cardronahotel.co.nz* ⇙*16 rooms* ⚒*In-hotel: spa, pool* ⊟*AE, MC, V.*

$$ 🏨**Lake Hawea Station.** Since 1912, the Rowley family has run this vast working sheep station which comprises 28,000 acres from lake level to 5,000 feet and has more than 10,000 merino sheep! Choose between two historic musterer cottages: the Packhorse Cottage or the Homespur Cottage. The cottages have modern amenities (kitchen facilities) and rustic charm (patchwork quilts). The Homespur is heated with a cozy woodstove, and the Packhorse has a gas heater. Both have decks with views of the mountains and lake. Go fishing in the lake, or explore the beautiful homestead garden. **Pros:** Very friendly hosts and outstanding location. **Con:** Real working farm means barking dogs real early. ⊠*20 mins north of Wanaka, 22 Timaru River Rd., Lake Hawea* ☎*03/443–1744* ⊕*www.lakehaweastation.co.nz* ⇙*2 units* ⚒*In-room: kitchen* ⊟*No credit cards* ⑩*CP.*

¢–$ 🏨**Purple Cow Backpackers.** Shoot pool with a view of the mountains and lake. This is the best known and most well-liked backpackers in town. The Purple Cow, not to be mistaken with The Cow, a pizza joint on Post Office Lane, is within walking distance of shops and stumbling distance from the bars. While the cost of a bed is relatively cheap, frills are extra: towels, duvets, and bicycles are for rent. And be sure you have an extra pocketful of "shrapnel" as the laundry, Internet, and BBQ are all coin-operated. **Pros:** Best location, well run. **Con:** You'll get nickel-and-dimed for extras. ⊠*94 Brownston St.* ☎*03/443–8153* 🖷*03/443–8163* ⊕*www.purplecow.co.nz* ⚒*In-hotel: laundry,* ⊟*AE, DC, MC, V.*

NIGHTLIFE

Down the lane next to the Post Office on Ardmore Street, a roaring out-door fireplace warms a trio of hotspots: **Woodys Pool Bar** (✉*Post Office La.* ☎*03/443–5551*) sees a local crowd shooting pool and watching rugby. **Barluga** (✉*Post Office La.* ☎*03/443–5400*) is a bit sophisti-cated with leather sofas and a fine wine list. If you want a bite, pop into The Cow next door for good garlic bread and pizza, and feel free to add commentary to their restroom chalkboard walls.

Longtime local favorites include **Red Rock** (✉*68 Ardmore St.* ☎*03/443–5545*), which crosses the line from cozy to crowded some nights, and the slightly scruffy **Bullock Bar** (✉*71 Ardmore St.* ☎*03/443–7148*). Serious Guinness drinkers lurk at **Scruffy Murphy's** (✉*21 Dunmore St., across from New World* ☎*03/443–7645*), and a plaque on the wall lists drinkers in the hundred-pints club.

Speights Ale House (✉*155 Ardmore St.* ☎*03/443–2920*) is always buzzing; head upstairs to the **& Bar** for a game of pool. Upstairs above Kai Whaka Pai, the **Pa Runga Wine Bar** (✉*Ardmore St. at Helwick St.* ☎*03/443–7795*) comes alive at sunset. Bar meals are available, and there's a lounge bar, a nice cozy fire, and a balcony overlooking the lake.

If you've worked up an appetite dancing with twentysomething back-packers at **Shooters** (✉*145 Ardmore St.* ☎*03/443–4345*), stop by the Doughbin, open until all hours, for a tasty meat pie. ■TIP➡**Bar staff will call a cab for you, but if it's a hopping night in town, it can be a drama getting a taxi to pick you up along the main drag (some drivers balk at the chaotic atmosphere, and even if they do arrive a bunch of trollied bullies might hijack your ride), so ask the cab to meet you a block inland from the busy lakefront area.**

★ The local institution **Cinema Paradiso** (✉*1 Ardmore St.* ☎*03/443–1505* ⊕*www.paradiso.net.nz*) is not your usual movie house—its seating includes couches, recliners, pillows, and even a yellow Morris Minor car. During intermission you can snack on homemade ice cream and warm cookies or have dinner with a glass of wine. Like a well-loved teddy bear, the seating has become a bit worn over the years. The shows include all the latest releases.

QUEENSTOWN

Fodor'sChoice
★

103 km (64 mi) southeast of Wanaka, 480 km (300 mi) southwest of Christchurch.

Set on the edge of the glacial Lake Wakatipu, with stunning views of the sawtooth peaks of the Remarkables mountain range, Queenstown is the most popular tourist stop in the South Island. Once prized by the Māori as a source of greenstone, the town boomed when gold was discovered in the Shotover River during the 1860s; the Shoto-ver quickly became famous as "the richest river in the world." By the 1950s Queenstown had become the center of a substantial farming area, and with ready access to mountains, lakes, and rivers, the town has since become the adventure capital of New Zealand. Its shop windows are crammed with skis, Polartec, Asolo walking boots, and Marin mountain bikes. Along Shotover Street, travel agents tout white-water rafting, jet-boating, caving, trekking, heli-skiing, parachuting, and parapenting (paragliding). Queenstown unabashedly caters to adrenaline junkies, so height, G-force, thrill factor, and danger are emphasized. Want to go on a nice rope swing? Queenstown has the world's highest—109 meters long—in the Shotover Canyon, the ride is 149 kph and deliver 3 Gs of force. New Zealanders' penchant for bizarre adventure sports culminates in Queenstown; it was here that the sport of leaping off a bridge with a giant rubber band wrapped around the ankles—bungy jumping—took root as a commercial enterprise. In late June and early July, the 10-day Queenstown Winter Festival brings the winter-sport frenzy to a climax, with musical performers, ski-slope antics and races, and serious partying.

If you're *not* an extreme adventure enthusiast, you might recoil a bit and view the city with a cynical eye. *Tacky gimmicky tourist trap!* you might think. Relax! There's a side to Queenstown that doesn't run on pure adrenaline: find a nice café, have wine by the lake, and sample the cuisine. Just because everyone and their grandma is jumping off a bridge here doesn't mean you have to! But, while you staunchly sip your Quartz Reef pinot, consider this: Queenstown *does* live up to its Adventure Capital moniker and the activities are genuinely thrilling. As for tacky, *you* try to design an elegant activity booth! While the rest of the country is decidedly low-key about its beauty, Queenstown shouts at you to park, pay, jump, scream, and then buy the DVD of yourself doing it. So maybe while you're here. you might want to do as the Queenstowners do, and get amongst it!

GETTING HERE & AROUND
Highway 6 enters Queenstown from the West Coast; driving time for the 400-km (250-mi) journey from Franz Josef is eight hours. It takes approximately an hour and a half to drive between Queenstown and Wanaka; the drive between Queenstown and Te Anau generally lasts a little over two hours. Bus and airplane service are also available between Christchurch and Queenstown.

ESSENTIALS
Airport Queenstown Airport (⊠ *Frankton Rd. Queenstown* ☎ *03/442–2670* ⊕ *www.queenstownairport.co.nz*).

Airport Transfers Super Shuttle Queenstown (☎ *03/442–3639 or 0800/748–8853*).

Bus Companies InterCity (☎ *03/443–7885 in Wanaka, 03/249–7559 in Te Anau, 03/442–8238 in Queenstown* ⊕ *www.intercitycoach.co.nz*). **Newmans** (☎ *09/913–6188 or 0508/353–947* ⊕ *www.newmanscoach.co.nz*).

Bus Depot Queenstown (⊠ *Athol St.*).

Medical Assistance Queenstown Medical Centre (⊠ *9 Isle St.* ☎ *03/441–0500*). **Wilkinson's Pharmacy** (⊠ *The Mall at Rees St., Queenstown* ☎ *03/442–7313*).

Rental Cars **Apex** (⊠ *Terminal Bldg., Queenstown Airport* ☎ *03/442–8040 or 0800/531–111*). **Avis** (⊠ *Terminal Bldg., Queenstown Airport* ☎ *03/442–7280*).

Visitor Info **Queenstown Visitor Information Centre** opens daily from 7 AM to 7 PM (⊠ *Clocktower Centre, Shotover St. at Camp St.* ☎ *03/442–4100 or 0800/668–888* ⊕ *www.queenstown-nz.co.nz*).

WHAT TO SEE

Get the lay of the land by taking the **Skyline Gondola** up to the heights of Bob's Peak, 1,425 feet above the lake, for a smashing panoramic view of the town and the Remarkables. You can also walk to the top on the **One Mile Creek Trail** and watch the paragliders jump off the summit for their slow cruise back down to lake level. There are restaurants at the summit, plus a *haka, or* Māori song and dance, show in the evening. For something a little faster, there's a luge ride, weather permitting—start with the scenic track, and then work your way up to the advanced track. If even that isn't exciting enough, you can bungy jump from the summit terminal (▷ *AJ Hackett Bungy in Sports & the Outdoors, below*). ⊠ *Brecon St.* ☎ *03/441–0101* ⊕ *www.skyline.co.nz* ⊠ *Gondola $19, $26 for gondola and basic luge package* ⊙ *Daily 9 AM–9:30 PM.*

☼ The steamship *T.S.S. Earnslaw* runs across Lake Wakatipu to Walter Peak Station on a 1½-hour cruise. Additional options allow a stopover for several hours at **Walter Peak High Country Farm** to see how a high-country sheep station works, and to enjoy a good farmhouse morning or afternoon tea. The steamship boilers are still stoked by hand, and the steam engines chuff noisily away just as they did 90 years ago. ⊠ *Steamer Wharf* ☎ *03/442–7500 or 0800/656–503* ⊕ *www.realjourneys.co.nz* ⊠ *$40 cruise, $60 with farm visit.*

One of the enduring attractions in the area is the drive up **Skippers Canyon.** Harking back to the days when the hills were filled with gold diggers, the Skippers Road was hand carved out of rock, and it reaches into the deep recesses of the Shotover Valley. It's breathtakingly beautiful but you could also be breathtakingly scared: if you're not confident about navigating a twisty, narrow, unsealed road fraught with slips and vertical drops, we suggest you take a tour. **Nomad Safaris** (☎ *03/442–6699 or 0800/688–222* ⊕ *www.queenstown4wd.com*) runs two trips a day up the Skippers Canyon in specialized four-wheel-drive vehicles. **Queenstown Heritage Tours** (☎ *03/442–5949* ⊕ *www.queenstown-holiday.co.nz*) gives historical tours with the comforts of air-conditioned vehicles, gourmet snacks, and local wines.

☼ Some of the best views of the town, lake, and mountains are from the **Deer Park.** Not only will you have outstanding views, some of which you may recognize from the *Lord of the Rings* films, but you'll also find yourself an object of attention from the resident creatures, which include thars (goatlike animals), goats, bison, and llamas. The animals are used to being fed by people, so they're not skittish. Keep your car window rolled down if you want to find out what bison breath is like. Bring some $1 coins for the food dispensers and wear something you won't mind getting nuzzled. ⊠ *Peninsula Rd.* ☎ *0800/843–333*

⊕*www.thedeerpark.co.nz* ✉*$20 self-drive tour, $59 guided tour* ⊙*Daily 9–dark.*

The public **Queenstown Gardens** on the waterfront peninsula are always worth a quiet stroll. It is one of the few places in Queenstown that hasn't changed. There's an easy path to wander along to wear off some of those calories you've consumed during your stay. Bring a disc and have a toss at the country's first Frisbee golf course.

WINERIES

The vineyards across Central Otago and into the Queenstown and Wanaka areas constitute the world's southernmost wine region. Specifically, Bannockburn, Gibbston Valley, and Lowburn are home to big plantings. More than 75 wineries are in the region. The 177 local vineyards have 2,250 acres in production, producing more than 3,500 tons of grapes each year. The predominant variety is pinot noir. Each year, in February, the region showcases its prowess at the Central Otago Wine & Food Festival, held in the Queenstown Gardens down by the lake. Check ⊕*www.winetastes.com* for details and ticket sales.

Into oenology? Don't know what that means? Touring Otago might make you wish you knew more about the great grape. The answer lies at **The Big Picture: Essential Wine Adventure,** an entertaining "Wine 101" that includes an interactive film and an "aroma room" where you educate your nose. The 40-minute drive from Queenstown showcases some beautiful wineries, including the Peregrine Winery, designed to look like a falcon's wing, and the famous Gibbston Valley Vineyard. Admission to the Big Picture includes a wine tasting/presentation. A restaurant is on the premises. ✉*Corner of Sandflat Rd. and State Hwy. 6, Cromwell* ☎*03/445–4052* 🖷*03/445–4053* ⊕*www.wineadventures.co.nz* ✉*$20* ⊙*Closed Christmas Day.*

Wine Tastes provides a winery tour with no driving! Purchase a wine card, peruse 84 tasting machines featuring New Zealand wines, insert the card into your chosen machine, and voilà, the machine debits your card and squirts a taste into your glass. You can buy any value card you like; $10 buys 6–10 tastes. If Woody Allen had imagined the future of wine tasting, this might be it. ✉*14 Beach St.* ☎*03/409–2226* 🖷*03/409–2290* ⊕*www.winetastes.com* ⊙*Daily 10–10.*

Amisfield Winery & Bistro is the latest hot-shot winery to join the Queenstown scene. Both the wines and the restaurant, which serves French Basque cuisine, have earned a strong reputation. The restaurant, in a huge stone-and-timber building with a sunny courtyard and reflection pool, opens for early dinners as well as lunch, although it closes around 8 PM. Pinot noir, aromatic whites such as Riesling and pinot gris, and the methode traditionelle are all worth sampling. ✉*10 Lake Hayes Rd.* ☎*03/442–0556* ⊕*www.amisfield.co.nz* ⊙*Bistro closed Mon.*

At **Gibbston Valley Wines,** the best-known vineyard in central Otago, you can taste wines in a cool, barrel-lined cave. The showcase wine is pinot noir, but you can sip Rieslings and a pinot gris as well. At the cheesery, you can watch sheep's-milk and goat's-milk cheeses being made. The attached restaurant offers tempting preparations of mostly local produce and wines by the glass. ⊠ *State Hwy. 6, Gibbston* ✛ *20-min drive east of Queenstown on SH6* ☎ *03/442–6910* ⊕ *www.gvwines.co.nz* ▦ *Wine-cave tour and tasting $9.50, less for larger groups* ⊙ *Tasting room daily 10–5, cave tours on the hr daily 10–4, restaurant daily noon–3.*

The **Chard Farm** vineyard perches on a rare flat spot on the edge of the Kawarau Gorge, not far from Gibbston Valley. The portfolio includes excellent varieties of chardonnay, sauvignon blanc, gewürztraminer, pinot gris, and pinot noir. They're also venturing into the champagne method. ⊠ *Chard Rd.* ⌖ *R.D. 1, Gibbston* ☎ *03/442–6110* ⊕ *www. chardfarm.co.nz* ⊙ *Weekdays 10–5, weekends 11–5.*

SPORTS & THE OUTDOORS

BUNGY JUMPING
AJ Hackett Bungy, the pioneer in the sport, offers a variety of jumps in the area. Kawarau Bridge is the original jump site, 23 km (14 mi) from Queenstown on State Highway 6 and offers a "Secrets of Bungy" tour, an interactive guided tour designed for those who are fascinated by bungy but just can't face the leap. Daredevils who graduate from the 142-foot plunge might like to test themselves on the 230-foot Skippers Canyon Bridge. Top that with the Nevis Highwire Bungy, suspended 440 feet above the Nevis River. With 8.5 seconds of free fall it's said to be the wildest bungy jump in the world. (Be advised that if your friends want to just go along and watch you jump, they will still be charged.) If you're short on time, head to the Ledge Urban Bungy and Ledge Urban Sky Swing, the jumping point by the Skyline Gondola; from April through September you can jump or swing by moonlight. Prices start at $140 for the Kawarau or Ledge jump, $199 for Nevis Highwire Bungy (all three include a T-shirt), and $75 for the Urban Sky Swing. Extra fees apply for DVDs of your exploits. Be sure to check the age, height, and weight requirements. Hours vary seasonally. ⊠ *The Station, Camp and Shotover Sts.* ☎ *03/442–4007 or 0800/286–495* ⊕ *www.ajhackett.com.*

FISHING
Note: *For information on trout-fishing guides around Queenstown, see Chapter 11.*

HIKING
Several scenic walks branch out from town. For a history lesson with your ramble, head to the **Time Walk,** entering through an iron gateway on the Queenstown Hill trail. Narrative panels line the route; it takes about two hours. The **Ben Lomond Track** takes you to one of the highest peaks in the basin. Take the gondola to the summit, then follow signs to the saddle and the steep climb to the peak (5,730 feet). This can be a full-day walk, so make sure you bring all the necessary supplies.

HORSE TREKKING
Moonlight Stables has a choice of full- or half-day rides with spectacular views of the mountains and rivers around the Wakatipu–Arrow Basin. Ride across its 800-acre deer farm. Novice and experienced riders are welcome. Transportation from Queenstown is provided. The company operates a clay-bird shooting range, and you can shoot in combination with the ride. ⌖ *Morven Ferry Rd., Arrow Junction, Queenstown* ☎ *03/442–1229* ⊕ *www.moonlightcountry.co.nz* ▦ *½-day trip $95 per person.*

9

JET-BOAT
RIDES

With **Dart River Safaris** you can get a nonpareil look at rugged Mt. Aspiring National Park, one of the most spectacular parts of South Island. The Safari route includes jet-boating on the upper and lower Dart River, along with a bit of walking. The longer Heritage Trail takes private charters on a jet boat and walking trip with a historic focus. The Funyak option takes you upstream by jet boat, then you paddle gently downstream, exploring the Rockburn Chasm on the way. Shuttle buses depart daily from Queenstown for the 45-minute ride to the boats. Costs range from $179 plus transfer to $255 plus transfer. ⌖27 *Shotover St., Queenstown* ☎03/442–9992 ⏛*www.dartriver.co.nz.*

Shotover Jet leads high-speed, heart-stopping rides in the Shotover River canyons; it's got exclusive rights to operate in these waters. The boat pirouettes within inches of canyon walls around full 360-degree spins. The boats are based at the Shotover Jet Beach beneath the historic Edith Cavell Bridge, a 10-minute drive from Queenstown. If you don't have transport, a free shuttle makes frequent daily runs. Reservations are essential. Costs start at $99. ✉*Shotover River Canyon, Queenstown* ☎*03/442–8570* ⏛*www.shotoverjet.co.nz.*

RAFTING

Rafting is an adult thrill; children must be at least 13 to participate. You'll need your swimsuit and a towel, but all other gear, including wet suit, life jacket, helmet, and wet-suit booties, are provided by the rafting companies. Instructors spend quite a bit of time on safety issues and paddling techniques before you launch.

Queenstown Rafting runs various half-, full-, and three-day white-water rafting trips in the Queenstown area year-round, advertising trips on the Shotover and Kawerau rivers. The Kawerau is pitched as a more scenic first-timer river. But hey, if you're gonna be a bear, be a grizzly: enjoy scenery later and go rafting on the more exciting and satisfying Shotover. With rapids named Pinball and Jaws, you should have a hint of what you're in for. Or go all out with the Nevis Triple Challenge, which includes a jet-boat ride, a helicopter trip, rafting on the Shotover, and a bungy jump, all in one day. Rates start at $145 and go above $1,000 for the multi-activity trips. ✉*35 Shotover St., Queenstown* ☎*03/442–9792 or 0800/442–9792* ⏛*www.rafting.co.nz.*

Mad Dog River Boarding proves that looks can be deceiving. The Kawerau seems calmer than the Shotover; but certainly not if you're in it. The Mad Dog crew loves their job, which essentially is to enable adults to turn into Tarzans and Peter Pans. In addition to riding down the Kawerau River on a body board, there's a giant waterslide, big rope swing, and good old rock jumping (beat your chest and holler). ✉*37 Shotover St., Queenstown* ☎*03/442–7797* ⏛*www.riverboarding.co.nz.*

SAILING

Lake Wakatipu gets very windy, and sailing is a popular pastime. **Sail Queenstown** (☎*03/442–7517* ⏛*www.sailqueenstown.co.nz*) runs a two-hour lake cruise on *NZL 14,* an America's Cup–class boat that was built for the 1992 challenge in San Diego and sailed by Russell Coutts. The boat is fitted with full safety gear and gives a very comfortable ride on these almost-waveless waters. It's a great way to feel the alpine environment as you tack up the lake then run back down before the wind. Trips leave from the Convelle Wharf in central Queenstown every day at 2—more often in summer, if necessary.

SCENIC **Over the Top Helicopters** (☎ *03/442–2233 or 0800/123–359* ⊕ *www.*
FLIGHTS *flynz.co.nz*) runs a diverse selection of flights, including glacier and alpine snowfield landings, and scenic tours above Queenstown, the Remarkables, Fiordland, and Milford and Doubtful sounds. They'll also deliver you to fly-fishing spots absolutely miles from anywhere, or take you heli-skiing or on ecotours as far away as Stewart Island. Jumping off a mountain isn't everyone's idea of fun, but it's a fantastic way to see Queenstown. These huge sails swoop down over the town like pterodactyls, whirling out over the lake and back in to a gentle landing in a nearby park. **Paraglide** (☎ *03/441–8581 or 0800/759–688* ⊕ *www.*
paraglide.co.nz) leads jumps from the peak above the top of the gondola every day that weather permits. For the adrenaline hooked, **Fly By**
Wire (☎ *03/442–2116* ⊕ *www.flybywire-queenstown.co.nz*) runs a six-minute flight through a deep canyon just out of town. You're strapped into a motorized machine that looks like a rocket, and off you go—at speeds that can reach 106 mph!

SKIING **Coronet Peak** (☎ *03/442–4620* ⊕ *www.nzski.com*), 10 minutes from Queenstown along Gorge Road, rocks day and night to a ski and snowboard crowd that returns year after year. Queenstown's original ski resort now has a skiable area of 700 acres, a vertical drop of 1,360 feet, and six tows and chairlifts, including a quad lift. The season usually runs June to October, and night skiing is available from mid-July to mid-September. Adult day passes cost $84. Just across the valley **the Remarkables** (☎ *03/442–615* ⊕ *www.nzski.com*) is a newer ski area that is good for beginner and intermediate skiing and hard-core off-piste runs. The vertical drop here is 1,160 feet, there are five tows and chairlifts, and 30% of the terrain is classified advanced. It's a 45-minute drive from Queenstown to the ski area parking lot on State Highway 6. Adult day passes cost $79.

WHERE TO EAT

At first glance Queenstown's little side streets seem full of party bars and pizza joints, but that's because all the really great spots are hidden away or down at Steamer Wharf, which juts out into Lake Wakatipu. Some places aren't easy to find, so ask if you can't find what you're looking for.

$$$$ ✕**The Bunker.** Log fires, leather armchairs, and a clubby atmosphere
★   make the Bunker especially cozy. Whet your appetite with an aperitif at the bar before heading downstairs for a meal that will likely include some of the finest lamb, venison, scampi, duck, and quail you'll find in Queenstown. The wine list is equally impressive. The Bunker stays open very late and is often booked days in advance for dinner. ✉ *Cow*
La. ☎ *03/441–8030* ⊕ *www.thebunker.co.nz* ✍ *Reservations essential*
🍴 *AE, DC, MC, V.*

$$$–$$$$ ✕**The Boardwalk.** You might want to eat here just for the view. The
★   restaurant looks over Lake Wakatipu toward the Remarkables from the second floor of the Steamer Wharf building. Seafood is the strong

9

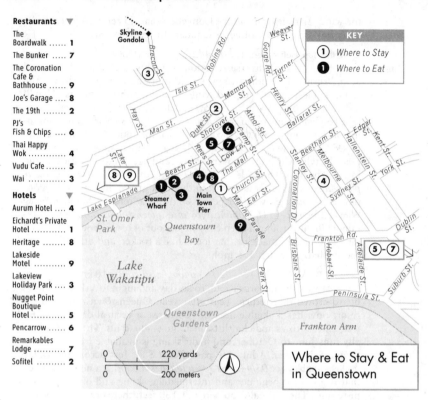

Where to Stay & Eat
in Queenstown

suit; try the fillet of grouper or the wonderful seafood platter with whole crayfish, blue cod, salmon, prawns, scallops, mussels, and oysters. There's also a good selection of dishes made with lamb, beef, and venison. ⊠*Steamer Wharf* ☎*03/442–5630* ⌖*Reservations essential* ▤*AE, DC, MC, V* ⊙*No lunch.*

$$$–$$$$ ✕**Coronation Café & Bathhouse.** Originally, it was exactly that—a 1911 Victorian bathhouse, right on the beach, built to commemorate the coronation of Britain's King George V. Now, it's a casual café in the mornings and afternoons, and a full-fledged restaurant for dinner. The surroundings remain Victorian, but the kitchen is up-to-date, offering starters such as a mille-feuille of wild rabbit ragout and main courses such as the sea-run salmon and the wild Blenheim hare. The waterfront location is superb. ⊠*28 Marine Parade* ☎*03/442–5625* ▤*AE, DC, MC, V* ⊙*Closed Mon. in winter, 6 wks in May/June.*

$$$–$$$$ ✕**The 19th.** This bright and breezy eatery sits at the town end of Steamer Wharf. The regularly changing and ambitious menu might include river-run salmon with colcannon (a traditional Irish mash made with leek, potato, and kale) or char-grilled Denver leg of venison. Reservations are recommended. ⊠*Steamer Wharf* ☎*03/442–4006* ⊕*www.19th. co.nz* ▤*AE, DC, MC, V.*

$$$–$$$$ ✕**Wai.** Occupying a corner spot on Steamer Wharf, Wai has one of the best views, and reputations, in town. The fillet of grouper, oven roasted and wrapped in prosciutto, is a standout. You also might enjoy the rack of lamb, venison, salmon, or veal. The degustation menu and the fabulous oyster menu are worth a second visit. ✉*Steamer Wharf* ☎*03/442–5969* ⊕*www.wai.net.nz* ▭*AE, DC, MC, V.*

¢–$$$ ✕**Vudu Café.** One of the best spots for breakfast in Queenstown, the petite Vudu is up and running when everyone is still sleeping off last night's party. The specially roasted coffee is a treat, and the breakfast choices include lots of home-baked goodies. Later in the day they transform into a dinner restaurant and carry on until late. Reservations aren't accepted, so come early to snag a table. ✉*23 Beach St.* ☎*03/442–5357* ▭*DC, MC, V.*

$ ✕**Joe's Garage.** Don't be fooled by the name; this place is one of the country's best cafés. The all-day menu includes simple pleasures such as bacon and eggs, pancakes, and paninis. But it's the trifecta of a laid-back atmosphere, quick and friendly service, and outstanding coffee that really puts Joe's on the map. The place is popular with locals, but it's worth the wait for a table. ✉*Searle La.* ☎*03/442–5282* ▭*AE, MC, V* ⊗*No dinner.*

$ ✕**PJ's Fish & Chips.** If it's good, old-fashioned crispy fish wrapped in newspaper you're after, this is the place to go. Brits and Aussies flock here, and the locals love it, too. The $10 meal with a big chunk of fresh fish, some chips, and salad or mushy peas is hard to beat, but there are also burgers, hot dogs, and other delightfully unhealthful choices. ✉*37 Camp St.* ☎*03/442–6080* ▭*AE, MC, V.*

$ ✕**Thai Happy Wok.** There are several Thai places in Queenstown, but the Happy Wok is a favorite with locals for consistently good food paired with BYO wine and reasonable prices. While not all fluent in English, the staff is competent and friendly. Open every day 5–10 PM for dinner. ✉*43 Beach St.* ☎*03/442–4415* ▭*MC, V* ⊗*No lunch.*

WHERE TO STAY

$$$$ ⌂**Eichardt's Private Hotel.** Once patronized by miners during the 1860s
Fodor'sChoice gold rush, the pricey Eichardt's now welcomes flush travelers drawn
★ by the rush of adventure sports. Guest rooms are done in rich cocoa brown and cream; all have sitting areas with fireplaces, dressing rooms, and bathrooms with heated floors and double vanities. You can request a lake or mountain view. The staff is exceptionally helpful and can arrange anything from a massage to a helicopter ride. The House Bar has delicious takes on lamb and salmon, along with an impressive selection of Otago and other New Zealand wines. **Pros:** Centrally located, great service. **Con:** A bit pricey for a small B&B. ✉*Marine Parade* ☎*03/441–0450* ⎙*03/441–0440* ⊕*www.eichardtshotel.co.nz* ⇆*5 rooms* ⌕*In-room: dial-up. In-hotel: bar* ▭*AE, DC, MC, V* ⏐◎⏐*BP.*

$$$$ ⌂**Nugget Point Boutique Hotel.** Check out the open-air whirlpool here,
★ perched on the edge of Shotover Valley; it's perfect with a glass of champagne. Rooms are luxuriously large, and each has a balcony and a separate seating area. The lodge is a 10-minute drive from Queenstown on the road to Coronet Peak, one of the top ski areas in the country.

9

The bright glassed-in public rooms give it an especially cheerful atmosphere, even if the weather outside is less than gorgeous. The views up and down the Shotover River are to die for. **Pro:** Excellent restaurant. **Con:** You'll need a car as this is outside town. ⊠ *146 Arthur's Point Rd.* ☎ *03/441–0288* 🖷 *03/442–7308* ⊕ *www.nuggetpoint.co.nz* 🛏 *35 rooms* △ *In-room: kitchen. In-hotel: restaurant, bar, tennis court, pool, spa* ☰ *AE, DC, MC, V.*

$$$$
★ 🏨 **Pencarrow.** It's not just the hillside setting by Lake Wakatipu, or the gardens, or the spacious guest rooms—the friendliness and service of the hosts, Bill and Kari Moers, set this place apart. Less expensive than many lodges in this neck of the woods, Pencarrow has all kinds of thoughtful details, from a special "concierge" room, stocked with information on local attractions, to the welcoming teddy bears on the beds. You can have breakfast in the dining room or on a tray in your room. You can also arrange to go gold panning in a local river, if you're feeling lucky. **Pro:** First-rate hospitality. **Con:** It's outside town, so you'll need a car. ⊠ *678 Frankton Rd.* ☎ *03/442–8938* 🖷 *03/442–8974* ⊕ *www.pencarrow.net* 🛏 *4 suites* △ *In-room: VCR. In-hotel: restaurant, bar, laundry service* ☰ *AE, DC, MC, V* ⍣⍣*BP.*

$$$$
★ 🏨 **Remarkables Lodge.** Sitting almost right under the mountains, Remarkables Lodge has extensive views of the jagged grandeur of the Remarkables Range. Out the windows deer wander in the nearby paddocks. A splendid evening meal is included in the high-end rate, and may include prawn ravioli for a starter, Moroccan rack of lamb, and poached pears for dessert. The Remarkables ski area is nearby, and if you can drag yourself away from the outdoor fireplace in the garden, Queenstown activities are a 10-minute drive away. **Pro:** Unbeatable views. **Con:** You'll want a vehicle as it's outside of town. ⊠ *595 Kingston Rd., about 6 km (3.5 mi) south of Queenstown toward Invercargill* ☎ *03/442–2720* 🖷 *03/442–2730* ⊕ *www.remarkables.co.nz* 🛏 *3 rooms, 4 suites* △ *In-hotel: bar, pool, spa* ☰ *AE, MC, V* ⍣⍣*MAP.*

$$$–$$$$
🏨 **Aurum Hotel and Suites.** Wide, floor-to-ceiling windows with views over the town, lake, and across to the mountains are the best part of these modern, spacious rooms. It's a short walk downhill to the town center (though a rather steep one on the way back). The neighboring A-Line, a more modestly priced sister hotel, shares the reception area, restaurant, and bar. **Pro:** Nice big rooms. **Con:** Steep (but short) walk from town. ⊠ *27 Stanley St.* ☎ *03/442–4718* 🖷 *03/442–4715* ⊕ *www.scenic-circle.co.nz* ✒ *aurum@scenic-circle.co.nz* 🛏 *42 rooms, 42 suites* △ *In-room: kitchen (some). In-hotel: restaurant, bar* ☰ *AE, MC, V.*

$$$–$$$$
🏨 **Sofitel.** With a commanding position in the center of town overlooking the lake, Sofitel embodies luxury, right down to the L'Occitane face products in the bathroom. The rooms have every comfort—even in-room espresso machines. Rooms also have private, but tiny, balconies, and TVs over the bathtubs (and a bathologist on hand to run your bath *just so* for a fee). Downstairs the Nue Bar is for feeling sophisticated. The in-house Vie Restaurant has a new world-renowned chef and a fantastic menu. **Pros:** Totally luxurious, conveniently located. **Con:** Doesn't always live up to its five stars, sometimes hovers around 4.8.

✉8 Duke St. ☎*03/450–0045* 🖷*03/450–0046* ⊕*www.sofitelqueens town.com* 🛏*70 rooms, 10 suites* ♿*In-room: Ethernet. In-hotel: restaurant, bar.*

$$–$$$ 🏨**Heritage Queenstown.** On Fernhill, just a few minutes from the town center, the Heritage is quieter than other local hotels and has great views of the Remarkables and Lake Wakatipu. The hotel was built almost entirely out of South Island materials, including central Otago schist and wooden beams from old local railway bridges. Rooms are notably spacious and are fitted with writing tables and comfortable sitting areas. **Pros:** Great service, nice rooms. **Con:** Ten-plus minute walk to downtown. *✉91 Fernhill Rd.* ☎*03/442–4988* 🖷*03/442–4989* ⊕*www.heritagehotels.co.nz* 🛏*137 rooms, 41 suites, 36 3-bedroom villas* ♿*In-hotel: restaurant, bar, pool, gym* 🖃*AE, DC, MC, V.*

$–$$ 🏨**Lakeside Motel.** At the economy end of the spectrum this homey motel has a premium lakefront location. The interior is plain, but there are some nice amenities for the price. Two two-bedroom family units come with full cooking and laundry facilities, but book well in advance for these. **Pro:** Great value. **Con:** On the edge of town. *✉18 Lake Esplanade* ☎*03/442–8976* 🖷*03/442–8930* ⊕*www.queenstownaccommodation. co.nz* 🛏*13 studios, 2 family units* ♿*In-room: kitchen (some). In-hotel: laundry facilities* 🖃*AE, DC, MC, V.*

$ 🏨**Queenstown Lakeview Holiday Park.** With everything from spic-and-span, fully equipped apartments to studios, cabins, and campsites, this park is a varied budget pick. It's right near the Skyline Gondola terminal, with good views of the Remarkables. The staff can help you get good deals on tours and activities. **Pro:** Centrally located. **Con:** Can get a bit crowded. *✉Brecon St.* ☎*03/442–7252* ⊕*www.holidaypark. net.nz* 🛏*16 rooms, 22 lodges, 8 cabins* ♿*In-room: kitchen (some). In-hotel: public Internet* 🖃*AE, MC, V.*

NIGHTLIFE

After days spent testing limits, visitors cram Queenstown's clubs and bars. Don't be surprised to encounter more than one "hens' party" or "stag do" on any given weekend night. Kiwi guys are notoriously vile to their groom-to-be mates, so steer clear if you see a pack of rowdy bachelors as things often get messy in their midst. All the popular venues are in the center of town, within easy walking distance of one another. Grab a copy of *The Source* weekly gig guide, available in most cafés and bars.

The "after-work" scene takes place at **Pig & Whistle** (*✉19 Camp St.* ☎*03/442–9055*), **Brazz on the Green** (*✉1 Athol St., Village Green* ☎*03/442–4444*), and **Monty's** (a Monteith Ale's brew bar) (*✉12 Church St.* ☎*03/441–1081*). **Dux de Luxe** is a popular brewery-restaurant and hosts local bands (*✉14–16 Church St.* ☎*03/442–9688*). **Chicos** (*✉The Mall* ☎*03/442–8439*) holds jam nights on Wednesday. It's also a rowdy late-night dance spot. **Surreal** (*✉7 Rees St.* ☎*03/441–8492*) goes for anything as long as it's not pop music—they'll spin trance, techno, reggae, house, or drum 'n' bass. The upstairs **Winnies** (*✉The Mall* ☎*03/442–8635*) slings pizza before transforming into a happening nightspot. **Bardeux** (*✉The Mall* ☎*03/442–8284*) is a wine bar that's good for an intimate, subdued evening; ditto **Skybar** (⊠*26 Camp St.* ☎*03/442–4283*), where you can munch on whitebait fritters in front of the fireplace, and Queenstown's smallest bar **Mini-bar** (⊠*Eureka Arcade* ☎*03/441–1324*). **Minus 5°** (⊠*Steamer Wharf* ☎*03/442–6050*) is literally a place for chilling out—with ice chairs, an ice bar, and ice glasses. However, warm gear—boots, big Eskimo-style jackets, and gloves—is supplied for you. Be prepared to spend $25 for admission—this includes a drink. Then go next door to warm up in the intimate **Boiler Room** (⊠*Steamer Wharf* ☎*03/441–8066*). End your night in classic Queenstown style with a famous **Fergberger** (⊠*42 Shotover St.* ☎*03/441–1232*). If they're closed you know you've had a big night—this institution is open until 5 AM! Prostitution is legal in New Zealand, and Queenstown has its share of brothels. Mind you, these are not establishments with blinking neon BROTHEL signs in the window; so be aware if you're seeking a massage that some parlors might not offer exactly what you had in mind. And Candy's on Shotover Street ain't sellin' jellybeans.

ARROWTOWN

22 km (14 mi) northeast of Queenstown, 105 km (66 mi) south of Wanaka.

Another gold-mining town, Arrowtown lies northeast of Queenstown. Jack Tewa, or Māori Jack, as he was known, found gold along the Arrow River in 1861, and when William Fox, an American, was seen selling large quantities of the precious metal in nearby Clyde shortly afterward, the hunt was on. Others attempted to follow the wily Fox back to his diggings, but he kept giving his pursuers the slip, on one occasion even abandoning his tent and provisions in the middle of the night. Eventually a large party of prospectors stumbled on Fox and his team of 40 miners. The secret was out, miners rushed to stake their claims, and Arrowtown was born. At the height of the rush there were more than 30,000 hardy souls in this tiny settlement.

After the gold rush ended in 1865, the place became another sleepy rural town until tourism created a new boom. This village at the foot of the steep Crown Range, with weathered-timber shop fronts and white stone churches shaded by ancient sycamores, was simply too gorgeous to escape the attention of tour buses. It has become a tourist trap, but a highly photogenic one, especially when autumn gilds the hillsides. Each April, Arrowtown celebrates the Autumn Festival when the trees are at their most spectacular. On a stroll along the main street, **Buckingham Street,** you can stop in the old post and telegraph office, still open for business. Take time to explore some of the lanes and arcades, filled with cafés and boutique shops.

There are several walks—**Tobin's Track, the Loop, Sawpit Gully,** and the **Lake Hayes Walk**—to raise the fitness levels and give you a feeling for where you are. Some investigate the old gold history, but others give nice views. You can get details on all of them from the Lakes District Museum Information Centre.

To get the full story, stop by the **Lakes District Museum,** which has artifacts of the gold-rush days, an information center, and a small bookstore and gallery. You can even rent pans and get gold-panning tips to try your luck in the Arrow River. When your patience frays and your hands go icy, keep in mind that a hobby prospector found a 275g nugget in this very river in 2006! (He sold it on eBay for US$15,000.) ⊠*Buckingham St.* ☎*03/442–1824* ⊕*www.museumqueenstown.com* ⊠*$5* ⊙*Daily 8:30–5.*

In a less-visited part of the town is the former **Chinese settlement.** Chinese miners were common on the goldfields, brought in to raise a flagging local economy after the gold rush abated, but local prejudice from resident Europeans forced them to live in their own separate enclave. Some of their tiny 19th-century buildings, which have been restored, were built of sod, which endures well in the dry climate; others were built of layered schist stone, with roofs of corrugated iron or tussock thatch. Ah Lum's store (also now restored) was built in a style typical of the Canton delta region of China and operated until 1972. ⊠*Bush Creek, west end of town* ⊠*Free* ⊙*Daily 9–5.*

WHERE TO STAY & EAT

¢–$$$$ ✕**Saffron.** With its dark wood and elegant atmosphere, this place is
★ much more chichi than you'd expect to find in the heart of rural New Zealand. The evening menu features the best of local foods—venison, lamb, snapper, pheasant, beef, local wines, and beautiful fresh vegetables. The rack of Southland lamb with mint-and-onion sauce is heavenly. Lunch takes a lighter spin with omelets, stir-fries, and egg dishes. Reserving is wise. (Its sister restaurant **Pesto** is a more casual eatery offering pizza and pasta, and if you want a drink in a really cool, comfortable bar, duck across the alley and poke your nose behind the **Blue Door.**) ⊠*18 Buckingham St.* ☎*03/442–0131* ⊟*AE, DC, MC, V.*

$$$ ✕**Cafe Mondo.** Tucked into a sheltered courtyard off the main street, this is the place for refreshing, slightly quirky cold drinks like the Mondo Combo, a blend of orange, carrot, and apple juices with a hint of ginger. You could also dig into a substantial lunch or dinner of salmon or chicken with couscous. There's a kids' menu as well. ⊠*4 Ballarat Arcade* ☎*03/442–0227* ⊟*AE, DC, MC, V.*

¢–$ ✕**Joe's Garage.** Sitting above Blue Moon in the Mall, this branch of the Queenstown's café provides a sunny, quiet spot away from the tour-bus crowd. The menu of casual sandwiches and great coffee is the same as in the main branch. ⊠*Arrow La.* ☎*03/442–1116* ⊟*AE, MC, V* ⊙*No dinner.*

$$$$ ☷**Millbrook Resort.** A 20-minute drive from Queenstown, this glamorous resort has a special appeal for golfers: an 18-hole championship golf course that was designed by New Zealand professional Bob Charles. A luxurious spa pampers you whether or not you've taken advantage of the extensive exercise options. Accommodations range from rooms in the resort's main hotel to villas and multi-bedroom cottages. Standard rooms have private balconies and fireplaces. The villas have kitchens, laundry facilities, and large lounge/dining rooms. **Pros:** The golf course, the location. **Cons:** Big, sprawling, and impersonal.

9

✉*Malaghans Rd.* ☎*03/441–7000 or 0800/800–604* 🖷*03/441–7007* ⊕*www.millbrook.co.nz* ➫*13 villas, 70 villa suites, 51 rooms, 24 cottage apartments* ♿*In-room: no a/c, kitchen (some). In-hotel: 2 restaurants, bar, golf course, tennis court, pool, gym, spa, bicycles* ▭*AE, DC, MC, V* ⑩*BP, CP.*

$$ ⚏**Arrowtown Lodge.** Designed to blend in with Arrowtown's historic buildings, these four cottage-style suites are just a two-minute walk from the center of town. All have views toward the Arrow River gorge, which ideally will inspire you to go on a day hike, the hosts' expertise. **Pro:** Delicious breakfast. **Con:** A block from the fire station so the siren might wake you. ✉*7 Anglesea St.* ☎*03/442–1101 or 0800/258–802* 🖷*03/442–1108* ⊕*www.arrowtownlodge.co.nz* ➫*4 rooms* ♿*In-room: dial-up. In-hotel: laundry facilities, public Internet* ▭*AE, MC, V* ⑩*BP.*

NIGHTLIFE

★ It may not have a flashy marquee, but **Dorothy Brown's Boutique Cinema and Bar** is a truly memorable movie house. The theater doesn't seat many people, but the chairs are cushy and have plenty of legroom. Better yet, you can get a glass of wine at the fireplace bar and bring it with you. The schedule mixes Hollywood releases with art and international films. ✉*Off Buckingham St., upstairs* ☎*03/442–1968 or 03/442–1964* ⊕*www.dorothybrowns.com.*

FIORDLAND

Fiordland, the name generally given to the southwest coast, is a majestic wilderness of rocks, ice, and beech forest, where glaciers have carved mile-deep notches into the coast. Rivers, sounds, and lakes eat away at the land, and it rains hard and often, so that the area seems to strike a tenuous balance between earth and water. Most of this terrain is officially designated Fiordland National Park, and in conjunction with South Westland National Park, is a designated UNESCO Te Wahipounamu World Heritage Area. Parts of the park are so remote that they have never been explored, and visitor activities are mostly confined to a few of the sounds and the walking trails. Te Anau serves as the base, with lodgings and sports outfitters. The most accessible scenic highlight of this area—and perhaps of the whole country—is Milford Sound, where tremendous green slopes plunge into the sea, and rare species of coral wait just below the water's surface.

The park is exceptional from a naturalist's point of view. More than 700 plants are found only here, and several rare birds as well. The flightless, blue-green takahē, for instance, was long thought to be extinct until one was found in Fiordland's Murchison Mountains in 1948. The last of the kākāpo, flightless nocturnal parrots, were also found in the park.

The winged creature you're far more likely to encounter is the pernicious sandfly. The swarms of sandflies never let up, and they've become the groaning punch line of many a Fiordland tale. (Paua—NZ abalone—divers in the area have them coming down their snorkels!) Bring tons of insect repellent and keep slathering it on. Interestingly the flies don't usually make it offshore to boats—one more reason why cruises have definite appeal.

The extreme landscape and the soggy climate have prevented much development; neither the first Māori, the early European explorers, sealers, whalers, nor modern arrivals have made many inroads here. If you really want to take in the raw grandeur of Fiordland, hike one of the many trails in the area, among them the famous four-day Milford Track, long considered one of the finest walks in the world.

Fiordland National Park Visitor Centre (✉*Lakefront Dr., Te Anau* ☎*03/249–7924*) hours vary a bit seasonally; summer hours are 8:30–6 and winter hours are 8:30–4:30.

TE ANAU

175 km (109 mi) southwest of Queenstown.

Lake Te Anau (tay-*ah*-no), which is 53 km (33 mi) long and up to 10 km (6 mi) wide, is the largest lake in New Zealand after Lake Taupo. The town of Te Anau, on the southern shores, serves as a base for Fiordland National Park. From Te Anau, you can set out on sightseeing trips by bus, boat, or plane to Milford and Doubtful sounds, or take off on one of the park's world-class hiking trails. (Of these, the most accessible to town is the Kepler Track.) The town itself is not much to write home about, but it does have a few attractions. It's busiest in summer; in winter, some cafés and shops close or reduce their hours.

ESSENTIALS

Bus Companies InterCity (☎*03/443-7885 in Wanaka, 03/249-7559 in Te Anau, 03/442-8238 in Queenstown* ⊕*www.intercitycoach.co.nz*). **Newmans** (☎*09/913-6188 or 0508/353-947* ⊕*www.newmanscoach.co.nz*). **Wanaka Connexions** (☎*03/443-9122* ⊕*www.time2.co.nz/transport/wanaka_connexions*) .

Bus Depot Te Anau (✉*Miro St.*).

Internet Café e-Stop Internet (✉*Jailhouse Mall, Town Centre, Te Anau* ☎*03/249-9461*).

Mail Te Anau (✉*102–104 Town Centre* ☎*03/249-7348*).

WHAT TO SEE

At **Te Anau Caves,** boats and walkways take you through a maze of caves containing underground whirlpools, waterfalls, and gushing streams. On the cave walls, glowworms shine like constellations in a clear night sky. The caves can be reached only by water, and the entire trip takes 2½ hours. There are three trips per day during summer and two per day the rest of the year. ✉*Real Journeys, Lakefront Dr.* ☎*03/249–7416 or 0800/656-502* ⊕*www.realjourneys.co.nz* 🎫*$50.*

The lakeshore **Te Anau Wildlife Centre** gives you the chance to preview some of the wildlife you're likely to encounter when hiking in Fiordland. The center houses one of New Zealand's rare flightless birds, the takahē, which was once thought to be extinct. The lakeside walk to the center makes for a pleasant one-hour stroll. ⊠ *Manapouri Rd., 1 km (½ mi) west of Te Anau* ☎ *03/249–7921* 🏷 *Donation requested* 🕐 *Daily dawn–dusk.*

SPORTS & THE OUTDOORS

CRUISING Doubtful Sound is three times as long as Milford Sound and sees far fewer visitors. **Real Journeys** (⊠ *Lakefront Dr.* ☎ *03/249–7416 or 0800/656–502* ⊕ *www.realjourneys.co.nz*) runs a range of combined bus and boat trips there. Tours include a 2-km (1-mi) bus trip down a spiral tunnel to the Lake Manapouri Power Station machine hall, an extraordinary engineering feat built deep beneath the mountain. On the sound itself, you may see bottlenose dolphins or fur seals. Most people take an eight-hour day trip from Lake Manapouri; there are bus connections from Te Anau and Queenstown. Between October and May you can overnight on the sound, aboard the *Fiordland Navigator.* Rates for the day excursion are $225 per person, and for the overnight cruise, $325 (for a quad share) to $499 (twin share).

HIKING Information, transport options, and maps for the plethora of hikes near Te Anau, including the Kepler Track, can be obtained from the **Fiordland National Park Visitor Centre** ⊠ *Lakefront Dr.* ☎ *03/249–7924* 🖷 *03/249–7613* ⊕ *www.doc.govt.nz*).

★ The 60-km (37-mi) **Kepler Track** loops from the south end of Lake Te Anau, starting just 4 km (2½ mi) from Te Anau township. It skirts the lakeshore, climbs up to the bush line, passing limestone bluffs and going through extensive beech forest, and has incredible views of the South Fiord and Te Anau Basin. An alpine crossing takes you to the high point near the peak of Mt. Luxmore. It's a moderate walking trail that takes three to four days to complete. If you're on a tight schedule, it's possible to take day hikes to the Luxmore and Moturau huts.

The track has some very good-quality trails, three huts, and two camps, and is relatively easy, with only one steep climb to the alpine section up Mt. Luxmore. Hikers should beware, however, of high wind gusts while crossing the exposed saddle above the bush line. In winter and spring the alpine section may be impassable because of snow. Although the trail can be walked in either direction, most people walk it counterclockwise.

In summer, from late October through late April, the three huts are serviced (which means they have gas for cooking and heating, toilets that are cleaned daily, and daily visits from a warden) and cost $40 per night for adults. In winter, when huts are unserviceable, this charge drops to $10. Reservations are required for the huts and the campsites and made with the **Great Walks Booking Office** (☎ *03/249–8514* ⊕ *www. doc.govt.nz*).

JET-BOATING **Luxmore Jet** ☎*03/249–6951 or 0800/253–826* ⊕*www.luxmorejet. co.nz)* zips you up the Upper Waiau River, where the forest comes down to the river's edge. Once on lovely Lake Manapouri, you'll stop to experience the serene quiet. The company also pairs its jet-boat rides with flights by Wings and Water *(see below)* or Southern Helicopters Heli-jet. Once you reach Manapouri, you could take off on a floatplane to see Doubtful Sound or Lake Te Anau by air, or be whisked back to base by helicopter. Costs start at $85 for the jet boat, $205 for the jet-boat-and-flight option, and $395 for jet-boat-and-helicopter option.

KAYAKING **Fiordland Wilderness Experiences** ⊠*66 Quintin Dr.* ☎*03/249–7700* ⊕*www.fiordlandseakayak.co.nz)* runs kayaking day trips and multi-day tours on Milford and Doubtful sounds and on Lakes Te Anau and Manapouri. Beginners are welcome. They operate from September to May, with some differences according to location, so call ahead; costs start around $100. <CLASS TAG="Tour–Sports"/>

SCENIC **Air Fiordland** ⊲*Ticket Centre, 70 Town Centre* ☎*03/442–3404 or*
FLIGHTS *0800/107–505* ⊕*www.airfiordland.co.nz)* offers a range of scenic flights on its fixed-wing aircraft to Milford Sound and Doubtful Sound, with prices hovering around $195–$299. It also has combined packages offering the option of flying to Milford Sound and then taking a cruise boat or kayaking before returning to either Te Anau or Queenstown ($335–$375). **Wings and Water Te Anau Ltd.** ⊠*Lakefront Dr.* ☎*03/249– 7405* 🖷*03/249–7939)* offers scenic flights with a floatplane that takes travelers to some of the region's most inaccessible areas, including a 10-minute trip over Lake Te Anau, Lake Manapouri, and the Kepler Track and longer flights over Doubtful, Dusky, and Milford sounds. Costs range from $65 for a 10-minute flight to $135 for 20 minutes.

WHERE TO EAT

$$$–$$$$ ✕**Fat Duck Cafe.** This relatively new restaurant has been receiving rave reviews from satisfied visitors and locals. The ambience, service, and cuisine are excellent. Try the venison. ⊠*164 Milford Rd..* ☎*03/249– 8480* ▭*MC, V.*

$$$–$$$$ ✕**Redcliff Café & Bar.** Te Anau might not strike you as a crème brûlée kind of place, but Redcliff pulls it off. Among the dishes served in this cottage setting, the Fiordland crayfish and the wild venison on the Fiordland platter are excellent. Reservations aren't accepted—so try to arrive by 6 if you don't want to join the wait list. ⊠*12 Mokonui St.* ☎*03/249–7431* ▭*MC, V* ⊗*Closed July and Aug.* No lunch.

$$$–$$$$ ✕**Settlers Steakhouse.** A carnivore's friend, Settlers revolves around red meat. Choose your own steak, perhaps porterhouse or a T-bone. It's not all beef—you can also choose from grilled lamb, venison, local salmon, or blue cod. The all-you-can-eat salad bar is the counterpoint. ⊠*Town Centre* ☎*03/249–8454* ▭*AE, DC, MC, V* ⊗*No lunch. Reduced hrs June and July.*

$$–$$$ ✕**Keplers Restaurant.** The view is magnificent, as are the lamb, venison, and seafood at this popular eatery. Tandoori prawns are the standout starter, and the beef Wellington, orange roughy, and blue cod main courses are always in demand. Crayfish arrives live in season and is

9

offered simply grilled or with Mornay sauce at the hefty cost of $65. ⊠*23 Town Centre* ☎*03/249–7909* ▭*AE, MC, V* ☽*Closed June–late Aug. No lunch.*

WHERE TO STAY

$$$$ 🏨**Fiordland Lodge.** A few kilometers out of Te Anau on the road to Milford Sound, glass, stone, and timber blend together to make a stylish place to spend a few days. Each room has a wide-ranging lake view, and there are two B&B log cabins, especially well suited for families. **Pro:** B&B price also includes dinner. **Con:** Considering the price, the staff could be sweeter. ⊠*State Hwy. 94, 472 Te Anau–Milford Hwy.* ☎*03/249–7832* 🖷*03/249–7449* ⊕*www.fiordlandlodge.co.nz* ⇆*10 lodge rooms, 2 cabins* ⚐*In-room: dial-up. In-hotel: restaurant, bar* ⍾*BP, MAP.*

$$$$ 🏨**Murrell's Grand View House.** Twenty minutes south of Te Anau, this B&B sits on one of New Zealand's prettiest and most pristine lakes—Lake Manapouri. The Murrell family has run this historic property since 1889. Play croquet, walk over to the wharf for a boat tour of Doubtful Sound, or curl up in the library by the fire. **Pro:** A perfect launching point to explore crystal clear Lake Manapouri or incredible Doubtful Sound. **Con:** It's a bit of a detour from the usual tourist circuit. ⊠*Murrell Ave., Manapouri* ☎*03/249–6642* 🖷*03/249–6966* ⊕*www.murrells.co.nz* ⇆*4 rooms* ⚐*In-hotel: restaurant, bar* ⍾*BP.*

$$$–$$$$ 🏨**Radfords Lakeview Motel.** This reasonably priced lakefront motel has clean, spacious rooms and is located a few minutes' walk from town. Five units have spa baths. **Pros:** Great location, good value. **Con:** Forgettable ambience. ⊠*56 Lakefront Dr.* ☎*03/249–9186* 🖷*03/249–9187* ⊕*www.radfordslakeviewmotel.co.nz* ⇆*6 studios, 10 rooms* ⚐*In-room: kitchen, Wi-Fi. In-hotel: laundry service, parking* ▭*AE, DC, MC, V.*

$$ 🏨**Cats Whiskers.** Hosts Anne Marie and Lindsay Bernstone keep things homey at their modern lakefront B&B, complete with, you guessed it, a resident cat (there's also a small dog). Each room has pluses such as tea-making facilities and hair dryers; ask for the one with a lake view. The house is a 10-minute walk from the town center and is opposite the National Park Visitor Centre. A courtesy car can take you to any of the local restaurants. **Pros:** Friendly hosts, cheerful place. **Con:** Fills up quickly, so try to book in advance. ⊠*2 Lakefront Dr.* ☎☎*03/249–8112* ⊕*www.catswhiskers.co.nz* ⇆*4 rooms* ⚐*In-hotel: laundry facilities, public Internet* ▭*MC, V* ⍾*BP.*

¢–$$ 🏨**Te Anau Top 10 Holiday Park Mountain View.** Ideally set across from the lakefront and just a couple of blocks from the town's commercial strip, this well-serviced park offers motel rooms, cabins, and campervan and camping sites. For the cabins, you'll need to rent linens for a small extra cost. The Matai Lodge also offers basic rooms with private baths. Their architecture is reminiscent of upmarket tramping huts, with exposed ceiling beams. **Pro:** Popular, well-run facility with options for everyone. **Con:** Very busy during high season, so book ahead. ⊠*Te Anau Terr.* ☎*03/249–7462 or 0800/249–746* 🖷*03/249–7262* ⊕*www.teanautop10.co.nz* ⚐*In-hotel: bicycles, laundry facilities, public Internet.*

CLOSE UP

Lake Manapouri & Doubtful Sound

Just 20 minutes south of Te Anau, Lake Manapouri has long had the reputation as one of New Zealand's prettiest lakes. The subject of contentious debate back in the 1970s when hydroelectricity producers wanted to raise the level of the lake and submerge the town, it is now a very down-to-earth spot. The lake is unspoiled, hemmed by high mountains and studded by many bush-covered islands. Cruises run several times a day to the head of the lake, where you can join a tour of the West Arm hydro-station, deep underground. West Arm is also the departure point for those traveling on to Doubtful Sound, a stunning stretch of water, largely untouched by visitors. A connecting bus crosses you over the 2,177-foot Wilmot Pass before dropping steeply down to sea level at Deep Arm, the head of Doubtful Sound.

Real Journeys (✉ *Pearl Harbour, Manapouri* ☎ *03/249–660 or* 0800/656–502 ⊕ *www.realjourneys. co.nz*) runs daily cruise options on Lake Manapouri, providing scenic cruises, a visit to the power station, or connections to their Doubtful Sound cruises. Costs for these tours start at $59 per person. **Fiordland Expeditions** (✉ *Deep Cove, Doubtful Sound* ☎ *03/442–2996* ⊕ *www. fiordlandexpeditions.co.nz*) offers a truly New Zealand experience on their great little boat, *Tutuko.* Skipper Richard Abernethy is totally at home on these waters and will take you to the most inaccessible reaches of Doubtful Sound, or out and around the coast, weather permitting (which doesn't happen often). This is the tour to do if you want to do a bit of fishing, dive some of the world-class water beneath the boat, or just soak up the scenery, of which there is plenty. Tours are run by arrangement, rather than on a set schedule, so you'll need to make a group, or join one.

EN ROUTE

The **Milford Road,** from Te Anau to Milford Sound, winds through deep, stony valleys where waterfalls cascade into mossy beech forests. It's a spectacular route, but if you're making the trip between May and November, check local information for avalanche warnings and come equipped with tire chains. You can rent these in any of the Te Anau service stations. The road is narrow and winding at times, so allow at least 2½ hours.

The 120-km (75-mi) road starts with a fast 29-km (18-mi) stretch along the shores of Lake Te Anau to Te Anau Downs. This is where the ferry leaves for those wishing to hike the Milford Track. Past Te Anau Downs, the road cuts away from the lake and after 20 km (12½ mi) enters Fiordland National Park. You'll pass some great photo ops at Mirror Lakes, Knobs Flat, and Lake Gunn before reaching the Divide, a watershed between rivers flowing both east and west and the starting point for the Routeburn Track. A few miles farther on, you'll come to the **Homer Tunnel.** After the lengthy tunnel, the road descends sharply in hairpin turns down the Cleddau Valley for 16 km (10 mi) before reaching the small settlement at Milford Sound.

Note: In 2008, Te Anau police expressed dismay at the high number of fatalities and injuries caused by head-on car crashes on this road.

Most of these incidents are caused by overseas drivers driving reck-lessly or inattentively. Please be careful on this road, pay attention, and slow down!

MILFORD SOUND

120 km (75 mi) northwest of Te Anau, 290 km (180 mi) west of Queenstown.

Fodor's Choice
★ Fiordland National Park's most accessible and busiest attraction is **Mil-ford Sound,** the sort of overpowering place where poets run out of words and photographers out of film or memory card. Hemmed in by walls of rock that rise from the waterline sheer up to 4,000 feet, the 13-km-long (18-mi-long) fiord was carved by a succession of glaciers as they gouged a track to the sea. Its dominant feature is the 5,560-foot pin-nacle of **Mitre Peak,** which is capped with snow for all but the warm-est months of the year. Opposite the peak, Bowen Falls tumbles 520 feet before exploding into the sea. On a clear day or after rain this is a spectacular place. Luxuriant rain forest clings to the sheer precipices washed with waterfalls. You'll often see seals on rocks soaking up the sun; dolphins sometimes flirt with the boats. But Milford Sound is also spectacularly wet: the average annual rainfall is around 20 feet, and it rains an average of 183 days a year. In addition to a raincoat you'll need insect repellent—the sound has voracious sandflies.

Even in heavy rain and storms Milford Sound is magical. Rainfall is so excessive that a coat of up to 20 feet of fresh water floats on the surface of the saltwater fjord. This creates a unique underwater environment similar to that found at a much greater depth in the open ocean. You can observe this at the **Milford Deep Underwater Observatory,** a 15-minute boat ride from the wharf in Milford at Harrison Cove. From the under-water windowed gallery you'll see rare red and black corals and a range of deepwater species. The 30-minute visit and round-trip shuttle boat trip from Milford takes about one hour. Several boating companies, such as Real Journeys and Mitre Peak Cruises, make regular trips to the observatory. ✉ *Milford Sound* ☎ *03/249–9442 or 0800/329–969* ⊕ *www.milforddeep.co.nz* ⊙ *Daily 8:30–5.*

SPORTS & THE OUTDOORS

CRUISING The gorgeous views from the water account for the popularity of cruising here. It's essential to book ahead between mid-December and March. Some include a visit to the Milford Sound Underwater Obser-vatory *(⇨ above)*. All boats leave from the Milford wharf area. Avoid the midday sailings, as they link with tour buses and are most crowded. Milford Sound Red Boat Cruises and Real Journeys run more than a dozen cruises a day between them, with extra options in summer.

Real Journeys (✉ *Lakefront Dr., Te Anau* ☎ *03/249–7416 or 0800/656–501* ⊕ *www.realjourneys.co.nz*) offers daily cruises on the *Milford Mon-arch* and its companion the *Milford Haven*. These trips cruise the full length of Milford Sound to the Tasman Sea, with views of waterfalls, rain forest, mountains, and wildlife. There's a choice of 1½-hour scenic cruises and 2½-hour nature cruises, at $60 and $80, respectively. To have the most intense experience on the sound, sign up for one of the three overnight cruise options that are offered from October to April. The *Milford Mariner* sleeps 60 passengers in private cabins with bathrooms ($350 per person twin share, September–May), the *Milford Wanderer* has bunk-style accommodation for 61 passengers ($210 per person quad share, October–April), and the M.V. *Friendship* has bunks for just 12 passengers ($210 per person; multishare, November–March). **Milford Sound Red Boat Cruises** (✉ *Milford Sound Wharf* ☎ *03/441–1137*

⊕ *www.redboats.co.nz*) offers frequent daily scenic cruises on its catamarans to Milford Sound or to the Milford Deep Underwater Observatory. The basic tour, which lasts less than two hours, loops through the sound to the Tasman Sea; the fare starts at $50 and goes up to $79 if you include a stop at the observatory.

HIKING
Fodor's Choice
★

If you plan to walk the **Milford Track**—a wholly rewarding, four-day bushwalk through Fiordland National Park—understand that it is one of New Zealand's most popular hikes. The 53½-km (33-mi) track is strictly one-way, and because park authorities control access, you can feel as though you have the wilderness more or less to yourself. Independent and guided groups stay in different overnight huts. Be prepared for rain and snow, but also for what many call the finest walk in the world. This is still wild country, largely untouched by humanity. Mountains rise vertically for several thousand feet out of valleys carved by glaciers. Forests tower above you, and myriad cascading waterfalls plunge into angry, fast-flowing rivers.

The trailheads for the track are remote. Both guided and unguided walks begin with a two-hour ferry ride to Glade Wharf on Lake Te Anau and end with a ferry taking you from Sandfly Point over to the Milford Sound wharf. Because of the good condition of the track, the walk is rarely demanding. But because the trail is often blocked by snow in winter, there is a restricted hiking season from late April until late October. Reservations are essential through the season, and there are no camping sites winter or summer. You can make a reservation with the **Great Walks Booking Office** (☎ *03/249–8514* ⊕ *www.doc.govt. nz*). If you don't have enough time for the whole Milford Track, try a day trip with **Real Journeys** (☎ *03/219–7416 or 0800/656–501* ⊕ *www. realjourneys.co.nz*), which includes a Lake Te Anau cruise and a guided day walk on the Milford Track. The 33-km (20½-mi) **Routeburn Track,** like the Milford Track, is designated one of the country's Great Walks.

Routeburn goes between Lake Wakatipu, near Glenorchy, and the road between Milford and Te Anau; it takes about three days to hike. The alpine landscape is stunning, and once you're above the tree line, the sandflies back off. As on the Milford, be prepared for rain and mud.

To hike independently of a tour group for either the Milford, Kepler, or Routeburn Track, call the **Great Walks Booking Desk** at the **Fiordland National Park Visitor Centre** (⊠ *Lakefront Dr., Te Anau* ☎ *03/249–8514* 🖶 *03/249–8515* ⊕ *www.doc.govt.nz*) or book online through the Web site. Reservations for the coming season can be made starting on the first of July every year. Book well in advance—especially if you plan to go in December or January. Independent walking, without a guide, requires that you bring your own food, utensils, bedding, and other equipment. You stay in clean, basic Department of Conservation huts. From October to April, the prime-booking time, the huts cost $40 per person per night. Campsites on the Routeburn and Kepler tracks are $15 and must also be reserved in advance. *For more details on these tracks, see Chapter 11.*

If you're itching to see some coastline during your hike, consider the **Hollyford Track** (⊠ *Lakefront Dr., Te Anau* ☎ *03/249–8514* 🖶 *03/249–8515* ⊕ *www.doc.govt.nz*). At 56 km (35 mi), it's a four-day endeavor, taking you from the Hollyford Road down to Martins Bay by roughly following the Hollyford River. You'll pass a couple of lakes and waterfalls on your way; at the coastline you'll likely spy seals and penguins. Be particularly careful of flooded creek crossings. For DOC huts on the track, book in advance through the **Fiordland National Park Visitor Centre.** Going with a guide from **Ultimate Hikes** (⊠ *1st fl., AJ Hackett Station Bldg., Camp St. at Duke St., Queenstown* ☎ *03/441–1138 or 0800/659–255* 🖶 *03/441–1124* ⊕ *www.ultimatehikes.co.nz*) requires deep pockets but provides comfortable beds and a cook. For the Milford Track, it'll cost $1,750 in high season (in multishare accommodation), $1,590 in low season, including a cruise on Milford Sound and transport to and from Queenstown; the Routeburn is a bit cheaper at $1,090 in the high season, $950 in low. If you're not up for a multiday trek, you can take a single-day "encounter" hike on either the Milford or Routeburn Track for $135.

KAYAKING   **Milford Sound Sea Kayaks** (⊠ *Milford Sound* ☎ *03/249–8500, 0800/476–726 in New Zealand* ⊕ *www.kayakmilford.co.nz*) offers guided double kayaking on the sound that includes a hike along part of the Milford track. Prices range from $69 to $169 per person. No experience is required.

SCENIC   "Flightseeing" combines a round-trip flight from Queenstown to Mil-
FLIGHTS   ford with a scenic cruise. Flights are weather-dependent. **Milford Sound Scenic Flights** (☎ *03/442–3065 or 0800/207–206* ⊕ *www.milfordflights. co.nz*) start with one-hour flights for $275. The **Glacier Southern Lakes Helicopters Ltd.** (☎ *03/442–3016* ⊕ *www.heli-flights.co.nz*) will get you buzzing over Milford Sound; the Milford Sound Fantastic trip has at least two landings and costs $610.

WHERE TO STAY & EAT

Accommodations are scant at Milford Sound, and it's best to stay in Te Anau and make your visit a long day trip.

$$–$$$ ✕**Blue Duck Café & Bar.** The view out the front window, across Milford Sound to Mitre Peak and the mountains beyond, is amazing—and the food's not bad, either. Lunch choices include wraps, rolls, and sandwiches, as well as a full buffet; there are even options for various dietary requirements and vegetarians. Dinner goes à la carte, and the restaurant and bar stay open until late. And if you're brave and don't mind a few sandflies, you can even eat outside. ✉*Milford Sound* ☎*03/249–7982* ▭*MC, V.*

¢ 🏨**Milford Sound Lodge.** Just 1 km (½ mi) out of the Milford settlement, on the banks of the Cleddau River, this backpacker hostel offers basic but relatively fresh accommodations. A few years ago the guest rooms were completely revamped, from the heating system to the mattresses and curtains. The range of rooms includes twin and double units with linen for $67 per person, four-person bunk rooms at $27 per bed, and dormitories for six people also at $27 a bed. All bathrooms are shared. The lodge serves inexpensive breakfast, or people can cook for themselves in the on-site kitchen. Powered and nonpowered campsites are also available. **Pros:** Clean bathrooms, good value. **Con:** No power 11 PM–6 AM. ✉*Milford Sound* ☎*03/249–8071* 🖷*03/249–8075* ⊕*www.milfordlodge.com* ⤶*23 rooms with shared bath* ⌂*In-room: no TV. In-hotel: restaurant, bar, laundry facilities, public Internet* ▭*MC, V.*

TOURS

ADVENTURE
TOURS

Mid Southern Tracks (✉*14 Pioneer Dr., Lake Tekapo* ☎*03/680–6774*) organizes and provides experienced guides for fishing trips and nature tours both locally and to destinations all over New Zealand. **Nomad Safaris** (✉*19 Shotover St., Queenstown* ☎*03/442–6699 or 0800/688–222* ⊕*www.queenstown4wd.com*) offers four-wheel-drive "safari" trips to old gold-rush settlements (or their remains), such as Skippers Canyon and Macetown. Another off-roading trip takes you to see some of the areas filmed for the *Lord of the Rings* trilogy. Costs start at $110. For a wide choice of fly-drive-cruise tour options to Milford and Doubtful sounds from Queenstown, Te Anau, and Milford, check out **Real Journeys** (✉*Lakefront Dr., Te Anau* ☎*03/249–7416 or 0800/656–501* 🖷*03/249–7022* ✉*Steamer Wharf, Queenstown* ☎*03/442–4846 or 0800/656–503* ⊕*www.realjourneys.co.nz*).

BOAT TOURS

Glacier Explorers (✉*Aoraki/Mount Cook Village* ☎*03/435–1077* ⊕*www.glacierexplorers.com*) leave from the Hermitage Hotel, the visitor center, or the Mount Cook YHA for guided boat trips on the Tasman Glacier Lake ($105). Tours run at 10 and 2, October–April, and last three hours.

9

BUS TOURS   The **Double Decker** *(☎0800/668–888)* is an original London bus that makes a three-hour circuit from Queenstown to Arrowtown and the bungy-jumping platform on the Karawau River. Leaving Queenstown, it goes via Frankton, Lake Hayes, and Gibbston Valley Wines before heading for a break at Arrowtown. The return trip to Queenstown goes by the Shotover River valley. Tours (about $38) depart Queenstown daily at 9:30 and 1:30 from The Mall outside McDonald's.

Otago, Invercargill & Stewart Island

WORD OF MOUTH

"We really love the Catlins but weather there is quite rough most of the time. You will get to see seals, sea lions and penguins if blessed with good weather at the right season."

–Chenoa

"Stewart Island is truly one of the most unique places I have ever been. This is not your typical 'island experience'. Although bird watching, snorkeling, fishing and beach combing for shells may sound like everyday activities on an island, each had an underlying element of true wildness and that is what makes Stewart Island so special…"

–Liza Smith, Savannah

Updated by
Jessica Kany

THE PROVINCE OF OTAGO OCCUPIES much of the southeast quadrant of the South Island. During the first three decades of the 1800s, European whaling ships cruised its coast and ventured ashore, yielding a mixed response from the Māori, who had been living here for hundreds of years. In 1848 Dunedin was settled, and all the land from the top of the Otago Peninsula south to the Clutha River and sections farther inland were purchased from the Māori. By the mid-1860s Dunedin was the economic hub of the Otago gold rush. Dunedin's historical wealth endures in such institutions as the University of Otago, the oldest in the country.

Invercargill, to the south, was born out of different economic imperatives. After the Dunedin settlers bought swaths of the Southland for their sheep, they needed a local port to bring in more stock from Australia. The town of Bluff, already familiar to sealers, was selected as an ideal location. Invercargill became the administrative center to the port and then the whole region. Until recent years, the town's economic focus remained that of raising sheep and other livestock and crops; it is now becoming a more diverse metropolis.

Hanging off the bottom of South Island, Stewart Island is a study in remoteness. Commercial-fishing settlements give way to bushland that the kiwi bird still haunts. At night, the birds can be seen wandering the beaches. On some nights the aurora australis, the southern hemisphere equivalent of the northern lights, light up the sky.

Note: *For more information on outdoor activities in lower South Island, see Chapter 11.*

ORIENTATION & PLANNING

ORIENTATION

The region is bordered by the snowcapped Southern Alps to the west and a string of golden, albeit chilly, beaches to the east. The north is met by the wide Canterbury Plains and the south by the timeless Catlins region. The two major hubs of civilization in the "deep south" are both coastal cities: Dunedin to the east and Invercargill to the south. The Otago Peninsula stretches east from "Dunners" into the Pacific and is home to the Royal Albatross and yellow-eyed penguins. Take the rugged coastal route west of Dunedin to explore the Catlins, where farms and forest meet the sea. Invercargill is flat and doesn't feel particularly coastal, as you can't see the sea from within the city. To avoid any "civilization hub," continue south, across Foveaux Strait, to Stewart Island.

Dunedin. A university town, Dunedin has the austere seriousness that old stone academic buildings lend a city. At the same time, it has the fresh, creative brio of young academics (aka partying 20-year-olds). The backdrop is just as interesting: the port clangs and squeals with the busy work of massive international freighters, while across the har-

TOP REASONS TO GO

Bird-Watching: If any region can bring out the bird-watcher in you, this is it. Seeing a yellow-eyed penguin or an albatross out on the peninsula or a kiwi on Stewart Island is undeniably special.

Kiwi Sports: Dunedin's Carisbrook Rugby Stadium is home to the Highlanders team, and they're the reason for the swaths of blue and yellow team colors around town and for the near-rabid crowds of fans. In Invercargill, Southland Stadium is home to the netball team the Southern Sting. (Netball is akin to outdoor basketball and almost always played by women.) Hence the Go Sting! slogans you'll see everywhere.

Pubs & Clubs: With its resident population of 20,000 university students during the academic year the city of Dunedin is full of funky bars, late-night pubs, value-for-the-money cafés, and rocking music venues.

The Southern Sea: The lower coast of the South Island is wild and woolly, bordering the great Southern Ocean that swirls around the base of the globe. Head south along the Catlins section of the Southern Scenic Route for ocean views, diving seabirds, and sandy beaches. At Bluff and Stewart Island, you can watch fishermen unloading their catches of oysters, cod, and lobsters (called crayfish here)—and then sample the catch in a local restaurant.

bor, albatross chicks learn to fly, and penguins waddle anxiously past snoozing elephant seals.

Invercargill. Cast your gaze upward! The architecture of Invercargill is a treat to behold. Due to its proximity to the sea, "Invers" has been called the "City of Water and Light." The wide flat roads of downtown and the enormous sweep of Oreti Beach were perfect training grounds for homegrown hero Burt Munro (motorcycle land speed record holder).

Stewart Island. If your hand represents the island, your pinky fingernail would be the amount that is actually inhabited. Roads link the main township, Halfmoon Bay, to the other "neighborhoods"—a few homes nestled around one bay or another. Beaches are pristine; the sea is crystal green and bountiful. Many residents are garden-proud—flowers spill from grounded dories, broken buoys, and old gumboots. Beyond town is wilderness, filled with wonderful birds and accessed by a network of walking trails.

10

PLANNING

Most people start in Dunedin and migrate south via State Highway 1. Once you reach Balclutha, you can continue south either by staying on the highway and heading straight for Invercargill or by turning off and going via the Catlins on the Southern Scenic Route. The Catlins route is more demanding—but also more rewarding, scenery-wise. Whichever route you take, by the time you hit the Southland border all roads are wide, flat, and point to Invercargill.

GETTING HERE & AROUND

Most flights to Dunedin and Invercargill go via Christchurch. Fog occasionally causes delays; fortunately Christchurch Airport has a decent food court, a pool table, *and* an air hockey table to amuse you. Stewart Island Flights operates from Invercargill, or you can take a boat to the island. (One local described the choices as "either 60 minutes of fear or 20 minutes of terror," but that's true only on a bad day—both journeys offer beautiful views.)

InterCity's two daily runs between Christchurch and Dunedin take about five to six hours. The company makes an extra run on Friday and Sunday. One daily InterCity bus continues on from Dunedin to Invercargill; this takes another four hours. Other bus companies operating in the region include Atomic Shuttles, Citibus, and Bottom Bus.

The best way to explore is by car, particularly if you want to take your time seeing the Catlins. You cannot ferry your rental car to Stewart Island; there is secure parking in Invercargill and Bluff. Buses serve most places of interest, including daily routes between South Island cities. They go the direct route between Dunedin and Invercargill, so you won't see the Catlins on the ride. Dunedin and Invercargill each have a bus system, but they are both pedestrian-friendly cities.

WHEN TO GO

Dunedin gets more visitors in summer, but during the university vacations the city is quieter, which has its pros and cons. Inland Otago remains dry year-round, and you can expect crisp, sunny days in winter, but the coast gets its share of rain, and Dunedin can have day after day of clouds and showers. Southland in winter isn't any colder, but it is wetter, and this can put a damper on things.

It's often said of New Zealand that you experience all four seasons in one day—but on Stewart Island you may experience all of them in an hour. Even in summer you can expect blustery and wet periods. In winter, there's a better chance of seeing the aurora australis, but some of the island's walking trails may be closed.

ABOUT THE RESTAURANTS

Dunedin has the area's highest concentration of good restaurants. Seafood is a big player, in part because of Dunedin's coastal location but also because of its proximity to Bluff, the home of New Zealand's great delicacy, the Bluff oyster. Many of the least-expensive options are café-like Asian restaurants; these tend to close early, around 9 PM. Locals don't usually dress up or make reservations for anything other than the most exclusive establishments.

Invercargill has a more limited selection of mostly moderately priced restaurants. Stewart Island has a reasonable selection considering its location, but in winter some places limit their hours or close.

WHAT IT COSTS IN NEW ZEALAND DOLLARS				
¢	$$$$	$$	$$$	$$$$
Restaurants	under $10	$10–$15	$15–$20	$20–$30	over $30

Prices are per person for a main course at dinner, or the equivalent.

ABOUT THE HOTELS

Dunedin has a full range of accommodations, from modest hostels to luxury hotels, whereas Invercargill has more motels than anything else. (Local motels generally offer clean rooms with kitchens and TVs.) Stewart Island's lodging options tend to be smaller, boutique establishments, and usually on the expensive side. Throughout the region, air-conditioning is a rarity, but given the cool climate, this isn't a problem. Heating, on the other hand, is standard in most places.

It's a good idea to make reservations, especially in summer. In Dunedin, rooms can be scarce around special events, such as graduation ceremonies and high-profile rugby games.

WHAT IT COSTS IN NEW ZEALAND DOLLARS				
¢	$	$$	$$$	$$$$
Hotels	under $75	$75–$125	$125–$200	$200–$300	over $300

Prices are for a standard double room in high season, including 12.5% tax.

DUNEDIN

280 km (175 mi) east of Queenstown, 362 km (226 mi) south of Christchurch.

Clinging to the walls of the natural amphitheater at the west end of Otago Harbour, the South Island's second-largest city is enriched with inspiring nearby seascapes and wildlife. Because Dunedin's a university town, floods of students give the city a vitality far greater than its population of 122,000 might suggest. Its manageable size makes it easy to explore on foot—with the possible exception of Baldwin Street, the world's steepest residential street and home to the annual "gutbuster" race, in which people run up it, and the "Jaffa" race, in which people roll the namesake spherical chocolate candy down it.

Dunedin, the Gaelic name for Edinburgh, was founded in 1848 by settlers of the Free Church of Scotland, a breakaway group from the Presbyterian Church. The city's Scottish roots are still visible; you'll find the only kilt shop in the country, the first and only (legal) whisky distillery, and a statue of Scottish poet Robert Burns. The Scottish settlers and local Māori came together in relative peace, but this wasn't true of the European whalers who were here three decades before, as places with names such as Murdering Beach illustrate.

10

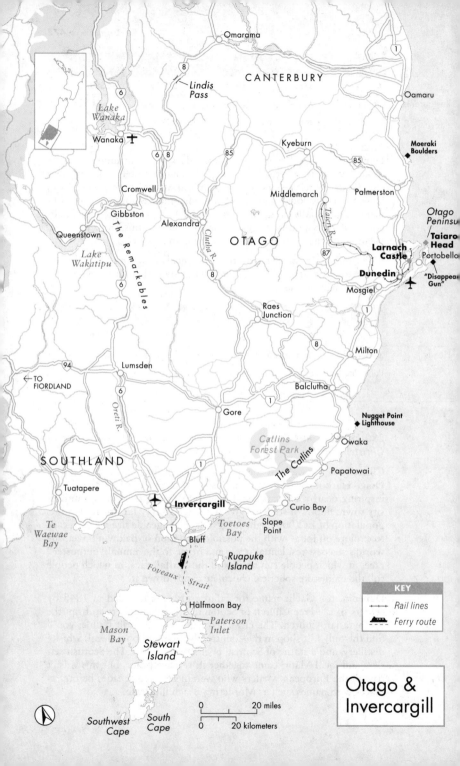

Omarama

8
*Lindis
Pass*

CANTERBURY

Oamaru

6
*Lake
Wanaka*

Wanaka ✝

6   8

Cromwell

Kyeburn

85

♦ Moeraki
  Boulders

Middlemarch

Palmerston

Gibbston

Alexandra

OTAGO

Taieri R.

85

Queenstown

The Remarkables

6

*Lake
Wakatipu*

Clutha R.

8

87

**Larnach
Castle**

**Taiaro
Head**

Portobello

*Otago
Peninsu*

Dunedin

"Disappear
Gun"

Mosgiel

1

Raes
Junction

94

Lumsden

8

Milton

← TO
FIORDLAND

6

Oreti R.

Clutha R.

1

Balclutha

Gore

♦ **Nugget Point
  Lighthouse**

SOUTHLAND

*Catlins
Forest Park*

1

The Catlins

Owaka

Tuatapere

Papatowai

✈ **Invercargill**

Curio Bay

*Te
Waewae
Bay*

1

*Toetoes
Bay*

Slope
Point

Bluff

Foveaux   Strait

*Ruapuke
Island*

Halfmoon Bay

*Paterson
Inlet*

*Mason
Bay*

*Stewart
Island*

KEY

✝──┼── *Rail lines*

🚢 *Ferry route*

*Southwest
Cape*

*South
Cape*

0 ────── 20 miles

0 ────── 20 kilometers

Otago &
Invercargill

Dunedin has always had a reputation for the eccentric. Wearing no shoes and a big beard here marks a man as bohemian rather than destitute, and the residents wouldn't have it any other way. The University of Otago was the country's first university and has been drawing writers ever since its founding in 1871, most notably Janet Frame and the poet James K. Baxter. Dunedin also has a musical heritage, which blossomed into the "Dunedin Sound" of the 1970s and '80s. The movement, which included the Chills and the Verlaines, is making a comeback.

GETTING HERE & AROUND
Newly upgraded Dunedin Airport, with the unfortunate code of DUD, lies 20 km (13 mi) south of the city. Both Qantas and Air New Zealand link Dunedin and Christchurch; the flight takes just under an hour. Air New Zealand also flies regularly from Dunedin to Auckland and Wellington Taxi fare from Dunedin's airport to the city center is about $60. Kiwi Shuttles and similar companies charge about $20 for a trip between the city and the airport.

Confusing, one-way roads and twisting hills in the suburbs make driving in Dunedin a challenge. Street parking is limited. Local buses to the peninsula depart from Stand 5, Cumberland Street. Stewart Island Experience operates buses to Bluff, which connect with the ferry. They pick up at the Southland Museum and at accommodations. The fare to Bluff is $15.

ESSENTIALS
Airport **Dunedin International Airport** (⊠ *25 Miller Rd., Momona* 🕿 *03/486–2879* ⊕ *www.dnairport.co.nz*).

Bus Depot **Dunedin** (⊠ *205 St. Andrew St.*).

Bus Information **Citibus** (🕿 *03/477–5577* ⊕ *www.citibus.co.nz*). **InterCity** (🕿 *03/471–7143* ⊕ *www.intercitycoach.co.nz*).

Medical Assistance **Dunedin Hospital** (⊠ *201 Great King St., Dunedin* 🕿 *03/474–7930*). **Urgent Pharmacy** (⊠ *95 Hanover St., Dunedin* 🕿 *03/477–6344*).

Rental Cars **Budget** (🕿 *03/474–0428* ⊕ *www.budget.co.nz*). **National** (🕿 *03/477–8801 or 0800/800–115* ⊕ *www.nationalcar.co.nz*). **Thrifty** (🕿 *03/477–7087 or 0800/737–070* ⊕ *www.thrifty.co.nz*).

Visitor Info **Dunedin Visitor Information Centre** ⊠ *48 The Octagon* 🕿 *03/474–3300* 🖷 *03/474–3311* ⊕ *www.cityofdunedin.com*. The Web site ⊕ *www.dunedinnz.com* has good information on Dunedin.

10

WHAT TO SEE
The city's hub is the **Octagon,** an eight-sided town center. It's lined with several imposing buildings, and a smattering of market stalls, cafés, and bars with tables spilling onto the pavement. In summer it's a meeting place, and it's also the site for the occasional student demonstration. A **statue of Robert Burns** sits in front of **St. Paul's Cathedral,** a part-Victorian Gothic, part-modern building with an imposing marble staircase

leading up to a towering facade of Oamaru stone. On Stuart Street at the corner of Dunbar, check out the late-Victorian **Law Courts.** Their figure of Justice stands with scales in hand but without her customary blindfold (she wears a low helmet instead).

The **Dunedin Public Art Gallery** has lovely exhibit spaces. The shell of an original municipal building has been paired with a sweeping, modern glass facade. The collection includes European masters Monet, Turner, and Gainsborough, as well as New Zealand and Otago artists. A special gallery highlights Dunedin native Frances Hodgkins, whose work won acclaim in the 1930s and '40s. Hodgkins's style changed through her career, but some of her most distinctive works are postimpressionist watercolors. ⊠ *30 The Octagon* ☎ *03/474–3240* ⊕ *www.dunedin.art. museum* 🖂 *Free* ⊙ *Daily 10–5.*

The **Otago Settlers Museum** tells the stories of all Otago settlers, from Māori and early European and Chinese to later Pacific Islanders and Asians. On display are documents, works of art, technological items, and forms of transport. The museum has changing exhibits, events, and historical walking tours of the city. ⊠ *31 Queens Gardens* ☎ *03/477–5052* ⊕ *www.otago.settlers.museum* 🖂 *$4* ⊙ *Daily 10–5.*

♻ Relax and enjoy the birdsong at the **Botanic Gardens** amid 70-acres of international and native flora. In addition to the seasonal gardens with their 6,800 plant species are the year-round attractions: an aviary, a winter garden hothouse, a native plant collection, and a rhododendron garden. Parking at the lower part of the gardens, off Cumberland Street, has easier access than the Opoho end, which is steeper, but both parts are worth visiting. ⊠ *Great King St. at Opoho Rd.* ☎ *03/477–4000* 🖂 *Free* ⊙ *Gardens dawn–dusk, buildings 10–4.*

★ The 1906 **Dunedin Railway Station,** a cathedral to the power of steam, is a massive bluestone structure in Flemish Renaissance style, lavishly decorated with heraldic beasts, nymphs, scrolls, a mosaic floor, and even stained-glass windows of steaming locomotives. This extravagant building earned its architect, George Troup, a knighthood from the king—and the nickname Gingerbread George from the people of Dunedin. The station is also home to the **Sports Hall of Fame** (☎ *03/477–7775* ⊕ *www.nzhalloffame.co.nz* 🖂 *$5* ⊙ *Daily 10–4*), the country's only sports museum. ⊠ *Anzac Ave. at Stuart St.* ☎ *03/477–4449* ⊙ *Daily 7–6.*

The **First Presbyterian Church** on the south side of Moray Place is not vast, but it's still impressive, with a base of Oamaru stone topped by a delicate 200-foot spire. Check out the leaf patterns, dragon, and other carved details around the windows. ⊠ *415 Moray Pl.*

♻ The **Otago Museum** demonstrates what galleries and museums were like in Victorian times. In this museum's 1877 building, you can visit the "Animal Attic," a restored, magnificent skylighted gallery. The museum's first curator was a zoologist, and many of the original animals collected from 1868 are still on display. "Southern Land, Southern People" explores the cultural heritage of this region, and other galleries focus on Māori and Pacific Island artifacts, animal and insect specimens, and nautical items, including ship models and a whale skeleton. ✉ *419 Great King St.* ☎ *03/474–7474* ⊕ *www.otagomuseum.govt.nz* 💲 *Free, Discovery World $6, special galleries and visiting exhibitions $10* ⏱ *Daily 10–5.*

🔄 Which came first, the Cadbury factory or the Cadbury Creme Egg? At **Cadbury World** you can watch chocolate candy in the making; keep an eye out for the chocolate waterfall. Kiwis from as far away as Stewart Island have memories of school field trips here and ensuing tummy aches (the tour includes free samples of candy). It's best to prebook a tour. ✉ *280 Cumberland St.* ☎ *03/467–7967 or 0800/223–287* ⊕ *www.cadburyworld.co.nz* 💲 *$16* ⏱ *Daily 9–4, 9–7 in summer.*

For more tasty indulgences, head to the **Speight's Brewery Heritage Centre** for a tour of the South's top brewery, which dates back to 1876. Here you can see the various stages of gravity-driven brewing, learn the trade's lingo such as *wort* and *grist,* and taste the results. Speight's makes several traditional beers, the most common being its Gold Medal Ale. The company claims that this is the drink of choice for every "Southern Man," which isn't far from the truth. Watch a video of various Speights television ads and learn to say the tough Southern way, *Good on ya, mate.* ✉ *200 Rattray St.* ☎ *03/477–7697* ✉ *tours@ speights.co.nz Reservations essential* 💲 *$17* ⏱ *Weekend tours at 10, noon, and 2 (sometimes an additional 4 PM tour is added on busy days); weekday tours at 10, noon, 2, and 7.*

🔄 The **Taieri Gorge Railway** tourist train runs from Dunedin through the now-closed Otago Central Railway to Pukerangi and Middlemarch (home of the annual Middlemarch Singles' Ball; each year this very train imports young city gals up to a dance with lonely Otago sheep shearers). Also available is a seasonal *Seasider* route from Dunedin up the coast to Palmerston. The train runs every day; check the timetable for its destination. Reservations are essential. (Attention cycling enthusiasts: connections can be made at Middlemarch to the wonderful Otago Central Rail Trail; *see further information in Chapter 11.*) ✉ *Dunedin Railway Station* ☎ *03/477–4449* ⊕ *www. taieri.co.nz* 💲 *$59–$75.*

SPORTS & THE OUTDOORS

Rugby is followed with cultish devotion in Dunedin, and **Carisbrook Stadium** (✉ *Burns St.* ☎ *03/466–4010 or 0800/227–472* ⊕ *www.orfu. co.nz*), also known as the "House of Pain," is where fans go to worship. (Fans of the local Super 14 team, the Highlanders, paint themselves blue and yellow on match days.) Games are played on weekends. Terrace tickets start at $12, and the main stand is just $27. Walking with the crowds out to the stadium for night games is an event unto itself, and can be a hasty pub crawl out of the city (got to get to the game in time for the opening haka!).

10

The Northern Otago Coast & Oamaru

Driving south from Timaru, **Oamaru** is the first stop of interest. Described as the best example of Victorian architecture in use in New Zealand today, the ornate Oamaru limestone facades of the buildings in the port precinct gleam. During the second week of November the town hosts the Victorian Heritage Celebrations. Festivities include the New Zealand Penny Farthing Championships, a Heritage Golf Classic, a Heritage Ball, and a Victorian Garden Party. The town's visitor center has information about the festival and the buildings themselves. ⌷ *Oamaru I-Site Info Centre, 1 Thames St., Oamaru* ☎ *03/434–1656* ⊕ *www.tourismwaitaki.co.nz.*

Oamaru's other claim to fame is penguins. Each evening, enthusiastic blue penguins—the world's smallest penguin breed—emerge from the sea and waddle up the beach to their nests. The **Oamaru Blue Penguin Colony** (⌷ *Waterfront Rd.* ☎ *03/433–1195* ⊕ *www.penguins.co.nz* 🕮 *Tour $15*) can be visited any time of the year, and providing penguins are present, tours and viewing opportunities run day and evening. **Pen-y-bryn Lodge** (⌷ *41 Towey St.* ☎ *03/434–7939* ⊕ *www.penybryn.co.nz*) offers entry to the penguin colony as part of the hotel's room rate. Each night, between the appetizer and the main course in the dining room, guests are encouraged to leave the table and head down to the ocean to watch the penguins come in, before returning to their meal and a quiet port afterward.

An even more significant population of **yellow-eyed penguins,** or *hoiho,* come ashore south of Oamaru. The best places to view them are Bushy Beach and Katiki Point, where hides (camouflaged viewing huts) have been constructed. These penguins are one of the world's rarest breeds, and they are considered an endangered species. Ask at the **local information office** (☎ *03/434–1656* ⊕ *www.tourismwaitaki.co.nz*) for details on viewing them.

Along the coast north of Dunedin, you can stop to see the striking **Moeraki Boulders.** These giant spherical rocks are concretions, formed by a gradual buildup of minerals around a central core. Some boulders have sprung open, revealing—no, not alien life forms, but—interesting calcite crystals. The boulders stud the beach north of the town of Moeraki and south as well at Katiki Beach off Highway 1, about 60 km (37 mi) above Dunedin, or 40 km (25 mi) south of Oamaru. Unfortunately, the boulders at Moeraki Beach have become a bit of a tourist item, and there are often whole busloads of people wandering the beach. Watch for little dolphins jumping in the surf just offshore; they're as interesting as the boulders. If you're feeling a bit peckish after the sea air, pop into **Fleurs Place** (⌷ *169 Haven St., Moeraki* ☎ *03/439–5980*) out on the old jetty. Here you can enjoy fish straight out of the sea, which is the highlight of the lunch and dinner menus. **Harbour to Ocean** (⌷ *Waterfront Rd., South Hill, Oamaru* ☎ *03/434–3400* ⊘ *Closed Mon.*),aka H2O, is a new waterfront all-day eatery that offers tasting plates for $15—mix and match among venison, risotto, lamb, and crab dishes, or drop in for a canapé and glass of wine. The presentation is elegant and the food is delicious. Kids can play in the big sandpit while grown-ups relax on the deck.

To get to **St. Clair beach** either drive south on State Highway 1 or hop on the Normanby–St. Clair bus from George Street or the Octagon. The sea at Dunedin can be a little wild; in summer an area between flags is patrolled by lifeguards. St. Clair has some good surfing; it hosts some prestigious competitions. Don't be too spooked by the shark bell on the Esplanade: a fatal attack hasn't occurred for 30 years, just the occasional nibble.

Signal Hill, to the northeast, with good views of the city below and the hills surrounding it, is a popular walking destination and an excellent mountain-biking venue. At the opposite end of town, Saddle Hill looks southward to Mosgiel and the Taieri Plain. Also south of town is the **Tunnel Beach walk,** which heads through a sandstone tunnel to a secluded beach (this walk is closed from August through October for lambing).

WHERE TO EAT

$$$–$$$$ ✕ **Bell Pepper Blues.** Inside a converted historic hotel, this casual restau-
★ rant with its mullioned bay windows and dark-wood interior is where Michael Coughlin, one of the country's most respected chefs, brings an inventive flair to his dishes. His lamb, beef, and *cervena* (farmed venison) dishes are well known; the pan-seared beef sirloin with a spring roll of slow-braised veal shin and aromatic Asian vegetables is a particular standout. Pre- and postdinner drinks can be had next door at the restaurant's Chilé Club Bar. ⊠*474 Princes St.* ☎*03/474–0973* ⊟*AE, DC, MC, V* ⊘*Closed Sun. No lunch.*

$–$$$$ ✕ **The Black Dog Café and Bar.** Along with the usual offerings of pancakes and beef fillet, the menu has some jazzier items such as venison sausages, paua samosas, and whitebait patties. Jazzier still: live jazz and blues on the weekend. Dinner reservations are recommended. ⊠*109 Princes St. (1 block from Octagon)* ☎*03/471–8180* ⊟*AE, MC, V* ⊘*No dinner Sun. and Mon.*

$$–$$$ ✕ **The Esplanade.** At one of the best locations in Dunedin—on the waterfront in St. Clair's—the Esplanade serves terrific pizzas and great views. The pizza choices are traditional, with some unusual extras such as artichokes and capers. About a third of the space is a bar, with the rest devoted to tables next to the pizza oven and, in winter, a roaring open fire. The long hours (9 AM to midnight daily) mean you can even have pizza for breakfast. One large pie is enough for two people. ⊠*5/250 Forbury Rd., St. Clair's* ☎*03/456–2544* ⊟*AE, DC, MC, V.*

$$–$$$ ✕ **Salt Bar Restaurant.** Located in an iconic art deco building, this is St. Clair's newest place to dine and take in the salty sea views. Sate yourself with shepherd's pie, pumpkin-sage risotto, or bacon-wrapped scallops, or sip an Oranjeboom on tap. The bar's cool ambience of chrome finishing and art deco decor is warmed by the dining area which features a brick fireplace. The service is extremely friendly. The Salt Bar serves breakfast, lunch, and dinner. ⊠*240 Forbury Rd., St. Clair's* ☎*03/455–1077* ⊟*AE, DC, MC, V.*

¢–$$$ ✕ **The Ale House Bar & Restaurant.** A rugged interior with heavy wood
★ furniture, old brewing equipment, and a huge schist fireplace makes the

10

Speight's brewery restaurant welcoming. Its hub, naturally, is the bar. The menu includes a "drunken" steak (steak marinated in dark, malty porter) and beer-battered fish. You also get recommendations for the best Speight's ale to match your meal. Several special seasonal beers are released each year; in the past, these have included Harvest (an apricot beer), Chocolate, and Samradh (a ginger-and-pimiento beer). ⊠*200 Rattray St.* 🕾📠*03/471–9050* ⊟*AE, DC, MC, V.*

$-$$ ✕ **Thai Hanoi.** This popular Thai restaurant has some Vietnamese influence. Try one of the green or red Thai curries, or a yellow or jungle (hot) Vietnamese curry. Because it's opposite the Rialto Cinema, Thai Hanoi makes for a convenient pre- or post-movie dinner spot—but reserving a table is a good idea. ⊠*24 Moray Pl.* 🕾*03/471–9500* ⊟*AE, DC, MC, V* ⊙*No lunch.*

¢-$$ ✕ **Anarkali.** Once named Ananda, Anarkali has retained the same chef and still serves the authentic Indian vegetarian *thalis* (meals made up of several small individual servings) served on traditional metal platters. You can choose from (in order of ascending size) the Prince, Rani, Raja, or Maharaja thali. Anarkali is best suited for lunches and early dinners. Although it has a liquor license, you're welcome to bring your own bottle. ⊠*365 George St.* 🕾*03/477–1120* ⊟*MC, V.*

¢-$ ✕The growing Asian community in Dunedin includes a Cambodian enclave, which has spawned a few noodle shops—most notably **Apsara** (⊠*380 George St.*) and **Sampan** (⊠*362 George St.*), a few doors down. These are both crowded with students and offer yummy, filling soups starting at about $5.

WHERE TO STAY

$$$$ 🏨 **Corstorphine House.** This restored Edwardian mansion, surrounded
Fodor$Choice   by private gardens, exudes luxurious gentility. The lavish interior
★   extends from the public areas, with carved fireplaces and custom-made furniture, to the themed rooms, which include the Egyptian Room and the Indian Room. Bathrooms have de-misting mirrors and heated floors, and your bed comes with a pillow menu. Organic produce grown on the property appears in the highly acclaimed conservatory restaurant's dishes, so your meals include free-range eggs, and fresh vegetables, all seasoned with handpicked herbs. The room rate includes a full breakfast. **Pros:** Beautiful rooms and grounds. **Con:** On the outskirts of the city, car required to get here. ⊠*23 Milburn St.* 🕾*03/487–1000* 📠*03/487–6672* ⊕*www.corstorphine.co.nz* 🖙*7 rooms* ☽*In-room: VCR, dial-up, Wi-Fi. In-hotel: restaurant* ⊟*AE, DC, MC, V* ⊧⊙⊧*BP, EP.*

$$-$$$ 🏨 **Brothers Boutique Hotel.** This centrally located historic building once housed members of the Christian Brothers Order. The priciest room is the old chapel with a super-king bed and stained-glass windows. Three rooms have balconies with city and harbor views. All rooms were refurbished in 2005 and have new bathrooms. The owners are friendly and helpful; free broadband Internet is offered in the lounge and a complimentary breakfast is provided. **Pros:** Clean rooms, quirky decor, and friendly staff. **Con:** Standard rooms on the small side. ⊠*295 Rattray*

St. ☎*03/477–0752* 🖷*03/477–0043* ⊕*www.brothershotel.co.nz* ⮌*15 rooms. In-hotel: public Internet, parking* ▤*AE, DC, MC, V.*

$$-$$$ 🛏 **Lisburn House.** This Victorian-Gothic inn is a romantic retreat amid
★ lovingly tended gardens. Many of its 1865 details are intact, including decorative Irish brickwork and fishtail slate roof tiles. Inside are high molded plaster ceilings, an impressive turn-of-the-20th-century stained-glass entrance, and a welcoming fireplace. The three sumptuous bedrooms have four-poster queen beds. At the Claddagh Restaurant ($$$), with its extensive wine list and plush interior, the venison and seafood chowder are always delicious. Dining reservations are essential, and Claddagh is open Tuesday–Saturday. **Pros:** Charming rooms and fabulous dining. **Con:** On the outskirts of city center. ⌧*15 Lisburn Ave.* ☎*03/455–8888* 🖷*03/455–6788* ⊕*www.lisburnhouse. co.nz* ⮌*3 rooms* ⟐*In-room: VCR. In-hotel: restaurant, bar* ▤*AE, DC, MC, V* ⏣*BP.*

$$ 🛏 **Bluestone on George.** One of Dunedin's newest hotels (opened March 2007) offers its guests all the nice amenities in spanking-clean new rooms. Rooms include bathrobes, heated bathroom floors, and kitchen facilities, and most rooms have spa baths. **Pros:** Centrally located, relatively new. **Con:** Not terribly Dunediny—a bit of an impersonal business-trip atmosphere. ⌧*571 George St.* ☎*03/477–9201* 🖷*03/477–9203* ⊕*www.bluestonedunedin.co.nz* ⮌*15 rooms* ⟐*In-hotel: gym, executive floor, parking* ▤*AE, DC, MC, V.*

$-$$ 🛏 **Hulmes Court Bed & Breakfast.** In an 1860 house built for one of the founders of the Otago Medical School, this bed-and-breakfast maintains its scholarly ties: the host, Norman Wood, employs University of Otago students and graduates. The complex includes a 1907 house next door. Rooms are characterized by their architectural elements, such as large bay windows. From Hulmes Court it's a short walk to the center of town. Children are welcome. There's a resident cat named Solstice. Some of the rooms have shared bathrooms, so make sure you inquire if you want a private toilet. **Pros:** Friendly staff, interesting decor. **Con:** Not ideal for folks with cat allergies. ⌧*52 Tennyson St.* ☎*03/477–5319* 🖷*03/477–5310* ⊕*www.hulmes.co.nz* ⮌*14 rooms, 8 with bath* ⟐*In-room: VCR, Ethernet (some). In-hotel: bar, bicycles, public Internet* ▤*AE, DC, MC, V* ⏣*CP.*

¢ 🛏 **Next Stop Backpackers.** A short walk from the Octagon, Next Stop Backpackers has double rooms and dorms with shared bathrooms. **Pro:** Nice downhill walk when you leave. **Con:** Steep uphill coming home from the Octagon. ⌧*2 View St.* ☎*03/477–0447* 🖷*03/477–0430* ⊕*www.nextstop.co.nz* ⮌*9 rooms, 4 dorms without bath* ⟐*In-room: kitchen, no TV. In-hotel: bar, public Internet* ▤*DC, MC, V.*

NIGHTLIFE & THE ARTS

Many venues are on or near George and Princes streets, often down dark alleys with no signs, so follow the crowd. Information about what's going on can be found on ⊕*www.fink.net.nz*, Radio One (91 FM), and in the student paper, *The Critic.*

ART GALLERIES   The **Marshall Seifert Gallery** (⊠*1 Dowling St.* ☎*03/477–5260*) is in a triangular-shape building with a dizzying spiral staircase. It's overflowing with fine art, antiques, prints, and contemporary New Zealand art. It's open weekdays 11–5:30, and Saturday 11–2. **Milford Galleries** (⊠*18 Dowling St.* ☎*03/477–7727* ⊕*www.milfordgalleries.co.nz*), a major fine-art dealer, presents solo and group exhibitions of New Zealand paintings, drawings, sculpture, glasswork, ceramic art, and photography. Among the artists are Neil Frazer (who does large-scale abstract expressionist paintings) and Elizabeth Rees (whose oils explore New Zealand machismo).

THEATER   Since 1961, the **Globe Theatre** (⊠*104 London St.* ☎*03/477–3274*) has produced high-quality plays, beginning with local author James K. Baxter. The **Regent Theatre** (⊠*17 The Octagon* ☎*03/477–6481, 03/477–8597 ticket reservations* ⊕*www.regenttheatre.co.nz*), in a historic building, holds large-scale musicals, dance, and theater performances, and the Royal New Zealand Ballet, the New Zealand Film Festival, and the World Cinema Showcase each year. The highly rated **Bean Scené** café, in the same building, is a nice stop for dinner (don't be fooled by the tired decor—the food is excellent).

You could spend all night bar-hopping and never leave the Octagon, with its many drinking establishments, from the swank upstairs wine bar **Bacchus** to the rowdy live music of Irish pub **The Craic.**

The **Arc Café** (⊠*135 High St.* ☎*03/474–1135*) is a bar, performance venue, café, and gallery all rolled into one. This very informal and affordable joint is probably the only place in town you can ask for a cognac with your morning coffee without raising an eyebrow.

★   Possibly the snuggest bar in Dunedin, **Pequeno** (⊠*Savoy Bldg., lower ground fl., 50 Princes St.* ☎*03/477–7830*) came to notoriety as the hangout of choice for Gwyneth Paltrow and Chris Martin, of the band Coldplay, during the Dunedin shoot of the film *Sylvia*. The wine list is good, if pricey, and there's live jazz on Thursday evenings. **Refuel** (⊠*640 Cumberland St.* ☎*03/479–5309* ⊕*www.dunedinmusic.com*), in the heart of the university campus, has a predominantly student clientele, though everyone is welcome. Nights are split between local or national (or even international) live rock acts and DJ-driven nights of '80s hits, hip-hop, house, and drum 'n' bass music.

SHOPPING

Nearly all the good shops are clustered around George Street and Moray Place.

Koru (⊠*Lower Stuart St., opposite Dunedin Railway Station* ☎*03/477–2138* ⊕*www.nzartandjade.co.nz*) is a local artists' co-op gallery and interactive studio, which sells crafts made of *pounamu* (New Zealand greenstone), *paua* (abalone shell), and wood, as well as weaving and pottery. Bargain hunting bibliophiles will be in heaven (or a level closer to it) on the second floor of the **University Bookshop** (✉*378 Great King St.* ☎*03/477–6976* ⊕*www.unibooks.co.nz*), where there is a constant sale. More Kiwi spirit can be found at **Outré** (✉*380 Great King St., opposite University Bookshop* ☎*03/471–7005*), where New Zealand–made crafts are mixed in with clothing, trinkets, and ecofriendly goods (possibly inspired by the Green Party offices across the street). **Plume** (✉*310 George St.* ☎*03/477–9358*) carries major international and New Zealand designer clothes. Great New Zealand labels abound, such as Nom D, Zambesi, Kate Sylvester, and Workshop. Girls: if you're looking for fun, funky sundresses, **Slick Willy's** (✉*323 George St. [upstairs]* ☎*03/477–1406*) has a great selection. For sweets, drop by **Guilty by Confection** (✉*44–46 Stuart St.* ☎*03/474–0835*) for a hot chocolate or some homemade fudge.

TOURS

One way to see Dunedin is via the **Double Decker Bus Tour** (✉*630 Princes St., Dunedin* ☎*03/477–5577* ⊕*www.citibus.co.nz*), which takes in numerous historic buildings in central Dunedin, the hillside suburbs, and the university. The one-hour tour costs $18.

Twilight Tours (✉*25 Coolock St., Dunedin* ☎*03/474–3300* ⊕*www.wilddunedin.co.nz*) organizes minibus tours of Dunedin and its surroundings, including one that focuses on the albatross, penguins, and seals of the Otago Peninsula. The tour costs $65 but doesn't include admission to the Royal Albatross Center *(see Otago Peninsula, below)*. (You can still see albatross flying free without entering the observation area.)

Another way to experience the area's prolific wildlife is to take a boat trip to Taiaroa Head with **Monarch Wildlife Cruises** (✉*Wharf St. at Fryatt St., Dunedin* ☎*03/477–4276* ⊕*www.wildlife.co.nz*).A guided hour-long cruise includes visits to the breeding sites of the northern royal albatross, New Zealand fur seals, and up to 20 species of coastal and pelagic birds. Very likely, an albatross will fly over your boat— their huge wingspan makes it a spectacular sight. Other trips include landing stops at the yellow-eyed penguin reserve or the Taiaroa visitor center. The basic cruise costs $32.

10

OTAGO PENINSULA

The main items of interest along the claw-shaped peninsula that extends northeast from Dunedin are an albatross colony and Larnach Castle. The road on the west side of the peninsula consists of 15 km (9½ mi) of tight curves along the harbor, so be careful while driving, or you could find yourself having an impromptu marine adventure. Along the road are a handful of settlements; these get progressively more rustic as you near the peninsula's tip. On the east side of the peninsula there's a string of rugged beaches; some are accessible via walking paths. On the journey back to Dunedin, the Highcliff Road, which turns inland at the village of Portobello, is a scenic alternative to the coastal Porto-

The Southern Scenic Route—Catlins Sections

The Southern Scenic Route, 440 km (273 mi) long, follows the coast south of Dunedin, picks up the highway to Balclutha, and swings around the Catlins coast before pushing through Invercargill to Milford Sound. The Catlins stretch (200 km, or 125 mi) is a treat, although some side roads are rough. Split your journey over two days. The *Southern Scenic Route* brochure, available at the Dunedin visitor center, describes the sights; attractions are signposted. Visit ⊕ *www. southernscenicroute.co.nz.*

When you leave the highway at Balclutha, you'll notice that the native bush is dense and relatively untouched. This, coupled with rich birdsong, gives the countryside a tropical feel.

The first stop is **Nugget Point.** Its Māori name, Tokatā, means "rocks standing up out of water." Wildlife abounds, including yellow-eyed penguins, fur and elephant seals, and sea lions. The town at Nugget Point is **Kaka Point.** There are several places to stay the night, and you should spend time at the "hide" observing the yellow-eyed penguins coming in from the sea. If you want a coffee served with an excellent sea view, stop in the **Point** at Kaka Point. Inland is **Owaka,** the Catlins' only town. With a population of roughly 400, Owaka has a cluster of shops, a Department of Conservation Field Centre, a small museum, and basic services.

At the settlement of **Papatowai,** there's a convenient picnic spot behind a tidal inlet. Here you can enjoy rock pools with bush on one side and coastline on the other. Just south of here, stop at the **Florence Hill Lookout.** The view of Tautuku

Bay is one of the best coastal views in New Zealand. There's a 30-minute loop walk onto the estuary at Tautuku Bay.

Farther on is **Curio Bay,** home to a petrified forest visible at low tide. From Curio Bay a back road runs over to **Slope Point,** mainland New Zealand's southernmost point. Heavy rains or unusually high tides can make the road impassable. Slope Point is a bit of a disappointment—just some farmland sloping to the sea. However, it gets plenty of visitors. There is no access during the lambing season in September and October. (If you skip Slope Point and continue on the main road, stop at the general store in Waikawa, where the art of the meat pie has been perfected.)

By now the rugged Catlins landscape smoothes out into gentle green hills. From the township of Fortrose the roads are straight once more across the wide flats of Southland; before you know it, you've reached Invercargill. The road continues westward to Tuatapere, the self-proclaimed "sausage capital of New Zealand." Stops along the way include a surf at Colac Bay, a try at the "Bull Ring" in Dusty's Pub, and a nosy in at Cosy Nook.

On the edge of Balclutha, the **Garvan Hotel** ($$–$$$) looks like a pleasant B&B with pretty gardens, nothing more. But luxury awaits: perfect hollandaise, crackling fires, accommodating hosts. The menu is divine. (What could be richer than beef fillet with merlot–blue cheese sauce? Answer: their chocolate dessert.) ⊠ *State Hwy. 1, Lovells Flat, Milton* ☎ *03/417–8407* ⊕ *www.garvan.co.nz* ⤶ *4 rooms* ▭ *MC, V* ⦿ *BP.*

bello Road and gives easiest access to Larnach Castle. Allow an hour to drive from the city.

ESSENTIALS

Visitor Info **Dunedin Visitor Information Centre** ✉ *48 The Octagon* ☎ *03/474–3300* 🖶 *03/474–3311* ⊕ *www.cityofdunedin.com).*

WHAT TO SEE

★ High on a hilltop with commanding views from its battlements, **Larnach Castle** is the grand baronial fantasy of William Larnach, an Australian-born businessman and politician. The castle, built in the mid-1870s, was a vast extravagance even in the free-spending days of the gold rush. Larnach imported an English craftsman to carve the ceilings, which took 12 years to complete. The solid marble bath, marble fireplaces, tiles, glass, and even much of the wood came from Europe. The mosaic in the foyer depicts Larnach's family crest and the modest name he gave to his stately home: the Camp. Larnach rose to a prominent position in the New Zealand government of the late 1800s, but in 1898, beset by a series of financial disasters and possible marital problems, he committed suicide in Parliament House. According to one version of the story, Larnach's third wife, whom he married at an advanced age, ran off with his youngest son; devastated, Larnach shot himself. The 35 acres of grounds around the castle include lodging, a rhododendron garden, a rain-forest garden with kauri, *rimu*, and *totara* trees, statues of *Alice in Wonderland* characters, a herbaceous walk, and a South Seas Walkway lined with palms and aloe plants. ✉ *Camp Rd.* ☎ *03/476–1616* 🖶 *03/476–1574* ⊕ *www.larnachcastle.co.nz* 🎫 *$20* ☉ *Daily 9–5.*

Fodor'sChoice **Taiaroa Head,** the wild and exposed eastern tip of the Otago Peninsula, ★ is the site of a breeding colony of royal albatrosses. Among the largest birds in the world, with a wingspan of up to 10 feet, they can take off only from steep slopes with the help of a strong breeze. With the exception of this colony and those in the Chatham Islands to the east, the birds are found only on windswept islands deep in southern latitudes, far from human habitation. Under the auspices of the **Royal Albatross Centre,** the colony is open for viewing all year, except during a two-month break between mid-September and mid-November when the birds lay their eggs; the visitor center is open year-round. The greatest number of birds are present shortly after the young albatrosses hatch near the end of January. Between March and September parents leave the fledglings in their nests while they gather food for them. In September, the young birds fly away, returning about eight years later to start their own breeding cycle. Access to the colony is strictly controlled, and you must book in advance. From the visitor center you go in groups up a steep trail to the Albatross Observatory, from which you can see the birds through narrow windows.

Overlooking the albatross colony is the **"Disappearing" Gun at Fort Taiaroa,** a 6-inch artillery piece installed during the Russian Scare of 1886, when Russia was making hostile maneuvers through the Pacific. The gun was shot in anger only once, during World War II, when it

10

was fired across the bow of a fishing boat that failed to observe correct procedures. Tours range from 30 to 90 minutes and can include albatross viewing, Fort Taiaroa, and an Albatross Insight presentation. ⊠*Taiaroa Head* ☎*03/478–0499* ⊕*www.albatross.org.nz* ⊠*Prices range from $8 for Insight presentation to $33 for Unique Taiaroa Tour* ☉*Royal Albatross Centre opens at 8:30; tours run 9* AM*–dusk in summer, 10* AM*–dusk in winter.*

☾ If you'd like to observe the world's most endangered penguin in its natural habitat, visit the **Yellow-Eyed Penguin Reserve,** also called the **Penguin Place,** where a network of tunnels has been disguised so that you can get close. The penguins, also known as *hoiho,* are characterized by their yellow irises and headbands. Reservations are essential. ⊠*Harrington Point* ☎*03/478–0286* 🖷*03/478—0257* ✐*penguin. place@clear.net.nz* ⊕*www.penguinplace.co.nz* ⊠*$33* ☉*Daily 9–5.*

OFF THE BEATEN PATH   **The Mole,** at the end of the Aramoana peninsula, is a 1-km-long (½-mi-long) breakwater protecting the entrance to Otago Harbour. A dozen or so small ships were sunk between 1920 and 1950 to protect the breakwater from the relentless Southern Ocean. You can check these ships out, and the tall kelp forest that protects them, with **Dive Otago** (⊠*2 Wharf St., Dunedin* ☎*03/466–4370* ⊕*www.diveotago. co.nz*), which run trips when the weather allows.

WHERE TO STAY & EAT

$$$ ✕ **Bay Café and Bar.** In the first settlement you reach on the peninsula, this well-known café has fine views across the harbor. Scallops, prawns, blue cod, and mussels are popular, as are the tasty gourmet pizzas with smoked salmon and prawns. The brunch menu is served between 11 and 3, and the dinner menu kicks in at 5. In summertime, reservations are essential. ⊠*494 Portobello Rd.* ☎*03/476–1357* ⊟*MC, V.*

$$–$$$ ✕ **1908 Café & Bar.** There are good views from this converted post office "where the high road meets the low road." The interior still feels Edwardian, and classic seafood dishes and steaks lead the menu. Hours can be changeable in winter, and crowds come in summer. ⊠*7 Harrington Point Rd.* ☎*03/478–0801* ⊟*AE, DC, MC, V.*

$$$ 🛏*Larnach Lodge.* It's hard to beat panoramic sea views, 35 acres of
★ gardens, the Larnach Castle next door, and luxury theme rooms. The Scottish Room has classic tartan bedcovers and curtains, heavy brass bedsteads, and a Robbie Burns rug; the Enchanted Forest Room has 19th-century William Morris wallpaper. Rooms with shared bathrooms in a converted 1870 coach house are about half the regular rate. Entry to the castle is included in the room rate. **Pro:** How often do you get to stay at a castle? **Con:** The food is not consistently good. ⊠*Camp Rd.* ☎*03/476–1616* 🖷*03/476–1574* ⊕*www.larnachcastle.co.nz* ⇥*12 rooms* ⚅*In-hotel: restaurant* ⊟*MC, V* ⏍*BP.*

The Southern Man

The laconic "Southern Man" has a special niche in the Kiwi mind—the typical specimen lives in the country, has a trusty dog by his side, is a rabid rugby fan, and adheres to a rugged lifestyle of farmwork, fixing the ute (pickup truck), and hitting the bars for pool and beer. Speight's beer has gotten a lot of mileage from this icon, using it for a successful Southern Man ad campaign, complete with a Southern Man theme song. ("Cuz here we just know/what makes a Southern boy tick/and it ain't margaritas/with some fruit on a stick…"). But this stereotype is rooted in reality. There are plenty of good, hardy blokes in Otago and Southland who dress in shorts and Swannies (Swanndri woolen bush shirts), drink Speight's beer, and work on farms. Before long some visitors may develop similar traits. If you find yourself saying things like "She's a hard road" and "She'll be right" when the going gets tough, then the process is well under way. To help the Southern Man find the right lady there is an annual Perfect Woman competition, with challenges such as digging in a fence post, backing a trailer loaded with hay, fitting snow chains, tipping a 242-pound ram, and opening a bottle of Speight's without a bottle opener. As the ad says, "It's a hard road to find the perfect woman."

–Joseph Gelfer & Sue Farley

TOURS

Natures Wonders Naturally (✉ *Harrington Point, Portobello* ☎ *03/478–1150* 🖨 *03/478–0714* ⊕ *www.natureswondersnaturally.com*) uses an all-terrain vehicle to get you to hard-to-reach parts of the Otago Peninsula. Tours include visits to colonies of shags (cormorants), seals, and blue penguins, and you may even catch up with some yellow-eyed penguins coming ashore. The one-hour trip starts at $40.

Earl Matheson at **Catlins Natural Wonders** (☎ *0800/353–941* ⊕ *www. catlinsnatural.co.nz*) provides day trips focusing on Catlins flora and fauna. Tours departing from Dunedin cost $140 (including lunch and refreshments), with lower prices for trips departing from Balclutha and Owaka. For a more immersiing experience, try **Catlins Wildlife Trackers Ecotours** (✉ *5 Mirren St., Papatowai* ☎ *03/415–8613* ⊕ *www. catlins-ecotours.co.nz*), operated by Fergus and Mary Sutherland. The two- and four-night tours include day and night walks and conservation activities. Tours cost $345 for two nights and $690 for four nights. Their Catlins Traverse Walk is $395.

10

INVERCARGILL

182 km (113 mi) south of Queenstown, 217 km (135 mi) southwest of Dunedin.

Originally settled by Scottish immigrants, Invercargill has retained much of its turn-of-the-20th-century character, with broad main avenues (Tay Street and Dee Street) and streetscapes with richly embellished buildings. You'll find facades with Italian and English Renaissance styles,

Gothic stone tracery, and Romanesque designs on a number of its well-preserved buildings.

Invercargill was featured in the movie *The World's Fastest Indian* (2005) starring Sir Anthony Hopkins as Invercargill-bred Burt Munro, who raced his Indian motorcycle on Oreti Beach in preparation for breaking a world land speed record. Mayor Tim Shadbolt had a cameo in the film, which is worth seeing. Invercargill has a reputation to this day for "boy racers," and you'll notice them roaring up and down the city streets in tricked-out cars. Indignant Invercargillites blame the epidemic on *Gorons,* boy racers from neighboring city Gore. You might have a '50s flashback if you're waiting at a light and a lowrider next to you starts to rumble and rev its engine.

GETTING HERE & AROUND

Invercargill's airport (IVC) is 3 km (2 mi) from city center. From Invercargill, Air New Zealand offers direct flights to Christchurch, and Stewart Island Flights hops over to Stewart Island. Several rental car companies operate in the terminal. Taxis from Invercargill Airport into town cost $8–$9. A shuttle run by Executive Car Services costs $8–$14 per person, and there's usually a shuttle waiting for each flight. Executive Car Service also offers secure car storage. Invercargill is extremely walkable, and also very driver-friendly. One daily InterCity bus continues on from Dunedin to Invercargill; this takes another four hours.

ESSENTIALS

Airport **Invercargill Airport** (⊠ *106 Airport Ave.* ☎ *03/218–6920* ⊕ *www. invercargillairport.co.nz*).

Bus Companies **InterCity** (☎ *03/471–7143* ⊕ *www.intercitycoach.co.nz*).

Bus Depot **Invercargill** (⊠ *Queens Park, 108 Gala St.*).

Stewart Island Experience (☎ *03/212–7660 or 0800/000–511* ⊕ *www. stewartislandexperience.co.nz*).

Medical Assistance **Southland Hospital** (⊠ *Kew Rd., Invercargill* ☎ *03/218–1949*).**Urgent Doctor Service** (⊠ *103 Don St., Invercargill* ☎ *03/218–8821*). **Donna Kerr Unichem Pharmacy** (⊠ *172 Tay St., Countdown Arcade, Invercargill*).

Rental Cars **Budget** (☎ *03/474–0428* ⊕ *www.budget.co.nz*). **National** (☎ *03/477–8801 or 0800/800–115* ⊕ *www.nationalcar.co.nz*). **Thrifty** (☎ *03/477–7087 or 0800/737–070* ⊕ *www.thrifty.co.nz*).

Visitor Info **Invercargill Visitor Information Centre** (⊠ *Southland Museum and Art Gallery, Victoria Ave., Queens Park* ☎ *03/214–6243* ☐ *03/218–4415* ⊕ *www. invercargill.org.nz*).

WHAT TO SEE

☼ The **Southland Museum and Art Gallery** contains the largest public display of live *tuatara*, New Zealand's extremely rare and ancient lizards. The museum has also established a successful captive-breeding program for the creatures. It's usually easy to spot these mini-dinosaurs, but they do a successful job of hiding themselves if it gets too noisy. Southland also contains fine displays of Māori and settler artifacts. The gallery has both older and modern New Zealand art on permanent display as well as temporary exhibits. It's set in Queens Park, with an on-site café and information center. ✉*108 Gala St.* ☎*03/218–9753* ⊕*www. southlandmuseum.com* ✎*Donation suggested; Tuatara and Gallery tours $3* ☉*Daily 10–5.*

The **Anderson Park Art Gallery** is set in a splendid 1925 Georgian-style house. The 60 acres of surrounding gardens and lawns include a traditionally carved Māori house and short bushwalks. The gallery displays New Zealand art, sculpture, and pottery. ✉*McIver Rd.* ☎*03/215– 7432* ✎*Donation* ☉*Daily 10:30–5.*

Shearing South provides an insider's look into the sheep-shearing profession and the industry that's led New Zealand's agricultural development for the past 150 years. On display are a collection of shearing artifacts, an exhibit of a woolshed along with DVD presentations (including "150 Years of Pain, Sweat and Shears"), a shearers' Hall of Fame, and even a collection of shearing-inspired art. Guided tours are available. ✉*Arcade 55, Dee St.* ☎*03/214–9155* ✎*$12* ☉*Weekdays 10–4, weekends 1–4.*

★ The 200 acres in the center of town that make up **Queens Park** create a
☺ fine layout of public gardens. Include are two rose gardens with both modern and "antique" rose varieties; a Japanese garden complete with meditation area; and an impressive hothouse, which acts as a sanctuary on a wet day. The park has miles of gentle walking paths and waterways, an 18-hole golf course, and a decent café. There's also a small zoo area and an aviary with a walk-through section that children love. The main entrance is next to the Southland Museum. ✉*Queens Dr. at Gala St.* ☎*03/217–7368.*

Invercargill's most famous store is a 100-year-old hardware store! **E. Hayes and Sons** (✉*168 Dee St.* ☎*03/218–2059*) has every little thing you can think of. It's very yin-yang (grandma-grandpa) with one half devoted to little glass lemon juicers and whisks and the other half filled with tools and wheelbarrows.

10

SPORTS & THE OUTDOORS

It would be a brave person who swims at **Oreti Beach,** 11 km (7 mi) southeast of town, but people do surf and windsurf, taking advantage of the wind and swells that whip the coast almost constantly. Another good walking spot is **Sandy Point**, which can be reached by taking a left after crossing the Oreti River on the way out to Oreti Beach. A 13-km (8-mi) network of easygoing trails covers the riverbanks, estuary, and the bush. A leaflet detailing the paths is available from the visitor information center in town. On the western side of the Southern Scenic Route, the **Tuatapere Hump Ridge Track** (☎*03/226–6739 or 0800/486–774* ✎*03/226–6739* ⊕*www.humpridgetrack.co.nz*) is a challenging circular three-day/two-night walk that combines beach, bush, and subalpine environments in its 53 km (33 mi). The track starts near Tuatapere, about two hours' drive west of Invercargill and right on the edge of the Fiordland National Park. It's no amble; you'll spend about nine hours walking each day, but two good huts each sleep about 40 people. You will need to buy hut tickets in advance. If you want to experience what rural New Zealand is all about, then **Waiau Downs Farm Adventures** (⊠*1609 Tuatapere–Orepuki Rd., Tuatapere* ☎*03/226–6622* ⊕*www.farmadventures.co.nz*), on the western side of the Southern Scenic Route, is worth getting your gumboots out for. Working dogs Perk and Dan demonstrate how to "head" or "back" sheep, or you can "throw" a fleece, "handle" some wool—or just learn what all that jargon actually means. Tours start at $15.

WHERE TO EAT

Many of Invercargill's motels are on Tay Street, handy if you're coming from Dunedin, and North Road, convenient if you're arriving from Queenstown.

$$$-$$$$ ✕ **Cabbage Tree.** For his ideal restaurant, owner Neville Kidd revamped this old store on the way to Oreti Beach. Resembling a vineyard restaurant, the inside is spacious and lined with wood and brick. Popular dishes are Stewart Island blue cod, lamb shanks, prawns, and pan-seared venison. The wine list includes mostly New Zealand wines, with the occasional European bottle for the stubborn. The outdoor garden bar is a perfect place to enjoy the Southland sun with a glass of wine. ⊠*379 Dunns Rd.* ☎*03/213–1443* ☐*AE, DC, MC, V.*

$$-$$$$ ✕ **The Rocks Café.** An urban-chic-meets-Tuscany ambience is achieved here, where the decor features terra-cotta, brick, and river stone. The kitchen employs local seasonal ingredients. Try the flaming-hot Southland squid starter and the yummy although unfortunately named "Beef Ron Jeremy" with Tuscan potatoes. As chef and owner Mark Elder says, the restaurant likes to do "everything that's good about Southland." ⊠*101 Dee St., at Courtville Arcade* ☎*03/218–7597* ☐*AE, DC, MC, V* ⊙*Closed Sun. No lunch Sat.*

$$-$$$ ✕ **Ziff's Café and Bar.** This enormously popular restaurant on the way to Oreti Beach (past the airport) is a local favorite. Ziff's does steak, blue cod, chicken, and pasta, and customers love the home-smoked salmon and the venison hot pot. The establishment offers a taxi service for $2 per person, so you can indulge in their excellent wines and cognacs, too. Some nights it can be noisy, so if you want a *sotto* dining experience have lunch here on the way to the "World's Fastest Indian's" training grounds. The house seafood chowder, flavored with capers, lime, and smoky bacon, is quite good. Breakfast is served until 2 PM. ⊠*143 Dunns Rd.* ☎*03/213–0501* ☐*AE, DC, MC, V.*

$$ ✕ **Sopranos Wood Fired Pizzeria.** The tasty pizzas here are named after various fictional and nonfictional mobsters and gangsters. It makes sense that "Meadow" is the vegetarian option and that "Dr. Melfi" is the smoked salmon, but how "Tony" became a Thai green curry–chicken topping we'll never know. There's a good local wine list. ⊠*33 Tay St.* ☎*03/218–3464* ☐*MC, V.*

$-$$ ╳ Invercargill is home to the world's southernmost Starbucks so you might want to pop in for the mug saying so, but as for cafés there are many other, more interesting options. Good coffee and fresh baked goodies and sandwiches can be found at **Café Amici** (corner of Dee and Don) and **Rain Espresso** (corner of Kelvin and Don).

WHERE TO STAY

$-$$$$ ▦ **Ascot Park Hotel.** This rambling complex is a welcome sight if you've just battled the rugged gravel roads of the Catlins. The largest hotel in town is just a five-minute drive from the town center. Spacious, modern rooms come with small balconies. An on-site restaurant serves traditional and contemporary New Zealand fare. **Pro:** Big rooms. **Cons:** Restaurant pricey; pool tiny. ⊠ *Tay St. at Racecourse Rd.* ☎ *03/217–6195* 🖷 *03/217–7002* ☟ *64 rooms, 24 motel rooms, 2 suites, 4 studio rooms* ☖ *In-room: no a/c. In-hotel: restaurant, bar, pool, gym* ▱ *AE, DC, MC, V.*

$$ ▦ **Kelvin Hotel.** The big advantage of this modern, rather bland hotel is that it's very central, and just about ideal if you're not driving. The rooms facing the back are quieter. **Pro:** couldn't be more centrally located. **Con:** rooms a bit shabby. ⊠ *16 Kelvin St.* ☎ *03/218–2829* 🖷 *03/218–2287* ☟ *58 rooms, 2 suites* ☖ *In-room: no a/c. In-hotel: restaurant, bar, laundry facilities* ▱ *AE, DC, MC, V.*

$$ ▦ **Kereru Cottage.** If you're traveling to Invercargill via the Southern Scenic Route, and want to break your stay in the middle, this one-bedroom self-catering cottage is a good choice. It's got lovely wild coastal views from the outdoor hot tub, especially with a glass of wine in hand. (Just remember to bring your own bottle.) **Pro:** Totally relaxing, beautiful spot. **Con:** It's not for sale. ⊠ *5 Mirren St., Papatowai* ☎ *03/415–8613 or 0800/228–5467* 🖷 *03/415–8613* ⊕ *www.catlins-nz.com/kereru.html* ☟ *1 cottage* ☖ *In-room: kitchen* ▱ *MC, V.*

¢–$ ▦ **Tuatara Backpackers Lodge.** The world's southernmost YHA hostel is in the center of Invercargill, next door to the Speight's Ale House and the main city library. The Tuatara has the usual group of bunks, twins, and double rooms, along with a couple of "executive suites" (with private bathrooms, TVs, and DVD players). It's on the main drag near some popular hangouts for bored teens, so the noise from the street can be high at night. **Pros:** Inexpensive, centrally located. **Con:** Can be noisy at night. ⊠ *30–32 Dee St.* ☎ *03/214–0954 or 0800/488–282* 🖷 *03/214–0956* ☟ *23 rooms, 3 suites* ☖ *In-hotel: laundry facilities, public Internet* ▱ *MC, V.*

10

EN ROUTE In the tiny township of **Bluff** (*the Bluff* to locals) you can taste its coveted namesake oysters. An annual festival, held in late April at the town's wharf, wallows in seafood delicacies; oyster-opening and oyster-eating competitions and cook-offs are part of the fun. If you miss the festival, the most spectacular place for oysters, in season, is **Lands End Restaurant** (⊠ *10 Ward Parade* ☎ *03/212–7575*) overlooking the sea. The Lands End Inn is also the best place to stay the night. The bakery on Gore Street is open from 5:30 AM and has nice pastries and meals. Don't miss the Maritime Museum on the Foreshore Road (the

Oyster boat *Monica* sits beside it). Bluff is also home to the frequently photographed **Stirling Point** signpost, at the southern end of State Highway 1, which gives directions to places all over the world, including the South Pole. If it's a nice day follow the signs up to Bluff Lookout: the views encompass the Catlins and Stewart Island, and give you an excellent lay of the land. Good walking tracks are around Bluff; many begin at Stirling Point. The town is also the main jumping-off point for Stewart Island. It's about 30 km (19 mi) from Invercargill to Bluff, an easy ½-hour drive south on State Highway 1. For more on Bluff go to ⊕*www.bluff.co.nz.*

TOURS

Lynette Jack, of **Lynette Jack Scenic Sights** (⊠*22 Willis St., Invercargill* ☎*025/338–370 or 03/215–7741*), draws on an extensive knowledge of Invercargill and the surrounding area to illuminate local history during an exploration of gardens, beaches, historic houses, local hero Burt Munro, and even a smeltery. A two-hour tour costs $59 per person.

STEWART ISLAND

The third and most southerly of New Zealand's main islands, Stewart Island is separated from the South Island by the 24-km (15-mi) Foveaux Strait. Its original Māori name, Te Punga O Te Waka a Maui, means "the anchor stone of Maui's canoe." Māori mythology says the island's landmass held the god Maui's canoe secure while he and his crew raised the great fish—the North Island. Today the island is more commonly referred to by its other Māori name, Rakiura, which means "the land of the glowing skies." This refers to the spectacular sunrises and sunsets and to the southern lights, or aurora australis. The European name of Stewart Island dates back to 1809. It memorializes an officer on an early sealing vessel, the *Pegasus,* who was the first to chart the island.

The island covers some 1,700 square km (650 square mi). It measures about 75 km (46 mi) from north to south and about the same distance across at its widest point. On the coastline, sharp cliffs rise from a succession of sheltered bays and beaches. In the interior, forested hills rise gradually toward the west side of the island. Seals and penguins frequent the coast, and the island's prolific birdlife includes a number of species rarely seen in any other part of the country. In fact, this is the surest place to see a kiwi. The Stewart Island brown kiwi, or *tokoeka,* is the largest species of this kind of bird. Unlike their mainland cousins, these kiwis can be seen during the day as well as at night. It's a rare and amusing experience to watch these pear-shaped birds scampering on a remote beach as they feed on sand hoppers and grubs.

Māori have visited Stewart Island for centuries. Archaeologists' studies of 13th-century Māori middens (refuse heaps) indicate that the island was once a rich, seasonal resource for hunting, fishing, and gathering

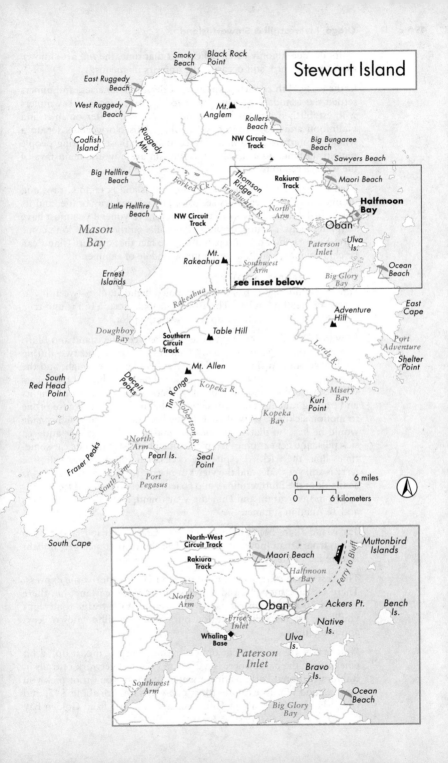

seafood. A commonly eaten delicacy at that time, the *titi*, also known as the muttonbird, still occasionally appears on menus.

In the early 19th century, explorers, sealers, missionaries, and miners settled the island. They were followed by fishermen and sawmillers who established settlements around the edges of Paterson Inlet and Halfmoon and Horseshoe bays. In the 1920s Norwegians set up a whaling enterprise, and many descendants of these seafaring people remain. Fishing, aquaculture, and tourism are now the mainstays of the island's economy.

Even by New Zealand standards, Stewart Island is remote, raw, and untouched. The appeal is its seclusion, its relaxed way of life, and its untouched quality. Stewart Island is not for everyone: if you must have shopping malls, casinos, or umbrella drinks on the beach, don't come here. Visitors should be prepared for the fact that Stewart Island can be chilly, windy, and rainy, even in the middle of summer.

GETTING HERE & AROUND

Stewart Island Flights has three scheduled flights daily between Invercargill and Halfmoon Bay. The 20-minute flight costs $155 round-trip; for the best views ask to sit up front with the pilot.

Stewart Island Experience runs the ferry between the island and Bluff. There are three departures daily October to April, and two during the low season. At times, Foveaux Strait can be quite rough, and the crossing might seem like an Irish wake: some folks bowed over seats while other folks stand casually in the back, drinking cans of Speights and trading raucous tales (those would be the locals). If you're prone to motion sickness, sit well back in the boat (ask the crew which side would be best on that day), consider taking some ginger or anti–sea sick pills, and get ear plugs from crew members (stuffing one ear sometimes does the trick). Despite the occasional roller-coaster ride, the ferry is still very safe, and the views are beautiful. Secure car parking is available at the Bluff terminal, and coach connections to and from Bluff run from Invercargill and Dunedin year-round, and from Queenstown and Te Anau in summer.

The island's bare-bones but paved Ryan's Creek Airstrip is about 2 km (1 mi) from Oban (population 390). The shuttle that meets each flight is included in the airfare.

The best mode of transportation on the island is the 10-toe express. There are cars, mopeds, and bicycles for rent on the island, but there are only 20 km (13 mi) of paved road (most of the traffic road signs you'll see are big yellow caution ones depicting silhouettes of kiwi and penguins.)

Water taxis are an excellent option if you want to "mix it up" a bit when seeing the park. There is a 200-km (124-mi) network of trails in Rakiura National Park; having a water taxi drop you off or pick you up is a good way to explore. Most one-way fares are about $45, and Ulva Island return is about $30. Four taxis operate from Golden Bay

Wharf, a scenic 15-minute walk from town. The visitor center can make a booking for you.

The Stewart Island Visitor Information Centre and the **Department of Conservation Rakiura National Park Visitor Centre** are open daily. The **Environment Centre,** located next to the Glowing Sky T-shirt shop, has information about the habitat recovery projects on the Island. The **Library** in the **Community Centre** has a complete collection of books about Stewart Island, and field guides of native flora and fauna. (The Library is open only five hours per week, but the librarian's number is on the door and she will open upon request.) For biased, vulgar, and amusing information about island goings-on ("the goss"), belly up to the bar at the Pub and do some earwigging.

ESSENTIALS
Air Carrier **Stewart Island Flights** (☎ *03/218–9129* ⊕ *www.stewartisland flights.com*).

Boat Company **Stewart Island Experience** (✉ *Stewart Island Visitor Terminal, Main Wharf, Halfmoon Bay* ☎ *03/212–7660 or 0800/000–511* 📠 *03/212–8377* ⊕ *www.stewartislandexperience.co.nz*).

Medical Assistance **Stewart Island Health Centre** (✉ *Argyle St.* ☎ *03/219–1098 or 0800/100–776*).

Visitor Info **Department of Conservation Rakiura National Park Visitor Centre** (✉ *Main Rd., Oban* ☎ *03/219–0002* ⊕ *www.doc.govt.nz*).**Stewart Island Visitor Information Centre (i-Site)** (✉ *12 Elgin Terr., Oban* ☎ *03/219–1400* ⊕ *www. stewartisland.co.nz*).

WHAT TO SEE
In spring 2002, about 85% of Stewart Island was designated as **Rakiura National Park.** The park encompasses areas that were formerly nature reserves and the like. More than 200 walking trails thread through the park, and a dozen huts give shelter for overnight stays.

For information on Rakiura as well as the rest of Stewart Island, contact the **Department of Conservation** or the **Stewart Island Visitor Centre.**

10

Apart from the tiny township of **Oban** at **Halfmoon Bay** on Paterson Inlet, Stewart Island is practically uninhabited. Directly behind Oban's waterfront is a short main street with a small collection of establishments. A handful of roads head up the surrounding hills. The hills are mostly thick bush, with houses poking their heads out for a view of the bay. You can see plenty of birds in Halfmoon Bay. Here are some of their hangouts: walk up Argyle Street, which dead-ends into a drive. Continue up (it turns into a path) and you'll be certain to see the noisy parrots (kaka) clowning in the trees around you. Ducks loiter at Mill Creek (locals have named many of them) and a little kingfisher often sits on the phone wire above them. Rare albino wood pigeons (kereru) reside in the rimu tree by the "rimu tree phone" on the road leading down into Horseshoe Bay. Little blue penguins are seen in Paterson Inlet, ditto yellow-eyed penguins and Stewart Island shags. Mollymawks soar past Acker's Point. Tūī, bellbirds, fantails, and robins can be seen throughout Halfmoon Bay gardens and on day walks. Weka have been recently reintroduced to the area and favor the gardens of Deep Bay Road (they cut through homes if residents leave the door open!). Oystercatchers live on every town beach, and pied oystercatchers like grazing the schoolyard. Kiwis are rarely seen around town but they are there, telltale tracks have been seen at Traill Park and their shrill unmistakable cry is heard some nights.

One of the best places for bird-watching is **Ulva Island** ⊕*www.stew-artisland.co.nz)* , 620 acres of thick native bush. The rare birds that live here have no predators, so they have an excellent survival rate. Among the resident species are the *weka,* saddleback, *kaka* (a parrot), and kiwi. The forest, which has walking paths accessible to the public, is made up primarily of *rimu, rata,* and *kamahi* trees. To get here, take a boat or water taxi from Halfmoon or Golden Bay, or paddle a kayak from Thule Bay. You can also join a tour, the best guide is the aptly named Ulva Goodwillie *(see Tours, below).*

The **Rakiura Museum** has an eclectic collection of Māori artifacts, ambergris, old school memorabilia, tools from gold and tinning prospectors, and a china "moustache cup" (there's a story behind every item). The museum also forgivingly includes an old world globe that doesn't include Stewart Island! ⊠*Ayr St. across from Community Centre* ⊠*$2* ☉*Mon.–Sat. 10–noon, Sun. noon–2.*

SPORTS & THE OUTDOORS

Are you the kind of traveler who packs running shoes? Stewart Island is paradise for **trail running.** Try out trails leading to Acker's Point, Deep Bay, Fern Gully, Little River and beyond.

FISHING

Your catch will likely be the succulent Stewart Island blue cod, and the guide will fillet and bag it for you, some will cook it for your lunch! If you want to go out with real salt dogs who have fished these waters all their lives, call upon John Leask of the *Rawhiti,* Squizzy of the *Lo Loma,* or Colin Hopkins of *Aurora Charters.* All three fishermen are capable, knowledgeable, and safe, and cater to people of all ages and abilities. John aka Hurricane Johnny (featured in the book *On the Next Tide*), has been fishing Foveaux Strait for 60 years. Like John, Squizzy runs an "old-school" operation, with a historic wooden boat and handlines. Colin uses rods-and-reels and his boat is a modern catamaran, so he can bring you farther afield in comfort.

Note: *For information on deep-sea fishing out of Halfmoon Bay, see Chapter 11.*

GOLF

Ringaringa Heights Golf Course is Australasia's most southerly course. It overlooks Ringaringa Bay and Paterson Inlet. Play a round at this six-hole course as kakas screech overhead, then relax at the new clubhouse (BYOB). The Flight Centre/Post Office rents clubs; the course is a 20-minute walk by road or bush track from there.

HIKING

Numerous day walks on well-maintained trails are in and around the township. Free maps are available at the Flight Centre/Post Office and Visitor Centre, and detailed maps and information are found at the Department of Conservation Office. Some walks, such as the Observation Rock and Fuchsia walks, are measured in minutes; others, such as the walks to Fern Gully, Ryan's Creek, and Horseshoe Point, are measured in hours. If you only have a few hours, the walk from town out to the **Acker's Point** lighthouse is beautiful and encompasses town, boat sheds, a historic homestead, lush forest, and ocean views. This is nesting ground for titi (sooty shearwaters or muttonbirds), and little blue (fairy) penguins, which can often be seen from the lookout, along with albatross and fishing boats.

There are also some outstanding multiday treks. The **Rakiura Track,** one of New Zealand's Great Walks, takes three days. Day 1 goes from Halfmoon Bay to Port William Hut via Horseshoe and Lee bays. Day 2 heads inland through native bush and wood across the ridge, allowing for good views of Paterson Inlet and the Tin Range. Day 3 connects back to Halfmoon Bay via *rimu* and *kamahi* forest. The huts accommodate up to 30 people on a first-come, first-served basis. They come with mattresses, a wood-burning stove, running water, and toilets. (If you're relatively fit and you leave early, you can do this track in one day, but you will be sore.) Another popular trek, a big step up in both distance and difficulty, is the **North West Circuit,** a 9- to 11-day walk from Halfmoon Bay that circles the north coast and then cuts through the interior. If that's not enough for you, five days can be tacked on by including the Southern Circuit. Stewart Island's climate is notoriously changeable, so be prepared for sun, wind, rain, and lots of mud. Take the usual safety precautions for these hikes: bring suitable boots, clothing, food, and a portable stove; complete an intentions form at the DOC office before setting out; and, ideally, bring along with you a locator beacon and/or a guide who knows the trails. For information on these walks, contact the **Department of Conservation Visitor Centre** (⊠*Main Rd., Oban* ☎*03/219–0002* ⊕*www.doc.govt.nz*).

SEA KAYAKING

You will share the water with raucous fairy penguins, yellow-eyed penguins, elephant seals, leopard seals, Stewart Island shags, and occasionally dolphins. The mostly uninhabited Paterson Inlet is 100 square km (38 square mi) of bush-clad, sheltered waterways. It has 20 islands, four DOC huts, and two navigable rivers.

Kayak rentals and gear (including bathyscopes for underwater viewing) are available from Liz Cave, a lifelong islander and paddler (a circumnavigation of Rakiura is under her belt). Contact **Rakiura Kayaks** (⊠*Argyle St., Oban* ☎*03/219–1160* ⊕*www.rakiura.co.nz*). Prices start at $35 for a half-day rental to $90 for two days; guided trips are available and might include hand-lining for cod and trumpeter from a kayak, starting at $55 for a half day. Liz's family owns one of the few homes on a Paterson Inlet island: the old Norwegian whalers' cookhouse makes a perfect base for your adventure. Ask for recommendations

10

on reliable water taxi operators and guides for kayak-hiking combos. Liz knows Paterson Inlet intimately, she can tell you where to spot baby oystercatchers, or where to best find a paua.

WHERE TO STAY & EAT

There are only a few places to dine on Stewart Island, but scores of places to stay catering to every budget and fancy. All lodging is guaranteed to have a beautiful view of bush, sea, or both. Many accommodations are online at ⊕ *www.stewartisland.co.nz*, and most are included in a binder at the visitor center. The term "visitor center" is used a bit loosely around the Bay—for unbiased information and bookings go to the i-Site Visitor Centre at 12 Elgin Terrace (in the red building by the animal bollards at the wharf). Around Christmas time and New Years every available bed is often taken, including the DOC huts, so prebooking is a must.

$$$–$$$$ ✕ **Church Hill Cafe Bar & Restaurant.** You know this is the islanders' "fancy restaurant" when you see the sign on the door: *No gumboots please.* The meat melts off the bone of the lamb shank, and they have a cook-it-yourself hot stone with pork, chicken, venison, and steak options. The seafood salad and the house smoked salmon are standouts. Dinner reservations are recommended. ⊠ *36 Kamahi Rd. (next to red-steeple church on hill), Oban* 🕾 *03/219–1323* ▤ *MC, V.*

$$–$$$ ✕ **Kai Kart.** Come here for good old-fashioned fish 'n' chips wrapped in a newspaper. There isn't an ounce of pretense in this cheerful little place between the museum and the "skateboard park" (a wooden ramp). The owner has a mussel farm in Paterson Inlet, and the cod comes from the Halfmoon Bay fishery. Try the bacon-wrapped mussels or Hilli's divine mussel chowder. ⊠ *Ayr St., Oban* 🕾 *03/219–1225* ▤ *MC, V.*

¢–$$$ ✕ **Wharfside Café.** Located upstairs in the ferry terminal, this café shudders and squeaks as boats dock. It is a perfect spot for grabbing coffee, breakfast, or a meat pie before setting out to tackle the island. Lunch dishes include seafood, pastas, and salads. ⊠ *Main Wharf, Halfmoon Bay, Oban* 🕾 *03/219–1470* ▤ *MC, V.*

¢–$ ✕ **Justcafé.** American Britt Moore has set up her cybercafe in this faraway outpost. Stop in for great coffee, muffins, waffles, and cold smoked-salmon sandwiches—and surf the Net (broadband) while you nibble and sip. Britt also makes and sells paua jewelry, and runs a day spa (make a booking at the café). ⊠ *Main Rd., Oban* 🕾 *03/219–1422* ▤ *MC, V* ☺ *Closed June–Sept. No dinner.*

$$–$$$ 🏠 **Port of Call.** Philippa Fraser-Wilson and sixth-generation islander Ian Wilson opened this modern B&B overlooking Halfmoon Bay and the Foveaux Strait. You can wander the trails through their 20 acres of native bush, which border a lush wilderness teeming with birdlife leading to Acker's Point. This friendly couple owns and operates Stewart Island Water Taxi & Eco-guiding, which offers guided and nonguided trips around the island. They also have two other fully equipped and totally charming properties: **the Bach** and **Turner Cottage**, where you can choose to "self-cater," or have Philippa spoil you with baskets of homemade breakfast goodies. **Pros:** Beautiful, historic properties.

Cons: PoC and Bach are a 15-minute walk from town. ✉ *Leask Bay Rd., Halfmoon Bay* ☎📠*03/219–1394* ⊕*www.portofcall.co.nz* ⚲*1 room* ⊟*MC, V* ⑂*CP.*

$$ 🛏 **Bay Motel.** Above town, this place has comfortable rooms, each with a deck. The view takes in Halfmoon Bay so you can observe the comings and goings of the wharf and pub, and the antics of the kakas from this "busybody" perch. For an extra 10 bucks choose the "honeymoon suite," the two-person Jacuzzi bath is nice after a day tramping. **Pros:** Relatively new, nice and clean. **Con:** A wee walk from town. ✉*9 Dundee St.* ☎*03/219–1119* ⊕*www.baymotel.co.nz* ⚲*11 rooms* ⚐*In-room: kitchen.*

$$ 🛏 **Glendaruel.** At this B&B, a short walk from town, you can have private views over Golden Bay. There are two double rooms and a cozy wee single. Kaka (parrots) are frequent visitors to the deck, and the gorgeous garden is nice for strolling. If you're homesick for your pets, you can take their adorable cairn terrier for a walk. Continental or cooked breakfasts are available, as is dinner by arrangement. **Pros:** Lovely garden and views. **Con:** A bit of a walk from town. ✉*38 Golden Bay Rd., Oban* ☎📠*03/219–1092* ⊕*www.glendaruel.co.nz* ⚲*3 rooms* ⚐*In-room: kitchen. In-hotel: bar* ⊟*MC, V* ⑂*BP, CP.*

$$ 🛏 **Tree-House B&B.** High costs of living have forced many young islanders away, so this is an opportunity to meet a rare breed here: a young working family. Kyle and Jo Learmonth own this architecturally contemporary home with sea and forest views. Kyle, a lifelong islander and keen outdoorsman, is a great source of information about the local terrain. Jo is a gourmet cook who will cater to any dietary needs, and for a bit extra dough you can have more than the inclusive breakfast. Jo's delicious meals often feature fresh venison and seafood (her hunter-husband's wedding vows included a proviso to provide) and produce from their garden. Your queen bedroom with en suite has a private deck and entrance, and you can relax on one of their three decks or snuggle by the fire in the lounge. Luggage transfers are provided. **Pros:** Very comfortable new home with friendly hosts. **Con:** Two-hill walk from town. ✉*3 Hicks Rd., Oban* ☎📠*03/219–1555* ✎*learmonthbb@ xtra.co.nz* ⚲*1 room* ⚐*In-hotel: kitchen* ⊟*Checks, cash, or MC, V accepted through i-Site or Vianet Travel* ⑂*BP*

$–$$ 🛏 **South Sea Hotel.** This handsome, historic building dominates the main road in Oban. Containing the only real pub on the island, it bustles with visitors and locals. Next to the main bar is a lounge with Internet facilities and comfy couches by the window. On sunny days patrons sit outside, or wander across the street with their drinks to play the giant waterfront chess set. (An irascible sea lion occasionally disrupts these games, much to everyone's delight.) Stewart Island blue cod is on the menu for breakfast, lunch, and dinner at the hotel restaurant ($$–$$$). Menu favorites are the perfectly flaky cod either panfried or battered, and the seafood chowder. The hotel rooms are comfortable, and the three at the front of the building have sea views. This is an old-fashioned hotel, which means that you share a bathroom with other guests if you stay upstairs and you're privy to a bit of noise from the pub (a basket of earplugs is in the upstairs lobby). If you'd like your own bathroom and a more peaceful room, ask for a studio unit behind the hotel. **Pro:** Great value for a real island experience. **Cons:** Can be noisy some nights; shared bathroom in hotel. ⊠ *Main Rd., Oban* ☎ *03/219–1059* 🖷 *03/219–1120* ⊕ *www.stewart-island.co.nz* ➽ *9 studios, 8 rooms with shared bath* ☰ *MC, V.*

$ 📺 **Beach House Holiday Home.** You couldn't be in a more prime location at the old postmaster's house, which sits next door to the Post Office/Flight Centre. Hosts Brenda and Roger Hicks have ties to the Island that go back generations, and they will happily help you book your activities. This three-bedroom waterfront home sleeps up to seven; there is a $25 per person charge after two. **Pro:** Very conveniently situated. **Con:** The house is a bit dated. ☎ *03/219–1348* ➽ *1 unit* ♿ *In-house: laundry, kitchen.*

¢ 📺 **Stewart Island Backpackers.** A five-minute walk from the ferry, this backpacker accommodation is the least expensive place to stay on the island, and also has the town's only campground (the $8 site fee includes use of all facilities). The rooms are small and clean, and linen is provided. **Pros:** Inexpensive, conveniently located. **Con:** If a school group, stag party, or rugby club happens to be staying, it's a bit noisy. ⊠ *Ayr St. past Community Centre and Garage Halfmoon Bay* ☎ *03/219–1114* ⊕ *www.stewart-island.co.nz* ➽ *66 beds* ♿ *In-hotel: kitchen* ☰ *MC, V.*

TOURS

Stewart Island Flights (☎ *03/218–9129* ⊕ *www.stewartislandflights.com*) and **Seaview Enterprises** (☎☎ *03/219–1014*) jointly offer a flying, hiking, and boating adventure called Coast to Coast. For $155 per person (with a three-person minimum) you can view the east and west coasts of the island, including Paterson Inlet and Mason Bay. The trip includes an easy four-hour hike on the North West Circuit and a water-taxi ride on the meandering Freshwater River. There's also an exciting plane landing on the beach and the chance to see kiwi birds. It's an interchangeable trip, so you can fly-hike-boat or boat-hike-fly.

Aurora Charters (⊠ *Halfmoon Bay Wharf, Oban* ☎ *03/219–1126* ⊕ *www.auroracharters.co.nz*) offers the popular "Experience Stewart Island" trip and the "Pelagic Bird Trip," but will take you farther afield to Lord's River or Port Pegasus aboard the comfortable catamaran *Aurora.*

Herbie Hansen of **Southern Isle Charters** (☎ *03/219–1133*) offers Paterson Inlet cruises. A descendent of Stewart Island whalers, Herbie has keen insight into the history of the old whaling base.

Stewart Island Experience (⊠ *Main Wharf, Halfmoon Bay, Oban* ☎ *03/212–7660 or 0800/000–511* ⊕ *www.stewartislandexperience. co.nz*) runs Underwater Explorer Cruises with semisubmersible craft. The large viewing windows give you a close-up look at dozens of fish species, and the mesmerizing kelp forests alone are worth the trip. There are several departures daily, the 45-minute cruise costs $37.

CLOSE UP

Stewart Island Nightlife

The Nature. As the last natural light fades at the lighthouse, you'll begin to hear the whir of wings and strange cries. These are the muttonbirds (aka sooty shearwater or titi) coming home to roost—they call to their ground nesting partner to locate their burrow, and their partner answers from their subterranean dwelling. Like the royal albatross, the muttonbirds are spectacular fliers and clumsy landers so beware, they have been known to hit people and your travel insurance may not cover muttonbird-impact injuries to your nose.

After a half hour the homecomings peter out, and it is time to walk back. Go slowly. The pound of the waves down the cliffs won't drown out the rustlings and weird sounds in the forest all around you: little blue penguins are coming home now, too, and you can often see them walking their funny penguin walk along the trail. Straggler muttonbirds crawl along making an odd forlorn noise. Long harsh screeches might be Fiordland crested penguins. The glimmer of enormous Gollum-like eyes in the trees belongs to possums (bane of native birds). Huge sudden crashes of foliage will be Virginia white-tailed deer (bane of Phillipa's Port-of-Call garden). When you return to the parking area it will take a while for your heart to slow down, and when you try to compose a postcard the next day you might find it hard to describe the experience. ■TIP➜**Please do not touch any of these creatures, don't use flash photography, and don't shine light directly in their eyes. For more information contact the Department of Conservation or the administrator at the Environment Centre.**

The Pub has plenty of character and plenty of characters. At Happy Hour you'll encounter the "five o'clockers," retired fishermen who gather for a "few pints" and trade improbable yarns. After a lifetime on the deck of storm-tossed boats, the sea stance remains—legs apart and knees slightly bent. There's almost an anti-dress code here: short-sleeved sweaters that are long in the back and often have burn holes from leaning against galley coal ranges and gumboots prevail. During oyster season, it's not uncommon to see customers in full wet suits squish-squashing around the bar. On Friday nights a crowd gathers when the kitchen sends out platters of free greasy "nibbles"—heaps of fried mussels, cod, chips, and pies. The pool table is free. Be aware that folks play by "Island rules," which are posted on the wall. Locals take the "down-trow" seriously, and if you lose without sinking a ball and you are not willing to circle the table with your pants down, you ought to buy your opponent a drink. Highly competitive and sometimes absurd Quiz Nights entail high spirits and high jinks, and visitors are always welcome to play. If you leave the jukebox idle, a certain resident will invariably play Three Dog Night and grab you for a whirl (whether you're a bloke or a lady) roaring "Jeremiah Was a Bullfrog." And that's on a quiet night! The Pub is a great place to enjoy a couple "coldies," hear some local lore, and have a laugh. (Those sensitive to rough language might want to bring ear plugs.) If you need a ride home, or help up the stairs, ask the bar staff for assistance.

10

For tour information and bookings, contact the Stewart Island Visitor Centre (⊕*www.stewart island.co.nz*).

Village & Bay Tours (⊠*Oban Visitor Centre, Main Rd.* ☎*03/219–0056*) provides entertaining insight into the community, history, and environment of Stewart Island. It's $35 for the 1½-hour tour, which takes in Horseshoe Bay and Observation Rock. For a more intimate tour, ask longtime islanders Peter and Iris Tait of **Sails Experience** (⊠*11 View St.* ☎*03/219–1151* ⊕*www.sailsashore.co.nz*) to show you around.

Kiwi Wilderness Walks (☎*03/226–6739* 🖷*03/442–8342* ⊕*www. nzwalk.com*) leads all-inclusive hiking and kayaking trips from the mainland. The four-day guided trips around Stewart Island cost $1,495 and are usually held between November and April.

For a unique Rakiura Māori interpretation of Ulva Island's flora and fauna, contact **Ulva's Guided Walks** (⊠*Elgin Terr., Oban* ☎*03/219–1216* ⊕*www.ulva.co.nz*). Ulva Goodwillie gives half-day and full-day tours of the island she was named after; the cost, including water-taxi fare, starts at $85.

Phillip Smith, of **Bravo Adventure Cruises** (⊠*Box 104, Stewart Island* ☎*03/219–1144* ✎*philldismith@xtra.co.nz*), takes you on an evening cruise and guided bushwalk to spot kiwis as they forage on the beach. Phillip is extremely knowledgeable about Island lore and local Māori history. The trip is $100 per person and limited to 15 people—you should have a reasonable level of fitness. Advance bookings are a must, but the trip may be canceled if the weather seems dodgy.

Adventure Vacations

Updated by
Jessica Kany

LAST YEAR, A VISITOR at the Stewart Island Pub excused herself from her friends, put her handle of Speights down, propped the pool cue against the wall, and went across the hall to the ladies room. There, she encountered a medium-size sea lion, which seemed supersized in the confines of the washroom and even larger when it made a loud woofing sound at her. Much screaming and excitement ensued, and eventually the local sea lion cowboy was summoned and the cheeky pinniped corralled back to the sea. The point of this anecdote is not to scare you away from the Pub toilets (you'll find grumpier creatures at the bar) but to illustrate that in New Zealand, even going to the loo can be an adventure.

Yes, the New Zealand experience is intrinsically exciting. You don't have to sign up for a tour to have a hair-raising trip; try to navigate Auckland motorways (challenging), grab a bite to eat in Hokitika (surprising), or just plain breathe in Rotorua (different). This is the birthplace of jet-boating and bungy jumping: both activities send you plunging, surreally, into the country's postcard-perfect scenery.

You can always choose to travel without a guide, but in unfamiliar territory you'll learn more about what's around you by having a knowledgeable local by your side. The material in this chapter complements information in the rest of the book on what to do in different parts of the country. If you're interested in a multiday excursion, such as a fishing tour or hike, book at least several weeks in advance. For a day's shot at an extreme-sport activity, such as bungy jumping, you'll generally need to make a reservation only a day in advance.

With most adventure-tour companies, the guides' knowledge of the environment is matched by a level of competence that ensures your safety even in dangerous situations. The safety record of adventure operators is very good. Be aware, however, that most adventure-tour operators require you to sign waivers absolving the company of responsibility in the event of an accident. Courts normally uphold such waivers except in cases of significant negligence.

BICYCLING

If you're a cyclist at heart and find yourself traveling via motor vehicle, you will suffer an aching yen for your bike. Long ribbons of asphalt unfurl throughout New Zealand's spectacular landscape: these roads seem tailor-made for the satisfying click of gears and happy whir of bicycle tires. On multiday trips, the average daily riding distance is about 60 km (37 mi), and support vehicles are on hand. These back-up vehicles are large enough to accommodate all riders and bikes. Some tours combine cycling with kayaking, hiking, or other outdoor pursuits. *For information on day trips or urban bike rentals, see the Outdoor Activities or Sports & the Outdoors sections in the appropriate destination chapters.* Wherever you cycle, remember that helmets are mandatory, and to ride on the left.

11

Bike to the Light

From Dunedin Railway Station, take the Taieri Gorge Train to Middlemarch (or Pukerangi, 19 km [12 mi] from Middlemarch), one end of the **Otago Central Rail Trail**. This 150-km (93-mi) pleasantly undulating bicycle path follows the old railway line and includes a dizzying wooden viaduct, a 150-meter-long tunnel, and places to eat, sleep, and drink along the way. The only traffic you'll encounter is the occasional herd of muddy-bottomed sheep. The ride takes about five days to complete, passing through sheep farms and lovely wee towns such as Ranfurly, an "oasis of art deco," and Alexander, one of the busier hubs in Central Otago on the banks of the paint-green Clutha River. The trail

eventually ends in thyme-scented Clyde. The route can be traversed in either direction; Clyde is approximately 80 km (50 mi) from Queenstown. The Otago Central Rail Trail is a great way to experience the sheep stations, sheep station gates with puzzling locks (a couple dozen of them), mud, wind, rivers, dags, pubs, and old gold fields of the South Island on a bicycle-friendly path. ⊕ *www.otagocentralrail trail.co.nz and* ⊕ *www.taieri.co.nz.*

In the summer season, some ski mountains open lifts so mountain bikers can access a network of trails. Check out ⊕ *www.treblecone.co.nz/ Summer/mountain-biking.asp* and ⊕ *www.dirtparknz.com.*

Traditionally, the South Island, with its central alpine spine, has been the most popular cycling destination. Rides in the South Island extend from the ferry port of Picton to Queenstown, the center of a thriving adventure day-trip industry. From Picton southward, the eastern route takes you through Kaikoura, with its dramatic mountain backdrop, then into the flat Canterbury Plains. From there, you can either cross the Alps at Arthur's Pass or head through the dry, barren, but beautiful, Mackenzie Country to Aoraki/Mt. Cook, New Zealand's highest mountain, before reaching Queenstown. From Queenstown, rides run down to Fiordland with lakes and glacier-formed valleys.

The western route through the South Island takes you through the Marlborough and Nelson wine regions, then follows the Buller River to the West Coast. Continuing southward, you're in for some spectacular mountain and coastal scenery as you head for the Franz Josef and Fox glaciers. Farther south, you cross the Alps over the rugged Haast Pass and then travel from the rain forest to the parched Otago interior within just a few miles. From there, you can cycle past blue-green lakes and on into Queenstown. The southernmost route explores the Catlins and down to Bluff, the beginning (or end) of the road.

The North Island has plenty of terrific biking terrain as well. The stunning Coromandel Peninsula is easily accessible from Auckland, where most travelers arrive. The areas around the Waitomo Caves and the hot mud pools of sulfurous Rotorua are other highlights.

Season: October–March.
Best Locations: Countrywide.

Cost: Multiday tours start around $1,500 per person, including food, lodging, and guide services. Supplemental fees are commonly charged for single riders.

TOUR OPERATORS
One advantage of touring New Zealand with a biking company is that you'll travel with a knowledgeable guide who can tell you about the terrain, flora, and fauna that you see along the way. Some trips include en route visits to wineries, but taste in moderation—remember that you have to cycle afterward! Depending on the route and type of trip, accommodations can range from camping to farm stays, motels, or lodges. Serious riders may wish to bring their own bikes, but bikes are typically available for rent; if you prefer, you can bring your own seats and/or pedals. Trip operators generally provide helmets and safety flags (to attach to the bikes). Most trips don't have minimum or maximum age limits—just be realistic about your cycling abilities. Most tours are limited to between 10 and 14 people.

Adventure South trips get you onto the quiet South Island back roads for 5 to 21 days. Tours are offered for all levels of cyclist and might include detours for wine tastings, hikes, or lake excursions. Accommodations are generally in comfortable inns and lodges. Price starts at $995 for a five-day tour. *17 Disraeli St., Addington, Box 33153, Christchurch* *03/942–1222* *03/942–4030* *www.advsouth.co.nz.*

New Zealand Pedaltours operates on both islands, with tours of 4 to 22 days. Tour options include the Coromandel Peninsula, the Southern Alps, and the Banks Peninsula. *Box 37–575, Parnell, Auckland* *09/585–1338 in N.Z.* *09/585–1339* *www.pedaltours.co.nz.*

Pacific Cycle Tours operate road- and mountain-bike trips that include Christchurch-to-Queenstown tours, and a three-week trip across both islands. They also offer a weeklong bike-and-ski combination trip and a four-day independent ride through the Marlborough wine region. Accommodations include hotels, inns, or farm stays. *14 Kennaway Rd.* *Christchurch* *03/329–9913* *09/329–9911* *www.bike-nz.com.*

CANOEING

There are many rivers to canoe in New Zealand, but one of the most popular rivers for day- and multiday canoeing trips is the Whanganui, which journeys through some of the most isolated and rugged parts of the North Island. The river starts 290 km (180 mi) above the small city of Wanganui, on the flanks of Mt. Ruapehu in Tongariro National Park, and then winds through the 700-square-km (270-square-mi) Whanganui National Park, with 249 named rapids to traverse on its descent to the Tasman sea.

Season: Year-round.
Best Locations: Whanganui River, North Island.
Cost: From $70 per person for single-day tours to $220 per person for five-day trips. Tents, sleeping bags, and bedrolls can be rented for an additional fee.

11

TOUR OPERATOR

Blazing Paddles Canoe Adventures runs one- to five-day trips on the Whanganui River, during which you can ride mild rapids, and see waterfalls, pristine forests, and birdlife. Overnight stays are spent camping or in huts, depending on the trip. Costs from $80 for day trip, $150 for two-day trip, $200 for three- and four-day trips. ✉ *1033 State Hwy. 4, R.D. 2, Taumarunui* ☎ *07/895–5261 or 0800/252–9464* 🖷 *07/895–5263* ⊕ *www.blazingpaddles.co.nz.*

CROSS-COUNTRY SKIING

Cross-country skiing is arguably the best way to appreciate the winter landscape here. Cross-country skiing is hard adventure—the joy of leaving the first tracks across new snow and the pleasure afforded by the unique scenery of the ski slopes is tempered by your fatigue at the end of the day. Multiday tours are arranged so that you stay in lodges every night.

Season: July–September.
Best Location: Aoraki (Mt. Cook), South Island.
Cost: Around $480 for two days, $1,150–$1,500 for five days high on Mt. Cook alpine skiing, which includes equipment, meals, hut accommodation, a guide, and transport.

TOUR OPERATOR

Alpine Recreation Canterbury runs multiday cross-country skiing trips on Aoraki (Mt. Cook) and its attendant Murchison and Tasman glaciers, with terrains to suit all reasonably fit skiers. Tours typically start with a flight to the alpine hut that becomes your base; from there the group sets out each day. 🖃 *Box 75, Lake Tekapo* ☎ *03/680–6736* 🖷 *03/680–6765* ⊕ *www.alpinerecreation.co.nz.*

DIVING

The Bay of Islands, in the Northland arm of the North Island, is perhaps New Zealand's best diving location. In the waters around Cape Brett, you have moray eels, stingrays, grouper, and other marine life. Surface-water temperatures rarely dip below 15°C (60°F). One of the highlights of Bay of Islands diving is the wreck of the Greenpeace vessel *Rainbow Warrior,* which French agents sank in 1985. It is about two hours from Paihia by dive boat. From September through November, a plankton bloom cuts down on underwater visibility.

Another top diving destination is the Poor Knights Islands Marine Reserve, a World Heritage area with crystal clear waters approximately 15 km (9 mi) off the Northland coast. Among the highlights are Rikiora Cave, the world's largest sea cave; the northern arch, where you sometimes see manta rays; and bubble caves, air pockets 45 feet down, where you can remove your regulator and breathe air. The small town of Tutukaka is the main jumping-off point for the reserve.

The clear waters around New Zealand make for good diving in other areas as well, such as Whangamata, with three islands just off the coast. While diving these waters, you are liable to encounter schools of snapper, giant kingfish, tuna, marlin, dolphins, and even sharks.

Remember that you cannot fly within 24 hours of scuba diving.

Season: Year-round.
Best Locations: Bay of Islands and the Coromandel Peninsula, North Island.
Cost: A two-dive day trip without rental gear runs about $90, with gear around $160.

TOUR OPERATORS

Cathedral Cove Dive brings groups to dive in the Cathedral Cove Marine Reserve of the Coromandel Peninsula; PADI courses are available. From $95. ⊠ *48 Hahei Beach Rd., Hahei* ☝ *R.D. 1, Whitianga* ☎ *07/866–3955* 🖷 *07/866–3053* ⊕ *www.hahei.co.nz.*

Dive Tutukaka runs trips to the Poor Knights Islands Marine Reserve off the Northland coast. Their comfortable dive boats have hot showers on board. $130 per day. ⊠ *Poor Knights Dive Centre, Marina Rd., Tutukaka* ☝ *R.D. 3, Whangarei* ☎ *0800/288–882 or 09/434–3867* 🖷 *09/434–3884* ⊕ *www.diving.co.nz.*

Knight Diver Tours makes the rounds at the Poor Knights Islands Marine Reserve, which is a great place to see colorful subtropical fish and underwater caves and tunnels. Although the outfit does not give PADI training courses, it can take noncertified people on guided dives. ⊠ *30 Whangarei Heads Rd., Whangarei* ☎ *0800/766–756, 027/499–9611 mobile* 🖷 *09/433–8664* ⊕ *www.poorknights.co.nz.*

Pacific Hideaway Charters runs dives at the Poor Knights Islands, Mokohinau Islands, and the coastal regions around Tutukaka—all of which are home to manta rays, large kingfish, and lots of other sea life. Day trips include tea, coffee, and snacks, as well as kayaks to borrow if you want to stay on the surface. ⊠ *Tutukaka Marina, R.D.3, Whangarei* ☎ *09/434–3762 or 0800/693–483* ⊕ *www.divenz.co.nz.*

Paihia Dive Hire and Charter organizes Bay of Islands dives to the wreck of the *Rainbow Warrior,* now an artificial reef; it also offers PADI courses. ☝ *Box 210, Paihia* ☎ *0800/107–551 or 09/402–7551* 🖷 *09/402–7110* ⊕ *www.divenz.com.*

Tairua Dive & Fishinn dives around the Aldermen Islands 19 km (12 mi) off the coast from Tairua, including Slipper, Shoe, Penguin, and Rabbit islands. Expect to see a large variety of fish, scallops, seals, black coral, and nudibranchs (sea slugs). $105 per day. ⊠ *The Esplanade, Paku Boat Ramp, Tairua* 🖷 *07/864–8054* ⊕ *www.divetairua.co.nz.*

FISHING

Fishing in New Zealand is as good as it gets. Most harbor towns have reasonably priced fishing charters available. They are generally very good at finding fish, and most carry fishing gear you can use if you do not have your own. Inland areas usually have streams, rivers, or lakes with great trout fishing, where guides provide their knowledge of local conditions and techniques. With the aid of a helicopter, you can get into places few people have ever seen. Catch-and-release practices are becoming more prevalent, especially in wilderness areas. As for equipment, visitors can bring their own gear into the country except for flies, which are forbidden. Equipment can also be rented or provided by a guiding company once you're there.

Licenses and Limits: Different districts in New Zealand require different licenses when fishing for trout, so it pays to check at the local tackle store; for example, Rotorua is not in the same license area as nearby Lake Taupo. Fees are approximately $60 per year, but at most tackle shops, you can purchase a daily or weekly license. No license is needed for saltwater fishing, but there are limits on the size and numbers of fish that you are allowed to take daily.

Publications: *How to Catch Fish and Where,* by Bill Hohepa, and *New Zealand Fishing News Map Guide,* edited by Sam Mossman, both have good information on salt- and freshwater fishing countrywide. A useful book on trout fishing is *New Zealand's Top Trout Fishing Waters,* by John Kent.

Season: Generally October–June in streams and rivers; year-round in lakes and at sea.

Best Locations: Countrywide.

Cost: Big-game fishing: $275 per person, per day. Heli-fishing: from $545 per person, per day. Trolling and fly-fishing for lake trout: from $75 per hour (one to four people), on rivers and streams from $75 per hour. Costs for fishing charters vary widely; contact operators for specifics.

FRESHWATER FISHING

Trout and salmon, natives in the northern hemisphere, were introduced into New Zealand in the 1860s and '80s. Rainbow and brown trout in particular have thrived in the rivers and lakes, providing arguably the best trout fishing in the world. Salmon do not grow to the size that they do in their native habitat, but they still make for good fishing. There is free access to all water. You may have to cross private land to fish certain areas, but a courteous request is normally well received.

The three methods of catching trout allowed in New Zealand are fly-fishing, spinning or threadlining, and trolling. In certain parts of the South Island using small fish, insects, and worms as bait is also allowed. Deep trolling using leader lines and large-capacity reels on short spinning rods is widely done on Lakes Rotoma, Okataina, and Tarawera around Rotorua and on Lake Taupo, with the most popular lures being tobies, flatfish, and cobras. Streamer flies used for trolling are normally the smelt patterns: Taupo tiger, green smelt, ginger mick, Jack Sprat,

Parsons glory, and others. Flies, spoons, or wobblers used in conjunction with monofilament and light fly lines on either glass fly rods or spinning rods are popular on all the other lakes.

The lakes in the Rotorua district—Rotorua, Rotoiti, and Tarawera are the largest—produce some of the biggest rainbow trout in the world, which get to trophy size because of an excellent food supply, the absence of competition, and a careful and selective breeding program. In Lake Tarawera, fish from 2.7 to 4.5 kg (6 to 10 lbs) can be taken, especially in autumn and winter, when bigger trout move into stream mouths before spawning.

The season around Rotorua runs from October 1 to June 30. In the period between April and June, just before the season closes, flies work very well on beautiful Lake Rotoiti. From December to March, fly-fishing is good around the stream mouths on Lake Rotorua. The two best areas are the Ngongotaha Stream and the Kaituna River, using nymph, dry fly, and wet fly. Lake Rotorua remains open for fishing when the streams and rivers surrounding the lake are closed.

Lake Taupo and the surrounding rivers and streams are world renowned for rainbow trout—the lake has the largest yields of trout in New Zealand, an estimated 500 tons. Trolling on Taupo and fishing the rivers flowing into it with a guide are almost surefire ways of catching fish. Wind and weather on the lake, which can change quickly, will determine where you can fish—and going with local knowledge of the conditions on Taupo is essential. The streams and rivers flowing into the lake are open for fly-fishing from October 1 to May 31. The lower reaches of the Tongariro, Tauranga-Taupo, and Waitahanui rivers, and the lake itself, remain open year-round. Lake Waikaremoana in Urewera National Park, southeast of Rotorua, is arguably the North Island's most scenic lake, and its fly-fishing and trolling are excellent. The South Island has excellent rivers with very clear water. Some hardly ever see anglers. South Island's best areas for trout are Marlborough, Westland, Fiordland, Southland, and Otago. Good trout fishing can also be found on Lake Dunstan east of Queenstown, Lake Poerua on the West Coast, and near Wanaka on Lake Hawea, the Hunter River, and the Timaru and Dingle creeks, all of which branch out from Lake Hawea. The rivers in the Motueka and Buller Gorge areas in northern South Island produce outstanding brown trout, too. The fishing season for the South Island runs from October 1 through April 30 for rivers going out of lakes, and from November 1 through April 30 for rivers going into lakes.

The Canterbury district has some productive waters for both trout and salmon—along with the West Coast it is the only part of New Zealand where you can fish for salmon, the quinnat, or Pacific chinook salmon introduced from North America. Anglers use large metal spoons and wobblers on long, strong rods with spinning outfits to fish the rivers around Christchurch, often catching salmon of 9 to 13.5 kg (20 to 30 lbs). In particular, top fishing spots include the Waimakariri and Hurunui rivers, both north of Christchurch, for excellent salmon and trout fishing; and the Rangitata River, south of Christchurch, for its sparkling rapids, oily glides, smooth pools, and clean gravel with good stocks of trout and salmon.

Trout fishing is normally tougher than in the North Island, with trout being a little smaller on average. You can catch brown and rainbow trout in South Island lakes using flies or by wading and spinning around lake edges or at stream mouths.

NORTH ISLAND FRESHWATER FISHING OPERATORS

Bryan Colman Trout Fishing fishes for trout in the Rotorua district's lakes and in the streams feeding these lakes. $120 per hour, one–four people. ✉ *32 Kiwi St., Rotorua* ☎ *07/348–7766* 🖷 *07/348–0832* ⊕ *www. TroutFishingRotorua.com.*

Central Plateau Fishing offers wilderness fly-fishing trips to rivers and streams often accessible only with 4X4 vehicles (or, in some cases, helicopters). There are single- and multiday packages available, for both beginners and seasoned anglers. ✉ *21 Glen Mohr, Acacia Bay, Taupo* ☎ *07/378–8192 or 027/681–4134* ⊕ *www.cpf.net.nz.*

Chris Jolly Outdoors takes clients trout fishing on the lakes and rivers in the Taupo region. The company also runs hunting trips for deer, boar, goats, and turkeys. ⬠ *Box 1020, Taupo* ☎ *07/378–0623* 🖷 *07/378–9458* ⊕ *www.chrisjolly.co.nz.*

Clark Gregor Trout Fishing specializes in fishing on Lake Rotorua and surrounding lakes for rainbow and brown trout. $95 per hour up to four people. ✉ *33 Haumoana St., Rotorua* ☎ *07/347–1123* 🖷 *07/347–1313* ⊕ *www.troutnz.co.nz.*

Lake Tarawera Launch Services will take you out on Lake Tarawera for trout fishing (or just sightseeing). They'll drop you off at a remote shore where you can fish, and they'll pick you up later in the day. ✉ *The Landing, Lake Tarawera, R.D. 5, Rotorua* ☎ *07/362–8595* 🖷 *07/362–8883.*

SOUTH ISLAND FRESHWATER FISHING OPERATORS

Dean Harrison leads fishing trips in the Canterbury and West Coast regions. ⬠ *Box 21192, Edgeware, Christchurch* ☎ *021/324–229* ⊕ *www.flyfishingadventures.co.nz.*

Fish Fiordland specializes in fly-fishing for trout on Fiordland's many stunning lakes and rivers. ⬠ *Box 75, Manapouri* ☎ *03/249–6855* ☎ *021/241–0815* ⊕ *www.fishfiordland.co.nz.*

Fishing & Hunting Amongst Friends takes you fishing for brown and rainbow trout in the rivers, streams, and lakes in central Otago and Southland. ⬠ *Box 312, Wanaka* ☎ *03/443–9257* ☎ *027/535–6651 mobile* ⊕ *www.flyfishhunt.co.nz.*

The guides at **Fly Fishing New Zealand Ltd.** will take you fly-fishing, lake trolling, drift-boat fishing, and heli-fishing on the rivers, streams, and lakes in the Lake Wakatipu basin. Two hours $100, full day $645 ⬠ *Box 1061, Queenstown* ☎ *03/442–5363* 🖷 *03/442–2734* ⊕ *www. wakatipu.co.nz.*

Based in Queenstown, **Harvey Maguire** fishes the rivers, lakes, and streams of the central Otago and Southland regions. DOC approved. Member NZ Professional Fishing Guide Association. ✉ *334 Littles Rd., Queenstown* ☎ *03/442–7061* ⊕ *www.flyfishing.net.nz.*

Strike Adventure fish for brown trout on local and wilderness rivers in the Nelson region and also run heli-fishing trips. 🏠 *Box 1619, Nelson 7040* ☎ *03/541–0020* 🖷 *03/541–0024* ⊕ *www.strikeadventure.com.*

SALTWATER FISHING

No country is better suited for ocean fishing than New Zealand. Its coastline—approximately as long as that of the mainland United States—has an incredible variety of locations, whether you like fishing off rocks, on reefs, surf beaches, islands, or harbors. Kiwi anglers have taken many world records over the years. All the big names are here—black, blue, and striped marlin, yellowfin and bluefin tuna, and mako, thresher, hammerhead, and bronze whaler sharks.

The most sought-after fish around the North Island are snapper (sea bream), kingfish, *hapuka* (grouper), *tarakihi*, John Dory, *trevally, maomao,* and *kahawai*. Many of these also exist around the top of the South Island. Otherwise, the South Island's main catches are blue cod, butterfish, hake, *hoki*, ling, *moki*, groper, greenbone, and trumpeter, which are all excellent eating fish.

Perhaps the most famous angler to fish New Zealand's waters was adventure novelist Zane Grey, who had his base on Urupukapuka Island in the Bay of Islands. On the North Island, the top areas are the Bay of Islands, the nearby Poor Knights Islands, Whangaroa in Northland, the Coromandel Peninsula and its islands, and the Bay of Plenty and White Island off its coast. The South Island does not have a well-established deep-sea game-fishing industry as yet, but places to fish include the Marlborough and Pelorus sounds at the northern tip.

NORTH ISLAND
SALTWATER
FISHING
OPERATORS

Baker Marine Charters is based in Whakatane in the Bay of Plenty, 1½ hours from Rotorua. Skipper John "Tuna" Baker, who has been charter fishing since the 1970s, targets marlin, tuna, sharks, and kingfish, and he bottom fishes for snapper and tereki. An experienced diver, John also runs dive trips to White Island. 🏠 *Box 473, Whakatane* ☎ *07/307–0015 or 0800/494–0324* 🖷 *07/307–1364* ⊕ *www.diven fish.co.nz.*

Blue Ocean Charters run half- or full-day fishing trips in the Bay of Plenty, as well as overnight reef-fishing excursions for snapper, trevally, kingfish, and kahawhai. ✉ *The Coronation Pier, Wharf St.* 🏠 *Box 13–100, Tauranga* ☎ *07/578–9685, 027/477–3339 mobile* 🖷 *07/578–3499* ⊕ *www.blueoceancharters.co.nz.*

Based in the Bay of Islands, **Earl Grey Fishing Charters** specializes in saltwater fly-fishing and light tackle fishing for a wide range of species. Fishing guide and captain Steve Butler particularly enjoys live-baiting for yellowtail kingfish. ✉ *23 Mission Rd., Kerikeri* ☎ *09/407–7165* 🖷 *09/407–5465* ⊕ *www.earlgreyfishing.co.nz.*

Tairua Dive & Fishinn fish the waters off the East Coast of the Coromandel Peninsula—Slipper and Shoe islands and the Aldermen Islands. You're liable to pull in snapper, kingfish, grouper, trevally, tereki, or kahawhai. ✉ *The Esplanade, Paku Boat Ramp, Tairua* ☎🖷*07/864–8054* ⊕*www.divetairua.co.nz.*

From its Coromandel Peninsula base, **Te Ra–The Sun** fishes the waters around Slipper and Mayor islands as well as the offshore reefs for snapper, kingfish, tereki, trevally, and kahawhai. ✉ *120 Moanuanu Ave., Whangamata* ☎🖷*07/865–8681* ⊕*tera.whangamata.co.nz.*

SOUTH ISLAND
SALTWATER
FISHING
OPERATORS **Anaru Accommodation and Charters** fishes the waters around French Pass, D'Urville Island, and the outer Marlborough Sounds. They target blue cod, groper, snapper, terakihi, sea perch; at times, you may catch kahawhai, kingfish, or barracuda as well. They also have backpacker-style accommodation in a comfortable lodge. ✉ *French Pass, R.D. 3, Rai Valley, Nelson* ☎*03/576–5260* 🖷*03/576–5090.*

Aurora Charters will take you on the seas around Stewart Island, with likely catches of blue cod and trumpeter. They also have great sightseeing trips. ✉*Halfmoon Bay Wharf, Stewart Island* ☎*03/219–1126* ⊕*www.auroracharters.co.nz.*

Chris Hobbs Snapper Fishing Charters targets large snapper in Pelorus Sound at the top of the South Island. Expect catches to average 4.5 kg (10 lbs); up to 9 kg (20 lbs) is not unheard of. ⬠*Box 21, Havelock* ☎*03/574–2911 or 025/397–178* 🖷*03/574–914.*

Takapu Charters fishes Preservation and Chalky inlets in Fiordland for blue cod, grouper, and trumpeter, all great eating fish. A trip here takes you to an especially wild and beautiful part of New Zealand. ⬠*Box 2013, Washdyke* ☎🖷*03/615–7574* ⊕*www.takapucharters.co.nz.*

Toa Tai Charters offers day- and multiday fishing trips to the Queen Charlotte, Pelorus, and Keneperu sounds, D'Urville Island, Port Underwood, Cook Straight, and Nelson areas. Up to 50 people can be accommodated for day trips; fewer spots are available for overnight trips. $70 per person. ✉*30 Buller St., Picton* ☎*03/573–7883* 🖷*03/573–7882* ⊕*www.soundsfishing.co.nz.*

HIKING

There isn't a better place on earth for hiking—called tramping here—than New Zealand. If you're looking for short tramps, you may want to head off on your own. "Freedom walking" means that you tramp without a guide and carry all your own food and equipment. For long treks, however, a guide can be a big help. With their knowledge of the native bush, guides can point out and discuss the country's fascinating flora and fauna. (They often have great senses of humor, too.) Although it varies by operator, most group hiking trips are limited to about 12 people. Book trips at least three weeks in advance.

In the peak months of January and February, trails can be crowded enough to detract from the natural experience. One advantage of a

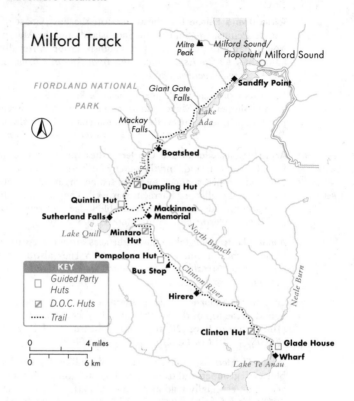

Milford Track

Mitre Peak

Milford Sound/
Piopiotahi Milford Sound

FIORDLAND NATIONAL

PARK

Giant Gate Falls

Sandfly Point

Lake Ada

Mackay Falls

Boatshed

Dumpling Hut

Quintin Hut

Mackinnon Memorial

Sutherland Falls

Lake Quill

Mintaro Hut

North Branch

Pompolona Hut

Bus Stop

Clinton River

Neale Burn

Hirere

KEY
☐ Guided Party Huts
☑ D.O.C. Huts
..... Trail

Clinton Hut

Glade House

Wharf

0 ———— 4 miles
0 ———— 6 km

Lake Te Anau

guided walk is that companies have their own tent camps or huts, with such luxuries as hot showers and cooks. For the phobic, it's worth mentioning one very positive feature: New Zealand has no snakes or predatory animals, no poison ivy, poison oak, leeches, or ticks. In the South Island, especially on the West Coast and in Fiordland, be prepared for voracious sandflies—some call it the state "bird." Pick up insect repellent in New Zealand; their repellent fends off their insects.

New Zealand's Department of Conservation (DOC) oversees a group of nine routes called Great Walks, which are outstanding both for their facilities and their incredible scenery. These routes are the Abel Tasman Coastal Track, the Heaphy Track, the Kepler Track, the Lake Waikaremoana Track, the Milford Track, the Rakiura Track, the Routeburn Track, the Tongariro Northern Circuit, and the Whanganui Journey. The Whanganui Journey, while technically a Great Walk, traces a canoeing trip. Most of the Great Walks are moderately difficult and take at least three days to complete. To overnight in a hut on a Great Walk route, you'll need to purchase a Great Walks pass from the local DOC office *(see the Great Walks chart)*.

There are also more than 50 routes the DOC dubs "major tracks," many of which go through national parks. These range from day hikes to challenging multiday tramps. At the start of each track, DOC signs outline a map of the route, as well as the track's degree of difficulty, distances, and estimated walking times. Most trail intersections are marked with informational signs as well. The DOC has a four-tier system grading track difficulty, as follows.

Grade 1: For well-formed, clearly marked, and graded tracks. This grade applies to many short walks as well as to longer walks that are suitable to a wide range of people.

Grade 2: For partly formed and marked tracks that are generally easy to follow. These may include bridge crossings and are often rough underfoot, requiring some tramping experience.

Grade 3: For marked, cairned, or poled routes with little or no cut or formed trail. For these you'll need reasonably advanced skill in route-finding and bush skills.

Grade 4: For unmarked or rarely marked routes crossing alpine passes or through deep bush. These are suitable only for experienced trampers with advanced bush and route-finding skills.

One of the top areas in the North Island for hiking and walking is the rugged Coromandel Peninsula, with 3,000-foot volcanic peaks clothed with semitropical rain forest and some of the best stands of the giant kauri tree and giant tree ferns. There is also gold-mining history on the peninsula, though the flicker of miners' lamps has given way to the steady green-blue light of millions of glowworms in the mines.

Tongariro National Park in central North Island has hiking with a difference—on and around active volcanoes rising to heights over 9,000 feet, the highest elevation on the island. It is a beautiful region of contrasts: deserts, forests, lakes, mountains, and snow.

The South Island, meanwhile, claims the most famous New Zealand walk—the Milford Track, a three- to four-day trek through Fiordland National Park. This track covers a wide variety of terrains, lakes, a glowworm grotto, and the spectacle of Milford Sound itself. As the track is strictly one-way (south to north), you rarely encounter other groups and so have the impression that your group is alone in the wild. Independent and escorted walkers stay in different huts about a half-day's walk apart. Escorted walkers' huts are serviced and very comfortable; independent walkers' huts are basic, with few facilities.

Elsewhere in the South Island, standouts are the three- to six-day routes on the beaches and in the forests of the Marlborough Sounds' Queen Charlotte Walkway and in Abel Tasman National Park. These are very popular, relatively easy, and well suited to family groups: your pack is carried for you, and you stay in lodges.

Alpine Guides has a renowned seven-day course on the basics of mountaineering around Aoraki (Mt. Cook), the highest point in the New Zealand Alps. There is also a 10-day technical course for experienced climbers.

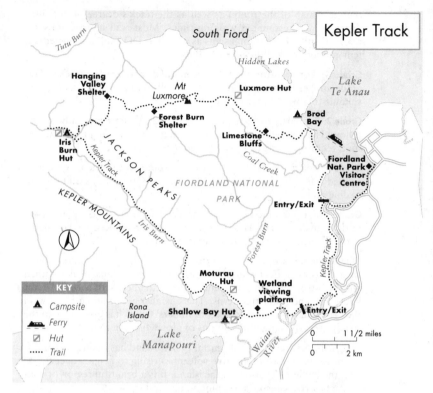

Your best bet at seeing a kiwi in the wild is on the 10-day Northern Circuit Track in Rakiura National Park on Stewart Island.

Season: October–March for high-altitude walks, year-round for others.
Best Locations: Coromandel Peninsula and Tongariro National Park in North Island; Aoraki, Westland, Abel Tasman, Fiordland parks in South Island; and Rakiura National Park on Stewart Island.
Cost: One- to three-day guided hikes range from $150 to $1,050. Prices for longer hikes vary widely; contact outfitters for specifics.

HUTS

New Zealand parks have an extensive range of huts for overnight use—they vary from well-equipped multiroom huts to small rough huts with only a few bunks and no facilities. You might hear of huts graded into categories; they're sometimes rated on a system of 1 (with heating and other facilities) to 4 (freebies with nothing much more than a roof over your head). Normally, backcountry huts are "first come, first served." However, on the more well-known tracks, you need to prebook. During the peak season, the huts can be full so you need to bring a small tent just in case things get overcrowded.

To pay for hut accommodations, purchase tickets in advance from DOC regional offices or at selected outlets (the DOC can direct you). You then deposit your ticket at each hut. During the high season there may be a hut warden who will take your fees, or you simply put the ticket into an envelope.

When using backcountry huts, leave them clean and tidy. Use gas, coal, or wood provided sparingly, and before leaving, replace any firewood you have used. Sign the hut book and include your planned itinerary; if anything goes amiss, the hut book will help locate you.

TOUR OPERATORS

Pioneers of tourism in the South Island's Abel Tasman National Park, **Abel Tasman Wilson's Experiences** run independent or guided walks ranging from a few hours to five days. "Cruise and walk" trips combine a boat tour with hiking, and sea-kayaking excursions are available as well. ⊠ *265 High St.* ✆ *Box 351, Motueka* ☎ *0800/221–888 or 03/528–2027* 🖷 *03/528–2029* ⊕ *www.abeltasmannz.com.*

Alpine Guides Ltd. lead 6- to 10-day ascents of New Zealand's highest peaks: Mt. Cook/Aoraki, Mt. Tasman, and Mt. Aspiring. You can also get private climbing instruction winter or summer. ✆ *Box 20, Mt. Cook* ☎ *03/435–1834* 🖷 *03/435–1898* ⊕ *www.alpineguides.co.nz.*

Alpine Recreation runs a 15-day minibus tour of the South Island, with two- to six-hour walks daily along the way. This scenic trip includes six national parks. The company also leads guided ascents of Mt. Cook and Mt. Tasman for experienced climbers. ✆ *Box 75, Lake Tekapo* ☎ *03/680–6736* 🖷 *03/680–6765* ⊕ *www.alpinerecreation.com.*

Bush & Beach operates half-day and overnight tours to the Waitakere Ranges and surrounding black-sand beaches, about a 30-minute drive from Auckland. These trips pair easy walks in the native rain forest and along the beach, with an optional overnight at a comfortable forest lodge. $125 half day, $185 full day, $545 Great Barrier Island tour. ⊠ *Shortland St.* ✆ *Box 121007, Henderson0650* ☎ *09/837–4130* 🖷 *09/837–4193* ⊕ *www.bushandbeach.co.nz.*

Guided Walks New Zealand Ltd. leads a variety of half- and full-day nature walks in the central Otago region that are designed for travelers of any age and ability. $98–$495. ✆ *Box 347, Queenstown* ☎ *03/442–7126* 🖷 *03/442–7128* ⊕ *www.nzwalks.com.*

Hike New Zealand runs 5- to 10-day hiking and camping tours in both the North and South islands for groups of up to 12. Tours include a trek to Franz Josef Glacier and the river country around the South Island's West Coast and a trip through the volcanic region of Tongariro National Park. From $595 for 5–10 days. ⊠ *Box 93, Lyttelton* ☎ *03/384–3706 or 0800/697–232* 🖷 *03/376–6483* ⊕ *www.Hiking NewZealand.com.*

Hollyford Track leads guided three-day walks on the wild and stunning Fiordland track of the same name. The track follows the Hollyford River to the Tasman Sea. The tours leave from Queensland and include

Continued on page 526

TRACK	LOCATION	LENGTH	DIFFICULTY	TERRAIN	
Abel Tasman Coastal Track	Near Nelson at top of South Island	50 km (31 mi) 3–5 days	Moderate fitness.	Beaches, rocks, forest. (Note tide schedules when crossing inlets.)	
Heaphy Track	Northwest tip of South Island	78 km (48 mi) 4–6 days	Moderate fitness. Most difficult section from Brown hut to Perry Saddle hut	Track begins in dense beech and podocarp forest in north; continues to high-level snow tussock plateaus midway; descends into palm-studded forests, rugged West Coast beaches.	
Kepler Track	Near Te Anau, Fiordland, South Island	67 km (41.5 mi) 3–4 days	Moderate fitness. Day one is steep climb from lake to tops.	Varies from beech forests to sometimes snow-covered tussock tops. Wonderful views in clear weather.	

*unless otherwise indicated, prices are per person per night.

DOC HUTS	CONDITIONS	SPECIAL ASPECTS	TRACK SAVVY	DOC INFO (www.doc.govt.nz)
4 huts; $30; toilets, bunks, mattresses, heating, filtered water. Bring cooking equipment. 20 campsites; $12.	Possible flooding at river and creek crossings in heavy rain.	Regenerating rainforest with nikau palms, ferns, forest giants; granite rocks; golden-sand beaches. May see seals and penguins.	Hut/camping passes required. In summer, bunks must be booked in advance with DOC. Pack sunscreen. In autumn and winter, walking and weather conditions are good; fewer people.	Nelson Regional Visitor Centre, Tel. 03/546-9339
7 huts; $20; toilets, bunks, mattresses, gas stoves. Gouland Downs hut: bunks, open fire 3 shelters. 9 campsites; $10	Normally a drier area, but be prepared for rain, especially on western slopes. Primarily a summer route; snow can block track in winter.	One of New Zealand's finest routes. Forests, limestone caves, snow tussock tops, nikau palms, many birds (including kiwis, rare pipits).	Nearest centers are Collingwood in north and Karamea in southwest. Several shuttles serve each end. Hut tickets required; carry a tent during Oct.–Apr. peak season.	Nelson Regional Visitor Centre, Tel. 03/546-9339
3 huts; $45; bunks, mattresses, running water, flush toilets, heating, gas stoves. 2 campsites; $15	Be prepared for rain. Watch weather on exposed mountaintops; snow is possible. Sandflies at lower altitude	Lovely forest scenery; may spot kea and other birds. Good for geology buffs, especially Mt. Luxmore. Detour to Iris Burn waterfall, 20-minute walk from Iris Burn hut.	Book huts in advance. Coal supplied to huts between Oct. and Apr.; other times, bring cooking gear. Pack insect repellent.	Great Walks Booking Desk, Tel: 03/249-8514; Fiordland National Park Visitor Centre, Tel: 03/249-7294

TRACK	LOCATION	LENGTH	DIFFICULTY	TERRAIN	
Lake Waikaremoana Track	In Te Urewera National Park, southeast of Rotorua, North Island	46 km (28.5 mi) 3–4 days	Moderate fitness required. Climb from lake edge to Panekiri Bluffs is toughest.	Much of track runs through podocarp forest. Generally in good condition.	
Milford Track	Near Te Anau, South Island	54 km (33.5 mi) 4–5 days	Moderately difficult; two strenuous climbs, one very steep descent.	Track follows Clinton River (gets muddy), crosses Mackinnon Pass, goes through alpine meadows, passes waterfalls. Thick forest at beginning and end.	
Northwest Circuit, Rakiura	Stewart Island	125 km (77.5 mi, full circuit); 102 km (63 mi) if you catch boat at Freshwater Landing. 10–12 days for full circuit	Difficult; requires good fitness, good equipment, bushcraft and survival skills.	Much of track is in dense forest, but it follows part of western coastline with some steep short climbs. Often muddy.	

*unless otherwise indicated, prices are per person per night.

11

DOC HUTS	CONDITIONS	SPECIAL ASPECTS	TRACK SAVVY	DOC INFO (www.doc.govt.nz)
5 huts; $25; bunks, mattresses, heating. Bring cooking gear. 5 campsites; $12	Can get very heavy rain at times. Bring repellent for mosquitoes and sandflies.	Great views from Panekiri Bluffs. Great birding: kaka, parakeets, paradise ducks, whiteheads, fantails, silvereyes, morepork (native owl), kiwi.	Advance booking advised. Don't miss short uphill side trip to Korokoro waterfall. Bus transport available from major centers, including Rotorua and Wairoa.	Urewera National Park Visitors Centre, Tel: 06/837–3803; Hawkes Bay Regional Visitor Centre, Tel: 06/834–3111
3 huts; $135 for all; ranger staff, gas stoves, cold running water, flush toilets.	Frequent rain. Sandflies below tree line. Beware of avalanche conditions at Mackinnon Pass in winter.	Sutherland Falls, country's highest waterfall. Lots of kea (mountain parrots).	New Zealand's most popular track; book at least 4 months ahead. Can only hike south to north); no backtracking allowed. Insect repellent a must.	Great Walks Booking Office, Tel: 03/249-8514; Fiordland National Park Visitor Centre, Tel: 03/249–7924
10 huts; $10; toilets (long drops), fireplaces. Bring your own cooking gear.	Wet weather, several river crossings—be prepared to get muddy. Lots of mosquitoes and sandflies.	Wild remote beaches and coastline; could see penguin and seals. Wonderful views from Mt. Anglem, a 3–4 hour side trip (one-way). Great birding; could see kiwi, bellbirds, tūī, fantails, tomtits and parakeets.	Hut tickets required; some camping possible. Regular flights from Invercargil (magical in good weather); also ferry service from Bluff. Pack extra food and insect repellent.	Rakiura National Park Visitor Centre, Tel: 03/219-0009

TRACK	LOCATION	LENGTH	DIFFICULTY	TERRAIN	
Routeburn Track	Western end of Lake Wakatipu, near Glenorchy, South Island	32 km (20 mi) 2–3 days	Moderate fitness required. Mountainous terrain, open tops; good equipment needed.	Track can be done in either direction. Either way runs through beech forest onto exposed mountaintops.	
Tongariro Northern Circuit	Tongariro National Park, central North Island.	49 km (30 mi) 3–4 days	Moderate fitness and good gear. Toughest section is "Staircase."	Most of track is out in open. Wonderful alpine and volcanic vistas	
Whanganui Journey	Near Taumarunui on Whanganui River, central North Island.	145 km (90 mi, full trip) 5 days, on average; 88 km (54.5 mi, shorter trip) 3 days	Moderate fitness; swimming, canoeing, kayaking skills.	Although a river journey, Whanganui is part of "Great Walks" network. A 3-day journey from Whakahoro to Pipiriki is also possible.	

*unless otherwise indicated, prices are per person per night.

DOC HUTS	CONDITIONS	SPECIAL ASPECTS	TRACK SAVVY	DOC INFO (www.doc.govt.nz)
4 huts; $30; toilets, bunks, mattresses, heating, filtered water. Bring cooking equipment. 20 campsites; $12.	Possible flooding at river and creek crossings in heavy rain.	Regenerating rainforest with nikau palms, ferns, forest giants; granite rocks; golden-sand beaches. May see seals and penguins.	Hut/camping passes required. In summer, bunks must be booked in advance with DOC. Pack sunscreen. In autumn and winter, walking and weather conditions are good; fewer people.	Nelson Regional Visitor Centre, Tel. 03/546–9339
7 huts; $20; toilets, bunks, mattresses, gas stoves. Gouland Downs hut: bunks, open fire 3 shelters. 9 campsites; $10	Normally a drier area, but be prepared for rain, especially on western slopes. Primarily a summer route; snow can block track in winter.	One of New Zealand's finest routes. Forests, limestone caves, snow tussock tops, nikau palms, many birds (including kiwis, rare pipits).	Nearest centers are Collingwood in north and Karamea in southwest. Several shuttles serve each end. Hut tickets required; carry a tent during Oct.–Apr. peak season.	Nelson Regional Visitor Centre, Tel. 03/546–9339
3 huts; $45; bunks, mattresses, running water, flush toilets, heating, gas stoves. 2 campsites; $15	Be prepared for rain. Watch weather on exposed mountaintops; snow is possible. Sandflies at lower altitude	Lovely forest scenery; may spot kea and other birds. Good for geology buffs, especially Mt. Luxmore. Detour to Iris Burn waterfall, 20-minute walk from Iris Burn hut.	Book huts in advance. Coal supplied to huts between Oct. and Apr.; other times, bring cooking gear. Pack insect repellent.	Great Walks Booking Desk, Tel: 03/249-8514; Fiordland National Park Visitor Centre, Tel: 03/249-7294

11

lodge accommodations en route. $1,655 for three-day walk. ⌂ *Box 360, Queenstown* ☎ *0800/832–226 or 03/442–7789* 🖷 *03/442–7781* 🌐 *www.hollyfordtrack.co.nz.*

Kapiti Island Alive tours include a boat trip to Kapiti Island, a bird sanctuary off the West Coast (north of Wellington). On these guided walks, you may see such rare birds as the kokako, kaka, saddleback, takahe, whitehead, weka, bellbird, tūī, and many seabirds. ⌂ *Box 28, Otaki* ☎ *06/364–8818, 027/288–3771 mobile* 🖷 *06/364–5828* 🌐 *www. kapitiislandalive.co.nz.*

A pioneer of nature tourism in New Zealand, **Kiwi Dundee Adventures, Ltd.** has been running guided walks and hikes since 1975. Their walking, touring, and hiking trips cover all aspects of the Coromandel Peninsula and New Zealand, from its history, flora, fauna, to its rugged mountains, glowworm caves, rain forests, and coastline and suit any age, fitness, and interests. They also lead multiday ecowalks in both the North and South islands away from the usual tourist spots. From $195. Qualmark endorsed. ⌂ *Box 198, Whangamata* ☎🖷 *07/865–8809* 🌐 *www.kiwidundee.co.nz.*

Marlborough Sounds Adventure Company runs four- to five-day guided and "freedom" (unguided but prearranged) walks on the 71-km (43-mi) Queen Charlotte walkway at the top of the South Island. The walkway, which follows a long, narrow ridge of mountains separating Queen Charlotte Sound from Kenepuru Sound. The company does sea-kayaking and mountain-biking trips as well. ✉ *London Quay, Picton* ☎ *03/573–6078 or 0800/283–283* 🖷 *03/573–8827* 🌐 *www. marlboroughsounds.co.nz.*

Ultimate Hikes leads guided trips of two of New Zealand's best-known treks: the Milford Track and the Routeburn Track. The spectacular **Milford Track,** frequently dubbed one of the world's greatest hikes, is a four-day walk that passes through Clinton Canyon's huge glacier-carved valleys before climbing over the McKinnon Pass and following the river out to Milford Sound. From $1,690. The **Routeburn Track,** a three- or four-day hike, takes you through lovely beech forest and river valleys before climbing over the main divide of the Southern Alps past waterfalls and small glacier-fed lakes. From $1,050. ⌂ *Box 259, Queenstown* ☎ *03/442–2800 or 0800/659–255* 🖷 *03/441–1124* 🌐 *www.ultimatehikes.co.nz.*

Wild West Adventure Co. operates wilderness hikes through the rain forests and valleys of the South Island's West Coast. Hikes range from two to five days, with accommodations in hotels, hostels, track lodges, or campsites. From $95. ✉ *8 Whall St., Greymouth* ☎ *03/768–6649 or 0508/286–877* 🖷 *03/768–9149* 🌐 *www.fun-nz.com.*

HORSE TREKKING

Operators all over New Zealand take people horseback riding along beaches, in native forests, on mountains, and up rivers through pine plantations. One of the best areas to explore on horseback is the sweep of the Canterbury Plains around Christchurch in the South Island—the surrounding mountain ranges create some of New Zealand's most dramatic scenery. The top of the South Island with its *nikau* palms, limestone cliffs, and sandy beaches also has some beautiful spots to ride. On the North Island, the rugged Coromandel Ranges and the Northland's vast stretches of white-sand beaches are popular riding territory as well. All of the outfitters listed here offer trips for inexperienced riders, and all provide the required protective headgear. Some companies will also supply suitable heeled footwear, but be sure to check with the outfitter about what you'll need to bring. On longer trips, you'll likely be expected to help with the horses and equipment.

Season: October–March.

Best Locations: Northland and the Coromandel Peninsula in the North Island, Nelson and Canterbury high country in the South Island.

Cost: Prices range from about $115 for two hours to $225 for a day trip, or $495 for overnight; contact outfitters for specifics on shorter or multiday trips.

TOUR OPERATORS

Cape Farewell Horse Treks operates horse treks from Puponga in Golden Bay at the northwest tip of the South Island, taking in beautiful beach scenery with giant limestone rocks and caves and lush palm-studded forests. They also lead four- to five-day treks down the isolated West Coast under cliffs full of huge fossils. From $45. ✆R.D. 1, Puponga, Collingwood ☎🖷03/524–8031 ⊕www.horsetreksnz.com.

Dart Stables Glenorchy, based near Queenstown, takes small groups out on trips ranging from two hours to three days; some of this South Island territory is where much of the *Lord of the Rings* was filmed. There are rides suitable for beginners and more advanced equestrians. $105 two hours, $215 full day. ✆Box 47, Glenorchy ☎03/442–5688 or 0800/474–3464 🖷03/442–6045 ⊕www.dartstables.com.

Hurunui Horse Treks has a variety of rides, including 8- and 10-day horse treks into remote backcountry, where the terrain varies from dense scrub to open meadows to alpine passes. Accommodation options include rustic huts (without electricity, showers, or flush toilets) or more comfortable farm stays; groups are generally limited to six or fewer. $150–$2,975. ✉757 The Peaks Rd. ✆R.D., Hawarden, North Canterbury ☎🖷03/314–4204 ⊕www.hurunui.co.nz.

Pakiri Beach Horse Rides, north of Auckland, runs trips from several hours to several days, all incorporating a ride on the namesake white-sand beach. You might ride through groves of pohutukawa, which are ablaze with red flowers in the summer, or across the sand dunes with inspiring views of islands on the horizon. $99 for half day, $199 full day. ✉Taurere Park, Rahuikiri Rd., Pakiri, Wellsford ☎09/422–6275 🖷09/422–6277 ⊕www.horseride-nz.co.nz.

Halfway between Whitianga and Tairua on the Coromandel Peninsula, **Rangihau Ranch** leads short rides of an hour or two; the routes follow pack-horse trails from the 1800s with wonderful views of the bush-clad

Coromandel mountains, Mercury Bay, and the Pacific Ocean. They specialize in working with inexperienced riders. ⊠*Rangihau Rd., Coroglen* ☎*07/866–3875* 🖷*07/866–3837.*

With **Stonehurst Farm Horse Treks,** trek through 1,000 acres of a working farm near Nelson with panoramic views over the mountains and Golden Bay. Their treks, for riders of all abilities, run from one hour to a half day. $55 per hour, $105 half day. ⊠*Stonehurst Farm, Clover Rd.* 🖅*R.D. 1, Richmond, Nelson* ☎*03/542–4121 or 0800/487–357* 🖷*03/542–4500* ⊕*www.stonehurstfarm.co.nz.*

RAFTING

After testing samples from New Zealand rivers, hydrologists have determined that the country's waterways contain high quantities of pure adrenaline.

OK, that's not actually true, but you might believe it if you sampled some rapids here. New Zealand, Aoteraroa, Land of the Long White Cloud, is also Land of the Longest White-water Waterfall Drop (not sure how that translates succinctly into Māori). The North Island's Kaituna River features the world's highest raftable waterfall—a 21-foot free fall.

The exhilaration of sweeping down into the foam-filled jaws of a rapid is always tinged with fear—white-water rafting is, after all, rather like being tossed into a washing machine. As you drift downriver during the lulls between the white water, it's wonderful to sit back and watch the wilderness unfold, whether it's stately *rimu* or *rata* trees overhanging the stream or towering cliffs with rain forest on the surrounding slopes. Rafting means camping by the river at night, drinking tea brewed over a fire, and going to sleep with the sound of the stream in the background. Rivers here are smaller and trickier than the ones used for commercial rafting in North America, and rafts usually hold only four to six people. Rafting companies provide all equipment—you only need clothing that won't be damaged by water (cameras are carried in waterproof barrels), a sleeping bag (in some cases), and sunscreen. Rafting qualifies as hard adventure.

In the North Island, near Rotorua, the Rangitaiki offers exciting Grade IV rapids and some good scenery. Nearby, the Wairoa offers Grade V—the highest before a river becomes unraftable. The Tongariro River flows from between the active 10,000-foot volcanic peaks of Tongariro National Park into the south end of Lake Taupo, New Zealand's largest lake. The Tongariro (Grade III) and the mighty Motu River (Grade V) are great for rafting.

In the South Island, the great majority of activity centers on Queenstown. The most popular spot here is the upper reaches of the Shotover River beyond tortuous Skippers Canyon. In winter, the put-in site for the Shotover is accessible only by helicopter, and wet suits are essential year-round, as the water is very cold. Some of the rapids are Grade V.

The Rangitata River south of Christchurch is fed by an enormous catchment basin, and rafting is serious at all water levels.

Season: Mainly October–May.

Best Locations: Rotorua and Taupo in the North Island, Canterbury and Queenstown in the South Island.

Cost: From $115 for two hours to $130 per person for three-hour trips; heli-rafting from $220 per person, three-day trips from $690 per person.

TOUR OPERATORS

Challenge Rafting operates half-day white-water raft and raft-combo trips on the South Island's Kawarau and Shotover rivers; the combo trips mix rafting with jet-boating or bungy jumping. The Kawarau offers exhilarating rafting for first timers, and the Shotover serves up extra excitement for the more experienced. Trips depart twice daily. The company also offers a heli-rafting option on the Shotover, which includes a helicopter flight to the Skipper Canyon launch site. *Box 634, Shotover and Camp Sts., Queenstown* ☎*03/442–7318 or 0800/423–836* ⊜*03/441–2983* ⊕*www.raft.co.nz.*

Kaituna Cascades does several rafting runs daily down the North Island's Kaituna River, with its 21-foot waterfall. They also raft the Rangitaiki (good for beginners) and Wairoa rivers (for the excitement seekers). From $72. ⊠*Trout Pool Rd., Okere Falls, Box 2217, Rotorua* ☎*07/345–4199 or 0800/524–8862* ⊜*07/345–9533* ⊕*www.kaituna cascades.co.nz.*

Queenstown Rafting runs raft trips on the South Island's Shotover and Kawarau rivers. Combo trips, pairing rafting with jet-boating, helicopter flights, or bungy jumping, are also available. From $155. ⊠*35 Shotover St., Queenstown* ☎*03/442–9792 or 0800/723–8464* ⊜*03/442–4609* ⊕*www.rafting.co.nz.*

Rangitata Rafts guides day trips through the Grade V rapids of the spectacular Rangitata Gorge on the South Island. Trips, which run September to May, include round-trip transport from Christchurch (about two hours each way) and finish with hot showers and a BBQ. From $185. Qualmark endorsed. ⊠*Rangitata Gorge Rd., Peel Forest, Geraldine, South Canterbury* ☎*0800/251–251* ⊜☎*03/696–3534* ⊕*www.rafts.co.nz.*

Wet 'n' Wild Rafting Company rafts several of the North Island's rivers: the Rangitaiki (Grade II–III, great for first timers), Kaituna (Grade IV–V, with the 21-foot waterfall), Wairoa (Grade IV–V, an ultimate white-water playground), Motu (Grade III–V, with wilderness camping for two to four days), and Mohaka (Grade III–V, with two to four days camping and fishing). From $75, with multiday trips from $375. ⊠*2 White St.* *Box 601, Rotorua* ☎*07/348–3191 or 0800/462–7238* ⊜*07/349–6567* ⊕*www.wetnwildrafting.co.nz.*

Wild West Adventure Co. operates wilderness white-water raft trips on several rivers on the South Island's West Coast. Another option is blackwater-cave rafting; these half-day trips take you through glowworm caves and down underground waterfalls. ⊠*8 Whall St., Greymouth* ☎*03/768–6649 or 0508/286–877* 🖷*03/768–9149* ⊕*www.fun-nz.com.*

SAILING

Varied coastline and splendid waters have made sailing extremely popular in New Zealand. Admittedly, your role as a passenger on a commercial sailing vessel is hardly strenuous. The best sailing areas in New Zealand are undoubtedly from the Bay of Islands south to the Coromandel Peninsula and the Bay of Plenty. This coastline has many islands and a wrinkled shoreline that make for wonderful, sheltered sailing.

The rugged Marlborough Sounds at the north end of the South Island are particularly beautiful when seen from the water. The islands and coves make ideal overnight moorings; it's easy to understand why Captain James Cook felt this was his favorite part of the country.

Season: Year-round.
Best Locations: Bay of Islands in the North Island, upper and lower South Island.
Cost: Bay of Islands from $75 for a day trip to $690 to $830 per night depending on the craft; Doubtful Sound from $1,725 for five days; Fiordland National Park area from $3,510 for eight days; sub-Antarctic islands of Australia and New Zealand from $2,467 for seven days.

TOUR OPERATORS

Abel Tasman Sailing Adventures, based at Kaiteriteri beach, between Motueka and Abel Tasman National Park, runs half-day, one-day, and two-day sailing tours with optional walks along the islands of Abel Tasman National Park. Fur seals, penguins, and dolphins are usually visible. ⊠*Sandy Bay/Marahau Rd., R.D.2, Motueka* ☎*0800/467–245 or 03/527–8375* 🖷*03/527–8374* ⊕*www.sailingadventures.co.nz.*

Catamaran Sailing Charters, based in Nelson, arranges sailing trips around Abel Tasman National Park, D'Urville Island, and the Marlborough Sounds. They specialize in skippered cruises, but experienced sailors can also hire their own boats. Short sails, day trips, and multiday trips are all available. ⊠*46 Martin St., Nelson* ☎*03/547–6666* 🖷*03/547–6663* ⊕*www.sailingcharters.co.nz.*

Heritage Expeditions runs voyages to the remote sub-Antarctic islands, to the Kermedec Islands (1,000 km [620 mi] northeast of New Zealand), and to Antarctica. You may see royal albatross, sea lions, elephant seals, and penguins. From $9,750. ✆*Box 7218, Christchurch* ☎*03/365–3500* 🖷*03/365–1300* ⊕*www.heritage-expeditions.com.*

Tauranga Sailing School and Yacht Charters sails to some of the islands in the Bay of Plenty. You can take a piloted launch or, if you have the experience, captain a sailboat yourself. ⊠*70 Omokoroa Rd., Tauranga* ☎*07/548–0689, 025/289–5594 mobile.*

SEA KAYAKING

Unlike rafting, sea kayaking is a calm adventure. The best places for it are in Northland and the Bay of Islands, the Coromandel Peninsula, the Whanganui River area, the top of South Island, Kaikoura, and as far south as Stewart Island. In the Bay of Islands and the Coromandel, you can kayak along stunning beaches in sheltered waters, whereas kayaking the sometimes mysterious Whanganui River takes you among deep forested gorges. On the South Island, the vast quiet waters and bush-lined bays of the Marlborough Sounds are also popular. If you opt to kayak the remote waters around Stewart Island, you may spot whales, dolphins, penguins, and seals. Kayaking outfitters usually take out small groups of no more than five kayaks at a time. The level of difficulty depends very much on the weather, so always talk to the operator to gauge the challenge.

Season: December–May.

Best Locations: Northland, the Coromandel Peninsula, and Whanganui River in the North Island; Marlborough Sounds, Kaikoura, Abel Tasman National Park, and Stewart Island's Paterson Inlet.

Cost: From $60 for a half-day excursion; contact kayaking outfitters for price information for longer trips.

TOUR OPERATORS

Cathedral Cove Kayaks offers beginner-friendly half-day guided kayak tours along the spectacular volcanic coast of the North Island's Hahei marine reserve. Explore offshore islands and sea caves, then wrap up the day with a cappuccino. $75 half day, $125 full day. ⊠88 *Hahei Beach Rd., Hahei* ☎07/866–3877 ⊜07 866–3876 ⊕*www.sea kayaktours.co.nz.*

Coastal Kayakers runs sea-kayaking excursions in the Bay of Islands, from four- to six-hour guided trips to Waitangi or Haruru Falls, to more leisurely three-day expeditions. On the overnight trips, you might camp on a deserted island after exploring lagoons, sea caves, and sandy beaches; you'll have time to swim, snorkel, or fish along the way. $55 half day to $480 for three days. ☖*Box 325, Paihia* ☎09/402–8105 ⊜09/403–8550 ⊕*www.coastalkayakers.co.nz.*

Fiordland Wilderness Experience provides one-day guided sea-kayaking tours in Milford Sound, departing daily. Other trips include two- to five-day tours in Doubtful Sound and one (or more) days kayaking on lakes Manapouri and Te Anau. Combination trips pair sea kayaking with hiking or diving. From $100 for day trips with multidays from $310. ⊠*66 Quintin Dr., Te Anau* ☎03/249–7700 or 0800/200–434 ⊜03/249–7768 ⊕*www.fiordlandseakayak.co.nz.*

The one- to three-day kayaking trips with the **Marlborough Sounds Adventure Company** explore the deeply indented, bush-clad coastline of the Marlborough Sounds. There is also a three-hour twilight excursion. ⊠*London Quay* ☖*Box 195, Picton* ☎03/573–6078 or 0800/283–283 ⊜03/573–8827 ⊕*www.marlboroughsounds.co.nz.*

New Zealand Sea Kayaking Adventures offers fully provisioned 3-, 6-, and 10-day guided sea-kayaking/camping trips in the Bay of Islands. They can provide instruction for novice and more advanced paddlers. $125 for a day, 3-day $525, 6-day $1,050, 10-day $1,500. ⌂ *Box 454, Paihia* ☎ *09/402–8596* ⊕ *www.nzkayaktours.com.*

Ocean River Adventure Company trips explore the Abel Tasman National Park by water. Their one- to three-day kayak trips follow the granite coastline. One tour visits the thriving seal colony in the Tonga Island Marine Reserve. ✉ *Abel Tasman National Park, Marahau* ⌂ *R.D. 2, Motueka* ☎ *03/527–8022 or 0800/732–529* 🖷 *03/527–8032* ⊕ *www. seakayaking.co.nz.*

With **Oceanix Sea Kayaking Expeditionz,** you kayak day or night in the Bay of Plenty. Tours typically last two or three hours. On daytime trips, you explore the offshore islands or the McLaren Falls waterway near Tauranga. On the nighttime trips, you can see glowworms in their natural environment. From $115. ⌂ *Box 4460, Mount Maunganui South* ☎ *0800/335–8004, 07/572–2226, or 0274/942–677* ⊕ *www.oceanix.co.nz.*

Rakiura Kayaks lets you kayak amidst the spectacular beauty of Stewart Island. Fur seals, penguins, and kiwis—oh my! Guided ($50 for half day, $75 for full day) and nonguided packages ($40 per day) are available. ✉ *Argyle St., Stewart Island* ☎ *03/219–1160* ⊕ *www.rakiura.co.nz.*

Ross Adventures, based at Matiatia Bay on Waiheke Island—just a 35-minute ferry ride from downtown Auckland, runs guided half-day, evening, full-day, and overnight kayaking trips with options for beginners and more advanced paddlers. Day trips explore the northwestern corner of Waiheke and its rock channels, archways, and sea caves. On their nighttime trips, you'll look for phosphorescence, where the water glows along your paddles or hands. ✉ *Matiatia Bay, Waiheke* ⌂ *Box 106037, Auckland* ☎ *09/372–5550* 🖷 *09/372–4422* ⊕ *www.kayakwaiheke.co.nz.*

UNDERSTANDING NEW ZEALAND

MĀORITANGA: AN INSIDER'S PERSPECTIVE

Ko au te whenua, ko te whenua, ko au.

I am the land, the land is me. (Māori proverb)

There is talk around New Zealand about the definition of the word *indigenous*. The argument concerns whether *Pākehā* New Zealanders (non-Māori, generally of European extraction) are as indigenous as Māori are to this country. After all, Pākehā New Zealanders' ancestors have been here for centuries—not quite as long as the Māori, but in some cases, for seven generations. Arriving in *waka* (canoes) or tall ships, 900 or 90 years ago—we're all immigrants, aren't we? Why is *Māoritanga* ("things Māori" or Māori culture) considered the only indigenous culture?

The concept of Māoritanga most likely took shape after the 1840 Treaty of Waitangi. Pretreaty, we identified ourselves tribally. Moreover, it's fairly certain that we did not use the word *Māori* to describe ourselves as a people. The term did exist, but as an adjective, meaning "normal, usual, ordinary," or "unadulterated." *Wai māori,* for example, meant "fresh water," as opposed to *wai tai,* "sea or salt water." When Pākehā first encountered Māori and asked the inevitable question, who are you? it's possible our ancestors replied, "*he tangata māori*," meaning "just a person." These days, there's a strong move back to tribal identification rather than the generic term *Māori.* Young people often refer to themselves as "T. W." or "Tee Dub," short for *tangata whenua* (people of the land), or they use their tribal names. (Ngāti Raukawa and Ngāi Tahu, for example, are two of my tribes.) But Māoritanga is still a common term, as it encompasses so many different activities and aspects of our lives.

Taonga tuku iho/treasures handed down

Our customs were, and are, based on certain life-sustaining philosophies and practices (*tikanga*), such as *utu* (a principle of reply or return, related to keeping things in balance) and *muru* (a concept related to forgiveness, literally meaning "to wipe out"). Two other important tikanga are *tapu* and its counterpart, *noa.* Although only our *tohunga* (experts, priests) can approach a thorough knowledge of these esoteric principles, the tikanga shape our daily lives.

Tapu is often translated as "sacred" or "set apart." One way I explain tapu to myself is this: if something or someone is "tapu," they are capable of invoking strong emotions. The body of someone who has died, for example, is considered very tapu.

Another way to understand the concepts of tapu and noa is to consider the potential something possesses. For instance, a tree growing in a forest may have a different kind of tapu, or potential, than a *waka* (canoe) made from that tree. If the tree is made into a waka, its potential has been reduced, as it can no longer become a *koauau* (traditional flute) or *maihi* (bargeboards for a meetinghouse). Noa has been enacted on the tree to reduce its potential.

The head, particularly for someone with great *mana* (status and/or sacred power), is considered the most tapu part of the human body, perhaps because of the unlimited potential of the mind and the imagination. Food is ritually used to counter or lift the tapu of many activities, people, places, or objects. This kind of ritual is rooted in centuries of spiritual knowledge and practice, entrusted to those who know what they're doing, the tohunga.

Ko tā te manuhiri/The role of the visitor

So how do these tikanga apply in everyday life? There are a few basic concepts worth remembering when visiting Māori homes or a community center or village, called a *marae*. (To many Māori, there is little difference between these two places.)

Certain customs in the home revolve around food both directly and indirectly, and they generally relate to food's entry and exit points. This determines the way *kai* (food) and dining utensils are handled. Avoid passing kai or plates over people's heads. Don't put your hat on the table or on a chair. Don't sit on tables, or on any surface on which food has or will be placed. Don't sit on pillows in the *wharenui* (the meetinghouse) or wherever people lay their heads. Walk around people's outstretched legs rather than over them.

Anything to do with food, even tea towels, will likely be treated differently from what you're used to. Most marae, for example, don't wash their kitchen linen with bed linen—often, not even in the same washing machine. In kitchens, there are sometimes separate towels for drying your hands; don't dry your hands on towels reserved only for dishes.

He whare, he tupuna/Our house is our ancestor

The area in front of the whare nui is known as the *marae ātea* and is considered the domain of the Tū Matāuenga, the Māori divinity of war. Out there, anything goes. This is where problems are thrashed out, debates are held, and disagreements resolved. Inside the whare nui, however, is the realm of Rongo-mā-Tane, the God of Peace. In recognition of this division, we leave our shoes at the door of the house so that the dust of the marae ātea is left outside.

The *whare whakāiro* (carved house) is the physical embodiment of a *tupuna* (ancestor) and as such commands respect. This connection echoes in the vocabulary of the house; the word for *veranda* (*roro*), for example, is the same as the word for *brain*. The *maihi* (bargeboards) are the outstretched arms of our loved one. The *heke* (rafters) in the ceiling are the ribs, descending from the spine, the *tāhuhu* (ridgepole of the ceiling).

Ngā kōrero o neherā/Ancient stories

The structure of the carved house incorporates the Māori genesis story. In the beginning was Te Kore, the void, from which arose Te Pō, the night. In this darkness lived Papatūānuku, the Earth Mother, and Ranginui, the Sky Father. Their children were cramped in their embrace and plotted their freedom. One of the sons, Tāne Mahuta (the divinity of the forest and its creatures), finally separated his parents by lying on his back and pushing Ranginui upward with his legs. In carved houses, the roof represents Ranginui, and the *poupou* (posts) represent the children, pushing him upward.

When Tāne separated his parents, he created the World of Light, Te Ao Mārama, the world of human beings. The first human being is also said to have been created by Tāne, when he sneezed life into Hine-ahu-one, the Woman Made of Earth. From this story comes the common blessing "Tihei mauri ora!" or "Behold the breath [or sneeze] of life!"

The descendants of Tāne and Hine-ahu-one increased generation by generation. Among their notable progeny is Hine-tītama, the Woman of the Dawn, who became Hine-nui-te-Pō, the Goddess of Death. She is the ancestor into whose embrace we deliver the spirits of our dead.

Māui is another major figure in our histories. Māui had humble beginnings as an aborted child, set adrift on the sea by his mother, wrapped in her topknot. Māui was saved by a favorable wind and a clump of seaweed, and became the legendary heroic figure who fished up the North Island (Te Ika a Māui, the Fish of Māui) from his canoe, the South Island (Te Waka a Māui). Māui was also a trickster with a penchant for playing practical jokes on his elders. He obtained the secret of fire, for example, by tricking his grandmother into giving up all the flames in her fingernails and toenails. Every tribe and subtribe among us has its own variations, big or small, on these stories.

Ko ngā mahi toi/The arts

In the Māori worldview, all objects have a *mauri* (spiritual essence), including those made by *tohunga toi* (expert artists). Objects were made to be beautiful, but also to serve a practical or symbolic function.

During your trip, you'll see all kinds of crafts made of indigenous materials, from *paua* (abalone) shell earrings and *pounamu* (greenstone) pendants to *kete whakairo* (finely woven flax bags). Perhaps the best known Māori visual art is **carving.** Carving was traditionally lavished on everything wooden, from massive poles in meetinghouses to waka paddles. Surfaces teem with stylized or organic forms such as spirals or waves. The human figure is also highly stylized. Pounamu carving is another major form; now artists use diamond-tipped instruments to carve the extremely hard jadelike stone. *Tā moko* is a variant of traditional carving as well: inked skin carving, or tattooing. These carvings historically indicated one's heritage or status.

A particularly high-profile Māori art form is the *haka,* now world famous thanks to our New Zealand All Blacks rugby team, as the players perform it before their opponents. The so-called "All Blacks haka" was actually composed by a Ngāti Toa Rangatira chief, Te Rauparaha. The opening words, "*ka mate, ka mate, ka ora ka ora*" ("I die, I die, I live, I live") refer to his imminent death at the hands of an enemy, searching for him as he hid in a kūmara (sweet

potato) pit. The search was in vain and Te Rauparaha lived to fight—and haka—another day. To haka is simply to dance. Ka mate is often wrongly called a war dance, but it's really more of a short free-form style.

There are many other movement-based art forms; at a cultural performance you might see *poi* dances (poi are balls on string swung in unison to music or rhythms). The *wero* (challenge), with its accompanying ritual choreography, is sometimes included in a *pōwhiri* (welcoming ceremony) for important guests.

Raranga (**weaving**) is a long-established craft that continues to flourish. The primary material is *harakeke* (flax); its fiber can be worked into *kete* (baskets), latticework wall panels, fine mats, ropes, string, nets, and even sandals and clothing. You might spot some harakeke sun hats and woven flowers in your browsings.

He aroha ki te tangata/Be sensitive

Māori are a colonized people, and many of us are unaware of our own tikanga. As a visitor, remember that Māori will more happily share what they know of their language and culture when they're approached without assumptions. Someone of Māori descent may not know their own tribal connections. We may not be able to tell you the "real" meaning of the greenstone pendant you've just bought. Rather than make the first move to *hongi,* the traditional greeting of pressing noses and foreheads, accept it if it is offered.

Another interesting point: not all of us are dark-skinned with dark eyes and black, curly hair. Some of us are fair-skinned with blue eyes and blonde hair. This is not only because of intermarriage, but because, as in so many countries, there are physical differences characteristic of certain regions.

It is safe to generalize, though, that Māori are extremely good at *manaakitanga* (hospitality). Looking after visitors, particularly *manuhiri tūārangi,* those who have come from far away, is a key part of our traditions.

Ko au te whenua/I am the land

Far back on one side of my *whakapapa* (genealogy), my roots stretch to England, Germany, and maybe even Holland (we're still working on that one). On the other side, too, my ancestry takes me offshore—to Hawaiiki, ancestral homeland in the Pacific. But the further back I trace my Māori whakapapa, the closer I get to the earth itself. On my Māori side, my grandmother is the earth under my feet. My grandfather is the sky above me. They are, literally, in my family tree. I am the land—as much as I am my Bavarian ancestors, as much as I am my mother and my father.

Tihei mauri ora, behold the breath of life.

—Hinemoana Baker

FLORA & FAUNA

New Zealand is a fascinating evolutionary case. Its islands are a chip off the one-time Gondwanaland supercontinent—a vast landmass that consisted of current-day South America, Africa, and Australia that started breaking up some 100 million years ago, well before the evolution of mammals. Since then, floating on its own some 1,920 km (1,200 mi) southeast of Australia, this cluster of islands might seem to have developed quietly on its own, away from the hungry, predatory jaws of the rest of the world.

But powerful forces of change have constantly worked on New Zealand. Plate tectonics created the rugged, 12,000-plus-foot mountains of the South Island. And the Pacific Rim's wild geothermal eruptions left their mark on the North Island. For eons volcanic activity has built mountainous cones and laid carpets of ash, making tremendously rich soil. The great, rumbling Mt. Ruapehu near Lake Taupo is a living reminder of this subterranean fury.

Animals on the islands were, at least until the arrival of humans, almost like living fossils. The only mammal was a tiny bat, and there were no predators until the Māori first came, around AD 700. Birdlife included the 12-foot flightless moa, which the Māori hunted to extinction. This happened relatively quickly, because the birds had never needed to develop evasive behavior to stay alive. The Māori brought dogs and rats, and Europeans brought deer, possums, goats, trout, and other fauna; some were used for their pelts, others for sport. In almost all cases, the alien fauna have done tremendous damage to the landscape. And, of course, the human presence has dramatically altered the land. Early Māori farming practices involved burning, which reduced a portion of the forests. When Europeans settled the country, they brought sheep, cattle, and the grasses that their livestock needed to eat. And they

cut down forests for, among other uses, ship masts. The kauri served this purpose better than any other wood in the world and paid for that virtue.

None of this makes the forests that cover New Zealand any less exotic, or any less fascinating. Some plants have adapted growth cycles in which the plant completely changes appearance—lancewood is an example—some of them two or three times until they reach maturity. If you have never been in a rain forest, the sheer density of vegetation in various subtropical areas will be dazzling. One-fifth of the country is set aside as parkland. In those wild woods, you will still find no predators, and native species are alive and well, in many cases making very dramatic comebacks.

Here is a short list of plants and animals that you might encounter in New Zealand.

The New Zealand forest has a sound that's different from any other—it's the welcoming, chiming song of the **bellbird,** together with that of the *tūī,* that makes it unique.

It's a lot easier to get into the grips of a **bush lawyer** plant than out of them. It is a thorny, viney thing that grows in dense forest, climbing in and out of whatever it chooses.

The odd plant clumps fastened to the sides of trees throughout forests are **epiphytes.** They grow on the trees and some are orchids—a marvelous sight in bloom.

The abundance of **ferns** may be what you most readily associate with the New Zealand bush. Two of the most magnificent are the *mamaku* and the *punga.* The former also goes by the English name black tree fern, and it's the one that grows as high as 60 feet and is found countrywide, with the exception of the East Coast of the South Island. The Māori used to cook and eat parts of the plant that are said to taste a bit like applesauce. The punga is shorter than the mamaku, reaching a height of 30 feet. Its English name, silver tree fern, comes from the color of the undersides of the fronds. Their silvery whiteness illuminates darker parts of the bush. The punga is the ferny emblem of New Zealand's international sports teams and Air New Zealand.

The **Hector's dolphin** is rare and confined to New Zealand waters. You might have the luck of seeing one near Kaikoura or off the Banks Peninsula. They have an unusual rounded dorsal fin, along with the distinction of being the world's smallest dolphin.

Endemic to New Zealand, the endangered *hoiho* or **yellow-eyed penguin** is the world's most rare penguin. There are approximately 1,500 breeding pairs but studies show that their numbers are dwindling. Hoiho can be seen along the southeastern coast of New Zealand and on Stewart Island.

The *horoeka* (also called lancewood) tree is one of the freakish New Zealand natives par excellence. In its youth, its long, serrated, almost woody leaves hardly look alive, hanging down from their scrawny trunk. Horoeka inch their way skyward like this for as many as 20 years before maturing, flowering profusely, and bearing black berries.

The towering *kahikatea* (ka-*hee*-ka-*tee*-ah) is the tallest tree in the country, reaching as high as 200 feet with its slender and elegant profile. A mature tree bears a tremendous amount of berries, which Māori climbers used to harvest by ascending 80 branchless feet and more to pluck.

It is a joy to watch the highly amusing **kaka.** These forest parrots are inquisitive, cheeky, and acrobatic. They are also beautiful, with olive feathers and a crimson underside. Kakas are most easily observed on Stewart Island where they are particularly prolific, roaming in noisy groups from balcony to balcony in the evening. The kaka has a hoarse shriek, but can also make waterlike glugging and burbling noises.

There are still **kauri** trees in Northland and the Coromandel Peninsula as much as 1,500 years old, with a girth of 30 feet and height upward of 150 feet. The lower trunks of the trees are branchless, and branches on an old tree begin some 50 feet above the ground. Lumberjacks in the 1800s spared some of these giants, and their presence is awesome. Like so many other native trees, kauri are slow growers—a mere 80-year-old will stand just 30 feet tall. Kauri were valued for their gum as well as their wood. The gum doesn't rot, so balls of gum of any age were usable to make varnish and paint. It is now illegal to cut down a kauri, and as a result the trees are making a solid comeback. Visitors can see impressive kauri trees in the Waitakere Ranges, just west of Auckland, but the oldest and largest examples are in the Waipoua Forest in Northland. The southernmost kauri trees are found just south of Katikati in the Bay of Plenty.

Much is said of the formidable South Island **kea** (*kee*-ah), a mountain parrot, which, because it has been accused of killing sheep, has in the last century barely escaped extinction. Its numbers are significant today, much to the dismay of campers and anyone who lives under a tin roof. Kea love to play, which means anything from ripping tents to shreds to clattering around on metal roofs at all hours to peeling out the rubber gaskets around car windows. They are smart birds, smart enough, perhaps, to delight in taking revenge on those who tried to wipe them out. Observe their behavior keenly; it may be the only way to maintain a sense of humor if harassed.

It takes effort and more than a fair share of luck to spot a **kiwi** in the wild. These nocturnal, bush-loving birds are scarce and shy, and their numbers had dwindled significantly with the felling of forests over the last 150 years. Predator eradication programs have helped them make a slight resurgence over the last few years. Along with the now-extinct giant moa and other species, the kiwi is one of the remarkable New Zealand natives that live (or lived) nowhere else on Earth. If you're keen on seeing one in the feather, plan a trip to Stewart Island and hire a guide to take you on a search, or have a look yourself at Mason Bay. Your best chance of sighting one on the North Island is to pitch a tent in the Waipoua forest campground.

The *mohua*, or **yellowhead**, is a small insect-eating bird found only in the forests of the South Island and Stewart Island. The bird is easily identifiable from the splash of bright yellow that covers its head and breast. The rest of the body is brown with varying tinges of yellow and olive. It is featured on the New Zealand $100 bill.

The **morepork** might be a good name for a ribs restaurant, but it is actually the common native owl, also known as the ruru.

The **manuka** is a small tree shrub found throughout the country in tough, impenetrable thickets. Early settlers made tea from the plant until something tastier came along. The tea tree's white or rosy blossoms attract bees in profusion, and they produce the popular, strong-tasting manuka honey found in stores just about everywhere.

The *nikau* **palm** is one of the country's most exotic-looking trees and grows about 30 feet high. The Māori used different parts of the leaves for food and for thatch in shelters.

Phormium tenax, also called **New Zealand flax**—even though it isn't a true flax—has been used in traditional and contemporary weaving. It favors damp areas and hillsides. Its thick, spiky, dark green leaves originate from a central saddle and

can grow to 6 feet. The telltale flower stalk can reach 15 feet and bears dark red flowers. A number of varieties are ornamental and are very popular in New Zealand gardens.

The **pohutukawa** (po-*hoo*-too-*ka*-wa) tree is a sight for its gnarly roots that like watery places and its red blossoms, which burst forth toward the end of December—hence its Kiwi name: New Zealand's Christmas tree.

Currently about 80 million in number, **possums,** an introduced species, are gobbling up New Zealand forests. Try as they may, New Zealanders are having a rough go getting rid of the tree dwellers. Their nickname, "squash 'ems," comes from seeing so many splayed out on roads throughout the country. ("Headlight delight possum pie" is featured on a menu in Pukekura and it's rather tasty.) Possum merino is a fine blend of possum fur and wool.

The *pukeko* (poo-*keh*-ko) is a bird that kicks around on farms and roadsides often enough that you're likely to see plenty of them. They're blue, with a red bill, and they stand about 15 inches tall.

You'll get to know the *rangiora* (rang-ee-*ohr*-ah) plant better if you remember it as "bushman's friend"—its soft, silvery underside is the forest's best tissue for your underside.

If you're in the country in November, you'll first see evidence of the **rewarewa** (*re*-wa-*re*-wa) tree in its fallen blossoms on the ground. They are tightly woven, magenta bottle-brush-like flowers, with touches of chartreuse and black, that are some of the most enchanting in the country.

The **rimu red pine** is a valuable source of timber. It spends its first stage in life as a delicate treelet, with pale green, weeping branches that look something like an upright moss. It then turns itself into a conical shape before finishing its growth as a soaring, 100-plus-foot wonder with a branchless trunk and a rounded head. Charcoal from rimu was used in traditional Māori tattooing.

Supplejack vines just hang about in the forest, so dense in places that they make passage next to impossible. You'll often find that their soft, edible tips have been nipped off by the teeth of wild goats (or peckish trampers). Some Stewart Islanders bend these branches into a conical shape and decorate the resulting "sculpture" as a Christmas tree. Believe it or not, this is a member of the lily family.

New Zealand's living dinosaur, the **tuatara,** is an ancient reptile found on protected islands such as Stephens Island in Marlborough Sounds. It feeds on insects, small mammals, and birds' eggs and has a vestigial third eye. They grow to about 2 feet and can live some 80 years in the wild. The combination of its nocturnal habits and its rarity means that the likelihood of seeing one in the wild is virtually nil. Your best bet is to see one in captivity at a zoo. Auckland Zoo has a particularly good tuatara display in its Kiwi House, and the Southland Museum in Invercargill features the country's only tuatarium.

Along with the bellbird, the **tūi** is the chanteuse extraordinaire that fills Aotearoa's woods with its magically clear melodies. It is also referred to as the parson bird for the little white "collar" at its throat. This bird is sometimes a mimic, and its repertoire includes groans, clicks, grunts and buzzes. At times it will seem to sing soundlessly—it is making notes too high for the human ear to register.

Weka (*weh*-kah) are funny birds. They can appear to be oblivious to what's going on around them as they walk about pecking at this or that. They are flightless rails, and they'll steal your food if you're camping, so hide it away. Weka are also attracted to small, shiny things, so keep a careful eye on your car keys if you're camping or picnicking! Generally speaking, though, they're pleasant to have around, particularly if you're looking for some entertainment.

Weta are large insects—some species are topped in size only by the African goliath beetle. If you chance upon one, it's likely to throw its spiny back legs up in the air as a defense, giving it a particularly ferocious look. However, weta are not as fearsome as they appear, and in the unlikely event that you do get nipped, it will result only in a slight stinging sensation. The largest species is found on Little Barrier Island near Auckland. You may well see specimens in forests such as the Waitakere Ranges near Auckland, but if you like your fierce-looking insects safely behind glass, they can be viewed at the Arataki Visitors Centre, west of Auckland, or the Karori Wildlife Sanctuary in Wellington.

You'll have no trouble figuring out that the *kereru,* or wood pigeon, is indeed a pigeon, but your jaw will drop at the size—they look like they've been inflated like balloons. They're beautiful birds but behave a bit daftly, which is not surprising considering their tiny head.

—Stephen Wolf, Barbara Blechman, and Stu Freeman

CHRONOLOGY

ca. AD 750 The first Polynesians arrive, settling mainly in the South Island, where they find the moa, a flightless bird and an important food source, in abundance.

950 Kupe, the Polynesian voyager, names the country Aotearoa, "land of the long white cloud." He returns to his native Hawaiki, believed to be present-day French Polynesia.

1300s A population explosion in Hawaiki triggers a wave of immigrants.

1642 Abel Tasman of the Dutch East India Company becomes the first European to sight the land—he names his discovery Nieuw Zeeland. But after several of his crew are killed by Māori, he sails away without landing.

1769 Captain James Cook becomes the first European to set foot on New Zealand. He claims it in the name of the British crown.

1790 Sealers, whalers, and timber cutters arrive, plundering the natural wealth and introducing the Māori to the musket, liquor, and influenza.

1814 The Reverend Samuel Marsden establishes the first mission station. Eleven years pass before the first convert is made.

1832 James Busby is appointed British Resident, charged with protecting the Māori people and fostering British trade.

1840 Captain William Hobson, representing the crown, and Māori chiefs sign the Treaty of Waitangi. In return for the peaceful possession of their land and the rights and privileges of British citizens, the chiefs recognize British sovereignty.

1840–41 The New Zealand Company, an association of British entrepreneurs, establishes settlements at Wanganui, New Plymouth, Nelson, and Wellington.

1852 The British Parliament passes the New Zealand Constitution Act, establishing limited self-government. The country's first gold strike occurs in Coromandel town in the Coromandel Peninsula.

1860–72 Māori grievances over loss of land trigger the Land Wars in the North Island. The Māori win some notable victories, but lack of unity ensures their ultimate defeat. Vast tracts of ancestral land are confiscated from rebel tribes.

1861 Gold is discovered in the river valleys of central Otago, west of Dunedin.

1882 The first refrigerated cargo is dispatched to England, giving the country a new source of prosperity—sheep. A century later, there will be 20 sheep for every New Zealander.

1893 Under the Liberal government, New Zealand becomes the first country to give women the vote.

1914 New Zealand enters World War I.

1931 The Hawke's Bay earthquake kills 258 and levels the city of Napier.

1939 New Zealand enters World War II.

1950 New Zealand troops sail for Korea.

1965 Despite public disquiet, troops are sent to Vietnam.

1973 Britain joins the European Economic Community, and New Zealand's loss of this traditional export market is reflected in a crippling balance-of-payments deficit two years later.

1981 Violent antigovernment demonstrations erupt during a tour by a South African rugby team.

1984 David Lange's Labour Government wins a landslide majority in the general election, partly because of its pledge to ban nuclear-armed vessels from New Zealand waters.

1985 The Greenpeace ship *Rainbow Warrior* is sunk by a mine in Auckland Harbour, and a crewman is killed. Two of the French secret-service agents responsible are arrested, jailed, transferred to French custody—then soon released.

Sir Paul Reeves is sworn in as the first Māori governor-general.

Relations with the United States sour when the government bans visits by ships carrying nuclear weapons. The U.S. government responds by ejecting New Zealand from the ANZUS (Australia/New Zealand/United States) alliance.

1986 Goods and Services Tax is introduced at 10% (later to be raised to 12.5%). Tourists are not exempt from the tax, although many exports and foreign exchange earners are.

1989 David Lange resigns as prime minister.

1990 The National Party replaces the Labour Party in government.

A mentally disturbed man named David Gray goes on a shooting rampage killing 13 citizens of a small town in what is known as the Aramoana Massacre.

1993 The country votes for a major constitutional change, replacing the "first past the post" electoral system inherited from Britain with a "mixed-member proportional" (MMP) system. The election sees the National Party clinging to power within a coalition.

1995 New Zealand's *Black Magic* wins the America's Cup yachting regatta. The country goes into party mode over the win, which signals both a sporting triumph and a coming-of-age technologically.

Mt. Ruapehu in the North Island's Tongariro National Park bubbles and sputters, attracting interested onlookers from around the world.

New Zealanders' abhorrence of all things nuclear comes to the fore again with major floating protests against France's resumed nuclear testing in the South Pacific.

1996   Noisy Ruapehu spews debris into the air, covering nearby towns with a few inches of ash.

New Zealand elects its first MMP government, having voted for constitutional change three years earlier. New Zealand First holds the balance of power and goes into government with the National Party.

1997   New Zealand starts to feel the effect of weakening Asian currencies, particularly as the number of Korean and Japanese tourists falls.

Jenny Shipley becomes the country's first woman PM.

1998   The government introduces a controversial "work for the dole" scheme, in which people on unemployment are required to work or train 20 hours a week or risk having their income slashed.

As the Asian economic crisis continues to bite, industrial strikes on Australia's waterfront also affect New Zealand's economy. The country's economic fundamentals remain strong, but these outside influences cause the N.Z. dollar to lose value against U.S. currency.

1999   The New Zealand cricketers record their first test-win over England at Lords, regarded as the spiritual home of the game. New Zealand goes on to win the series.

New Zealand contributes personnel and machinery to a United Nations peacekeeping force in Indonesia.

A Labour-Alliance coalition wins the general election, but a close vote means it still needs the support of the Green Party in matters of national importance. Helen Clark becomes New Zealand's second successive female prime minister.

2000   New Zealand successfully defends the America's Cup, becoming the first country outside the United States to do so.

The lone, 125-year-old pine at the top of Auckland's One Tree Hill, one of the city's defining features, is removed.

2001   National carrier Air New Zealand runs into financial troubles and is bailed out by an $885 million taxpayer-financed rescue package.

Sir Peter Blake, a yachting champion who led New Zealand to win and retain the America's Cup, is murdered by pirates while on a conservation expedition in the Amazon.

2002   A simmering dispute over sponsorship and control of corporate facilities culminates with the International Rugby Board's dropping New Zealand as a subhost of the 2003 Rugby World Cup. Australia becomes the event's sole host, and the rugby-mad New Zealand public is left fuming.

Internal wrangling sees the minor government partner, the Alliance, split in half, though both sides continue to support Labour. After an early election, Labour has to rely on the support of several minor parties rather than a single coalition partner.

2003 Debate flares up as Māori request a legal inquiry into their preco-
lonial customary ownership of the seabed and shore. Thousands of
protesters march on Parliament in support of Māori claims.

2004 *The Return of the King,* the final film in Peter Jackson's *Lord of
the Rings* trilogy, wins 11 Academy Awards. Keisha Castle-Hughes
becomes the youngest nominee in the Academy Awards' Best Actress
category for her work in *Whale Rider.*

Don Brash, leader of the National Party, ignites a furor with a speech
at Orewa. He argues that the Crown should own the foreshore and
the seabed, asserts that all claims based on the Treaty of Waitangi
should be settled by 2010, and attacks the welfare system.

The Seabed and Foreshore Act is passed, ensuring that as of January
2005 any territory below the high-tide mark belongs to the Crown.

Labour MP Tariana Turia resigns after opposing the Labour Party's
Seabed and Foreshore Act, going on to establish the Māori Party.

The Māori Television Service takes to the airwaves.

2005 Helen Clark's Labour Party wins a third term in Parliament, this time
in coalition with Jim Anderton's Progressive Party, with support from
Winston Peters's New Zealand First and Peter Dunne's United Future.

David Lange, 1984–89 Labour leader of New Zealand, dies of
complications associated with renal failure and blood disease on
August 13, 2005. He was perhaps best known for implementing New
Zealand's nuclear-free legislation.

The Lions, a British and Irish rugby team, tour New Zealand to play
against regional rugby teams as well as long-standing rivals the All
Blacks and the Māori All Blacks. The Lions are outstandingly beaten
by both the All Blacks and the Māori All Blacks.

2006 A flotilla of icebergs is seen off the New Zealand coast for the first
time since 1931.

National Party leader Don Brash resigns.

2007 New Zealand Prime Minister Helen Clarke announces that the
country intends to produce 90% of its electricity from renewable
resources by the year 2025. Further goals, such as reducing vehicle
emissions by half by 2040 and increasing forested areas to 617, 000
acres by 2020, are aimed at eventually making New Zealand a
carbon neutral country.

2008 Parliament bans party pills. The popular drug, which is illegal in the
United States, is known as "herbal e" and is considered by many to
be dangerous, especially when mixed with alcohol. Some politicians
criticize the ban, saying regulation is preferable to prohibition.

KIWI & MĀORI GLOSSARY

A Kiwi Glossary

Talking Kiwi is hardly a daunting prospect for people traveling abroad with the English language under their belt. You'll seldom be at a complete loss, and if a phrase does confuse you, the locals will delight in explaining its meaning. The word *kiwi* itself can be a source of confusion—it can mean the brown flightless bird that lives in New Zealand forests, the people of New Zealand, a furry fruit that is one of the country's best-known exports, a quick lottery ticket, or even a rugby league team. Despite being half a world away, New Zealanders are in many ways still protective of the Queen's English and have resisted the Americanization of the language to a greater extent than their Australian cousins. In newspapers and magazines you will read *colour* instead of *color, organise* instead of organize, and *programme* instead of *program*. New Zealanders are prone to shorten names and to give nicknames, but this isn't as prevalent as in Australia. Kiwis have developed a few quirky terms of their own. Here are a few translations that will help:

Across the Ditch: Over the Tasman Sea in Australia

Aubergine: Eggplant

Aussie: An Australian

Bach: Vacation house (North Island) (pronounced *batch*)

Battle on: Try hard with limited success

Bludger: Someone who lives off other people's effort

Bush: The outdoors, wilderness

Capsicum: Bell pepper

Carpark: Parking lot

Chilly bin: A cooler

Chocka (or chocka block): Full

Chunder: Vomit

Courgette: Zucchini

Crib: Vacation house (South Island)

Crook: Sick

Cuppa: Cup of tea or coffee

Dag: Amusing person or happening

Dairy: Convenience or corner store

Devonshire tea: Cream tea with scones (served morning and afternoon)

En suite: Bathroom attached to your hotel room

Entree: Appetizer (main course, or U.S. "entrée" is Mains)

Fair go: Fair chance

Fanny: Woman's privates (considered obscene)

Feed: Meal

Flat white: Coffee with milk (equivalent to a café au lait)

Footie: Rugby football

Footpath: Sidewalk

Give a wide berth: Leave alone

Greenie: Conservationist

Gumboots: Rubber boots, Wellies

Gutted: Very upset

Hard case: Unsentimental, tough, often amusing character

Home and hosed: Successful

Jandal: Open-topped footwear

Jersey: Sweater

Lemon: No good

Lemonade: Lemon-flavored soda

Lollies: Candy

Loo: Toilet (*bathroom* is only for bathing)

Mainlander: Resident of the South Island

Metal road: Gravel road

Motorway: Freeway or highway

Mozzie: Mosquito

Mug: Good-hearted to the point of being foolish

Nappie: Diaper

Pavlova: A meringue cake

Piss-crook: Hung over

Pissed: Drunk

Pom or pommie: Native of England

Pudding: Dessert

Rubber: Eraser (also condom)

Sealed road: Paved road

Serviette: Napkin

Shag: Have sex with

Shout: Buy a round of drinks

Sink a few: Drink some beer

Skite: Boast

Smoko: Tea or coffee break

Sticking plaster: Adhesive bandage

Stuffed up: Made a mistake

Ta: Thanks

Take-away: Food to go, takeout

Take the piss: Ridicule (Kiwis have tons of slang words involving piss)

Tall poppy: One who excels and stands out in doing so (often used to describe someone disparagingly, rather than in admiration)

Tea: Dinner (also the beverage)

Tidy: Attractive, fit (describing a woman)

Togs: Swimsuit

Torch: Flashlight

Track: Hiking trail

Tramping: Hiking

Trollied: Drunk

Up with the play: Knows what is going on

Ute: Pickup truck

Whinger: Whiner or moaner

A Māori Glossary

The use of the *Te Reo Māori* (Māori language) is experiencing a resurgence in contemporary New Zealand, with nearly 90% of Māori children enrolled in some form of Māori language early-childhood education. This is a heartening outcome for a language that has stood for decades tenuously at the brink of extinction.

Though the language was never officially legislated against, the great-grandparents of today's generation were beaten at school for speaking Māori. Not until the 1980s was government funding made available for Māori language education.

The realms of Māori language use are slowly moving out of the *marae* (gathering place) and into schools, parliament, and broadcasting. The advent of Māori TV, the recently established Māori television channel, has meant that a range of programs, from news, talk shows, and documentaries to soap operas and kids' shows, is now produced and broadcast in the Māori language. In terms of daily use, however, unless you're involved in a specifically Māori activity or event, you won't hear it much (though expressions such as "kia ora" have made their way into general Kiwi speech).

Still, knowing how to pronounce Māori words can be important when trying to say place-names in New Zealand. Even if you have a natural facility for picking up languages, you'll find many Māori words to be quite baffling. The West Coast town of Punakaiki (pronounced poon-ah-*kye*-kee) is relatively straightforward, but when you get to places such as Whangamata, the going gets tricky—the opening *wh* is pronounced like an *f,* and the accent is placed on the last syllable: "fahng-ah-ma-*ta.*" Sometimes it is the mere length of words that makes them difficult, as in the case of Waitakaruru (why-ta-ka-ru-ru) or Whakarewarewa (fa-ka-*re*-wa-*re*-wa). You'll notice that the ends of both of these have repeats—of "ru" and "rewa," which is something to look out for to make longer words more manageable. Town names like Waikanea (*why*-can-eye) you'll just have to repeat to yourself a few times before saying them without pause.

The Māori *r* is rolled so that it sounds a little like a *d*. Thus the Northland town of Whangarei is pronounced "fang-ah-day," and the word *Māori* is pronounced "mah-*aw*-dee," or sometimes "mo-dee," with the *o* sounding like it does in the word *mold,* and a rolled *r*. A macron indicates a lengthened vowel. In general, *a* is pronounced *ah* as in "car"; *e* is said as the *ea* in "weather." *O* is pronounced like "awe," rather than *oh,* and *u* sounds like the *u* of "June." *Ng,* meanwhile, has a soft, blunted sound, as the *ng* in "singing." All of this is a little too complicated for those who still choose not to bother with Māori pronunciations. So in some places, if you say you've just driven over from "fahng-ah-ma-*ta*," the reply might be: "You mean 'wang-ah-*ma*-tuh.'" You can pronounce these words either way, but more and more people these days are pronouncing Māori words correctly.

Āe: Yes

Ahau: I, me

Aotearoa: Land of the long white cloud (New Zealand)

Atua: Spirit, god

Awa: River

Awhi: Help

Haere atu: Go away, farewell, depart

Haere mai: Welcome, come here

Haere rā: Farewell, good-bye

Haka: Fierce rhythmical dance made internationally famous by the country's rugby team, the All Blacks, and performed before each game

Hākari: Feast, gift

Hāngi: Earth oven, food from an earth oven

Hapū: Subtribe

Harakeke: Flax leaf (also used to refer to woven flax items)

Heitiki: Greenstone pendant

Hongi: Press noses in greeting

Hui: Gathering

Ika: Fish

Iwi: People, tribe

Kāhore: No

Kai: Food, eat, dine

Kai moana: Seafood

Karakia: Ritual chant, prayer, religious service

Kaumātua: Elder

Kete: Flax bag

Kino: Bad

Koha: Customary gift, donation

Kōhanga reo: Māori preschool

Kōtiro: Girl

Kūmara: Sweet potato

Kura kaupapa: Total immersion Māori-language school

Mana: Influence, prestige, power

Manu: Bird

Manuhiri: Guest, visitor

Māoritanga: Māori culture, perspective

Marae: Traditional gathering place

Maunga: Mountain

Mauri: Life principle, source of vitality and mana

Mihi: To greet, congratulate

Moana: Sea, lake

Moko: Tattoo

Motu: Island

Pā: Fortress

Pai: Good

Pākehā: Non-Māori, European, Caucasian

Poi: Light ball attached to string

Rangatira: Chief, person of rank

Reo: Language

Roto: Lake

Taiaha: Long, two-handed weapon, with blade at one end and point at the other

Tama: Boy

Tāne: Man

Tangata whenua: People of the land, local people

Taniwha: Spirit-monsters living in the sea and inland waters

Taonga: Treasure

Tapu: Sacred, under religious restriction, taboo

Tauiwi: Foreigner

Tino rangatiratanga: Chief's authority, self-determination

Toa: Warrior

Tohunga: Priest, expert

Tupuna: Ancestor

Wahine: Woman

Wai: Water, liquid

Waiata: Sing, song

Wairua: Soul, spirit

Waka: Canoe

Whai kōrero: Speech

Whakapapa: Genealogy, cultural identity

Whānau: Family

Whare: House

Whenua: Land, country

Greetings & Expressions

E noho ra: Good-bye (from the person leaving to the person staying)

Kia ora: Hello, thank you

Tēnā koe (korua) (koutou): Hello to one person (to two people) (to three or more people)

Haere mai: Welcome

Haere rā: Good-bye (from the person staying to the one leaving)

Ka pai: Good, excellent

Kei te pehea koe: How are you? (to one person)

Māori Place-Names

Kirikiriroa: Hamilton

Ōtautahi: Christchurch

Ōtepoti: Dunedin

Rakiura: Stewart Island

Tāmaki-makau-rau: Auckland

Te Ika-A-Māui: North Island

Te Waipounamu–Te-Waka-A-Aoraki: South Island

Whanganui-a-tara: Wellington

BOOKS & MOVIES

Books

Because of the limited availability of many first-rate books on New Zealand outside the country, there is only so much that you'll be able to read before you go. So leave room in your suitcase for pick-up reading once you arrive, and bring something home to make your trip linger longer. One caveat: books in New Zealand tend to be expensive. That's one reason to do some secondhand shopping; another is the stores' usually knowledgeable staff, who can make recommendations.

Fiction. New Zealand's best-known short-story writer is Katherine Mansfield (1888–1923), whose early stories were set in and around the city of Wellington, her birthplace. *The Best of Katherine Mansfield* is a fine compilation of stories from five collections. Reading her journals will give you a sense of her passionate romantic side, and as much as she disliked the small-minded provincial qualities of New Zealand, she loved the country deeply.

One of New Zealand's most distinguished writers was Janet Frame (1924–2004). Her works are numerous, from novels such as her successful *The Carpathians* to a three-part autobiography, which is a lyrical evocation of growing up in small-town New Zealand in the 1920s and 1930s and of the gradual awakening of a writer of great courage. Kiwi filmmaker Jane Campion adapted part of it for the screenplay of *An Angel at My Table*. *The Goose Bath*, a collection of Frame's poetry, was published posthumously in 2006. Maurice Gee is another acclaimed novelist. His *Plumb* won the James Tait Prize for the best novel in Britain when it was published. *Plumb* reaches back to the early 20th century for its story of a renegade parson and his battle with old-world moral pieties. One particularly compelling scene is set in a mining town, where Plumb happens to be the man to hear the last testament of a notorious murderer. A more recent volume is *Ellie and the Shadow Man*. In *My Father's Den*, a suspenseful small-town drama that Gee wrote in 1972, was made into a movie in 2004.

Two of the finest and most exciting writers at work in the country today are Patricia Grace and Witi Ihimaera, both Māori. Grace's stories are beautifully and fluidly related, very much from inside her characters. Look for *The Dream Sleepers and Other Stories* and her novel *Mutuwhenua*. Her newest book, *Tu,* is a historical novel that recounts the life of a young boy who runs away to join the Māori Battalion and fight in World War II. Ihimaera (ee-hee-may-ra) also uses very clear prose and Māori experience. His early novel *Tangi* opens with the death of a father and moves through the 22-year-old son's experience of loss and innocence to his acceptance of his role as a man. Māori elements of the story are fascinating both culturally and emotionally. Also look for his *Bulibasha* and *Nights in the Garden of Spain*.

Keri Hulme's internationally celebrated *The Bone People* won the Booker McConnell Prize in 1985. Set on the isolated West Coast of the South Island, this challenging, vital novel weaves Polynesian myth with Christian symbolism and the powerful sense of place that characterizes modern Māori writing. More recently, Alan Duff's *Once Were Warriors* is a frank, uncompromising, and ultimately transcendent look at urban Māori society. Both the novel and the film were real sensations in New Zealand. The sequel, *One Night Out Stealing,* as well as *What Becomes of the Broken Hearted* and *Both Sides of the Moon,* has also been hugely successful. In a move to nonfiction, Duff addresses Māori issues in *Maori: The Crisis and the Challenge*.

Lloyd Jones, a hot current novelist, focuses on New Zealand while also looking beyond the country's borders. In *The Book of Fame* (2001), for instance, he fictionalizes the true story of New Zealand's All Blacks rugby team, who set out by steamer in 1905 to tour Great Britain. In *Here at the End of the World We Learn to Dance,* he brings tango music to the rural West Coast. His latest novel, *Mister Pip,* is a clever, modern-day nod to Charles Dickens's *Great Expectations.*

Margaret Mahy is a prolific children's-book writer; her books for kids under 10 include *Bubble Trouble* and *Down the Dragon's Tongue.* Lynley Dodd has delighted children for years with the beloved *Hairy Maclary from Donaldson's Dairy* and a variety of his scruffy pals. Joy Cowley's *Bow Down Shadrach* and *Mrs. Wishy-Washy* are favorites with Kiwi youth as well.

On a lighter note, cartoonist Murray Ball has created an amusing look at Kiwi country life with his *Footrot Flats* series.

History & Observations. Michael King's *Penguin History of New Zealand* (2003) became a runaway best seller in New Zealand. It's hard to find in the United States, but if you're interested in this topic, it's well worth buying once you get to New Zealand.

If you're interested in issues around the Treaty of Waitangi, *Healing Our History* (2001) by Robert Consedine focuses on New Zealand *Pākehā* identity, racism within New Zealand, and its intersection with the Treaty of Waitangi. Written from (and for) a non-Māori perspective, it aims to provide a better understanding of New Zealand's colonial history and the effect it's had on the Māori.

The *Oxford Illustrated History of New Zealand,* edited by Keith Sinclair, provides a comprehensive and highly readable account of the country's social, political, cultural, and economic evolution from the earliest Māori settlements until 1989. James Belich's *Making Peoples* looks at New Zealand history from

a 1990s perspective, with more emphasis on the Māori view than some earlier publications. His *Paradise Reforged: A History of the New Zealanders from the Beginning of the Twentieth Century* (2002) also pays particular attention to the Māori population. The *Colonial New Zealand Wars,* by Tim Ryan and Bill Parham, is a vivid history of the Māori-British battles. Lavishly illustrated with photographs of colonial infantry and drawings of Māori hill forts, flags, and weapons, the book makes far more compelling reading than the dry military history suggested by the title. Another highly readable military-historical book is James Belich's *The New Zealand Wars.* J. C. Beaglehole's *The Discovery of New Zealand* is an authoritative and scholarly analysis of the voyages of discovery, from the first Polynesians to the Europeans of the late 18th century. *A Traveller's History of New Zealand,* by John Chambers, is a suitcase-friendly reference.

As the title suggests, *New Zealand's Top 100 History-Makers* profiles 100 New Zealand icons, from politicians and artists to explorers and inventors. Author Joseph Romanos stretches back into the far reaches of New Zealand history before leading up to the present day, covering people made of the stuff from which local legends are made.

The terrific *Slipping Into Paradise,* by Jeffrey Moussaieff Masson (2004), is both memoir and commentary on the Kiwi culture. It includes his personal favorite-trip itinerary and a fun glossary of Kiwi words and expressions.

Poetry. *100 New Zealand Poems by 100 New Zealand Poets,* edited by New Zealand's current poet laureate, Bill Manhire, ranges from the country's earliest poems to the new poets of the 1990s. Greg O'Brien and Jenny Bornholdt's *My Heart Goes Swimming* is a charming selection of New Zealand love poems. A more wide-ranging and weighty collection is *An Anthology of New Zealand Poetry* *in English,* edited by Mark Williams, Greg O'Brien, and Jenny Bornholdt. Hone Tuwhare (too-fah-dee) is perhaps New Zealand's most distinguished Māori poet. With a background in trade-union organizations, Tuwhare's poetry highlights an ongoing commitment to working-class and Māori issues, combined with his lyrical love of the land. Born in 1922, Tuwhare is still writing. Look out for *Oooooo!!!,* a collection of new poems and previously unpublished work.

Specialized Topics. *Wine Atlas of New Zealand,* by Michael Cooper, is the first such tome devoted to New Zealand. It discusses all the key wine regions, with illustrations, tasting notes, and maps. *The Wines and Vineyards of New Zealand,* also by Cooper, is an exhaustive evaluation in words and pictures of every vineyard in the country. *A Field Guide to Auckland* is a wonderful introduction to the natural and historic attractions of the Auckland region. It includes an overview of natural and human history and details of more than 140 interesting places to visit within easy distance of the city. Hobbitheads and Frodofreaks will love the *Lord of the Rings Location Guidebook* by Ian Brodie. Kirk Hargreaves put together a marvelous collection of anecdotes of New Zealand fishermen in *On the Next Tide.* If you're interested in off-roading, *Classic New Zealand Mountain Bike Rides,* by Paul, Simon, and Jonathan Kennett, provides route information for more than 400 rides, ranging from as far north as Cape Reinga all the way to the deep south. The Kennett brothers organize numerous mountain-biking events throughout the year, and manage the popular New Zealand Mountain Bike Web site, ⊕ *www.mtbnz.org.nz.*

Published just days before his death, *David Lange: My Life,* is a memoir that chronicles the life of Lange, who became the country's youngest prime minister at age 41. His Labour government was responsible for groundbreaking legislation that established the world's first nuclear-free state, as well as for heralding many social and human rights reforms such as the New Zealand homosexual law reform and the bill of rights legislation. To learn more about the Māori New Year, read *Matariki* by Libby Hakaraia.

Art Books. Greg O'Brien's *Hotere: Out the Black Window* covers the work of one of the country's most respected artists. *The Art of Robyn Kahukiwa* presents the art of another well-known and loved artist. Kahukiwa explores sociocultural issues particular to Māori in New Zealand, intersecting Māori culture and mythology with colonialism through her often vibrant, always powerful works. For a broad sampling of New Zealand art, *Icons Ngā Taonga: From the Collections of the Museum of New Zealand Te Papa Tongarewa* is a glossy showcase of photographs of almost 400 *taonga* (treasures) from Te Papa Tongarewa, New Zealand's national museum. The art in this book covers Māori painting, carving, sculpture, and other cultural artifacts. Accompanying text is written in Māori and English.

Movies

New Zealand director Peter Jackson dazzled moviegoers with the imagery and creativity of his home country with the *The Lord of the Rings* film trilogy. Each movie was a knockout, winning Academy Awards and a huge following. The final film, *The Return of the King,* capped the accomplishment by sweeping the 2003 Academy Awards with 11 Oscars. Wellington-based Weta Workshop, which designed and achieved many of the films' special effects, won several Academy Awards for its phenomenal work. But some of the strongest visuals in the films came from the scenery. By shooting in New Zealand national parks and mountain ranges, Jackson introduced thousands of viewers to the stunning Kiwi landscape.

In 2006, Peter Jackson wrapped up another blockbuster, a $207 million remake of *King Kong*. Three hours long (as opposed to the 100-minute 1933 original), *Kong* was mostly shot in and around Wellington. Thanks once again to the Weta team, the movie is packed with the kind of special effects Jackson fans have grown accustomed to. The other major 2005 movie that was largely filmed in New Zealand (and worked on by the Weta Workshop) was *The Chronicles of Narnia: The Lion, the Witch & the Wardrobe* by New Zealand director Andrew Adamson (director of the *Shrek* movies).

But New Zealand films haven't always needed the Weta Workshop for success. *Whale Rider* (2002), a decidedly un-high-tech, grassroots film, also did tremendously well. Shot in rural eastern North Island and based on a novel by Witi Ihimaera, it's about a young Māori girl struggling to find a place in her family and society.

Until the past few years, New Zealand's film industry has had a relatively small output, but the quality of its films has been consistently high. Jane Campion's *The Piano* (1993) is a prime example, as are her earlier *An Angel at My Table* (1990) and *Sweetie* (1988), which was made in Australia. Roger Donaldson's 1977 thriller *Sleeping Dogs* was the first New Zealand film released in the United States, followed by the equally worthy *Smash Palace* (1982). The tough, urban portrayal of *Once Were Warriors* (1995) is also made it across the Pacific. Its portrait of urban Māori life makes New Zealand look a little too much like down-and-out Los Angeles. *Scarfies,* a black comedy about Otago University students, received positive feedback at the 2000 Sundance Film Festival, after success in local cinemas. Christine Jeffs's haunting depiction of troubled family dynamics, *Rain* (2001), was filmed on the North Island coast. Gwyneth Paltrow starred as the late poet Sylvia Path in *Sylvia* (2003), which was filmed in and around Dunedin.

Sir Anthony Hopkins' portrayal of Burt Munro put Invercargill on the map in *The World's Fastest Indian* (2005). Scenes from the story of the record-breaking motorcyclist were filmed on Oreti Beach and in downtown Invercargill, and Invercargill Mayor Tim Shadbolt had a cameo role in the film. *River Queen* (2005) stars Samantha Morton and Kiefer Sutherland. This drama was directed by New Zealander Vincent Ward and filmed in Whanganui. *Out of the Blue* (2006) explores a dark episode in recent Kiwi history, the Aramoana Massacre. Fans of campy horror flicks might find *Black Sheep* (2007) amusing (the trailer warns "Prepare for the violence of the lambs," how baaad can it be?)

Peter Jackson was having an effect on the industry long before *The Lord of the Rings*. His first foray into film was the splatter comedy *Bad Taste* (1987), followed by the intense murder drama *Heavenly Creatures* (1994), which introduced Kate Winslet to a worldwide audience. *The Frighteners* (1996), another dip into the horror pool, starred Michael J. Fox.

Hardly high culture, but still a major success for New Zealand's film and television industry, was the *Hercules* television series starring Kevin Sorbo. The show was axed in the United States in 1999, but its spin-off series, *Xena: Warrior Princess,* survived until 2001. Both series were filmed in West Auckland, doing its best to look like ancient Greece.

Travel Smart
New Zealand

WORD OF MOUTH

"The weather in NZ is unpredictable year round.
Personally, I prefer the off season and have visited
the SI in April, May, August and September—and
I'd definitely visit during those months again . . . plan
to dress in layers, pack a fleece and waterproof
jacket and go have yourself a grand old time."
—Melnq8

GETTING HERE & AROUND

▌ BY AIR

The least expensive airfares to New Zealand are priced for round-trip travel and must usually be purchased in advance. Airlines generally allow you to change your return date for a fee; most low-fare tickets, however, are nonrefundable. To expedite an airline fare search on the Web, check travel search engines with meta-search technology, such as ⊕*www.mobissimo.com*. These search across a broad supplier base so you can compare rates offered by travel agents, consolidators, and airlines in one fell swoop.

Although budget air travel within New Zealand is still expensive compared with the cost of bus or train travel, the one-way fare system does make it easy to get around, especially if you don't want to spend all your time on the road. These days, booking your domestic flights in conjunction with your international flight won't save you any money, but it allows you to travel with the international luggage allowance (2 x 23 kg bags when flying with Air New Zealand, 2 x 32 kg bags when flying with Qantas), significantly higher than domestic allowances (2 x 20 kg bags). Some airlines give great deals if you add stopovers to your flight itinerary. You'll need to stop in at a Pacific destination like Tahiti or Fiji for a limited time before heading to New Zealand. Check with the airline and see what they're offering; make sure that New Zealand is included in Pacific deals since sometimes it's the one exception.

If you hold an international student identification card, you'll save even more.

From New York to Auckland (via Los Angeles) flights take about 19 hours; from Chicago, about 17 hours; from Los Angeles to Auckland (nonstop), about 12 hours. From the United States and Canada, you will have to connect to a New Zealand–bound flight in L.A. or San Francisco.

When taking your return flight from New Zealand, you will need to pay a departure tax. This tax is already factored into your airfare on your way to New Zealand, but must be paid separately when leaving. It's NZ$25 and you pay it between checking in and going through the immigration checkpoint.

For domestic flights within New Zealand, check in at least a half hour before departure.

It is not required that you reconfirm outbound flights from or within New Zealand.

Long flights put you at a higher risk of deep vein thrombosis (DVT), otherwise known as "economy class syndrome." When you stay motionless for an extended period of time, blood can pool in your legs and clot; these clots can later lodge in a vital organ and cause major medical complications. So it's extremely important to flex your feet and walk around the cabin regularly to keep your blood flowing.

All New Zealand domestic flights and flights between New Zealand and Australia are no-smoking. Air New Zealand has banned smoking on all of its flights worldwide.

Airlines & Airports Airline and Airport Links.com (⊕www.airlineandairportlinks.com) has links to many of the world's airlines and airports.

Airline Security Issues Transportation Security Administration (⊕www.tsa.gov) has answers for almost every question that might come up.

AIRPORTS

The major airport is Auckland International Airport (AKL). It is usually a bit cheaper to fly into and out of this airport, but the supplemental fees for flights to Wellington (WLG) or Christchurch (CHC) are reasonable. New Zealand's airports are relatively compact and easy to negotiate. But if you're in Auckland's airport, **don't wait to hear your boarding announcement,** because it has adopted "the quiet airport" concept. There are usually no flight announcements made over a loudspeaker; instead, information on flight arrivals and departures appears on display boards and TV monitors.

A less quiet feature of Auckland's airport is its children's play areas, including a playground on the top floor of the terminal. Complimentary showers are also available to all passengers on the "Arrivals" side of the international terminal. Towels and toiletries can be rented at the nearby florist.

New Zealand has a dense network of domestic air routes, so hopping from one area to another is fairly easy, if not inexpensive. The regional airlines that service the smaller airports such as Picton and Kaikoura often partner with Air New Zealand or Qantas, so you can make these flight arrangements when booking your international flight. There are also numerous charter companies with planes carrying a dozen passengers or less. *For details on local services, see this guide's destination chapters.*

Airport Information **Auckland International Airport** (☎09/275–0789 ⊕www. auckland-airport.co.nz). **Christchurch International Airport** (☎03/358–5029 ⊕www. christchurch-airport.co.nz). **Wellington International Airport** (☎04/385–5100 ⊕www. wlg-airport.co.nz).

FLIGHTS
Air New Zealand flies two to three times a day from Los Angeles to Auckland and is the only carrier that extends a daily nonstop flight from San Francisco to Auckland. Qantas flies nonstop from Los Angeles to New Zealand. United and Air Canada connect from points in North America with flights of their own out of Los Angeles.

Within New Zealand, Air New Zealand, Pacific Blue, and Qantas compete on intercity trunk routes. Air New Zealand serves a wide network of provincial and tourist centers. *For more information about regional travel, see the Essentials sections within regional chapters.*

Pacific Blue provides direct flights between New Zealand, Australia, Vanuatu, the Cook Islands, and Samoa. Freedom Airlines operates low-cost flights between New Zealand and Australia, including direct flights from Dunedin.

Airline Contacts **Air Canada** (☎888/247–2262 in U.S. and Canada, 09/969–7470 in New Zealand, 0508/747–767 toll-free in New Zealand ⊕www.aircanada.ca). **Air New Zealand** (☎310/615–1111, 800/262–1234 in U.S., 800/663–5494 in Canada, 0800/028–4149 toll-free in U.K., 0800/737–000 toll-free in New Zealand ⊕www.airnewzealand.co.nz). **British Airways** (☎800/247–9297 in U.S., 0870/850–9850 in U.K., 09/966–9777 in New Zealand ⊕www.britishairways.com). **Cathay Pacific** (☎020/8834–8888 in U.K., 0800/800–454 toll-free in New Zealand ⊕www.cathay pacific.com). **Freedom Air** (☎0800/600–500 ⊕www.freedomair.co.nz) **Japan Airlines** (☎800/525–3663 in U.S., 845/774–7700 in U.K., 09/379–3202 or 0800/525–747 toll-free in New Zealand ⊕www.jal.com). **Pacific Blue** (☎0800/670–000 toll-free in New Zealand ⊕www.pacificblue.co.nz).**Qantas** (☎800/227–4500 in U.S. and Canada, 0845/774–7767 in U.K., 0800/808–767 toll-free in New Zealand ⊕www.qantas.com.au). **Singapore Airlines** (☎800/742–3333 in U.S., 0844/800–2380 in U.K., 0800/808–909 toll-free in New Zealand ⊕www.singaporeair.com). **United Airlines** (☎800/864–8331 for U.S. reservations, 800/538–2929 for international reservations, 0800/747–400 toll-free in New Zealand ⊕www.united.com).

▌BY BOAT

To travel between the North Island and the South Island take Tranz Scenic's Interislander ferry or the Bluebridge ferry between Wellington and Picton. Both ferries carry cars. They also connect with Tranz Scenic's trains, and a free shuttle is available between the railway station and ferry terminal in both Wellington and Picton. The Interislander travels four to five times a day; Bluebridge, twice daily. Standard one-way fare can be as much as $70, but there are off-peak deals to be had for as low as $39. The fare for a medium-size sedan costs around $200. Be sure to ask about specials, including ferry-train package deals through Tranz Scenic, when you book. *For package ideas that include ferry travel, see Discounts & Deals, below.*

Schedules are available at train stations and visitor-information centers around the country. Most will arrange Interislander ferry bookings. You can also check schedules and fares and book online via the Interislander Web site. Some fares allow you to make schedule changes up to the last minute and guarantee a full refund if you cancel prior to check-in. Discount fares can be booked once in New Zealand; these have some restrictions. No matter how you go about it, it's a good idea to reserve in advance, especially during holiday periods.

Information **Bluebridge** (☎0800/844–844 toll-free in New Zealand ⊕www.bluebridge. co.nz). **Tranz Scenic Interislander** (☎04/498–3302, 0800/802–802 toll-free in New Zealand ⊕www.interislander.co.nz).

▌BY BUS

New Zealand is served by an extensive bus network. InterCity and Newmans are the main bus lines. They operate under a collective marketing umbrella and are part of a larger shareholder group. Newmans differentiates itself by offering newer, spiffier vehicles, which conform to a strict criteria based upon vehicle age and amenities.

Some Newmans and InterCity bus routes overlap, but Newmans tends to have fewer stops and sticks to the key corridors, making travel times shorter. InterCity buses, on the other hand, cover more remote areas. Nevertheless, both services stop at small towns along the way.

Although Newmans and InterCity are the top national carriers, there are also many regional bus services. For instance, Bottom Bus runs around the Catlins and Southland; Atomic Travel also covers the majority of the South Island. *See the Essentials sections in regional chapters for more details on local services.*

Take a hop-on, hop-off bus if you prefer a more flexible itinerary. Although the buses run by companies like Kiwi Experience and Magic Travellers Network may not be as comfortable as Newmans and InterCity, they offer flexible coach passes, typically valid for 12 months. Some passes cover all of New Zealand, whereas others are limited to specific regions. Most of these backpacker buses have affiliations with hostels and hotels, and various combination packages are available. Stray Travel, operated by the people who founded Kiwi Experience, gives you the option of using the service as a tour or having unlimited stopovers for the duration of your chosen pass.

Putting a dent in even the most flexible schedule are unexpected road closings. It's a good idea to call ahead to confirm your itinerary. Otherwise, the buses tend to run on schedule.

Bus fares vary greatly. A standard full fare between Auckland and Wellington is $100 but can be obtained for as low as $48. A certain number of seats are offered at a discounted rate, so book your tickets as early as possible, especially during the holidays. Individual company Web sites are the best way to find out about special fares; both Newmans and InterCity have online reservation systems.

Look into the various flexible passes that allow coach travel over a set route in a given time frame, usually three or six months. You can travel whenever you like, without paying extra, as long as you stick to the stops covered by your pass. There is also the New Zealand Travelpass, which allows unlimited travel on buses and trains and on the Interislander ferries that link the North and South islands (⇨ *Discounts & Deals, below*). Both Newmans and InterCity offer a 20% discount to students and 15% for Youth Hostel members. Identification cards are required. Discounts are given to senior citizens and children, too.

The Flexi-Pass, ⊕*www.flexipass.co.nz*, is sold in blocks of time during which you're eligible to travel on regular InterCity bus routes or on any Newmans sightseeing packages, or both. This is such a good deal that locals even use this pass for their daily commute. Typically valid for a year, you can hop on and off, changing your plans without a penalty at least two hours prior to your departure. You must schedule in advance, as independent bus ticketing windows don't track your Flexi-Pass hours.

Kiwi Experience and Magic Travellers Network offer packages that combine one-way domestic flights with bus passes to help you cover a little more ground for a little less money.

Credit cards and traveler's checks are accepted by the major bus companies.

Bus Information **Atomic Travel** (☏03/349–0697 ⊕www.atomictravel.co.nz). **Bottom Bus** (☏03/434–7370 ⊕www.bottombus. co.nz). **InterCity** (☏ 09/623–1503 ⊕www. intercitycoach.co.nz). **Kiwi Experience** (☏09/366–9830 ⊕www.kiwiexperience. com). **Magic Travellers Network** (☏09/358–5600 ⊕www.magicbus.co.nz). **Newmans** (☏09/623–1504 ⊕www.newmanscoach.

co.nz). **Stray Travel** (☏09/309–8772 or 03/377–6192 ⊕www.straytravel.co.nz).

▌BY CAR

Nothing beats the freedom and mobility of a car for exploring. Even if you're nervous about driving on the "wrong" side of the road, driving here is relatively easy. Many rental cars will have a sticker right next to the steering wheel reading STAY TO THE LEFT.

Remember this simple axiom: drive left, look right. That means keep to the left lane, and when turning right or left from a stop sign, the closest lane of traffic will be coming from the right, so look in that direction first. By the same token, pedestrians should look right before crossing the street. Americans and Canadians can blindly step into the path of an oncoming car by looking left as they do when crossing streets at home. You'll find yourself in a constant comedy of errors when you go to use directional signals and windshield wipers—in Kiwi cars it's the reverse of what you're used to.

Japanese brands dominate rental agencies in New Zealand. For some local flavor, rent a Holden Commodore, a popular car in New Zealand. Most major agencies will have this as a luxury option and some even offer Lexus convertibles and other high-end hot rods. Domestic agency Smart Cars specializes in luxury rentals such as Mercedes and Audi convertibles. Stick shift tends to be the norm, so specify if you prefer an automatic.

Kiwi companies Maui Rentals and Kea Campers are best known for wide selections of campers, motor homes, and 4X4 vehicles. Other reputable domestic agencies are Apex Car Rental and Auto Rentals NZ Wide, which have several branches throughout the country.

Rates in New Zealand begin at $40 a day and $320 a week—although you can sometimes get even cheaper deals—for an economy car with unlimited mileage. This does not include tax on car rentals, which is 12.5%. Reserve a vehicle well in advance if renting during holiday peak seasons, especially Christmas.

Most major international companies (and some local companies) have a convenient service if you are taking the ferry between the North and South islands and want to continue your rental contract. You simply drop off the car in Wellington and on the same contract pick up a new car in Picton, or vice versa. It saves you from paying the fare for taking a car across on the ferry (and it's easier for the company to keep track of its rental fleet). Your rental contract is terminated only at the far end of your trip, wherever you end up. In this system, there is no drop-off charge for one-way rentals, making an Auckland–Queenstown rental as easy as it could be.

Check for rates based on a south-to-north itinerary; it may be less expensive as it's against the normal flow. Special rates should be available whether you book from abroad or within New Zealand.

In New Zealand your own driver's license is acceptable. Still, an International Driver's Permit is a good idea; it's available from the American Automobile Association. These international permits are universally recognized, and having one in your wallet may save you a problem with the local authorities.

For most major rental companies, the minimum age for renting a car in New Zealand is 21. With some local rental companies, however, drivers under 21 years old can rent a car, but may be liable for a higher deductible. Children's car seats are mandatory for kids under five years old. Car-rental companies may ask drivers not to take their cars onto certain roads, so ask about such restrictions.

Major Rental Agencies Avis (☎09/526–3256 or 0800/284–722 toll-free in New Zealand ⊕www.avis.com). **Budget**

(☎0800/283–438 toll-free in New Zealand ⊕www.budget.com). **Hertz** (☎ 0800/654–321 toll-free in New Zealand ⊕www.budget.com). **National** (☎09/275–0066 in New Zealand ⊕www.nationalcar.com).

Local Rental Agencies Apex Rental Car (☎03/379–6897, 0800/93–9597 toll-free in New Zealand ⊕www.apexrentals.co.nz). **Auto Rentals NZ Wide, Ltd.** (☎03/3717–343, 0800/736–893 toll-free in New Zealand ⊕www.autorentals.co.nz). **Kea Campers** (☎09/441–7833, 0800/520–052 toll-free in New Zealand ⊕www.keacampers.com). **Maui Rentals** (☎09/275–3013, 0800/651–080 toll-free in New Zealand ⊕www.maui-rentals.com). **Smart Cars** (☎09/307–3553, 0800/458–987 toll-free in New Zealand ⊕www.smartcars.co.nz).

GASOLINE

On main routes you'll find stations at regular intervals. However, if you're traveling on back roads where the population is sparse don't let your tank get low—it can be a long walk to the nearest farmer.

The price of gas (Kiwis say "petrol") in New Zealand is more volatile than the fuel itself. At this writing, prices had recently rocketed from 82¢ per liter to about $1.70 (NZD) a liter. Credit cards are widely accepted, though not necessarily at small country gas stations, so ask before you fill up.

Unleaded gas is widely available and is often referred to as 91. High-octane unleaded gas is called 96. The 91 is usually a couple of cents cheaper than 96; most rental cars run on 91. Virtually all gas stations will have staff on hand to pump gas or assist motorists in other ways; however, they tend to have self-service facilities for anyone in a hurry. These are simply operated by pushing numbers on a console to coincide with the dollar value of the gas required. When you pump the gas, the pump will automatically switch off when you have reached the stated amount. Pay at the counter inside the station after you fill your tank.

ROAD CONDITIONS

Roads are well maintained and generally not crowded. In rural areas, you may find some unpaved roads. On most highways, it's easier to use the signposted names of upcoming towns to navigate rather than route numbers.

Due to the less-than-flat terrain, many New Zealand roads are "wonky," or crooked. So when mapping out your itinerary, don't plan on averaging 100 kph (62 mph) very often. Expect two or three lanes; there are no special multi-occupant lanes on the major highways. In areas where there is only one lane for each direction, cars can pass, with care, while facing oncoming traffic, except where there is a double yellow center line. Rural areas still have some one-lane roads. One-lane bridges are common and are sometimes used by trains as well as cars; *see Rules of the Road, below.*

New Zealanders are seldom as good at driving as they think they are (they're terrible), so the best policy is just to keep at a safe distance. Dangerous overtaking, speeders, lack of indication, and slow drivers in passing lanes are all afflictions suffered on New Zealand highways. In saying that, driving has improved over recent years due to increased education about speeding, drunk driving, and bad driving in general.

ROADSIDE EMERGENCIES

In the case of a serious accident, immediately pull over to the side of the road and phone ☎111. Emergency phone boxes are not common; you may have to rely on a cellular phone. You will find New Zealanders quick to help if they are able to, particularly if you need to use a phone. Minor accidents are normally sorted out in a calm and collected manner at the side of the road. However, "road rage" is not unknown. If the driver of the other vehicle looks particularly angry or aggressive, you are within your rights to take note of the registration number and then report

the accident at the local or nearest police station.

The New Zealand Automobile Association offers emergency road service and is associated with the American Automobile Association (AAA). If you are an AAA member, you will be covered by the service as long as you register in person with a NZAA office in New Zealand and present your membership card.

Should you find yourself at a panel beater (repair shop) after a prang (minor car accident), talking about your vehicle might end up sounding like more of an Abbott and Costello routine if you're not prepared with the appropriate vehicle vernacular. For instance, you might hear the mechanic say, "Crickey dick! What are ya?! Doing the ton on loose metal when it was hosing down was two sammies short of a picnic. You have a chip in the windscreen, the fender has to be reattached under the boot, and your axle is puckeroo. Pop the bonnet and let's take a look." Translation: "Wow! Are you nuts?! Driving so fast on a gravel road in the rain was crazy (aka two sandwiches short of a picnic). You chipped the windshield, the bumper needs to be reattached under the trunk, and the axle is broken. Pop the hood."

Emergency Services New Zealand Automobile Association (✉99 Albert St., Auckland ☎09/966–8800, 0800/500–222, 0800/500–222 toll-free in New Zealand, *222 toll-free from cell phone ⊕www.aa.co.nz).

RULES OF THE ROAD

The speed limit is 100 km per hour (62 mi per hour) on the open road and 50 kph (31 mph) in towns and cities. A circular sign with the letters LSZ (Limited Speed Zone) means speed should be governed by prevailing road conditions but still not exceed 100 kph. Watch out for speed cameras, particularly in city suburbs and on approaches to and exits from small towns. The police force (not to mention the money counters) has taken to them with relish. Fines start at about $60 for speeds 10 kph (6 mph) over the speed limit.

Right turns are not permitted on red lights. The law states that you must always wear a seat belt in New Zealand, whether you are driving or a passenger in a car. You can be fined for any passenger under the age of 15 not wearing a seat belt or approved child restraint if under the age of 5. If you are caught without a seat belt and you are clearly not a New Zealander, the result is likely to be a friendly but firm warning. Drunk drivers are not tolerated in New Zealand. The blood alcohol limit is 0.05 (80 milligrams of alcohol per 100 milliliters of blood for adults), and it's safest to avoid driving altogether if you've had a drink. If you are caught driving over the limit you will be taken to the nearest police station to dry out and required to pay a high fine. Repeat offenses or instances of causing injury or death while under the influence of alcohol are likely to result in jail terms.

When driving in rural New Zealand, cross one-lane bridges with caution—there are plenty of them. A yellow sign on the left will usually warn you that you are approaching a one-lane bridge, and another sign will tell you whether you have the right-of-way. A rectangular blue sign means you have the right-of-way, and a circular sign with a red border means you must pull over to the left and wait to cross until oncoming traffic has passed. Even when you have the right-of-way, slow down and take care. Some one-lane bridges on the South Island are used by trains as well as cars. Trains always have the right-of-way.

Roundabouts can be particularly confusing for newcomers. When entering a roundabout, yield to all vehicles coming from the right. A blue sign with a white arrow indicates that you should keep to the left of the traffic island as you come up to the roundabout. In a multilane roundabout, stay in the lane closest to the island until ready to exit the circle.

You can only pass on the left if there are two or more lanes on your side of the center line, if the vehicle you are passing has stopped, or if the vehicle ahead is signaling a right turn. At all other times, you must pass on the right.

When you encounter fog, remember to drive with low-beamed headlights, as high beams refract light and decrease visibility. It is illegal to drive with only your parking lights on.

The usual fine for parking over the time limit on meters is $10–$15. In the last few years "pay-and-display" meters have been put up in cities. You'll need to drop a couple of dollars' worth of coins in the meter, take the dispensed ticket, and put it in view on the dashboard of your car. The fine for running over the time for these meters runs about $12, but if you don't display your ticket at all, the fine will be at least $40 and you may risk being towed. So carry a few coins at all times—any denomination will usually do. Make sure to observe all NO PARKING signs. If you don't, your car will almost certainly be towed away. It will cost about $100 to have the car released, and most tow companies won't accept anything but cash.

For more road rules and safety tips, check the Land Transport Safety Authority (LTSA) Web site, ⊕*www.ltsa.govt.nz.*

TRAFFIC

The only city with a serious congestion problem during rush hour is Auckland, particularly on inner-city highways and on and off ramps. Avoid driving between 7:30 AM and 9 AM, and 5 PM and 6:30 PM. Traffic around other cities, such as Wellington and Christchurch, builds up at these times, too, and it is worth taking this into account if you have important appointments or a plane to catch. Give yourself a spare 30 minutes to be on the safe side.

▌ BY CRUISE SHIP

Auckland's bright cruise depot, opened in 2001, reflects the upswing in the cruising industry in recent years. Since the 1990s more companies have been drawn to Auckland's superb harbor, as well as to the gorgeous scenery in places such as the Bay of Islands and Marlborough Sounds. New Zealand is now included on world-cruise itineraries by vessels such as Crystal Cruises' *Crystal Serenity and* Regent Seven Seas Cruises' *Seven Seas Voyager and Seven Seas Marine.* But some of the best cruising programs are those that concentrate entirely on the South Pacific and combine New Zealand with destinations such as Fiji, New Caledonia, Tonga, and Samoa. Generally, such cruises start and finish in Auckland and visit South Pacific islands in between.

P&O Cruises runs a couple cruises out of Auckland to the South Pacific. Another choice is the Holland America Line vessel *Volendam* with its cruises around New Zealand, Australia, and the South Pacific.

Cruise Lines **Crystal Cruises** (☎310/785–9300 or 888/722–0021 ⊕www.crystalcruises.com).**Holland America Line** (☎206/281–3535 or 877/724–5425 ⊕www.hollandamerica.com). **Norwegian Cruise Line** (☎305/436–4000, 800/327–7030, or 866/234–0292 ⊕www.ncl.com). **P&O Cruises** (☎0800/441–766, 0800/951–200 toll-free in New Zealand ⊕www.pocruises.com.au). **Princess Cruises** (☎ 800/774–6237, 0800/951–200 toll-free in New Zealand ⊕www.princess.com). **Regent Seven Seas Cruises** (☎954/776–6123 or 800/477–7500 ⊕www.rssc.com).

▌ BY TRAIN

New Zealand's Tranz Scenic trains travel, as a rule, north and south along the main trunk of New Zealand. If you want to crisscross the country, then you'll have to abandon the country's rail network. There are some exceptions, most notably the famous Tranz-Alpine Express, a spectacular scenic ride across Arthur's Pass and the mountainous spine of the South Island between Greymouth and Christchurch.

Even the most popular services tend to run only once daily. They do leave and arrive on time as a rule. Trains have one class, and they have standard, comfortable seats, and a basic food service offering light meals, snacks, beer, wine, and spirits. Special meals (diabetic/wheat free/vegetarian) can be arranged, but you have to order at least 48 hours before you board the train. Most carriages have large windows from which to view the spectacular passing scenery, and some routes have a commentary on points of interest. Most trains also have a viewing carriage at the rear.

Travelers can purchase a New Zealand Travelpass for unlimited travel by train, bus, and Interislander ferry for a variety of periods. *See Discounts & Deals, below, for more information.* For Youth Hostel Association members, InterCity provides a 15% discount on most train service, all InterCity coach service, and on Interislander ferries. Students with an International Student Identity Card (ISIC) get a 20% discount. Senior citizens (over 60) get a 20% discount with proof of age.

You can obtain both schedules and tickets at visitor-information centers and at train stations. Major credit cards are accepted, as are cash and traveler's checks. Reservations are advised, particularly in the summer months. Book at least 48 hours in advance.

Information **ATS Tours** (☎310/643-0044, 888/781-5170 in U.S. ⊕www.atstours.com). **InterCity Travel Centres** (☎09/623-1503 in Auckland, 03/365-1113 in Christchurch, 04/385-0520 in Wellington, 0508/353-947 toll-free in New Zealand).

Train Information **Tranz Scenic** (☎04/495-0775, 0800/872-467 toll-free in New Zealand for bookings, 0800/277-482 toll-free in New Zealand for train schedule and update information ⊕www.tranzscenic.co.nz).

▌ DISCOUNTS & DEALS

Look into the New Zealand Travelpass to save money by combining bus, ferry, and train costs. The Travelpass has no fixed itineraries and gives you 3,000 different stops to choose from. You choose from a certain number of days of travel and kinds of transportation; there's also an option to tack on air travel. Most Travelpasses are valid for one year, the bus-only version is valid for unlimited travel on InterCity and Newmans coaches over a one-, two-, or three-month period, with an incremental-rate structure. You can purchase an open-ended pass from your travel agent prior to leaving and then call the Travelpass reservations center to make reservations.

The Tranz Scenic rail service also has a couple of deals worth checking out, including ThroughFares, which combine Tranz Scenic train trips with SoundsAir flights and the Interislander ferries.

▌TIP➔**Ask the local tourist board about hotel and local transportation packages that include tickets to major museum exhibits or other special events.**

Discount Resources **New Zealand Travelpass** (☎09/638-5788 or 0800/339-966 toll-free in New Zealand ⊕www.travelpass.co.nz). **Tranz Scenic** (☎04/495-0775 or 0800/872-467 toll-free in New Zealand ⊕www.tranzscenic.com).

ESSENTIALS

■ ACCOMMODATIONS

Tourism New Zealand *(⇨ Visitor Information, below)* publishes an annual "Where to Stay" directory listing more than 1,000 properties. This directory lists all properties who register for it, but it gives priority to those accredited by Qualmark, the national tourism–quality assurance organization.

The lodgings we list are the cream of the crop in each price category. We always list the facilities but we don't specify whether they cost extra; when pricing accommodations, always ask what's included and what costs extra. Properties are assigned price categories based on the range from their least-expensive standard double room at high season (excluding holidays) to the most expensive. All rooms listed have an en suite or private bath unless otherwise noted. In New Zealand, the phrase "en-suite bathroom" means that the bathroom is connected directly with the bedroom, while a "private bath" often is outside the bedroom but is not shared with other guests.

■ TIP→Assume that hotels operate on the European Plan (EP, no meals) unless we specify that they use the Breakfast Plan (BP, with full breakfast), Continental Plan (CP, Continental breakfast), Full American Plan (FAP, all meals), Modified American Plan (MAP, breakfast and dinner) or are all-inclusive (AI, all meals and most activities).

BED & BREAKFASTS

There are some helpful resources on the Web for researching and booking B&B choices. On Web sites such as those maintained by SelectionsNZ and Jasons Travel Media, you'll find hundreds of listings and advertisements for B&Bs throughout the country. Heritage & Character Inns of New Zealand specializes in higher-end B&Bs.

Once in New Zealand you will find the *New Zealand Bed and Breakfast Book* in most major bookstores, or you can look at their listings online for free at ⊕*www.bnb.co.nz*. It lists about 1,000 B&Bs, but be aware that the editorial copy in the book has been provided by the property owners themselves, rather than providing independent assessments as this Fodor's guide does.

Reservation Services The New Zealand Bed & Breakfast Book (⊕www.bnb.co.nz). **Heritage & Character Inns of New Zealand** (⊕www.heritageinns.co.nz).

Jasons Travel Media (⊕www.jasons.com). **SelectionsNZ** (⊕www.selections.co.nz).

HOME & FARM STAYS

If you think green acres is the place to be, New Zealand has plenty of them. Home and farm stays offer not only comfortable accommodations but a chance to experience the countryside and the renowned Kiwi hospitality. Most operate on a B&B basis, though some also offer evening meals. Farm accommodations vary from modest shearers' cabins to elegant homesteads. Some hosts offer day trips, as well as horseback riding, hiking, and fishing. For two people, the average cost ranges from $90 to $200 per night, including meals.

Home stays, the urban equivalent of farm stays, are less expensive. Most New Zealanders seem to have vacation homes, called *baches* in the North Island, *cribs* in the South Island; these are frequently available for rent. New Zealand Vacation Homes lists houses and apartments for rent on both the North and South islands. Baches and Holiday Homes to Rent Ltd. publishes an annual directory of rental homes throughout the country, with color photos for each listing.

Another accommodation option is a home exchange. Intervac, one of the largest international home-exchange services, has a New Zealand representative on hand.

Contacts **Baches and Holiday Homes to Rent Ltd.** (⌂ Box 3107, Richmond, Nelson ☎ 03/544–4799 ⊕ www.holidayhomes. co.nz). **Farm Helpers in New Zealand** (⌂ 31 Moerangi St., Palmerston North ☎ 06/354–1104 ⊕ www.fhinz.co.nz). **Intervac** (⌂ 13 Zetland St., Wellington ⊕ www. intervac.co.nz). **New Zealand Farm Holidays Ltd.** (⌂ Box 74, Auckland ☎ 09/412–9649 ⊕ www.nzaccom.co.nz). **New Zealand Vacation Homes Ltd.** (⌂ Box 76112, Auckland ☎ 09/268–2161 ⊕ www.nzvacationhomes. co.nz). **Rural Holidays NZ Ltd.** (⌂ Box 2155, Christchurch ☎ 03/355–6218 ⊕ www. ruralholidays.co.nz).

HOME EXCHANGES

With a direct home exchange you stay in someone else's home while they stay in yours. Some outfits also deal with vacation homes.

Exchange Clubs **Home Exchange.com** (☎ 800/877–8723 ⊕ www.homeexchange. com); $99.95 for a 1-year online listing. **HomeLink International** (☎ 800/638–3841 ⊕ www.homelink.org); $110 yearly for online membership; $170 also includes printed directories. **Intervac U.S.** (☎ 800/756–4663 ⊕ www.intervacus.com); $95 for Web-only membership; $140 includes Web access and catalogs.

HOSTELS

The Youth Hostels Association of New Zealand (YHA NZ)—there's also an Australian YHA—is similar to Hosteling International (HI). A year's membership costs about $30, which taps you into a network of hostels throughout the country and discounts on various activities, tours, and transportation.

In addition to the YHA NZ, a network of low-cost, independent backpacker hostels operates in New Zealand. They can be found in nearly every city and tour-

ist spot, and they offer clean, twin- and small dormitory-style accommodations and self-catering kitchens, similar to those of the YHA NZ and HI-affiliated hostels, with no membership required.

Qualmark, New Zealand's official tourism quality-assurance company, rates backpacker hostels on a five-star system. You can check ratings on ⊕ www.qualmark.co.nz.

Information **Hostelling International—USA** (☎ 301/495–1240 ⊕ www.hiusa.org). **Youth Hostels Association of New Zealand** (☎ $$$$$800/278–299 toll-free in New Zealand ⊕ www.yha.co.nz).

HOTELS

When looking up hotel information, you'll often see a reference to Qualmark, New Zealand's official tourism quality-assurance agency. This nonprofit service grades hotels on a one- to five-star system and participation is voluntary. Each business applies and undergoes a strict assessment and licensing process to win Qualmark accreditation, shelling out some cash in the process. These ratings are generally fair gauges of each property's cleanliness and security. You can check a hotel's Qualmark rating on the Web site ⊕ www. qualmark.co.nz.

LUXURY LODGES

At the high end of the price scale, luxury lodges offer the best of country life, fine dining, and superb accommodations. Many specialize in fishing, but there is usually a range of outdoor activities for nonanglers. Tariffs run about $400–$2,000 per day for two people; meals are generally included. For information, visit the New Zealand Lodge Association's Web site, ⊕ *www.lodgesofnz.co.nz*, where you can download an electronic catalog of New Zealand lodges.

MOTELS

Motels are the most common accommodations, and most offer comfortable rooms for $70–$195 per night. They're usually open every day of the year. Unlike in the United States, motels in New Zealand are not always below the standard of hotels. For instance, "motel flats" are set up like apartments, with living areas as well as bedrooms. Accommodations with more basic facilities are called "serviced motels." All motel rooms come with tea- and coffee-making equipment; many have full kitchens. The Motel Association of New Zealand (MANZ) is an independent company with nearly 1,000 members. Its Web site, ⊕ *www.manz.co.nz*, allows you to find properties by region or by motel name.

MOTOR CAMPS

The least expensive accommodations are the tourist cabins and flats in most of the country's 400 motor camps. Tourist cabins offer basic accommodation and shared cooking, laundry, and bathroom facilities. Bedding and towels are not provided. A notch higher up the comfort scale, tourist flats usually provide bedding, fully equipped kitchens, and private bathrooms. Tent sites and caravan sites usually cost less than $10 and overnight rates for cabins range anywhere from $6 to $20. More fully equipped tourist flats will cost $25 to $70.

▌ COMMUNICATIONS

INTERNET

Traveling with a laptop does not present any problems in New Zealand, where the electricity supply is reliable. However, you will need a converter and adapter as with other electronic equipment (⇨ *Electricity, below*). It pays to carry a spare battery and adapter, since they're expensive and can be hard to replace.

City hotels and even provincial hotels and motels are well equipped to handle computers and modems. You may get a little stuck in family-run bed-and-breakfasts and farm stays in remote areas, but even these places can usually sort something out for you.

Contacts Cybercafes (⊕ www.cybercafes. com) lists more than 4,000 Internet cafés worldwide.

PHONES

The country code for New Zealand is 64. When dialing from abroad, drop the initial "0" from the local area code. Main area codes within New Zealand include 09 (Auckland and the North), 04 (Wellington), and 03 (South Island). Dialing from New Zealand to back home, the country code is 1 for the United States and Canada, 61 for Australia, and 44 for the United Kingdom. The prefixes 0800 and 0867 are used for toll-free numbers in New Zealand.

Dial 018 for New Zealand directory assistance. For international numbers, dial 0172. To call the operator, dial 010; for international operator assistance, dial 0170. To find phone numbers within New Zealand online go to ⊕ *www.whitepages.co.nz*.

CALLING OUTSIDE NEW ZEALAND

To make international calls directly, dial 00, then the international access code, area code, and number required. The country code for the United States is 1.

Access Codes AT & T Direct (☎ 000–911). **MCI WorldPhone** (☎ 000–912). **Sprint International Access** (☎ 000–999).

CALLING CARDS

Most pay phones now accept PhoneCards or major credit cards rather than coins.

PhoneCards, available in denominations of $5, $10, $20, or $50, are sold at post offices, dairies (convenience stores), tourist centers, and any other shops displaying the green PhoneCard symbol. To use a PhoneCard, lift the receiver, put the card in the slot in the front of the phone, and dial. The cost of the call is automatically deducted from your card; the display on the telephone tells you how much credit you have left at the end of the call. A local call from a public phone costs 70¢. Don't forget to take your PhoneCard with you when you finish your call or those minutes will be lost—or spent by a stranger.

Telecom offers a reliable card called Easy Call, which covers minutes to the United States for as low as 3¢ per minute. You can add minutes to the card by using your credit card; unlike a PhoneCard, you don't need to purchase a new one when you're running out of time. Other phone cards include Kia Ora and Talk 'n' Save (both offered by Compass Phone Cards), which operate in the same way; you can call the United States for as low as 3.9¢ per minute. You can buy these phone cards at gas stations, dairies, and most hostels.

The Net2Phone Direct Calling Card offers an affordable solution by utilizing local access numbers to make calls utilizing the Internet. This is used in the same manner as a regular calling card, but depending upon the area from which you are calling there is sometimes a slight voice delay. This type of technology has also made it possible to make phone calls right from your laptop computer. If you are going to have free access to the Internet, this can prove to be the most affordable means of making international calls, with rates from New Zealand to the United States being approximately 4¢ per minute with Net2Phone's PC2Phone plan. It is advisable to use a headset for the best clarity.

Calling Cards **Compass Phone Cards** (☎800/646–444 toll-free in New Zealand). **Telecom Easy Call** (☎0800/922–2248 toll-free in New Zealand).

MOBILE PHONES

If you have a multiband phone (some countries use different frequencies from what's used in the United States) and your service provider uses the world-standard GSM network (as do T-Mobile and Cingular), you can probably use your phone abroad. Roaming fees can be steep, however: 99¢ a minute is considered reasonable. And overseas you normally pay the toll charges for incoming calls. It's almost always cheaper to send a text message than to make a call, since text messages have a very low set fee (often less than 5¢).

If you just want to make local calls, consider buying a new SIM card (your provider may have to unlock your phone for you to use a different SIM card) and a prepaid service plan in the destination. You'll then have a local number and can make local calls at local rates. If your trip is extensive, you could also simply buy a new cell phone in your destination, as the initial cost will be offset over time.

■TIP→If you travel internationally frequently, save one of your old mobile phones or buy a cheap one on the Internet; ask your cell phone company to unlock it for you, and take it with you as a travel phone, buying a new SIM card with pay-as-you-go service in each destination.

There are both analog and digital mobile-communications networks covering most of the country, which operate on the GSM system. If you have a tri-band GSM phone you can rent a SIM card for about $10 per week. Keep in mind, however, that the phone must be unlocked, so you should be sure to get that number from your provider prior to leaving.

Cell phones can be rented at Auckland, Wellington, Queenstown, and Christchurch airports, starting at $6 a day. Look for a Vodafone stand in the arrival area of each airport. Prior reservations are a good idea, though not absolutely necessary. Make phone-rental arrangements

LOCAL DO'S & TABOOS

CUSTOMS OF THE COUNTRY

In general, Kiwis are accommodating folk who are more likely to good-naturedly tease you about a cultural faux pas than to take offense, but there are a few etiquette points to keep in mind. First, the word "kiwi" refers to either people (New Zealanders) or to the protected kiwi bird, but not the kiwifruit. Also, don't lump New Zealanders in with Australians. A New Zealand accent does not sound just like an Australian one, or a British accent for that matter, and a Kiwi will be the first to point this out. *For tips on how to distinguish between these accents, see Language, below.*

Be considerate of Māori traditions. For instance, *marae*, the area in front of a meetinghouse, should not be entered unless you are invited, or unless it's in use as a cultural center. Also, it's best not to use *hongi* (touching foreheads and noses in greeting) unless someone initiates it. *For more on Māori traditions, see the Understanding New Zealand. chapter*

If you're visiting someone's house, take along a small gift. Among gestures, avoid the "V" symbol with the first two fingers with the palm facing in—an offensive vulgarity.

LANGUAGE

Kiwi English can be mystifying. The colloquialisms alone can make things puzzling, not to mention rural slang. Known as "cow cockie" talk, this is what you'll hear when "girls" refers to someone's cows, and gummies (galoshes) are the favored footwear.

The Māori language has added many commonly used words to the New Zealand lexicon. For instance, the Māori greeting is *kia ora*, which can also mean "thank you," "good-bye," "good health," or "good luck." You'll hear it from everyone, *Pākehā* (non-Māori) and Māori alike. Many place names are Māori as well, and can be so long as to seem unpronounceable. (A Māori word stands as the longest place-name in the world.) *See the Kiwi and Māori Glossaries in the Understanding New Zealand chapter for guidance on pronunciation.*

Avoid the grave error of mistaking a Kiwi accent for an Australian one by listening for certain signature vowel sounds. For instance, New Zealanders often pronounce a short "e" as a short "i," making "pen" sound like "pin." And, vice versa, short "i" often sounds like a short "e." Both Aussies and Kiwis pronounce "day" as "die," but using more of an "oi" sound is an Australian twist. The easiest test to tell an Aussie from a Kiwi is to listen for the phrase "fish-and-chips." If it sounds like "feesh-and-cheeps," you're listening to an Australian but if it sounds like "fush-and-chups," you're with a Kiwi.

The biggest communication glitch between New Zealanders and visitors often involves the Kiwis' eloquent use of the understatement. This facet of Kiwi speech is both blessing and curse. Everything sounds relaxed and easygoing…but if you're trying to judge something like distance or difficulty you may run into trouble. No matter how far away something is, people often say it's "just down the road" or "just over the hill." Ask specific questions to avoid a misunderstanding.

SIGHTSEEING

If you are driving a road maggot (campervan), be considerate of the drivers behind you, pull over when safe and possible and let them pass.

There is etiquette when visiting a marae, best illustrated in the book *Te Marae: A Guide to Māori Protocol*, available through Raupo Publishing (⊕ www.raupopublishing.co.nz).

New Zealand is big on sheep, and you might lose smarty points if you ask dumb sheep questions. "When do you cut their fur?" or "When do their tails fall off?" will elicit laughter: sheep have wool, and their tails are cut off. And remember, there isn't a sheep joke here that hasn't been heard.

in advance so you can give family and friends your number before you leave.

CUSTOMS & DUTIES

New Zealand has stringent regulations governing the import of weapons, foodstuffs, and certain plant and animal material. Anti-drug laws are strict and penalties severe. In addition to personal effects, nonresidents over 17 years of age may bring in, duty-free, 200 cigarettes or 250 grams of tobacco or 50 cigars, 4.5 liters of wine, three bottles of spirits or liqueur containing not more than 1,125 mls, and personal purchases and gifts up to the value of US$440 (NZ$580).

The agricultural quarantine is serious business, and you'll be hit with an instant $250 fine if you're caught bringing in even an undeclared piece of fruit. The beagle is cute but he will bark if he smells a banana, he will put his paws on your bag and everyone will be staring at you like it's *Midnight Express,* and while that movie is a lot of things, cute is not one of them. And be truthful about your camping gear because they *will* take it into a back room, unravel your tent and sleeping bag and check for grass and muck. Do yourself a favor and make sure any camping gear and hiking boots are reasonably clean when entering the country. The authorities don't want any nonnative seeds (or popcorn kernels or honey) haplessly transported into the country.

Check the following Web sites for a more detailed description and explanations of no-nos. Since the foot-and-mouth-disease outbreak in the United Kingdom and Europe in 2000–01 and the terrorist attacks in the United States, airport officers have become even more vigilant and all bags coming into the country are X-rayed.

EATING OUT

Some restaurants offer a fixed-price dinner, but the majority are à la carte. Remember that "entrée" in Kiwi English is the equivalent of an appetizer. It's wise to make a reservation and inquire if the restaurant has a liquor license or is "BYOB" or "BYO" (Bring Your Own Bottle)—many places have both. By the way, this only pertains to wine, not bottles of beer or liquor. Be prepared to pay a corkage fee, which is usually a couple of dollars.

Many restaurants add a 15% surcharge on public holidays. Employers are required by law to pay staff a higher wage during these holidays. This amount will be itemized separately on your bill.

New Zealand's *Cuisine* magazine has a special annual issue devoted to restaurants throughout the country; hit their Web site, ⊕*www.cuisine.co.nz,* if you'd like to get a copy before your trip. There are also a few helpful New Zealand dining Web sites worth a look. Through some, you can make online reservations. These include ⊕*www.cup.co.nz,* an independent nationwide café guide; ⊕*www. dineout.co.nz,* a national database with customer reviews; and ⊕*www.menus. co.nz,* which posts photos and menus of restaurants in Auckland and Wellington.

For information on food-related health issues, see Health below.

MEALS & MEALTIMES

When in New Zealand, have a little lamb. No matter where you go in the country, it's sure to be there on the menu. Cervena, or farm-raised venison, is another local delicacy available all over New Zealand, and farmed ostrich is gaining popularity as well.

In New Zealand restaurants, many vegetables have two names, used interchangeably. Eggplants are often called aubergines, zucchini are also known as courgettes. The vegetable North Americans know as a bell pepper is a capsicum here. The tropical fruit papaya is known by its British name, pawpaw.

Don't miss a Māori *hāngi*. This culinary experience can be loosely compared to a family barbecue (hosted by a family that likes to do a lot of dancing and singing). The traditional preparation involves steaming meat, seafood, and vegetables in a large underground pit, and the meal is accompanied by Māori performances. *See the "Dinner on the Rocks" CloseUp box in Chapter 4.* Also be sure to try *kūmara*, an indigenous sweet potato that's sacred to the Māori. Many Kiwis view muttonbird as a special treat, but some outsiders balk at its peculiar smell and unusual flavor. It is an acquired taste, but if you're an adventurous eater it's definitely one to try.

Of course, seafood is a specialty, and much of the fish is not exported so this is your chance to try it! The tastiest fish around is snapper in the North, and blue cod (not a true cod relative) in the South. Grouper (often listed by its Māori name of *hapuku*), flounder, and salmon are also menu toppers, as is whitebait, the juvenile of several fish species, in spring. As for shellfish: try the Bluff oysters (in season March–August), Greenshell mussels (also known as green-lipped or New Zealand green mussels), scallops, crayfish (spiny lobster), and local clamlike shellfish, *pipi* and *tuatua*. *For more on native foods, see the "Something to Chew On" CloseUp box in Chapter 5.*

Burgers are a staple for a quick bite. However, you'll find there's a whole lot more than two all-beef patties between your bun—one of the most popular toppings is beetroot and a fried egg. Cheese on burgers (and sandwiches) is often grated bits sprinkled atop. Another Kiwi snack staple, meat pies, are sold just about everywhere. The classic steak-and-mince fillings are getting gussied up these days with combinations like steak and cheese and steak and oysters. And who could forget good ol' fish-and-chips in this former British colony? Appropriately called "greasies," this mainstay is often made of shark but called lemon fish or flake. You might notice bowls by the cash registers of take-out shops containing packets of tartar sauce or tomato sauce (catsup). Don't just grab a handful, these are usually not free for the taking; they cost about 45¢ each.

Be aware that the word "bacon" on a menu might not meet your expectations of bacon. If you love your bacon streaky and crisp, you might politely inquire what kind of bacon they serve before ordering a BLT...some places use a thick blubbery slice of ham, and some places use a processed fatty pink spongy substance that will upset you.

Lemon & Paeroa, otherwise known as L&P, is New Zealand's most famous soft drink. Keep in mind that if you order a lemonade you will be served a carbonated lemon-flavored drink. If you've a sweet tooth, nibble a chocolate fish, a chocolate-covered fish-shaped marshmallow. This treat has become so popular in New Zealand that it's now synonymous with success. You'll often hear someone say, "you deserve a chocolate fish!" in place of "job well done!" Hokey pokey, a lacy honey toffee, is another favorite candy. And if you're traveling in the heat of the summer, don't leave town until you've tried a hokey pokey ice cream, another New Zealand mainstay. If you want to try a truly unique bit of New Zealand grub, and we do mean grub, taste the larvae of the huhu beetle.

Restaurants serve breakfast roughly between 7 and 9:30. Lunch usually starts about noon and is over by 2. Dinners are usually served from 5 PM, but the most popular dining time is around 7. Restaurants in cities and resort areas will serve dinner well into the night, but some places in small towns or rural areas still shut their doors at around 9.

Unless otherwise noted, the restaurants listed in this guide are open daily for lunch and dinner.

PAYING

Credit cards are widely accepted in restaurants and even small cafés. You may find exceptions to this rule, so check first. In some areas, American Express and Diners Club cards are accepted far less frequently than MasterCard and Visa. *For guidelines on tipping see Tipping below.*

RESERVATIONS & DRESS

We only mention them specifically when reservations are essential or when they are not accepted. For popular restaurants, book as far ahead as you can (often 30 days), and reconfirm as soon as you arrive. (Large parties should always call ahead to check the reservations policy.) We mention dress only when men are required to wear a jacket or a jacket and tie.

Attire countrywide is pretty casual; unless you're planning to dine at the finest of places, men won't need to bring a jacket and tie. At the same time, the most common dinner attire is usually a notch above jeans and T-shirts.

WINES, BEER & SPIRITS

New Zealand is best known for its white wines, particularly sauvignon blanc, Riesling, and chardonnay. The country is now gaining a reputation for red wines such as cabernet sauvignon, pinot noir, and merlot. The main wine-producing areas are West Auckland, Hawke's Bay, Martinborough, Marlborough, and Nelson. Emerging regions include Canterbury and Central Otago. Restaurants almost without exception feature New Zealand products on their wine list. *For a rundown on New Zealand's wine industry, see "News from the Grapevine" in Chapter 7.*

When ordering a beer, you'll get either a handle (mug) or a one-liter jug (pitcher). In some Southland country pubs you'll see all the blokes drinking "big botts" of Speights (500 ml). To get beer served in a glass, you usually have to request it. Monteith's Brewery and Macs are South Island–based breweries that distribute around the country and have a strong local following. Steinlager, probably the most famous (but not the tastiest) of New Zealand beers, is brewed by Lion Breweries and is widely available. There are a number of boutique microbreweries in New Zealand, some of which have won international beer awards, such as Tuatara, West Coast Brewing, and Emersons; each brand has its own fan base. Most restaurants and liquor stores sell beers from Australia, the United States, Europe, and other parts of the world. Some of the beer in New Zealand is stronger than the 4% alcohol per volume brew that is the norm in the United States. Many go up to 7% or 8% alcohol per volume, so check that number before downing your usual number of drinks.

New Zealand only has a couple of spirits it can really call its own. One is Wilson's Whisky, distilled in Dunedin—a city with a strong Scottish heritage. Another popular drink is 42 Below. With its claim to fame as "the world's southernmost vodka," 42 Below incorporates local flavors: feijoa, manuka honey, passion fruit, and kiwifruit. Most inner-city bars will have it on the menu if you want to try before you buy a bottle; and having won a slew of gold and silver medals at international wine and spirit competitions around the world, it makes a cool duty-free gift to bring back to vodka connoisseurs back home. You'll also sometimes find sticky-sweet kiwifruit or feijoa liqueurs.

Use your judgment about ordering "off the drinks menu." If you're in a South Island country pub, don't try to order an umbrella cocktail. By insisting on a margarita from an establishment that doesn't have the mix, the recipe, or the right glass, you're not gaining anything except a lousy margarita and a reputation as an obnoxious customer.

Since 1999 it has been possible to purchase beer and wine in supermarkets as well as specialized shops and to do so seven days a week. People under 18 are not permitted by law to purchase alcohol, and shops, bars, and restaurants strictly enforce this. If you look younger than you are, carry photo identification to prove your age.

▌ELECTRICITY

If you forget to pack a converter, you'll find a selection at duty-free shops in Auckland's airport and at electrical shops around the city. The electrical current in New Zealand is 240 volts, 50 cycles alternating current (AC); wall outlets take slanted three-prong plugs (but not the U.K. three-prong) and plugs with two flat prongs set at a "V" angle.

Consider making a small investment in a universal adapter, which has several types of plugs in one lightweight, compact unit. Most laptops and mobile phone chargers are dual voltage (i.e., they operate equally well on 110 and 220 volts), requiring only an adapter. These days the same is true of small appliances such as hair dryers. Always check labels and manufacturer instructions to be sure. Don't use 110-volt outlets marked FOR SHAVERS ONLY for high-wattage appliances such as hair dryers.

Contacts Steve Kropla's Help for World Traveler's (⊕www.kropla.com) has information on electrical and telephone plugs around the world. **Walkabout Travel Gear** (⊕www.walkabouttravelgear.com) has a good coverage of electricity under "adapters."

▌EMERGENCIES

For fire, police, or ambulance services, dial ☎111.

In Auckland, the U.S. Consulate is open only from 9:30 until around 12:30 on weekdays.

In Wellington, the U.S. Embassy is open weekdays 10–noon and 2–4.

United States U.S. Consulate (✉Level 3, Citigroup Bldg., 23 Customs St., Auckland ☎09/303–2724). **United States Embassy** (✉29 Fitzherbert Terr., Thorndon, Wellington ☎04/462–6000).

▌HEALTH

The most common types of illnesses are caused by contaminated food and water. Especially in developing countries, drink only bottled, boiled, or purified water and drinks; don't drink from public fountains or use ice. You should even consider using bottled water to brush your teeth. Make sure food has been thoroughly cooked and is served to you fresh and hot; avoid vegetables and fruits that you haven't washed (in bottled or purified water) or peeled yourself. If you have problems, mild cases of traveler's diarrhea may respond to Imodium (known generically as loperamide) or Pepto-Bismol. Be sure to drink plenty of fluids; if you can't keep fluids down, seek medical help immediately.

Infectious diseases can be airborne or passed via mosquitoes and ticks and through direct or indirect physical contact with animals or people. Some, including Norwalk-like viruses that affect your digestive tract, can be passed along through contaminated food. If you are traveling in an area where malaria is prevalent, use a repellant containing DEET and take malaria-prevention medication before, during, and after your trip as directed by your physician. Condoms can help prevent most sexually transmitted diseases, but they aren't absolutely reliable and their quality varies from country to country. Speak with your physician and/or check the CDC or World Health Organization Web sites for health alerts, particularly if you're pregnant, traveling with children, or have a chronic illness.

Health Warnings National Centers for Disease Control & Prevention (CDC ☎877/394–8747 international travelers' health line ⊕wwwn.cdc.gov/travel). **World Health Organization** (WHO ⊕www.who.int).

SPECIFIC ISSUES IN NEW ZEALAND

General health standards in New Zealand are high, and it would be hard to find a more pristine natural environment.

The major health hazard in New Zealand is sunburn or sunstroke. Even people who are not normally bothered by strong sun should cover up with a long-sleeve shirt, a hat, and pants or a beach wrap. At higher altitudes you will burn more easily, so apply sunscreen liberally before you go out—even for a half hour—and wear a visor or sunglasses.

Dehydration is another serious danger that can be easily avoided, so be sure to carry water and drink often. Limit the amount of time you spend in the sun for the first few days until you are acclimatized, and avoid sunbathing in the middle of the day.

There are no venomous snakes, and the only native poisonous spider, the *katipo,* is a rarity. The whitetail spider, an unwelcome and accidental import from Australia, packs a nasty bite and can cause discomfort but is also rarely encountered.

One New Zealander you will come to loathe is the tiny black sandfly (some call it the state bird), common to the western half of the South Island, which inflicts a painful bite that can itch for several days. In other parts of the country, especially around rivers and lakes, you may be pestered by mosquitoes. Be sure to use insect repellent.

One of New Zealand's rare health hazards involves its pristine-looking bodies of water; don't drink water from natural outdoor sources. Although the country's alpine lakes might look like backdrops for mineral-water ads, some in the South Island harbor a tiny organism that can cause "duck itch," a temporary but intense skin irritation. The organism is found only on the shallow lake margins, so the chances of infection are greatly reduced if you stick to deeper water. Streams can be infected by giardia, a waterborne protozoal parasite that can cause gastrointestinal disorders, including acute diarrhea. Giardia is most likely contracted when drinking from streams that pass through an area inhabited by mammals (such as cattle or possums). There is no risk of infection if you drink from streams above the tree line.

Less common, but a risk nevertheless, is the possibility of contracting amoebic meningitis from the water in geothermal pools. The illness is caused by an organism that can enter the body when the water is forced up the nose. The organism is quite rare, but you should avoid putting your head underwater in thermal pools or jumping in them. Also remember not to drink geothermic water.

OVER-THE-COUNTER REMEDIES

Popular headache/pain/flu medicines are Nurofen (contains Ibuprofen), Panadol (contains Paracetamol), and Dispirin (contains Aspirin). Dispirin often comes as large tabs, which you must dissolve in water. Many Kiwi households and wheelhouses have a green tube of Berocca, the soluble vitamin supplement often taken the morning after a big night out.

▌ HOURS OF OPERATION

Banks are open weekdays 9–4:30, but some cease trading in foreign currencies at 4.

Gas stations are usually open, at the least, from 7 to 7 daily. Large stations on main highways are commonly open 24 hours.

Museums around the country do not have standard hours, but many are open daily from 10 to 5. Larger museums and government-run collections are generally open daily, but the hours of small local museums vary, as many are run by volunteers. The New Zealand Museums Web site (⊕ *www.nzmuseums.co.nz*) is a helpful information source; you can search by collection, region, or museum name.

Pharmacies are open from 9 to 5. In larger cities, you will find basic nonprescription drugstore items in supermarkets, many of which are open until 10 PM. During off-hours there will usually be emergency-hour pharmacies in the major cities. Phone the local hospital for details.

Shops are generally open Monday through Thursday 9–5:30, Friday 9–9, and Saturday 9–noon (until 5 in main cities). Sunday trading is becoming more common but still varies greatly from place to place. In many rural areas, stores are closed on Sunday, but most Auckland shopping centers are at least open Sunday morning. Liquor stores are often open daily. In major cities supermarkets and convenience stores, called "dairies," are usually open from 7 AM to 10 PM; a few stay open 24 hours.

HOLIDAYS

On Christmas Day, Good Friday, Easter Sunday, and the morning of ANZAC Day, everything closes down in New Zealand except for a few gas stations, some shops selling essential food items, and emergency facilities. On other public holidays (often referred to as bank holidays) many museums and attractions stay open, as do transportation systems, though on a reduced schedule. Local anniversary days, which vary regionally, pop up as once-a-year three-day weekends in each particular area; some businesses close but hotels and restaurants stay open. Around Christmas and New Year's Kiwis go to the beach, so seaside resorts will be difficult to visit unless you have booked well in advance. You'll get plenty of sunshine and far fewer crowds if you visit from late January through to the colder period of late March. Cities such as Auckland and Wellington are quite pleasant over Christmas and New Year's. Fewer cars are on the road, and you'll get good prices from hotels making up for the lack of corporate guests.

▌ MAIL

Airmail should take around six or seven days to reach the United Kingdom or the United States and two or three days to reach Australia.

Most post offices are open weekdays 8:30–5, and in some areas on Saturday 9–12:30 or 10–1. The cost of mailing a letter within New Zealand is 50¢ standard post, $1 fast post. Sending a standard-size letter by airmail costs $2 to North America, $2 to Europe, and $1.50 to Australia. Aerograms and postcards are $1.50 to any overseas destination.

If you wish to receive correspondence, have mail sent to New Zealand held for you for up to one month at the central post office in any town or city if it is addressed to you "c/o Poste Restante, CPO," followed by the name of the town. This service is free; you may need to show ID.

Postal Service New Zealand Post (☎ 0800/501–501 toll-free in New Zealand ⊕ www.nzpost.co.nz).

SHIPPING PACKAGES

Overnight services are available between New Zealand and Australia, but to destinations farther afield "overnight" will in reality be closer to 48 hours. Even to Australia, truly overnight service is only offered between major cities and can be subject to conditions, such as the time you call in. A number of major operators are represented in New Zealand and the services are reliable, particularly from cities.

You can use the major international overnight companies listed above or purchase packaging and prepaid mail services from the post office. Major duty-free stores and stores that deal frequently with travelers will be able to help with international shipping, but if you purchase from small shops, particularly in country areas, arrange shipping with a company in the nearest city.

Express Services DHL World Express (☎ 0800/800–020 toll-free in New Zealand ⊕ www.dhl.co.nz). **Federal Express** (☎ 0800/733–339 toll-free in New Zealand ⊕ www.fedex.com). **TNT International Express** (☎ 0800/275–868 toll-free in New Zealand ⊕ www.tnt.com).

▌ MONEY

For most travelers, New Zealand is not an expensive destination. The cost of meals, accommodation, and travel prove comparable to larger cities within the United States and somewhat less than in Western

Europe. At about $1.70 per liter—equal to about US$4.90 per gallon—premium-grade gasoline costs more than it does in North America; prices are much cheaper than in Europe.

Prices throughout this guide are given for adults. Substantially reduced fees are almost always available for children, students, and senior citizens.

Currency Conversion Google (⊕ www. google.com). **Oanda.com** (⊕ www.oanda.com). **XE.com** (⊕ www.xe.com).

▌TIP→ Banks never have every foreign currency on hand, and it may take as long as a week to order. If you're planning to exchange funds before leaving home, don't wait until the last minute.

ATMS & BANKS

Your own bank will probably charge a fee for using ATMs abroad; the foreign bank you use may also charge a fee. Nevertheless, you'll usually get a better rate of exchange at an ATM than you will at a currency-exchange office or even when changing money in a bank. And extracting funds as you need them is a safer option than carrying around a large amount of cash.

▌TIP→ PIN numbers with more than four digits are not recognized at ATMs in many countries. If yours has five or more, remember to change it before you leave.

EFTPOS (Electronic Fund Transfer at Point of Sale) is widely used in New Zealand stores and gas stations. Needless to say, ATMs are easily found in city and town banks and in shopping malls. The number of ATMs in small rural communities continues to grow, but there are still areas where ATMs or banks are few and far between. For example, there are no ATMs on Stewart Island. All the major banks in New Zealand (Bank of New Zealand, Westpac, and Auckland Savings Bank) accept cards in the Cirrus and Plus networks. The norm for PINs in New Zealand is four digits. If the PIN for your account has a different number of digits, you must change your PIN number before you leave for New Zealand.

CREDIT CARDS

Throughout this guide, the following abbreviations are used: **AE**, American Express; **DC**, Diners Club; **MC**, Master-Card; and **V,** Visa.

MasterCard and Visa are the most widely accepted cards throughout New Zealand. Discover Cards are not recognized.

Reporting Lost Cards **American Express** (☎800/992–3404 in U.S., 336/393–1111 collect from abroad, for New Zealand offices call 09/583–8300 or 0800/656–660 toll-free ⊕www.americanexpress.com). **Diners Club** (☎800/234–6377 in U.S., 303/799–1504 collect from abroad, for New Zealand offices call 09/359–7797 or 0800/657–373 toll-free ⊕www.dinersclub.com). **MasterCard** (☎800/622–7747 in U.S., 636/722–7111 collect from abroad, for New Zealand offices call 0800/449–140 toll-free ⊕www.master card.com). **Visa** (☎800/847–2911 in U.S., 410/581–9994 collect from abroad, for New Zealand offices call 0508/600–300 toll-free ⊕www.visa.com).

CURRENCY & EXCHANGE

New Zealand's unit of currency is the dollar, divided into 100 cents. Bills are in $100, $50, $10, and $5 denominations. Coins are $2, $1, 50¢, 20¢, and 10¢. At this writing the rate of exchange was NZ$1.32 to the U.S. dollar, NZ$1.30 to the Canadian dollar, NZ$2.59 to the pound sterling, NZ$2.05 to the Euro, and NZ$1.25 to the Australian dollar. Exchange rates change on a daily basis.

PACKING

In New Zealand, be prepared for weather that can turn suddenly and temperatures that vary greatly from day to night, particularly at the change of seasons. The wisest approach to dressing is to wear layered outfits. You'll appreciate being able to remove or put on a jacket. Take along a light raincoat and umbrella, but remember that plastic raincoats and non-breathing polyester are uncomfortable in the humid climates of Auckland and its northern vicinity. Many shops in New Zealand sell lightweight and mid-weight merino wool garments, which are expensive but breathe, keep you warm, and don't trap body odor, making them ideal attire for tramping. Don't wear lotions or perfume in humid places like Southland, either, since they attract mosquitoes and other bugs; carry insect repellent. Sandflies seem drawn to black and dark blue colors. Bring a hat with a brim to provide protection from the strong sunlight (⇨Health, above) and sunglasses for either summer or winter; the glare on snow and glaciers can be intense. There's a good chance you'll need warm clothing in New Zealand no matter what the season; a windbreaker is a good idea wherever you plan to be.

Dress is casual in most cities, though top resorts and restaurants may require a jacket and tie. Some bouncers for big city bars will shine a flashlight on your shoes; if you like these kinds of places bring some spiffy spats. In autumn, a light wool sweater and/or a jacket will suffice for evenings in coastal cities, but winter demands a heavier coat—a raincoat with a zip-out wool lining is ideal. Comfortable walking shoes are a must. You should have a pair of what Kiwis call "tramping boots," or at least running shoes if you're planning to trek, and rubber-sole sandals or canvas shoes for the beaches.

Weather **Accuweather.com** (⊕www. accuweather.com). **New Zealand Weather Today** (⊕www.weather.co.nz). **Weather.com** (⊕www.weather.com).

▌ RESTROOMS

Shopping malls in cities, major bus and train stations, gas stations, and many rest areas on main highways have public toilets. Look for a blue sign with white figures (ladies and gents) for directions to a public toilet. New Zealanders often use the word "loo," or, better yet, "super loo."

Most New Zealand public restroom facilities are clean and tidy and often have a separate room for mothers with young children.

Some gas stations, shops, and hotels have signs stating that only customers can use the restroom. Kiwis are generally fair-minded folk, so if you're genuinely caught short and explain the situation you will probably not be turned away.

Most gas stations in New Zealand have toilet facilities, but their standard is varied. As a rule of thumb, the newer and more impressive the gas station, the cleaner and better the toilet facilities.

Find a Loo **The Bathroom Diaries** (⊕www. thebathroomdiaries.com) is flush with unsanitized info on restrooms the world over—each one located, reviewed, and rated.

▌ SAFETY

New Zealand is safe for travelers, but international visitors have been known to get into trouble when they take their safety for granted. Use common sense, particularly if walking around cities at night. Stick around other people and avoid deserted alleys. Although New Zealand is an affluent society by world standards, it has its share of poor and homeless (often referred to as "street kids" if they are young), and violent gangs such as the Mongrel Mob have footholds in major cities. Avoid bus and train stations or city squares and parks late at night. The crowds in some pubs can get a bit rough late, so if you sense irritation, leave.

Hotels offer safes for guests' valuables, and it pays to use them. Don't flash your wealth, and remember to lock doors of hotel rooms and cars. Unfortunately, opportunist criminals stake out parking lots at some popular tourist attractions. Put valuables out of sight under seats or lock them in your trunk *before* you arrive at the destination.

Most visitors have no trouble and find New Zealanders among the friendliest people in the world. Nine times out of 10, offers of help or other friendly gestures will be genuine.

Women will not attract more unwanted attention than in most other Western societies, nor will they be immune from the usual hassles. In cities at night, stick to well-lighted areas and avoid being totally alone. Hotel staff will be happy to give tips on any areas to avoid, and the times to avoid them. New Zealand is relatively safe for women, but don't be complacent. Female travelers have been victim to sexual assault in New Zealand; hitchhiking is not recommended for solo females.

Some top Kiwi destinations have accommodations especially geared to women. Wellington, for instance, has a women-only guesthouse, and the Base Backpacker hostel chain (⊕*www.base-backpackers.com*), with locations in major New Zealand cities, created Sanctuary Floors, secure women-only zones with special amenities.

Contact **Transportation Security Administration** (TSA ⊕www.tsa.gov).

General Information & Warnings **Australian Department of Foreign Affairs & Trade** (⊕www.smartraveller.gov.au). **Consular Affairs Bureau of Canada** (⊕www.voyage. gc.ca). **U.K. Foreign & Commonwealth Office** (⊕www.fco.gov.uk/travel). **U.S. Department of State** (⊕www.travel.state.gov).

▌ TAXES

Many restaurants add a 15% surcharge to your bill on public holidays, reflecting the need to pay staff a higher wage on holidays. This tax will be itemized separately on your bill when applicable.

Visitors exiting New Zealand must pay a departure tax of $25. *(See By Air, above.)*

A goods and services tax (GST) of 12.5% is levied throughout New Zealand. It's usually incorporated into the cost of an item, but in some hotels and some restaurants it is added to the bill.

▌ TIME

Trying to figure out just what time it is in New Zealand can get dizzying, especially because of cross-hemisphere daylight-saving times and multi-time-zone countries. Without daylight saving time, Auckland is 17 hours ahead of New York; 18 hours ahead of Chicago and Dallas; 20 hours ahead (or count back 4 hours and add a day) of Los Angeles; 12 hours ahead of London; and 2 hours ahead of Sydney.

From the States, call New Zealand after 5 PM.

Time Zones **Timeanddate.com** (⊕www.timeanddate.com/worldclock).

▌ TOURS

Among companies that sell tours to New Zealand, the following are nationally known organizations with a proven reputation. The key difference between the categories listed below is usually in the accommodations, which run from budget to better, and better-yet to best.

LUXURY

Abercrombie & Kent, otherwise known as A&K, is the benchmark for pairing deluxe accommodations with soft adventure. Its itineraries can be combined with a visit to Australia or focus solely New Zealand. Sometimes better deals can be landed by booking a flight package with their affiliate airlines, Qantas. Tauck World Discovery offers trips with private chartered plane service. Antipodes Tours combed New Zealand for posh accommodations and tailors tours to individual requests. The

"Connoisseur Collection" tour series with Luxury Vacations New Zealand takes small groups of just eight people to both the North and South islands.

Luxury Tour Companies **Abercrombie & Kent** (✉1520 Kensington Rd., Oak Brook, IL ☏800/554-7016 or 630/954-2944 🖷630/954-3324 ⊕www.abercrombiekent. com). **Antipodes Tours** (✉5777 W. Century Blvd.Los Angeles, CA ☏800/354-7471 or 310/410-9734 🖷310/410-9451 ⊕www. antipodestours.com). **Luxury Vacations New Zealand** (✉121 Elliot St., 1st fl., Howick, Auckland ☏09/537-2325 🖷09/532-8825 ⊕www.luxuryvacationsnz.com). **Tauck World Discovery** (✉10 Norden Pl., Norwalk, CT ☏800/788-7885 or 203/899-6500 🖷203/221-6828 ⊕www.tauck.com).

MODERATE

Grey Line of Auckland and Pacific Travel of Christchurch formed a joint marketing venture to promote North and South Island tours called Scenic Pacific Tours. Their tours depart daily from Auckland, Wellington, Picton, Christchurch, and Queenstown. You can mix and match your tours and choose your level of accommodations to fit your budget. ATS Tours and Australian Pacific Touring (APT) both specialize in South Pacific vacations and can arrange everything from self-drive to fully escorted tours.

Moderate Tour Companies **ATS Tours** (✉300 Continental Blvd., Suite 350, El Segundo, CA ☏888/781-5170 or 310/643-0044 🖷310/643-0032 ⊕www. atstours.com). **Australian Pacific Touring (APT)** (✉2 Augustus Terrace, Parnell, Auckland ☏0800/278-687 toll-free in New Zealand, 800/290-8687 in U.S. 🖷09/279-8813 ⊕www.aptours.com). **Scenic Pacific Tours** (✉Box 14037, Christchurch ☏03/359-3999, 0800/500-388 toll-free in New Zealand 🖷03/359-9058 ⊕www.scenicpacific.co.nz).

BUDGET

Thrifty Tours New Zealand packaged holidays are flexible, combining regular bus, train, and ferry services with prebooked accommodation. Flying Kiwi Wilderness Expeditions Ltd. helps tie up loose ends for those on a shoestring budget. It's geared to camping rather than hotels and sometimes the major means of transit are your two feet, but this tour company has been a longtime Kiwi favorite.

Budget Tour Companies **Flying Kiwi Wilderness Expeditions Ltd.** (⌧4B Forests Rd., Nelson ☏03/547–0171 or 0800/693–296 🖷03/547–0173 ⊕www.flyingkiwi.com). **Thrifty Tours New Zealand** (⌧ Auckland ☏09/359–8380, 0800/803–550 toll-free in New Zealand 🖷09/358–5408 ⊕www.thriftytours.co.nz).

SPECIAL-INTEREST TOURS

Golf Wine New Zealand and Grape Escape Food and Wine Tours share astute insights on Hawke's Bay, Martinborough, and Marlborough vintages, the former with some time on the links as well. Homestay NZ Ltd. will arrange theme trips based upon your individual interests, be it wine or whale-watching. One of their more unique options includes having dinner at a local New Zealand family's home.

Lord of the Rings fans will find there are numerous companies offering tours of Middle Earth by helicopter, four-wheel drive, and bus. One of the most beautiful trips is a horseback tour around Glenorchy—contact Dart Stables about the "Ride of the Rings."

Serious outdoor enthusiasts can take a walk on the wild side, or bike, kayak, or bungy jump with Active New Zealand. *For more New Zealand–based outfitters who organize multiday sports trips, see Chapter 11.*

Theme-Tour Companies **Active New Zealand** (⌧Box 972, Queenstown ☏03/450–0414, 800/500–3398 and 800/661–9073, in U.S. 🖷03/409–0119, 603/251–1051 in U.S. ⊕www.activenewzealand.com). **Dart Stables** (⌧Box 47, Glenorchy ☏03/442–5688, 0800/474–3464 toll-free in New Zealand 🖷03/442–6045 ⊕ www.dartstables.com).

Golf Wine New Zealand (⌧10869 N. Scottsdale Rd., Suite 103 Scottsdale, AZ ☏888/607–1717, 480/607–1717, 09/445–3757 in New Zealand 🖷480/607–1771 ⊕www.golfwinenewzealand.com). **Grape Escape** (⌧Box 1058, Napier ☏0800//100–489 toll-free in New Zealand 🖷06/870–0451 ⊕ www.grapeescapenz.co.nz).**Homestay NZ Ltd.** (⌧Box 146, Auckland ☏09/411–9166 🖷09/411–9170).**New Zealand Wine Tourism Network** (⊕www.wtn.co.nz).

▎TIPPING

Tipping is not as widely practiced in New Zealand as in the United States or Europe, but in city restaurants and hotels it's appreciated if you acknowledge good service with a 10% tip.

Taxi drivers will appreciate rounding up the fare to the nearest $5 amount, but don't feel you have to do this. Porters will be happy with a $1 or $2 coin. Most other people, like bartenders, theater attendants, gas-station attendants, or barbers, will probably wonder what you are doing if you try to give them a tip.

▎VISITOR INFORMATION

Tourism New Zealand is a government agency that serves as a hub for the 28 different Regional Tourism Organizations (RTOs) based throughout the country. These locally funded RTOs run most of the 71 i-SITE visitor centers. Many of these have computerized booking systems in place, so rather than drive from lodge to B&B to hotel-making inquiries, the i-SITE can be a good place to let you know instantly which places are vacant. These centers are marked with blue signs and a lowercase white letter i. *Please see the individual chapter Essentials sections for details on local visitor bureaus.*

Contact **Tourism New Zealand** (⌧501 Santa Monica Blvd., Los Angeles, CA ☏310/395–7480 or 866/639–9325 🖷310/395–5453 ⊕www.newzealand.com).

ONLINE TRAVEL TOOLS

Tourism New Zealand's site includes city and regional overviews, travel journals, information on major events like the America's Cup, and cultural background. Stuff (⊕*www.stuff.co.nz*) and NZ Pages (⊕*www.nzpages.co.nz*) are also good catchall sites for Kiwi news, links to local resources, and more.

For the latest on the grape, Wine OnLine (⊕*www.wineonline.co.nz*) and New Zealand Wine (⊕*www.nzwine.com*), the official site for the country's wine and grape industry, post updates on some of the country's top wineries. NZ Gardens Online (⊕*www.gardens.co.nz*) cultivates information on New Zealand's public and private gardens. At ⊕*www.maori.org.nz,* you can find answers to cultural FAQs.

For detailed information on New Zealand's wilderness areas, visit the Department of Conservation's site (⊕*www.doc.govt.nz)*, which covers all the national parks, major walking tracks, campgrounds and huts, safety tips, and so forth. Snowco (⊕*www.snow.co.nz*) provides countrywide snow reports; the New Zealand Alpine Club (⊕*www.alpineclub.org.nz*) focuses on climbing. To get up to speed on rugby, check out the New Zealand Rugby Union's ⊕*www.allblacks.com* or the comprehensive Planet Rugby at ⊕*www.planet-rugby.com.*

Cuisine magazine's online presence (⊕*www.cuisine.co.nz)* includes restaurant reviews and discussions of local wines. If you're inspired, look up recipes for Kiwi dishes. For reviews from the public, check ⊕*www.dineout.co.nz.* The New Zealand Historic Places Trust site (⊕*www.historic.org.nz)* will give you the latest on heritage sights throughout the country. And at ⊕*www.nzmusic.com* you can get the scoop on New Zealand bands and shows.

INDEX

NOTES

NOTES

ABOUT OUR WRITERS

Sue Farley, a 14 year veteran of travel writing, has been to a diverse spectrum of environments, from deep, dark Fiordland nights to bright, sunny, tropical days on the beach. She most enjoys wild or remote places, especially ones of ecological significance. Australia has always been a favored spot and her recent foray up into the vastness of Cape York was a highlight. Closer to home she combines off-the-beaten track writing in NZ with a selection of quality guidebook work to keep her solvent. She updated the Upper South Island and Christchurch and Canterbury chapters for this edition.

Jessica Kany, who updated the Southern Alps & Fiordland, Otago & Invercargill, and Adventure Vacations chapters, as well as the front matter, was born in New York City, attended Washington University in St. Louis, and then spent a decade moving haphazardly around the U.S. Favorite locales include Wyoming, where she corrected "telemarkers" to "telemarketers" while working as the worst copyeditor ever for the *Jackson Hole News,* and Maui. Now a resident of Stewart Island, New Zealand, Jess is a freelance writer, an avid runner, an unskilled but enthusiastic paua diver, the editor of *S.I.N. (Stewart Island News),* and field scribe for the Yellow-eyed penguin team.

A writer by trade and a traveler by compulsion, **Alia Levine** enjoyed a stint working in the wilds of the publishing industry in New York City before heading back home to Aotearoa, New Zealand, where she now lives on the Kapiti Coast with her partner and daughter. Along with writing about the people and places she's seen, her background is in human rights, which has taken her to more than a few spots off the beaten track. For this edition, she updated Travel Smart New Zealand.

Bob Marriott was born in Nottingham, England but has lived in New Zealand for many years. He loves the harbor, the rivers, and the bush-clad hills around Wellington, which he calls home. A passion for travel has taken him to Europe, the Americas, Africa, South East Asia, and Australia and the South Pacific. His freelance writing and photography have been widely published. Bob contributes to several Fodor's guides, and for this edition he wrote the chapters on the East Coast & Volcanic Zone and Wellington & Wairarapa.

Kathy Ombler, updated the Western North Island chapter. Kathy is a freelance writer focusing on nature tourism. She has written several guide books, including *Where to Watch Birds in New Zealand* and *A Visitor's Guide to New Zealand National Parks.* Kathy grew up on a Waikato farm, has lived in many places throughout New Zealand from big cities to small rural settlements in national parks, and is now based in Wellington.

Richard Pamatatau was born in Auckland and grew up on the relaxed North Shore with a beach at the end of his street. As a child he spent some time mucking around in boats on the Waitemata Harbour, and as an enthusiastic surfer and triathlete, he loves playing outdoors. Richard is now Radio New Zealand's Pacific Issues Correspondent, and while he travels a lot, he still enjoys discovering new things in Auckland every day. For this edition he updated the Auckland, Coromandel, and Northland & Bay of Islands chapters.